MICROSOFT® OFFICE 97

— VISUAL SOLUTIONS —

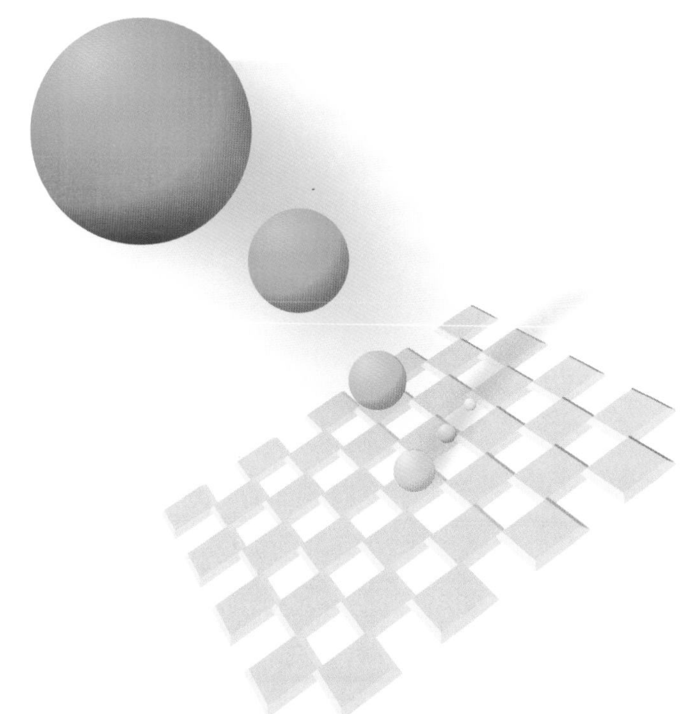

by: maranGraphics' Development Group

Corporate Sales
Contact maranGraphics
Phone: (905) 890-3300
(800) 469-6616
Fax: (905) 890-9434

Canadian Trade Sales
Contact Prentice Hall Canada
Phone: (416) 293-3621
(800) 567-3800
Fax: (416) 299-2529

Visit our Web site at:
http://www.maran.com

Microsoft® Office 97 Visual Solutions

Screen shots reprinted by permission from Microsoft Corporation.

Canadian Cataloguing in Publication Data

Maran, Ruth, 1970-
Microsoft Office 97

(Visual solutions)
Written by Ruth Maran.
Includes index.
ISBN 1-896283-27-6

1. Microsoft Office for Windows (Computer file).
2. Business – Computer programs. 3. Business presentations – Graphic methods – Computer programs. I. MaranGraphics Inc. II. Title. III. Series.

HF5548.4.M525M3715 1997 005.369 C97-930135-1

Printed in the United States of America

10 9 8 7 6 5 4 3 2 1

Trademark Acknowledgments

maranGraphics Inc. has attempted to include trademark information for products, services and companies referred to in this guide. Although maranGraphics Inc. has made reasonable efforts in gathering this information, it cannot guarantee its accuracy.

All other brand names and product names used in this book are trademarks, registered trademarks, or trade names of their respective holders. maranGraphics Inc. is not associated with any product or vendor mentioned in this book.

FOR PURPOSES OF ILLUSTRATING THE CONCEPTS AND TECHNIQUES DESCRIBED IN THIS BOOK, THE AUTHOR HAS CREATED VARIOUS NAMES, COMPANY NAMES, MAILING ADDRESSES, E-MAIL ADDRESSES AND PHONE NUMBERS, ALL OF WHICH ARE FICTITIOUS. ANY RESEMBLANCE OF THESE FICTITIOUS NAMES, COMPANY NAMES, MAILING ADDRESSES, E-MAIL ADDRESSES AND PHONE NUMBERS TO ANY ACTUAL PERSON, COMPANY AND/OR ORGANIZATION IS UNINTENTIONAL AND PURELY COINCIDENTAL.

The 3-D illustrations are the copyright of maranGraphics, Inc.

MICROSOFT®

OFFICE 97

VISUAL SOLUTIONS

maranGraphics™

Every maranGraphics book represents
the extraordinary vision and commitment of a unique family:
the Maran family of Toronto, Canada.

Back Row (from left to right): *Sherry Maran, Rob Maran, Richard Maran, Maxine Maran, Jill Maran.*

Front Row (from left to right): *Judy Maran, Ruth Maran.*

Richard Maran is the company founder and its inspirational leader. He developed maranGraphics' proprietary communication technology called "visual grammar." This book is built on that technology—empowering readers with the easiest and quickest way to learn about computers.

Ruth Maran is the Author and Architect—a role Richard established that now bears Ruth's distinctive touch. She creates the words and visual structure that are the basis for the books.

Judy Maran is the Project Coordinator. She works with Ruth, Richard, and the highly talented maranGraphics illustrators, designers, and editors to transform Ruth's material into its final form.

Rob Maran is the Technical and Production Specialist. He makes sure the state-of-the-art technology used to create these books always performs as it should.

Sherry Maran manages the Reception, Order Desk, and any number of areas that require immediate attention and a helping hand.

Jill Maran is a jack-of-all-trades and dynamo who fills in anywhere she's needed anytime she's back from university.

Maxine Maran is the Business Manager and family sage. She maintains order in the business and family—and keeps everything running smoothly.

CREDITS

Author & Architect:
Ruth Maran

Copy Development & Editor:
Alison MacAlpine

Project Coordinator:
Judy Maran

Copy Editor:
Brad Hilderley

Editors for Introduction, Word and PowerPoint Chapters:
Karen Derrah
Wanda Lawrie

Editors for Excel, Outlook and Internet Chapters:
Kelleigh Wing
Richard Warren

Layout Designers:
Christie Van Duin
Tamara Poliquin

Illustrations & Screens:
Chris K.C. Leung
Russell Marini
Ben Lee
Jeff Jones

Indexer:
Kelleigh Wing

Post Production:
Robert Maran

ACKNOWLEDGMENTS

Thanks to the dedicated staff of maranGraphics, including Karen Derrah, Francisco Ferreira, Brad Hilderley, Jeff Jones, Wanda Lawrie, Ben Lee, Chris K.C. Leung, Alison MacAlpine, Michael W. MacDonald, Jill Maran, Judy Maran, Maxine Maran, Robert Maran, Sherry Maran, Russ Marini, Tamara Poliquin, Christie Van Duin, Richard Warren, Paul Whitehead and Kelleigh Wing.

Finally, to Richard Maran who originated the easy-to-use graphic format of this guide. Thank you for your inspiration and guidance.

TABLE OF CONTENTS

INTRODUCTION

1 GETTING STARTED

2 SAVE, PRINT AND OPEN A DOCUMENT

3 CHANGE DOCUMENT DISPLAY

4 EDIT A DOCUMENT

5 FORMAT TEXT

6 FORMAT PAGES

7 WORKING WITH TABLES

TABLE OF CONTENTS

TABLE OF CONTENTS

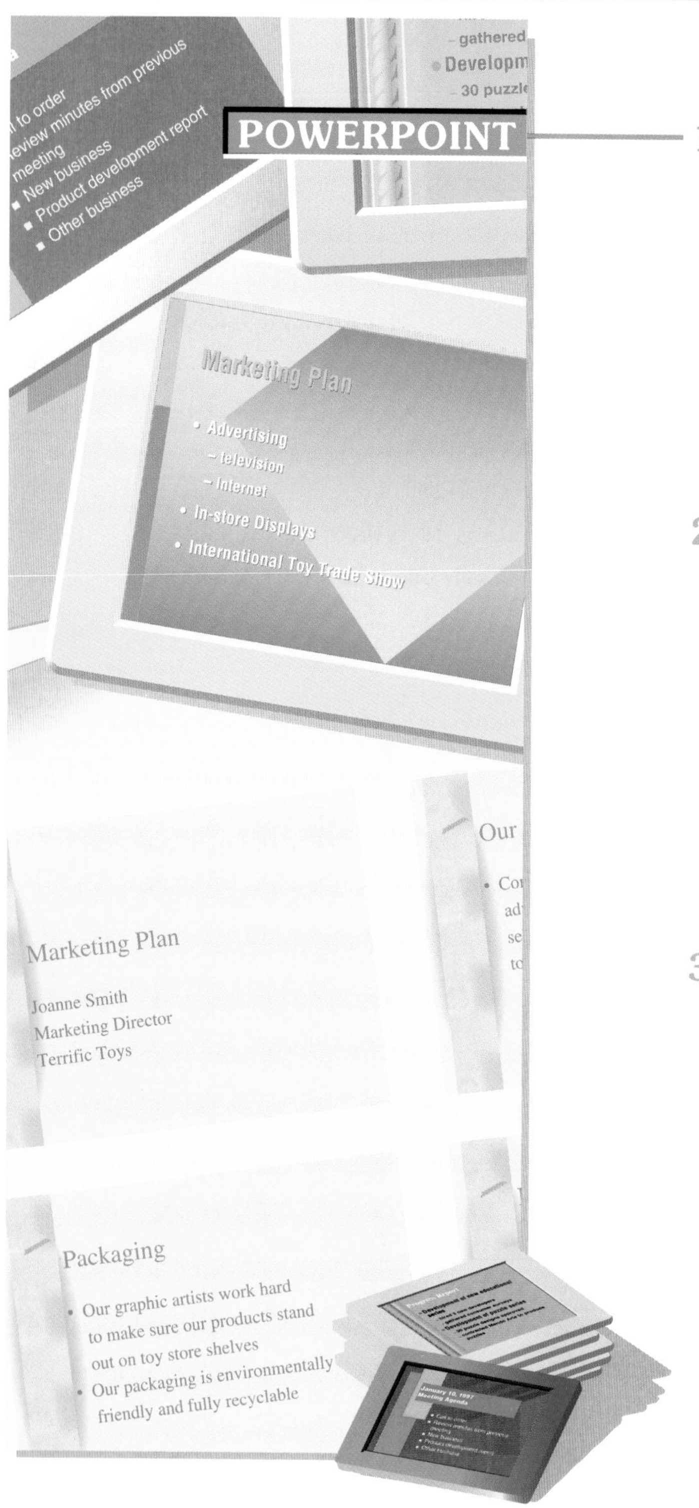

1 GETTING STARTED

2 EDIT SLIDES

3 ADD OBJECTS TO SLIDES

OUTLOOK

TABLE OF CONTENTS

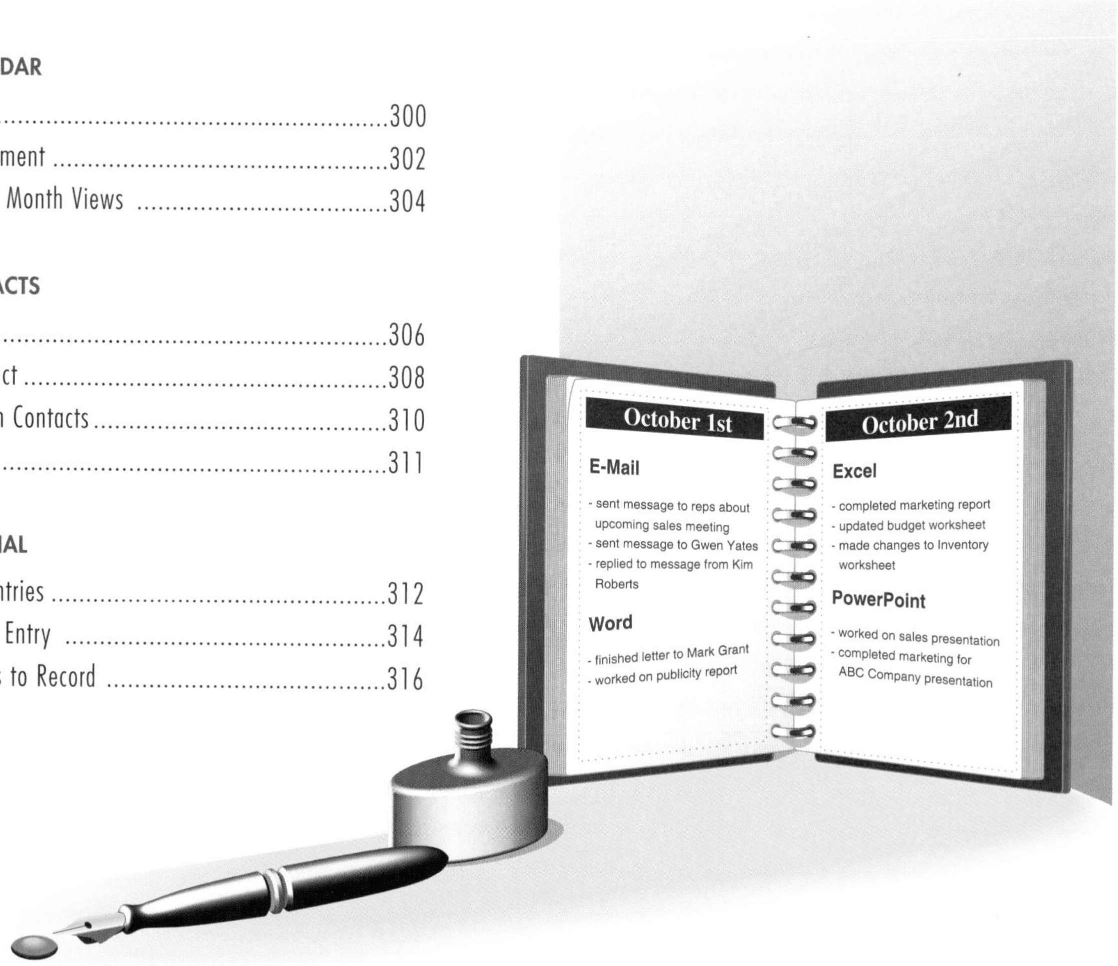

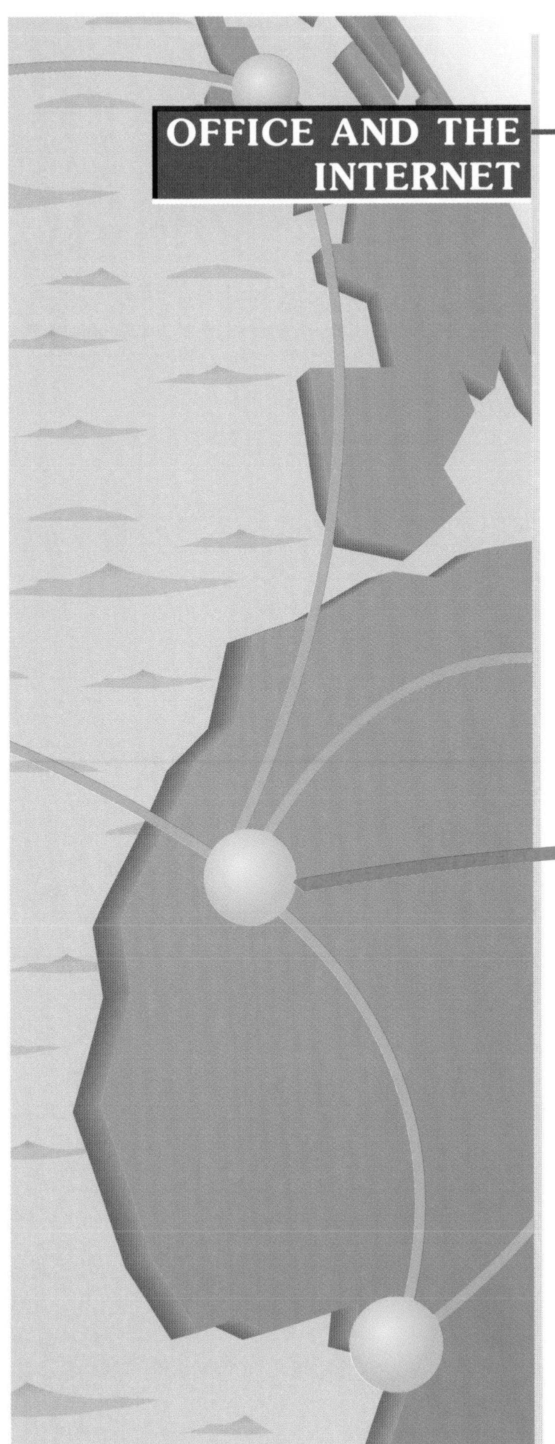

OFFICE AND THE INTERNET

ABC CORPORATION

	Jan	Feb
Revenue	8745	11500
Payroll	3850	4850
Rent	1750	1750
Supplies	1920	1980
Total Expenses		
Income		

January 10, 1997
Meeting Agenda
- Call to order
- Review minutes from previous meeting
- New business
- Product development report
- Other business

series
- hired 3 new developers
- gathered consumer surv
- Development of puzzle
- 30 puzzle designs appro
- contracted Mendo Arts
puzzles

Marketing Plan
- Advertising
  - Television
  - Internet
- In-store Displays
- International Toy Trade Show

Editor's Note...
Mountain Bike Tune-ups

This is my first year of mountain biking, and so far I've been doing my own tune-ups. But lately my bike hasn't performed well. For example, the chain slips when I switch gears. I'm wondering if I should pay a mechanic to do my tune-ups. Is it worth it?

George Arnoldson

Speaking of tune-ups, your friendly Mountain Mania Bike Stores are having one day seminars on bike tune-ups. Look below for the location nearest you!

Mountain Mania
Bike Store locations:

New York, NY
Boston, MA
Cincinnati, OH
Las Vegas, NV
Jacksonville, FL
Nashville, TN
Greenwich, CT
Salem, MA
Atlanta, GA
San Diego, CA
Los Angeles, CA
Denver, CO

Introduction

This section introduces you to the programs included in Microsoft Office 97. You will learn the basic skills required to use these programs and how to get help from the Office Assistant.

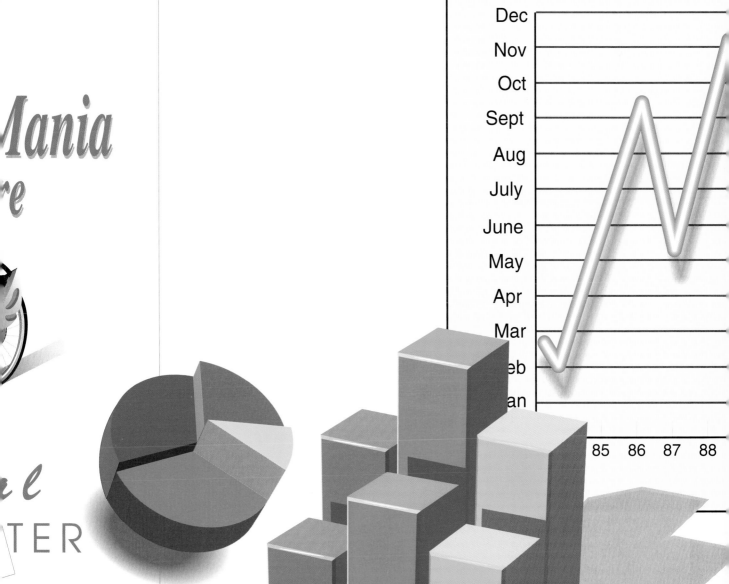

Microsoft Office includes several programs to help you accomplish many tasks.

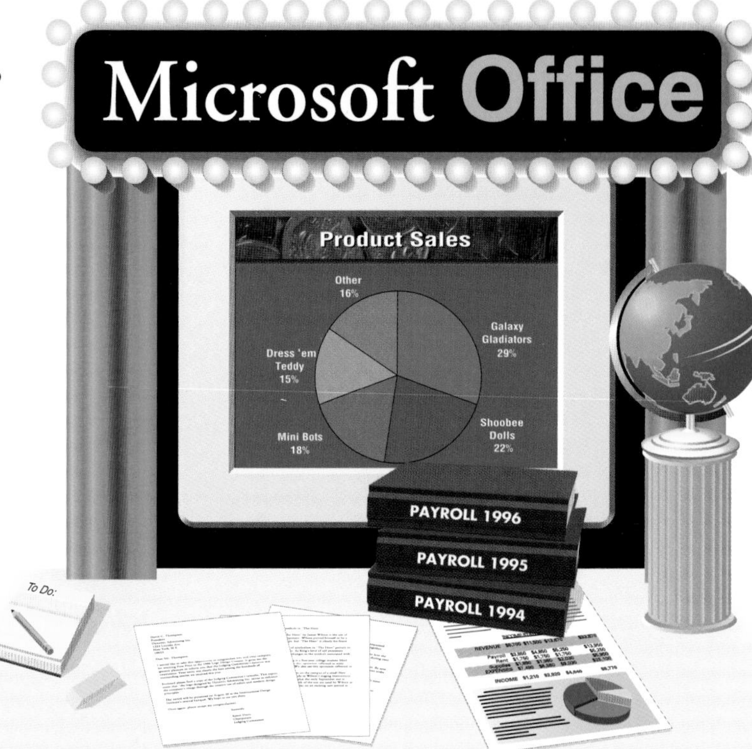

Each Office program has features that make it easy for you to take advantage of the World Wide Web.

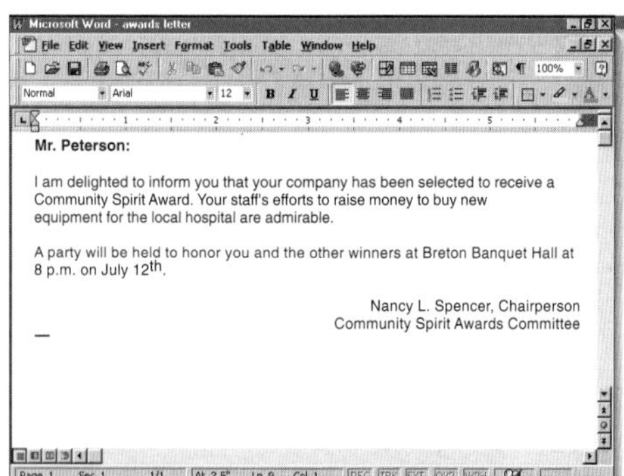

WORD

Word is a word processing program that helps you create letters, reports, memos and newsletters quickly and efficiently.

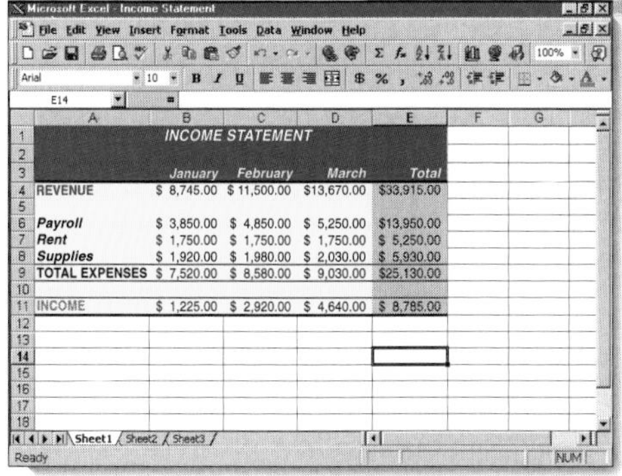

EXCEL

Excel is a spreadsheet program that helps you organize, analyze and present data.

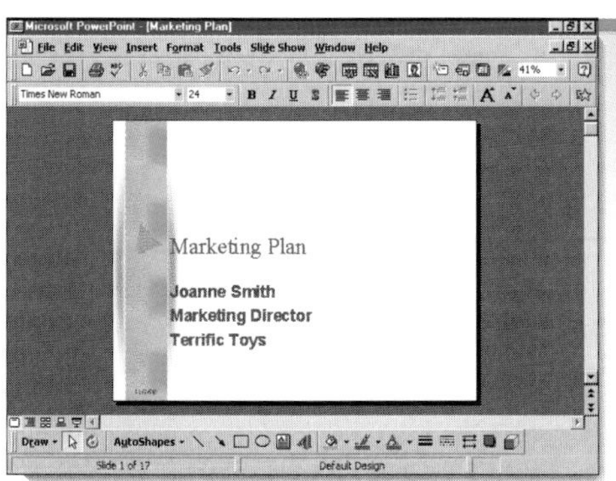

POWERPOINT

PowerPoint is a program that helps you plan, organize and design professional presentations.

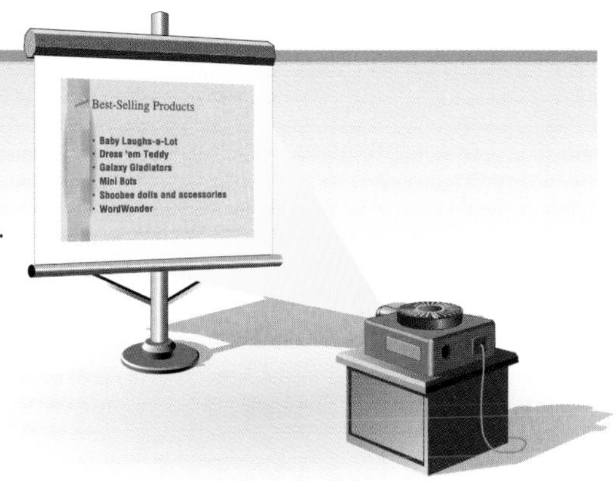

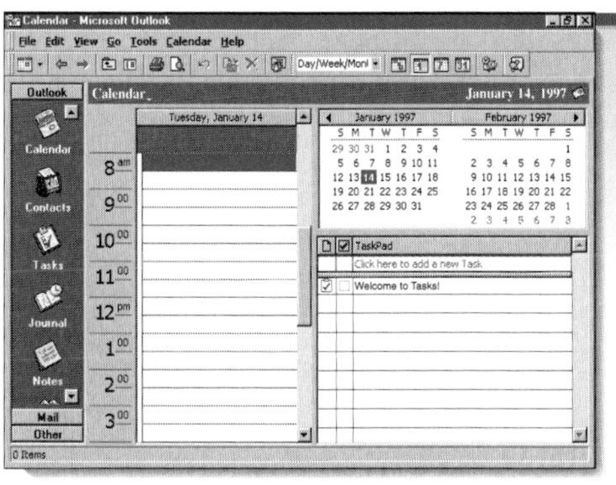

OUTLOOK

Outlook is an information management program that helps you organize messages, appointments, contacts, tasks and activities.

USING THE MOUSE

A mouse is a hand-held device that lets you select and move items on your screen.

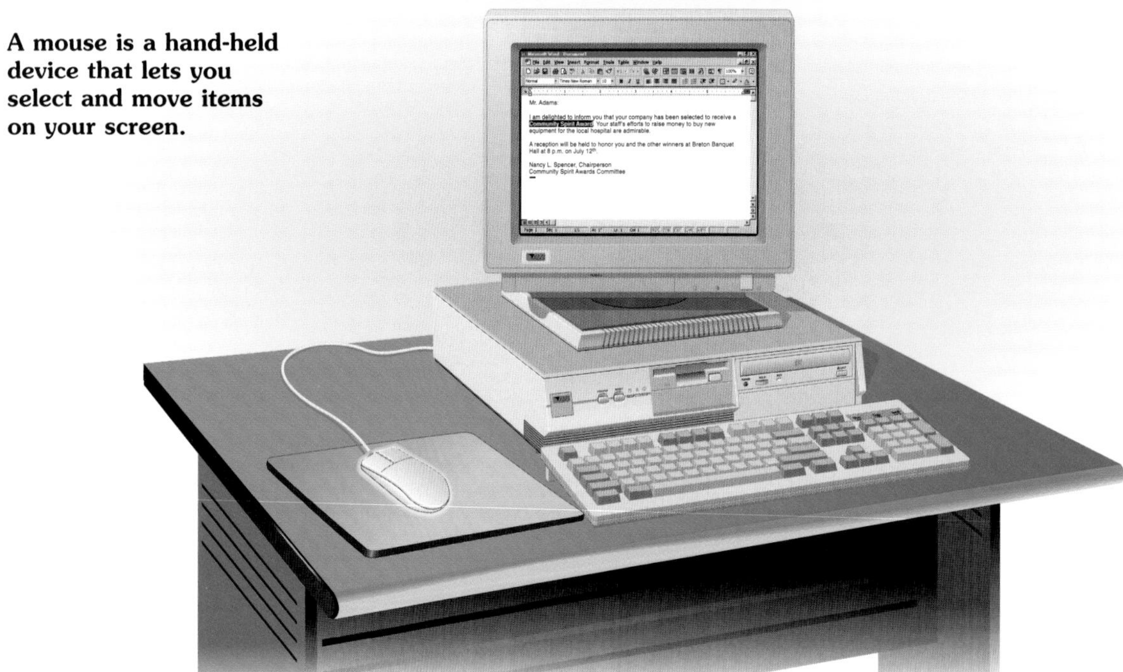

Mr. Adams:
I am delighted to inform you that your company has been selected to receive a Community Spirit Award. Your staff's efforts to raise money to buy new equipment for the local hospital are admirable.
A reception will be held to honor you and the other winners at Breton Banquet Hall at 8 p.m. on July 12th.
Nancy L. Spencer, Chairperson
Community Spirit Awards Committee

Holding the Mouse

Resting your hand on the mouse, use your thumb and two rightmost fingers to move the mouse on your desk. Use your two remaining fingers to press the mouse buttons.

Moving the Mouse

When you move the mouse on your desk, the mouse pointer on the screen moves in the same direction.

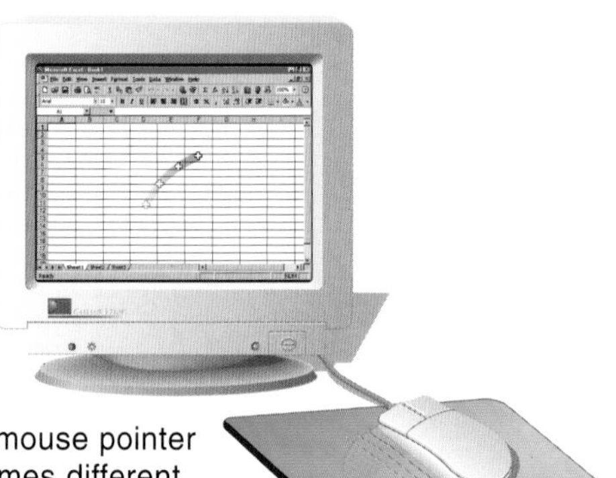

The mouse pointer assumes different shapes (examples: , or), depending on its location on the screen and the task you are performing.

Cleaning the Mouse

A ball under the mouse senses movement. You should occasionally remove and clean this ball to ensure smooth motion of the mouse.

MOUSE ACTIONS

Click

Press and release the left mouse button.

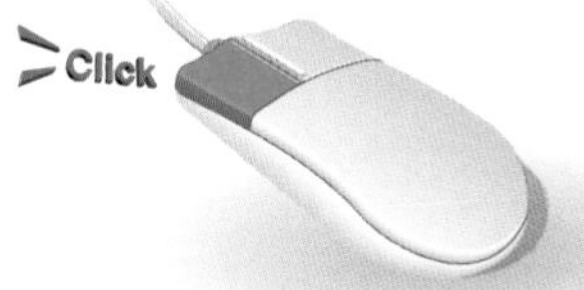

Double-Click

Quickly press and release the left mouse button twice.

Drag

Position the mouse pointer ( ) over an object on your screen and then press and hold down the left mouse button. Still holding down the mouse button, move the mouse to where you want to place the object and then release the mouse button.

MICROSOFT INTELLIMOUSE

The new Microsoft IntelliMouse has a wheel between the left and right mouse buttons. Moving this wheel lets you quickly scroll through information on the screen.

You can also zoom in or out with the Microsoft IntelliMouse by holding down Ctrl on your keyboard as you move the wheel.

START A PROGRAM

You can easily start a Microsoft Office program to create a letter, analyze finances, design a presentation or manage information.

START A PROGRAM

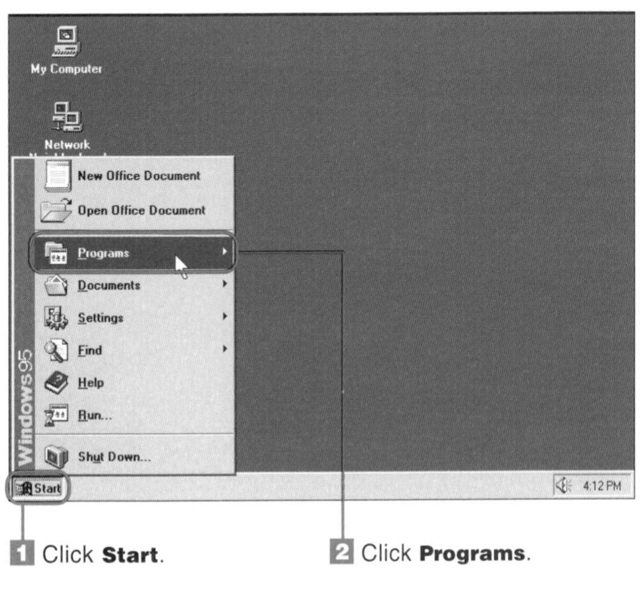

1 Click **Start**.

2 Click **Programs**.

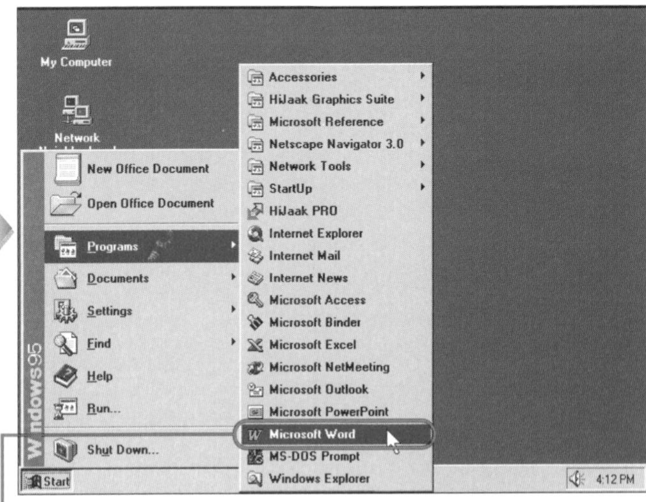

3 Click the program you want to start.

What is the difference between a toolbar and a menu bar?

Each button on a toolbar provides a fast method of selecting a command on a menu. For example, you can use the **Save** button to quickly select the **Save** command.

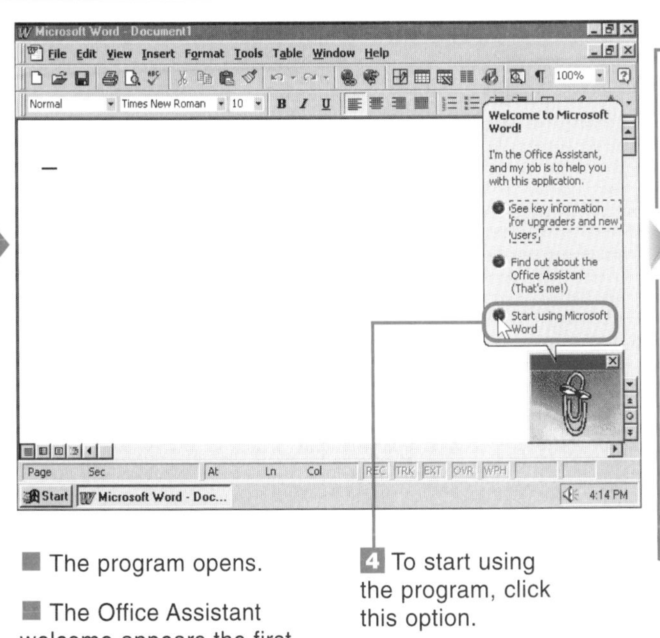

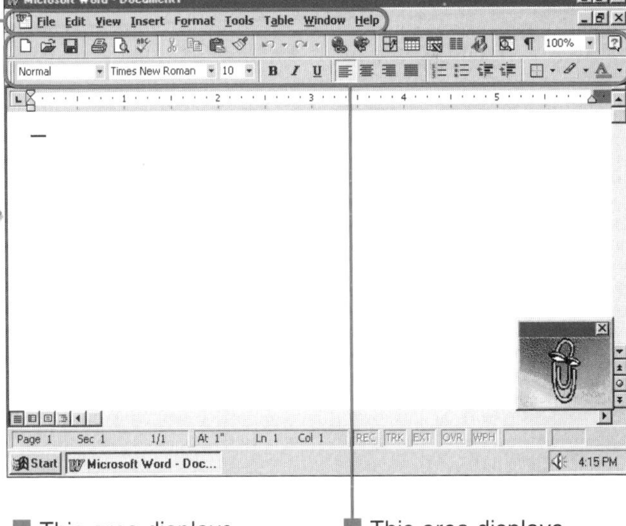

- The program opens.
- The Office Assistant welcome appears the first time you start a program. For information on the Office Assistant, refer to page 12.

4 To start using the program, click this option.

- This area displays a menu bar that lets you select commands to perform tasks.
- This area displays toolbars that let you quickly select common commands.

SWITCH BETWEEN PROGRAMS

You can have more than one program open at a time. You can easily switch between the open programs.

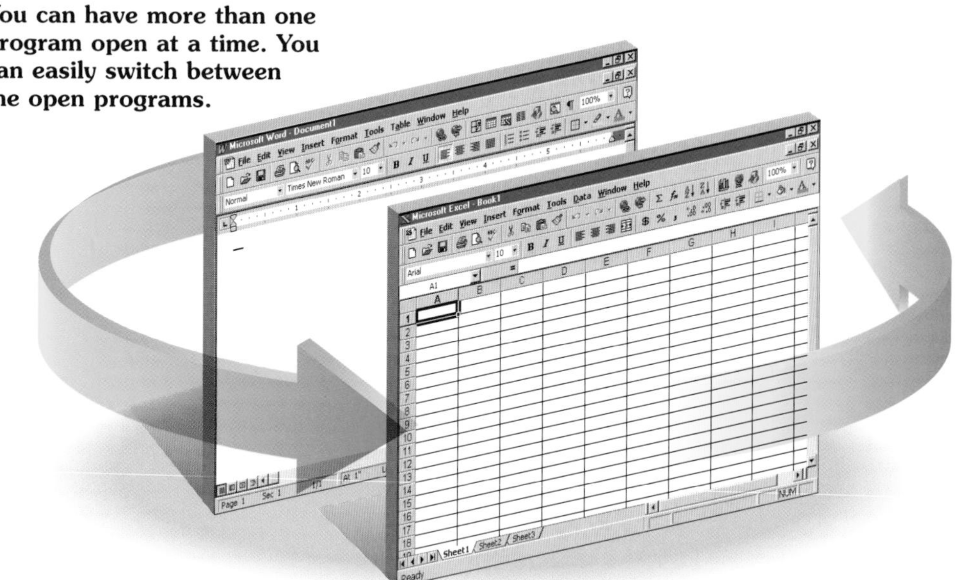

Think of each program as a separate piece of paper. Switching between programs lets you place a different piece of paper at the top of the pile.

SWITCH BETWEEN PROGRAMS

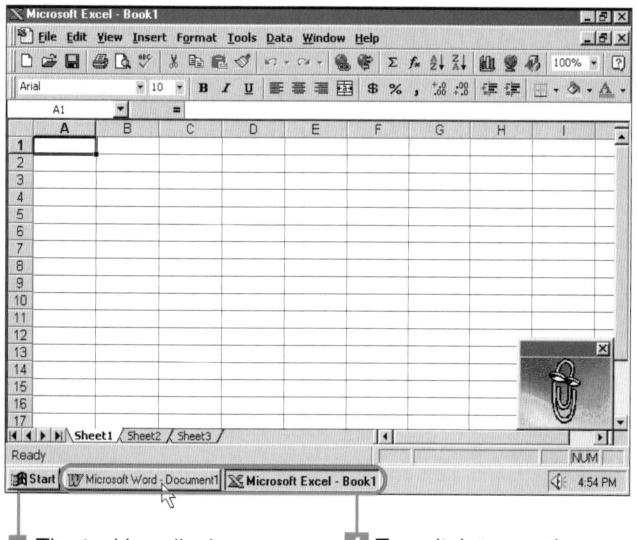

The taskbar displays the name of each program you have opened.

Note: To start a program, refer to page 8.

1 To switch to another program, click the name of the program.

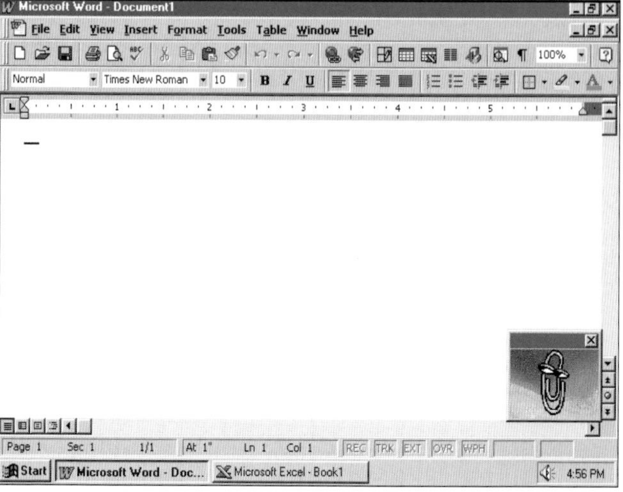

The program you selected appears on top of all other open programs.

EXIT A PROGRAM

When you finish using a program, exit the program.

You should always exit all programs before turning off your computer.

EXIT A PROGRAM

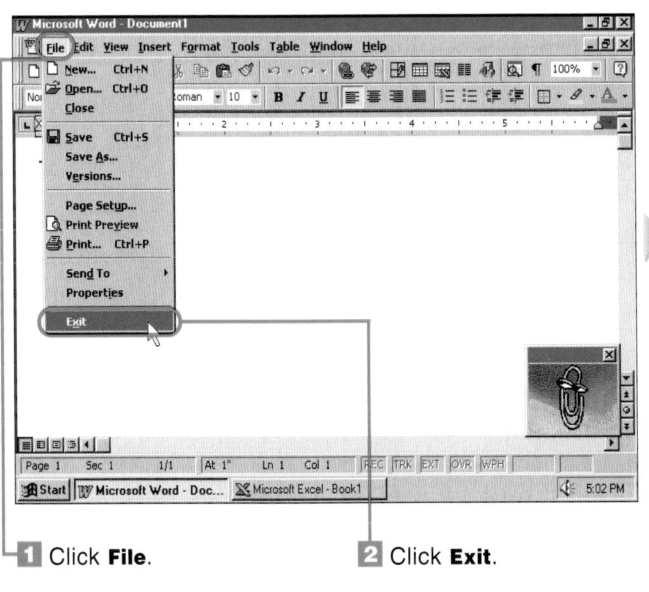

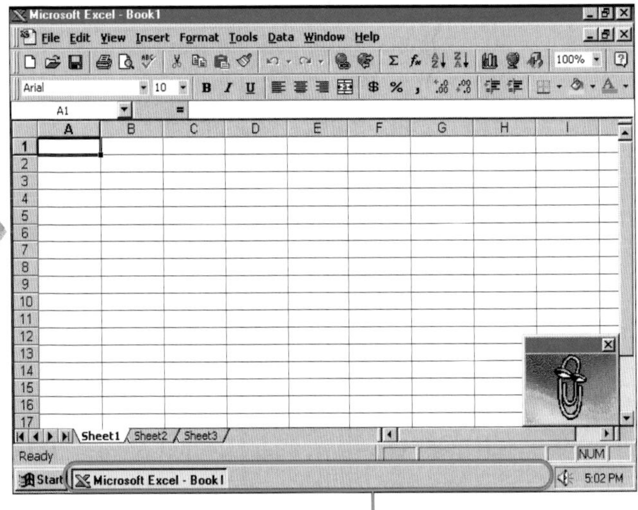

1 Click **File**.

2 Click **Exit**.

■ The program disappears from the screen.

■ The name of the program disappears from the taskbar.

GETTING HELP

If you do not know how to perform a task you can ask the Office Assistant for help.

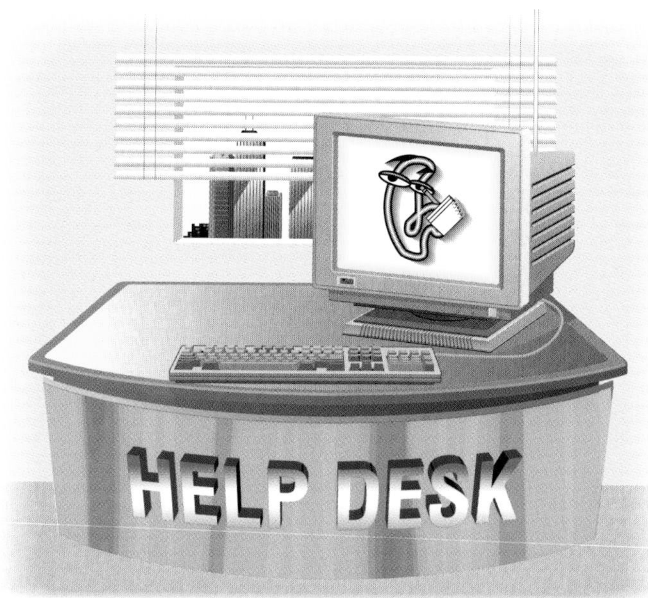

GETTING HELP

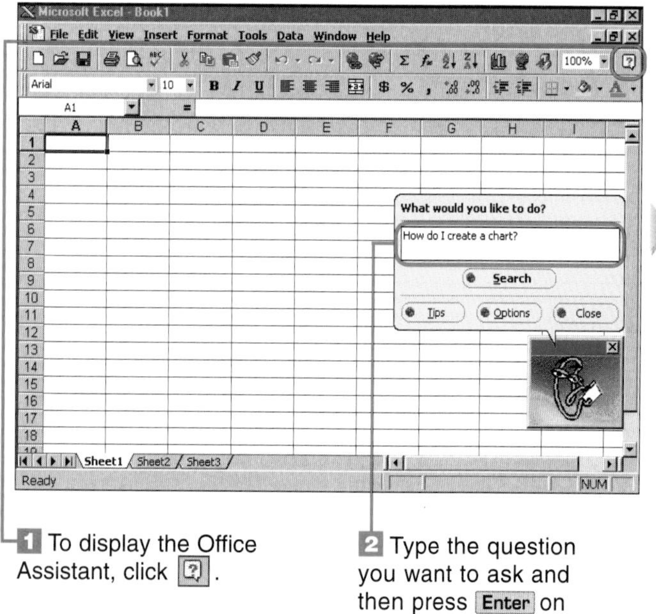

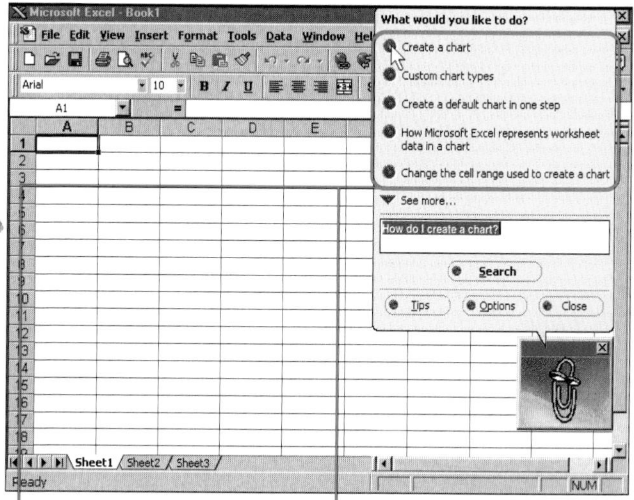

1 To display the Office Assistant, click [?].

2 Type the question you want to ask and then press Enter on your keyboard.

■ The Office Assistant displays a list of help topics that relate to the question you asked.

Note: If you do not see a help topic of interest, try rephrasing your question. Type the new question and then press Enter *on your keyboard.*

3 Click the help topic you want information on.

?

How do I display the name of each toolbar button?

To display the name of a toolbar button, position the mouse over the button. After a few seconds, the name of the button appears.

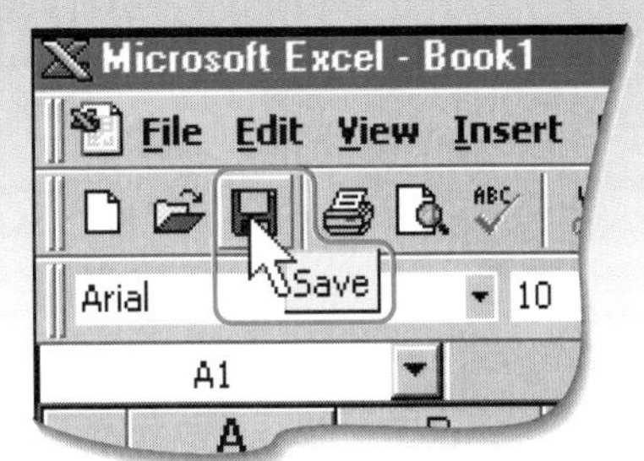

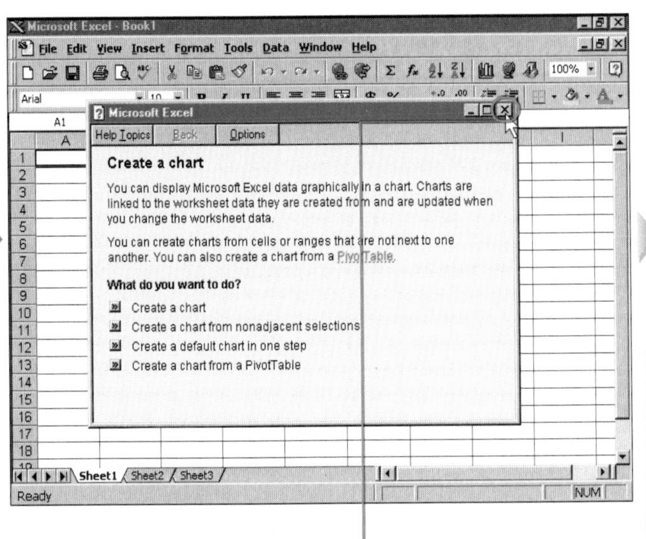

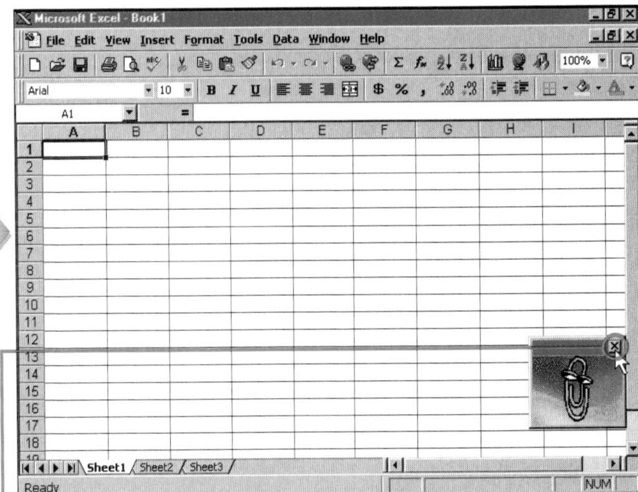

■ The Help window appears, displaying information about the topic you selected.

4 When you finish reading the information, click ☒ to close the Help window.

5 To hide the Office Assistant, click ☒.

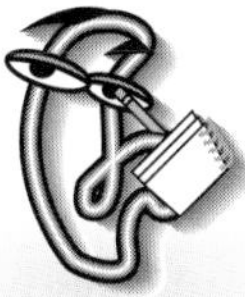

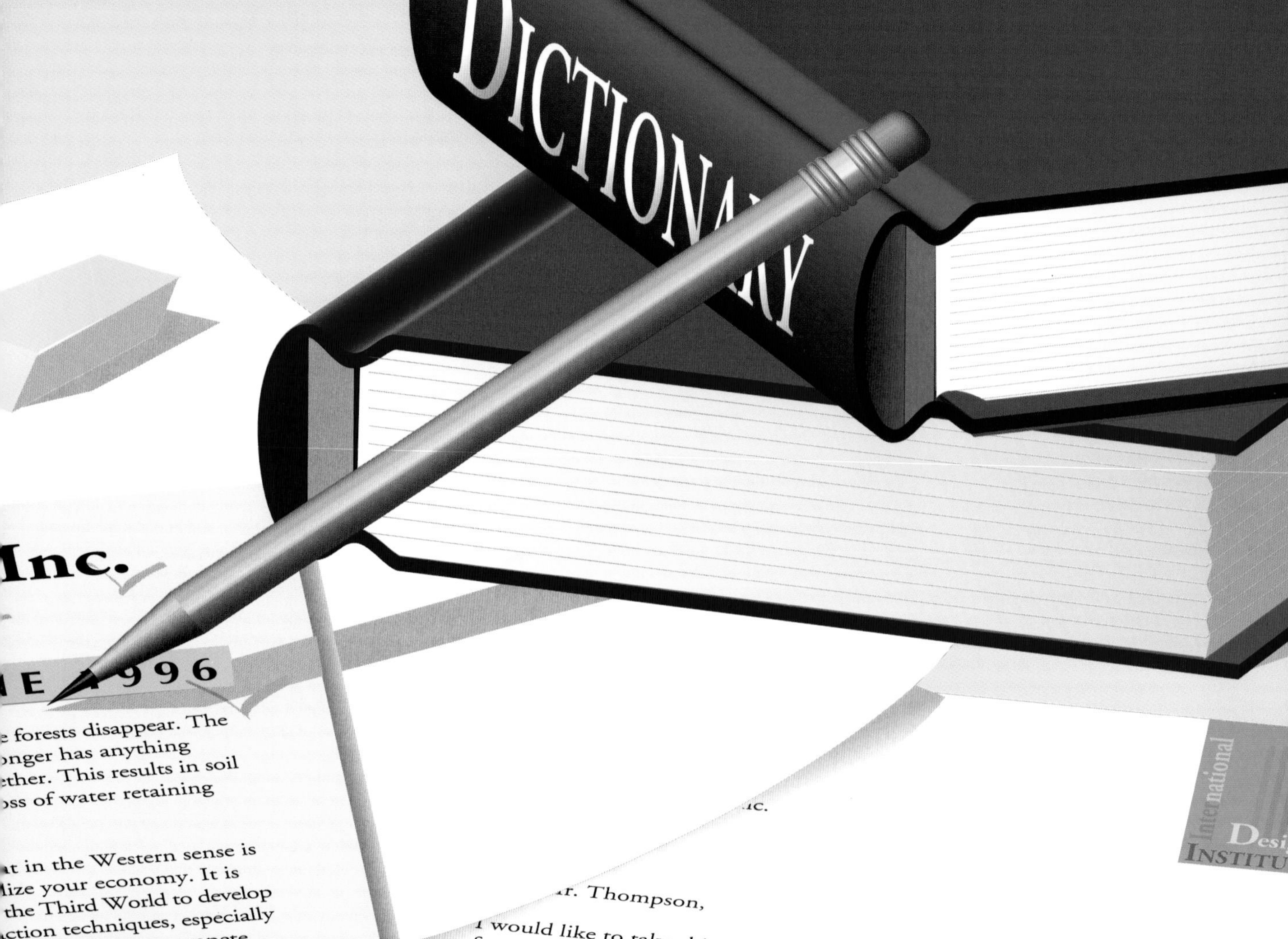

DICTIONARY
Inc.
996
forests disappear. The
onger has anything
ether. This results in soil
oss of water retaining
t in the Western sense is
lize your economy. It is
the Third World to develop
ction techniques, especially
ure, in order to compete
on the World Markets. This
velopment, however, requires
costly machinery, but
fossil fuels for operation.
International Design Institute
r. Thompson,
I would like to take this opportunity to congratulate you and your company
for winning First Prize in the 1996 Logo Design Contest. It gives me the
greatest pleasure to inform you that the Judging Committee's decision was
unanimous. Your entry was clearly the best among the hundreds of
outstanding entries we received this year.
Enclosed please find a copy of the Judging C
states that "the logo designed by Dynami
the company's image through the creative use of colors and modern design
principles."
The award will be presented on August 20 at the International Design
nstitute's annual banquet. We hope to see you there.
nce again, please accept my congratulations.
erely,
Karen Davis
Chairperson

Word

Includes:

1 Getting Started
This chapter introduces you to the Word screen and teaches you the basic skills needed to use Word, from starting the program to moving through your document.

2 Save, Print and Open a Document
Word allows you to save your document, preview your document before printing, create a new document and move between your open documents.

3 Change Document Display
You can change the appearance of your Word screen to make viewing and working on your documents easier.

4 Edit a Document
This chapter teaches you fast and easy ways to edit the text in your document.

5 Format Text
Word offers many features that allow you to emphasize information and enhance the appearance of text in your document.

6 Format Pages
There are many ways you can format the pages of your document, including adding page numbers, changing margins and centering text on a page.

7 Working with Tables
You can create and format a table to neatly display information in your document.

Word allows you to produce professional documents quickly and efficiently.

You can use Word to create letters, reports, manuals, newsletters and brochures.

Editing

Word offers many features that help you work with text in a document. You can easily edit text, rearrange paragraphs and check for spelling mistakes.

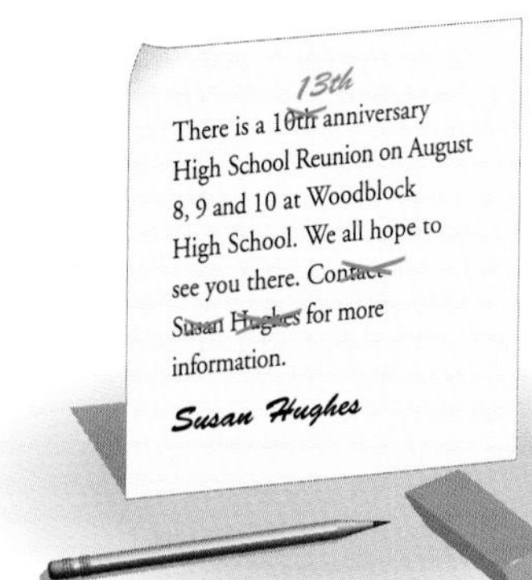

There is a ~~10th~~ 13th anniversary High School Reunion on August 8, 9 and 10 at Woodblock High School. We all hope to see you there. ~~Contact~~ ~~Susan Hughes~~ for more information.

Susan Hughes

Formatting

Word offers many features that help you to change the appearance of a document. You can add page numbers, center text and use various fonts in a document.

Save the World Inc.

NEWSLETTER - JUNE 1997

Seventy-five percent of the World's people live in the Third World. These nations supply the developed nations with a multitude of raw materials and natural resources, and also buy many of our exports, (40% of U.S. exports are bought by the Third World). Clearly the lives of the people in the developed and underdeveloped worlds are unavoidably interrelated. It is for this reason that it is important for the rich nations to study the problems in other countries and help them to overcome them. One major problem in most underdeveloped countries (UDC), is that since the Colonial period, exploitation of their arable land has rapidly increased. Companies from the developed countries (DC) are blamed for abusing the land, but the farmers and locals are often guilty as well. 75% of the energy supplied in the UDC's is produced by wood burning. To get this wood they must tear down trees, and eventually whole forests disappear. The land then no longer has anything holding it together. This results in soil erosion and loss of water retaining abilities.

Development in the Western sense is to industrialize your economy. It is essential for the Third World to develop their production techniques, especially in agriculture, in order to compete effectively on the World Markets. This kind of development, however, requires not only costly machinery, but expensive fossil fuels for operation.

1

Printing

You can produce a paper copy of a Word document. Word lets you see on the screen exactly what the printed document will look like.

START WORD

When you start Word, a blank document appears. You can type text into this document.

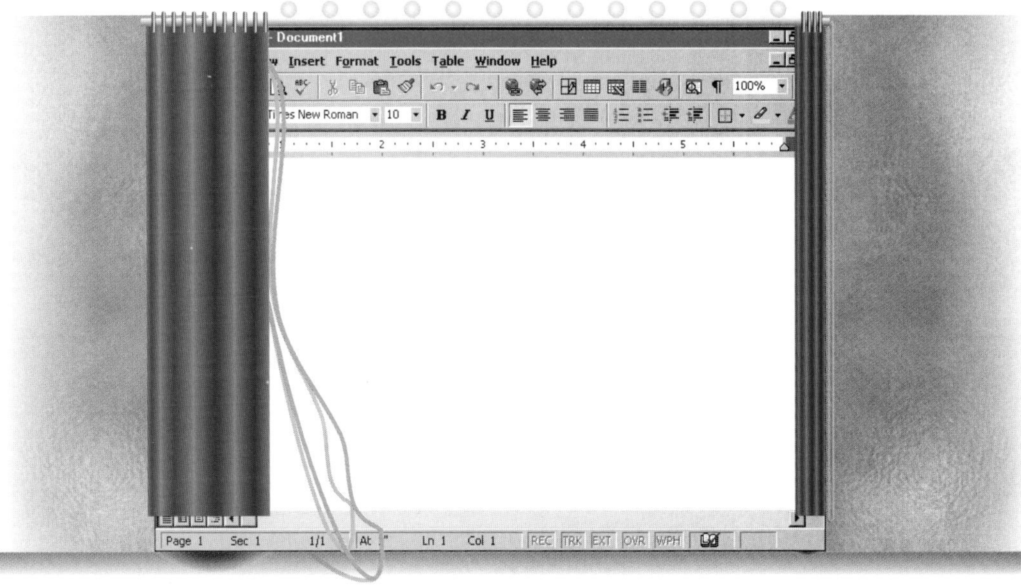

START WORD

1 Click **Start**.

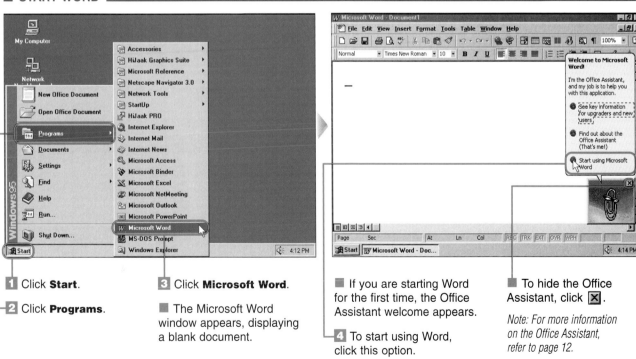

2 Click **Programs**.

3 Click **Microsoft Word**.

■ The Microsoft Word window appears, displaying a blank document.

■ If you are starting Word for the first time, the Office Assistant welcome appears.

4 To start using Word, click this option.

■ To hide the Office Assistant, click ☒.

Note: For more information on the Office Assistant, refer to page 12.

ENTER TEXT

Word lets you type text into your document quickly and easily.

ENTER TEXT

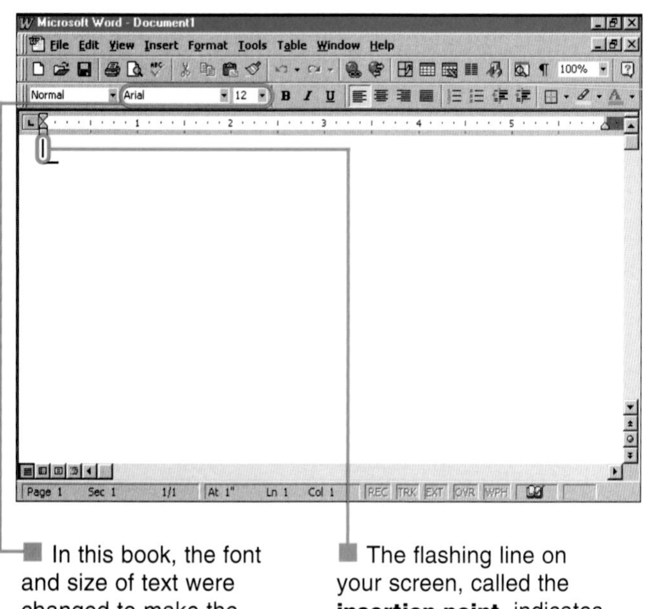

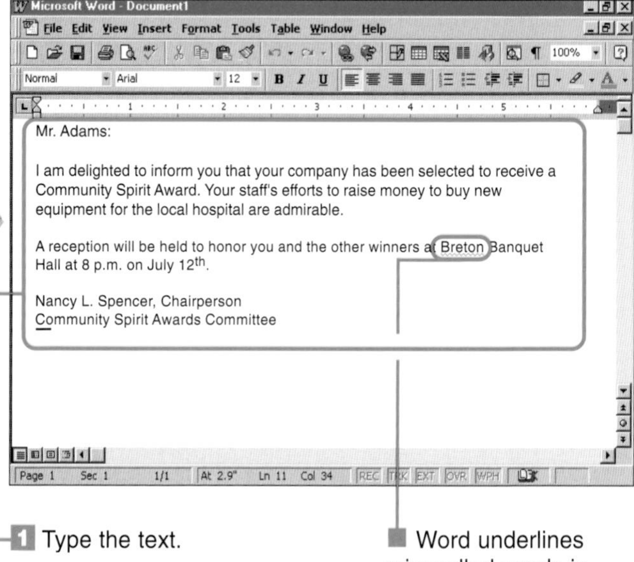

■ In this book, the font and size of text were changed to make the document easier to read. To change the font and size of text, refer to pages 62 and 63.

■ The flashing line on your screen, called the **insertion point**, indicates where the text you type will appear.

1 Type the text.

■ When you reach the end of a line, Word automatically wraps the text to the next line. You only need to press Enter when you want to start a new line or paragraph.

■ Word underlines misspelled words in red and grammar mistakes in green.

Note: For information on how to check spelling and grammar, refer to page 56.

THE WORD SCREEN

The Word screen displays several bars to help you perform tasks efficiently.

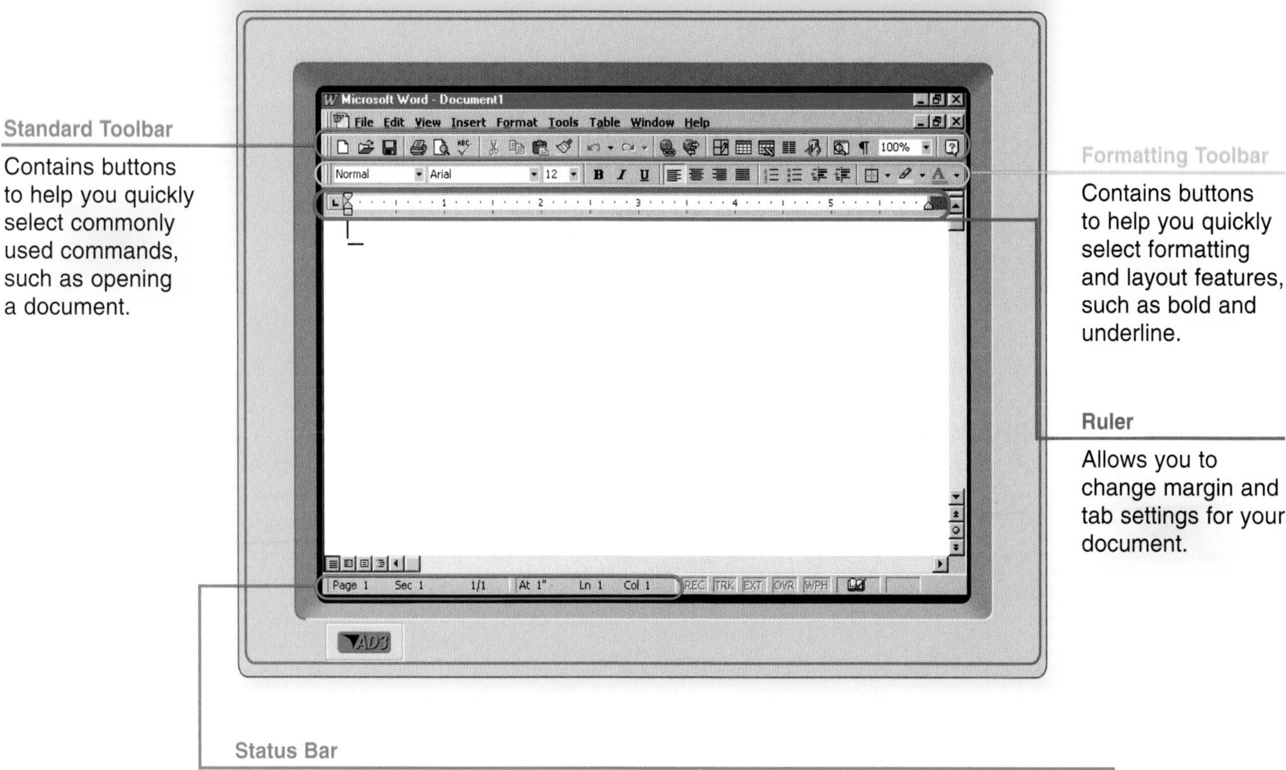

Standard Toolbar

Contains buttons to help you quickly select commonly used commands, such as opening a document.

Formatting Toolbar

Contains buttons to help you quickly select formatting and layout features, such as bold and underline.

Ruler

Allows you to change margin and tab settings for your document.

Status Bar

Displays information about the area of the document displayed on your screen and the position of the insertion point.

Page 1

The page displayed on your screen.

Sec 1

The section of the document displayed on your screen.

1/1

The page displayed on your screen and the total number of pages in the document.

At 1"

The distance from the top of the page to the insertion point.

Ln 1

The number of lines from the top of the page to the insertion point.

Col 1

The number of characters from the left margin to the insertion point, including spaces.

SELECT TEXT

Before performing many tasks in Word, you must select the text you want to work with. Selected text appears highlighted on your screen.

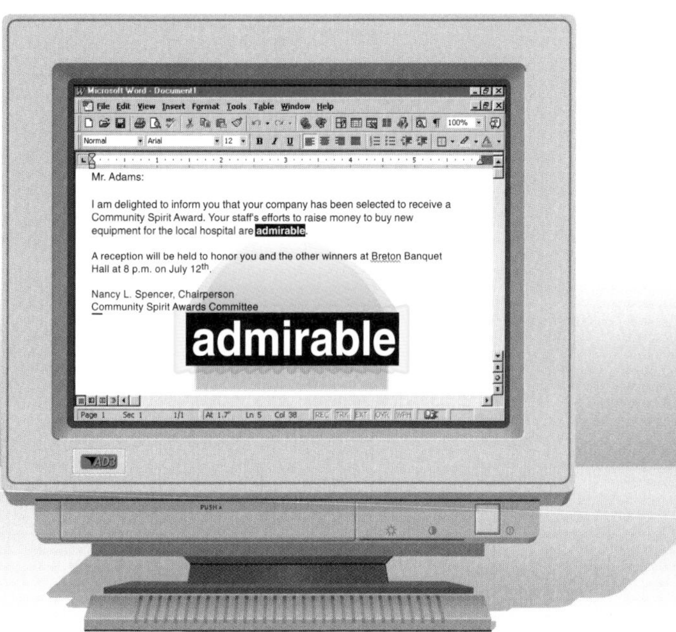
Mr. Adams:
I am delighted to inform you that your company has been selected to receive a Community Spirit Award. Your staff's efforts to raise money to buy new equipment for the local hospital are admirable.
A reception will be held to honor you and the other winners at Breton Banquet Hall at 8 p.m. on July 12th.
Nancy L. Spencer, Chairperson
Community Spirit Awards Committee
admirable

SELECT TEXT

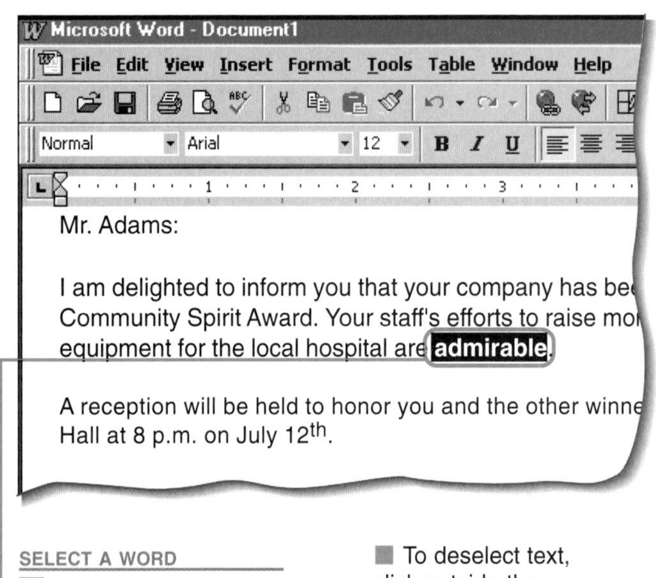
Microsoft Word - Document1
File Edit View Insert Format Tools Table Window Help
Normal
Arial
12
Mr. Adams:
I am delighted to inform you that your company has bee
Community Spirit Award. Your staff's efforts to raise mo
equipment for the local hospital are admirable.
A reception will be held to honor you and the other winne
Hall at 8 p.m. on July 12th.

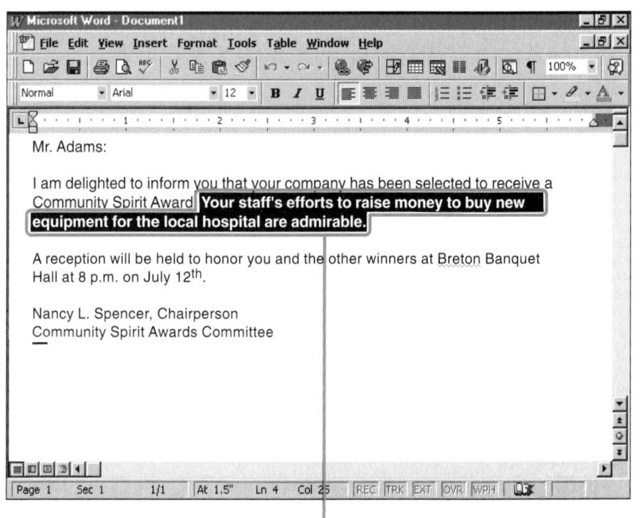
Microsoft Word - Document1
File Edit View Insert Format Tools Table Window Help
Normal
Arial
12
Mr. Adams:
I am delighted to inform you that your company has been selected to receive a
Community Spirit Award. Your staff's efforts to raise money to buy new
equipment for the local hospital are admirable.
A reception will be held to honor you and the other winners at Breton Banquet
Hall at 8 p.m. on July 12th.
Nancy L. Spencer, Chairperson
Community Spirit Awards Committee
Page 1 Sec 1 1/1 At 1.5" Ln 4 Col 25 REC TRK EXT OVR WPH

SELECT A WORD

1 Double-click anywhere over the word you want to select.

■ To deselect text, click outside the selected area.

SELECT A SENTENCE

1 Press and hold down Ctrl on your keyboard.

2 Still holding down Ctrl, click anywhere over the sentence you want to select. Then release Ctrl.

How do I select all the text in a document?

To quickly select all the text in your document, press and hold down Ctrl and then press A on your keyboard. Then release both keys.

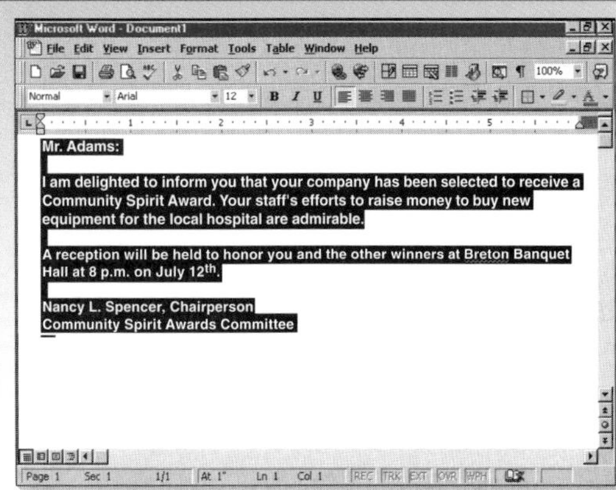

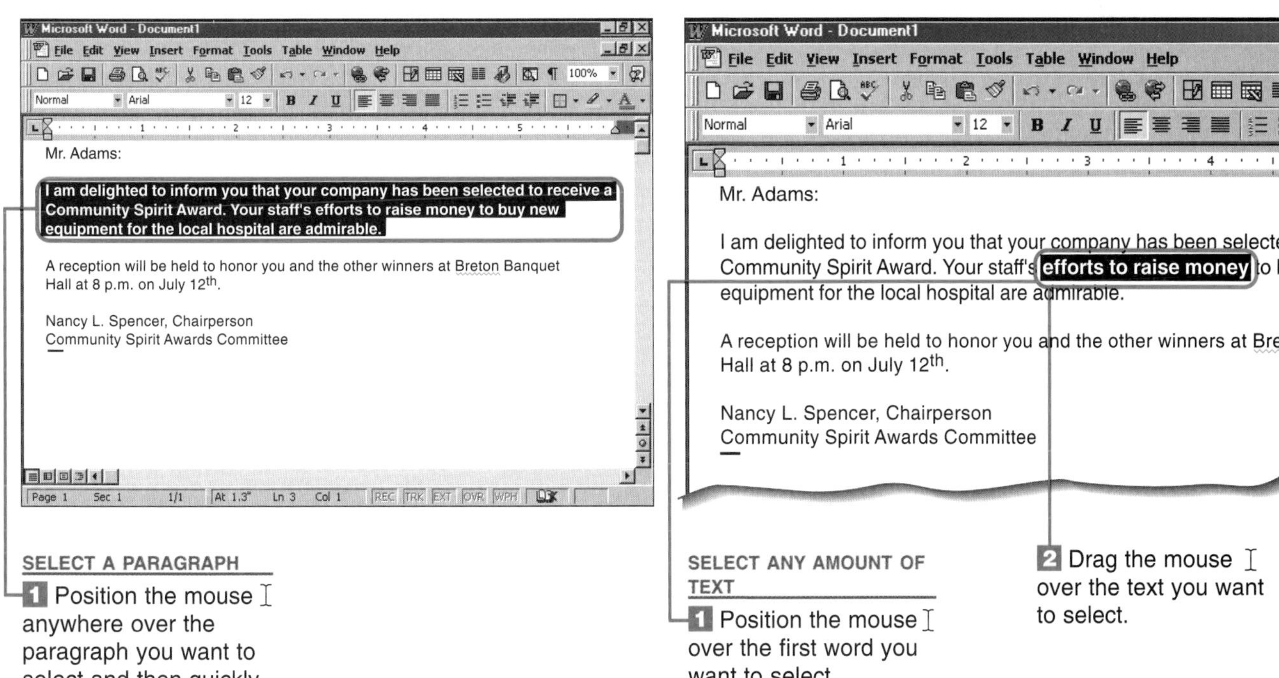

SELECT A PARAGRAPH

1 Position the mouse anywhere over the paragraph you want to select and then quickly click **three** times.

SELECT ANY AMOUNT OF TEXT

1 Position the mouse over the first word you want to select.

2 Drag the mouse over the text you want to select.

MOVE THROUGH A DOCUMENT

You can easily move to another location in your document.

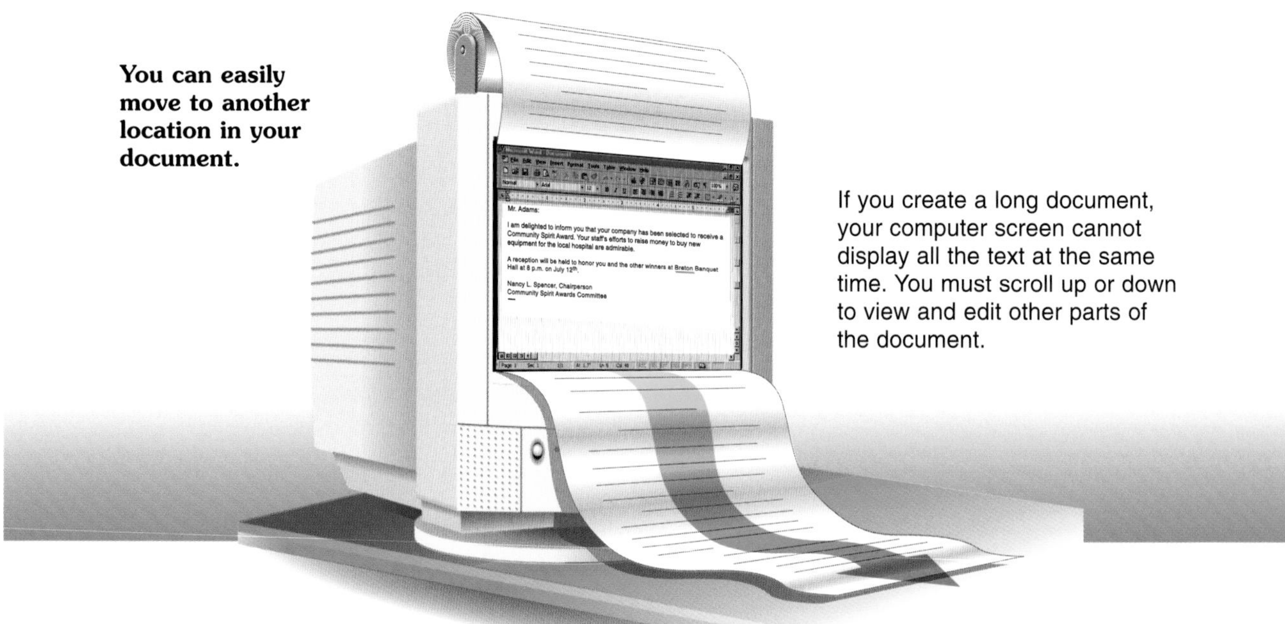

If you create a long document, your computer screen cannot display all the text at the same time. You must scroll up or down to view and edit other parts of the document.

MOVE THE INSERTION POINT

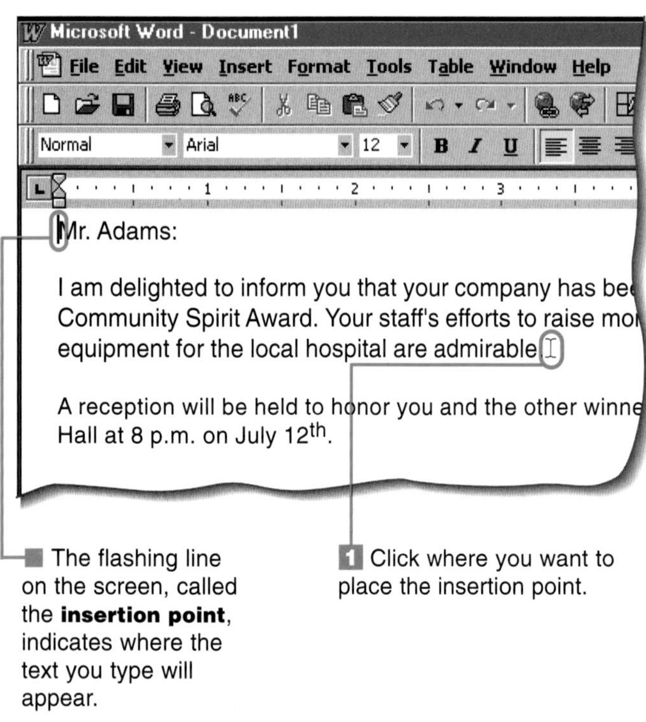

Microsoft Word - Document1
File Edit View Insert Format Tools Table Window Help
Normal
Arial
12
Mr. Adams:
I am delighted to inform you that your company has bee
Community Spirit Award. Your staff's efforts to raise mo
equipment for the local hospital are admirable
A reception will be held to honor you and the other winne
Hall at 8 p.m. on July 12th.

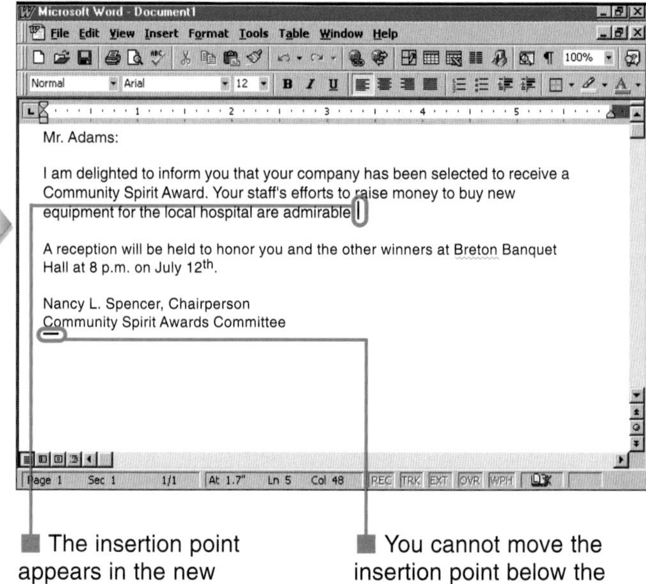

Microsoft Word - Document1
File Edit View Insert Format Tools Table Window Help
Normal
Arial
12
100%
Mr. Adams:
I am delighted to inform you that your company has been selected to receive a
Community Spirit Award. Your staff's efforts to raise money to buy new
equipment for the local hospital are admirable
A reception will be held to honor you and the other winners at Breton Banquet
Hall at 8 p.m. on July 12th.
Nancy L. Spencer, Chairperson
Community Spirit Awards Committee
Page 1 Sec 1 1/1 At 1.7" Ln 5 Col 48 REC TRK EXT OVR WPH

■ The flashing line on the screen, called the **insertion point**, indicates where the text you type will appear.

1 Click where you want to place the insertion point.

■ The insertion point appears in the new position.

Note: You can also press ↑, ↓, ← *or* → *on your keyboard to move the insertion point one line or character in any direction.*

■ You cannot move the insertion point below the horizontal line displayed on the screen. To move this line, position the insertion point after the last character in the document and then press Enter several times.

? How do I use the new Microsoft IntelliMouse to scroll?

The Microsoft IntelliMouse has a wheel between the left and right mouse buttons. Moving this wheel lets you quickly scroll through a document.

SCROLL UP OR DOWN

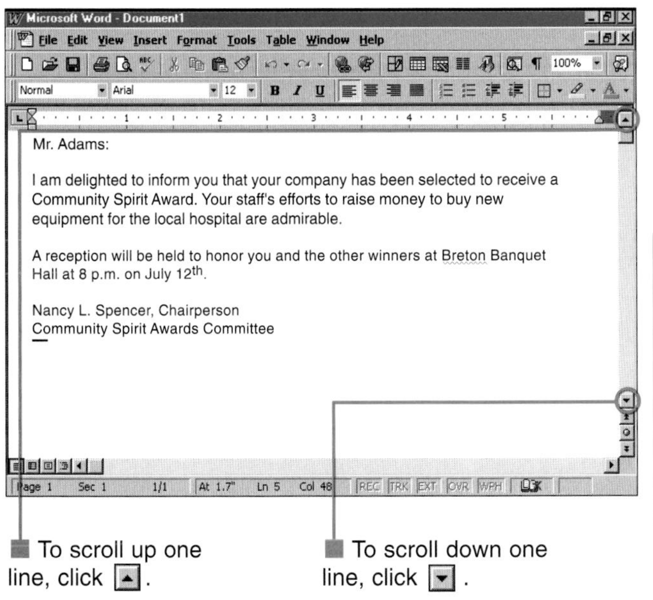

■ To scroll up one line, click ▲.

■ To scroll down one line, click ▼.

SCROLL TO ANY POSITION

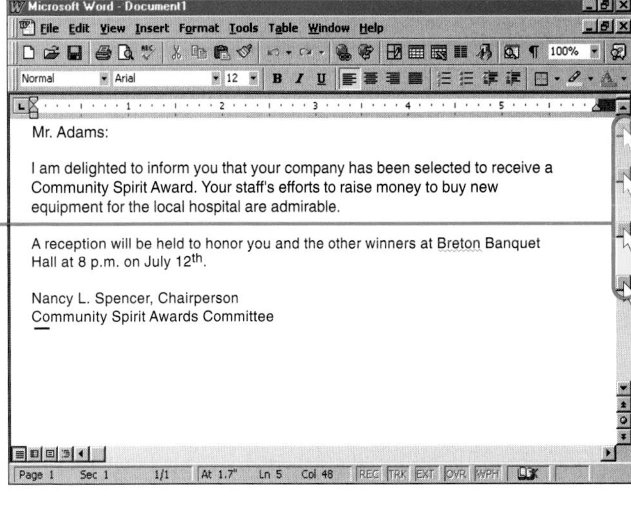

1 To quickly scroll through the document, drag the scroll box □ up or down the scroll bar.

■ The location of the scroll box indicates which part of the document you are viewing. To view the middle of the document, drag the scroll box halfway down the scroll bar.

SAVE A DOCUMENT

You should save your document to store it for future use. This allows you to later retrieve the document for reviewing or editing.

SAVE A DOCUMENT

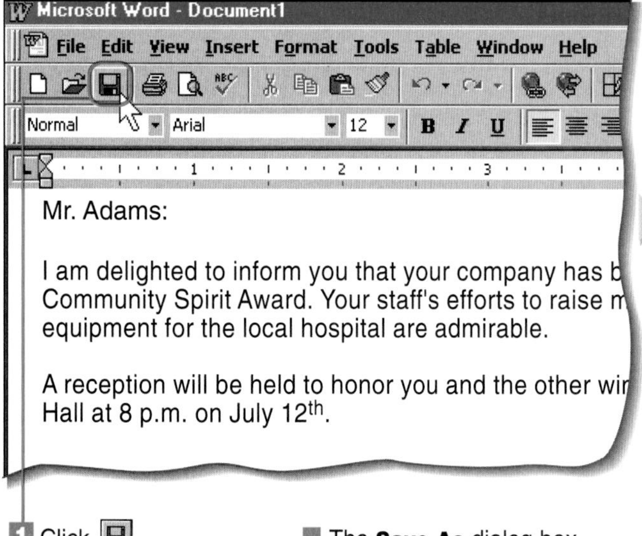

1 Click .

■ The **Save As** dialog box appears.

*Note: If you previously saved the document, the **Save As** dialog box will not appear since you have already named the document.*

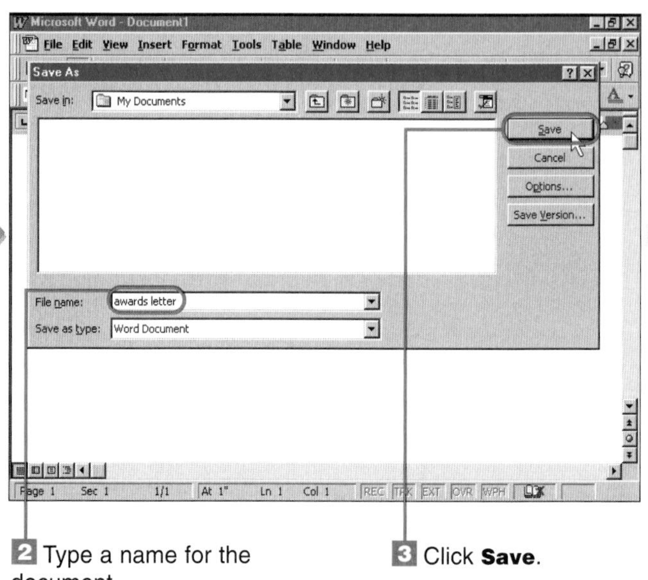

2 Type a name for the document.

Note: You can use up to 255 characters to name a document.

3 Click **Save**.

Before you make major changes to a document, save the document with a different name. This gives you two copies of the document—the original document and a document with all the changes.

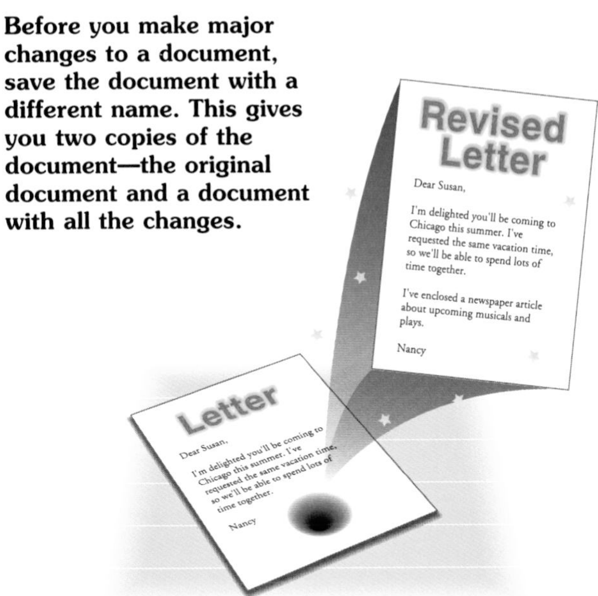

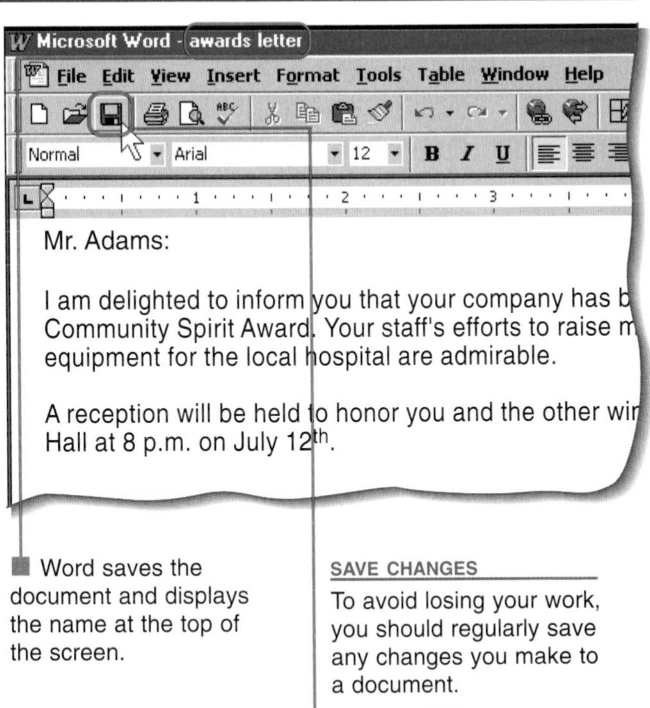

■ Word saves the document and displays the name at the top of the screen.

SAVE CHANGES

To avoid losing your work, you should regularly save any changes you make to a document.

1 Click 💾.

SAVE A DOCUMENT WITH A NEW NAME

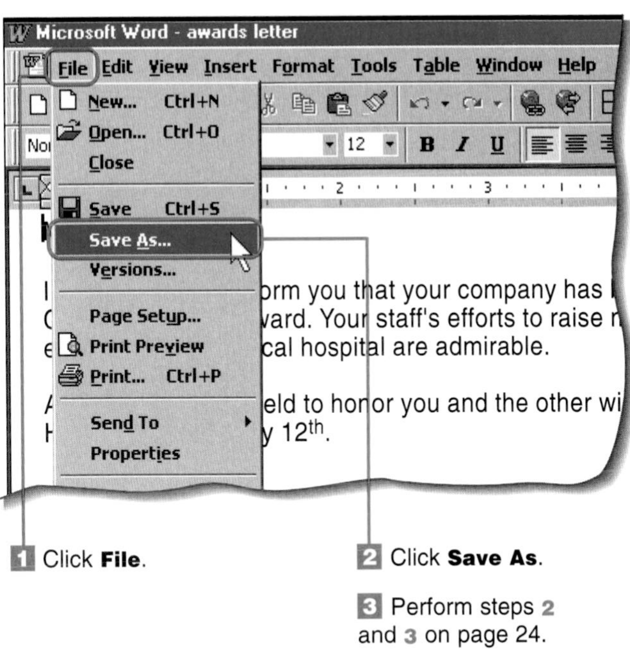

1 Click **File**.

2 Click **Save As**.

3 Perform steps 2 and 3 on page 24.

PREVIEW A DOCUMENT

You can use the Print Preview feature to see how your document will look when printed.

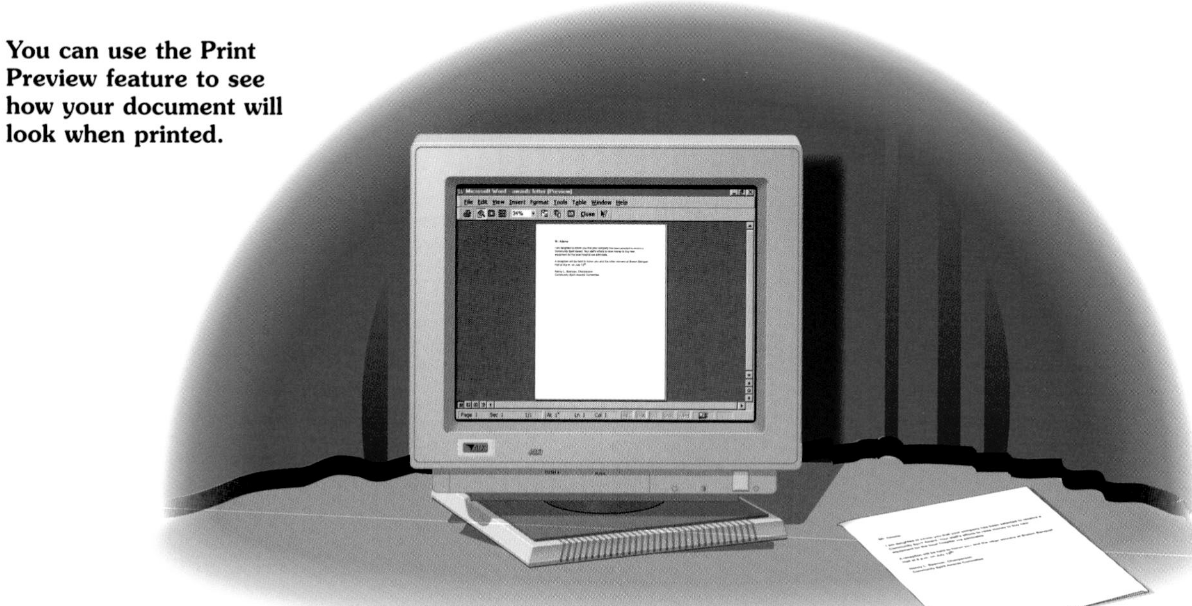

PREVIEW A DOCUMENT

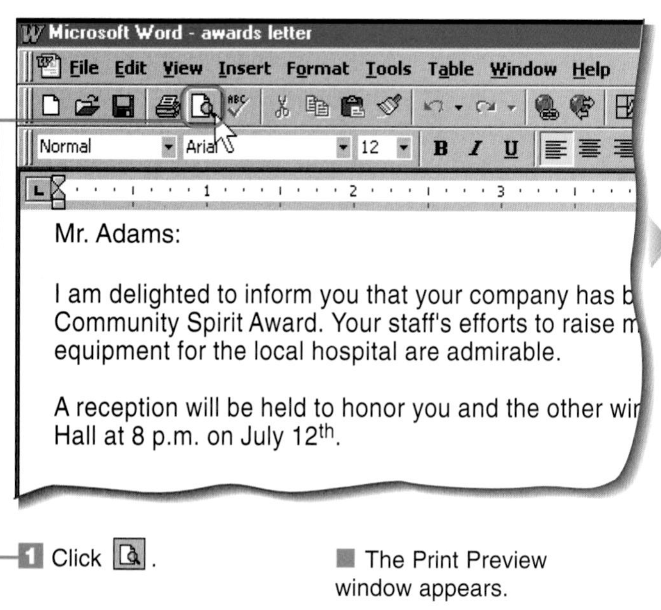

1 Click .

The Print Preview window appears.

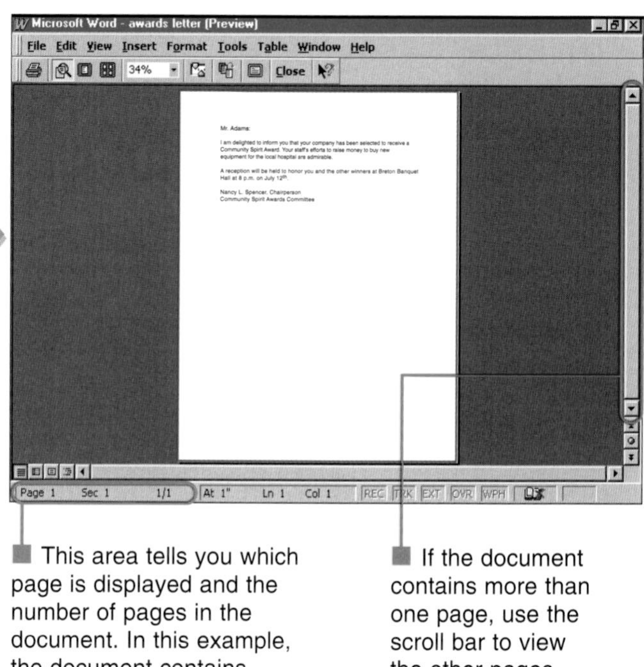

This area tells you which page is displayed and the number of pages in the document. In this example, the document contains one page.

If the document contains more than one page, use the scroll bar to view the other pages.

When can I edit my document in the Print Preview window?

If the mouse looks like I when over your document, you can edit the document.

If the mouse looks like ⊕ or ⊖ when over your document, you can magnify or shrink the page displayed on your screen.

Note: To change the shape of the mouse, perform step 3 below.

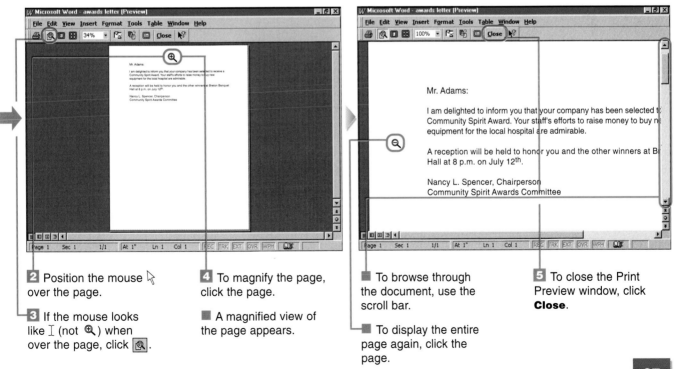

2 Position the mouse over the page.

3 If the mouse looks like I (not ⊕) when over the page, click the Magnifier button.

4 To magnify the page, click the page.

■ A magnified view of the page appears.

■ To browse through the document, use the scroll bar.

■ To display the entire page again, click the page.

5 To close the Print Preview window, click **Close**.

PRINT A DOCUMENT

You can produce a paper copy of the document displayed on your screen.

PRINT A DOCUMENT

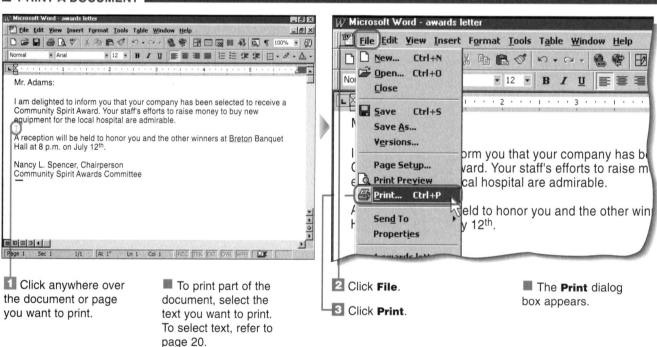

1 Click anywhere over the document or page you want to print.

■ To print part of the document, select the text you want to print. To select text, refer to page 20.

2 Click **File**.

3 Click **Print**.

■ The **Print** dialog box appears.

How do I prepare my printer to print documents?

Before printing, always make sure your printer is turned on and contains paper.

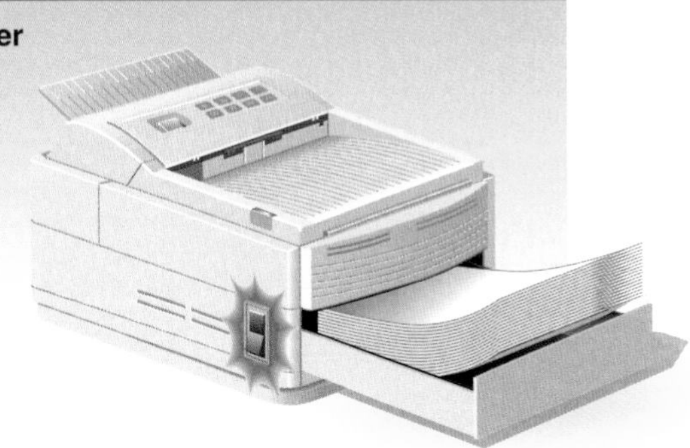

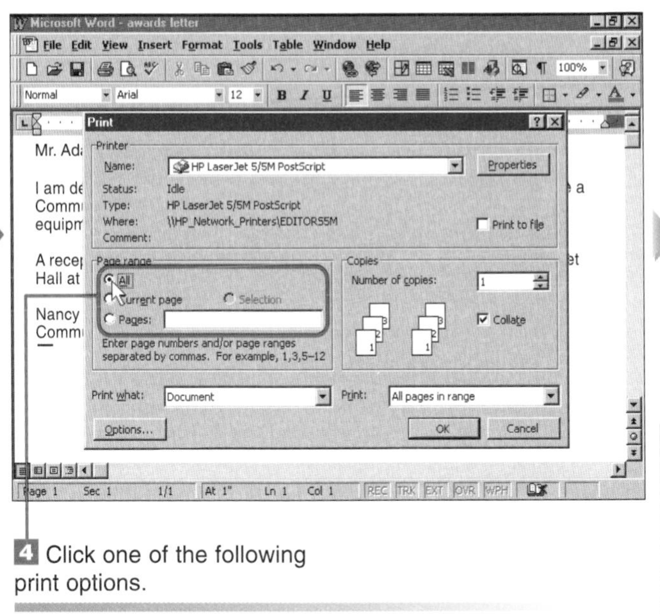

4 Click one of the following print options.

All - Prints every page in the document.

Current page - Prints the page containing the insertion point.

Pages - Prints the pages you specify.

Selection - Prints the text you selected.

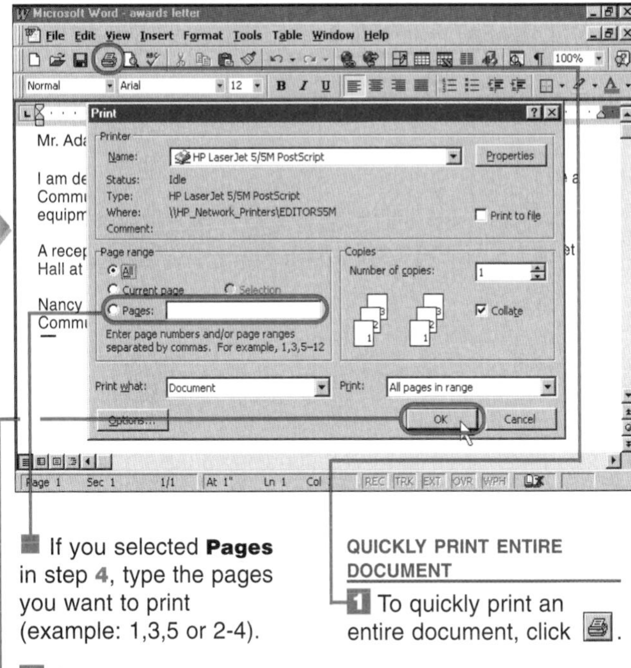

■ If you selected **Pages** in step 4, type the pages you want to print (example: 1,3,5 or 2-4).

5 Click **OK**.

QUICKLY PRINT ENTIRE DOCUMENT

1 To quickly print an entire document, click 🖨.

CREATE A NEW DOCUMENT

You can create a new document to start writing a letter, report or memo.

CREATE A NEW DOCUMENT

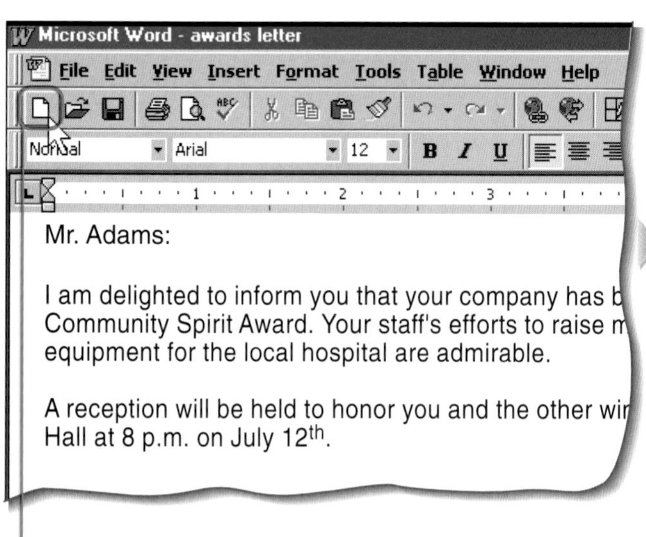

1 Click the New button.

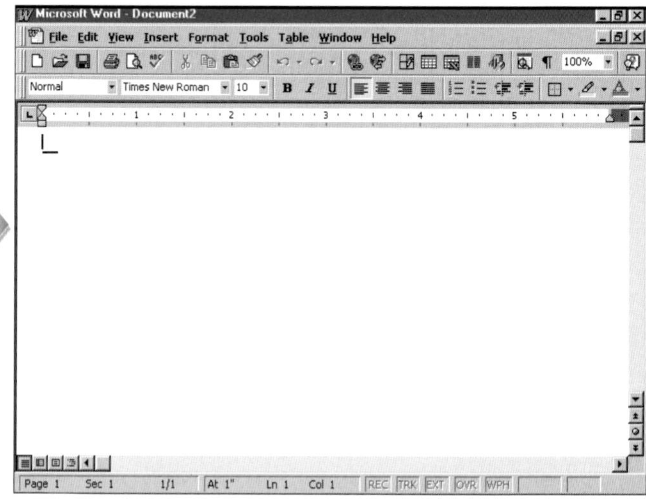

■ A new document appears. The previous document is now hidden behind the new document.

■ Think of each document as a separate piece of paper. When you create a document, you are placing a new piece of paper on the screen.

SWITCH BETWEEN DOCUMENTS

Word lets you have many documents open at once. You can easily switch from one open document to another.

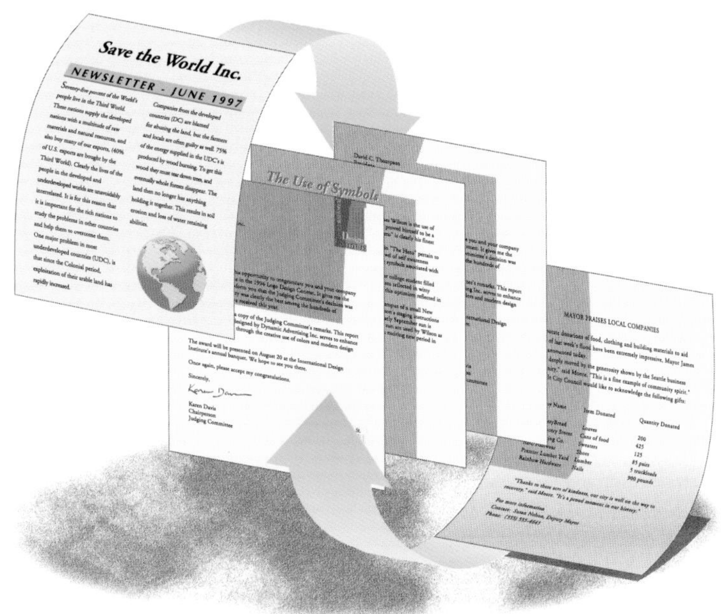

SWITCH BETWEEN DOCUMENTS

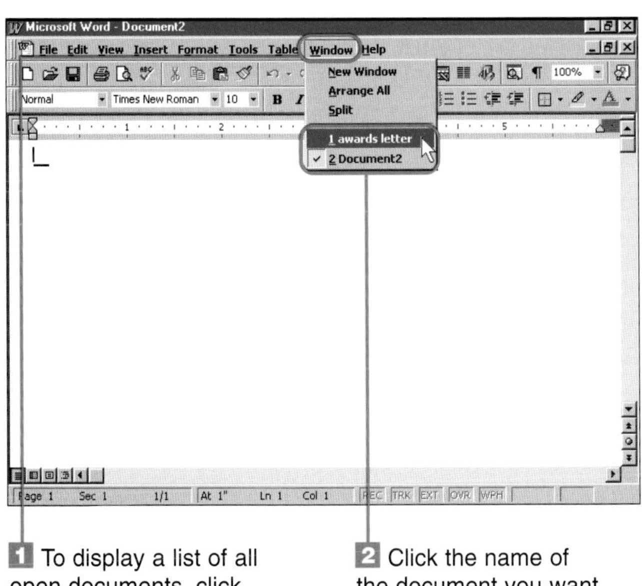

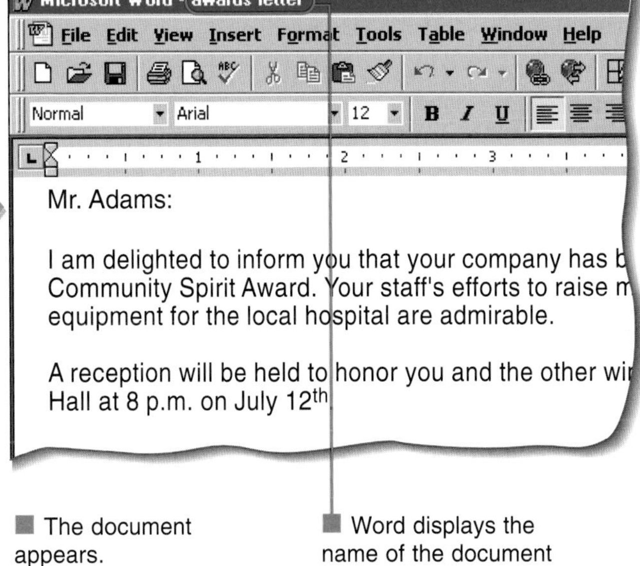
Microsoft Word - awards letter
Mr. Adams:
I am delighted to inform you that your company has b
Community Spirit Award. Your staff's efforts to raise m
equipment for the local hospital are admirable.
A reception will be held to honor you and the other wi
Hall at 8 p.m. on July 12th.

1 To display a list of all open documents, click **Window**.

2 Click the name of the document you want to display.

■ The document appears.

■ Word displays the name of the document at the top of the screen.

CLOSE A DOCUMENT

When you finish working with a document, you can close the document to remove it from your screen.

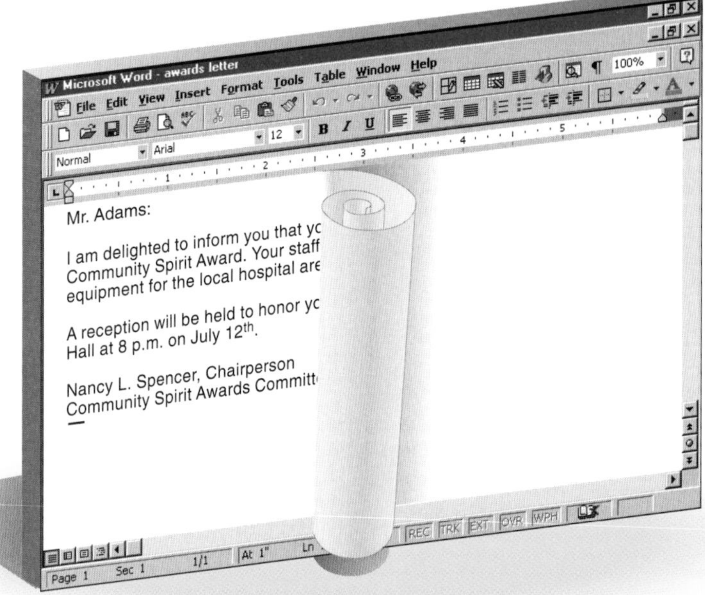

When you close a document, you do not exit the Word program. You can continue to work on other Word documents.

CLOSE A DOCUMENT

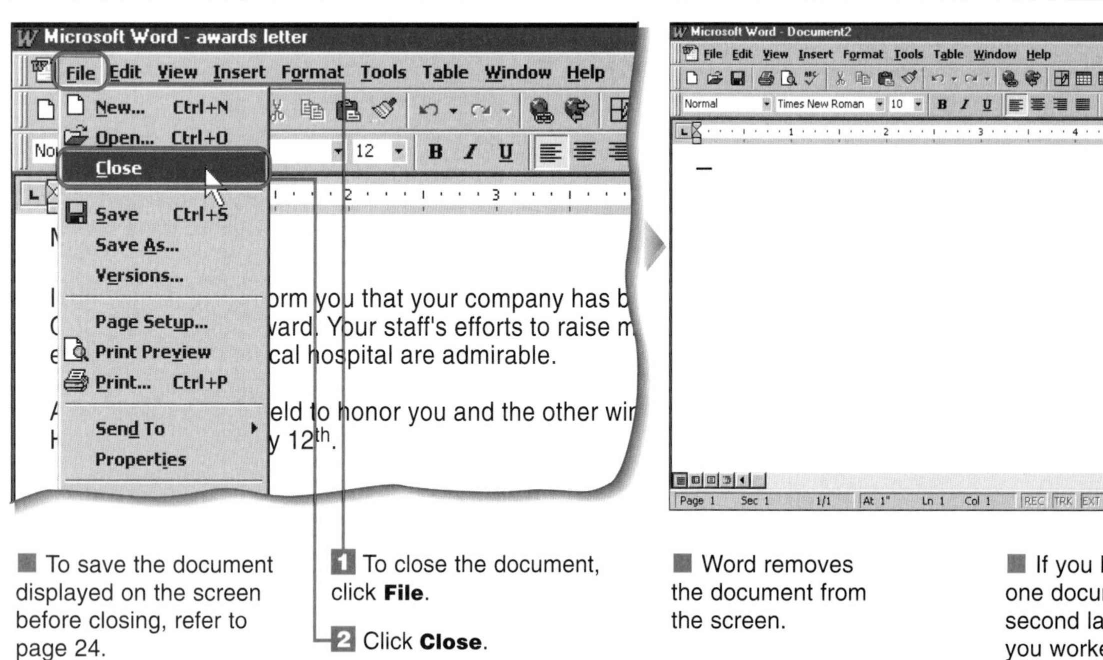

■ To save the document displayed on the screen before closing, refer to page 24.

1 To close the document, click **File**.

2 Click **Close**.

■ Word removes the document from the screen.

■ If you had more than one document open, the second last document you worked on appears on the screen.

EXIT WORD

When you finish using Word, you can exit the program.

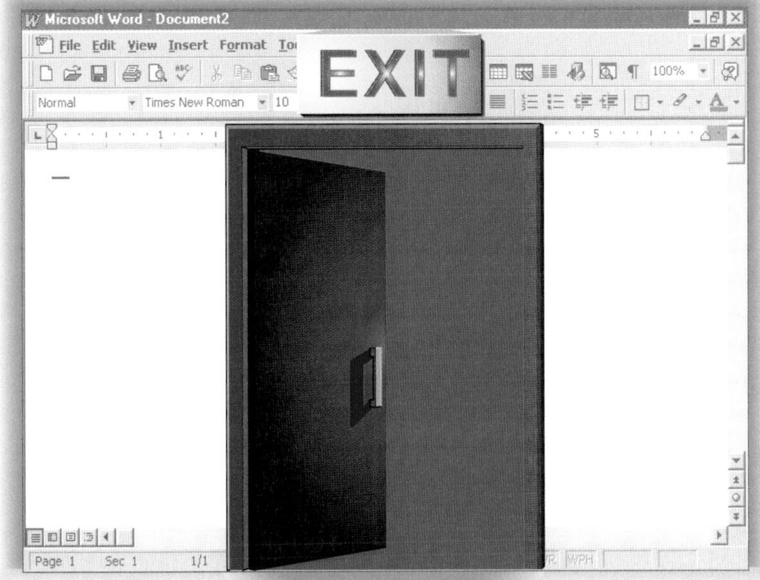

You should always exit all programs before turning off your computer.

EXIT WORD

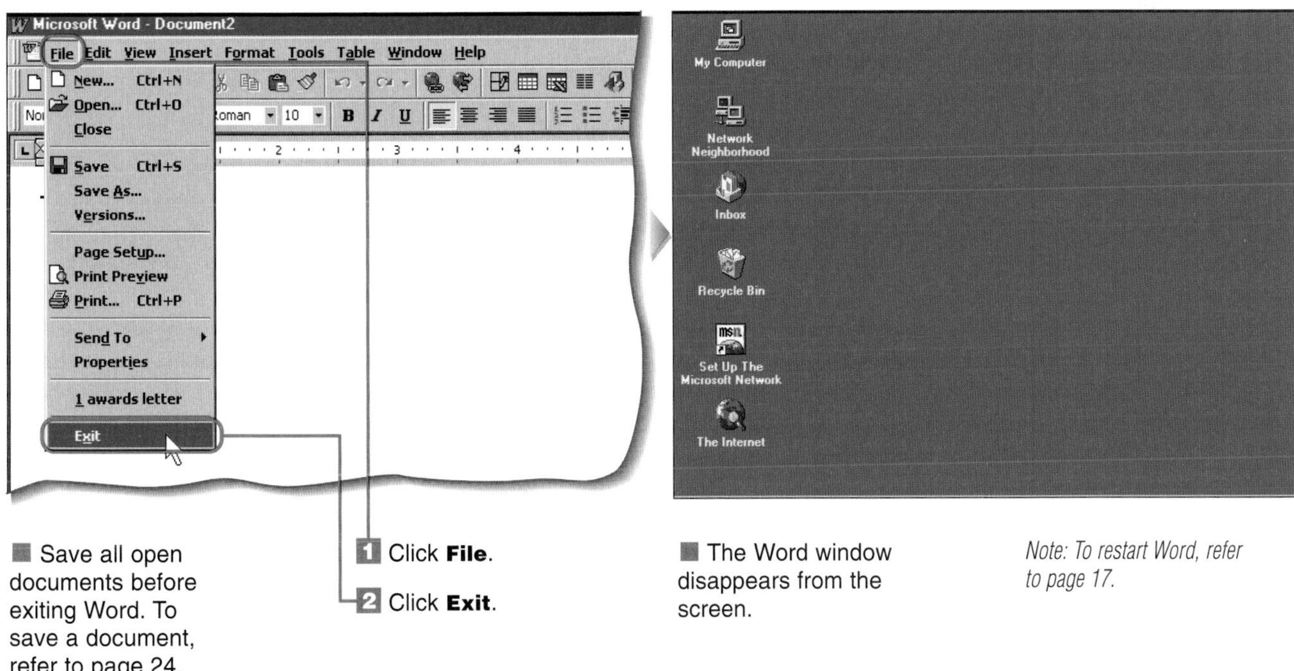

■ Save all open documents before exiting Word. To save a document, refer to page 24.

1 Click **File**.

2 Click **Exit**.

■ The Word window disappears from the screen.

Note: To restart Word, refer to page 17.

OPEN A DOCUMENT

You can open a saved document and display it on your screen. This allows you to review and make changes to your document.

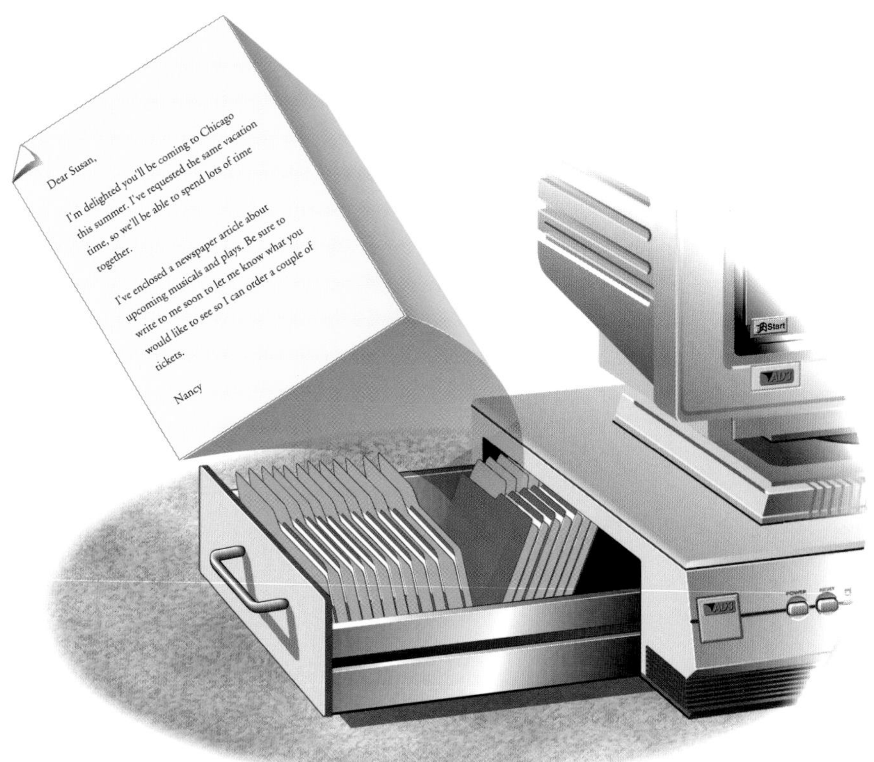

OPEN A DOCUMENT

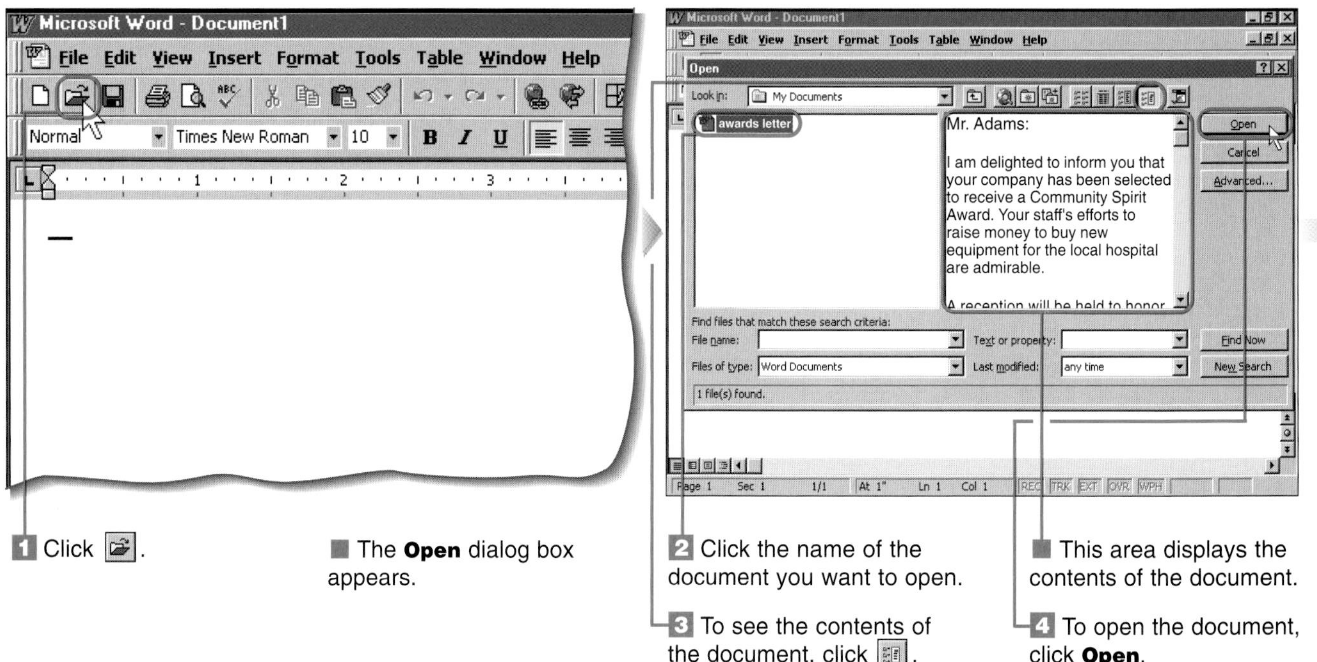

1 Click the Open button.

■ The **Open** dialog box appears.

2 Click the name of the document you want to open.

3 To see the contents of the document, click the Preview button.

■ This area displays the contents of the document.

4 To open the document, click **Open**.

Word remembers the names of the last four documents you worked with. You can quickly open any of these documents.

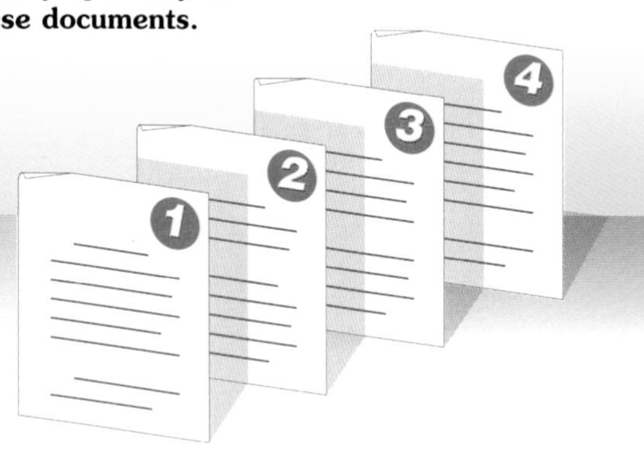

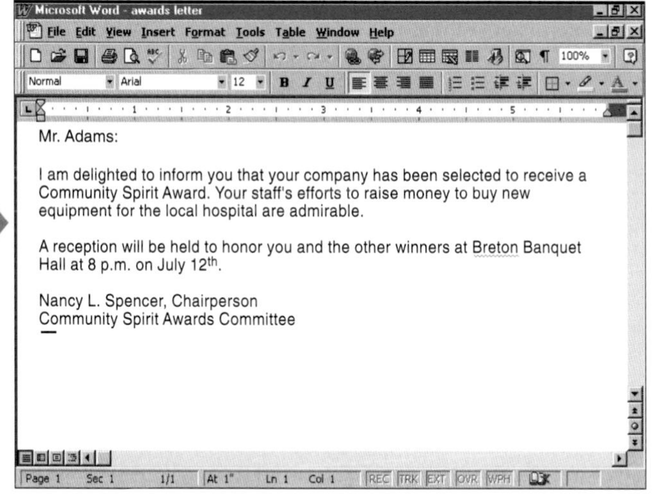

■ Word opens the document and displays it on the screen. You can now review and make changes to the document.

QUICKLY OPEN A DOCUMENT

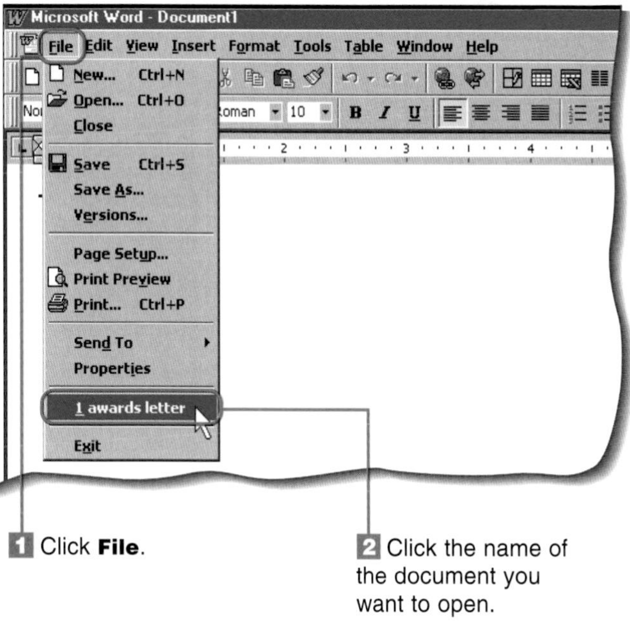

1 Click **File**.

2 Click the name of the document you want to open.

CHANGE THE VIEW

Word offers four different ways to display your document. You can choose the view that best suits your needs.

CHANGE THE VIEW

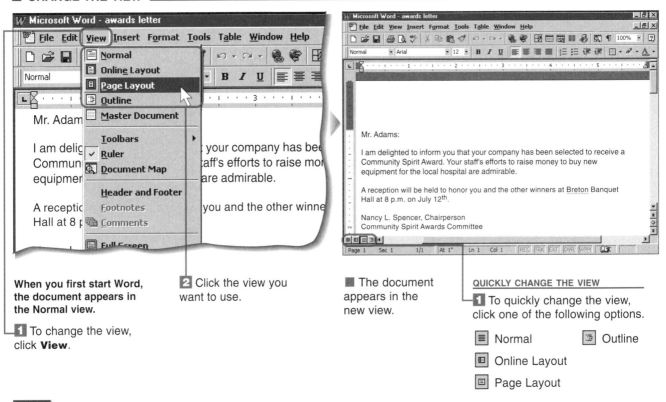

When you first start Word, the document appears in the Normal view.

1 To change the view, click **View**.

2 Click the view you want to use.

■ The document appears in the new view.

QUICKLY CHANGE THE VIEW

1 To quickly change the view, click one of the following options.

- Normal
- Online Layout
- Page Layout
- Outline

THE FOUR VIEWS

Normal View

This view simplifies the document so you can quickly enter, edit and format text. The Normal view does not display top or bottom margins, headers, footers or page numbers.

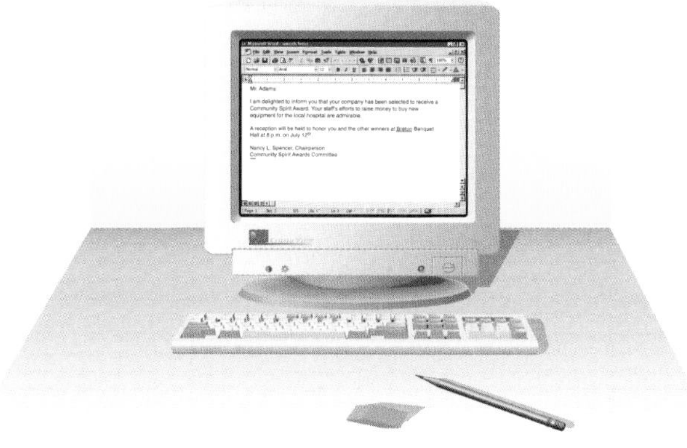

Outline View

This view helps you review and work with the structure of a document. You can focus on the main headings by hiding the remaining text.

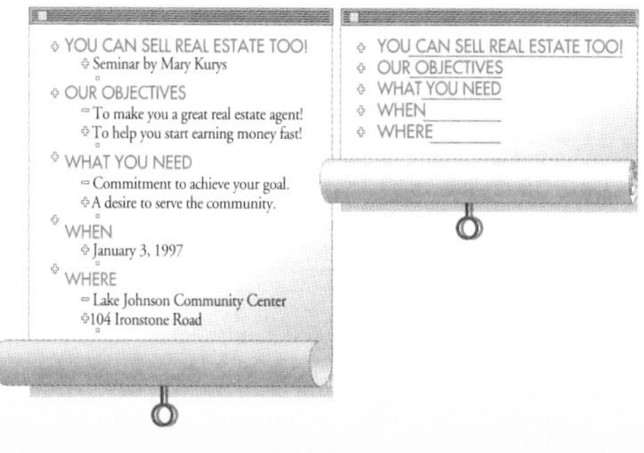

Page Layout View

This view displays the document as it will appear on a printed page. The Page Layout view displays top and bottom margins, headers, footers and page numbers.

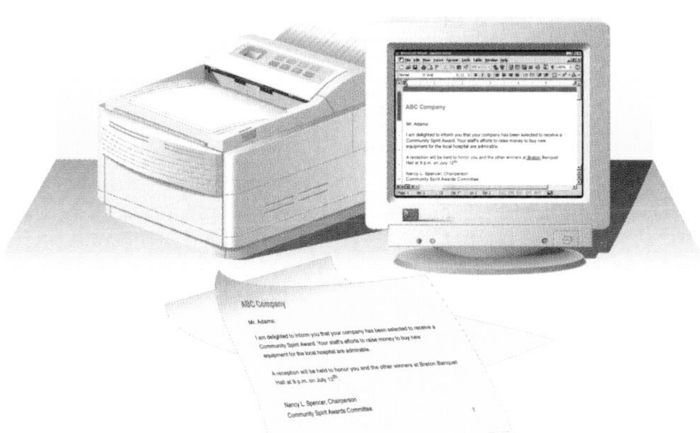

Online Layout View

This view displays documents so they are easy to read on the screen. The Online Layout view displays a document map, which lets you move quickly to specific locations in your document.

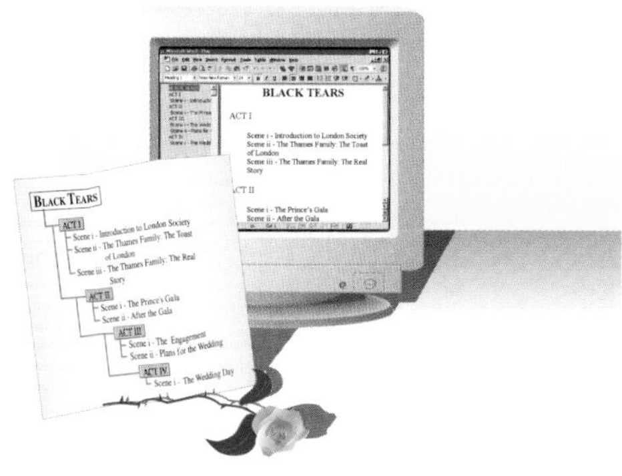

ZOOM IN OR OUT

Word lets you enlarge or reduce the display of text on your screen.

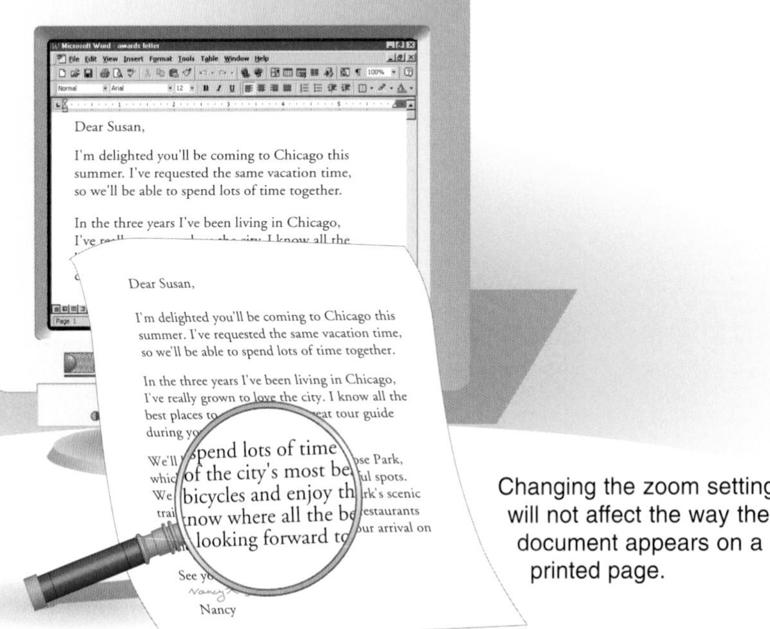

Changing the zoom setting will not affect the way the document appears on a printed page.

ZOOM IN OR OUT

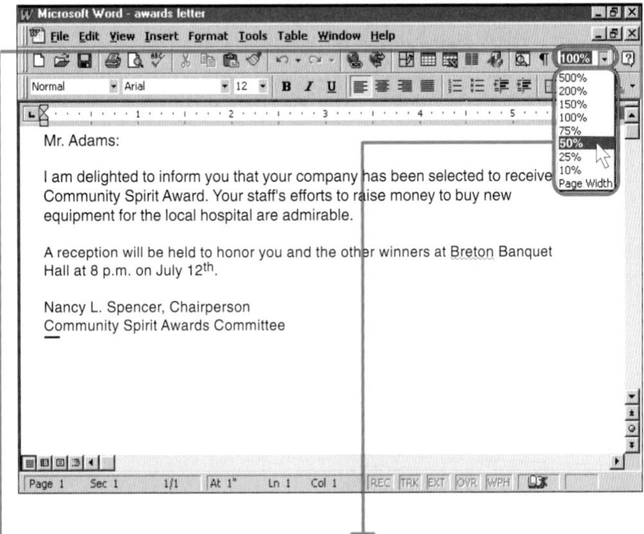

- When you first start Word, the document appears in the 100% zoom setting.

1. To display a list of zoom settings, click ▾ in this area.

2. Click the setting you want to use.

- The document appears in the new zoom setting. You can edit your document as usual.

- To return to the normal zoom setting, repeat steps 1 and 2, selecting **100%** in step 2.

DISPLAY OR HIDE THE RULER

You can use the ruler to position text on a page. You can display or hide the ruler at any time.

When you first start Word, the ruler is displayed on your screen. Hiding the ruler provides a larger and less cluttered working area.

DISPLAY OR HIDE THE RULER

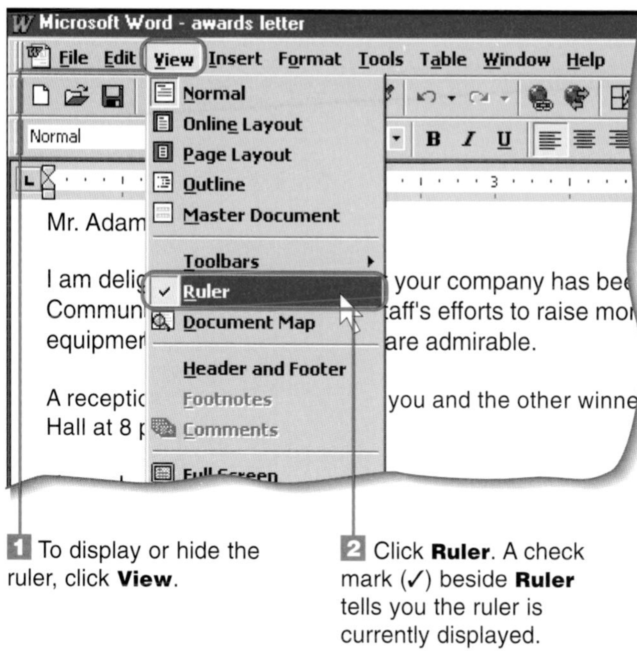

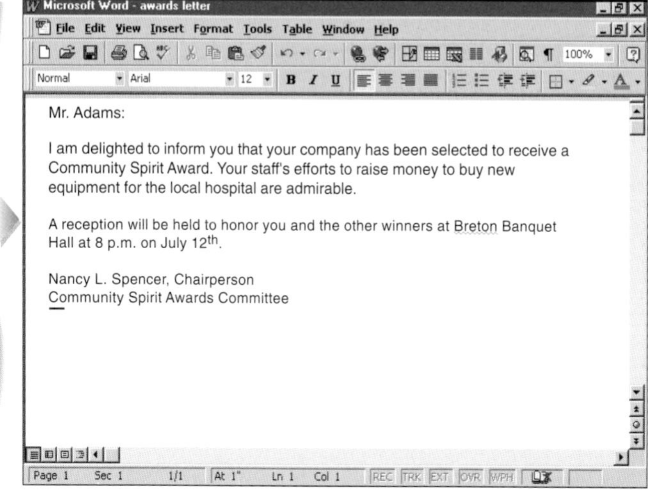

1 To display or hide the ruler, click **View**.

2 Click **Ruler**. A check mark (✓) beside **Ruler** tells you the ruler is currently displayed.

Word displays or hides the ruler.

DISPLAY OR HIDE TOOLBARS

Word offers several toolbars that you can hide or display at any time. Each toolbar contains buttons that help you quickly perform common tasks.

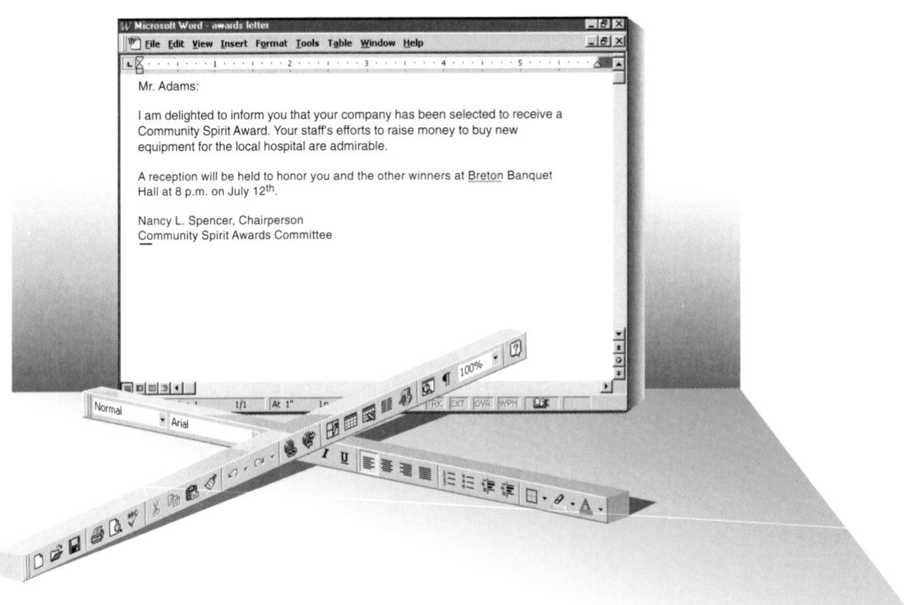

DISPLAY OR HIDE TOOLBARS

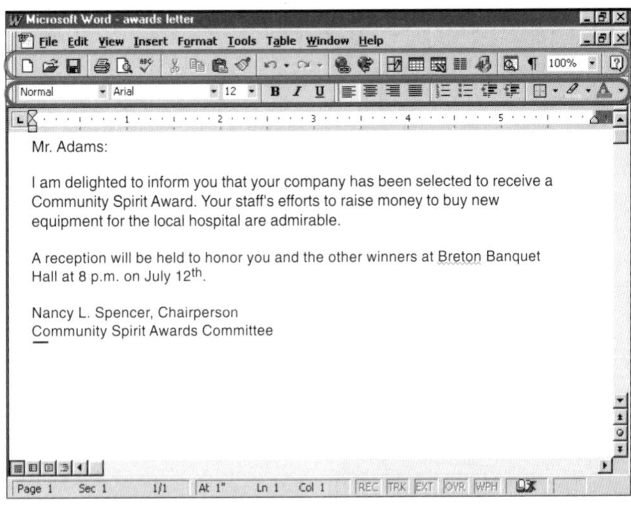

When you first start Word, the Standard and Formatting toolbars appear on the screen.

Standard toolbar

Formatting toolbar

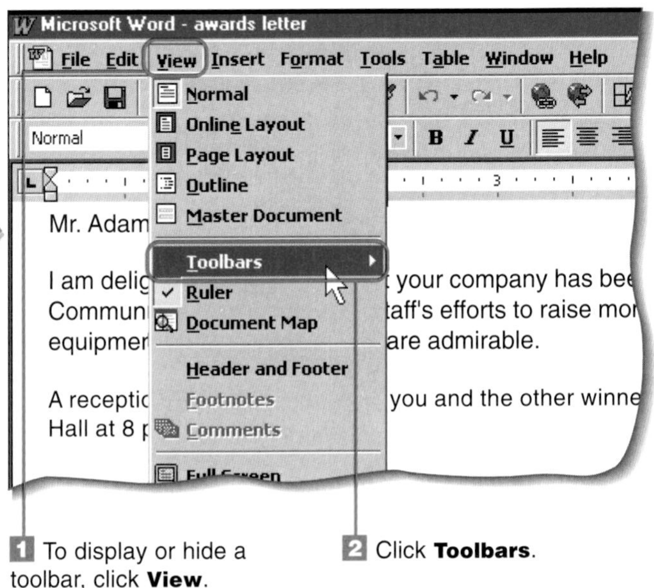

1 To display or hide a toolbar, click **View**.

2 Click **Toolbars**.

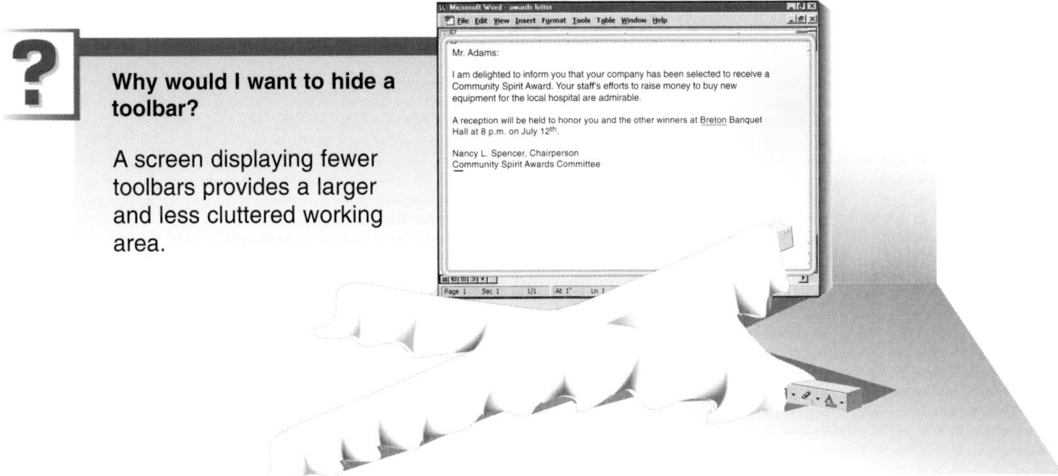

Why would I want to hide a toolbar?

A screen displaying fewer toolbars provides a larger and less cluttered working area.

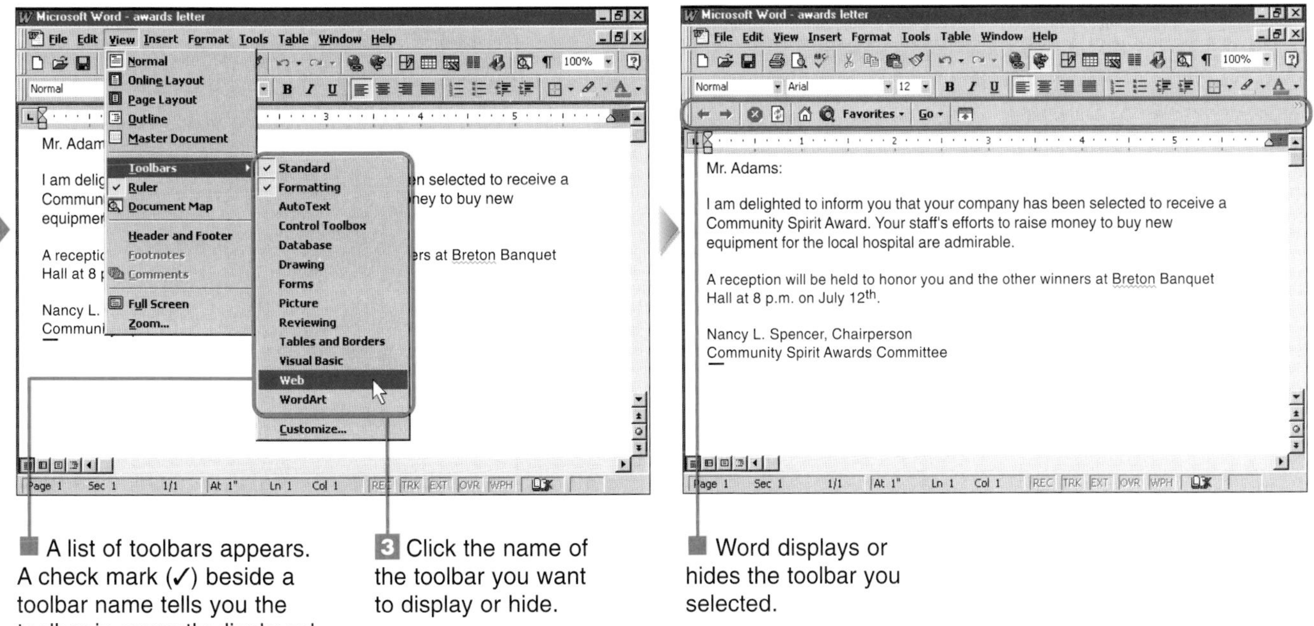

■ A list of toolbars appears. A check mark (✓) beside a toolbar name tells you the toolbar is currently displayed.

3 Click the name of the toolbar you want to display or hide.

■ Word displays or hides the toolbar you selected.

INSERT TEXT

You can easily add new text to your document. The existing text will move to make room for the text you add.

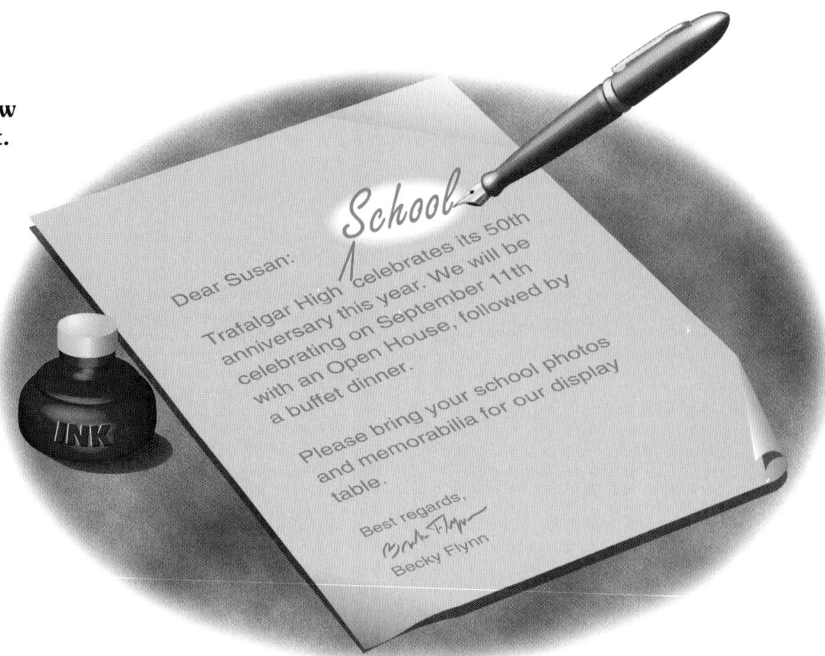

INSERT CHARACTERS

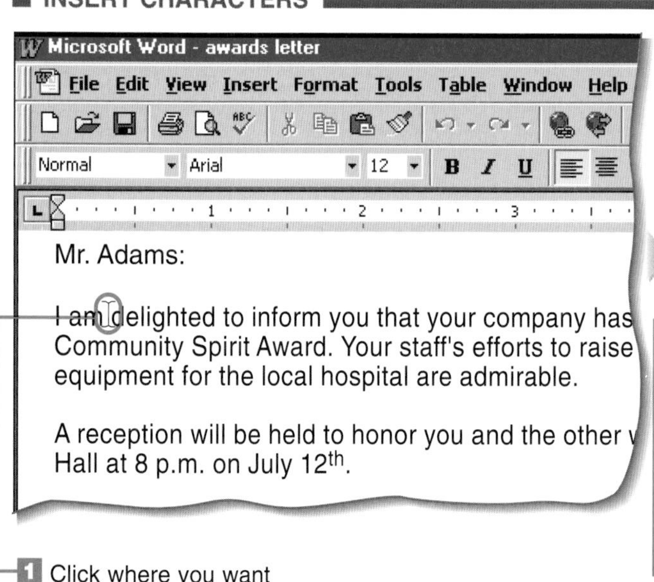

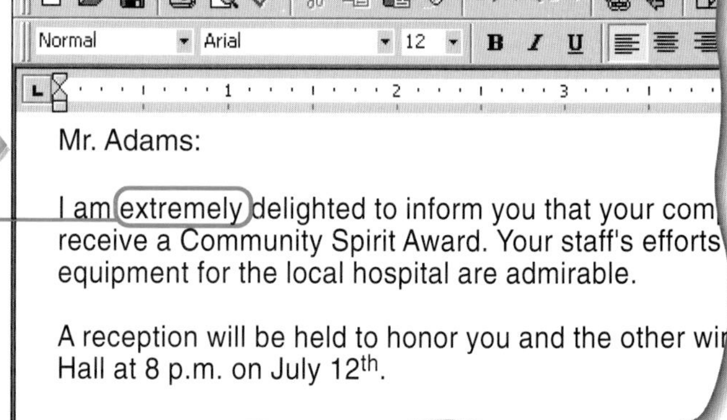

1 Click where you want to insert the new text.

2 Type the text you want to insert. To insert a blank space, press the **Spacebar**.

■ The words to the right of the new text move forward.

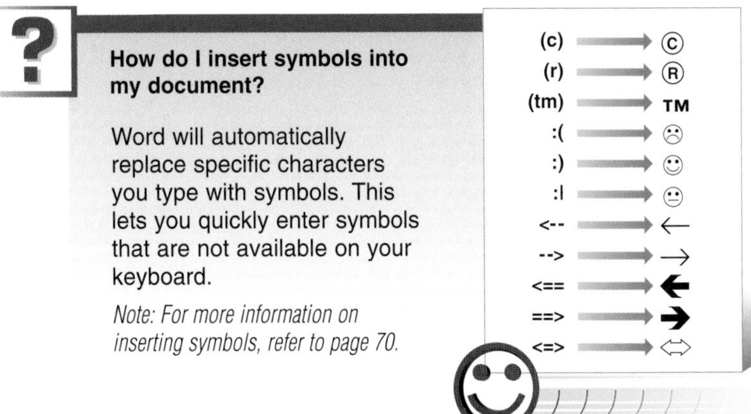

How do I insert symbols into my document?

Word will automatically replace specific characters you type with symbols. This lets you quickly enter symbols that are not available on your keyboard.

Note: For more information on inserting symbols, refer to page 70.

INSERT A BLANK LINE

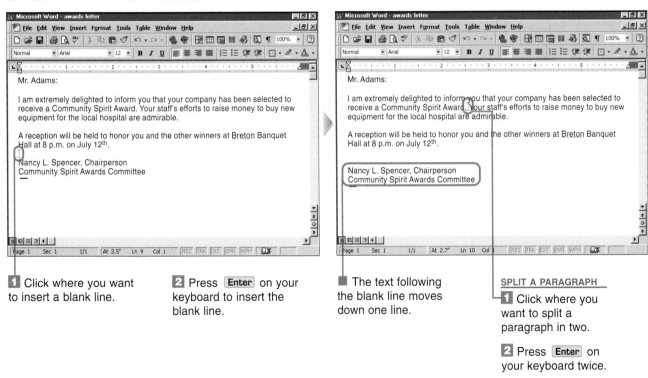

1 Click where you want to insert a blank line.

2 Press **Enter** on your keyboard to insert the blank line.

■ The text following the blank line moves down one line.

SPLIT A PARAGRAPH

1 Click where you want to split a paragraph in two.

2 Press **Enter** on your keyboard twice.

DELETE TEXT

You can easily remove text you no longer need. The remaining text moves to fill any empty spaces.

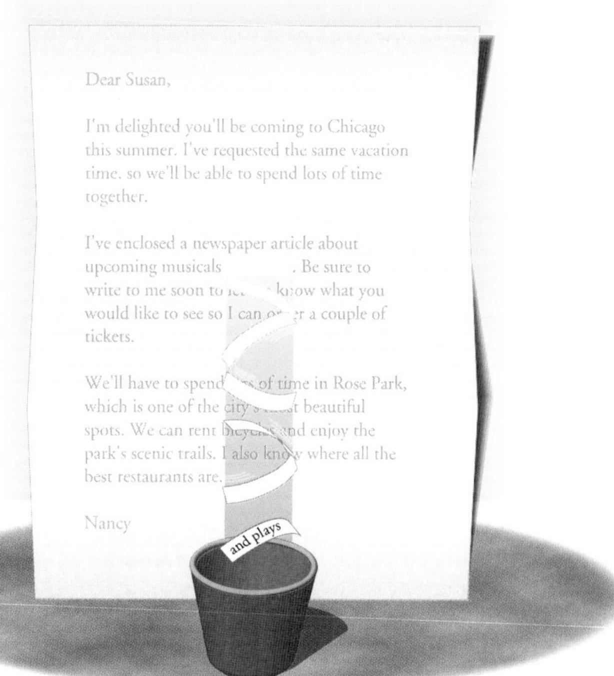

DELETE CHARACTERS

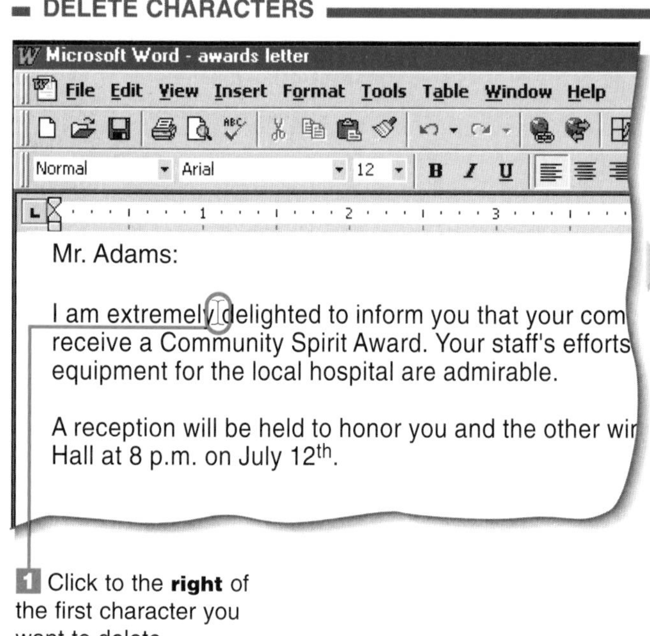

1 Click to the **right** of the first character you want to delete.

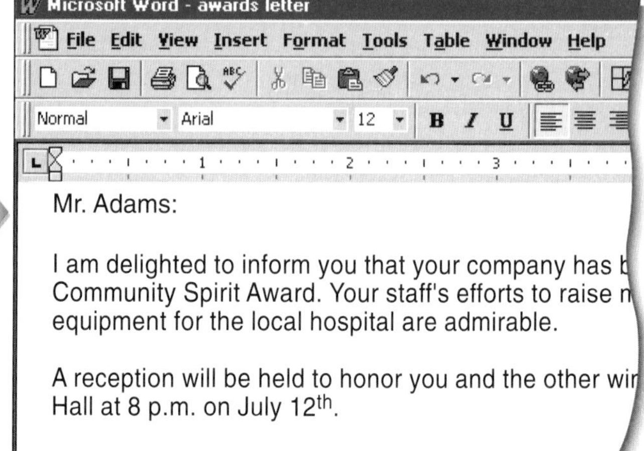

2 Press **←Backspace** on your keyboard once for each character or space you want to delete.

■ You can also use **Delete** on your keyboard to remove characters. Click to the **left** of the first character you want to remove. Press **Delete** once for each character or space you want to remove.

Can I recover text I accidentally delete?

Word remembers the last changes you made to your document. If you regret deleting text, you can use the Undo feature to undo the change.

Note: For information on the Undo feature, refer to page 47.

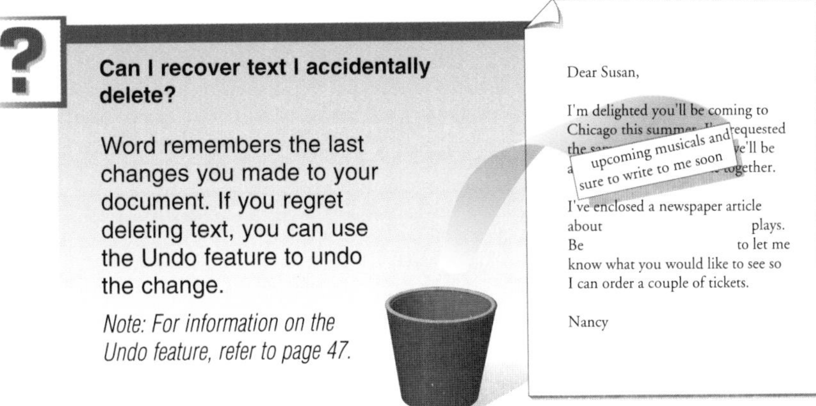

DELETE A BLANK LINE

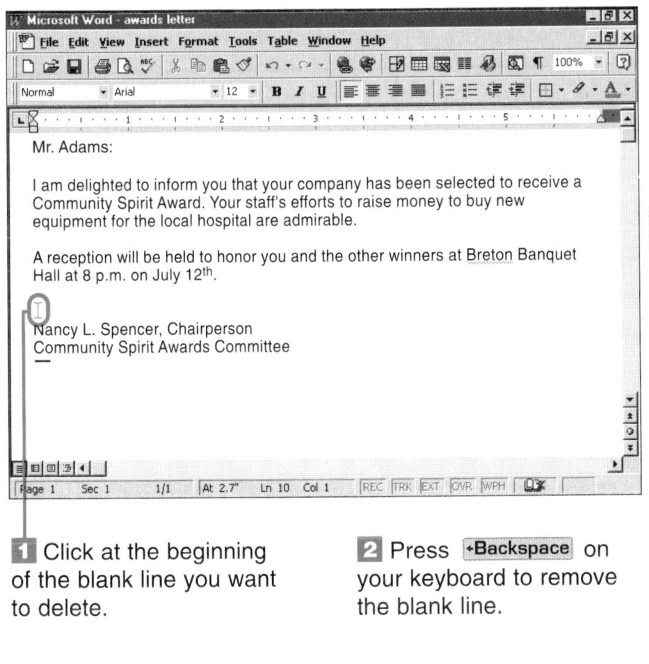

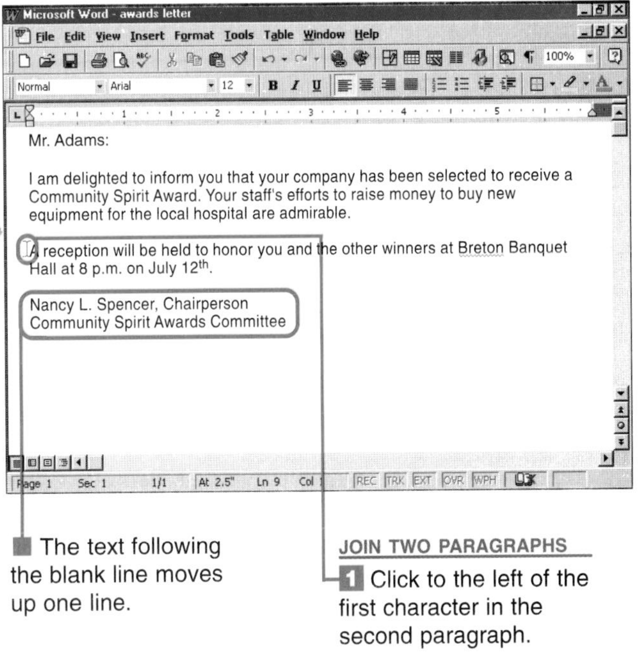

1 Click at the beginning of the blank line you want to delete.

2 Press ←Backspace on your keyboard to remove the blank line.

■ The text following the blank line moves up one line.

JOIN TWO PARAGRAPHS

1 Click to the left of the first character in the second paragraph.

2 Press ←Backspace on your keyboard until the paragraphs are joined.

DELETE TEXT

You can quickly delete a section of text you have selected.

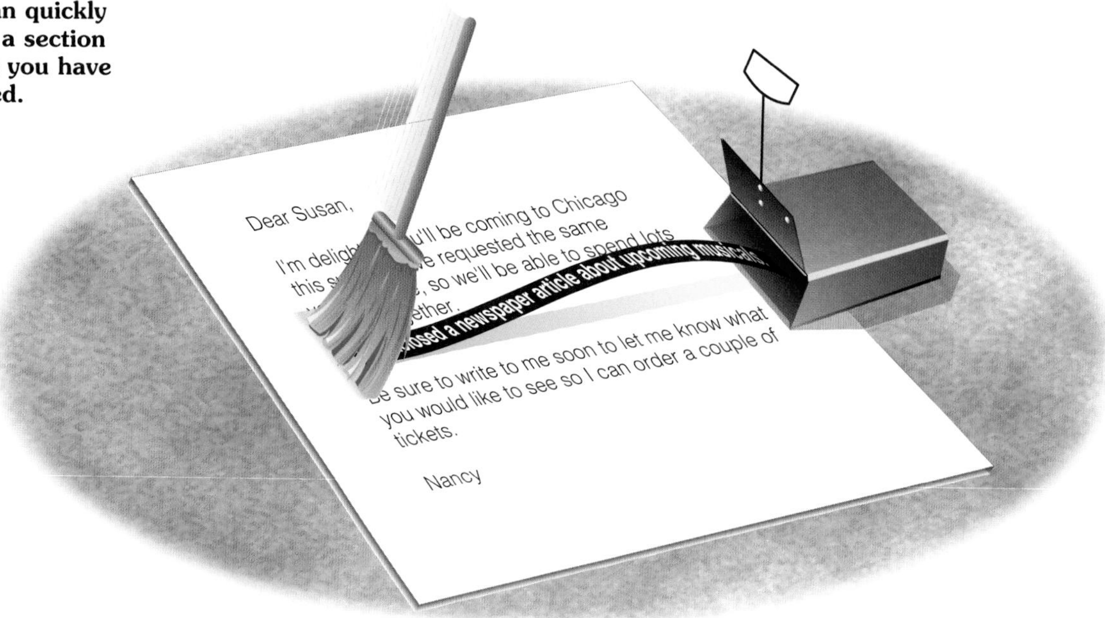

DELETE SELECTED TEXT

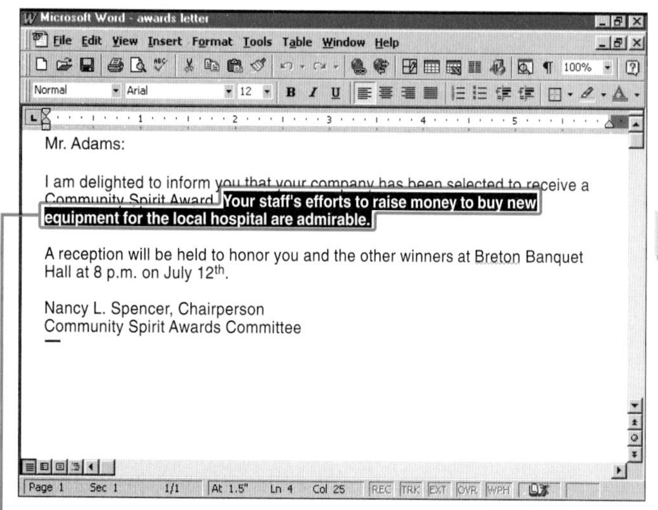

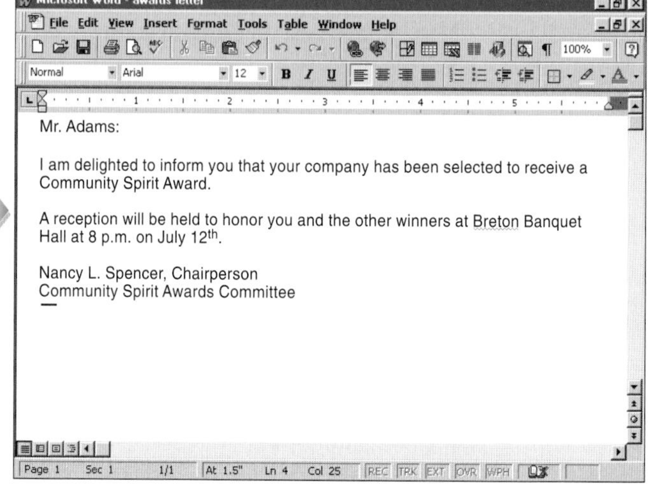

1 Select the text you want to delete. To select text, refer to page 20.

2 Press Delete on your keyboard to remove the text.

UNDO LAST CHANGE

Word remembers the last changes you made to your document. If you regret these changes, you can cancel them by using the Undo feature.

UNDO LAST CHANGE

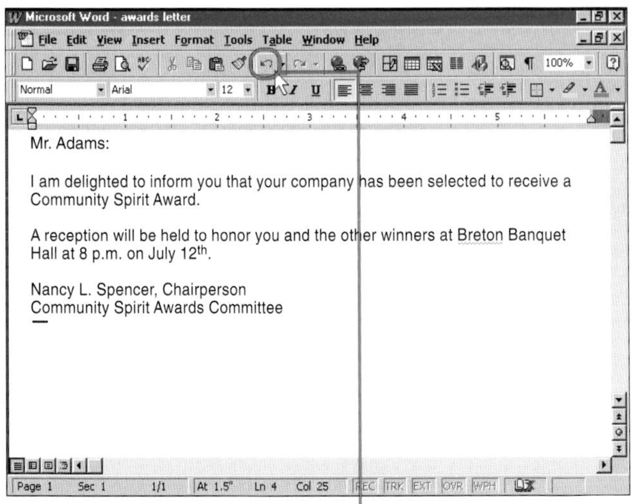

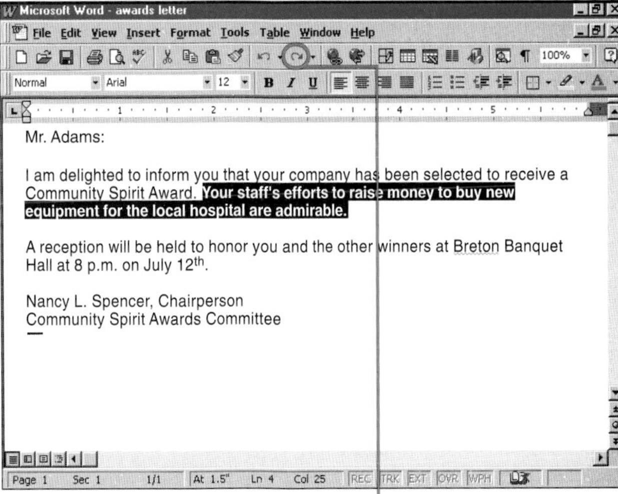

The Undo feature can cancel your last editing and formatting changes.

1 To undo your last change, click ↶.

■ Word cancels the last change you made to the document.

■ You can repeat step 1 to cancel previous changes you made.

■ To reverse the results of using the Undo feature, click ↷.

MOVE TEXT

You can reorganize your document by moving text from one location to another.

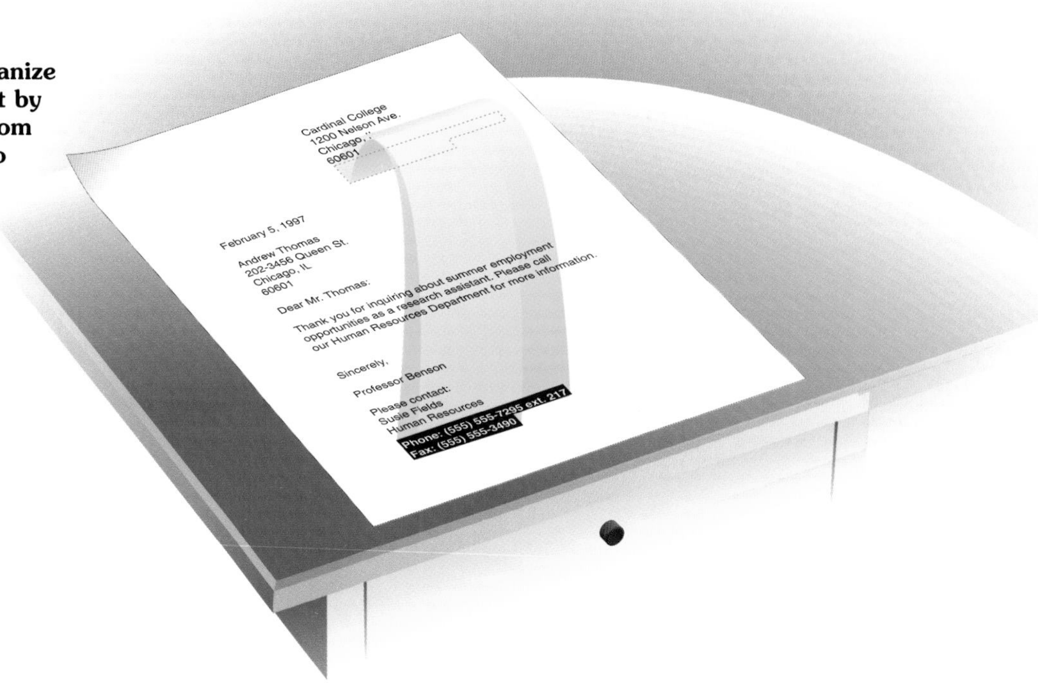

MOVE TEXT

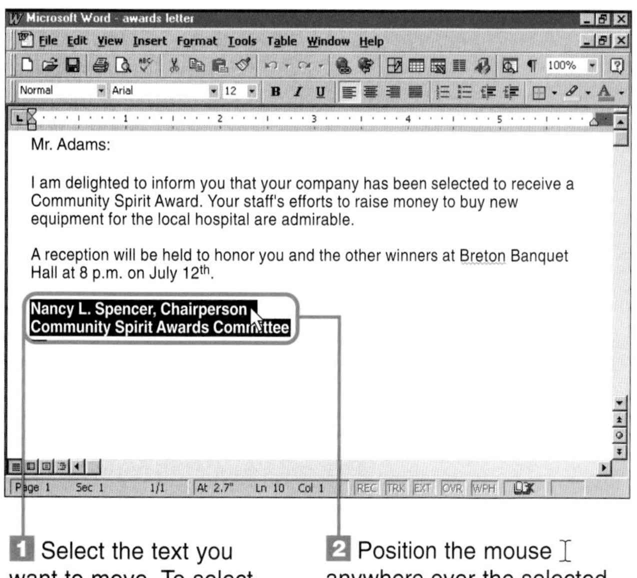

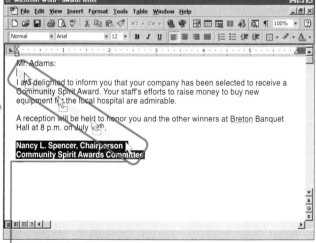

1 Select the text you want to move. To select text, refer to page 20.

2 Position the mouse I anywhere over the selected text (I changes to ↖).

3 Drag the mouse to where you want to place the text. The text will appear where you position the dotted insertion point on the screen.

? Can moving text help me edit my document?

Moving text lets you easily try out different ways of organizing the text in a document. You can find the most effective structure for your document by experimenting with different placements of sentences and paragraphs.

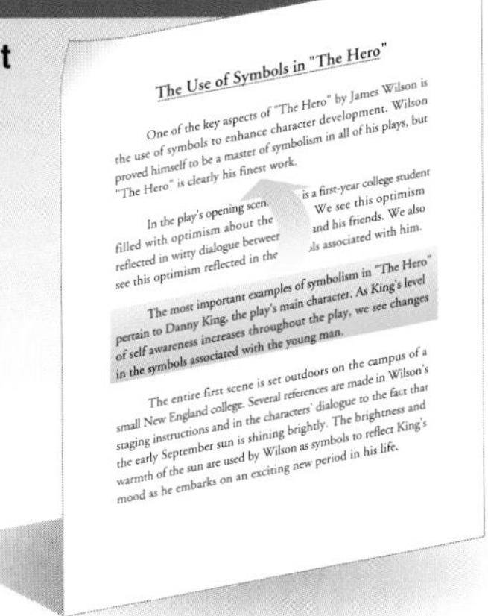
The Use of Symbols in "The Hero"

The text moves to the new location.

UNDO MOVE

1 To immediately move the text back click ↶.

MOVE TEXT USING TOOLBAR

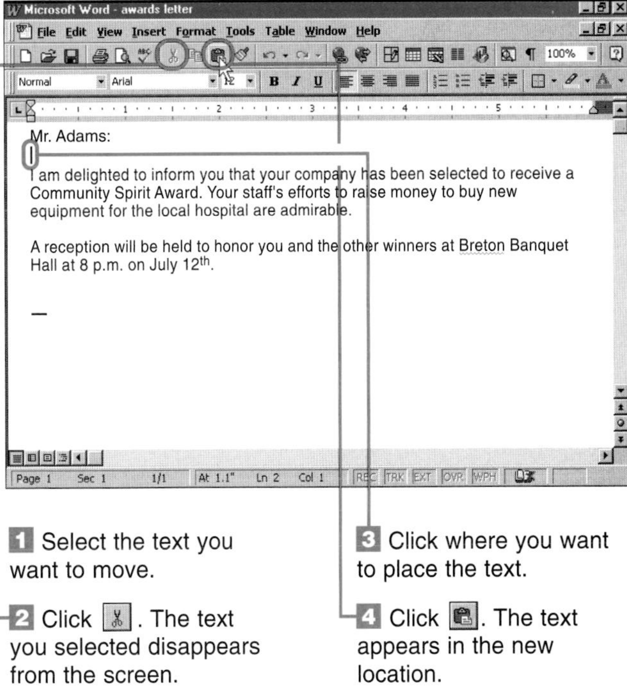
Microsoft Word - awards letter
Mr. Adams:
I am delighted to inform you that your company has been selected to receive a Community Spirit Award. Your staff's efforts to raise money to buy new equipment for the local hospital are admirable.
A reception will be held to honor you and the other winners at Breton Banquet Hall at 8 p.m. on July 12th.

1 Select the text you want to move.

2 Click ✂. The text you selected disappears from the screen.

3 Click where you want to place the text.

4 Click 📋. The text appears in the new location.

COPY TEXT

You can copy text to a different location in your document. This will save you time since you do not have to retype the text.

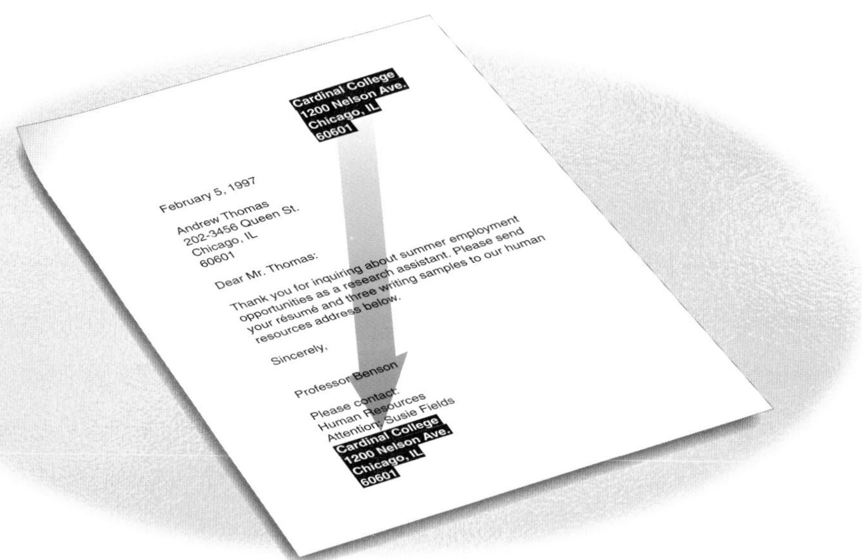

COPY TEXT

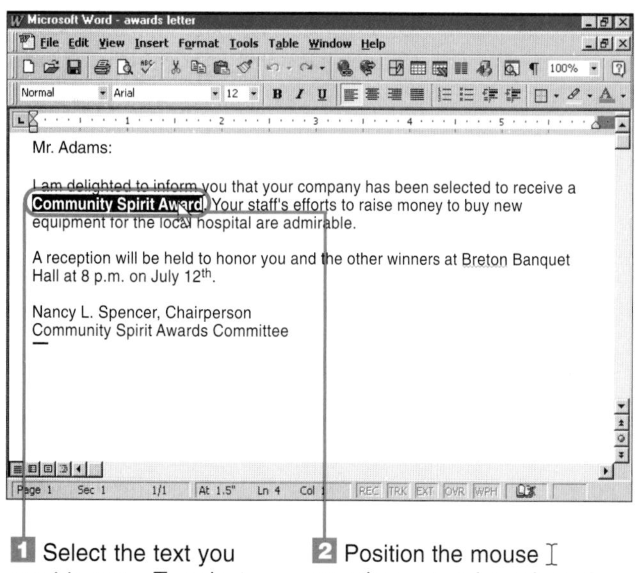

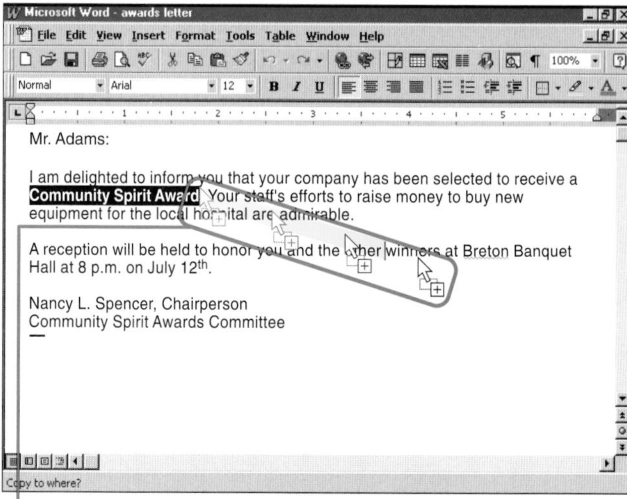

1 Select the text you want to copy. To select text, refer to page 20.

2 Position the mouse I anywhere over the selected text (I changes to ↖).

3 Press and hold down Ctrl on your keyboard.

4 Still holding down Ctrl, drag the mouse to where you want to place the copy. Then release Ctrl.

Note: The text will appear where you position the dotted insertion point on the screen.

? How can copying text help me edit my document?

If you plan to make major changes to a paragraph, you may want to copy the paragraph before you begin. This gives you two copies of the paragraph—the original paragraph and a paragraph with all the changes.

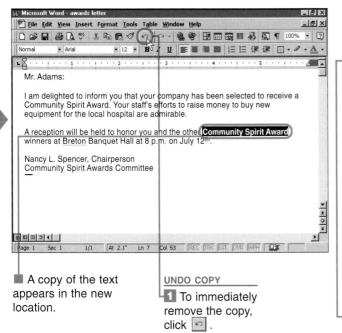

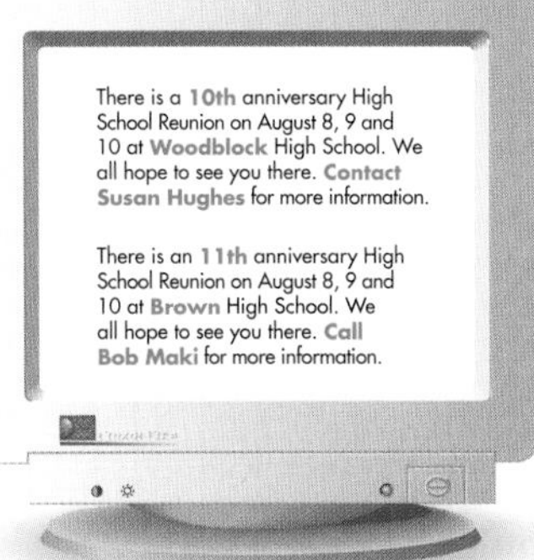

■ A copy of the text appears in the new location.

UNDO COPY

1 To immediately remove the copy, click ↶.

COPY TEXT USING TOOLBAR

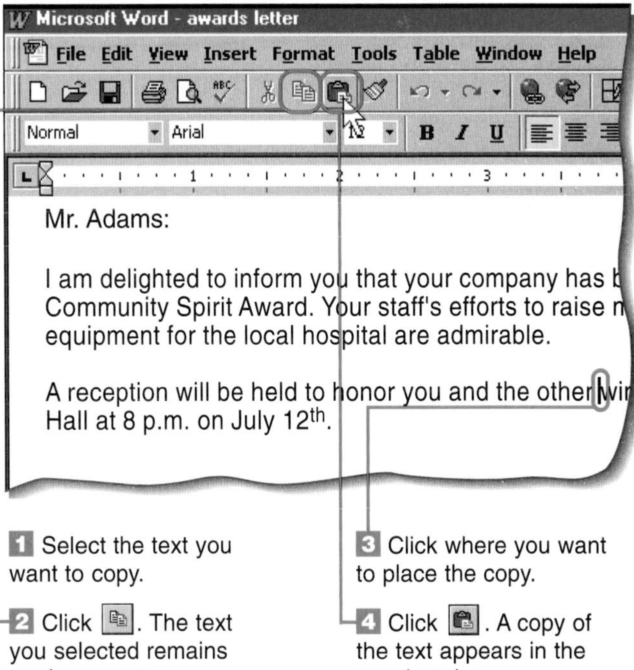

1 Select the text you want to copy.

2 Click 📄. The text you selected remains on the screen.

3 Click where you want to place the copy.

4 Click 📋. A copy of the text appears in the new location.

FIND TEXT

You can use the Find feature to locate a word or phrase in your document.

FIND TEXT

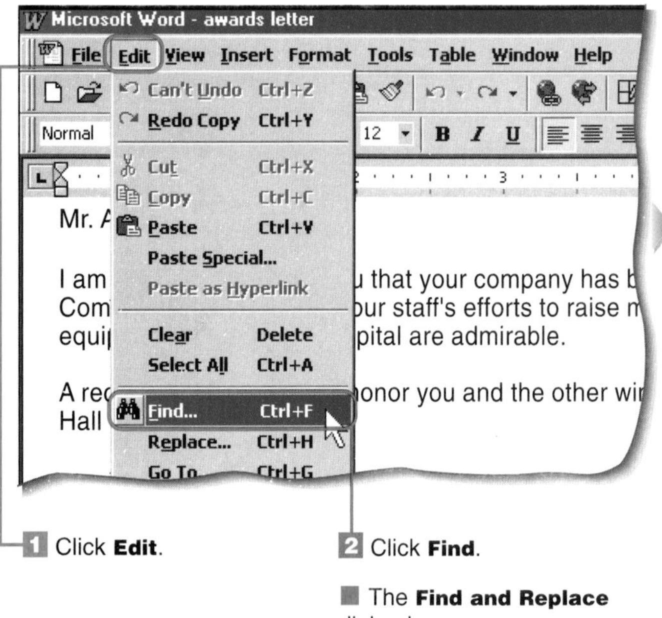

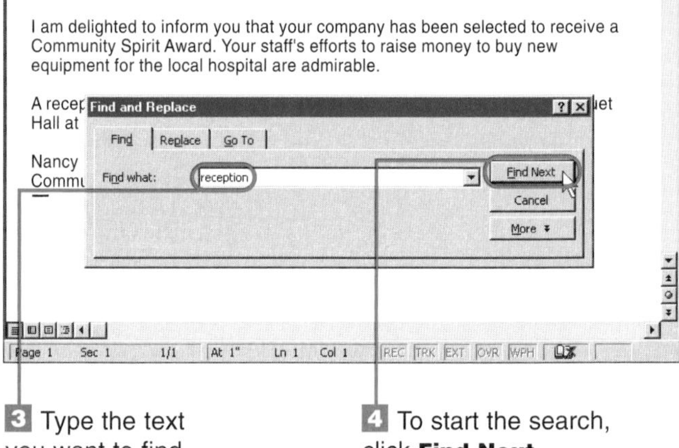

1 Click **Edit**.

2 Click **Find**.

■ The **Find and Replace** dialog box appears.

3 Type the text you want to find.

4 To start the search, click **Find Next**.

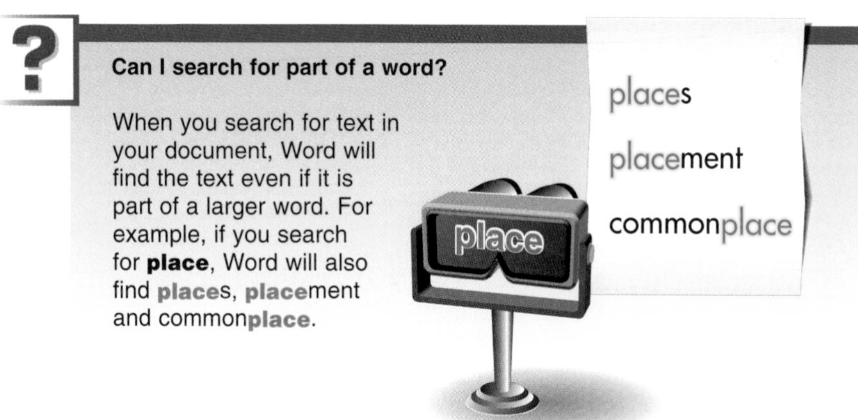

Can I search for part of a word?

When you search for text in your document, Word will find the text even if it is part of a larger word. For example, if you search for **place**, Word will also find **place**s, **place**ment and common**place**.

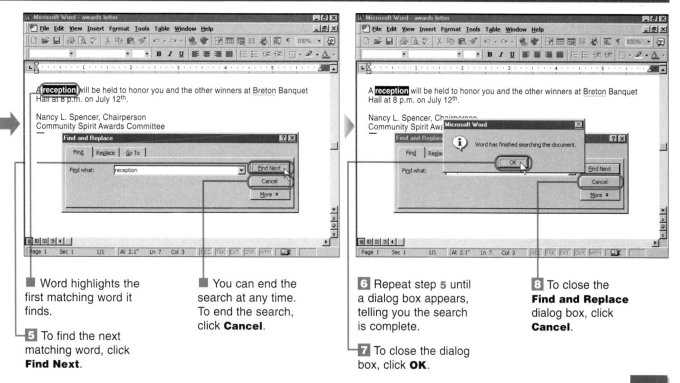

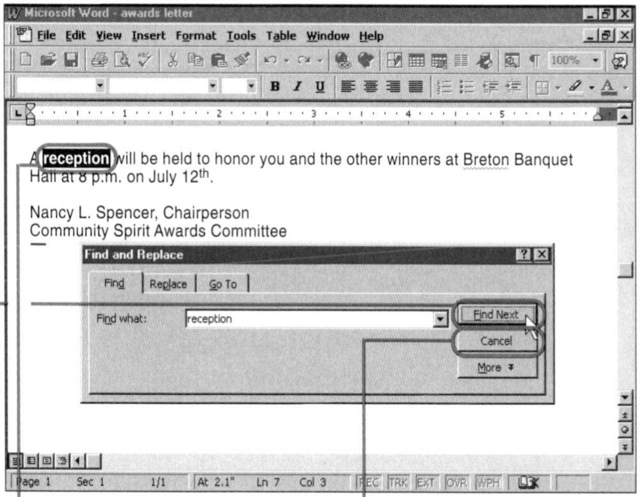

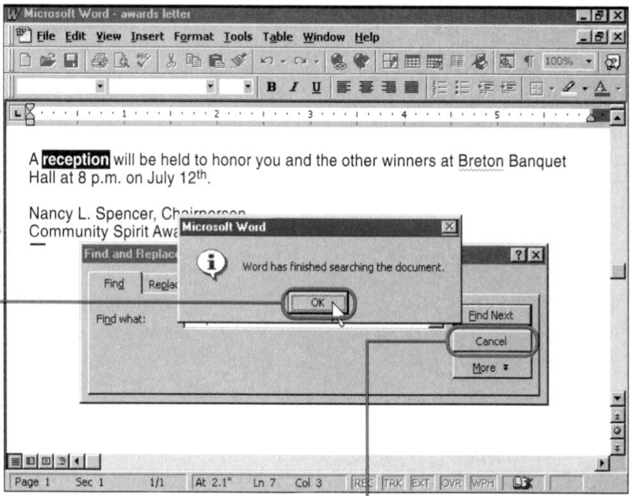

■ Word highlights the first matching word it finds.

5 To find the next matching word, click **Find Next**.

■ You can end the search at any time. To end the search, click **Cancel**.

6 Repeat step **5** until a dialog box appears, telling you the search is complete.

7 To close the dialog box, click **OK**.

8 To close the **Find and Replace** dialog box, click **Cancel**.

REPLACE TEXT

The Replace feature can locate and replace every occurrence of a word or phrase in your document. This is ideal if you have frequently misspelled a name.

REPLACE TEXT

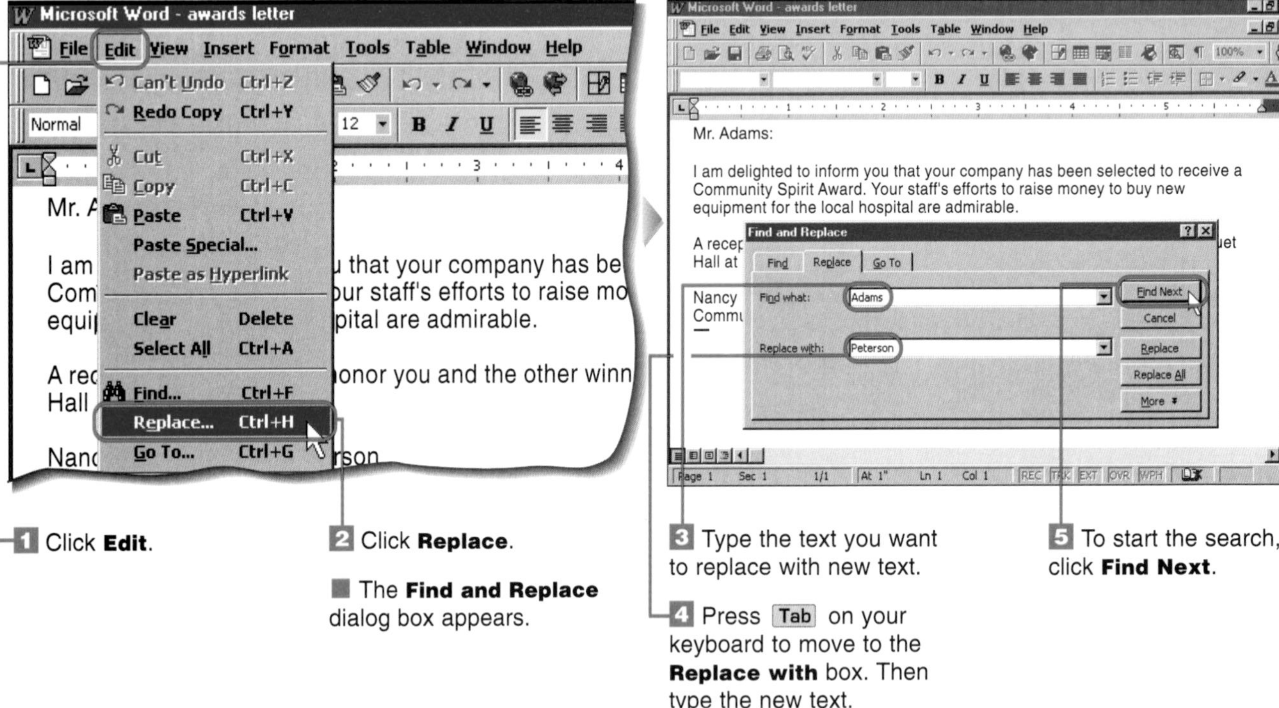

1 Click **Edit**.

2 Click **Replace**.

■ The **Find and Replace** dialog box appears.

3 Type the text you want to replace with new text.

4 Press Tab on your keyboard to move to the **Replace with** box. Then type the new text.

5 To start the search, click **Find Next**.

Can I use the Replace feature to enter text more quickly?

The Replace feature is useful if you have to type a long word or phrase (example: University of Massachusetts) many times in a document. You can type a short form of the word or phrase (example: UM) throughout your document and then have Word replace the short form with the full word or phrase.

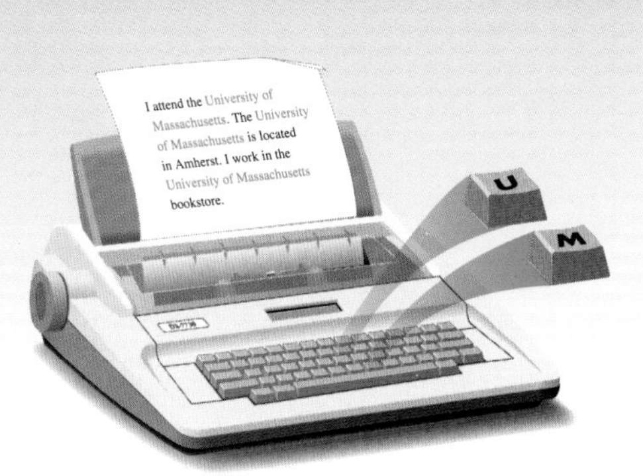

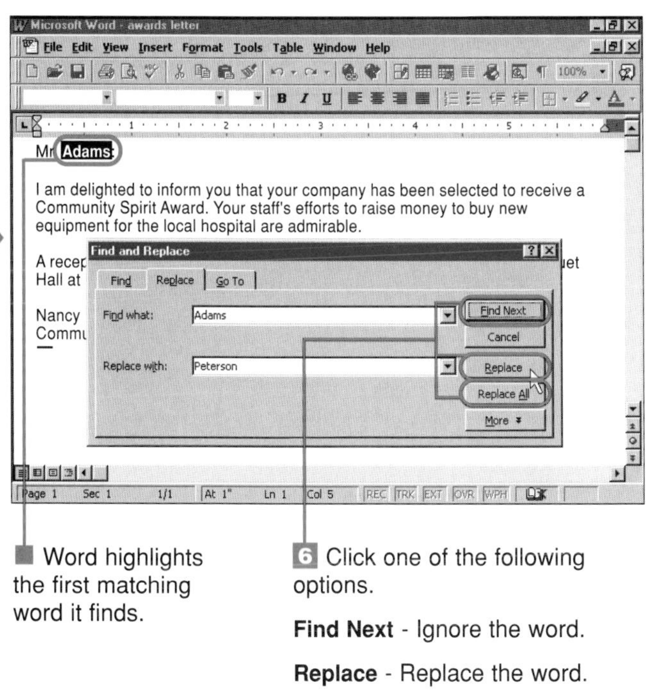

■ Word highlights the first matching word it finds.

6 Click one of the following options.

Find Next - Ignore the word.

Replace - Replace the word.

Replace All - Replace the word and all other matching words in the document.

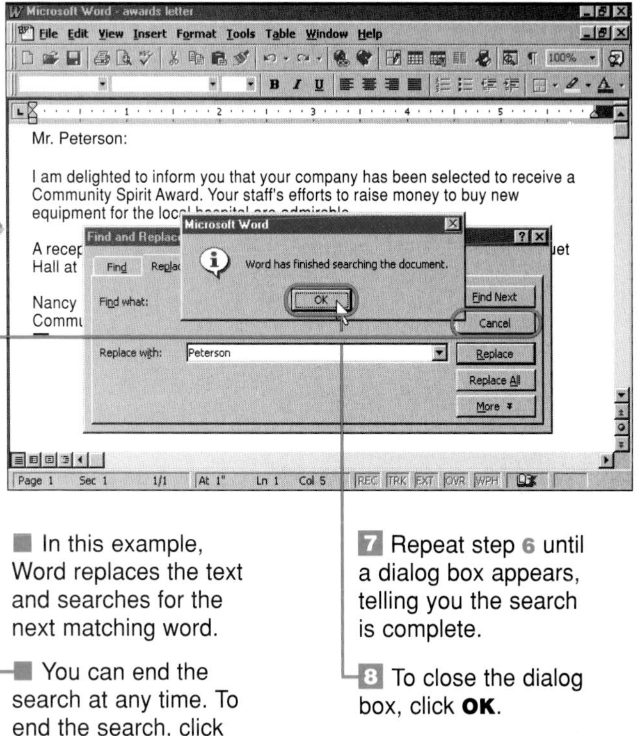

■ In this example, Word replaces the text and searches for the next matching word.

■ You can end the search at any time. To end the search, click **Cancel** or **Close**.

7 Repeat step 6 until a dialog box appears, telling you the search is complete.

8 To close the dialog box, click **OK**.

CHECK SPELLING AND GRAMMAR

Word offers a Spelling and Grammar feature to help you find and correct errors in your document.

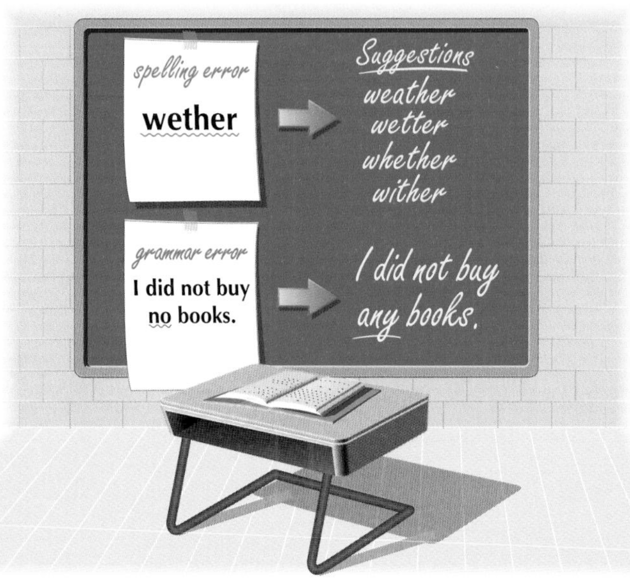

Word automatically underlines misspelled words in red and grammar mistakes in green. The red and green underlines will not appear when you print your document.

CHECK SPELLING AND GRAMMAR

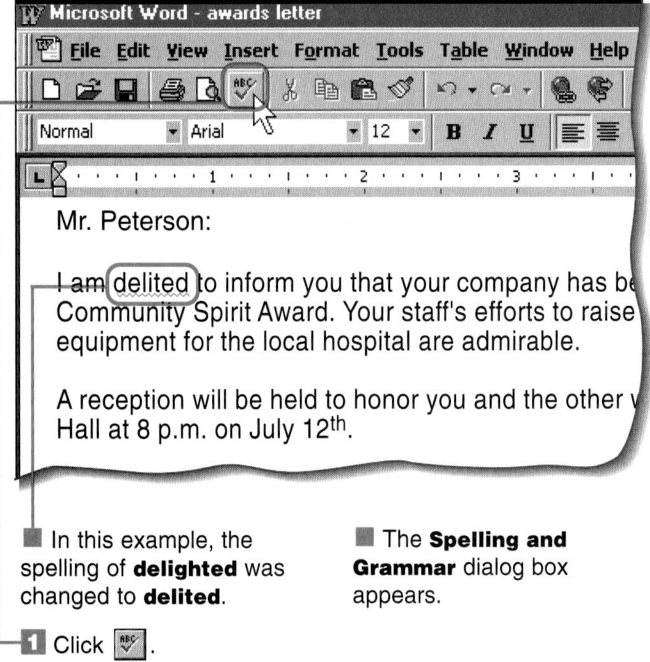

■ In this example, the spelling of **delighted** was changed to **delited**.

1 Click [icon].

■ The **Spelling and Grammar** dialog box appears.

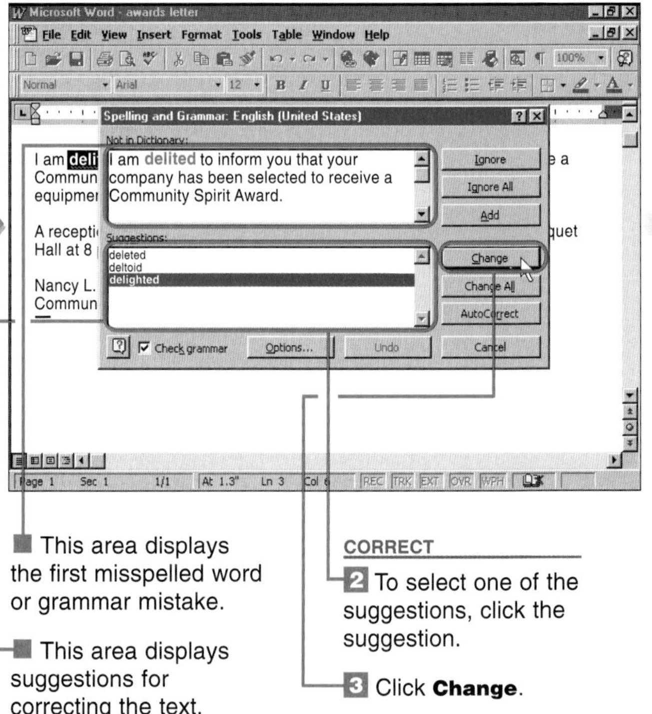

■ This area displays the first misspelled word or grammar mistake.

■ This area displays suggestions for correcting the text.

CORRECT

2 To select one of the suggestions, click the suggestion.

3 Click **Change**.

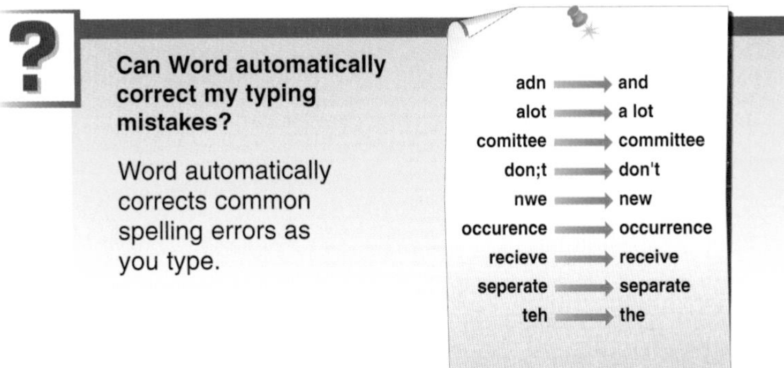

adn → and
alot → a lot
comitte → committee
don;t → don't
nwe → new
occurence → occurrence
recieve → receive
seperate → separate
teh → the

Can Word automatically correct my typing mistakes?

Word automatically corrects common spelling errors as you type.

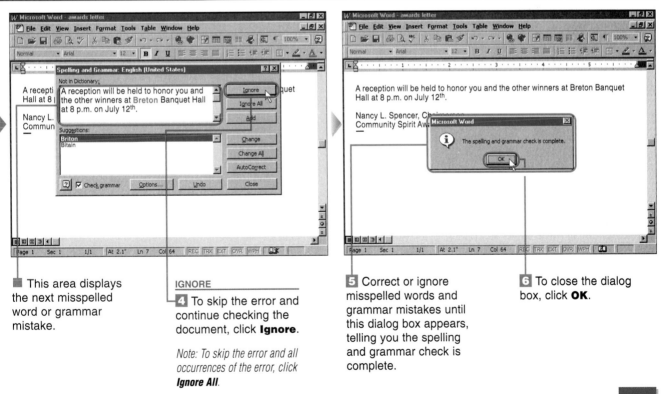

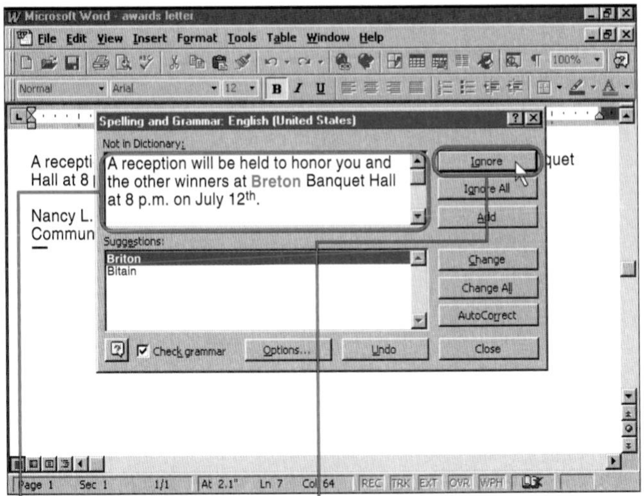

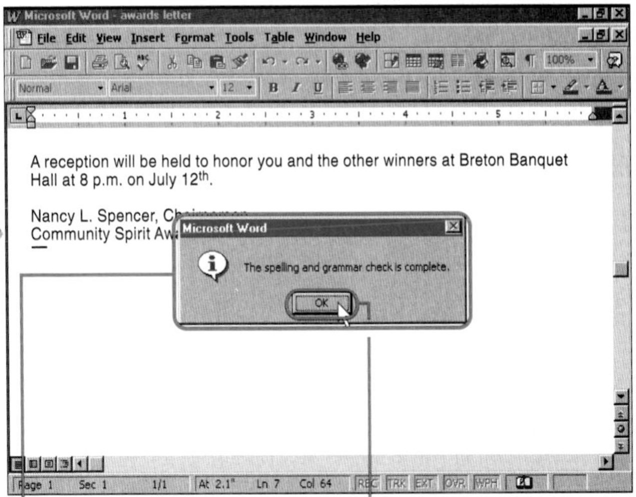

■ This area displays the next misspelled word or grammar mistake.

IGNORE

4 To skip the error and continue checking the document, click **Ignore**.

*Note: To skip the error and all occurrences of the error, click **Ignore All**.*

5 Correct or ignore misspelled words and grammar mistakes until this dialog box appears, telling you the spelling and grammar check is complete.

6 To close the dialog box, click **OK**.

USING THE THESAURUS

You can use the Thesaurus to replace a word in your document with one that is more suitable.

USING THE THESAURUS

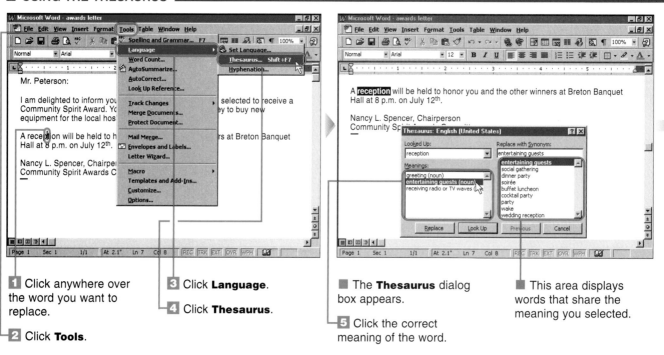

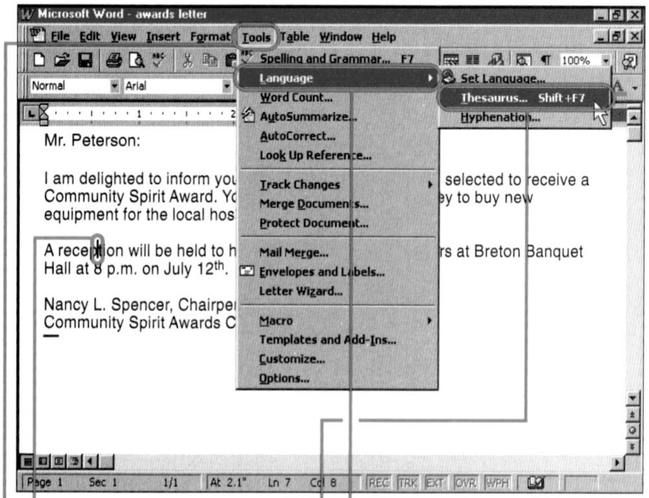

1 Click anywhere over the word you want to replace.

2 Click **Tools**.

3 Click **Language**.

4 Click **Thesaurus**.

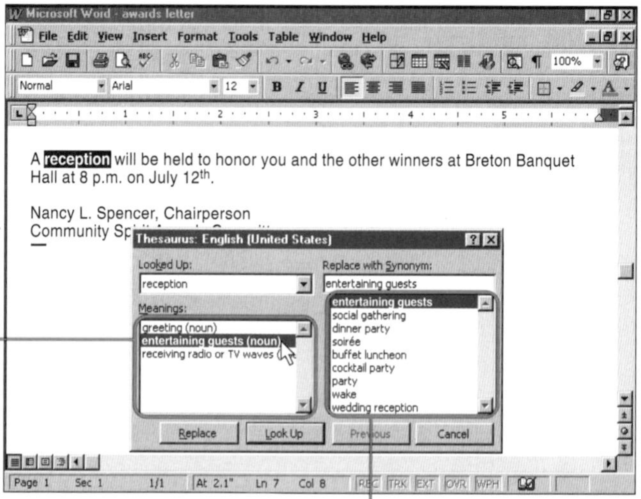

■ The **Thesaurus** dialog box appears.

5 Click the correct meaning of the word.

■ This area displays words that share the meaning you selected.

How can the Thesaurus feature help me?

Using the Thesaurus included with Word is faster and more convenient than searching through a printed thesaurus.

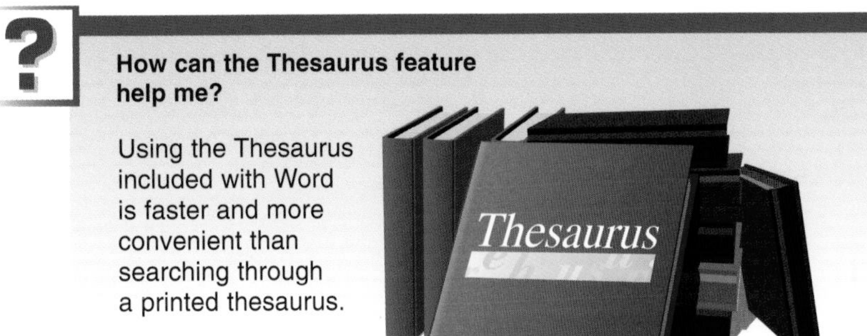

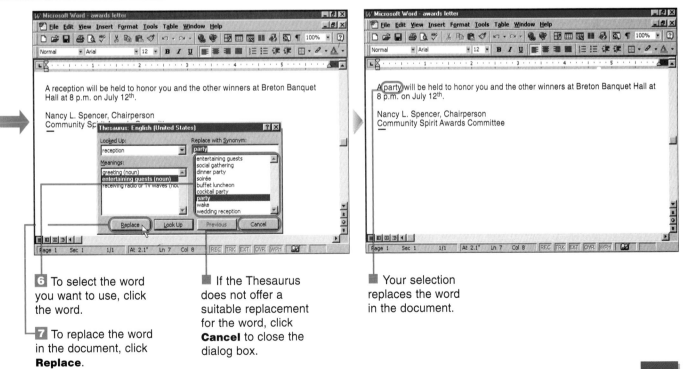

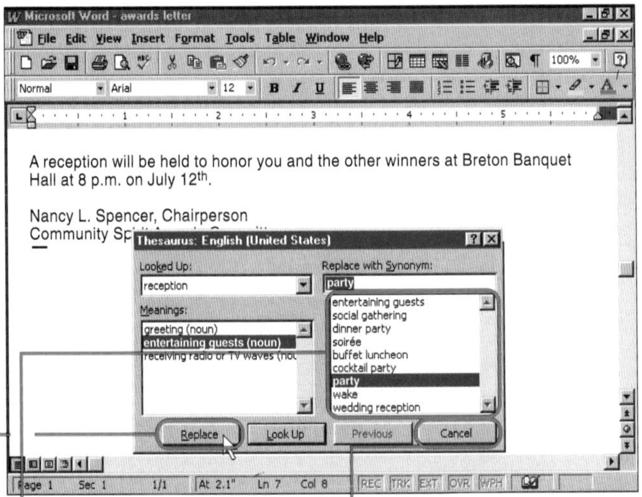

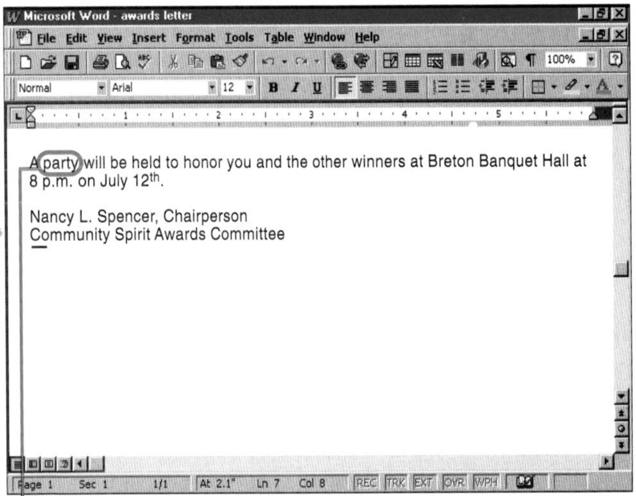

6 To select the word you want to use, click the word.

7 To replace the word in the document, click **Replace**.

■ If the Thesaurus does not offer a suitable replacement for the word, click **Cancel** to close the dialog box.

■ Your selection replaces the word in the document.

BOLD, ITALIC AND UNDERLINE

You can use the Bold, Italic and Underline features to emphasize information in your document.

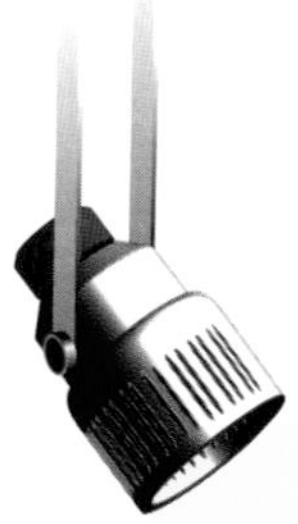

BOLD, ITALIC AND UNDERLINE

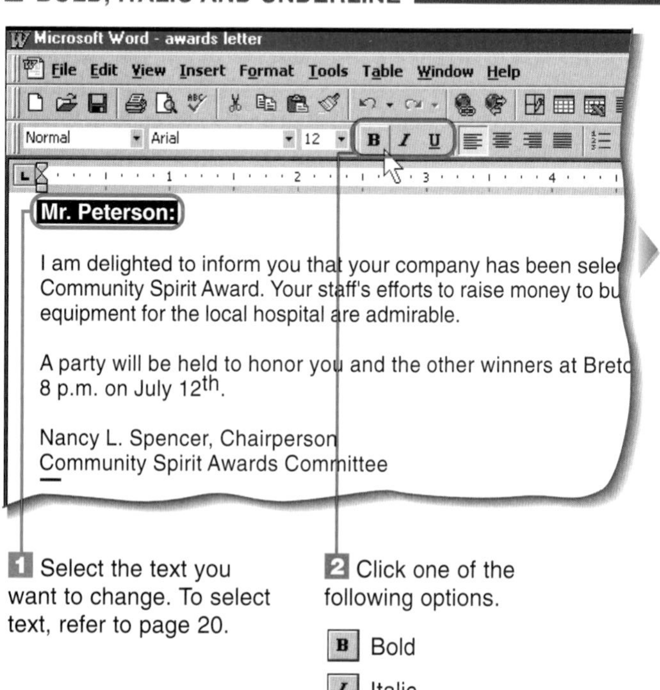

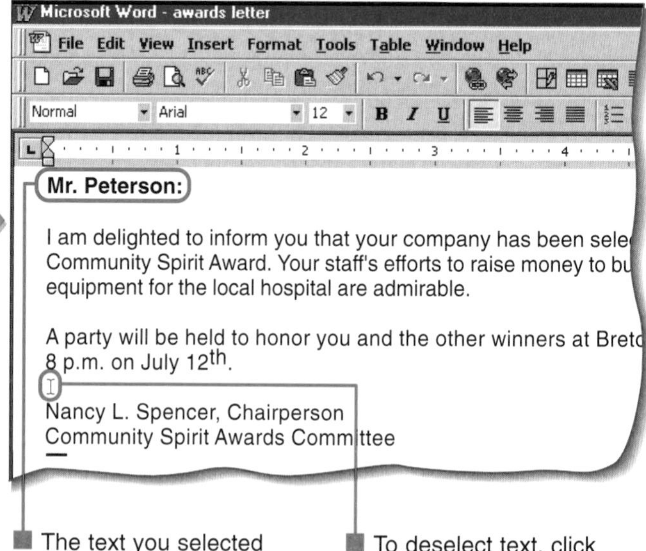

1 Select the text you want to change. To select text, refer to page 20.

2 Click one of the following options.

- **B** Bold
- *I* Italic
- U Underline

■ The text you selected appears in the new style.

■ To deselect text, click outside the selected area.

■ To remove a bold, italic or underline style, repeat steps **1** and **2**.

CHANGE ALIGNMENT OF TEXT

You can enhance the appearance of your document by aligning text in different ways.

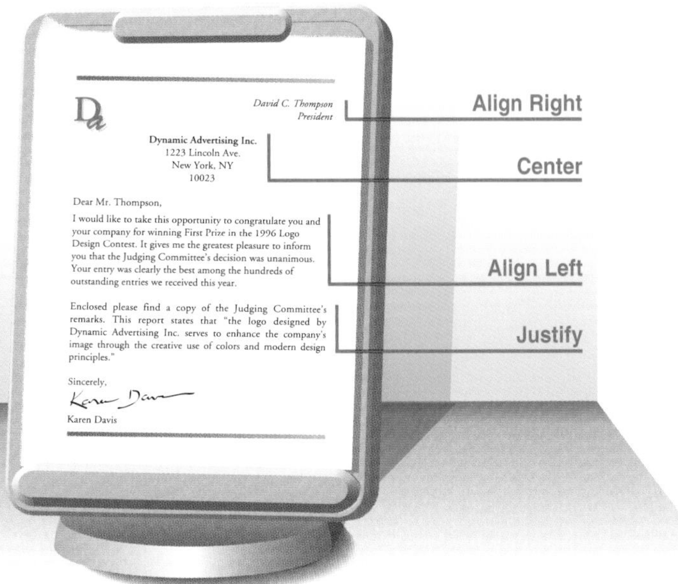

Align Right
Center
Align Left
Justify
David C. Thompson
President
Dynamic Advertising Inc.
1223 Lincoln Ave.
New York, NY
10023
Dear Mr. Thompson,
I would like to take this opportunity to congratulate you and your company for winning First Prize in the 1996 Logo Design Contest. It gives me the greatest pleasure to inform you that the Judging Committee's decision was unanimous. Your entry was clearly the best among the hundreds of outstanding entries we received this year.
Enclosed please find a copy of the Judging Committee's remarks. This report states that "the logo designed by Dynamic Advertising Inc. serves to enhance the company's image through the creative use of colors and modern design principles."
Sincerely,
Karen Davis

CHANGE ALIGNMENT OF TEXT

Microsoft Word - awards letter
File Edit View Insert Format Tools Table Window Help
Mr. Peterson:
I am delighted to inform you that your company has been selected to receive a Community Spirit Award. Your staff's efforts to raise money to buy new equipment for the local hospital are admirable.
A party will be held to honor you and the other winners at Breton Banquet Hall at 8 p.m. on July 12th.
Nancy L. Spencer, Chairperson
Community Spirit Awards Committee

Microsoft Word - awards letter
File Edit View Insert Format Tools Table Window Help
Mr. Peterson:
I am delighted to inform you that your company has been selected to receive a Community Spirit Award. Your staff's efforts to raise money to buy new equipment for the local hospital are admirable.
A party will be held to honor you and the other winners at Breton Banquet Hall at 8 p.m. on July 12th.
Nancy L. Spencer, Chairperson
Community Spirit Awards Committee

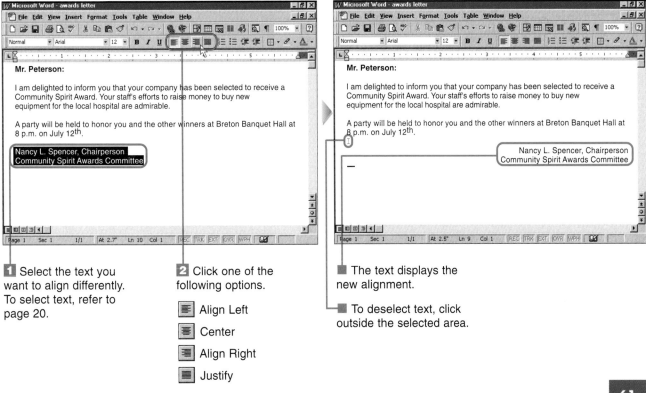

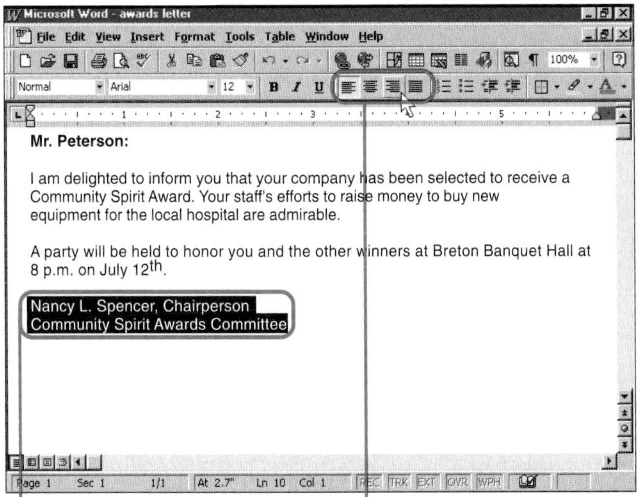

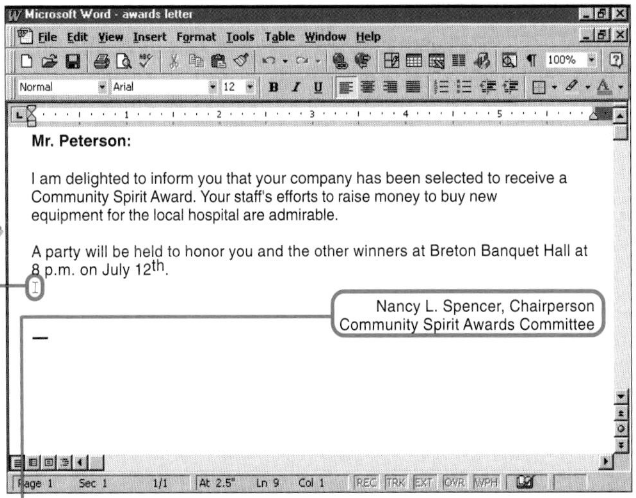

1 Select the text you want to align differently. To select text, refer to page 20.

2 Click one of the following options.

- Align Left
- Center
- Align Right
- Justify

■ The text displays the new alignment.

■ To deselect text, click outside the selected area.

CHANGE FONT OF TEXT

You can enhance the appearance of your document by changing the design of the text.

CHANGE FONT OF TEXT

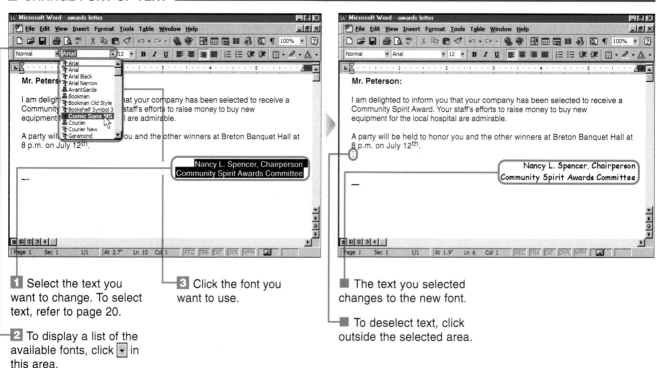

1 Select the text you want to change. To select text, refer to page 20.

2 To display a list of the available fonts, click ▾ in this area.

3 Click the font you want to use.

■ The text you selected changes to the new font.

■ To deselect text, click outside the selected area.

CHANGE SIZE OF TEXT

You can increase or decrease the size of text in your document.

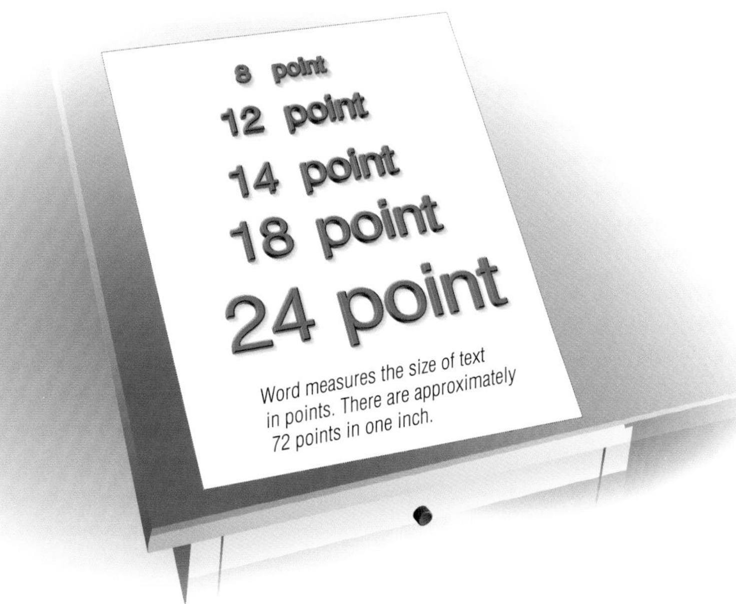

8 point
12 point
14 point
18 point
24 point
Word measures the size of text in points. There are approximately 72 points in one inch.

CHANGE SIZE OF TEXT

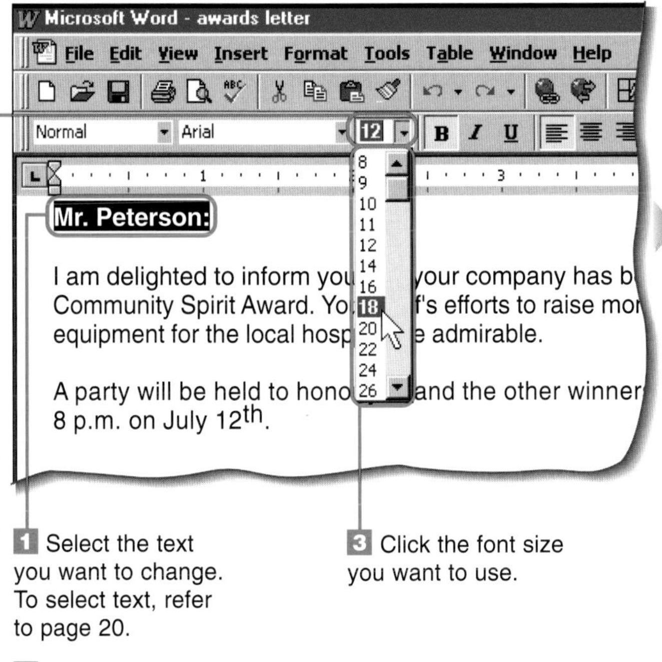

1 Select the text you want to change. To select text, refer to page 20.

2 To display a list of the available font sizes, click ▾ in this area.

3 Click the font size you want to use.

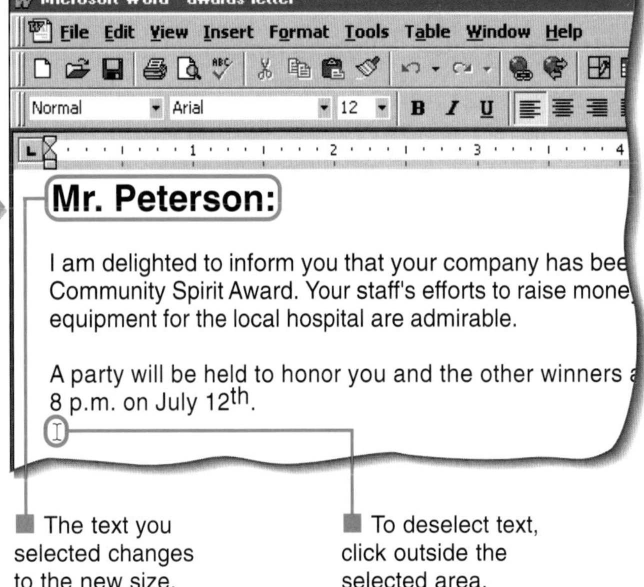

■ The text you selected changes to the new size.

■ To deselect text, click outside the selected area.

CHANGE APPEARANCE OF TEXT

You can make text in your document look attractive by using various fonts, sizes, styles, underlines and special effects.

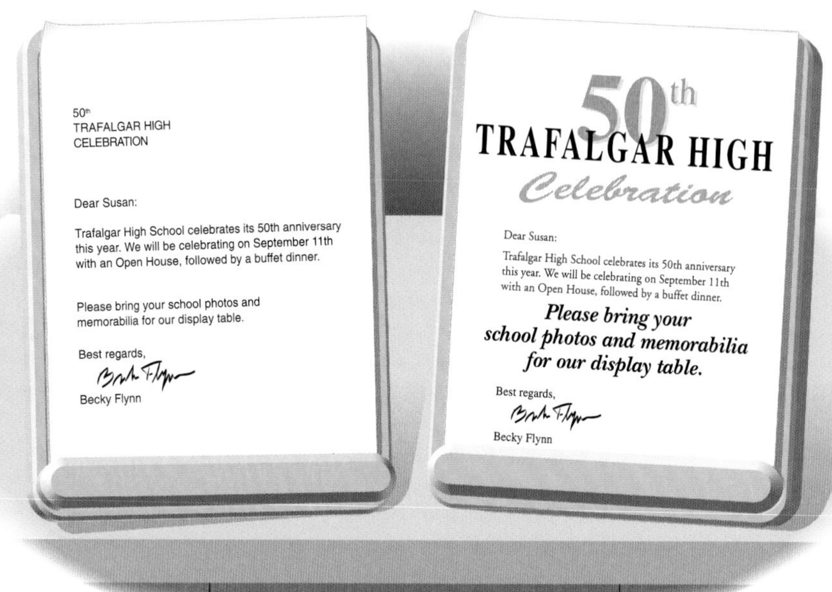

CHANGE APPEARANCE OF TEXT

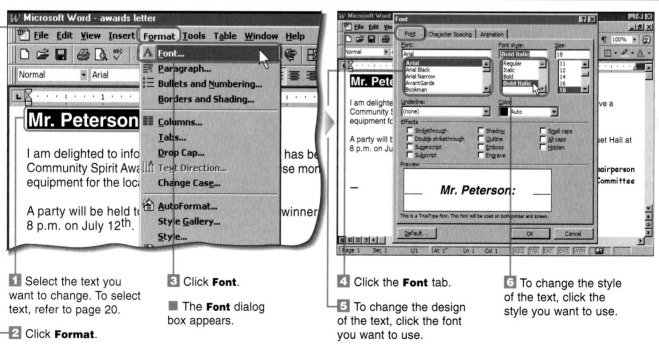

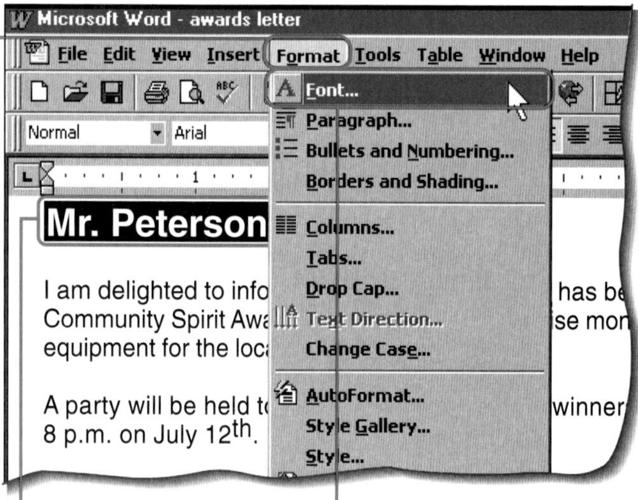

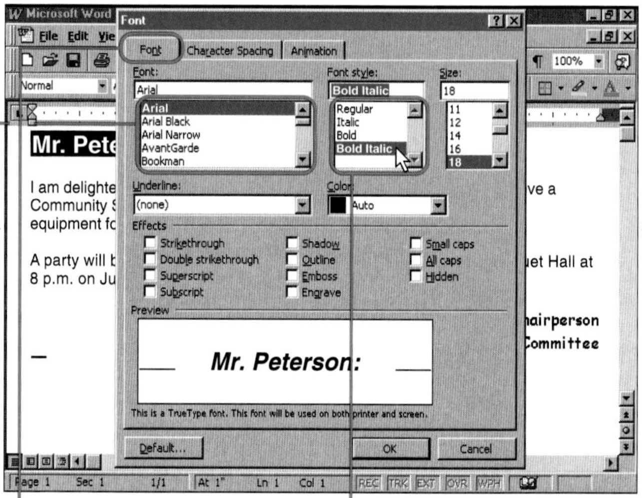

1 Select the text you want to change. To select text, refer to page 20.

2 Click **Format**.

3 Click **Font**.

■ The **Font** dialog box appears.

4 Click the **Font** tab.

5 To change the design of the text, click the font you want to use.

6 To change the style of the text, click the style you want to use.

What underline styles and special effects can I add to my document?

Word offers many underline styles and special effects.

Underline Styles	Effects
Single	Strikethrough
Double	Shadow
Dash	Emboss
Wave	Engrave

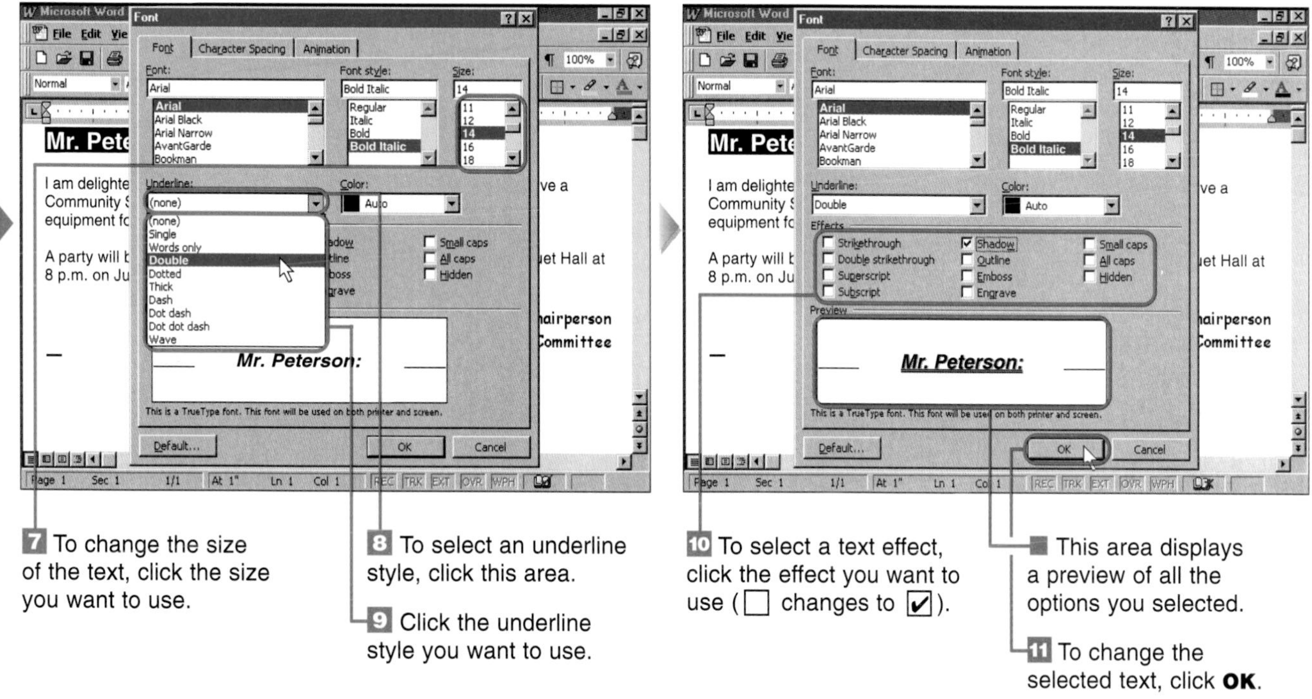

7 To change the size of the text, click the size you want to use.

8 To select an underline style, click this area.

9 Click the underline style you want to use.

10 To select a text effect, click the effect you want to use (☐ changes to ☑).

■ This area displays a preview of all the options you selected.

11 To change the selected text, click **OK**.

CHANGE TEXT COLOR

You can change the color of text to draw attention to headings or important information in your document.

CHANGE TEXT COLOR

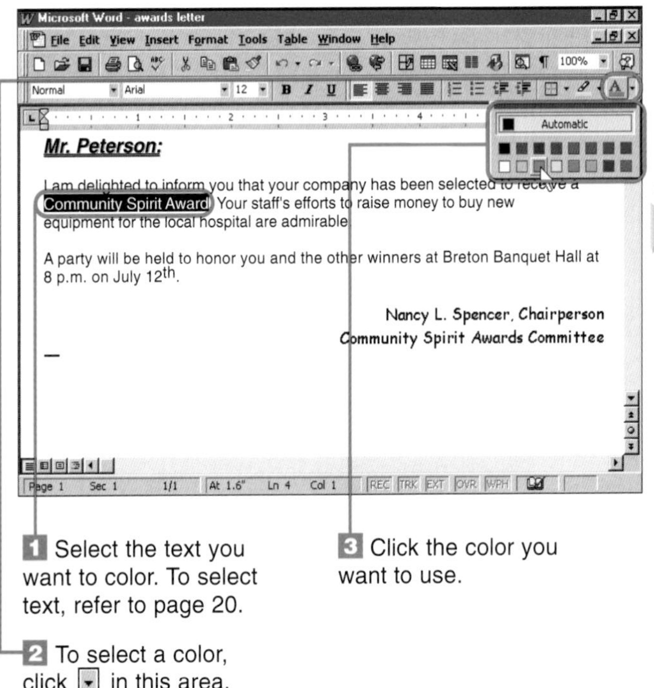

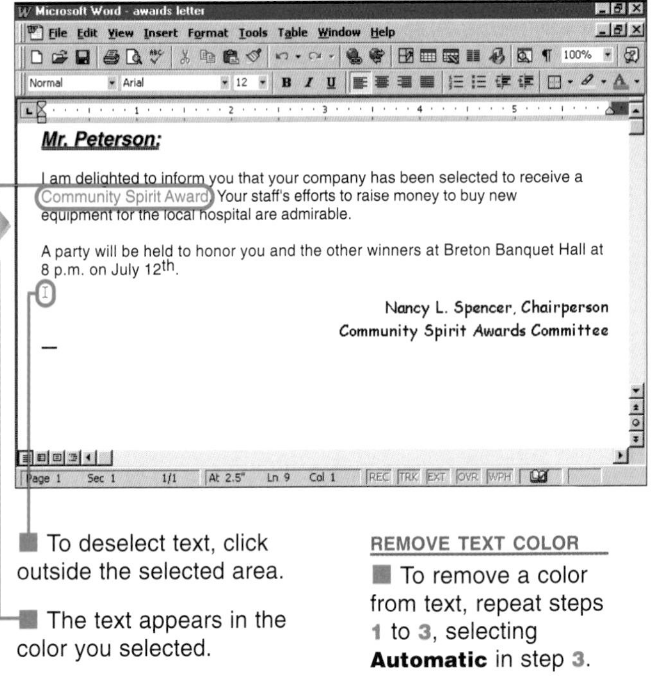

1 Select the text you want to color. To select text, refer to page 20.

2 To select a color, click ▾ in this area.

3 Click the color you want to use.

■ To deselect text, click outside the selected area.

■ The text appears in the color you selected.

REMOVE TEXT COLOR

■ To remove a color from text, repeat steps 1 to 3, selecting **Automatic** in step 3.

HIGHLIGHT TEXT

You can highlight important text in your document. Highlighting text is useful for marking text you want to verify later.

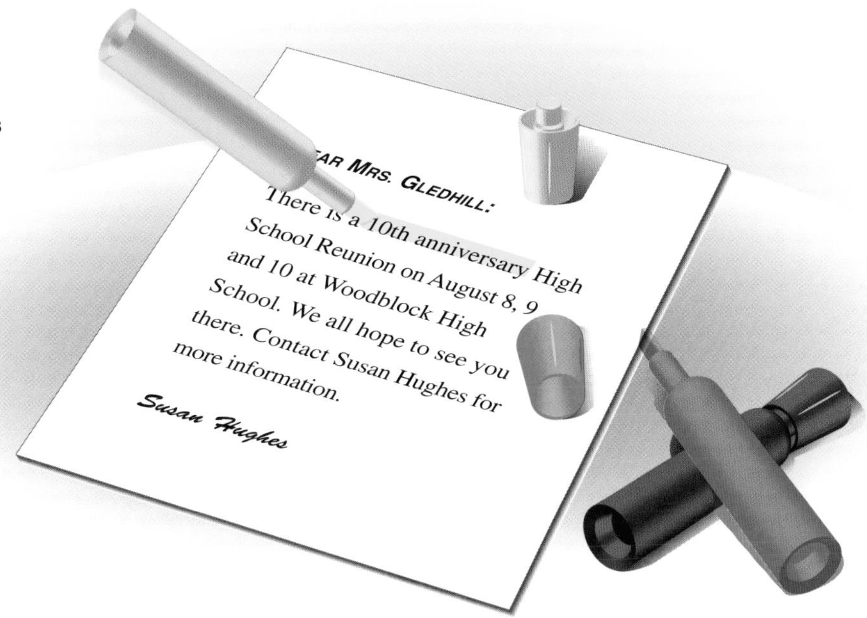
Dear Mrs. Gledhill:
There is a 10th anniversary High School Reunion on August 8, 9 and 10 at Woodblock High School. We all hope to see you there. Contact Susan Hughes for more information.
Susan Hughes

HIGHLIGHT TEXT

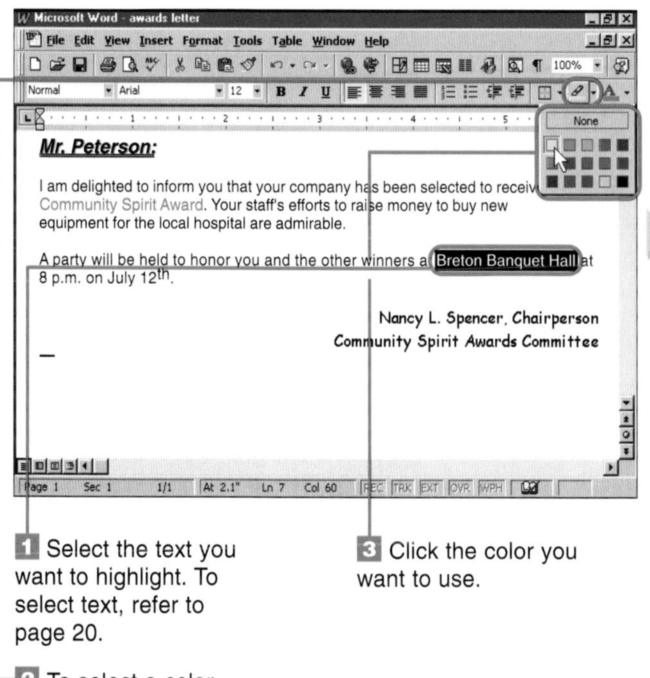
Microsoft Word - awards letter
File Edit View Insert Format Tools Table Window Help
None
Mr. Peterson:
I am delighted to inform you that your company has been selected to receive a Community Spirit Award. Your staff's efforts to raise money to buy new equipment for the local hospital are admirable.
A party will be held to honor you and the other winners at Breton Banquet Hall at 8 p.m. on July 12th.
Nancy L. Spencer, Chairperson
Community Spirit Awards Committee

1 Select the text you want to highlight. To select text, refer to page 20.

2 To select a color, click ▾ in this area.

3 Click the color you want to use.

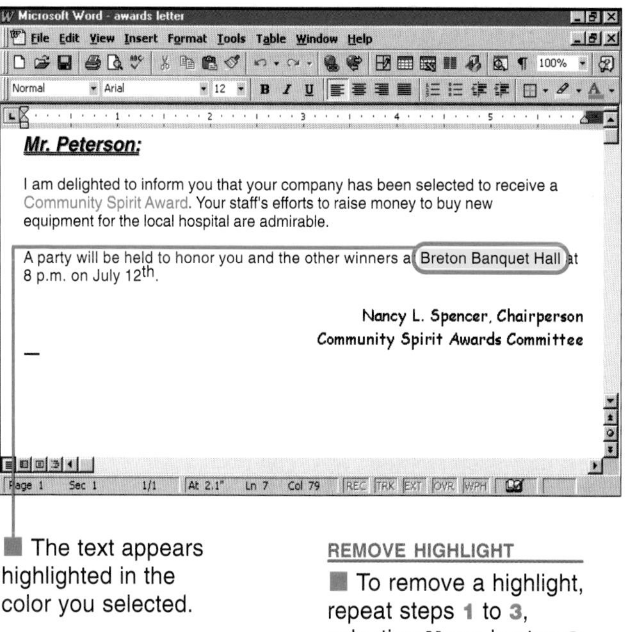
Microsoft Word - awards letter
File Edit View Insert Format Tools Table Window Help
Mr. Peterson:
I am delighted to inform you that your company has been selected to receive a Community Spirit Award. Your staff's efforts to raise money to buy new equipment for the local hospital are admirable.
A party will be held to honor you and the other winners at Breton Banquet Hall at 8 p.m. on July 12th.
Nancy L. Spencer, Chairperson
Community Spirit Awards Committee

■ The text appears highlighted in the color you selected.

REMOVE HIGHLIGHT

■ To remove a highlight, repeat steps 1 to 3, selecting **None** in step 3.

COPY FORMATTING

You can easily make one area of text look exactly like another.

Great Composers
Bach
Mozart
Beethoven
Vivaldi
Holst

COPY FORMATTING

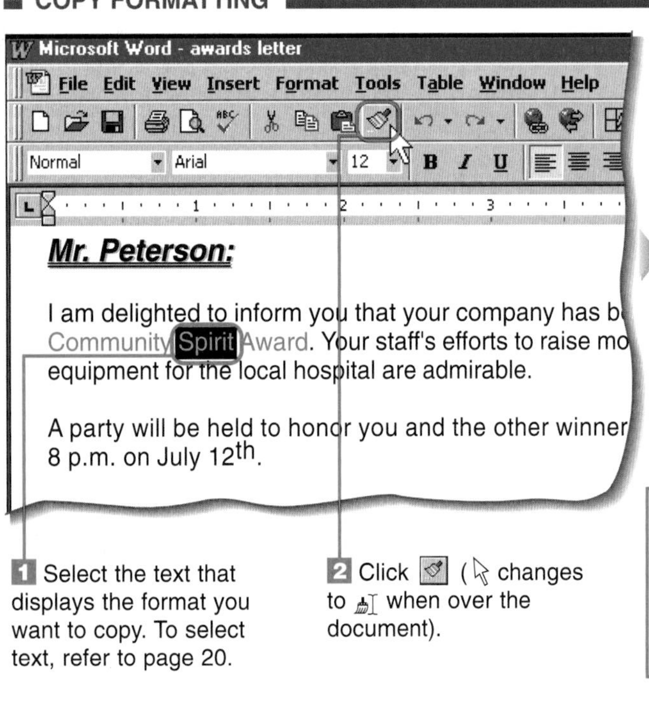

Microsoft Word - awards letter
File Edit View Insert Format Tools Table Window Help
Normal
Arial
12
Mr. Peterson:
I am delighted to inform you that your company has b
Community Spirit Award. Your staff's efforts to raise mo
equipment for the local hospital are admirable.
A party will be held to honor you and the other winner
8 p.m. on July 12th.

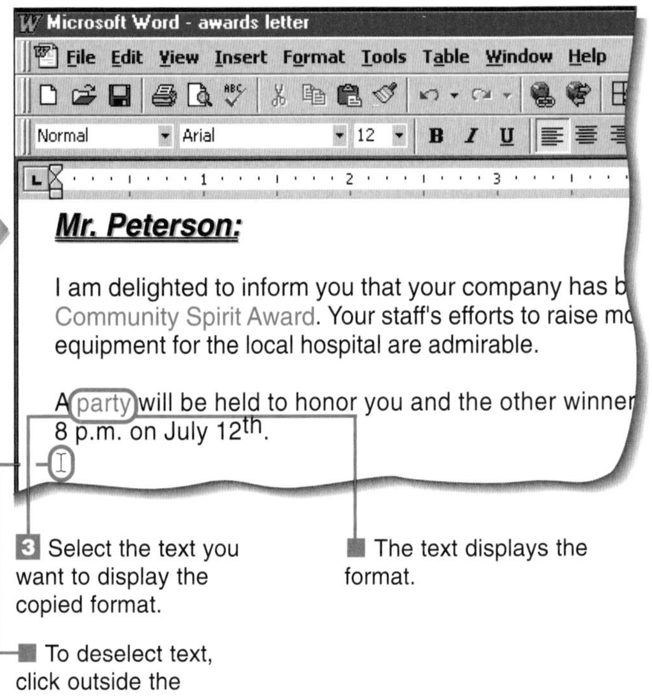

Microsoft Word - awards letter
File Edit View Insert Format Tools Table Window Help
Normal
Arial
12
Mr. Peterson:
I am delighted to inform you that your company has b
Community Spirit Award. Your staff's efforts to raise mo
equipment for the local hospital are admirable.
A party will be held to honor you and the other winner
8 p.m. on July 12th.

1 Select the text that displays the format you want to copy. To select text, refer to page 20.

2 Click (changes to when over the document).

3 Select the text you want to display the copied format.

■ To deselect text, click outside the selected area.

■ The text displays the format.

ADD A BORDER

You can add a border to emphasize an area of text in your document.

ADD A BORDER

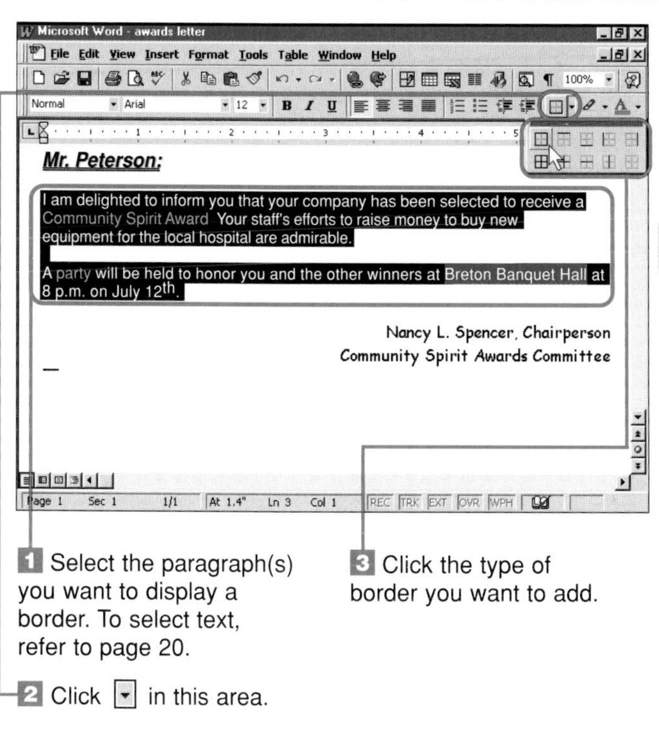

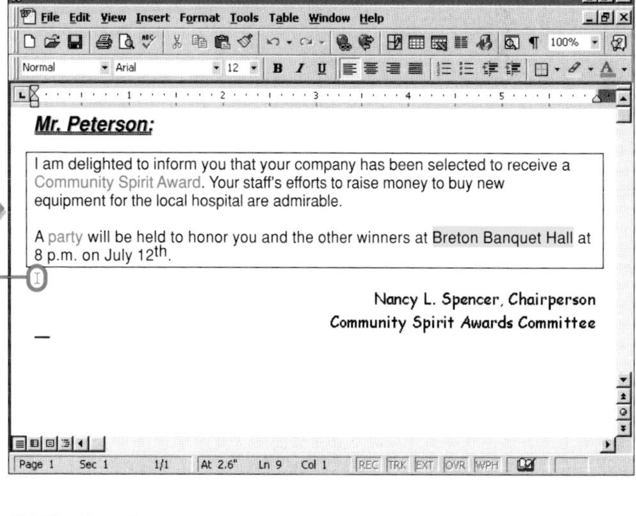

1 Select the paragraph(s) you want to display a border. To select text, refer to page 20.

2 Click ▾ in this area.

3 Click the type of border you want to add.

■ The border you selected appears.

■ To deselect text, click outside the selected area.

REMOVE A BORDER

■ Select the paragraph(s) you no longer want to display a border. Then perform steps **2** and **3**, selecting ▢ in step **3**.

INSERT A SYMBOL

You can insert symbols that do not appear on your keyboard into your document.

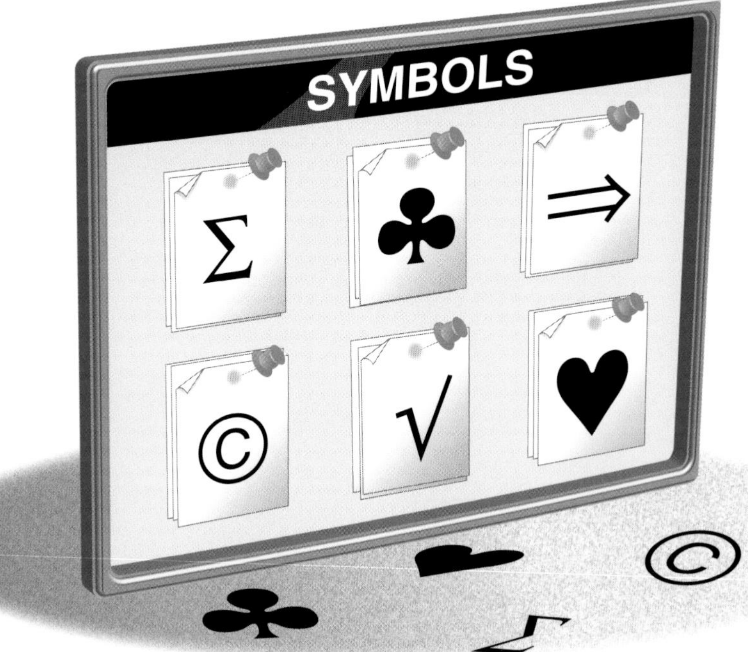

INSERT A SYMBOL

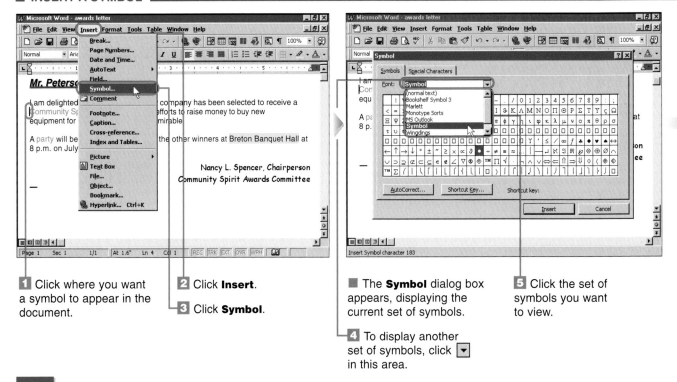

1 Click where you want a symbol to appear in the document.

2 Click **Insert**.

3 Click **Symbol**.

■ The **Symbol** dialog box appears, displaying the current set of symbols.

4 To display another set of symbols, click ▾ in this area.

5 Click the set of symbols you want to view.

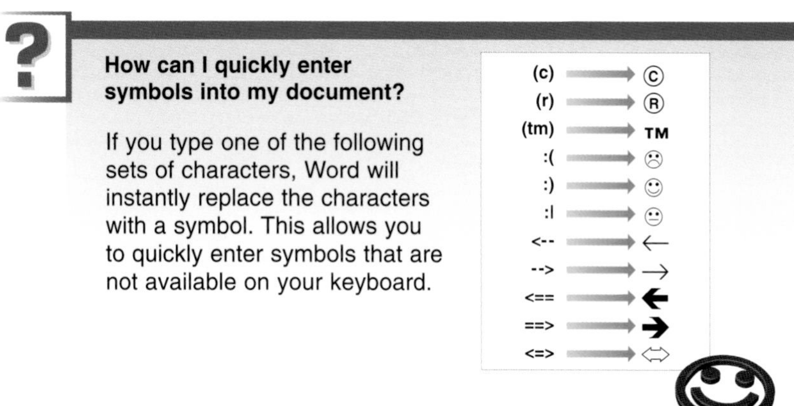

How can I quickly enter symbols into my document?

If you type one of the following sets of characters, Word will instantly replace the characters with a symbol. This allows you to quickly enter symbols that are not available on your keyboard.

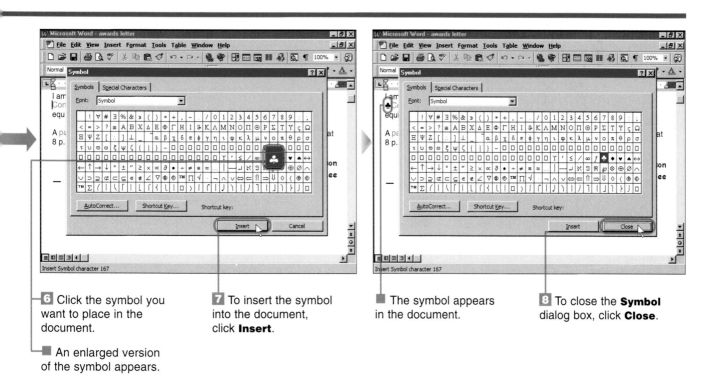

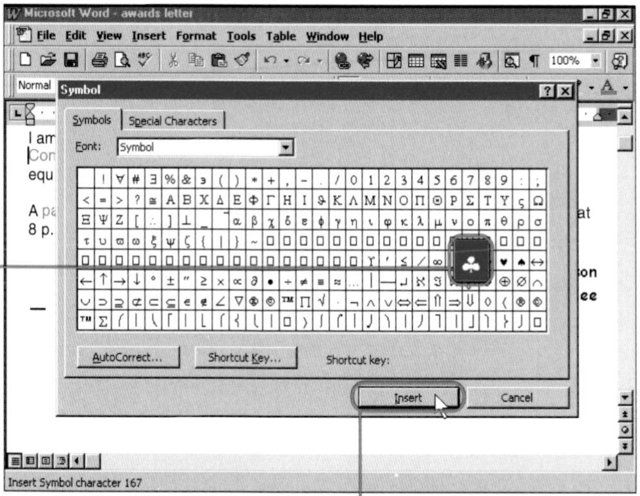

6 Click the symbol you want to place in the document.

■ An enlarged version of the symbol appears.

7 To insert the symbol into the document, click **Insert**.

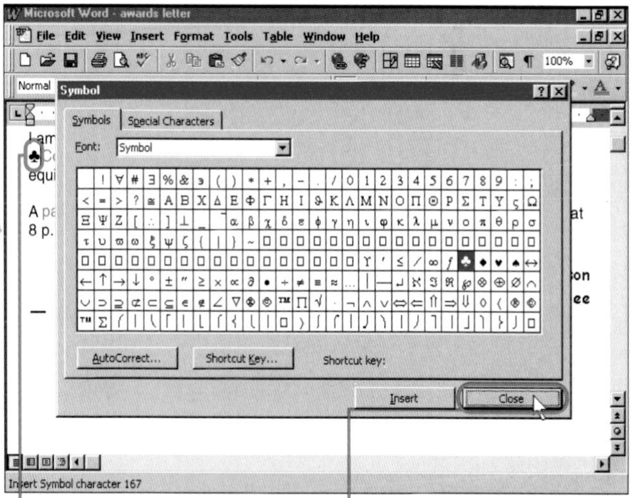

■ The symbol appears in the document.

8 To close the **Symbol** dialog box, click **Close**.

ADD BULLETS OR NUMBERS

You can separate items in a list by beginning each item with a bullet or number.

ADD BULLETS OR NUMBERS

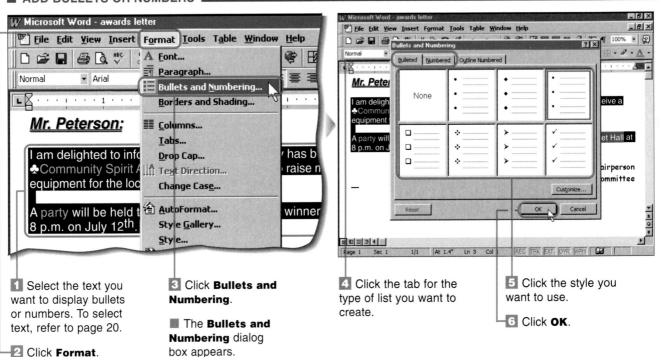

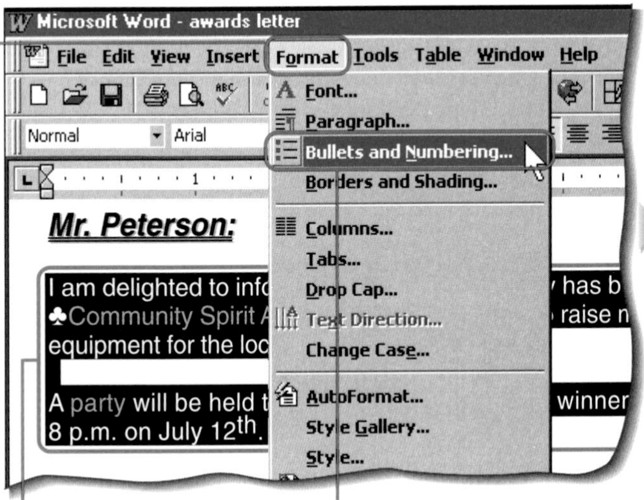

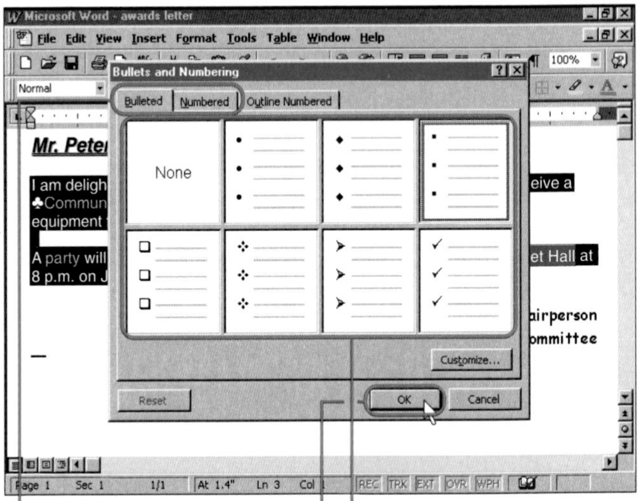

1 Select the text you want to display bullets or numbers. To select text, refer to page 20.

2 Click **Format**.

3 Click **Bullets and Numbering**.

■ The **Bullets and Numbering** dialog box appears.

4 Click the tab for the type of list you want to create.

5 Click the style you want to use.

6 Click **OK**.

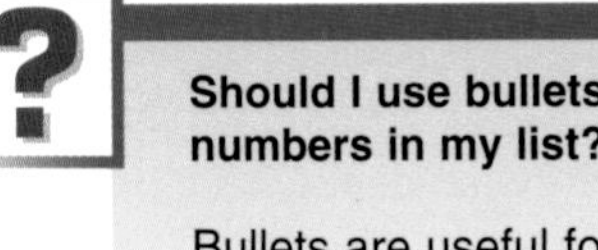

Should I use bullets or numbers in my list?

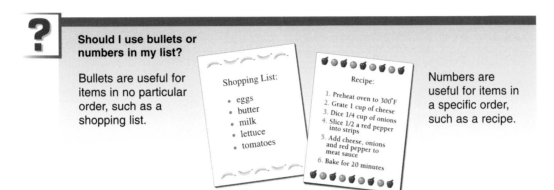

Bullets are useful for items in no particular order, such as a shopping list.

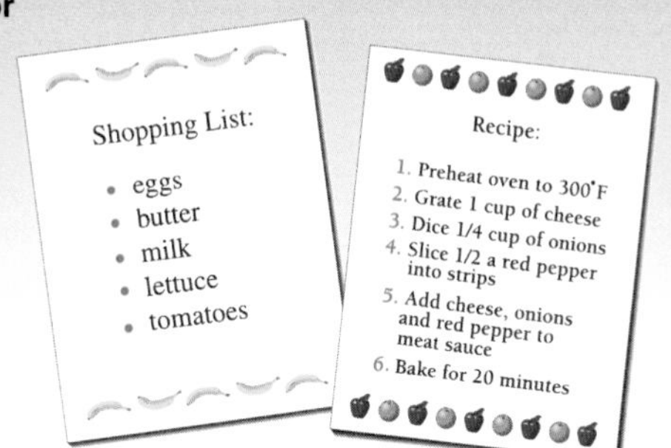

Shopping List:
eggs
butter
milk
lettuce
tomatoes
Recipe:
1. Preheat oven to 300°F
2. Grate 1 cup of cheese
3. Dice 1/4 cup of onions
4. Slice 1/2 a red pepper into strips
5. Add cheese, onions and red pepper to meat sauce
6. Bake for 20 minutes

Numbers are useful for items in a specific order, such as a recipe.

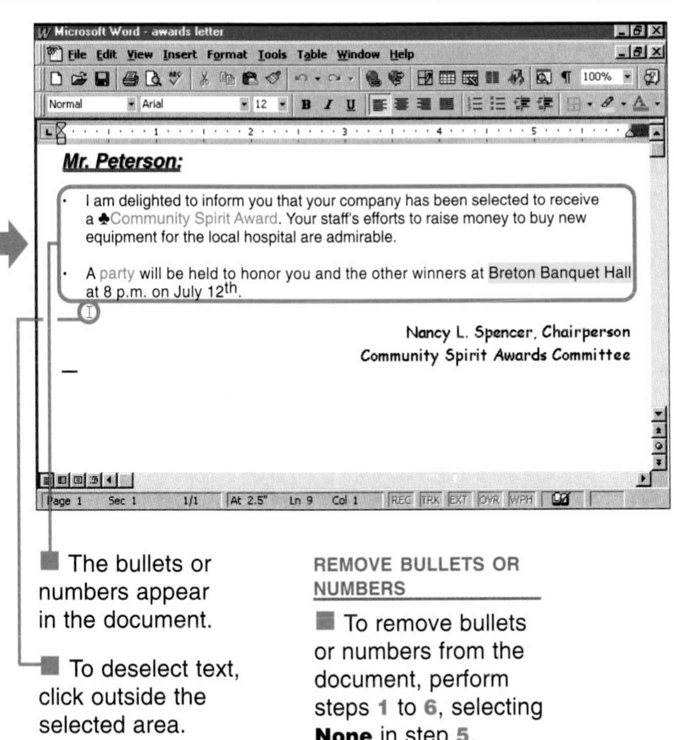

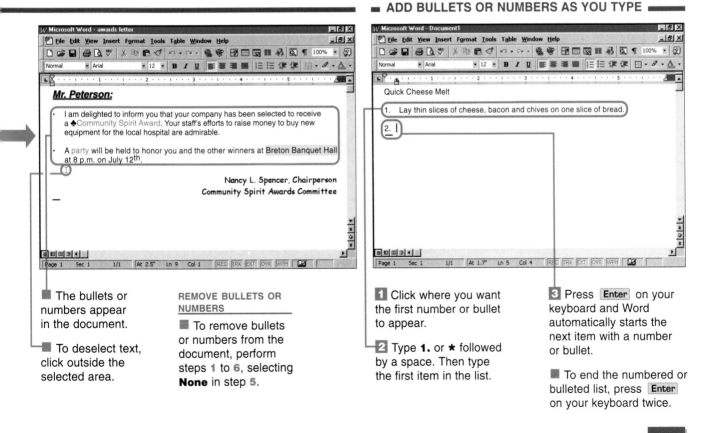

- The bullets or numbers appear in the document.
- To deselect text, click outside the selected area.

REMOVE BULLETS OR NUMBERS

- To remove bullets or numbers from the document, perform steps 1 to 6, selecting **None** in step 5.

ADD BULLETS OR NUMBERS AS YOU TYPE

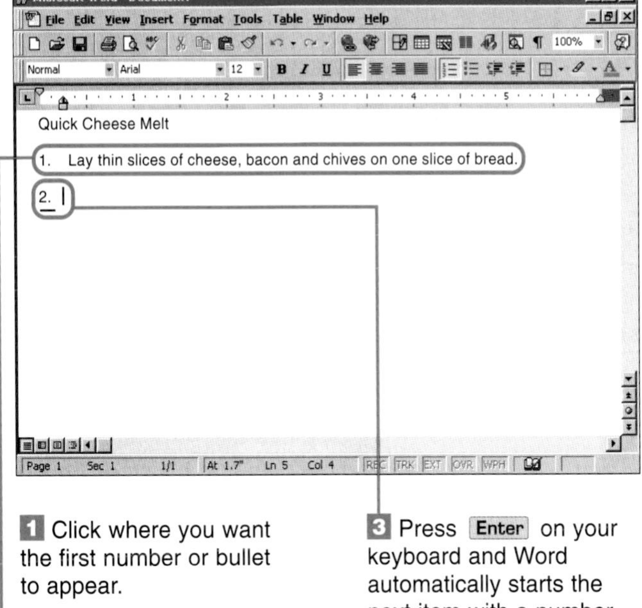

1 Click where you want the first number or bullet to appear.

2 Type **1.** or ***** followed by a space. Then type the first item in the list.

3 Press Enter on your keyboard and Word automatically starts the next item with a number or bullet.

- To end the numbered or bulleted list, press Enter on your keyboard twice.

CHANGE LINE SPACING

You can change the amount of space between the lines of text in your document to make your document easier to review and edit.

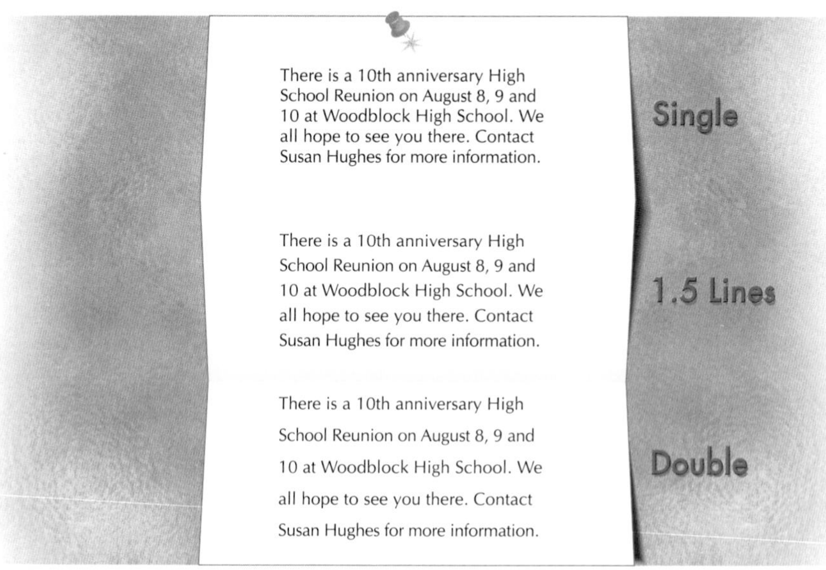

There is a 10th anniversary High School Reunion on August 8, 9 and 10 at Woodblock High School. We all hope to see you there. Contact Susan Hughes for more information.
Single
There is a 10th anniversary High School Reunion on August 8, 9 and 10 at Woodblock High School. We all hope to see you there. Contact Susan Hughes for more information.
1.5 Lines
There is a 10th anniversary High School Reunion on August 8, 9 and 10 at Woodblock High School. We all hope to see you there. Contact Susan Hughes for more information.
Double

CHANGE LINE SPACING

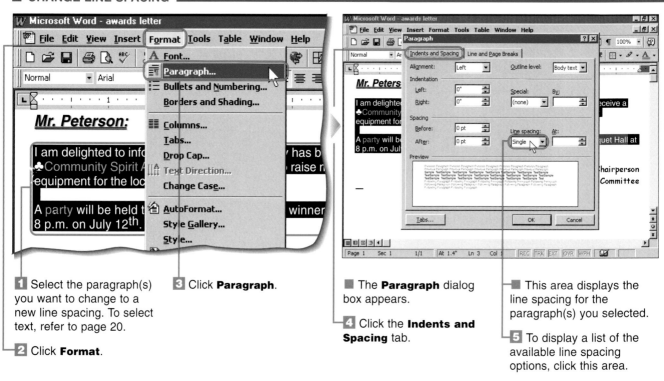

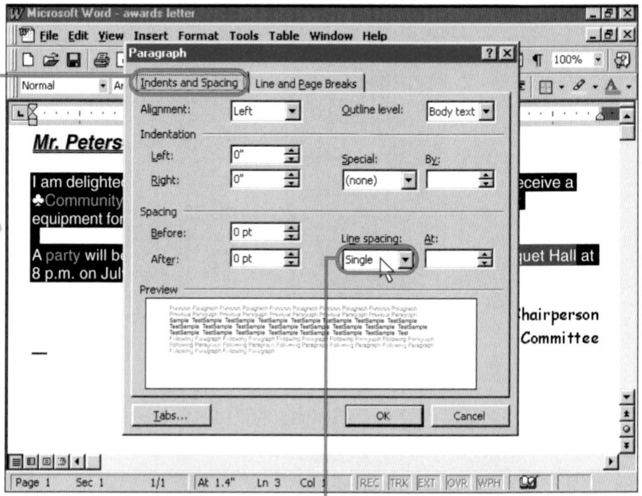

1 Select the paragraph(s) you want to change to a new line spacing. To select text, refer to page 20.

2 Click **Format**.

3 Click **Paragraph**.

■ The **Paragraph** dialog box appears.

4 Click the **Indents and Spacing** tab.

■ This area displays the line spacing for the paragraph(s) you selected.

5 To display a list of the available line spacing options, click this area.

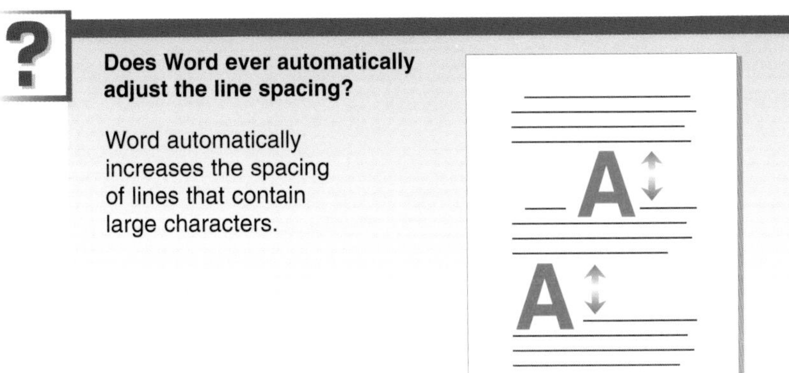

Does Word ever automatically adjust the line spacing?

Word automatically increases the spacing of lines that contain large characters.

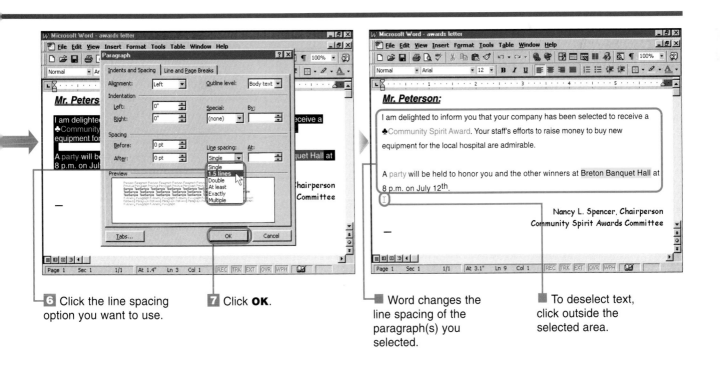

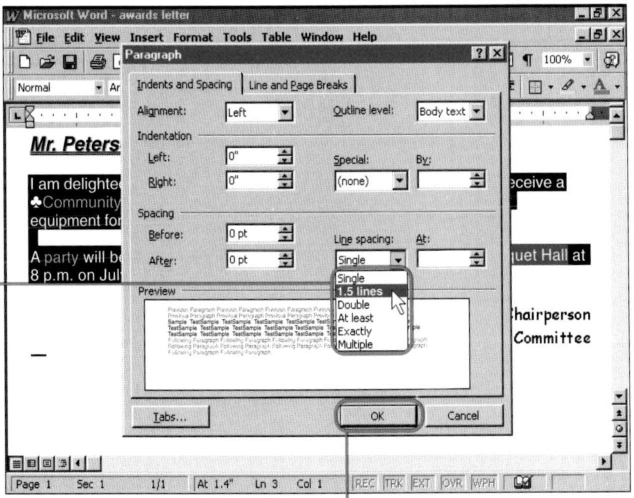

6 Click the line spacing option you want to use.

7 Click **OK**.

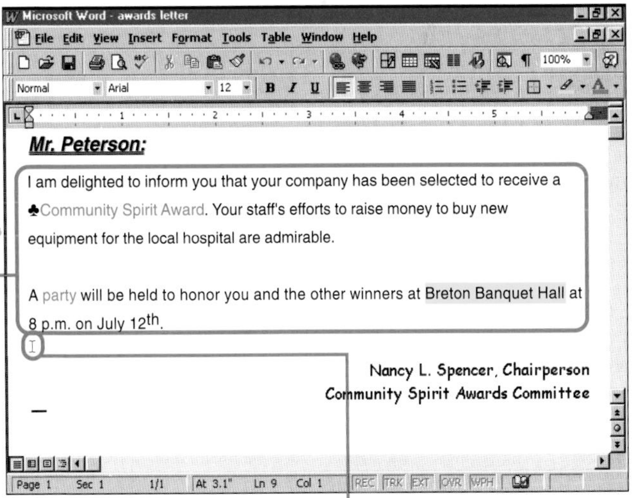

■ Word changes the line spacing of the paragraph(s) you selected.

■ To deselect text, click outside the selected area.

INDENT PARAGRAPHS

You can use the Indent feature to set off paragraphs in your document.

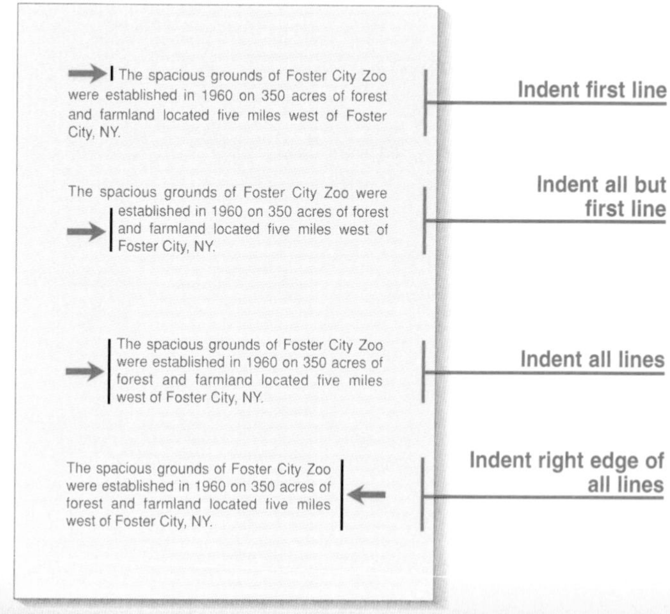

The spacious grounds of Foster City Zoo were established in 1960 on 350 acres of forest and farmland located five miles west of Foster City, NY.
Indent first line
The spacious grounds of Foster City Zoo were established in 1960 on 350 acres of forest and farmland located five miles west of Foster City, NY.
Indent all but first line
The spacious grounds of Foster City Zoo were established in 1960 on 350 acres of forest and farmland located five miles west of Foster City, NY.
Indent all lines
The spacious grounds of Foster City Zoo were established in 1960 on 350 acres of forest and farmland located five miles west of Foster City, NY.
Indent right edge of all lines

INDENT PARAGRAPHS

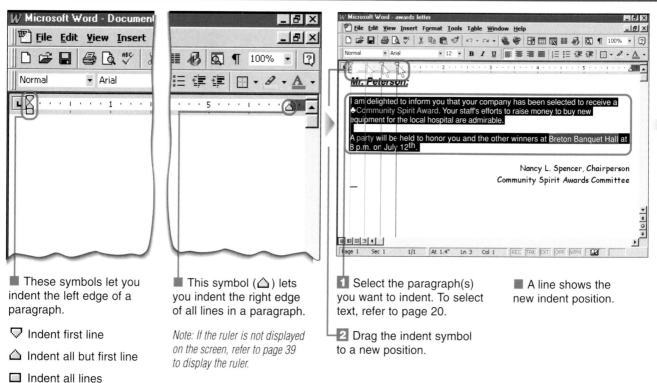

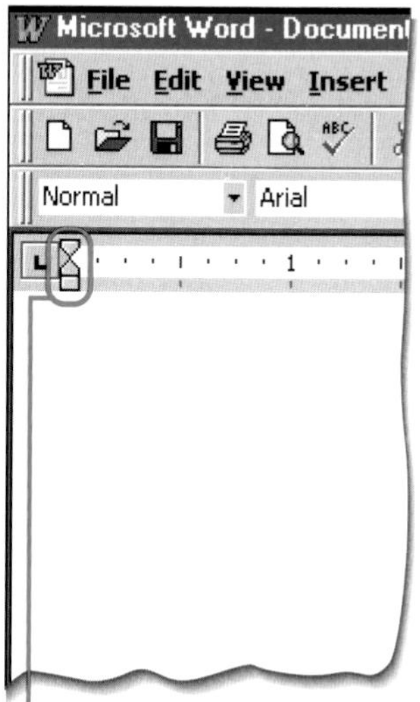

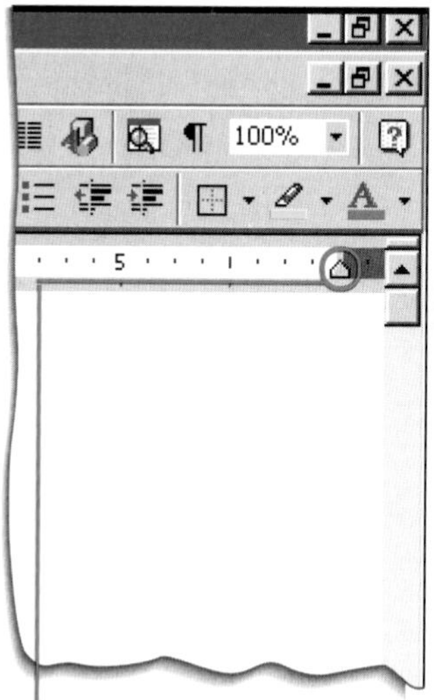

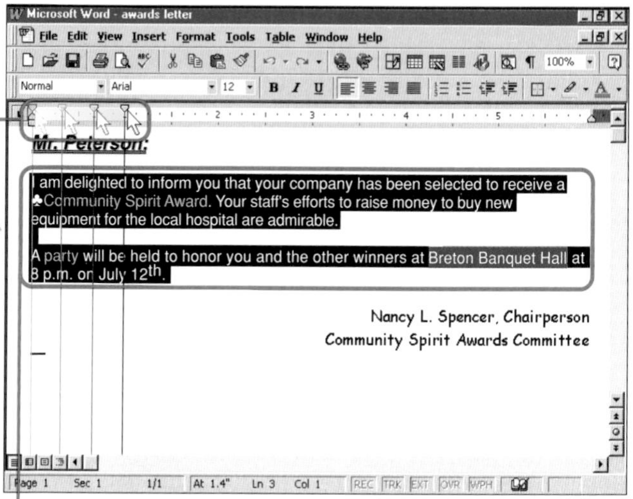

■ These symbols let you indent the left edge of a paragraph.

▽ Indent first line

△ Indent all but first line

□ Indent all lines

■ This symbol (△) lets you indent the right edge of all lines in a paragraph.

Note: If the ruler is not displayed on the screen, *refer to page 39* *to display the ruler.*

1 Select the paragraph(s) you want to indent. To select text, refer to page 20.

2 Drag the indent symbol to a new position.

■ A line shows the new indent position.

What is a hanging indent?

A hanging indent moves all but the first line of a paragraph to the right. Hanging indents are useful when you are creating a résumé, glossary or bibliography.

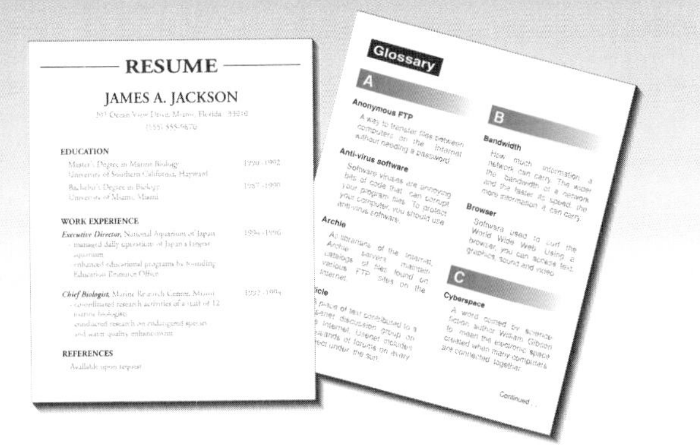

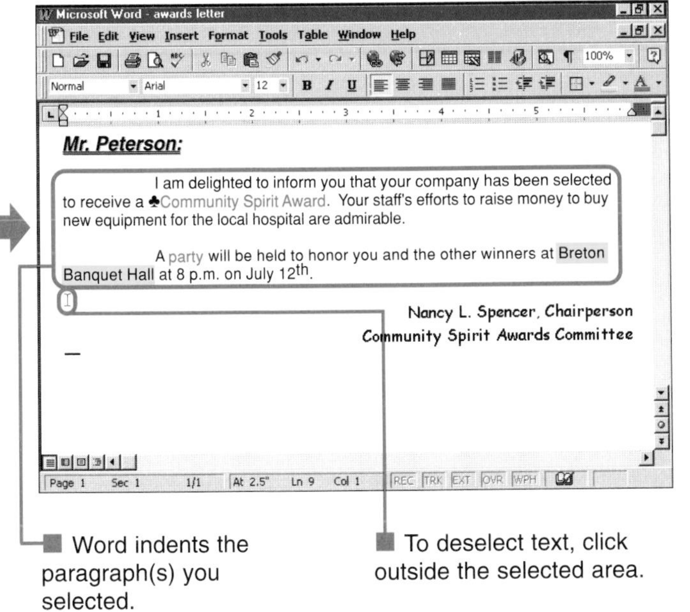

■ Word indents the paragraph(s) you selected.

■ To deselect text, click outside the selected area.

QUICKLY INDENT ALL LINES IN A PARAGRAPH

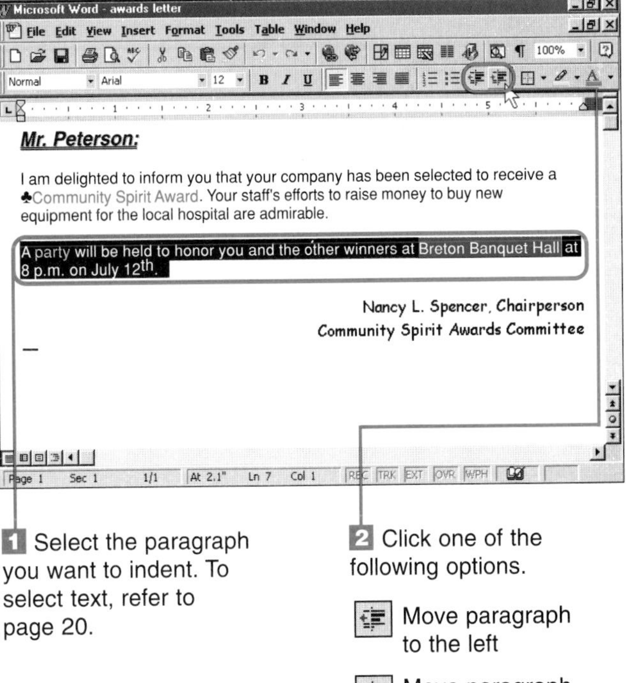

1 Select the paragraph you want to indent. To select text, refer to page 20.

2 Click one of the following options.

- Move paragraph to the left
- Move paragraph to the right

CHANGE TAB SETTINGS

You can use tabs to line up columns of information in your document. Word offers four types of tabs.

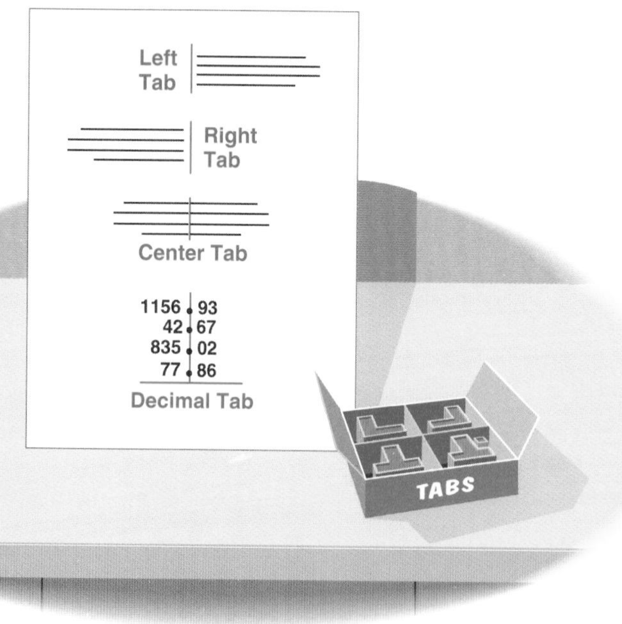

Word automatically places a tab every 0.5 inches across each page.

ADD A TAB

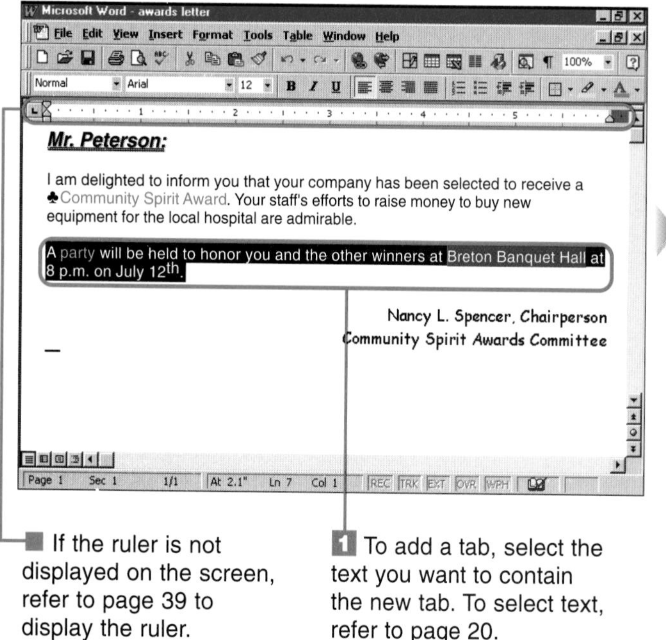

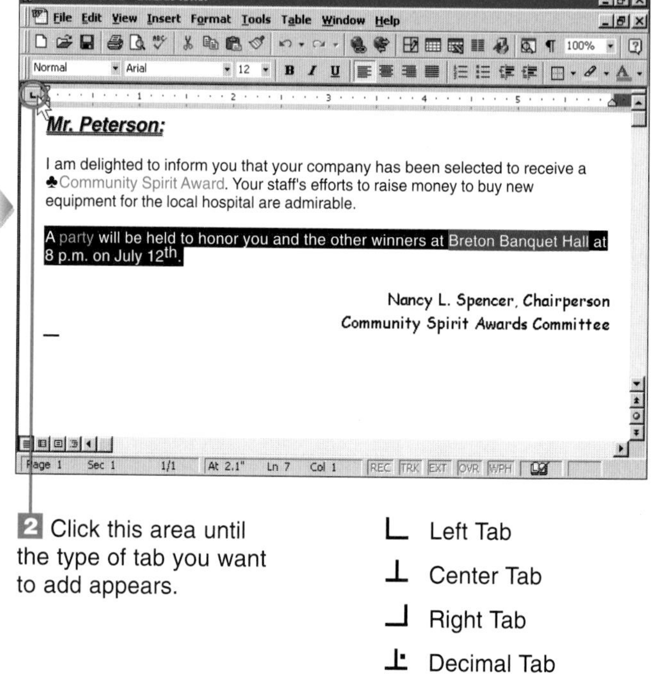

■ If the ruler is not displayed on the screen, refer to page 39 to display the ruler.

1 To add a tab, select the text you want to contain the new tab. To select text, refer to page 20.

■ To add a tab to text you are about to type, click where you want to type the text.

2 Click this area until the type of tab you want to add appears.

- ∟ Left Tab
- ⊥ Center Tab
- ┘ Right Tab
- ⊥· Decimal Tab

?

What happens if I use spaces instead of tabs to line up columns of text?

Your document may not print correctly if you use spaces instead of tabs to line up columns of text.

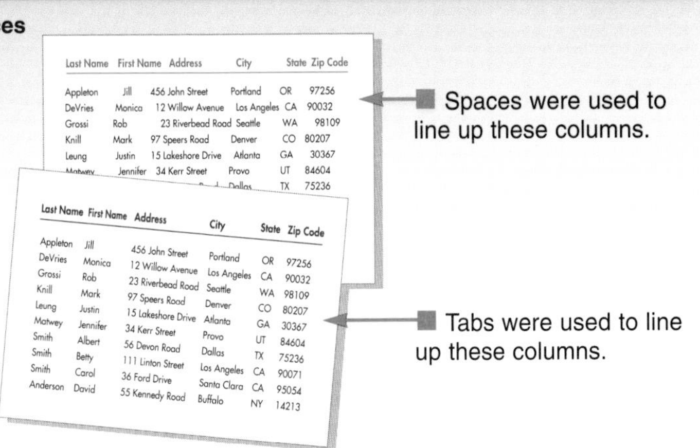

■ Spaces were used to line up these columns.

■ Tabs were used to line up these columns.

USING TABS

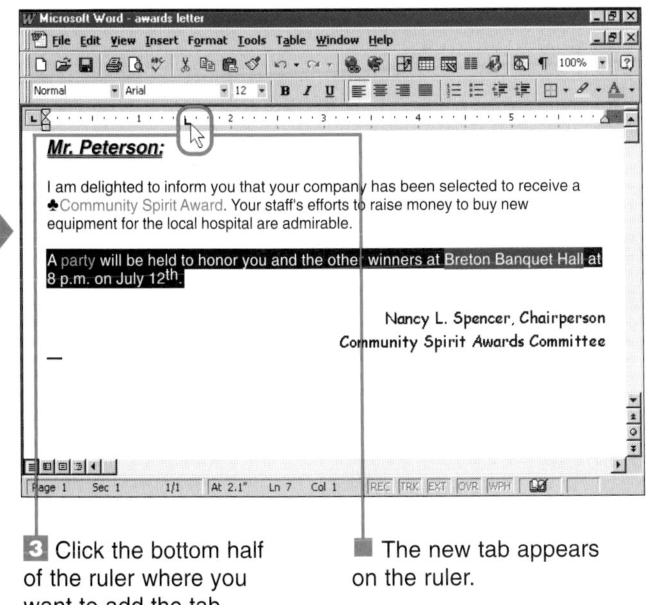

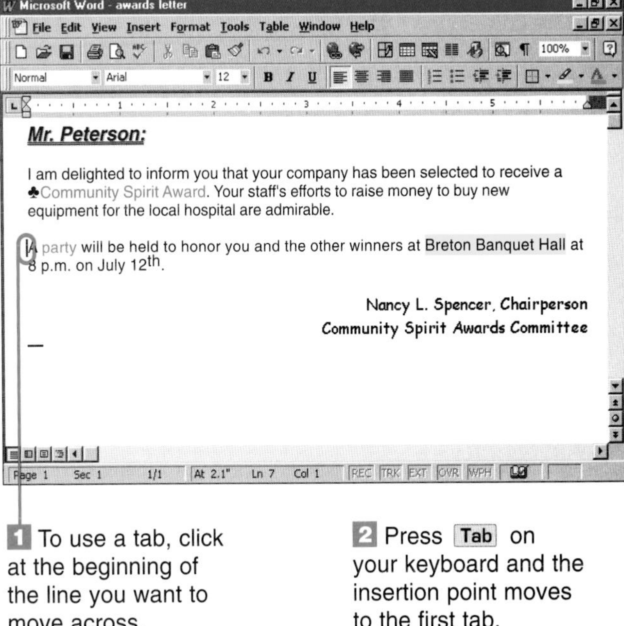

1 To use a tab, click at the beginning of the line you want to move across.

2 Press Tab on your keyboard and the insertion point moves to the first tab.

3 Click the bottom half of the ruler where you want to add the tab.

■ The new tab appears on the ruler.

You can easily move a tab to a different position on the ruler.

MOVE A TAB

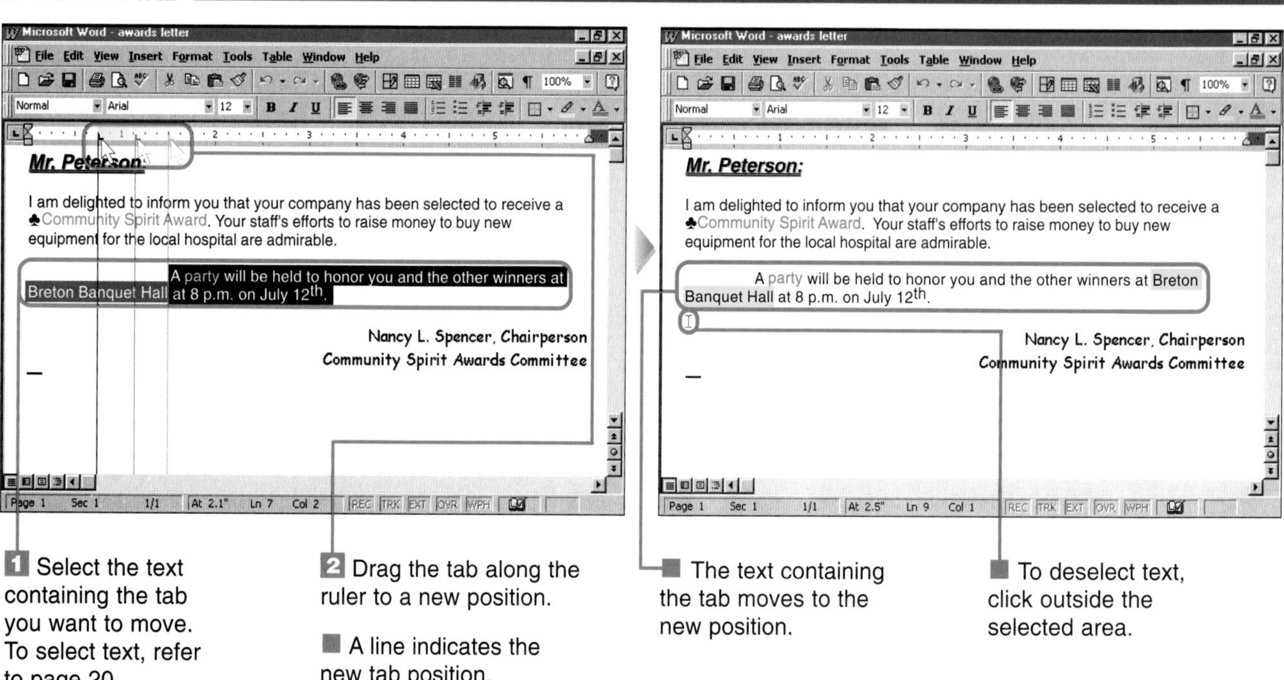

1 Select the text containing the tab you want to move. To select text, refer to page 20.

2 Drag the tab along the ruler to a new position.

■ A line indicates the new tab position.

■ The text containing the tab moves to the new position.

■ To deselect text, click outside the selected area.

When you no longer need a tab, you can remove it from the ruler.

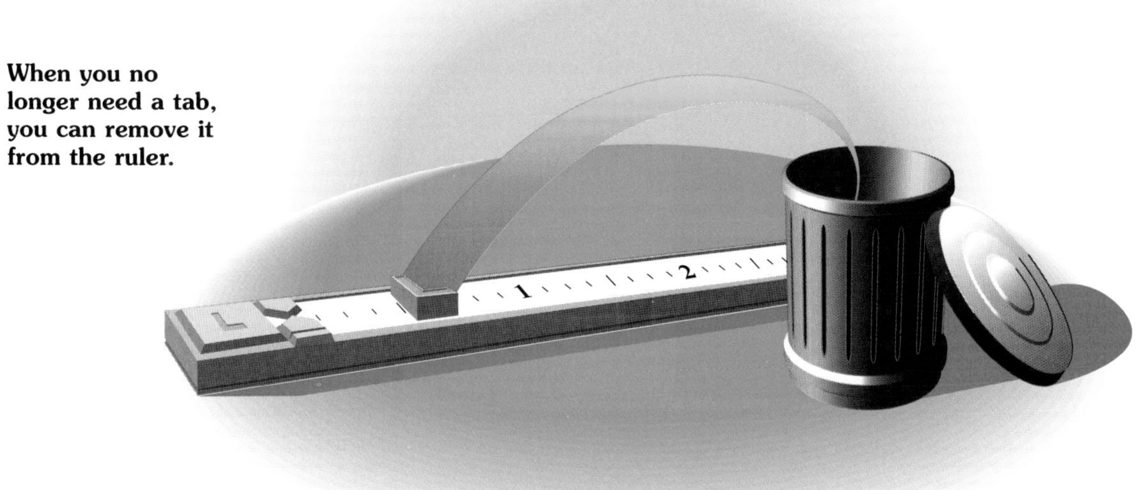

REMOVE A TAB

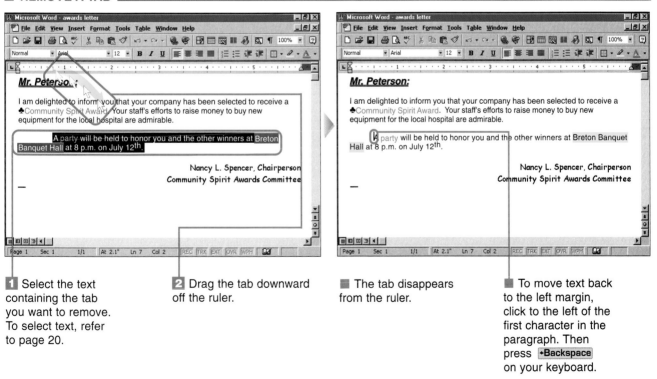

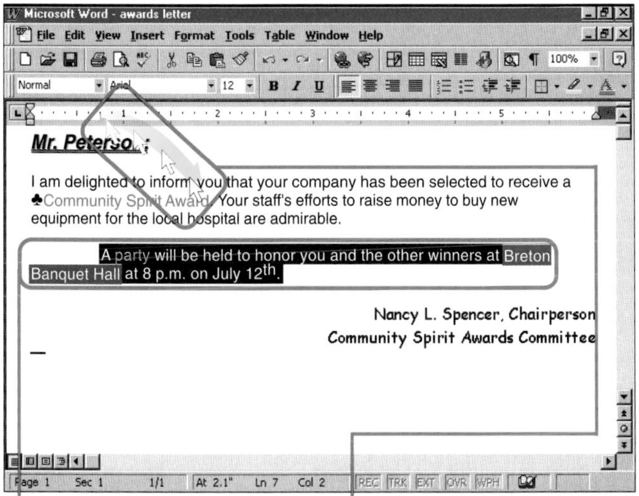

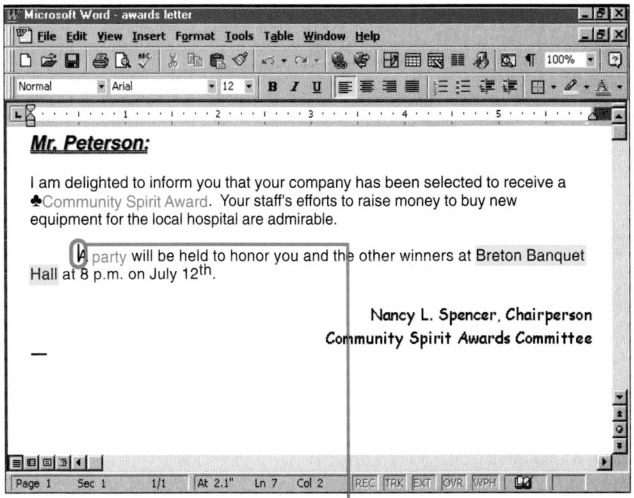

1 Select the text containing the tab you want to remove. To select text, refer to page 20.

2 Drag the tab downward off the ruler.

■ The tab disappears from the ruler.

■ To move text back to the left margin, click to the left of the first character in the paragraph. Then press Backspace on your keyboard.

ADD PAGE NUMBERS

You can have Word number the pages in your document.

ADD PAGE NUMBERS

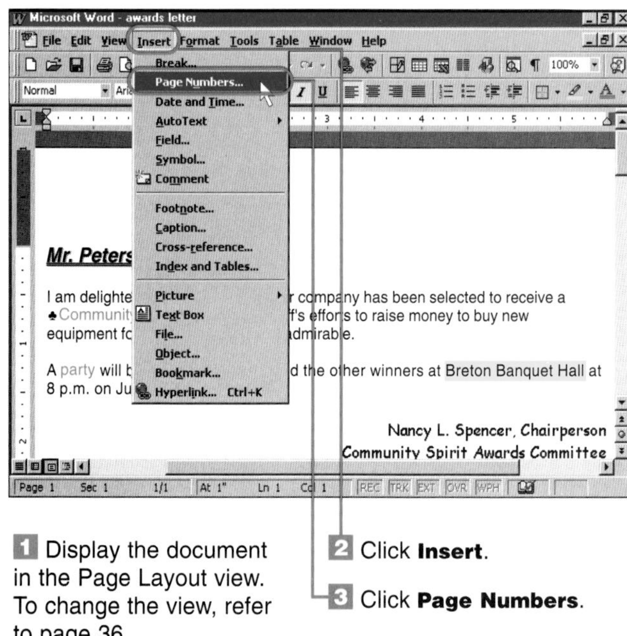

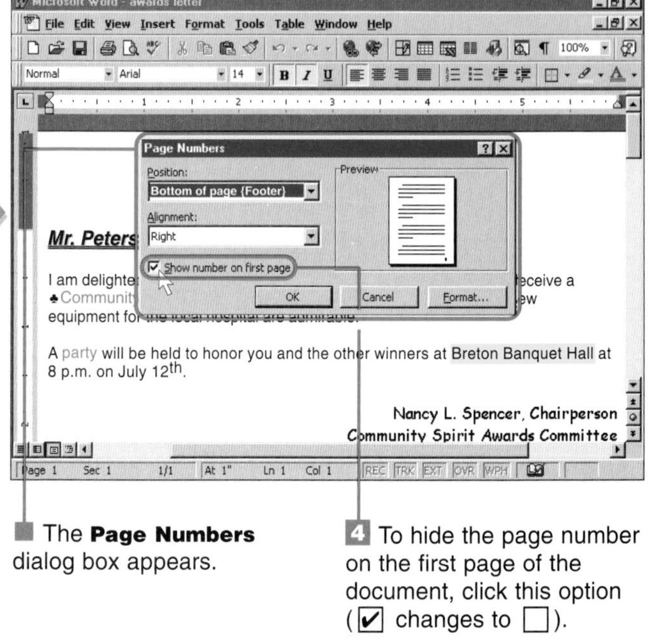

1 Display the document in the Page Layout view. To change the view, refer to page 36.

Note: Word does not display page numbers in the Normal view.

2 Click **Insert**.

3 Click **Page Numbers**.

■ The **Page Numbers** dialog box appears.

4 To hide the page number on the first page of the document, click this option (☑ changes to ☐).

Note: This option is useful if the first page of the document is a title page.

Will Word adjust the page numbers if I change my document?

If you add, remove or rearrange text in your document, Word will automatically adjust the page numbers for you.

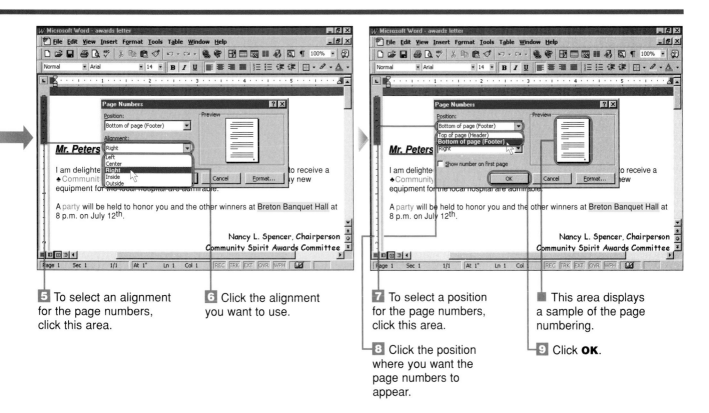

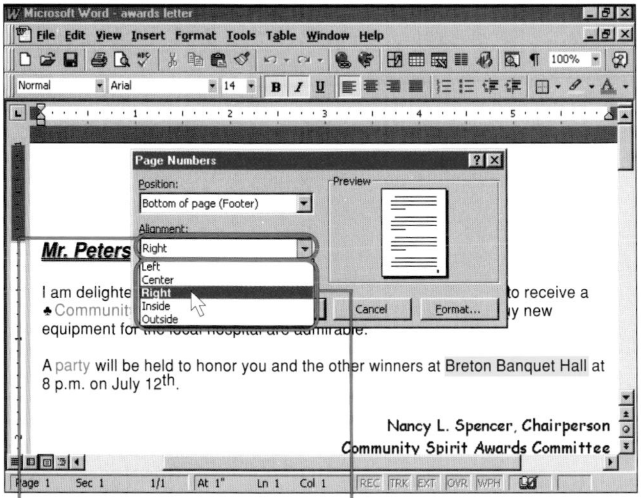

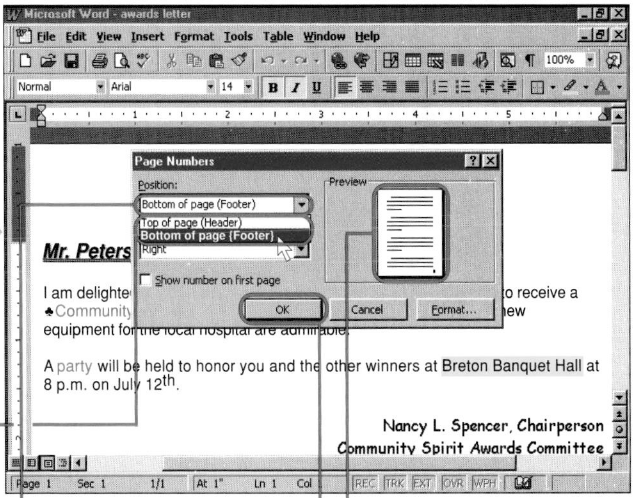

5 To select an alignment for the page numbers, click this area.

6 Click the alignment you want to use.

7 To select a position for the page numbers, click this area.

8 Click the position where you want the page numbers to appear.

■ This area displays a sample of the page numbering.

9 Click **OK**.

ADD FOOTNOTES

A footnote appears at the bottom of a page to provide additional information about text in your document.

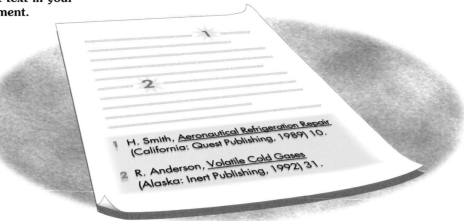

Word ensures that the footnote text always appears on the same page as the footnote number.

ADD FOOTNOTES

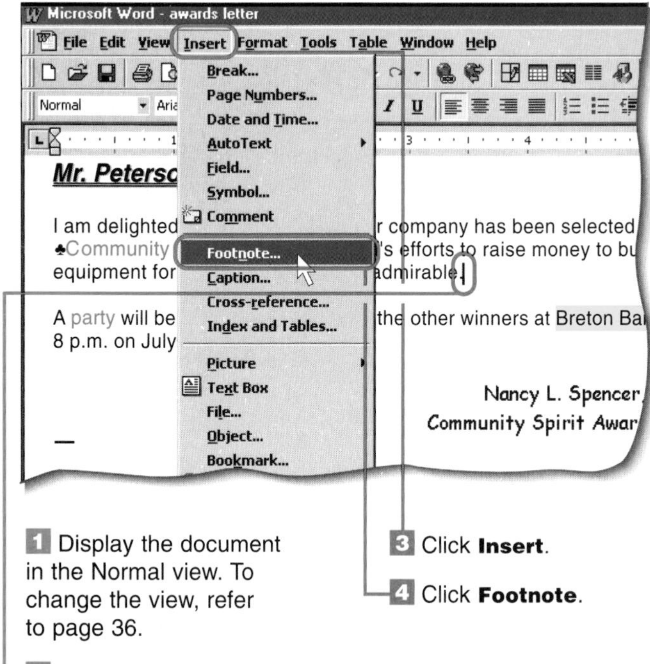

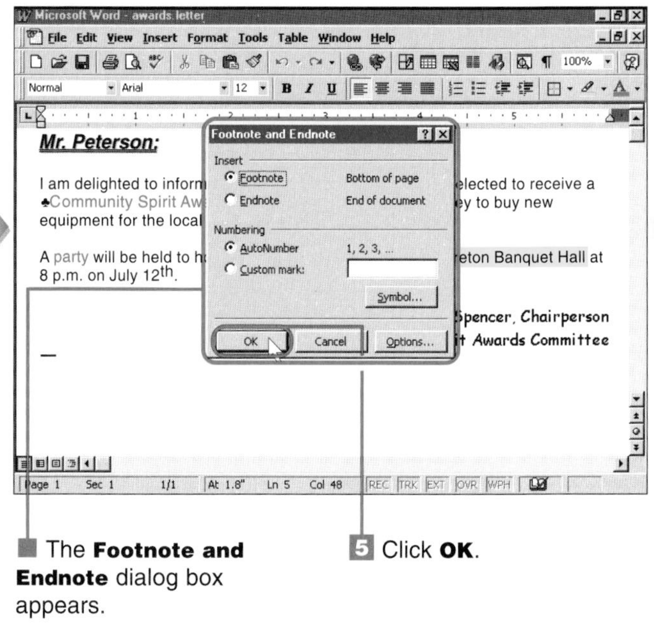

1 Display the document in the Normal view. To change the view, refer to page 36.

2 Click where you want the number of the footnote to appear.

3 Click **Insert**.

4 Click **Footnote**.

■ The **Footnote and Endnote** dialog box appears.

5 Click **OK**.

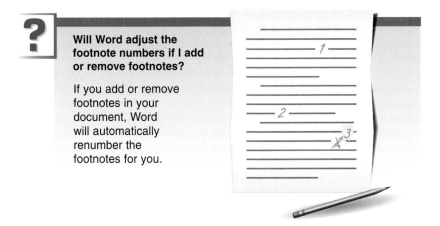

Will Word adjust the footnote numbers if I add or remove footnotes?

If you add or remove footnotes in your document, Word will automatically renumber the footnotes for you.

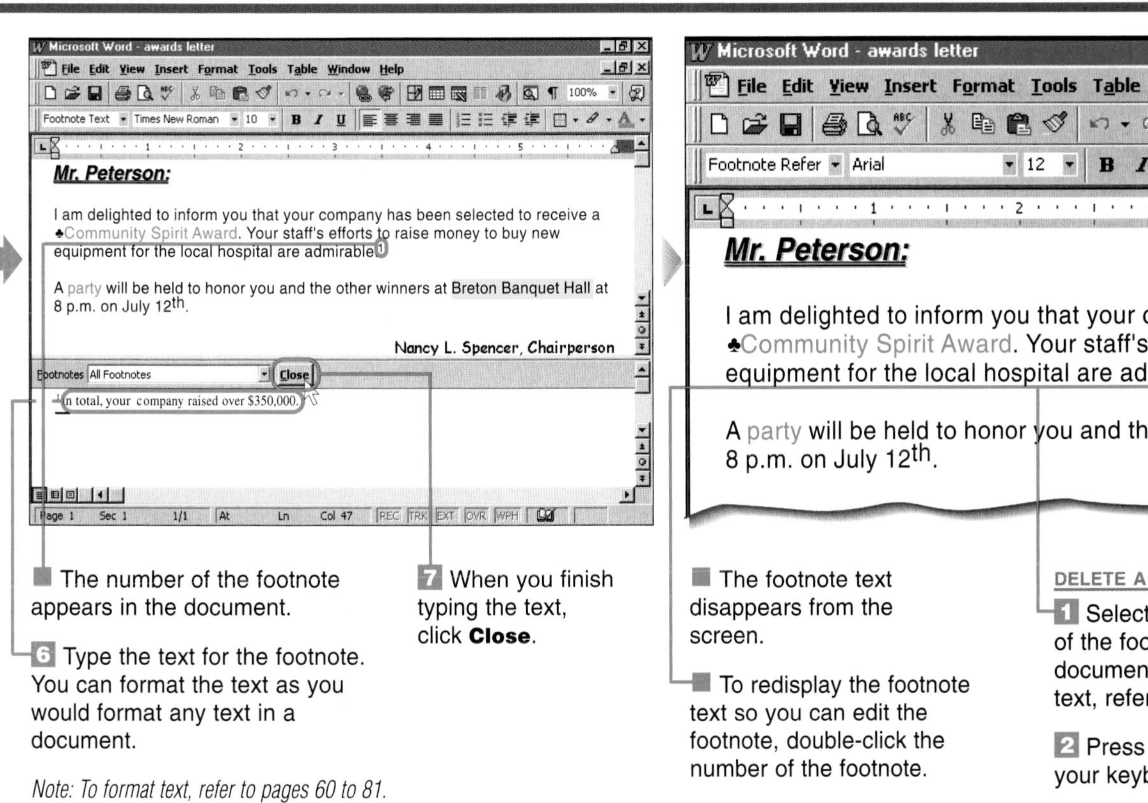

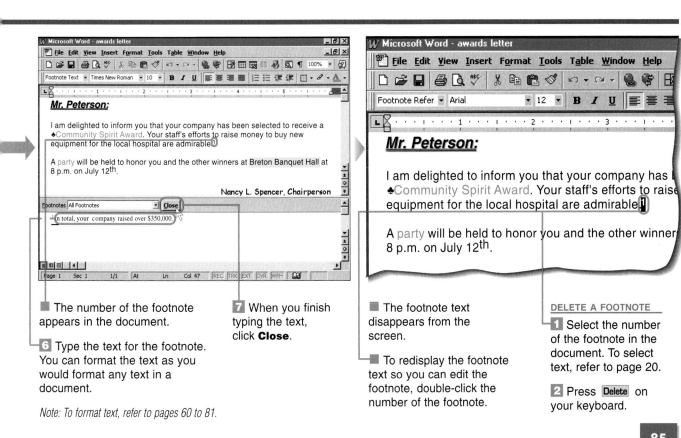

■ The number of the footnote appears in the document.

6 Type the text for the footnote. You can format the text as you would format any text in a document.

Note: To format text, refer to pages 60 to 81.

7 When you finish typing the text, click **Close**.

■ The footnote text disappears from the screen.

■ To redisplay the footnote text so you can edit the footnote, double-click the number of the footnote.

DELETE A FOOTNOTE

1 Select the number of the footnote in the document. To select text, refer to page 20.

2 Press Delete on your keyboard.

ADD A HEADER AND FOOTER

You can add a header and footer to each page of your document.

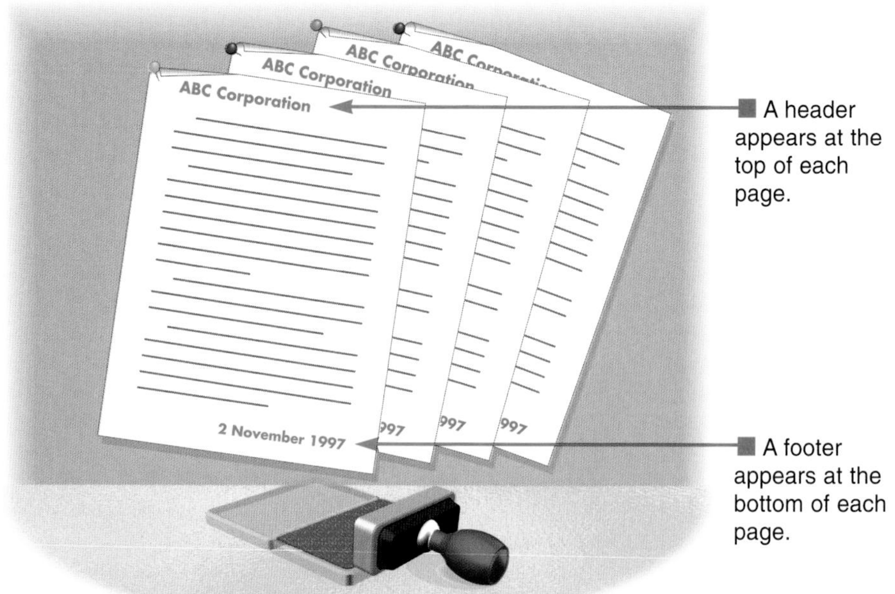

A header appears at the top of each page.

A footer appears at the bottom of each page.

ADD A HEADER AND FOOTER

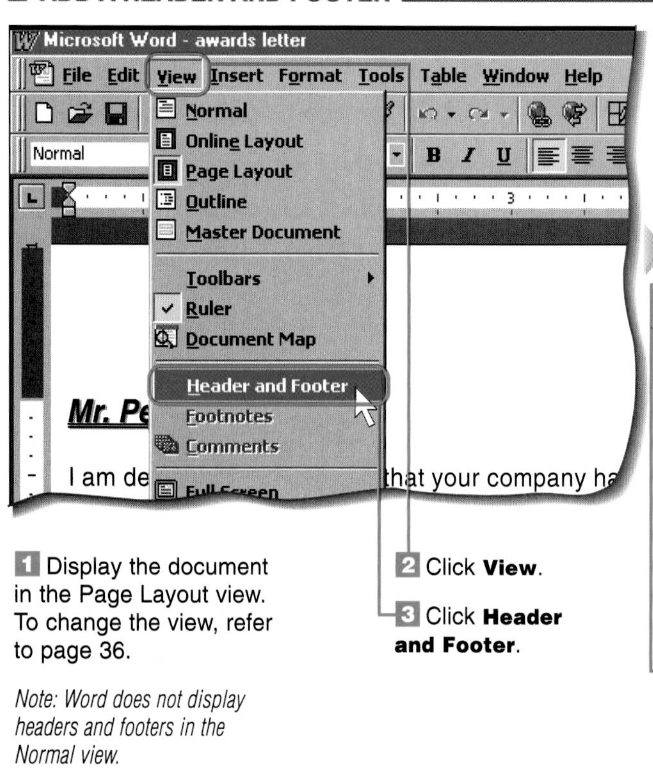

1 Display the document in the Page Layout view. To change the view, refer to page 36.

Note: Word does not display headers and footers in the Normal view.

2 Click **View**.

3 Click **Header and Footer**.

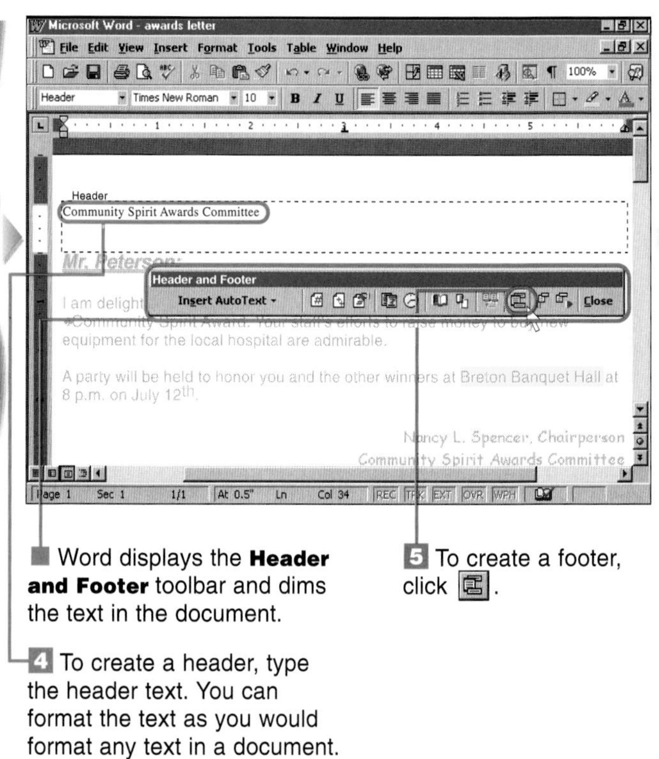

Word displays the **Header and Footer** toolbar and dims the text in the document.

4 To create a header, type the header text. You can format the text as you would format any text in a document.

5 To create a footer, click [icon].

? What information can a header or footer contain?

A header or footer can contain information such as the company name, author's name, chapter title or date.

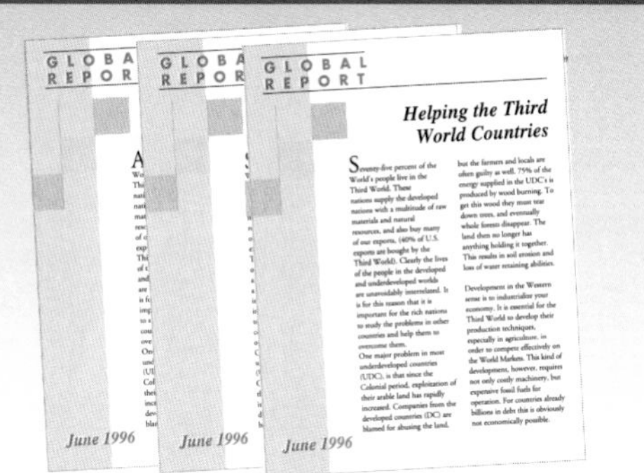

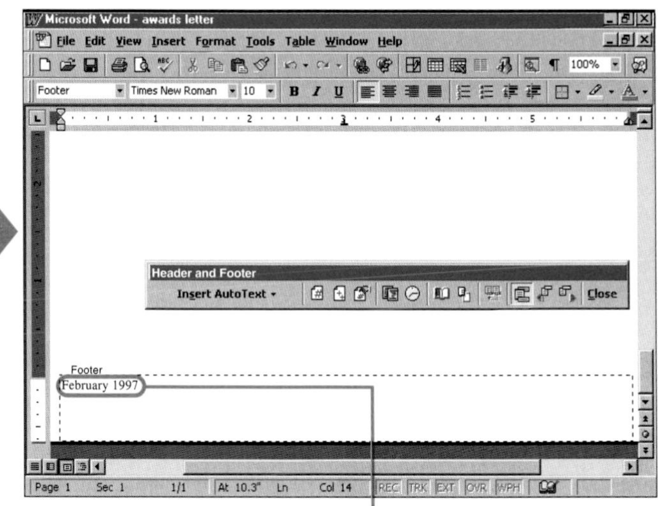

■ The **Footer** area appears.

Note: To return to the header area at any time, repeat step 5.

6 Type the footer text. You can format the text as you would format any text in a document.

Note: To format text, refer to pages 60 to 81.

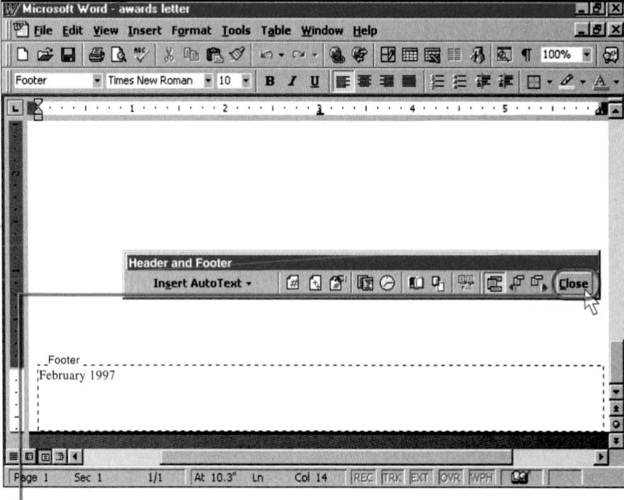

7 When you have finished creating the header and footer, click **Close**.

EDIT A HEADER OR FOOTER

1 To edit a header or footer, repeat steps 1 to 7.

INSERT A PAGE BREAK

If you want to start a new page at a specific place in your document, you can insert a page break. A page break shows where one page ends and another begins.

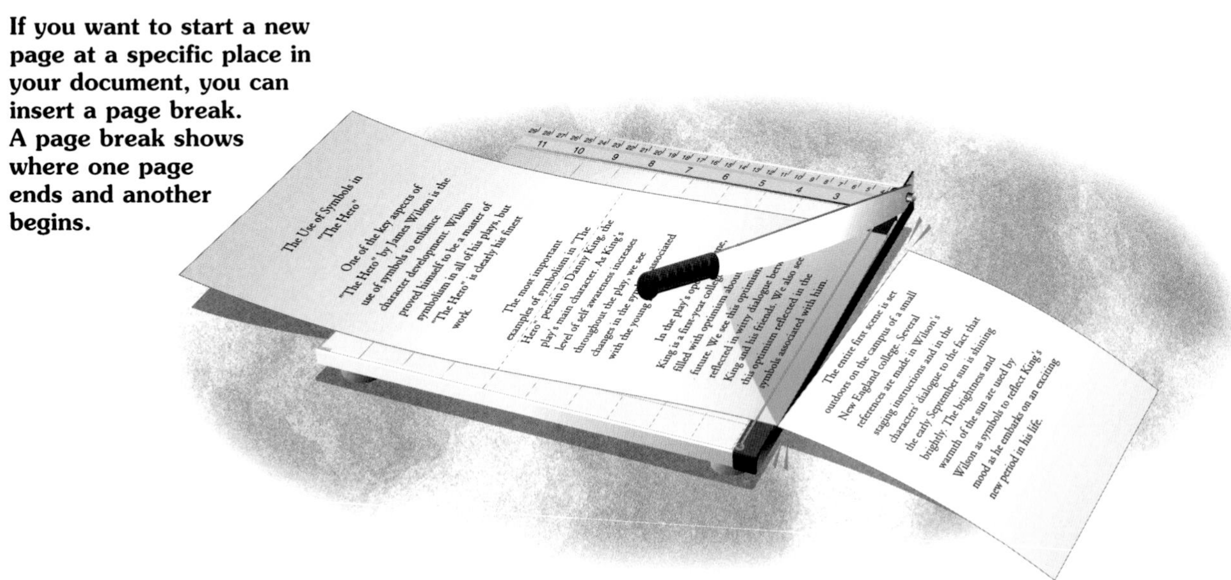

INSERT A PAGE BREAK

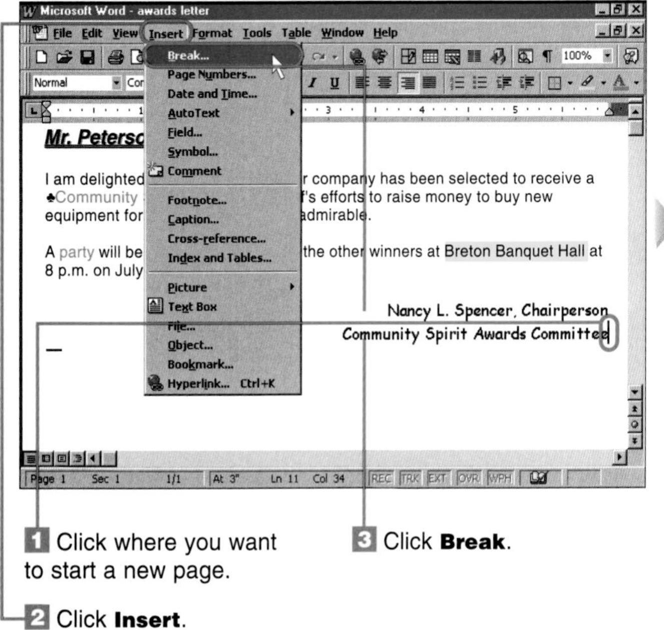

1 Click where you want to start a new page.

2 Click **Insert**.

3 Click **Break**.

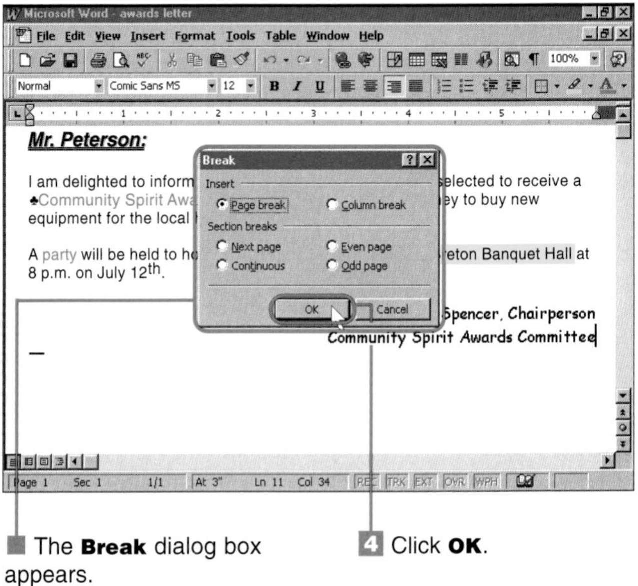

■ The **Break** dialog box appears.

4 Click **OK**.

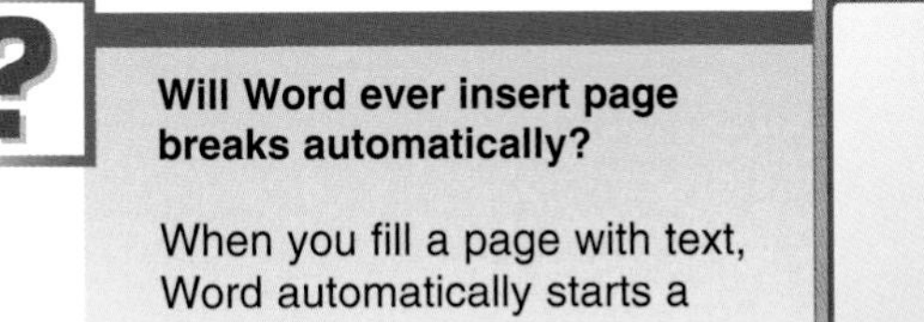

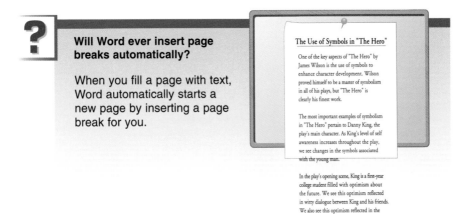

Will Word ever insert page breaks automatically?

When you fill a page with text, Word automatically starts a new page by inserting a page break for you.

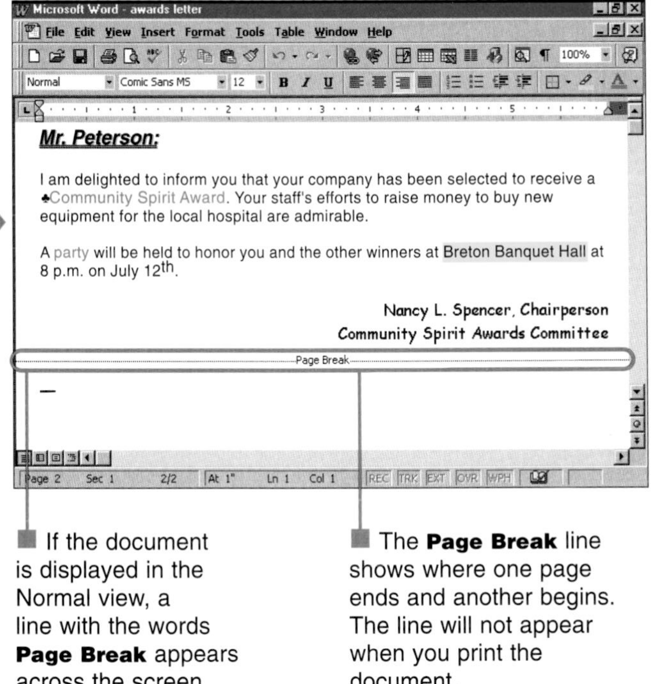

The Use of Symbols in "The Hero"
One of the key aspects of "The Hero" by James Wilson is the use of symbols to enhance character development. Wilson proved himself to be a master of symbolism in all of his plays, but "The Hero" is clearly his finest work.
The most important examples of symbolism in "The Hero" pertain to Danny King, the play's main character. As King's level of self awareness increases throughout the play, we see changes in the symbols associated with the young man.
In the play's opening scene, King is a first-year college student filled with optimism about the future. We see this optimism reflected in witty dialogue between King and his friends. We also see this optimism reflected in the symbols associated with him.

■ If the document is displayed in the Normal view, a line with the words **Page Break** appears across the screen.

■ The **Page Break** line shows where one page ends and another begins. The line will not appear when you print the document.

REMOVE A PAGE BREAK

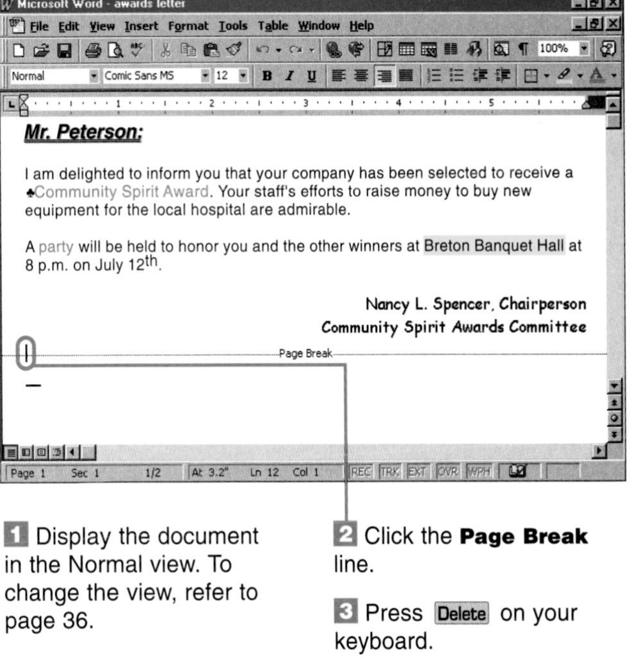

1 Display the document in the Normal view. To change the view, refer to page 36.

2 Click the **Page Break** line.

3 Press Delete on your keyboard.

INSERT A SECTION BREAK

You can divide your document into sections so you can format each section separately.

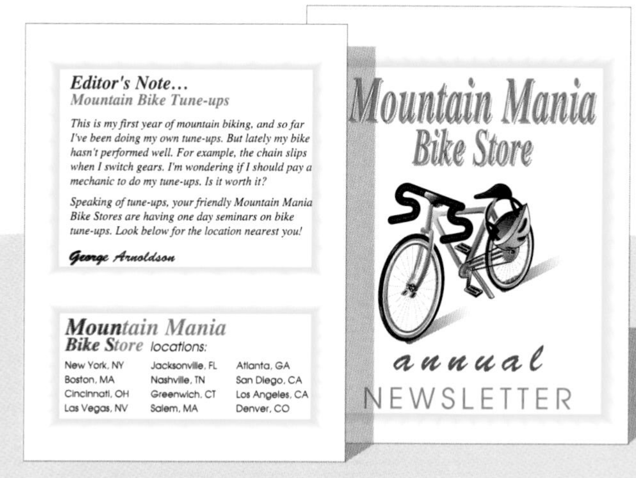

You need to divide a document into sections to change margins, create columns or vertically center text for only part of your document.

INSERT A SECTION BREAK

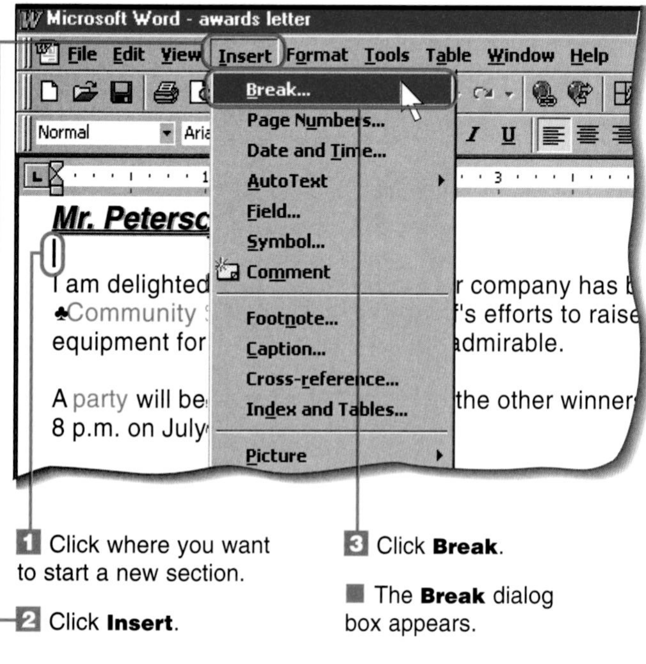

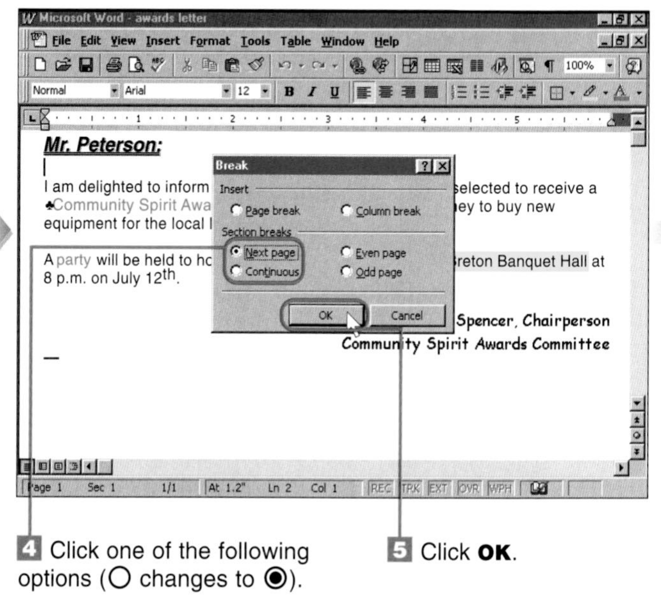

1 Click where you want to start a new section.

2 Click **Insert**.

3 Click **Break**.

■ The **Break** dialog box appears.

4 Click one of the following options (○ changes to ◉).

Next page - Creates a new section on a new page.

Continuous - Creates a new section on the current page.

5 Click **OK**.

?

If I remove a section break will my document change?

When you remove a section break, the text above the break assumes the appearance of the following section.

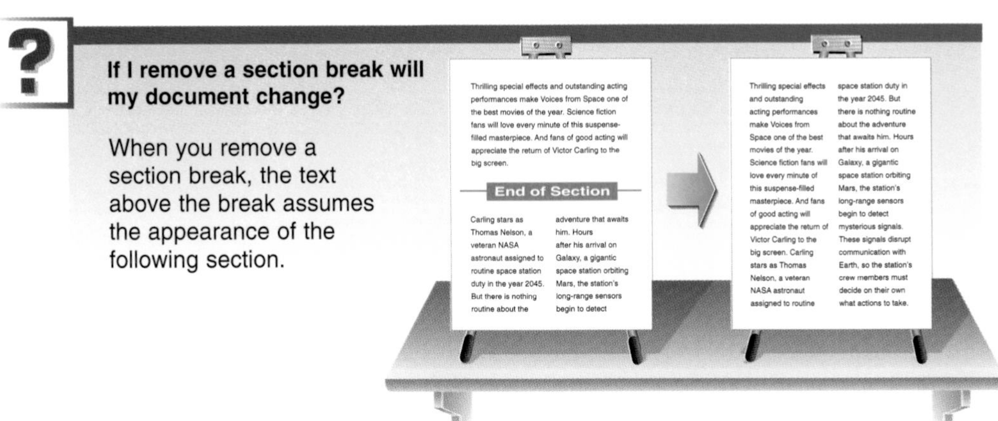

REMOVE A SECTION BREAK

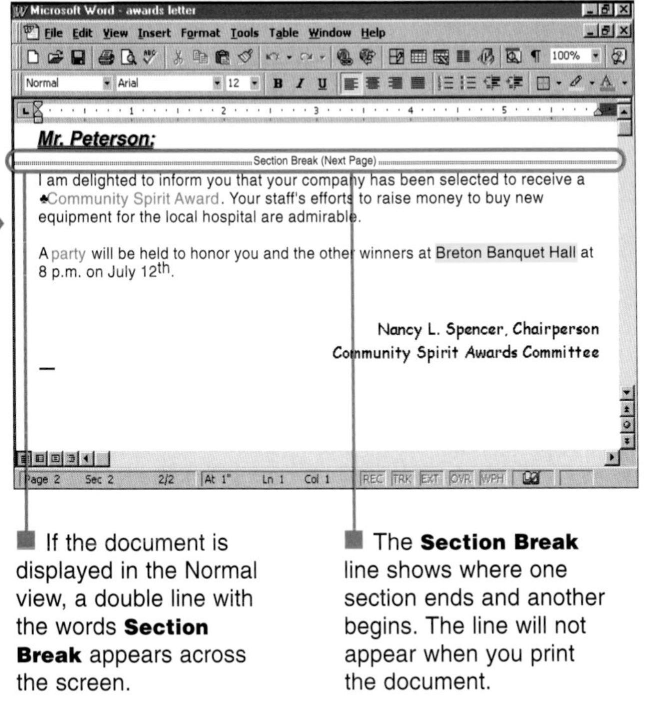

■ If the document is displayed in the Normal view, a double line with the words **Section Break** appears across the screen.

■ The **Section Break** line shows where one section ends and another begins. The line will not appear when you print the document.

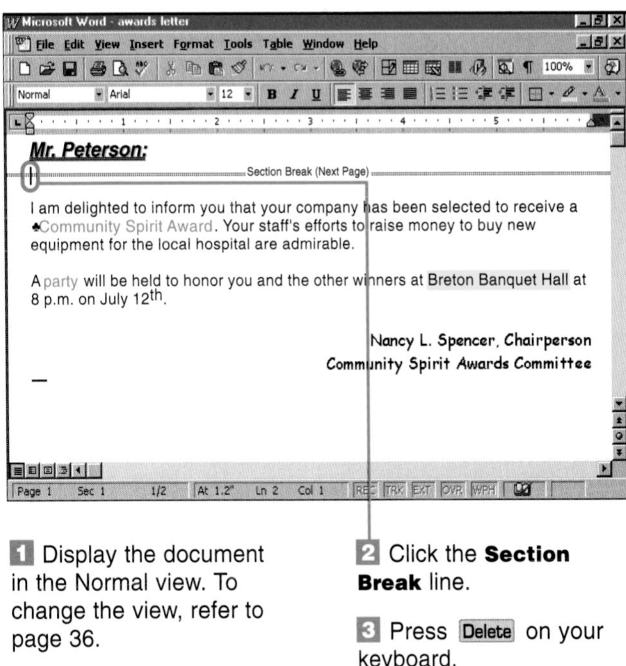

1 Display the document in the Normal view. To change the view, refer to page 36.

2 Click the **Section Break** line.

3 Press Delete on your keyboard.

CENTER TEXT ON A PAGE

You can vertically center text on each page of a document. This is useful for creating title pages or short memos.

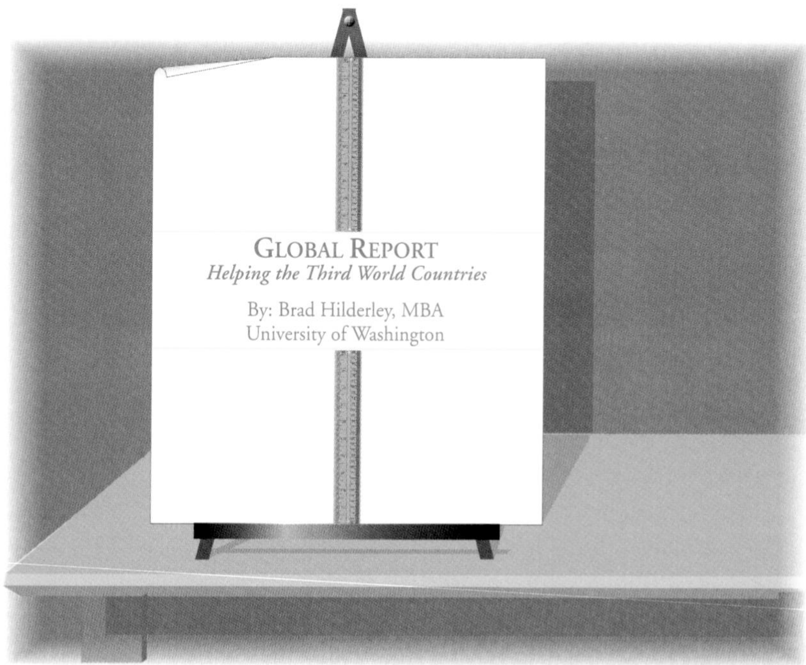

GLOBAL REPORT
Helping the Third World Countries
By: Brad Hilderley, MBA
University of Washington

CENTER TEXT ON A PAGE

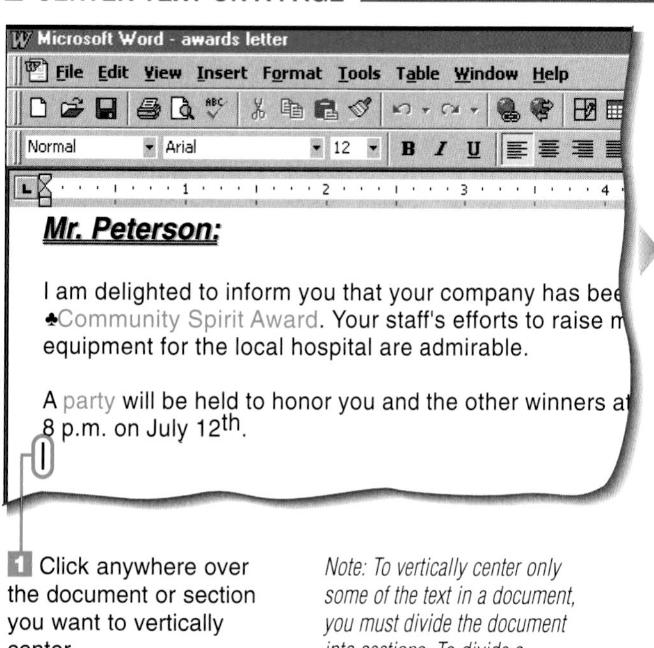

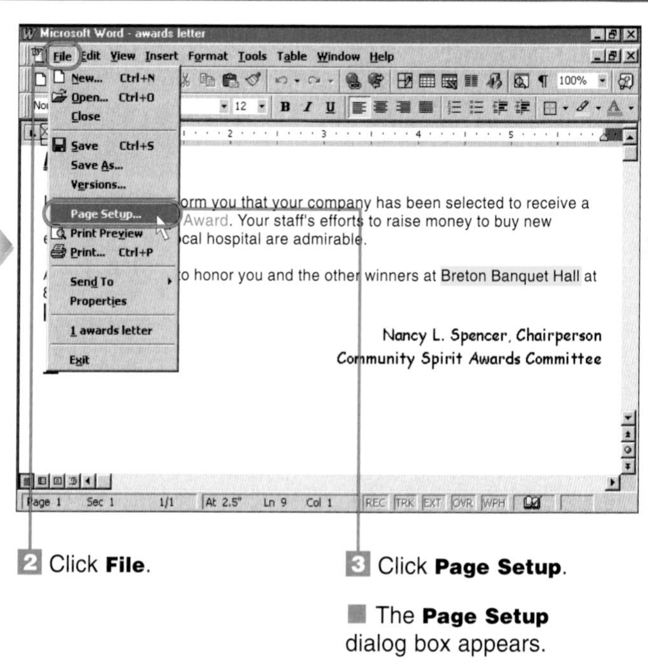

1 Click anywhere over the document or section you want to vertically center.

Note: To vertically center only some of the text in a document, you must divide the document into sections. To divide a document into sections, refer to page 90.

2 Click **File**.

3 Click **Page Setup**.

■ The **Page Setup** dialog box appears.

How can I see what text centered on a page will look like when printed?

You can use the Print Preview feature to display the page on your screen. This lets you see how the page will look when printed.

Note: For information on using Print Preview, refer to page 26.

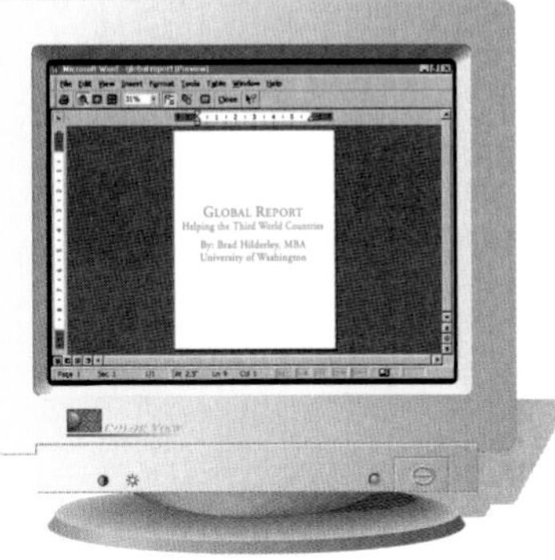

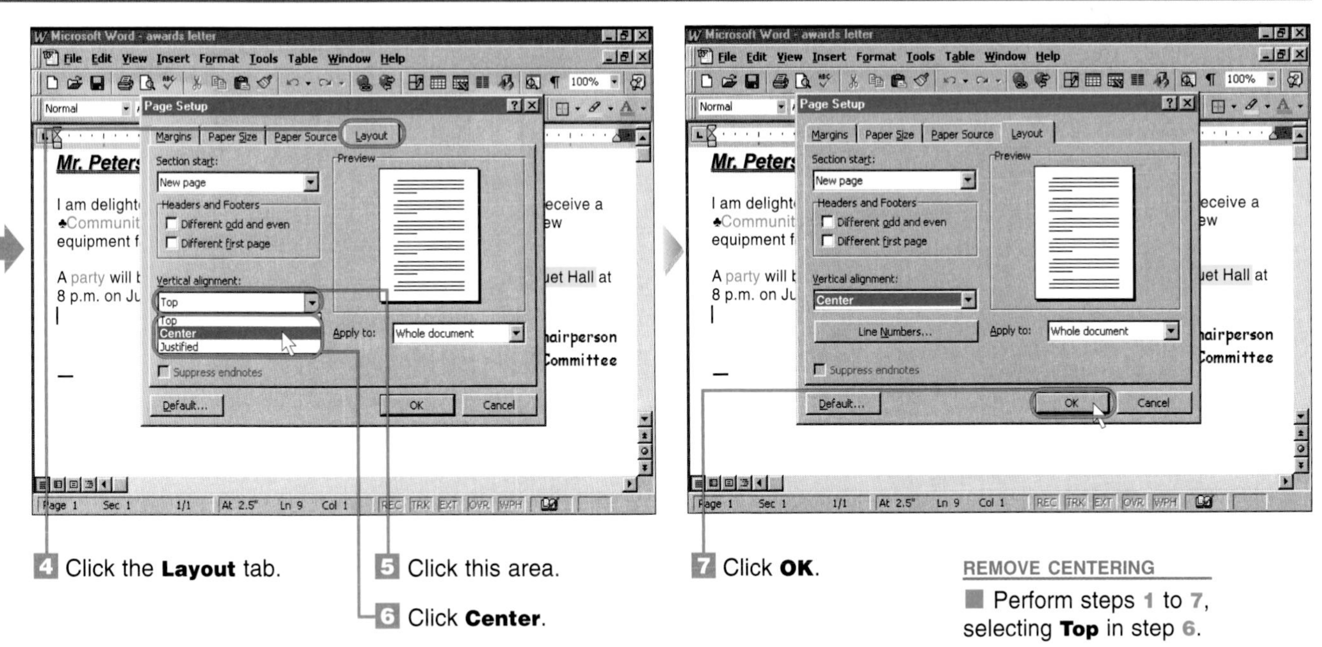

4 Click the **Layout** tab.

5 Click this area.

6 Click **Center**.

7 Click **OK**.

REMOVE CENTERING

■ Perform steps 1 to 7, selecting **Top** in step 6.

CHANGE MARGINS

A margin is the amount of space between text and an edge of your paper. You can easily change the margins to suit your document.

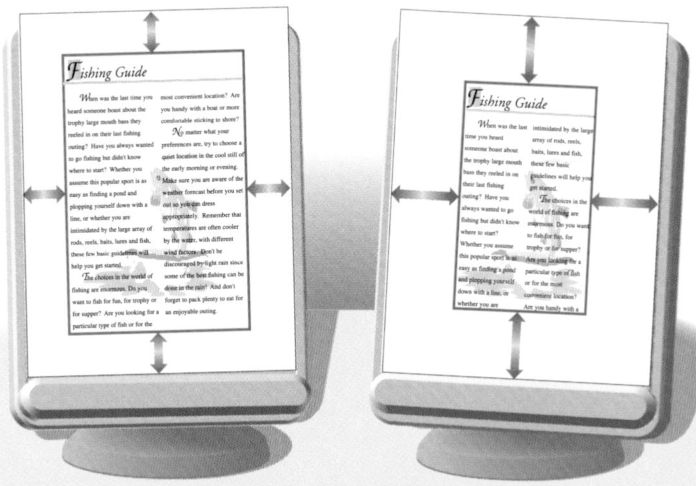

Changing margins lets you accommodate letterhead and other specialty paper.

CHANGE MARGINS

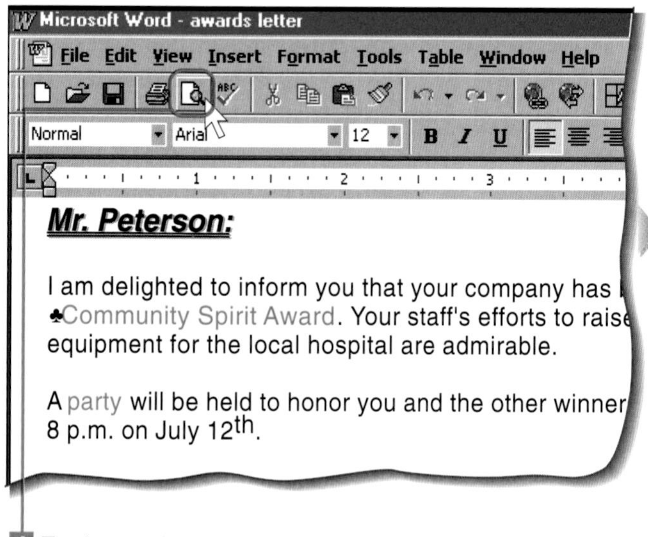

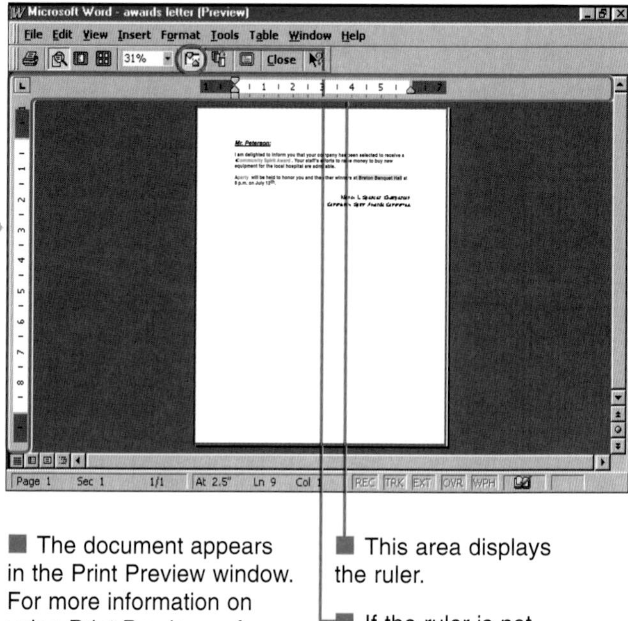

1 To change the margins for the entire document, click [Print Preview icon].

Note: To change the margins for only part of the document, refer to the top of page 95.

■ The document appears in the Print Preview window. For more information on using Print Preview, refer to page 26.

■ This area displays the ruler.

■ If the ruler is not displayed, click [View Ruler icon].

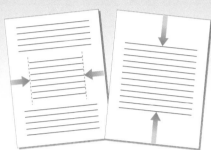

How can I change the margins for part of my document?

If you want to change the left and right margins for only part of your document, change the indentation of paragraphs. To indent paragraphs, refer to page 76.

If you want to change the top and bottom margins for only part of your document, you must divide the document into sections. To divide a document into sections, refer to page 90.

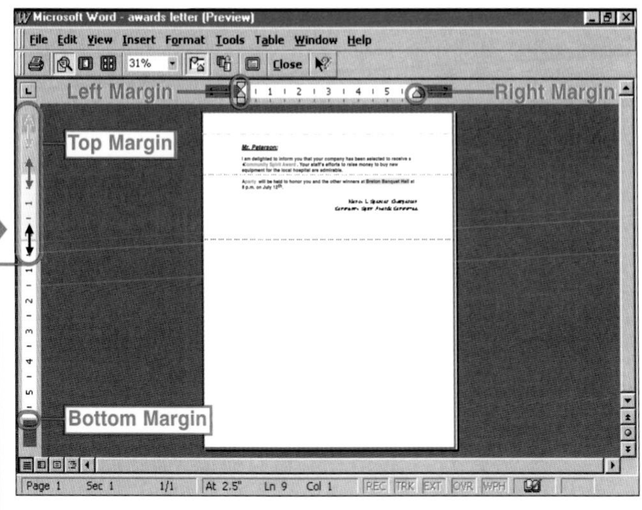

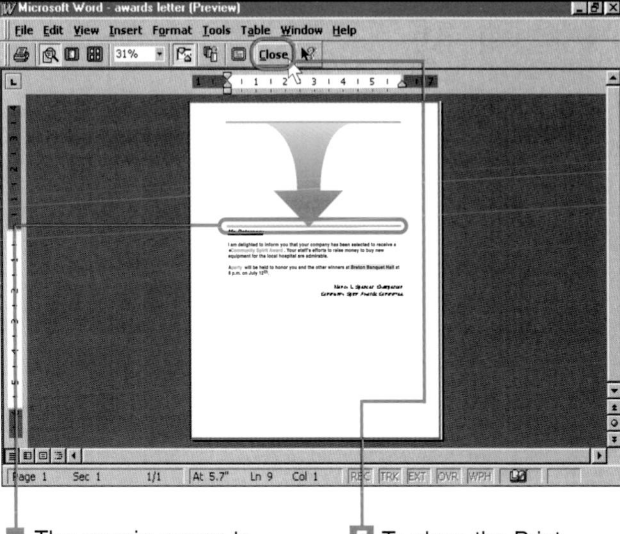

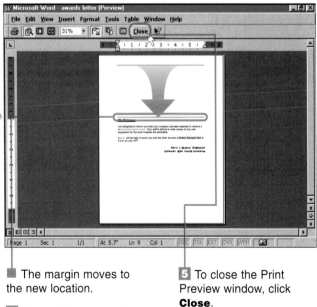

2 Position the mouse over the margin you want to change (changes to ↕ or ↔).

3 Drag the margin to a new location. A line indicates the new location.

*Note: To view the exact measurement of a margin, perform step **2** then press and hold down* Alt *on your keyboard as you perform step **3**.*

■ The margin moves to the new location.

4 Repeat steps 2 and 3 for each margin you want to change.

5 To close the Print Preview window, click **Close**.

CREATE NEWSPAPER COLUMNS

You can display your text in columns like those found in a newspaper. This is useful for creating newsletters and brochures.

CREATE NEWSPAPER COLUMNS

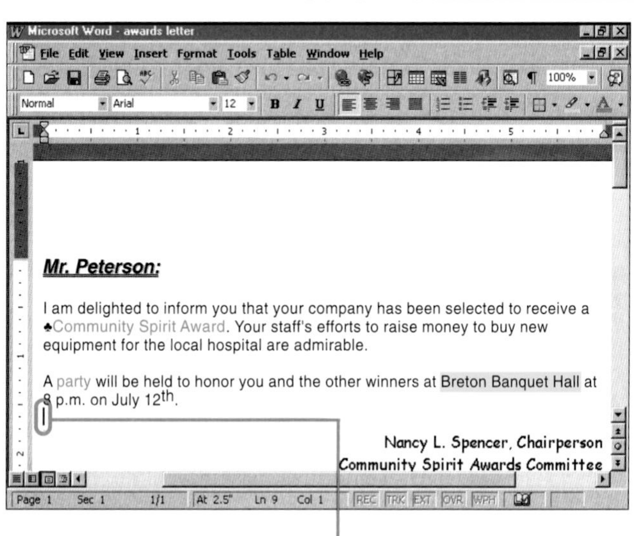

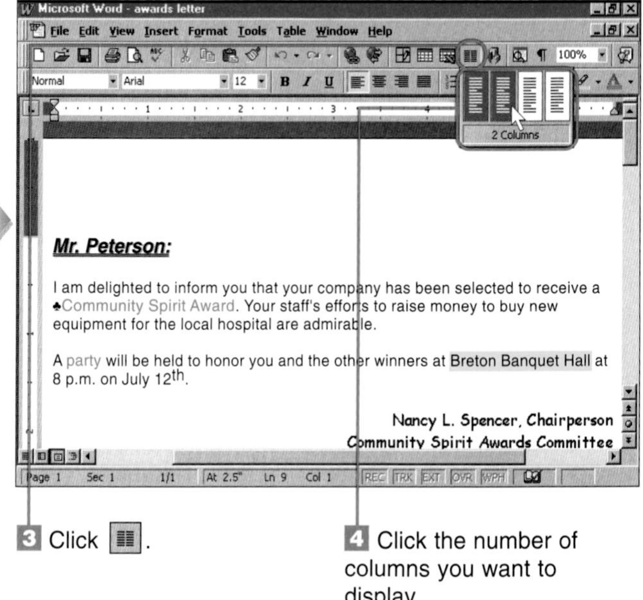

1 Display the document in the Page Layout view. To change the view, refer to page 36.

Note: Word does not display newspaper columns side-by-side in the Normal view.

2 Click anywhere over the document or section you want to display in newspaper columns.

Note: To create newspaper columns for only part of the document, you must divide the document into sections. To divide a document into sections, refer to page 90.

3 Click ▤.

4 Click the number of columns you want to display.

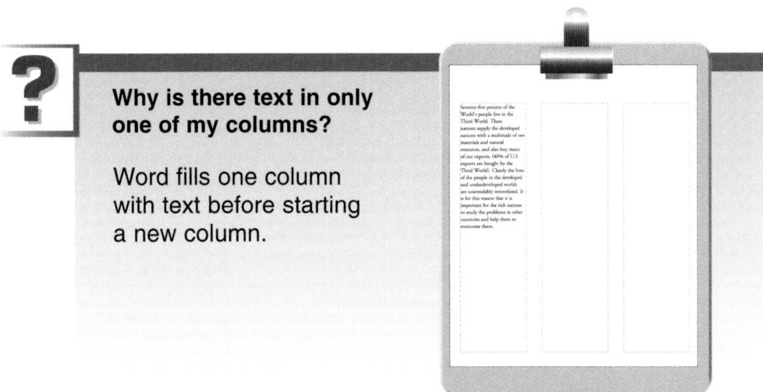

Why is there text in only one of my columns?

Word fills one column with text before starting a new column.

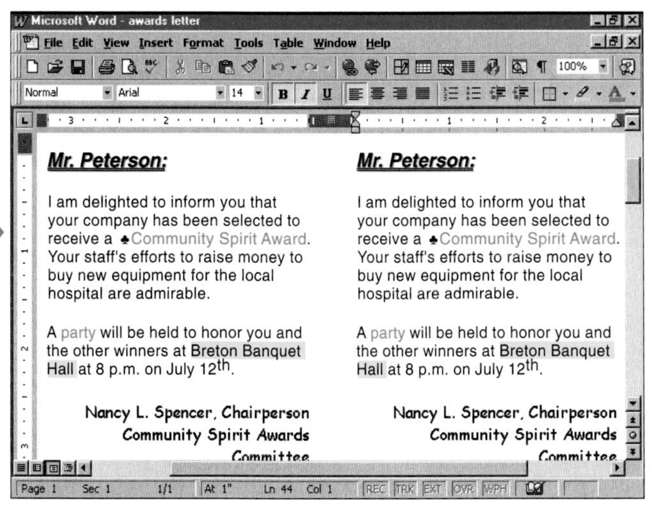

■ The text in the document appears in newspaper columns.

Note: In this example, the existing text was copied to show the newspaper columns. To copy text, refer to page 50.

REMOVE NEWSPAPER COLUMNS

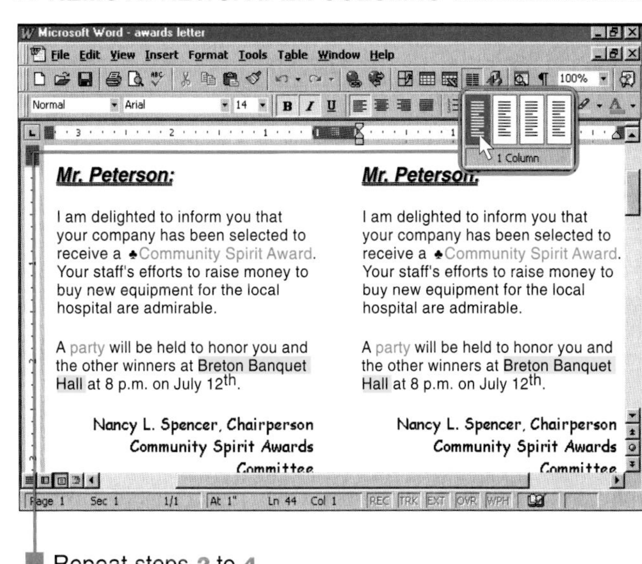

■ Repeat steps 2 to 4, selecting **1 Column** in step 4.

CREATE A TABLE

You can create a table to neatly display information in your document.

Word lets you draw a table on the screen as you would draw a table with a pen and paper.

CREATE A TABLE

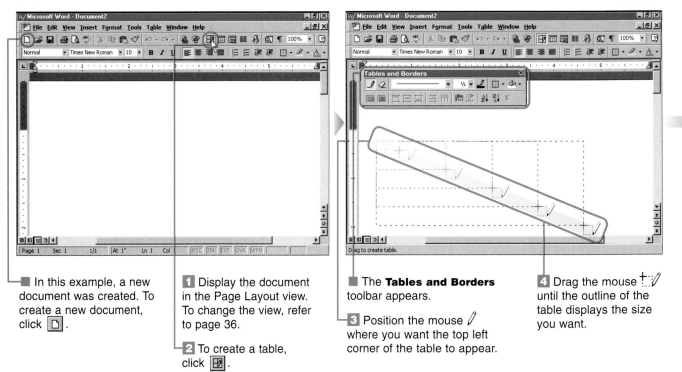

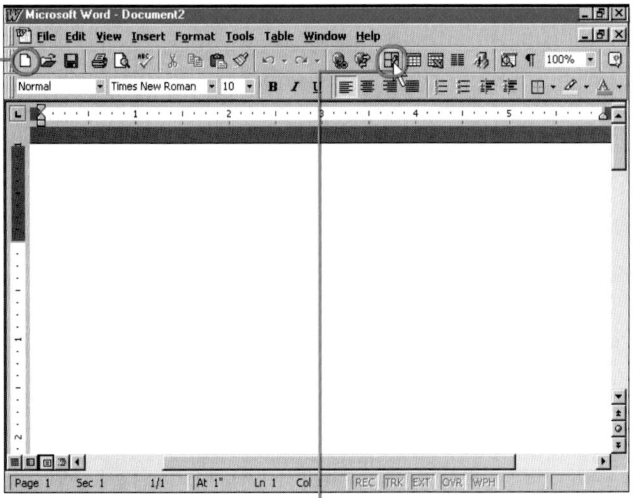

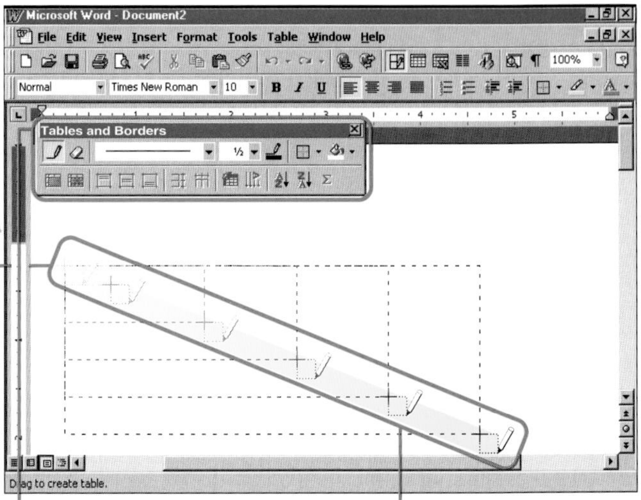

■ In this example, a new document was created. To create a new document, click 🗋.

1 Display the document in the Page Layout view. To change the view, refer to page 36.

2 To create a table, click ⊞.

■ The **Tables and Borders** toolbar appears.

3 Position the mouse ✎ where you want the top left corner of the table to appear.

4 Drag the mouse ✎ until the outline of the table displays the size you want.

Can I move a toolbar out of the way?

If a toolbar is in the way, you can easily move the toolbar to a new location.

1 Position the mouse over the title bar.

2 Drag the toolbar to a new location.

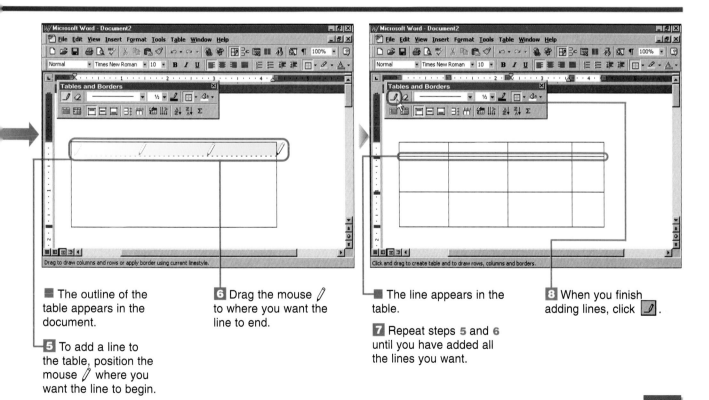

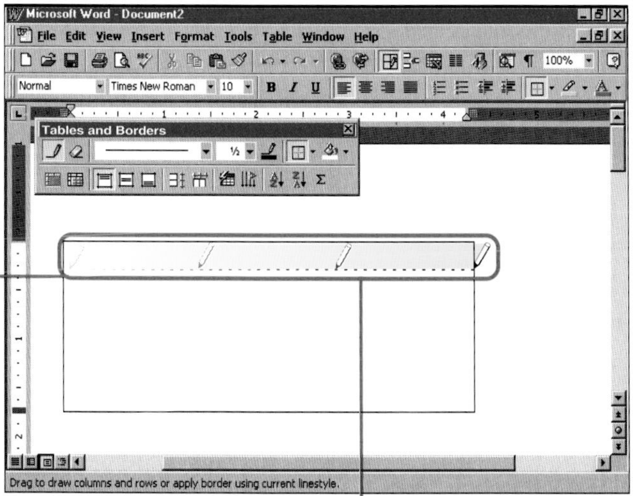

■ The outline of the table appears in the document.

5 To add a line to the table, position the mouse where you want the line to begin.

6 Drag the mouse to where you want the line to end.

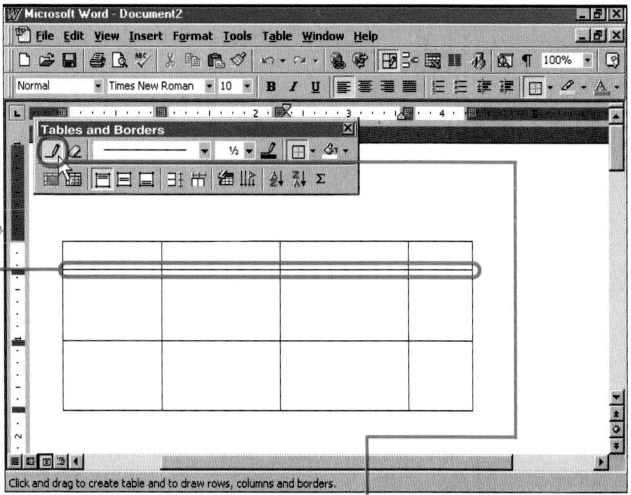

■ The line appears in the table.

7 Repeat steps 5 and 6 until you have added all the lines you want.

8 When you finish adding lines, click .

CHANGE ROW HEIGHT OR COLUMN WIDTH

After you have created a table, you can change the height of rows or the width of columns.

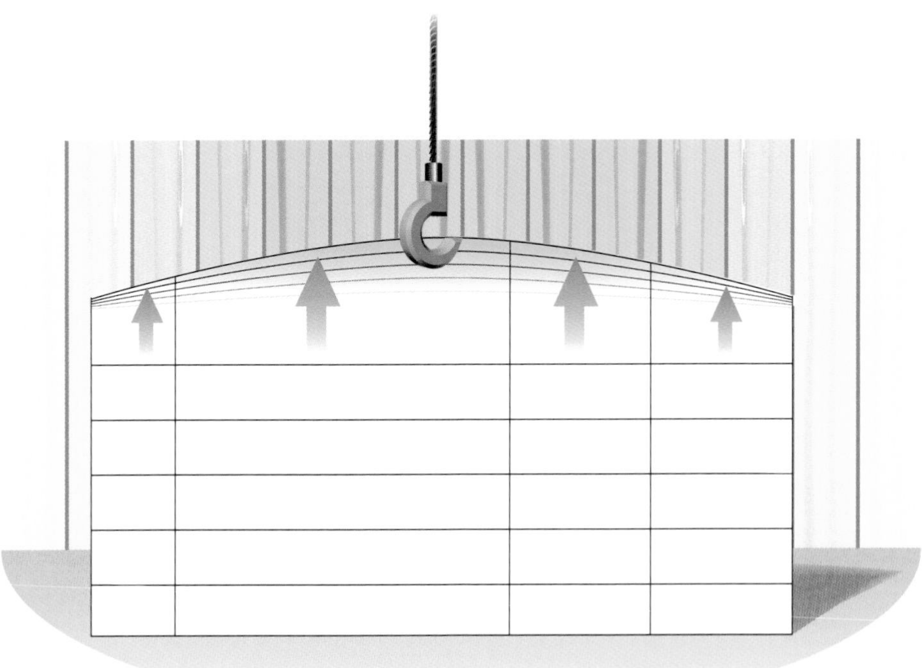

CHANGE ROW HEIGHT

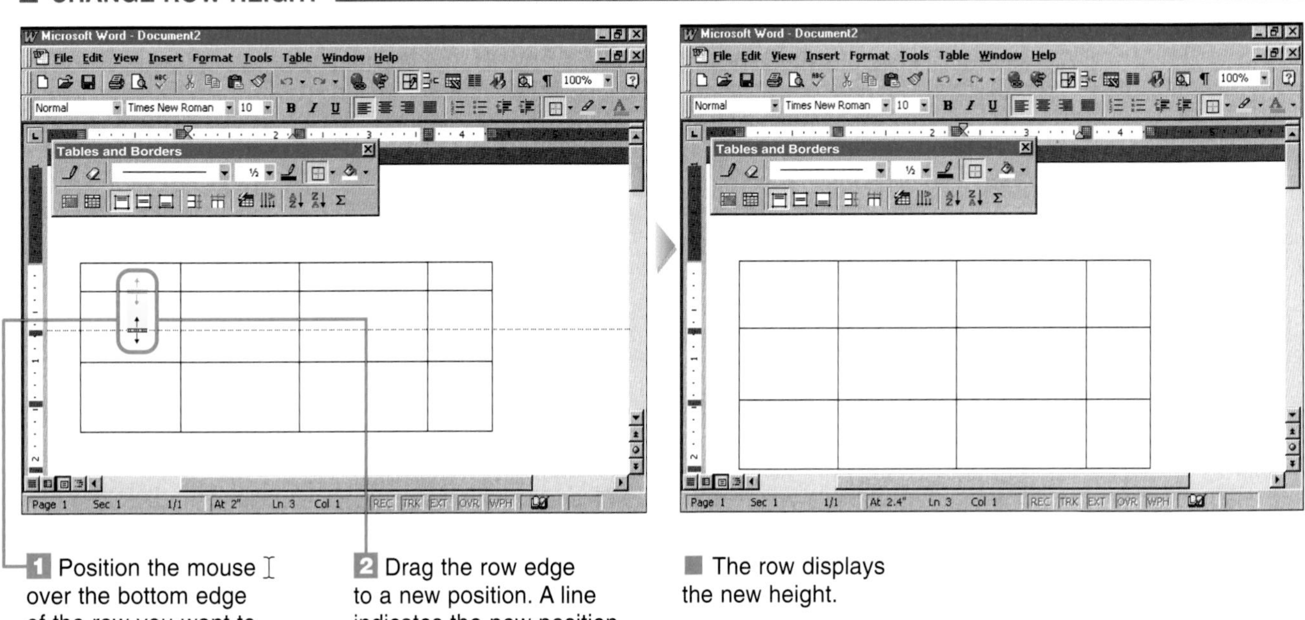

1 Position the mouse I over the bottom edge of the row you want to change (I changes to ╪).

2 Drag the row edge to a new position. A line indicates the new position.

■ The row displays the new height.

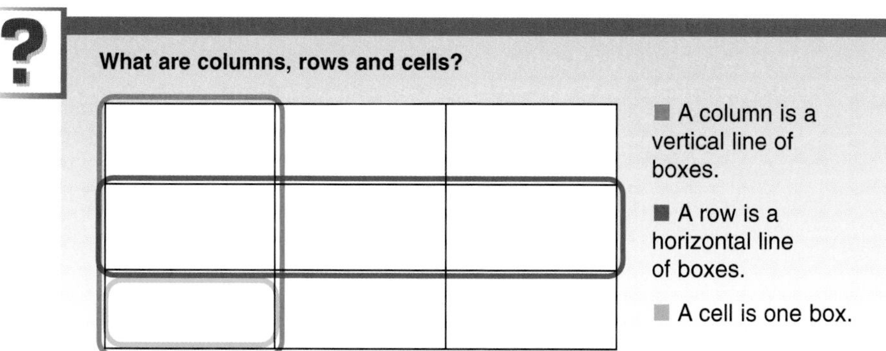

What are columns, rows and cells?

- A column is a vertical line of boxes.
- A row is a horizontal line of boxes.
- A cell is one box.

CHANGE COLUMN WIDTH

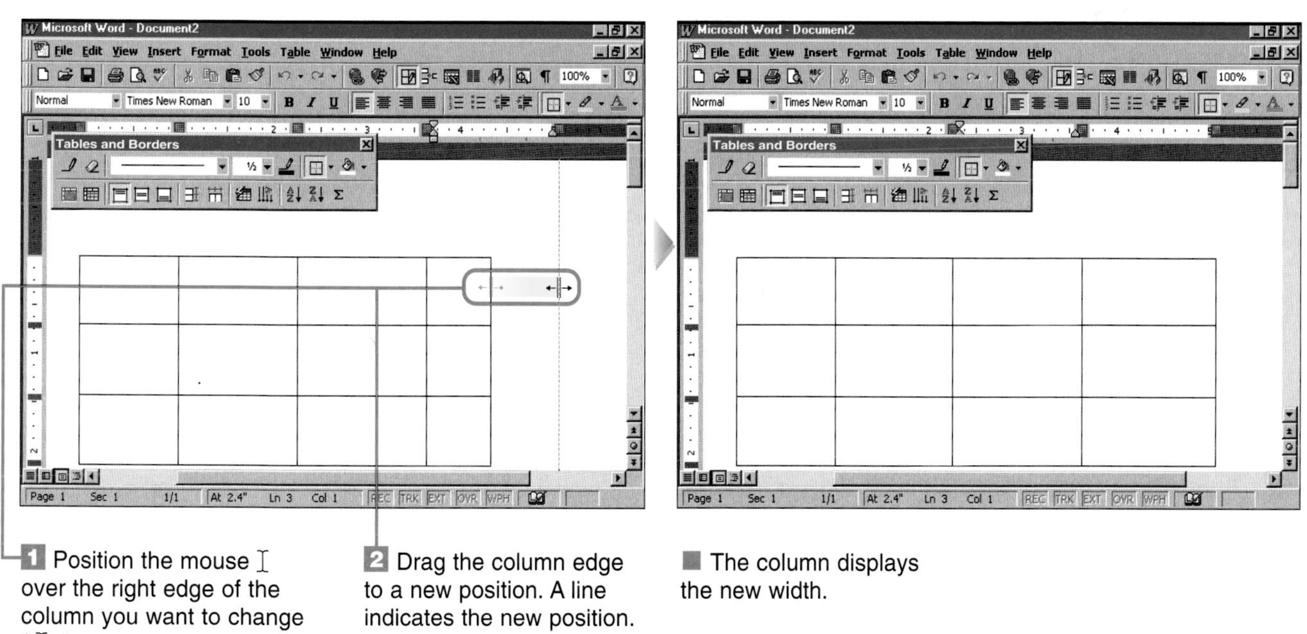

1 Position the mouse I over the right edge of the column you want to change (I changes to ‖).

2 Drag the column edge to a new position. A line indicates the new position.

■ The column displays the new width.

ERASE LINES

You can erase lines you do not need in your table.

ERASE LINES

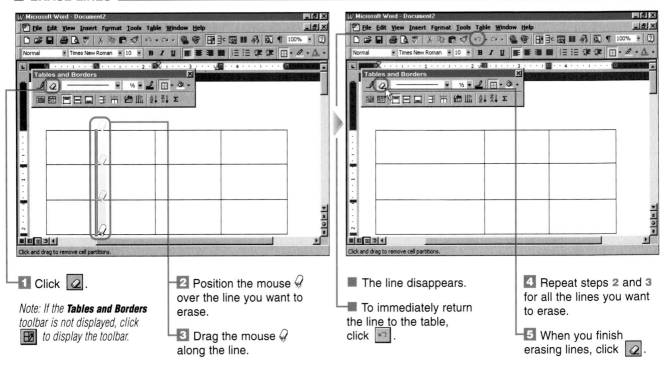

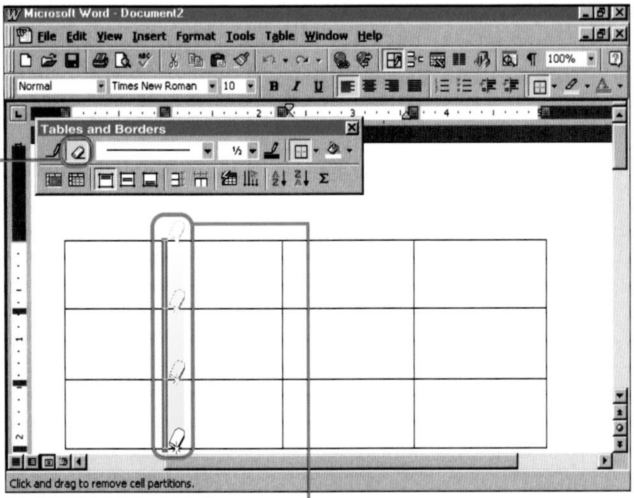

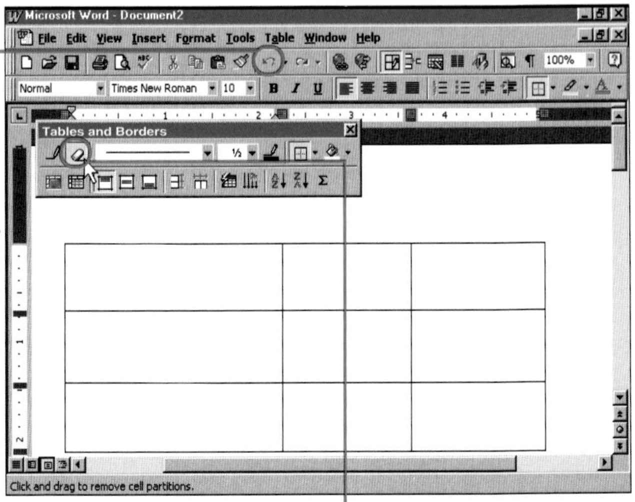

1 Click .

*Note: If the **Tables and Borders** toolbar is not displayed, click to display the toolbar.*

2 Position the mouse over the line you want to erase.

3 Drag the mouse along the line.

■ The line disappears.

■ To immediately return the line to the table, click .

4 Repeat steps 2 and 3 for all the lines you want to erase.

5 When you finish erasing lines, click .

ENTER TEXT

You can easily enter text into the cells of your table.

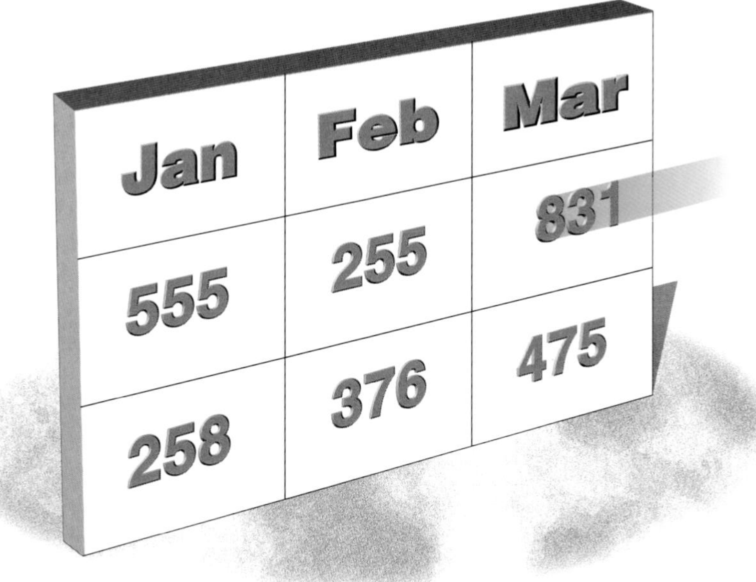

ENTER TEXT

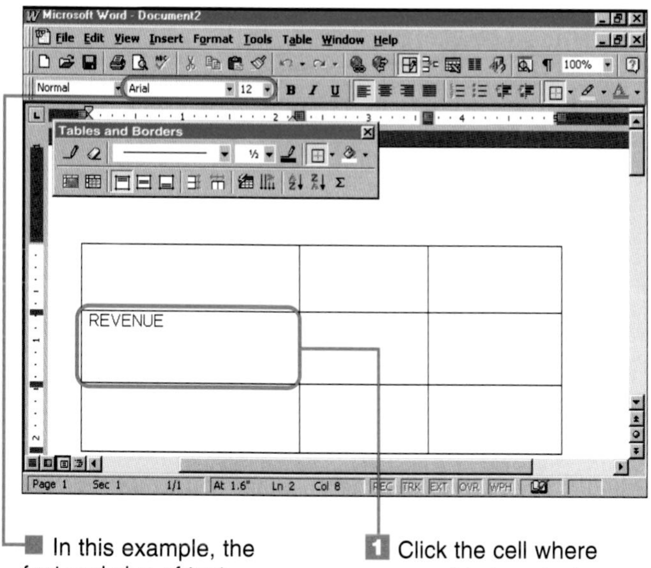

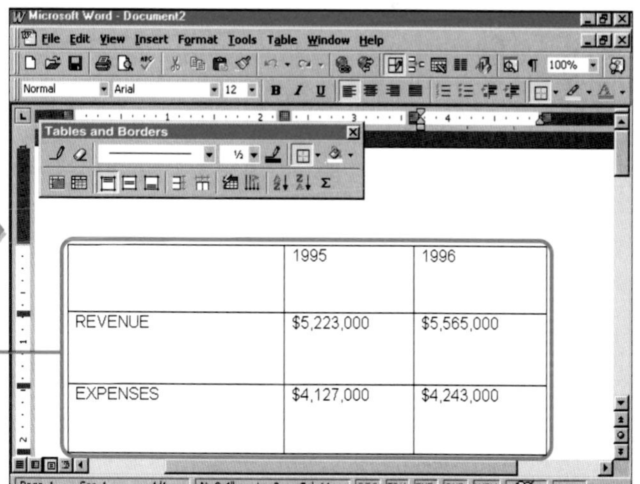

■ In this example, the font and size of text were changed to make the text easier to read. To change the font and size of text, refer to pages 62 and 63.

1 Click the cell where you want to type text. Then type the text.

Note: To quickly move through the cells in a table, press ←, ↑, ↓ or → on your keyboard.

2 Repeat step 1 until you have typed all the text.

■ You can edit and format the text in a table as you would edit and format any text in a document.

Note: To format text, refer to pages 60 to 81.

ADD A ROW OR COLUMN

You can add a row or column to your table to insert additional information.

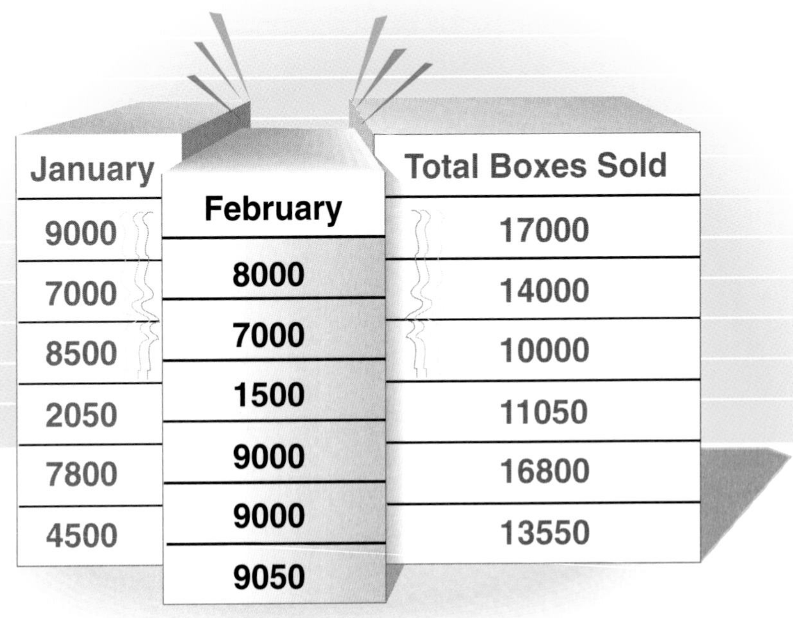

ADD A ROW

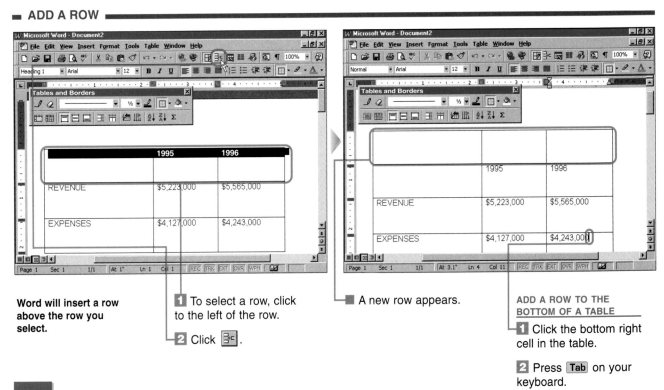

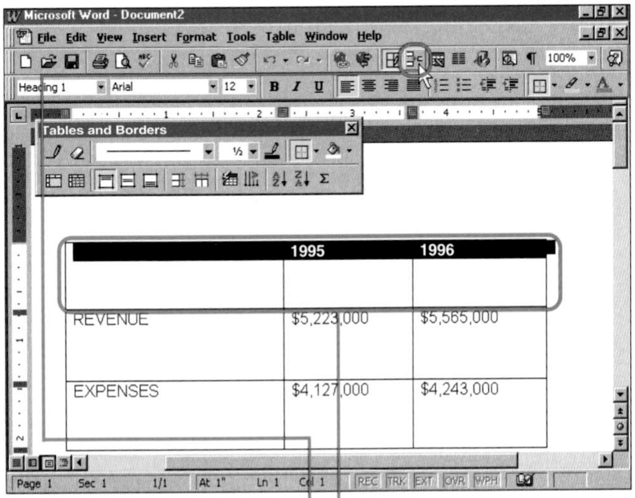

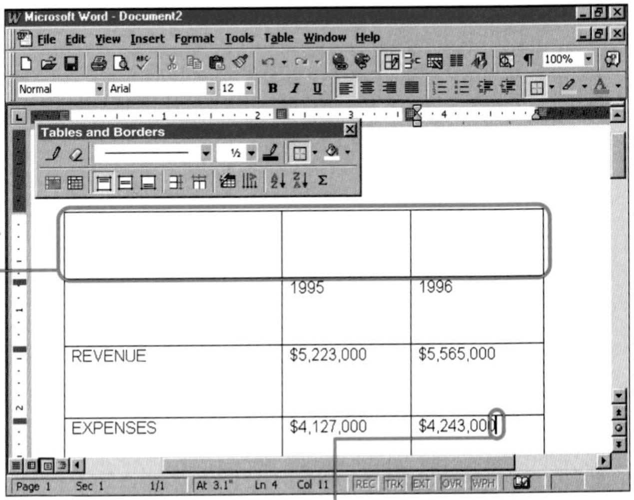

Word will insert a row above the row you select.

1 To select a row, click to the left of the row.

2 Click ⊞.

■ A new row appears.

ADD A ROW TO THE BOTTOM OF A TABLE

1 Click the bottom right cell in the table.

2 Press Tab on your keyboard.

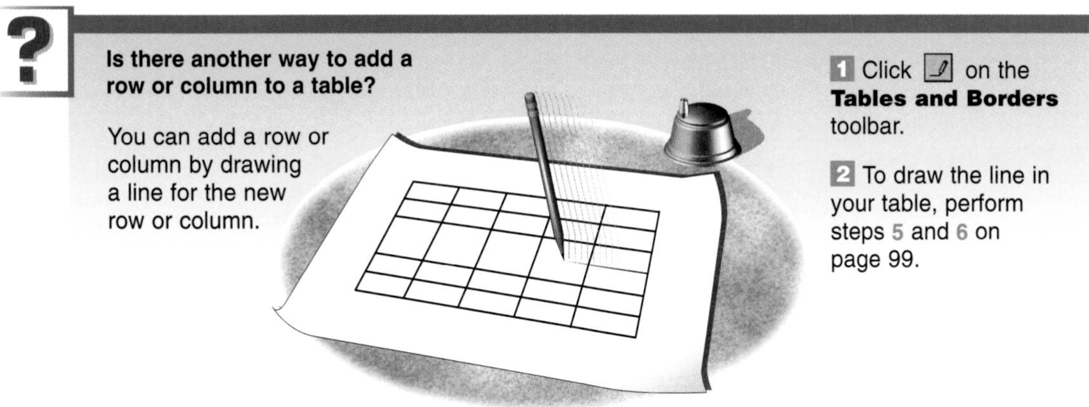

Is there another way to add a row or column to a table?

You can add a row or column by drawing a line for the new row or column.

1 Click on the **Tables and Borders** toolbar.

2 To draw the line in your table, perform steps 5 and 6 on page 99.

ADD A COLUMN

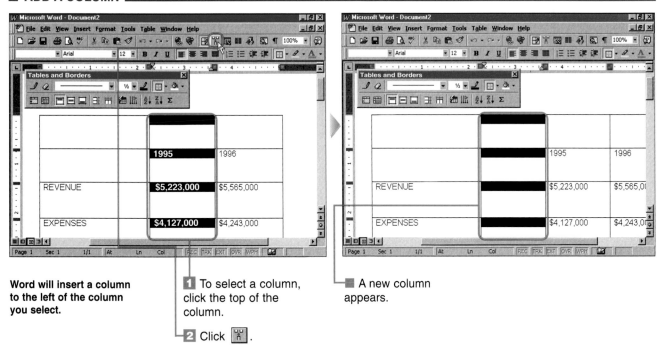

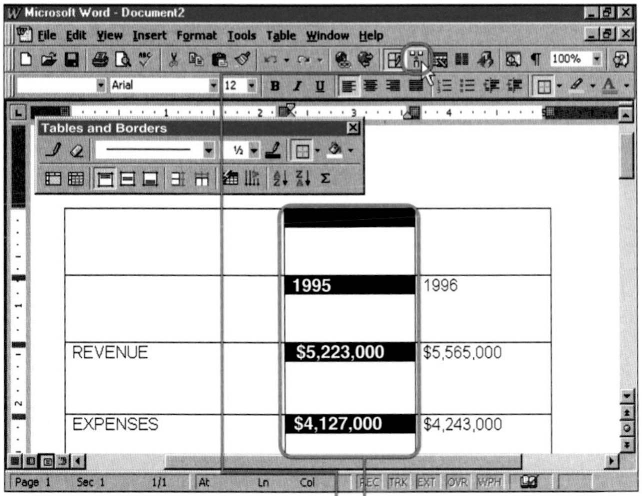

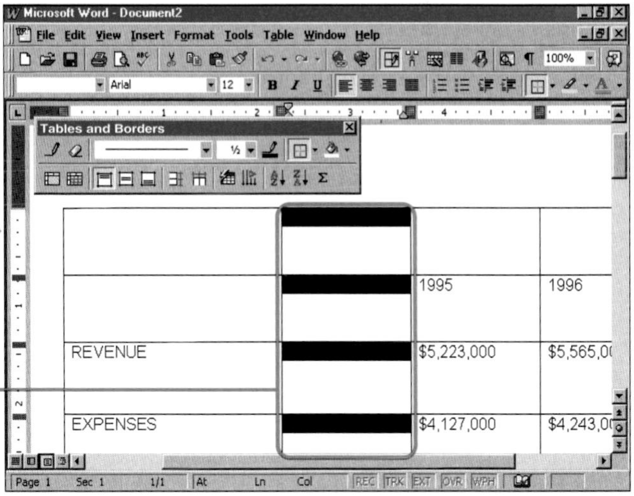

Word will insert a column to the left of the column you select.

1 To select a column, click the top of the column.

2 Click .

■ A new column appears.

DELETE A ROW OR COLUMN

You can delete a row or column you no longer need.

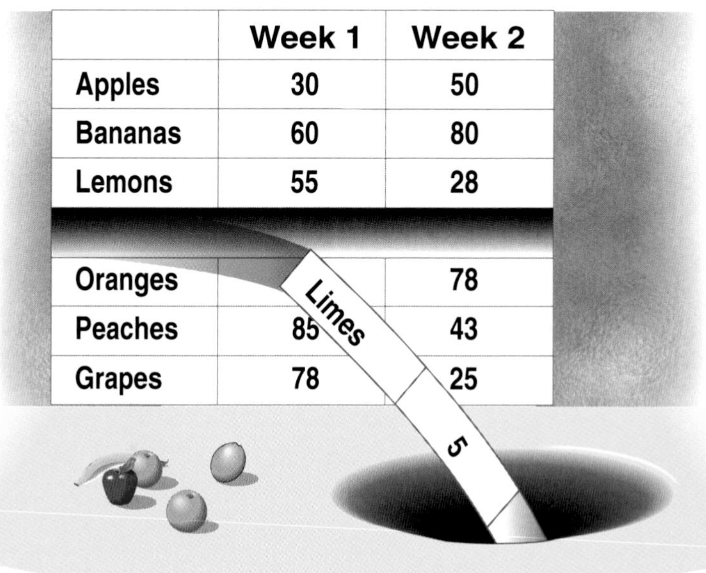

DELETE A ROW OR COLUMN

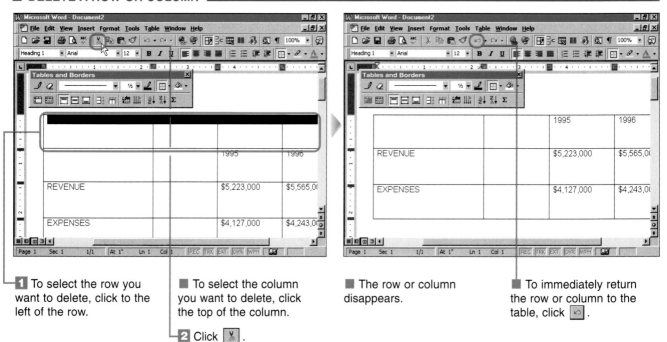

1 To select the row you want to delete, click to the left of the row.

■ To select the column you want to delete, click the top of the column.

2 Click ✂.

■ The row or column disappears.

■ To immediately return the row or column to the table, click ↶.

DELETE A TABLE

You can quickly remove an entire table from your document.

DELETE A TABLE

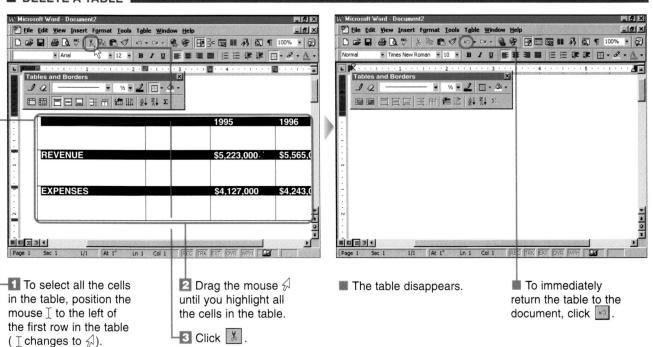

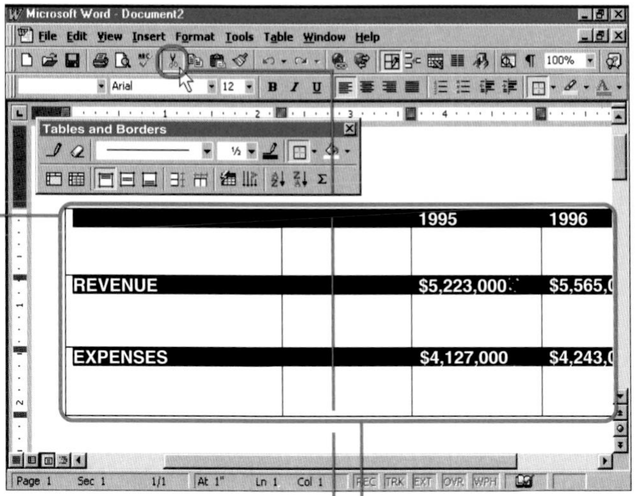

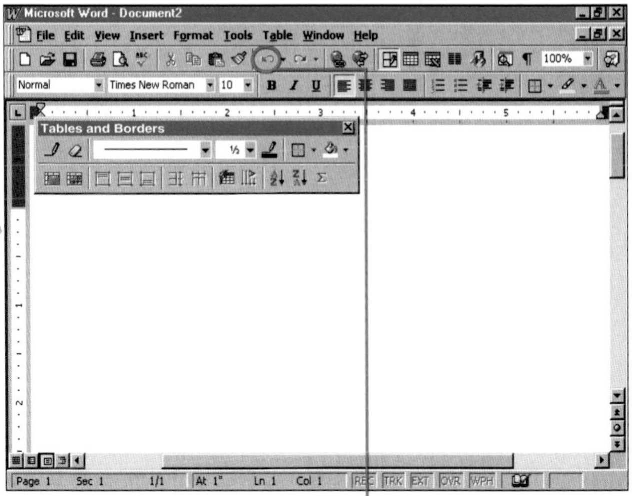

1 To select all the cells in the table, position the mouse I to the left of the first row in the table (I changes to ⇗).

2 Drag the mouse ⇗ until you highlight all the cells in the table.

3 Click ✂.

■ The table disappears.

■ To immediately return the table to the document, click ↶.

FORMAT A TABLE

Word offers many ready-to-use designs that you can choose from to give your table a new appearance.

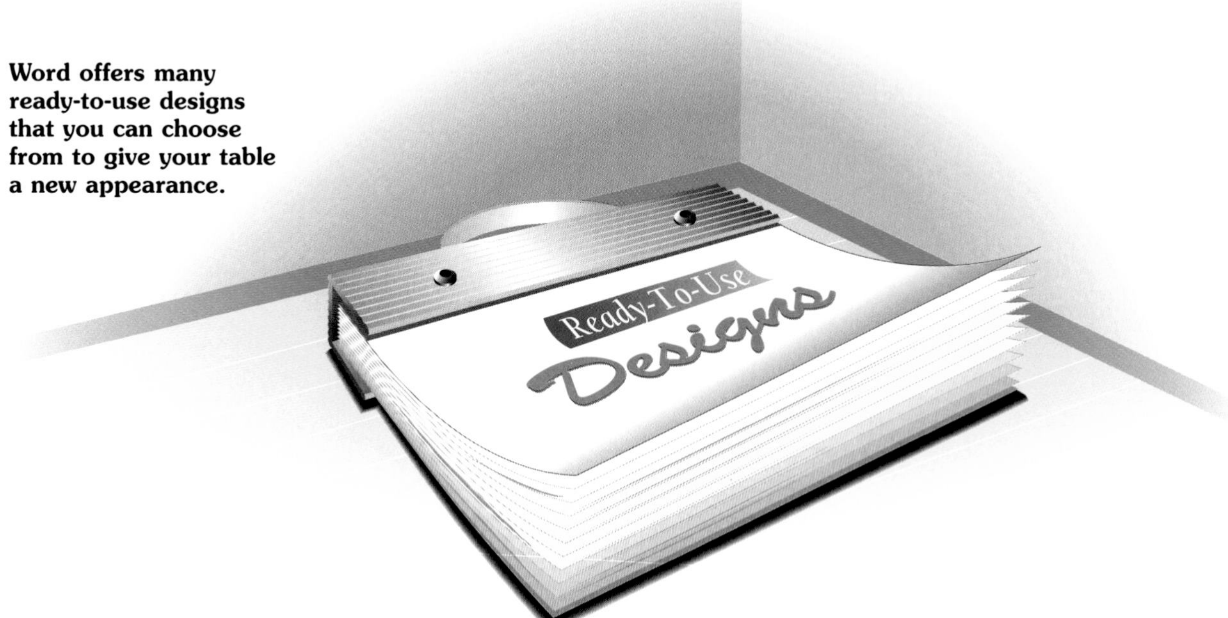

FORMAT A TABLE

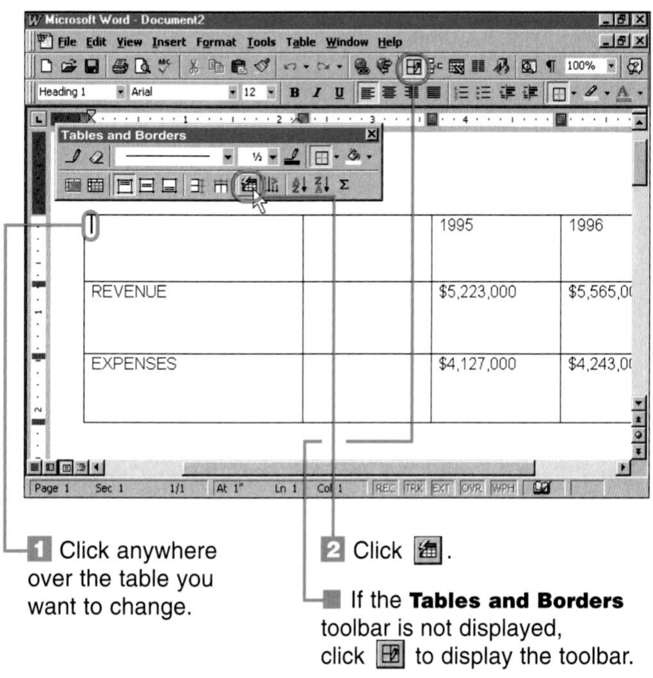

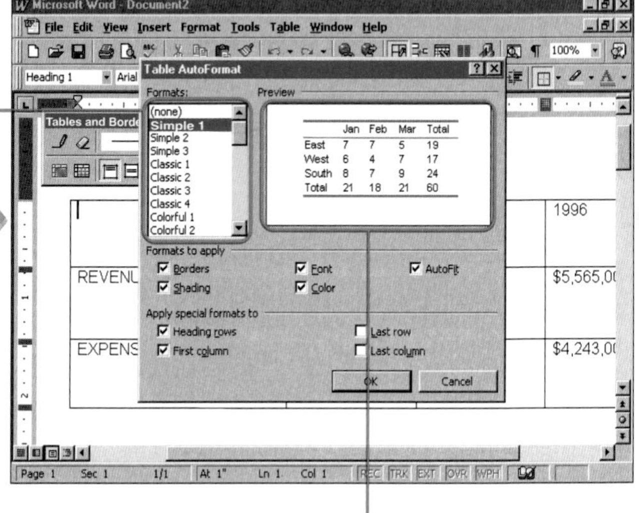

1 Click anywhere over the table you want to change.

2 Click .

■ If the **Tables and Borders** toolbar is not displayed, click to display the toolbar.

■ The **Table AutoFormat** dialog box appears.

■ This area displays a list of the available table designs.

■ This area displays a sample of the highlighted table design.

3 Press ↓ or ↑ on your keyboard until a design you like appears.

What are some of the table designs offered by Word?

	Jan	Feb	Mar	Total
East	7	7	5	19
West	6	4	7	17
South	8	7	9	24
Total	21	18	21	60

Colorful 1

	Jan	Feb	Mar	Total
East	7	7	5	19
West	6	4	7	17
South	8	7	9	24
Total	21	18	21	60

Grid 8

	Jan	Feb	Mar	Total
East	7	7	5	19
West	6	4	7	17
South	8	7	9	24
Total	21	18	21	60

Classic 3

	Jan	Feb	Mar	Total
East	7	7	5	19
West	6	4	7	17
South	8	7	9	24
Total	21	18	21	60

Columns 5

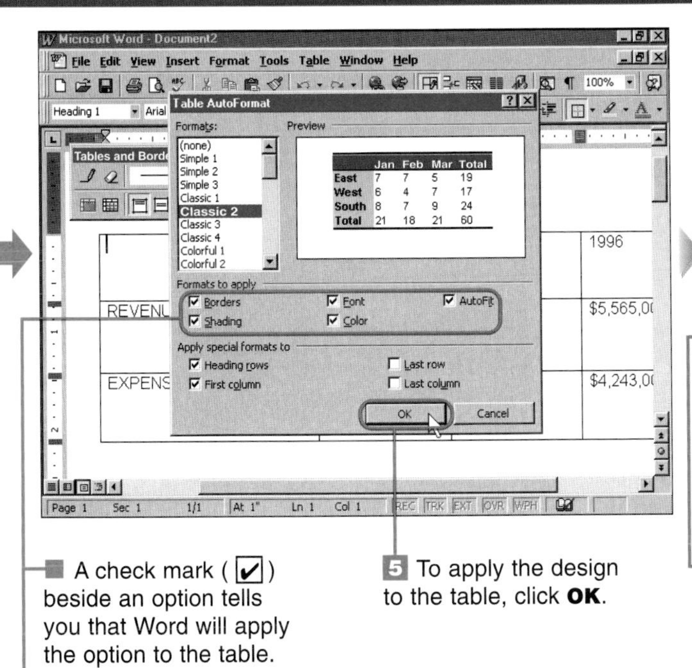

■ A check mark (☑) beside an option tells you that Word will apply the option to the table.

4 To add or remove a check mark (☑) for an option, click the check box beside the option.

5 To apply the design to the table, click **OK**.

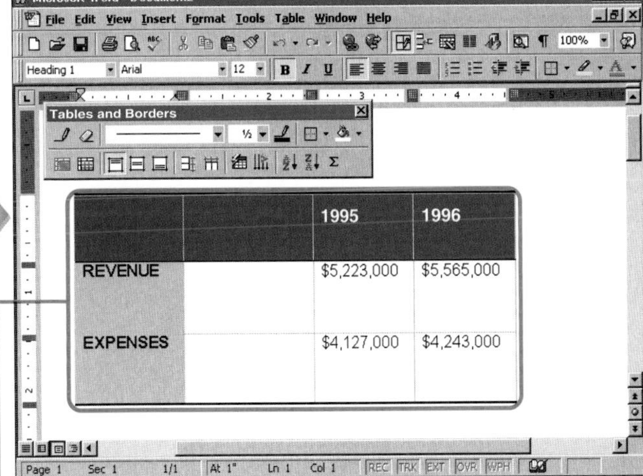

■ The table displays the design you selected.

REMOVE AUTOFORMAT

■ Perform steps 1 to 3, selecting **Grid 1** in step 3. Then press Enter on your keyboard.

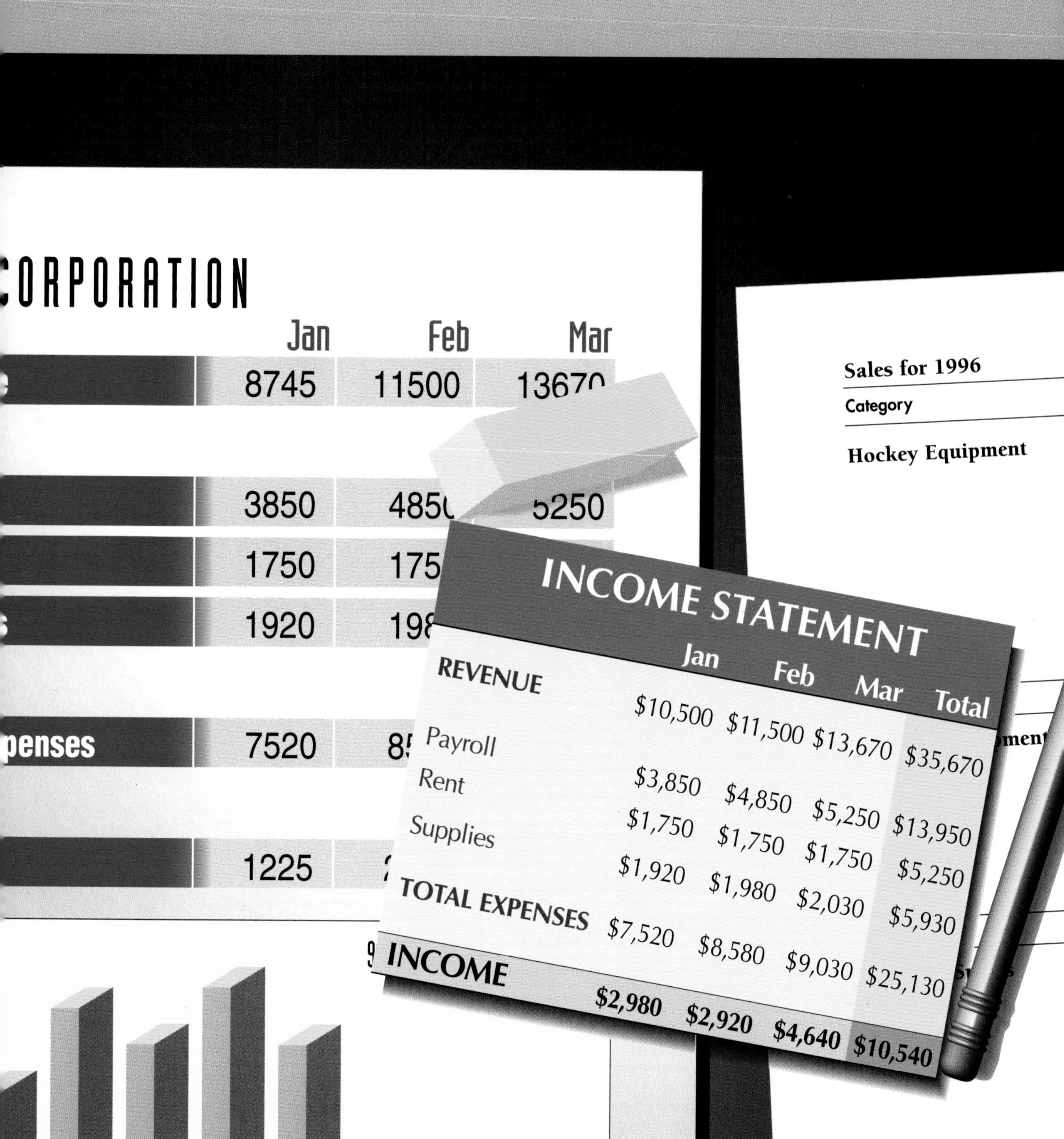
ORPORATION
Jan
Feb
Mar
8745
11500
3850
1750
1920
penses
7520
1225
Sales for 1996
Category
Hockey Equipment
INCOME STATEMENT
Jan
Feb
Mar
Total
REVENUE
$10,500
$11,500
$13,670
$35,670
Payroll
$3,850
$4,850
$5,250
$13,950
Rent
$1,750
$1,750
$1,750
$5,250
Supplies
$1,920
$1,980
$2,030
$5,930
TOTAL EXPENSES
$7,520
$8,580
$9,030
$25,130
INCOME
$2,980
$2,920
$4,640
$10,540

Excel

Includes:

1 **Getting Started**
This chapter teaches you the basic skills you need to use Excel, from starting the program to entering data and selecting cells.

2 **Save and Open a Workbook**
Learn how to create a new workbook, open an existing workbook, save your work and exit Excel.

3 **Edit a Worksheet**
Here you will learn how to edit data in your worksheet.

4 **Using Formulas and Functions**
Excel lets you easily perform calculations on the data in your worksheet using formulas and functions.

5 **Format a Worksheet**
From changing the column width to adding color, Excel provides many ways to change the appearance of data in your worksheet.

6 **Print a Worksheet**
Here you will learn how to print your worksheet and specify the way it will appear on a printed page.

7 **Using Multiple Worksheets**
This chapter teaches you how to work on many worksheets at one time.

8 **Working with Charts**
Learn how to use your worksheet data to create charts.

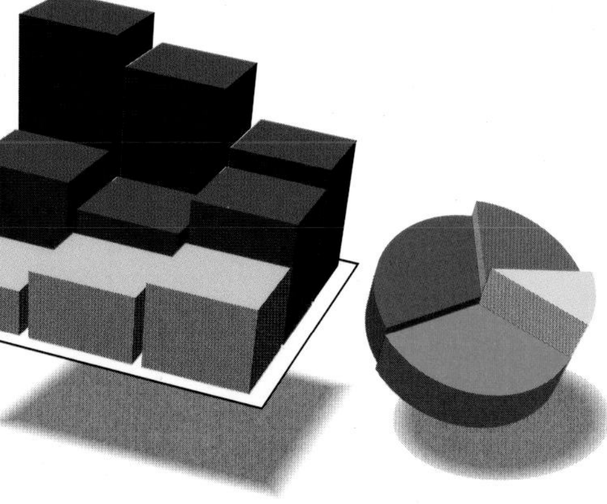

INTRODUCTION TO EXCEL

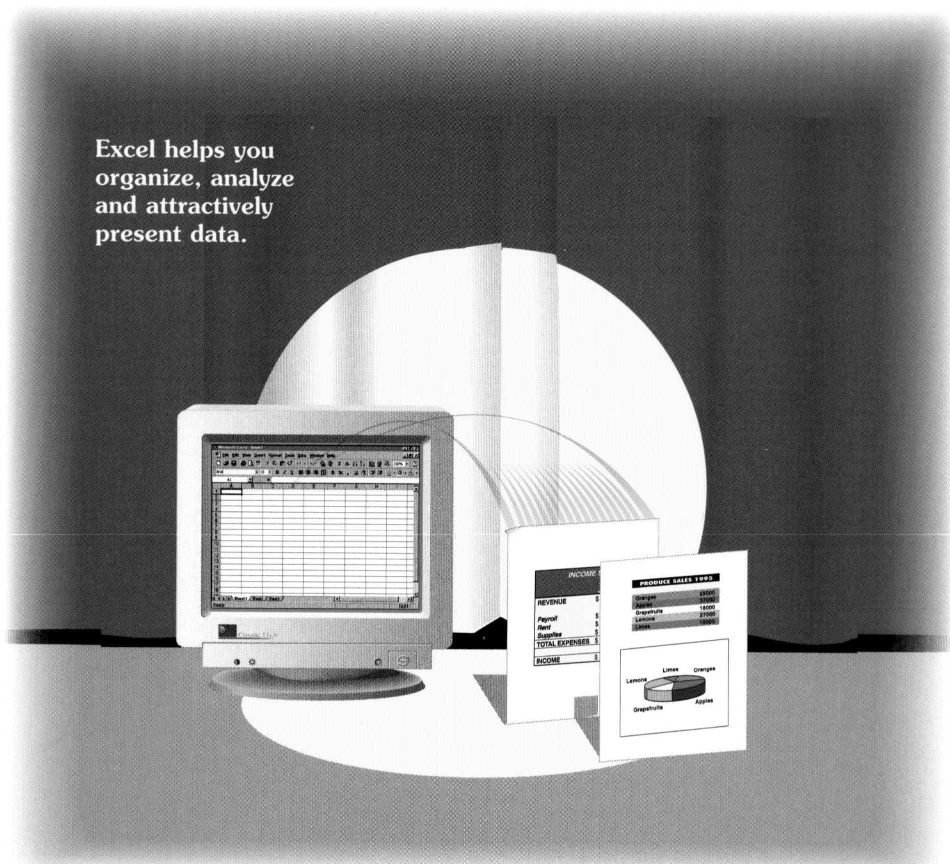

Formulas and Functions

Excel provides powerful tools to calculate and analyze data in your worksheets.

Edit and Format Data

Excel lets you efficiently enter, edit and change the appearance of data in your worksheets.

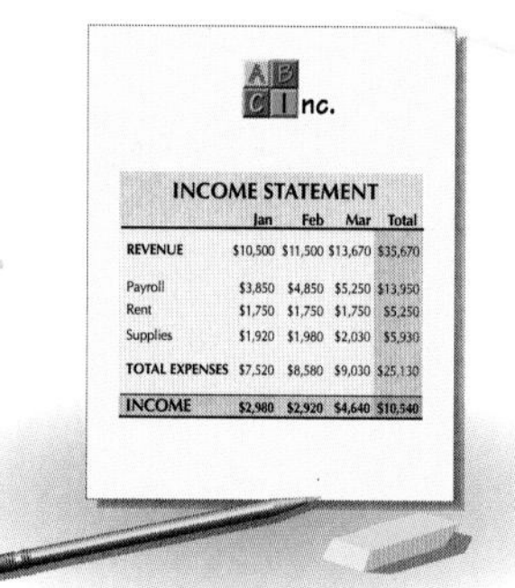

ABC Inc.

INCOME STATEMENT

	Jan	Feb	Mar	Total
REVENUE	$10,500	$11,500	$13,670	$35,670
Payroll	$3,850	$4,850	$5,250	$13,950
Rent	$1,750	$1,750	$1,750	$5,250
Supplies	$1,920	$1,980	$2,030	$5,930
TOTAL EXPENSES	$7,520	$8,580	$9,030	$25,130
INCOME	$2,980	$2,920	$4,640	$10,540

Charts

Excel helps you create colorful charts using your worksheet data.

START EXCEL

When you start Excel, a blank worksheet appears. You can enter data into this worksheet.

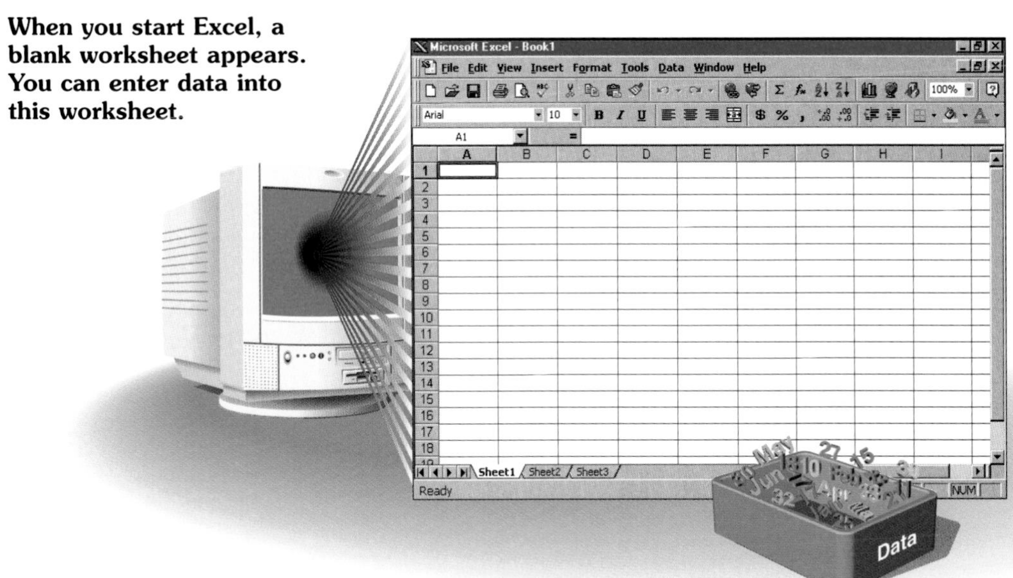

START EXCEL

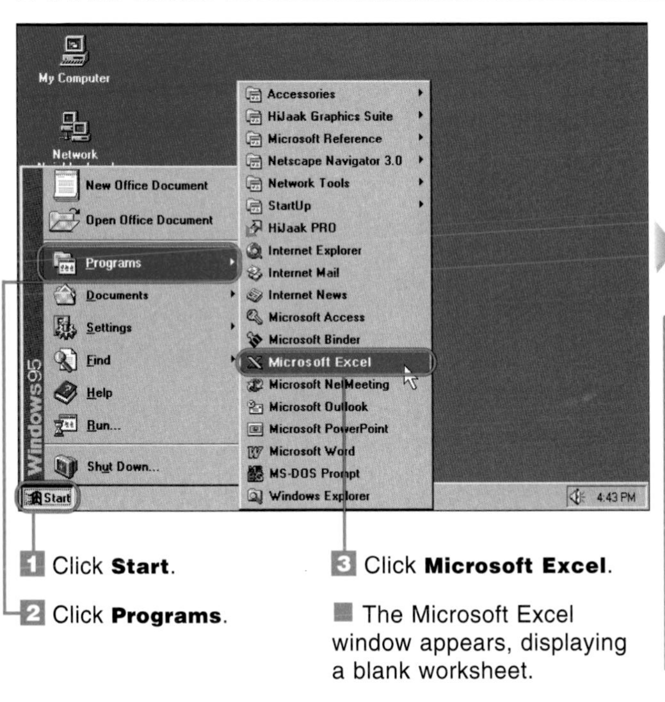

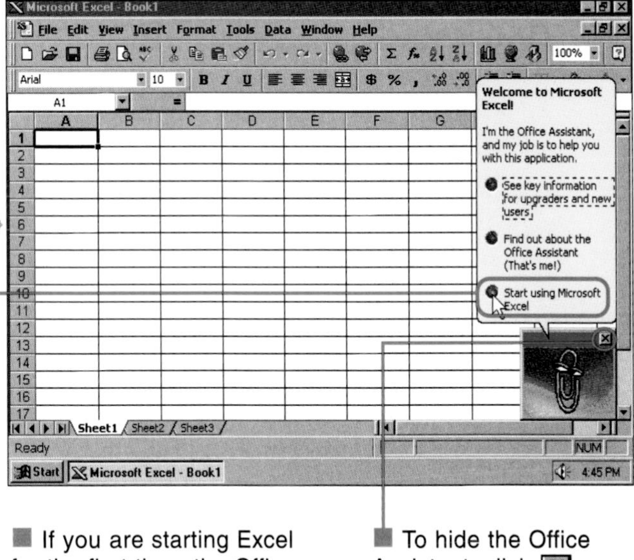

1 Click **Start**.

2 Click **Programs**.

3 Click **Microsoft Excel**.

- The Microsoft Excel window appears, displaying a blank worksheet.

- If you are starting Excel for the first time, the Office Assistant welcome appears.

4 To start using Excel, click this option.

- To hide the Office Assistant, click ☒.

Note: For more information on the Office Assistant, refer to page 12.

WORKSHEET BASICS

A worksheet consists of rows, columns and cells.

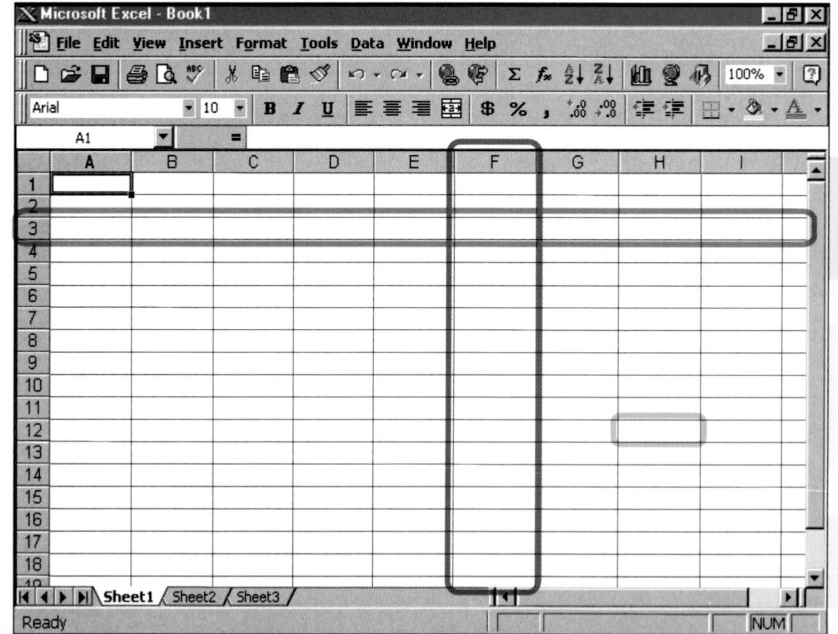

Row

A horizontal line of boxes. A number identifies each row.

Column

A vertical line of boxes. A letter identifies each column.

Cell

One box in a worksheet.

Cell Reference

A cell reference defines the location of each cell in a worksheet. A cell reference consists of a column letter followed by a row number (example: B3).

Active Cell

You enter information into the active cell. The active cell displays a thick border.

THE EXCEL SCREEN

The Excel screen displays several items to help you perform tasks efficiently.

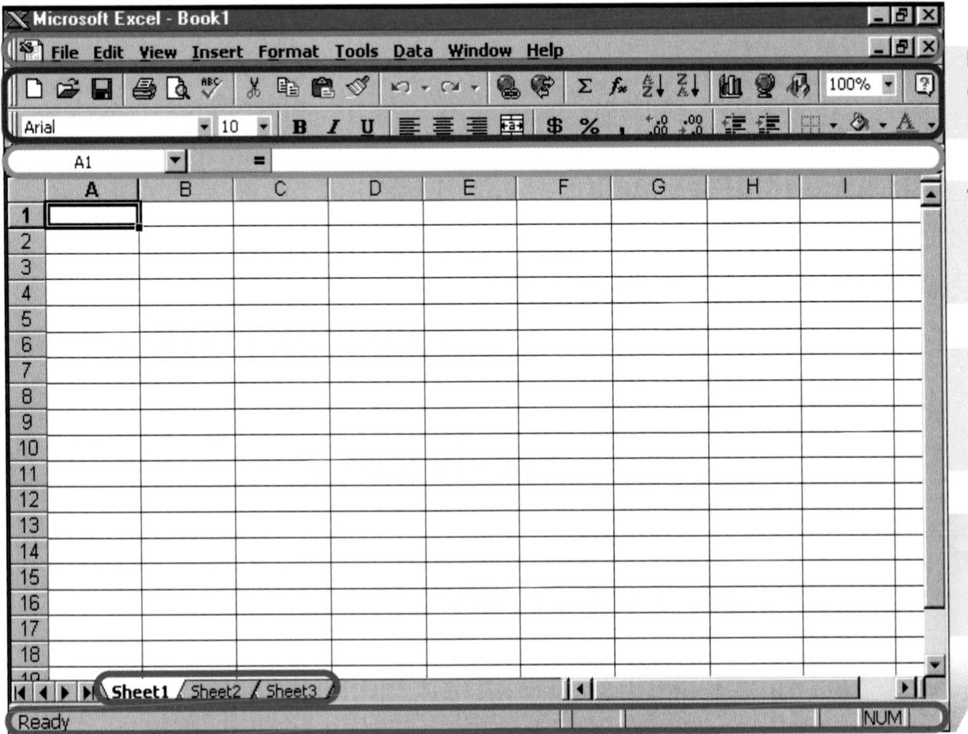

Menu Bar

Contains commands that let you perform tasks.

Toolbars

Contain buttons to help you quickly select common commands.

Formula Bar

Displays the cell reference and contents of the active cell.

Status Bar

Displays information about the task you are performing.

Worksheet Tabs

An Excel file is called a workbook. Each workbook is divided into several worksheets. Excel displays a tab for each worksheet.

A workbook is similar to a three-ring binder that contains several sheets of paper.

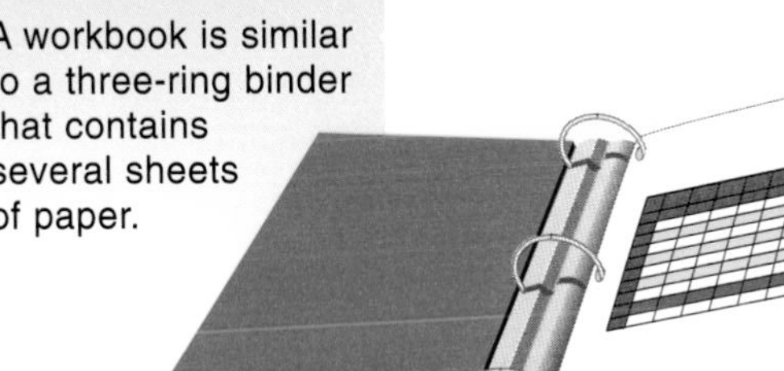

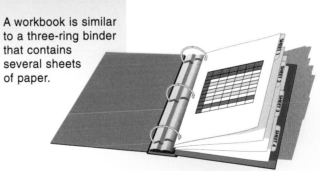

You can enter data into your worksheet quickly and easily.

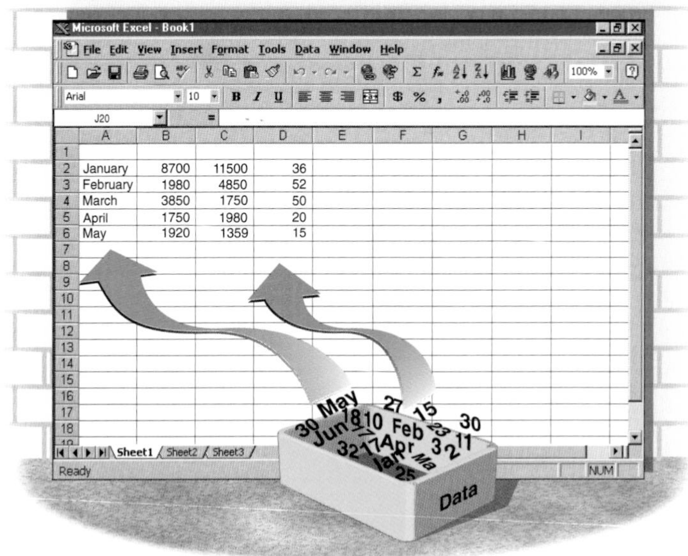

ENTER DATA

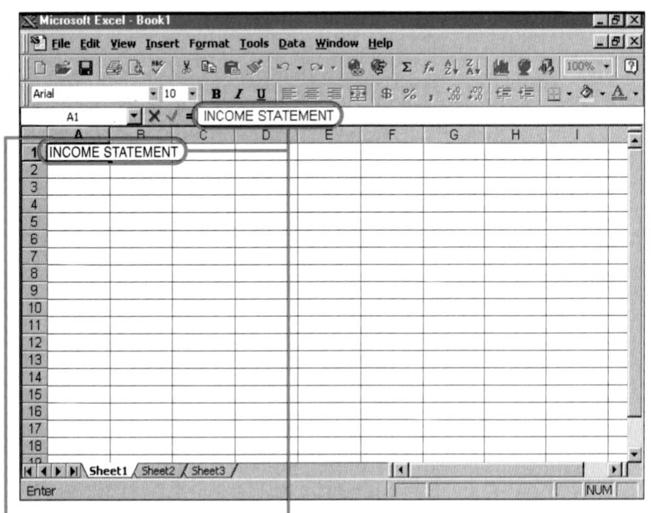

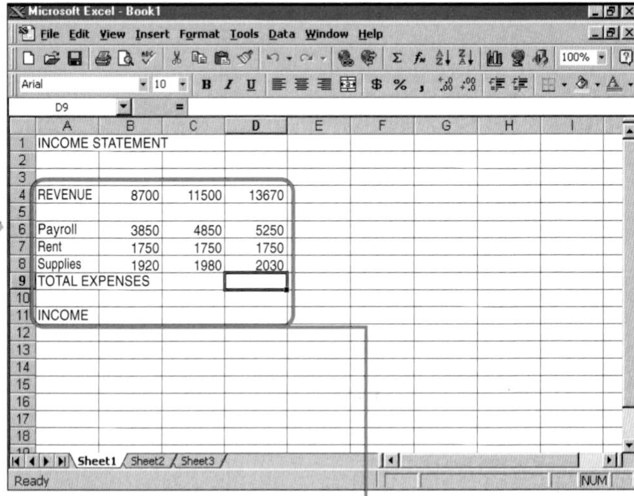

1 Click the cell where you want to enter data. Then type the data.

■ If you make a typing mistake, press **Backspace** on your keyboard to remove the incorrect data and then type the correct data.

■ The data you type appears in the active cell and in the formula bar.

2 To enter the data and move down one cell, press **Enter** on your keyboard.

Note: To enter the data and move one cell in any direction, press ↑, ↓, ← or → on your keyboard.

3 Repeat steps **1** and **2** until you finish entering all the data.

?

How do I use the number keys on the right side of my keyboard?

When **NUM** appears at the bottom of your screen, you can use the number keys on the right side of your keyboard to enter numbers.

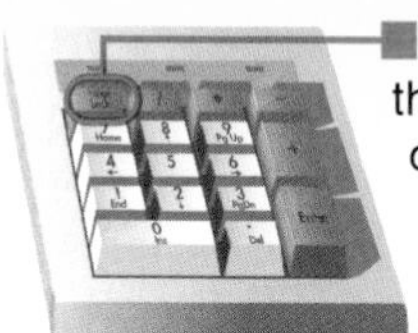

■ To turn on or off the display of **NUM** on your screen, press Num Lock on your keyboard.

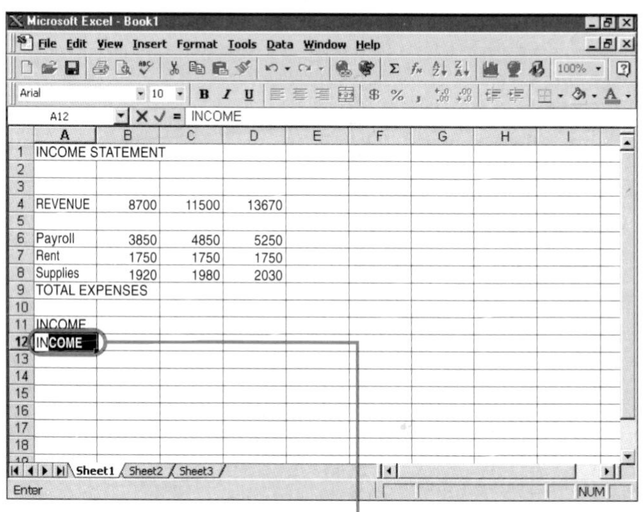

AUTOCOMPLETE

If the first few letters you type match another cell in the column, Excel will complete the text for you.

■ To keep the text Excel provides, press Enter on your keyboard.

■ To enter different text, continue typing.

4	TOTAL EXPENSES	
5		
6		

4	TOTAL EX	227
5		
6		

Long Words

If text is too long to fit in a cell, the text will spill into the neighboring cell.

If the neighboring cell contains data, Excel will display as much of the text as the column width will allow. To change the column width, refer to page 166.

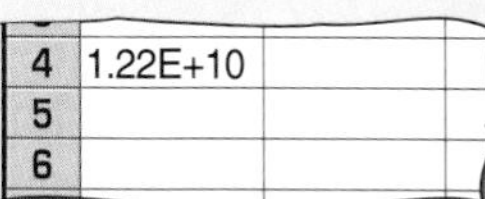

4	#####
5	
6	

Long Numbers

If a number is too long to fit in a cell, Excel will display the number in scientific form or as number signs (#). To change the column width to display the number, refer to page 166.

COMPLETE A SERIES

Excel can save you time by completing a text or number series for you.

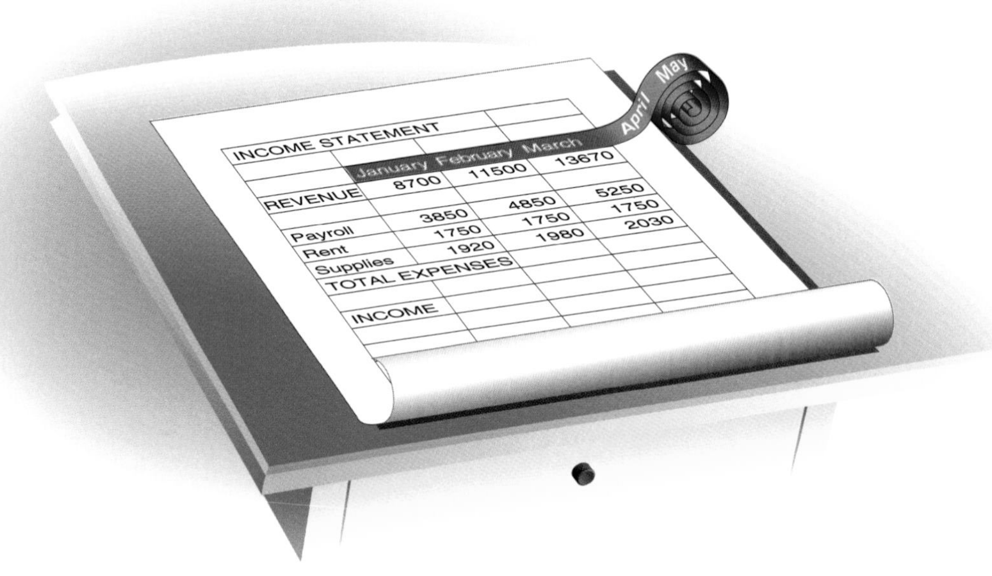

COMPLETE A SERIES

Text Series

Mon	Tue	Wed	Thu
Product 1	Product 2	Product 3	Product 4
1st Quarter	2nd Quarter	3rd Quarter	4th Quarter

■ Excel completes a text series based on the text in the first cell.

Number Series

1995	1996	1997	1998
5	10	15	20
202	204	206	208

■ Excel completes a number series based on the numbers in the first two cells.

These numbers tell Excel how much to add to each number to complete the series.

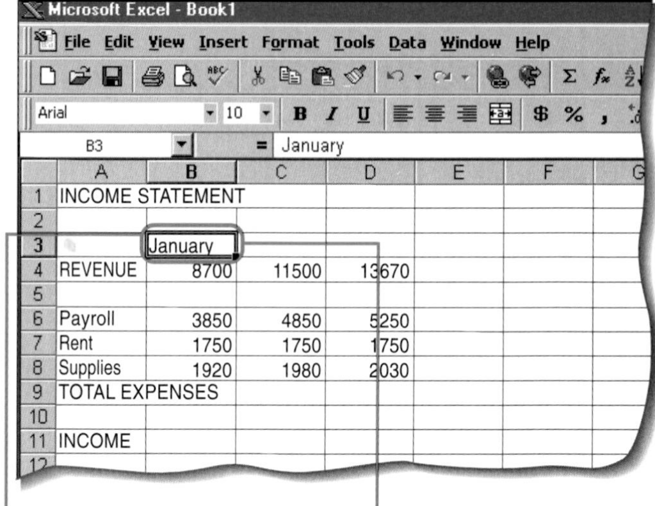

1 Enter the text or the first two numbers you want to start the series.

2 Select the cell(s) containing the text or numbers you entered. To select cells, refer to page 120.

?

Can I change the color of data in my worksheet?

You can easily change the color of data to make your worksheet more attractive. To do so, refer to page 176.

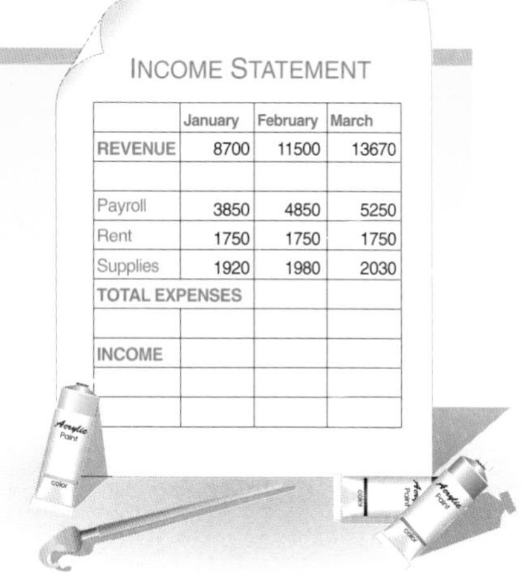

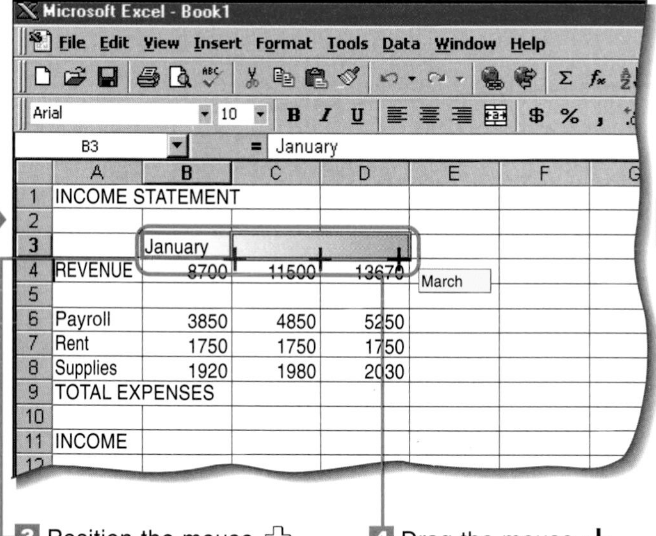

3 Position the mouse ✥ over the bottom right corner of the selected cell(s) (✥ changes to **+**).

4 Drag the mouse **+** over the cells you want to include in the series.

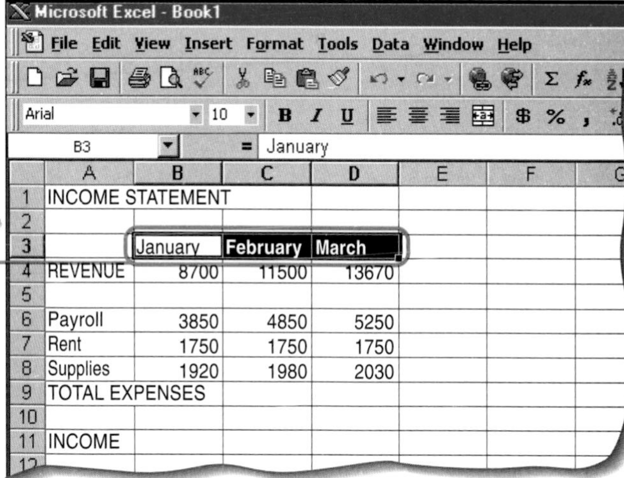

■ The cells display the series.

*Note: You can also perform steps **1** to **4** to complete a series in a column.*

SELECT CELLS

Before performing many tasks in Excel, you must select the cells you want to work with. Selected cells appear highlighted on your screen.

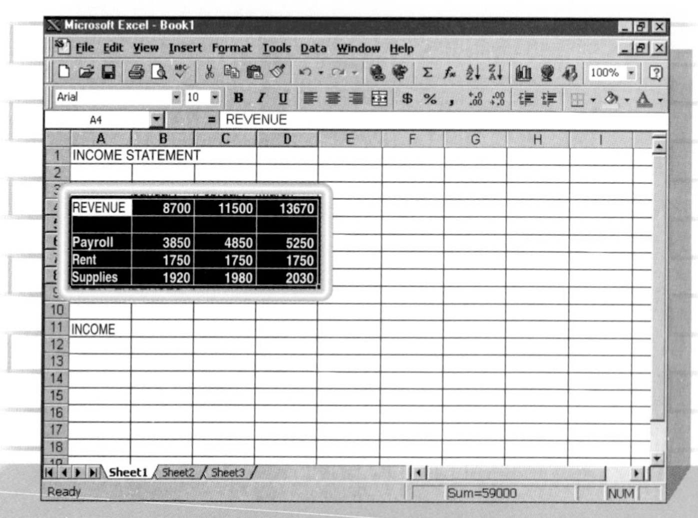

SELECT ONE CELL

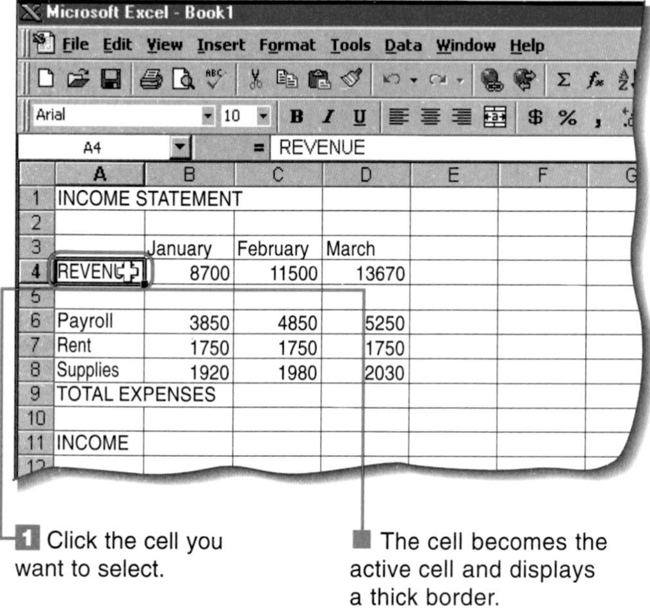

1 Click the cell you want to select.

■ The cell becomes the active cell and displays a thick border.

SELECT GROUPS OF CELLS

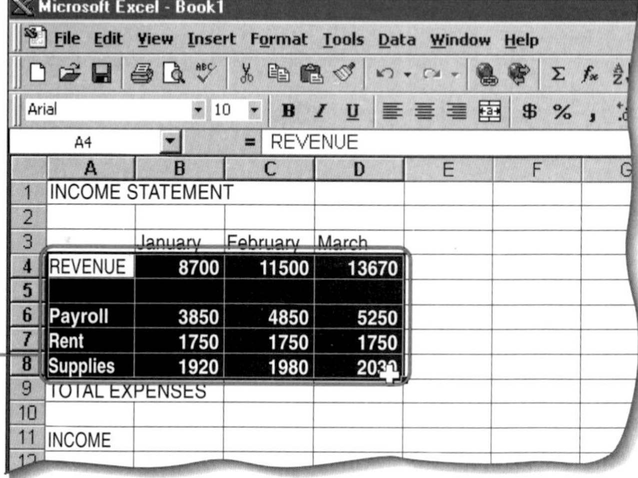

1 Position the mouse ✥ over the first cell you want to select.

2 Drag the mouse ✥ to highlight all the cells you want to select.

■ To select multiple groups of cells, press and hold down Ctrl on your keyboard as you repeat steps 1 and 2 for each group.

■ To deselect cells, click any cell.

?

How do I select all the cells in my worksheet?

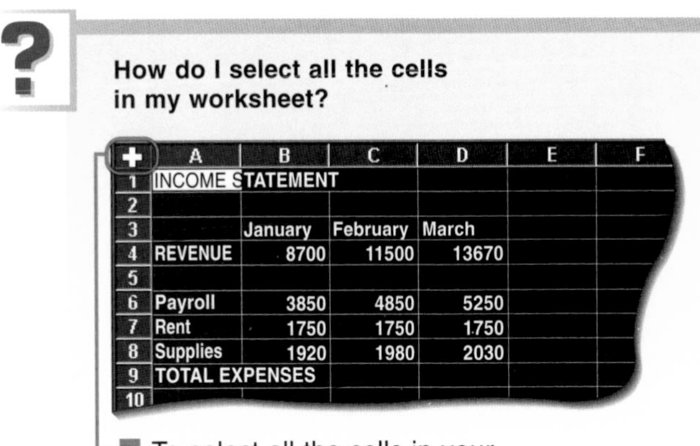

To select all the cells in your worksheet, click the area where the row and column headings meet.

SELECT A ROW

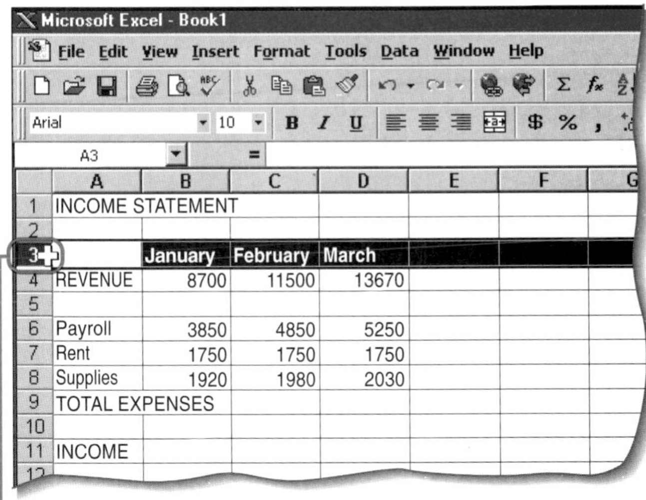

1 Click the number of the row you want to select.

SELECT A COLUMN

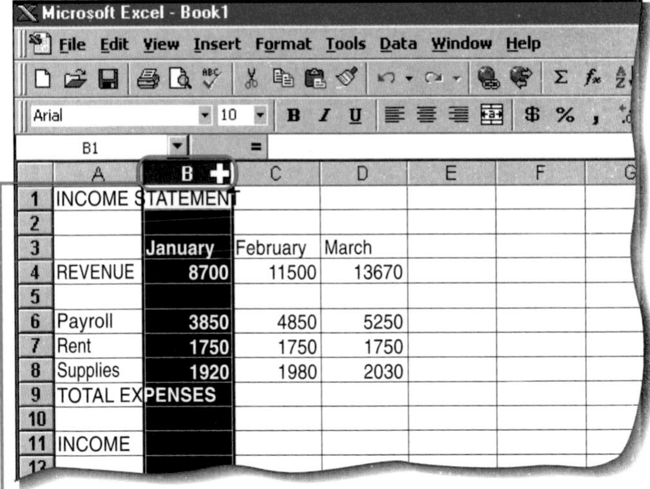

1 Click the letter of the column you want to select.

SCROLL THROUGH A WORKSHEET

If your worksheet contains a lot of data, your computer screen cannot display all the data at once. You must scroll through the worksheet to view other areas.

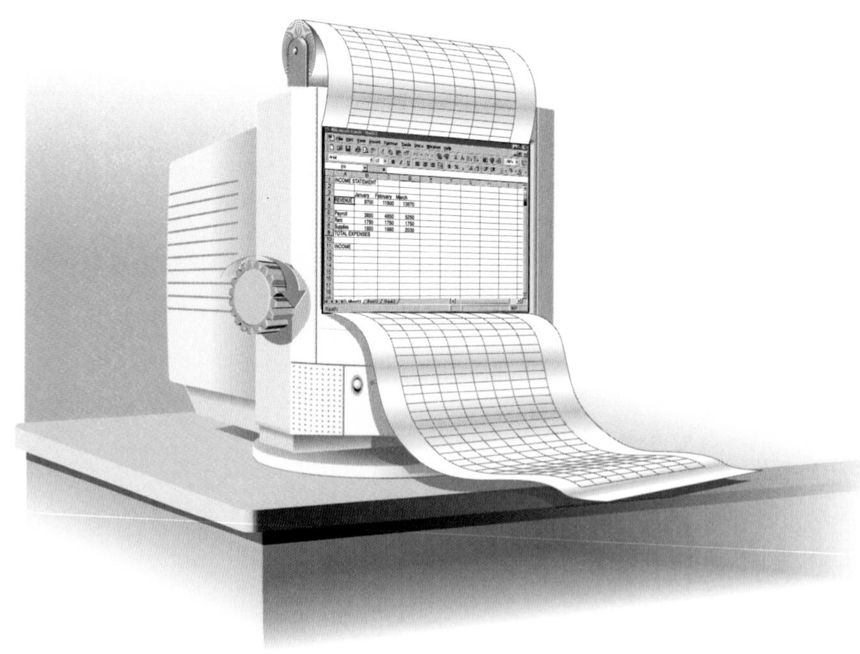

SCROLL UP OR DOWN

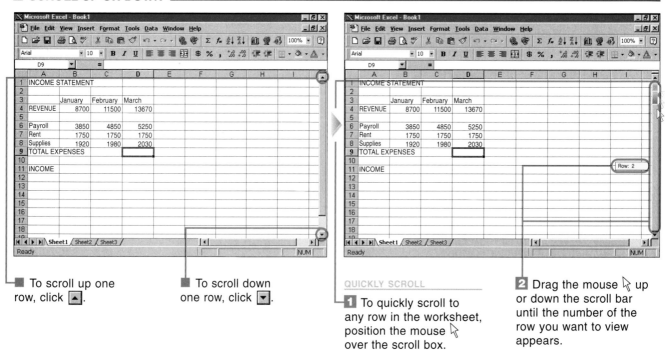

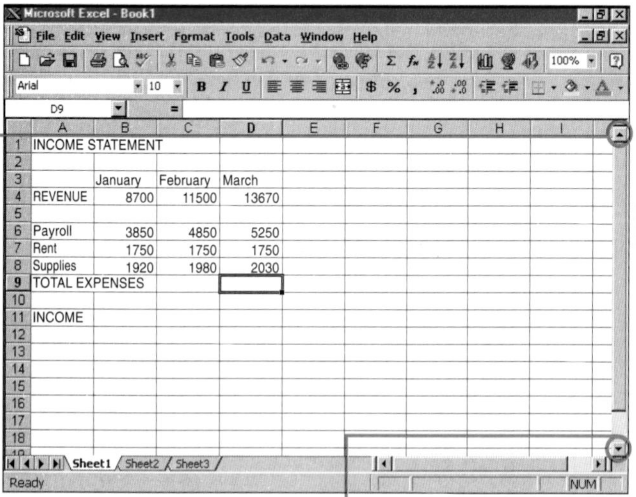

■ To scroll up one row, click ▲.

■ To scroll down one row, click ▼.

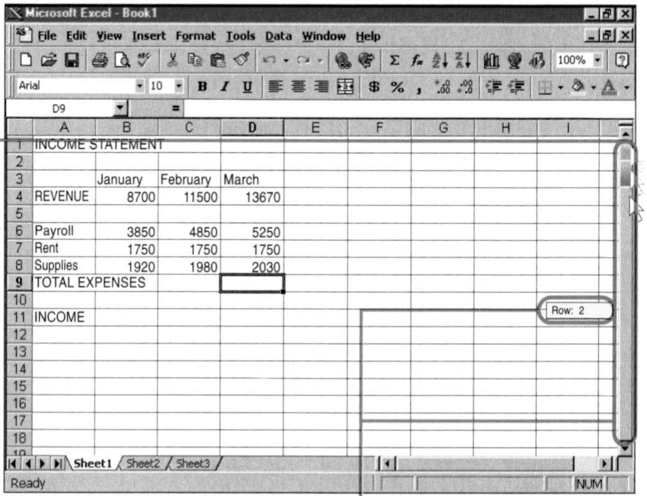

QUICKLY SCROLL

1 To quickly scroll to any row in the worksheet, position the mouse ↖ over the scroll box.

2 Drag the mouse ↖ up or down the scroll bar until the number of the row you want to view appears.

How do I use the new Microsoft IntelliMouse to scroll through a worksheet?

The Microsoft IntelliMouse has a wheel between the left and right mouse buttons. Moving this wheel lets you quickly scroll up and down through a worksheet.

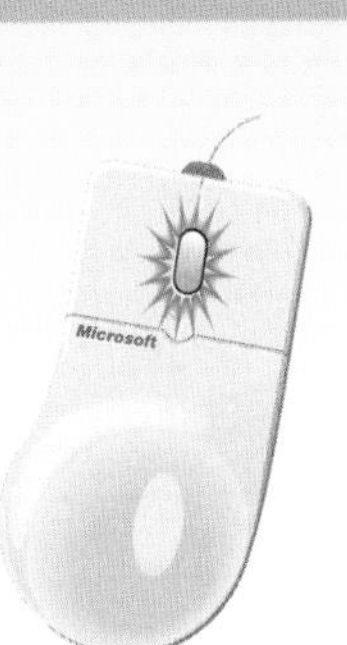

SCROLL LEFT OR RIGHT

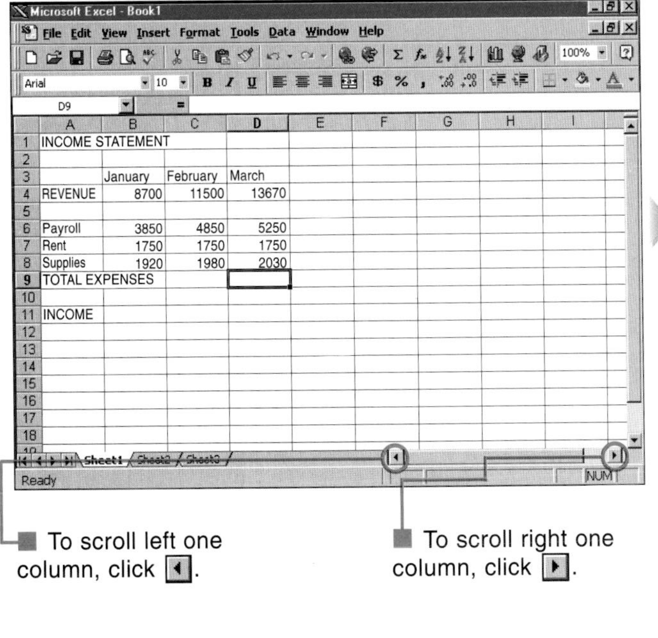

■ To scroll left one column, click ◂.

■ To scroll right one column, click ▸.

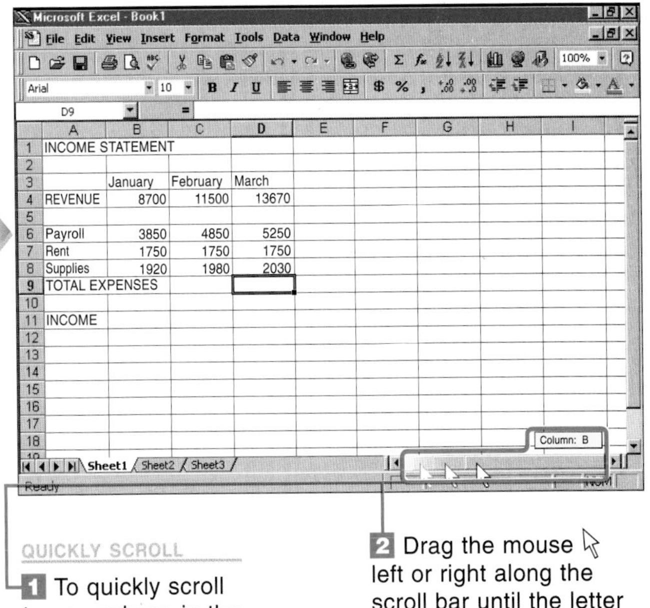

QUICKLY SCROLL

1 To quickly scroll to any column in the worksheet, position the mouse over the scroll box.

2 Drag the mouse left or right along the scroll bar until the letter of the column you want to view appears.

IN OR OUT

Excel lets you enlarge or reduce the display of data on your screen.

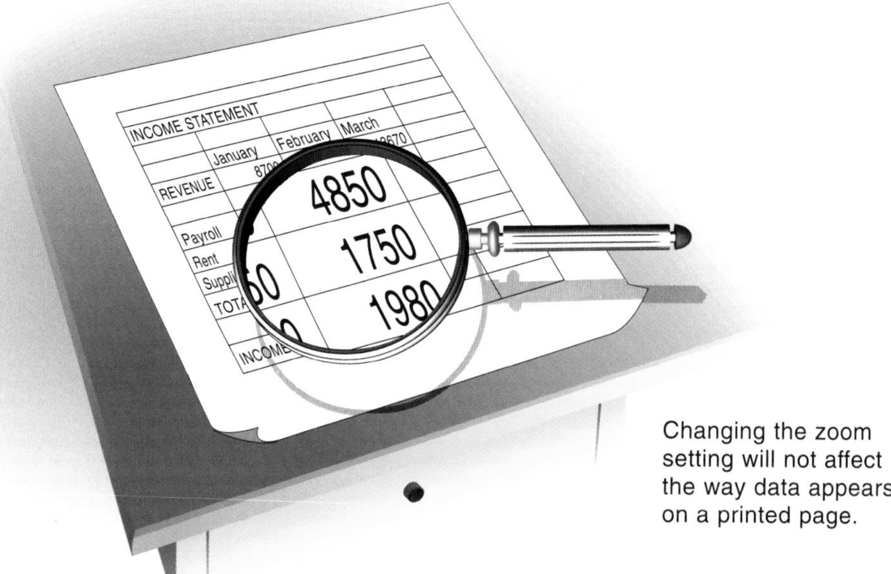

Changing the zoom setting will not affect the way data appears on a printed page.

ZOOM IN OR OUT

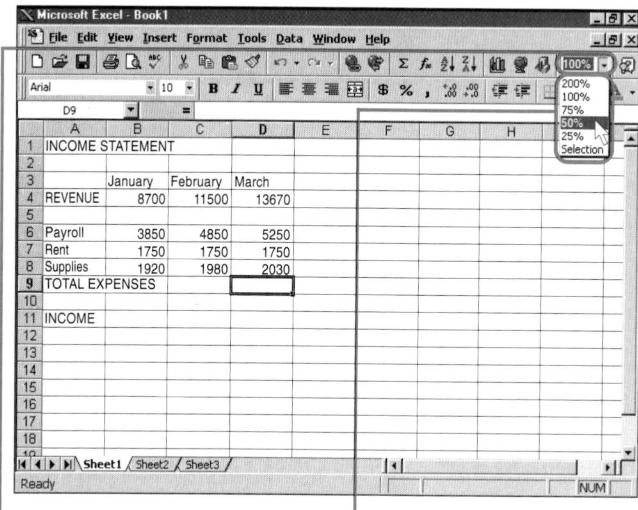

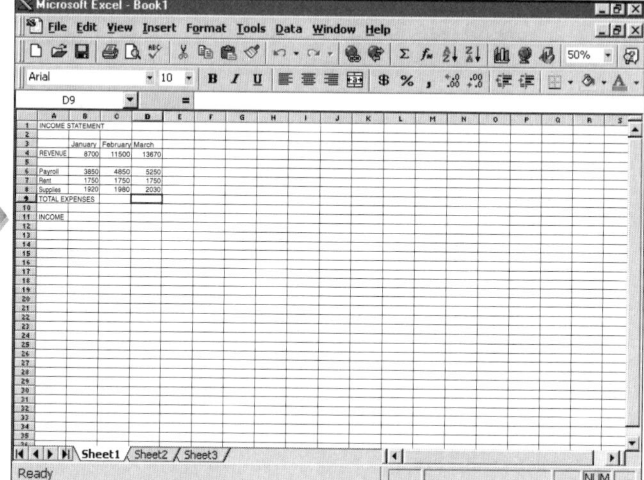

■ When you first start Excel, the worksheet appears in the 100% zoom setting.

1 To display a list of zoom settings, click ▾ in this area.

2 Click the zoom setting you want to use.

■ The worksheet appears in the new zoom setting. You can edit your worksheet as usual.

■ To return to the normal zoom setting, repeat steps **1** and **2**, selecting **100%** in step **2**.

DISPLAY OR HIDE TOOLBARS

Excel offers several toolbars that you can display or hide at any time. Each toolbar contains a series of buttons that help you quickly perform tasks.

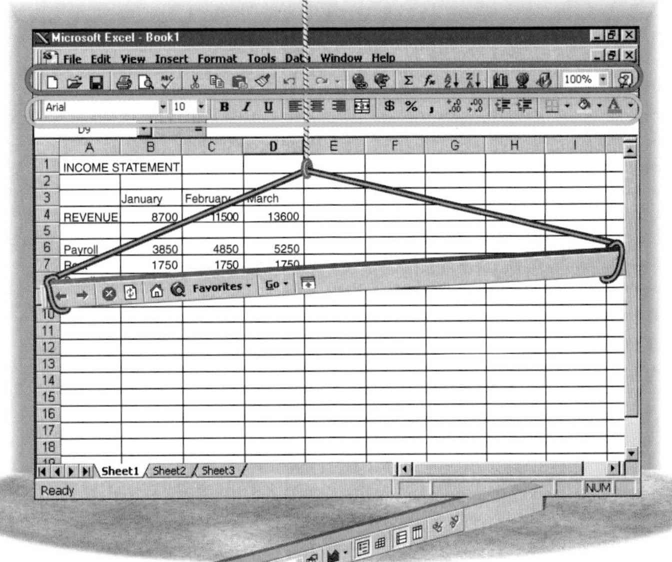

Standard

Formatting

When you first start Excel, the **Standard** and **Formatting** toolbars appear on your screen.

DISPLAY OR HIDE TOOLBARS

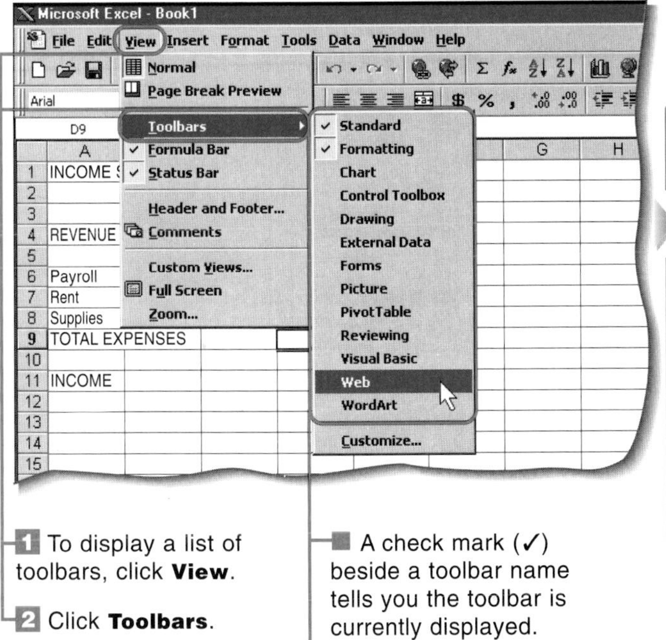

1 To display a list of toolbars, click **View**.

2 Click **Toolbars**.

■ A check mark (✓) beside a toolbar name tells you the toolbar is currently displayed.

3 To display or hide a toolbar, click the name of the toolbar.

■ Excel displays or hides the toolbar you selected.

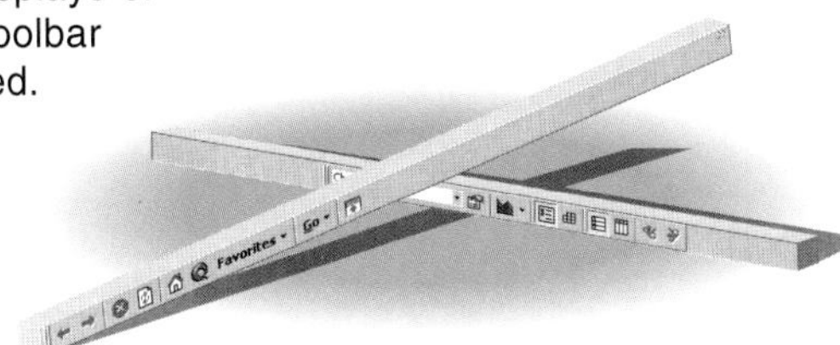

SAVE A WORKBOOK

You should save your workbook to store it for future use. This lets you later review and make changes to the workbook.

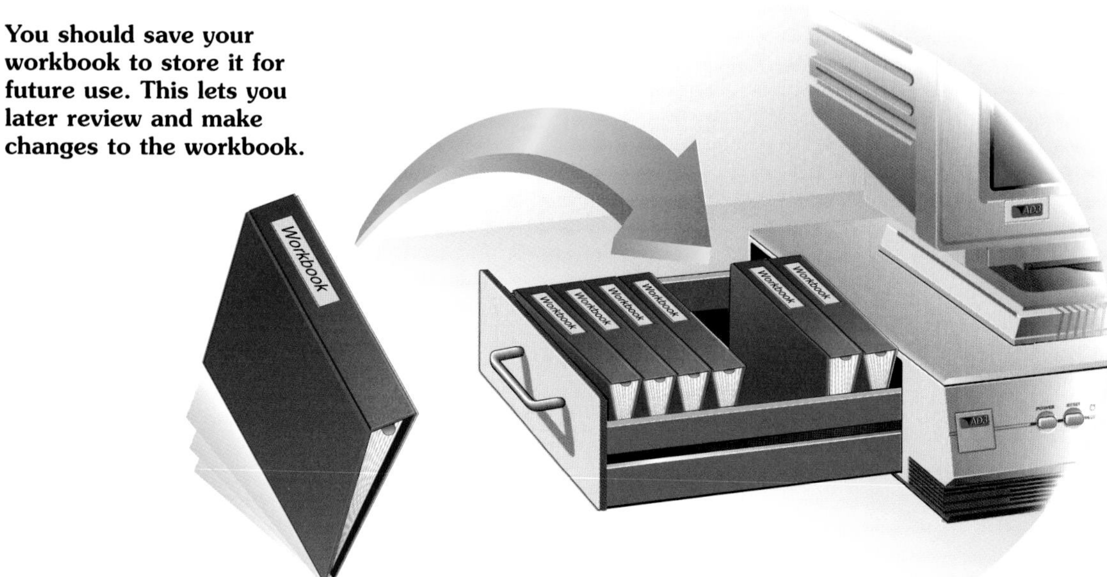

SAVE A WORKBOOK

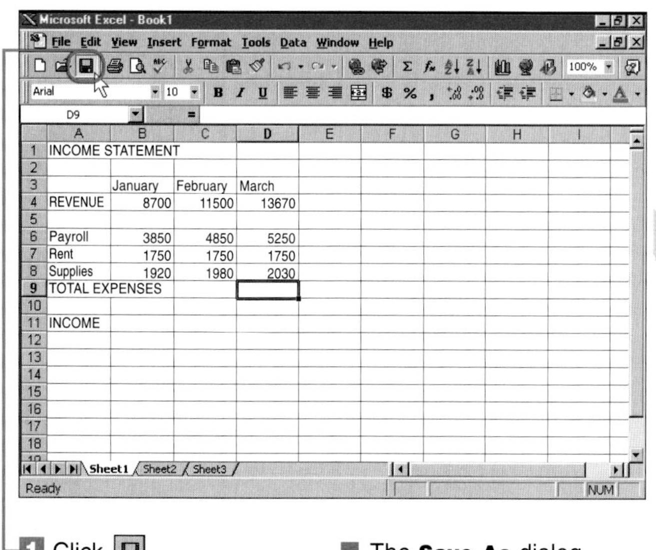

1 Click the Save button.

■ The **Save As** dialog box appears.

*Note: If you previously saved the workbook, the **Save As** dialog box will not appear since you have already named the workbook.*

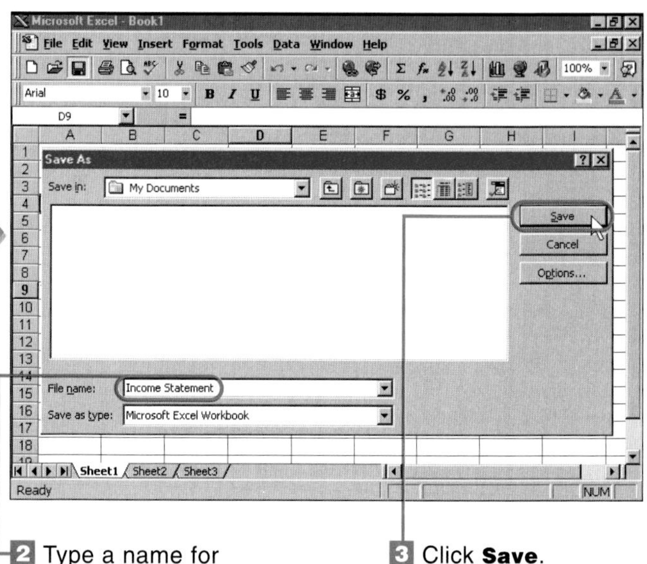

2 Type a name for the workbook.

Note: You can use up to 218 characters, including spaces, to name a workbook.

3 Click **Save**.

What is the difference between a workbook and a worksheet?

An Excel file is called a workbook. Each workbook is divided into several worksheets. A workbook is similar to a three-ring binder that contains several sheets of paper.

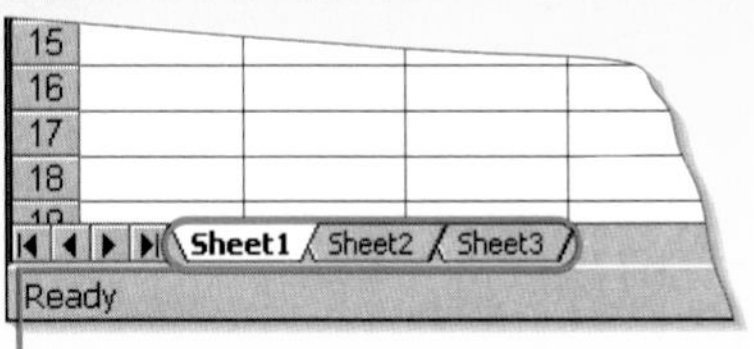

■ Excel displays a tab for each worksheet in your workbook.

Note: To use multiple worksheets in a workbook, refer to pages 194 to 199.

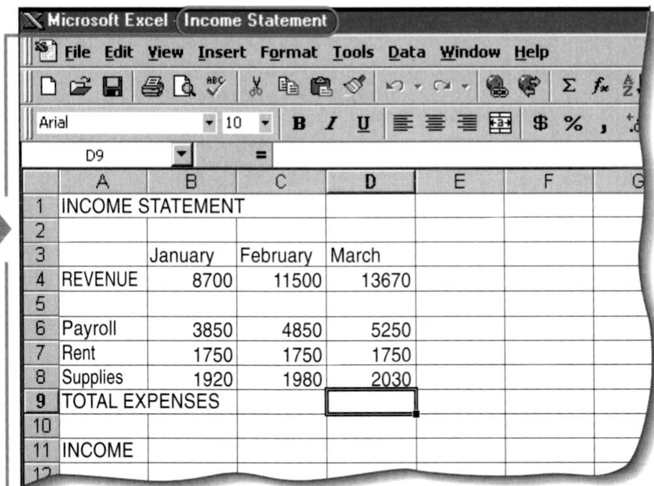

■ Excel saves the workbook and displays the name at the top of the screen.

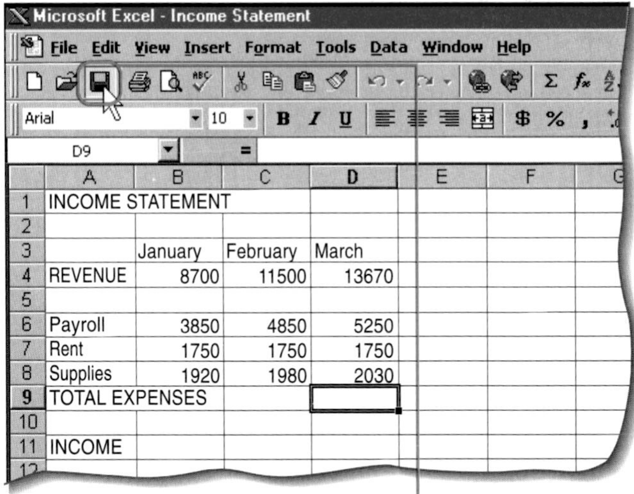

SAVE CHANGES

To avoid losing your work, you should regularly save changes you make to a workbook.

1 To save changes, click 💾.

CREATE A NEW WORKBOOK

You can easily create another workbook to store new data.

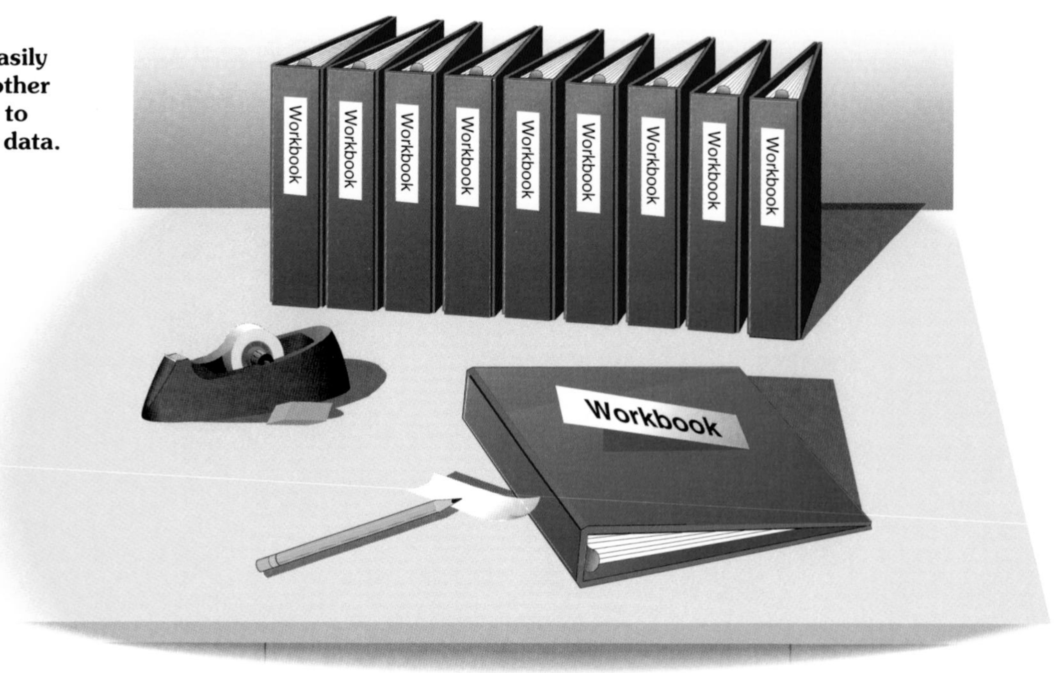

CREATE A NEW WORKBOOK

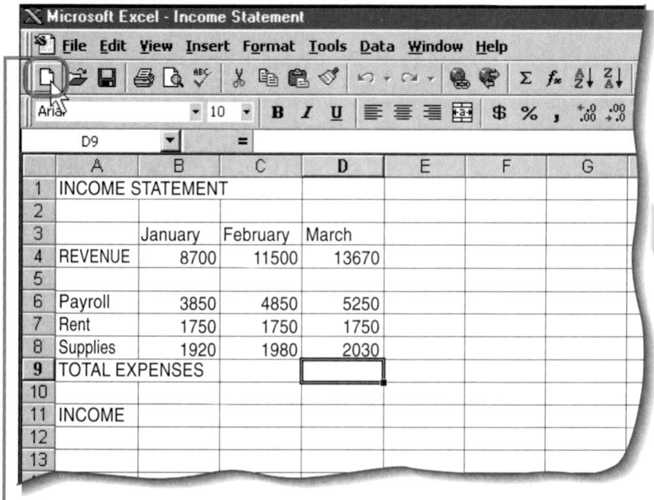

1 Click ▢.

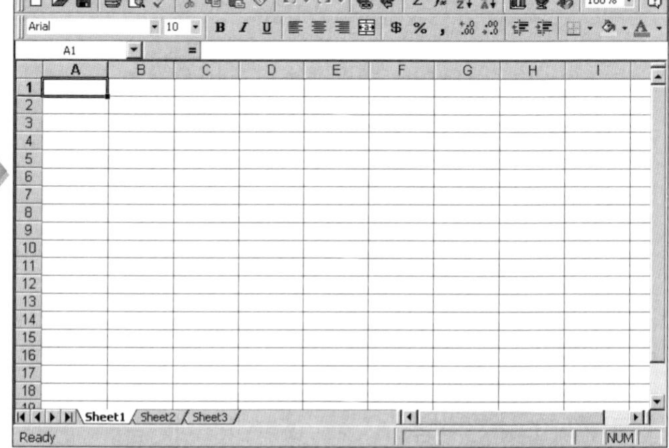

■ A new workbook appears. The previous workbook is now hidden behind the new workbook.

SWITCH BETWEEN WORKBOOKS

Excel lets you have many workbooks open at once. You can easily switch between all of your open workbooks.

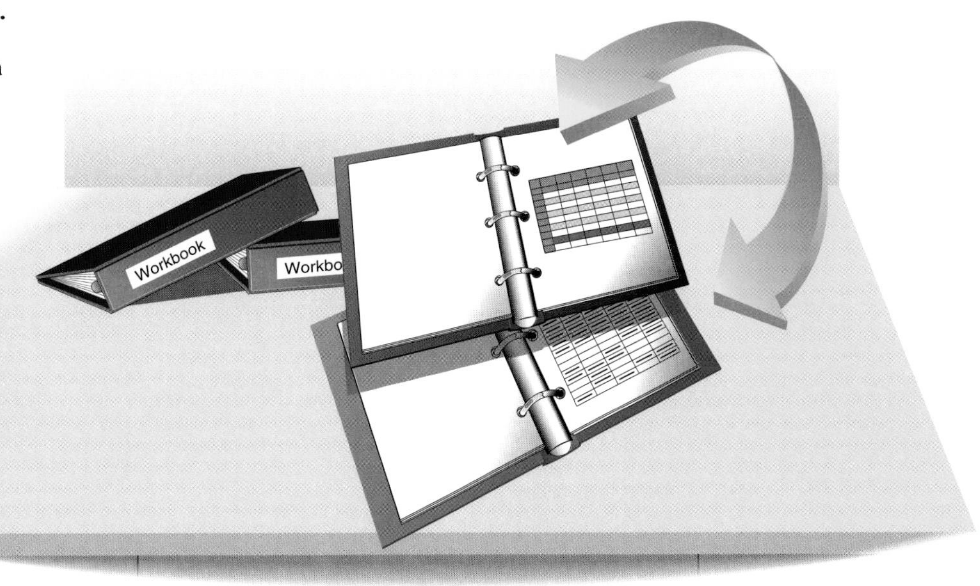

SWITCH BETWEEN WORKBOOKS

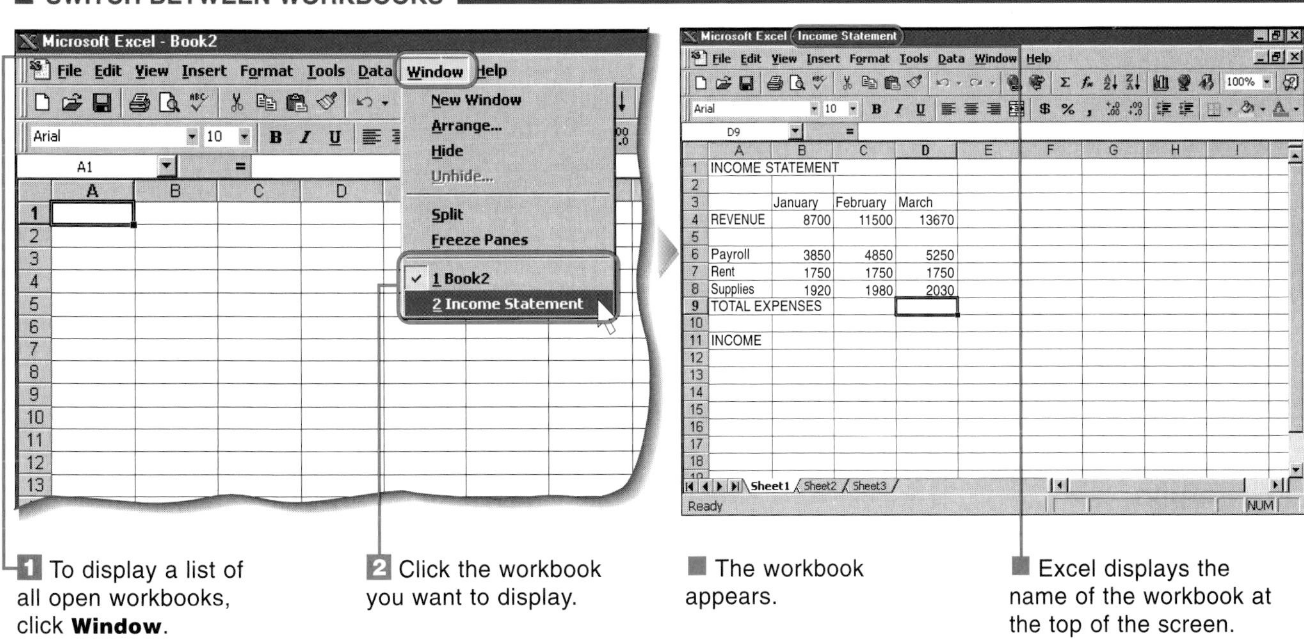

1 To display a list of all open workbooks, click **Window**.

2 Click the workbook you want to display.

■ The workbook appears.

■ Excel displays the name of the workbook at the top of the screen.

CLOSE A WORKBOOK

When you finish using a workbook, you can close the workbook to remove it from your screen.

CLOSE A WORKBOOK

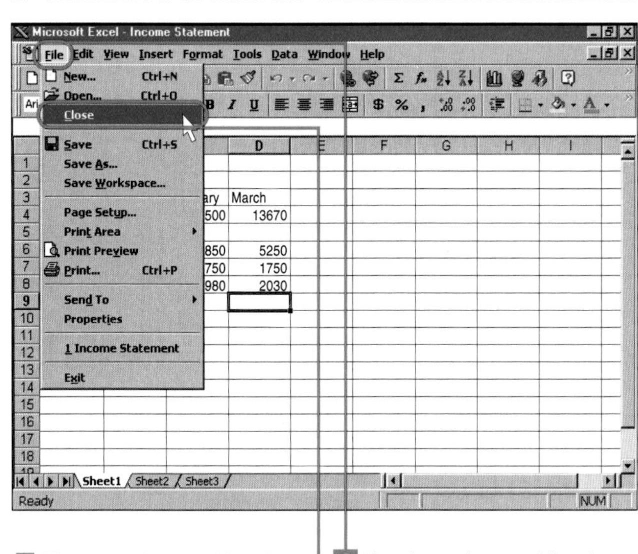

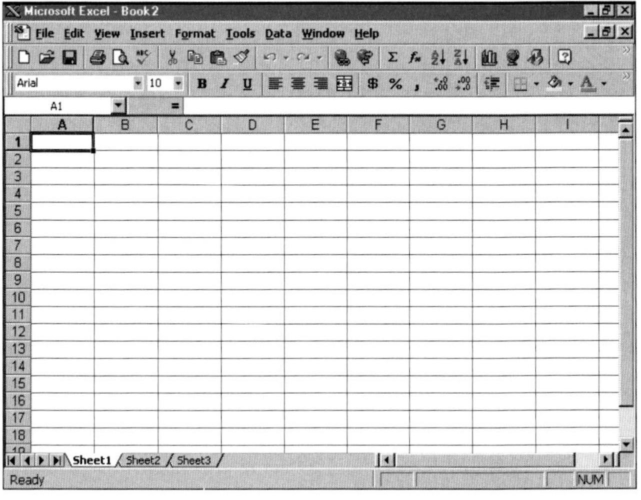

■ To save the workbook before closing, refer to page 126.

1 To close the workbook, click **File**.

2 Click **Close**.

■ Excel removes the workbook from the screen.

■ If you had more than one workbook open, the second last workbook you used appears on the screen.

EXIT EXCEL

When you finish using Excel, you can exit the program.

You should exit all programs before turning off your computer.

EXIT EXCEL

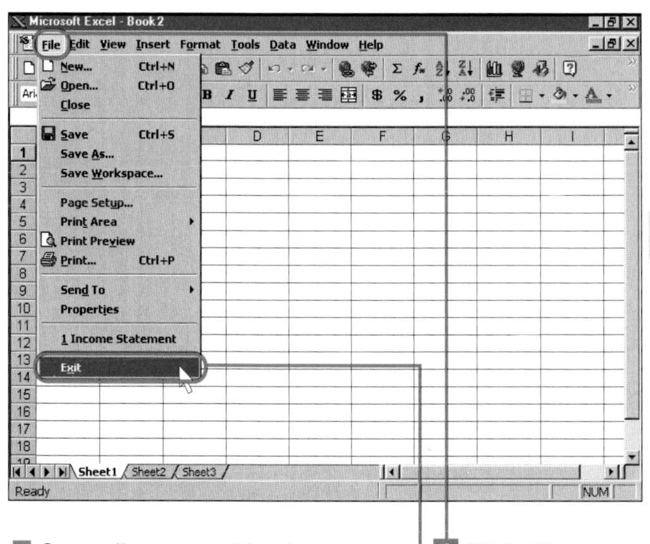

■ Save all open workbooks before exiting Excel. To save a workbook, refer to page 126.

1. Click **File**.
2. Click **Exit**.

■ The Excel window disappears from the screen.

Note: To restart Excel, refer to page 113.

You can open a saved workbook and display it on your screen. This lets you review and make changes to the workbook.

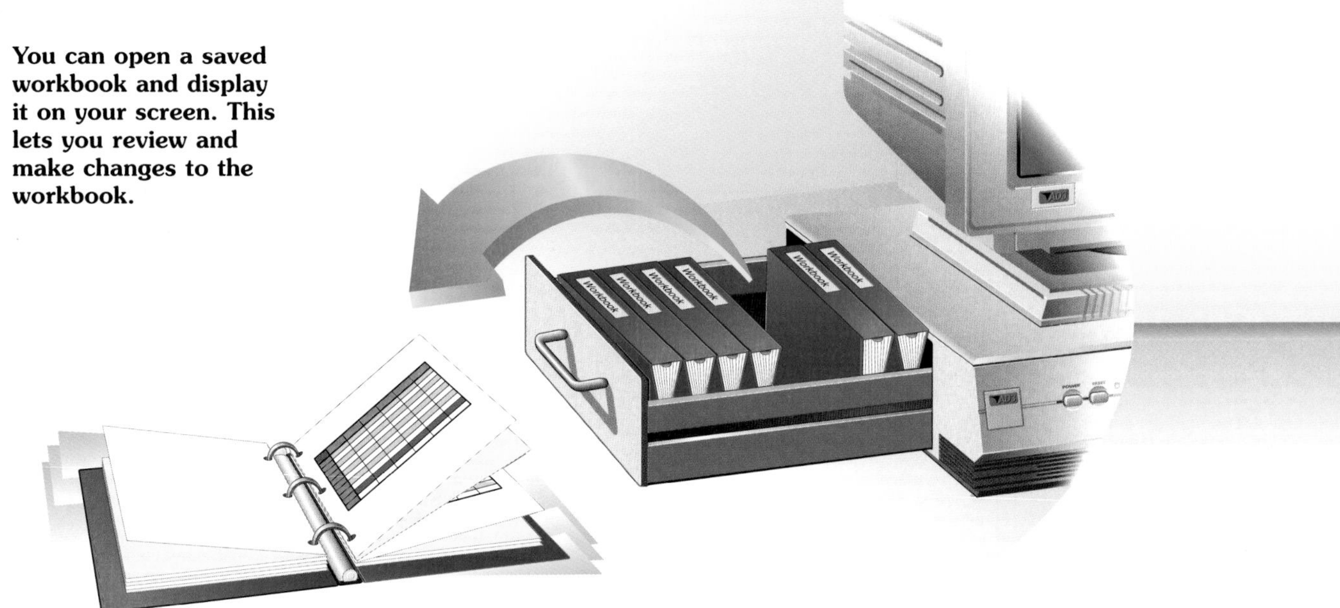

OPEN A WORKBOOK

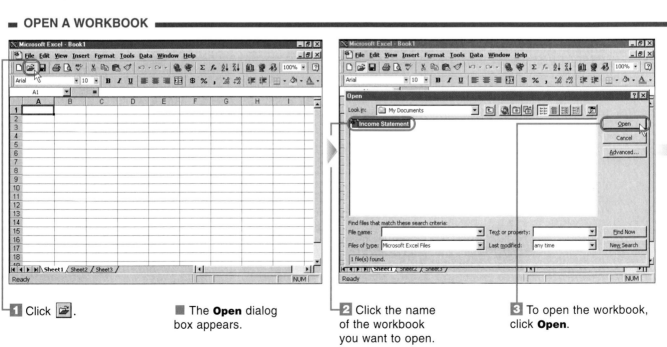

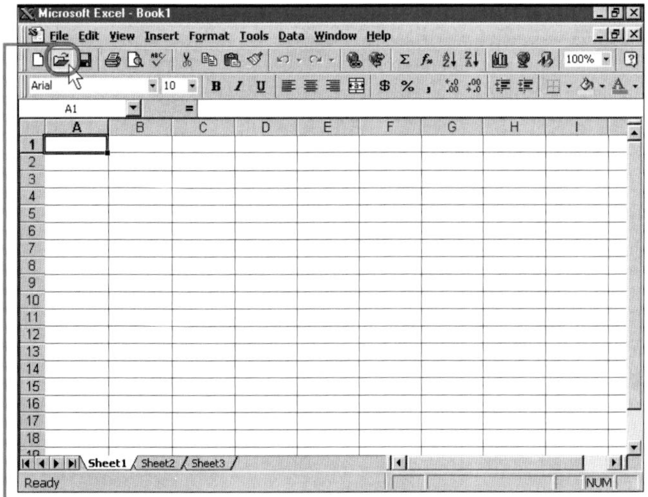

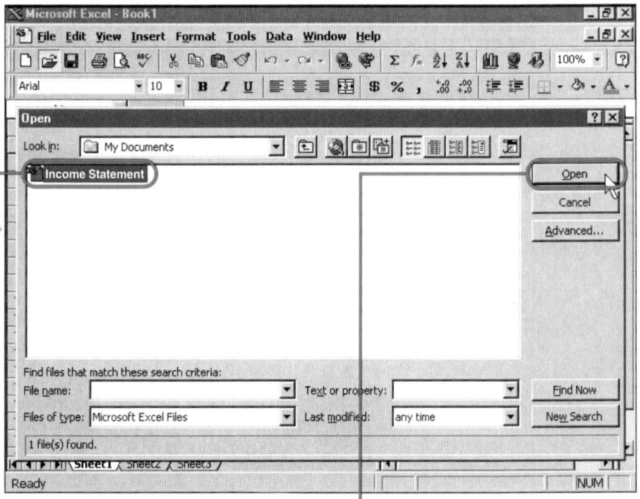

1 Click [Open button].

■ The **Open** dialog box appears.

2 Click the name of the workbook you want to open.

3 To open the workbook, click **Open**.

Excel remembers the names of the last four workbooks you opened. You can quickly open any of these workbooks.

Microsoft Excel - Income Statement

	A	B	C	D
1	INCOME STATEMENT			
2				
3		January	February	March
4	REVENUE	8700	11500	13670
5				
6	Payroll	3850	4850	5250
7	Rent	1750	1750	1750
8	Supplies	1920	1980	2030
9	TOTAL EXPENSES			
10				
11	INCOME			

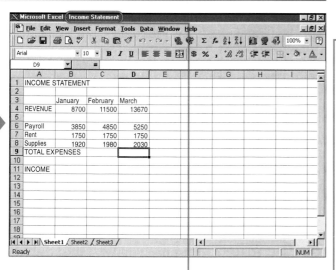

■ Excel opens the workbook and displays it on the screen. You can now review and make changes to the workbook.

■ The name of the workbook appears at the top of the screen.

QUICKLY OPEN A WORKBOOK

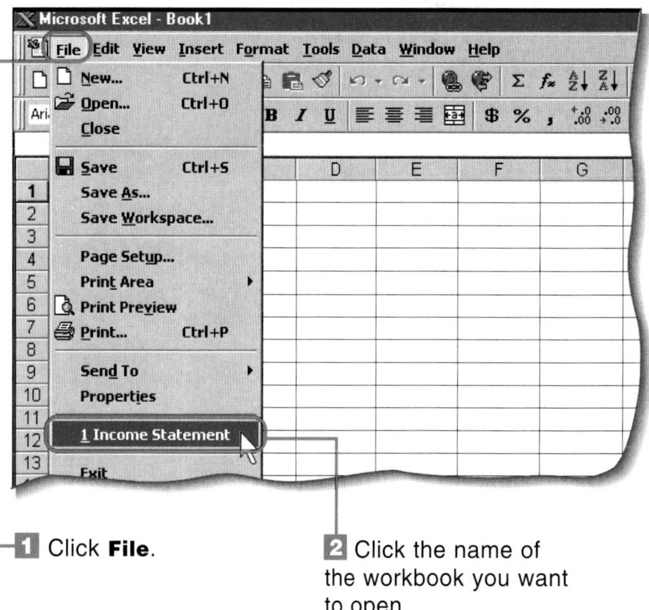

1 Click **File**.

2 Click the name of the workbook you want to open.

EDIT DATA

After you enter data into your worksheet, you can change the data to correct a mistake or update the data.

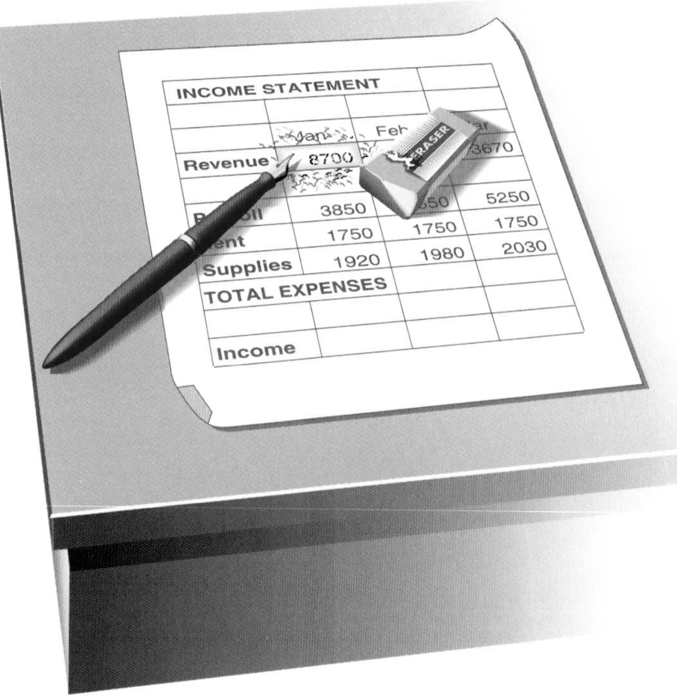

INCOME STATEMENT
Revenue
8700
3670
3850
5250
1750
1750
1750
Supplies
1920
1980
2030
TOTAL EXPENSES
Income
ERASER

EDIT DATA

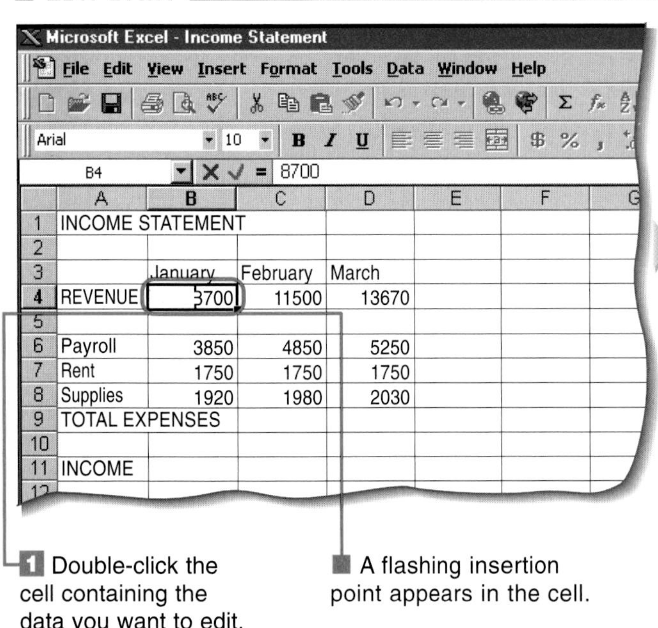

1 Double-click the cell containing the data you want to edit.

■ A flashing insertion point appears in the cell.

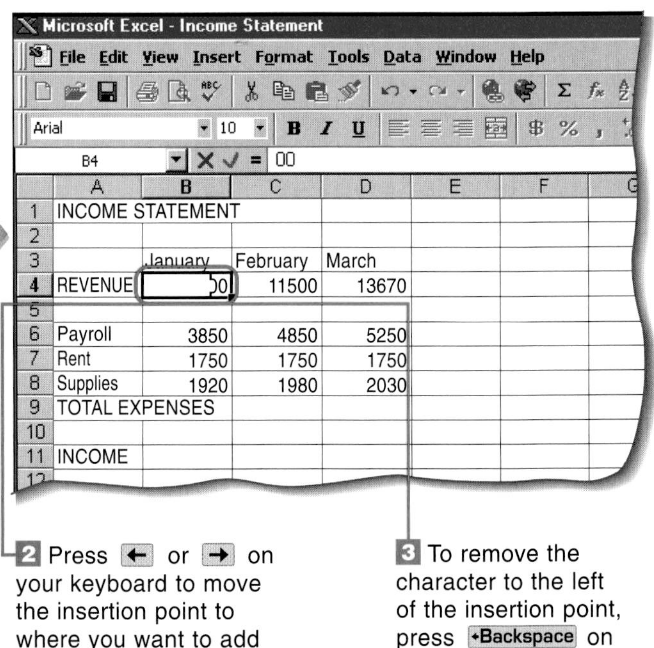

2 Press ← or → on your keyboard to move the insertion point to where you want to add or remove characters.

3 To remove the character to the left of the insertion point, press Backspace on your keyboard.

Can Excel automatically correct my typing mistakes?

Excel automatically corrects common spelling errors as you type.

adn → and
alot → a lot
comittee → committee
don;t → don't
nwe → new
occurence → occurrence
recieve → receive
seperate → separate
teh → the

Microsoft Excel - Income Statement

File Edit View Insert Format Tools Data Window Help

Arial 10

B4 = 9200

	A	B	C	D	E	F
1	INCOME STATEMENT					
2						
3		January	February	March		
4	REVENUE	9200	11500	13670		
5						
6	Payroll	3850	4850	5250		
7	Rent	1750	1750	1750		
8	Supplies	1920	1980	2030		
9	TOTAL EXPENSES					
10						
11	INCOME					

4 To insert data where the insertion point flashes on the screen, type the data.

5 When you finish making changes to the data, press Enter on your keyboard.

REPLACE ALL DATA IN A CELL

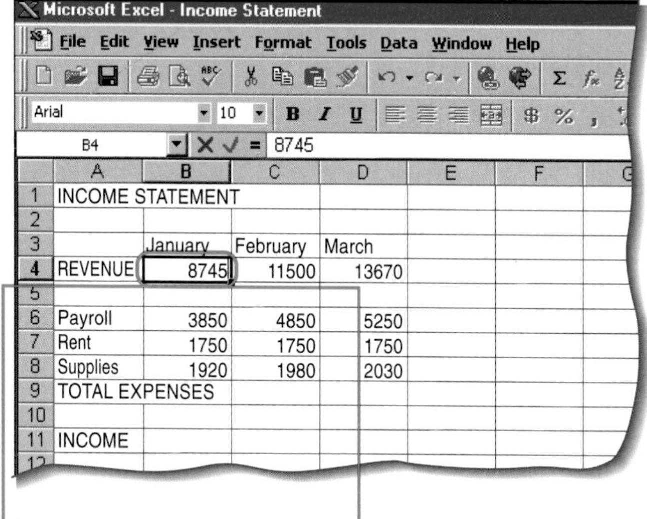

1 Click the cell containing the data you want to replace with new data.

2 Type the new data and then press Enter on your keyboard.

DELETE DATA

You can easily remove data you no longer need from cells in your worksheet.

INCOME STATEMENT
January
February
March
REVENUE
Payroll
Rent
Supplies
TOTAL EXPENSES
INCOME
3850
4850
5250
1750
1750
1750
1920
1980
2030
8745
11500
13670
3765
1284

DELETE DATA

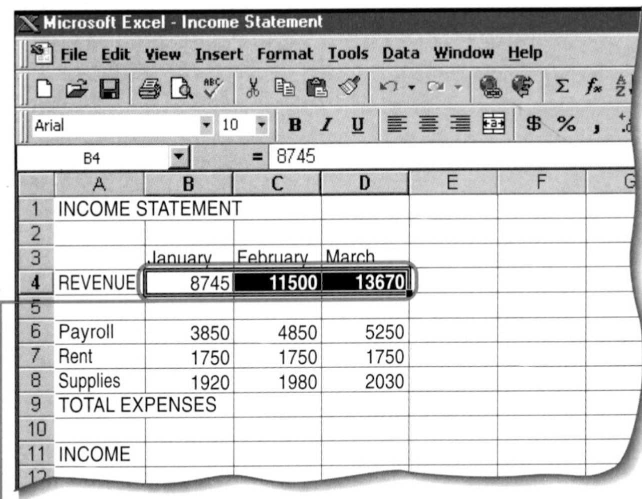

1 Select the cells containing the data you want to delete. To select cells, refer to page 120.

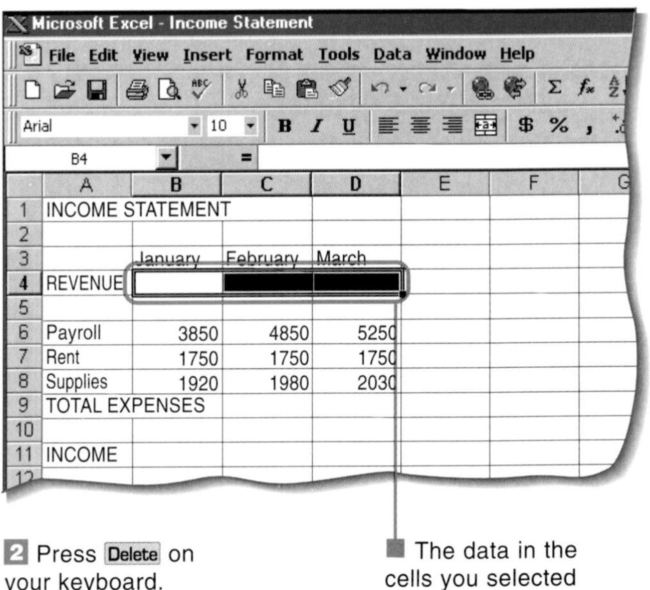

2 Press Delete on your keyboard.

■ The data in the cells you selected disappears.

UNDO LAST CHANGE

Excel remembers the last changes you made to your worksheet. If you regret these changes, you can undo them.

UNDO LAST CHANGE

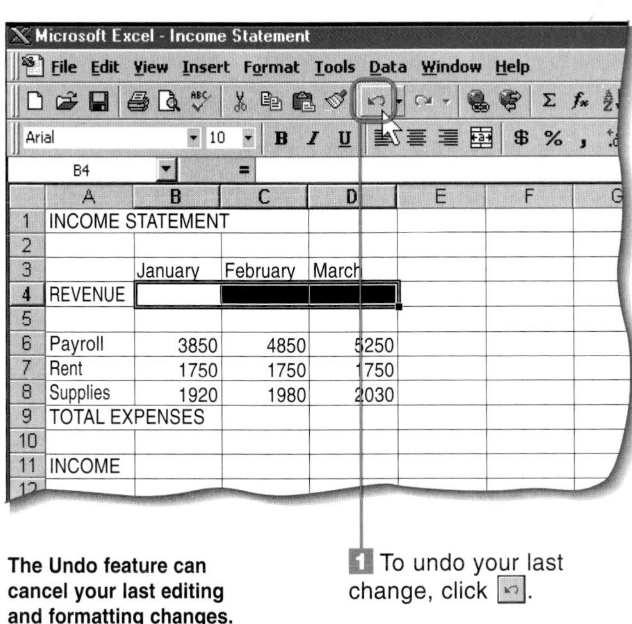

The Undo feature can cancel your last editing and formatting changes.

1 To undo your last change, click .

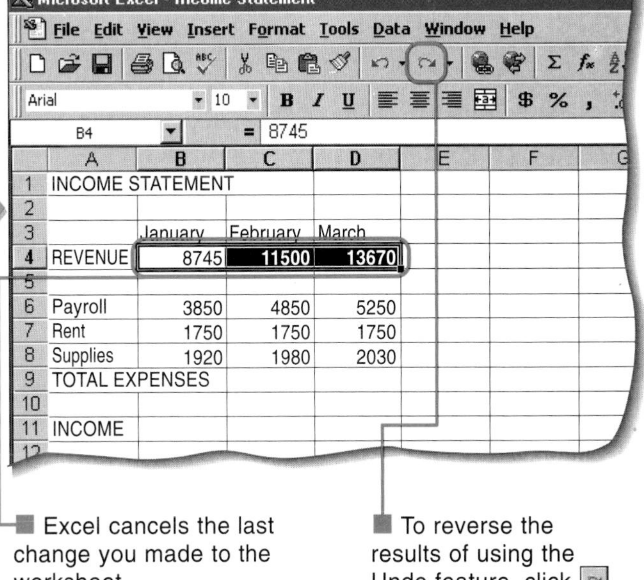

■ Excel cancels the last change you made to the worksheet.

■ You can repeat step 1 to cancel previous changes you made.

■ To reverse the results of using the Undo feature, click .

You can reorganize the data in your worksheet by moving data from one location to another.

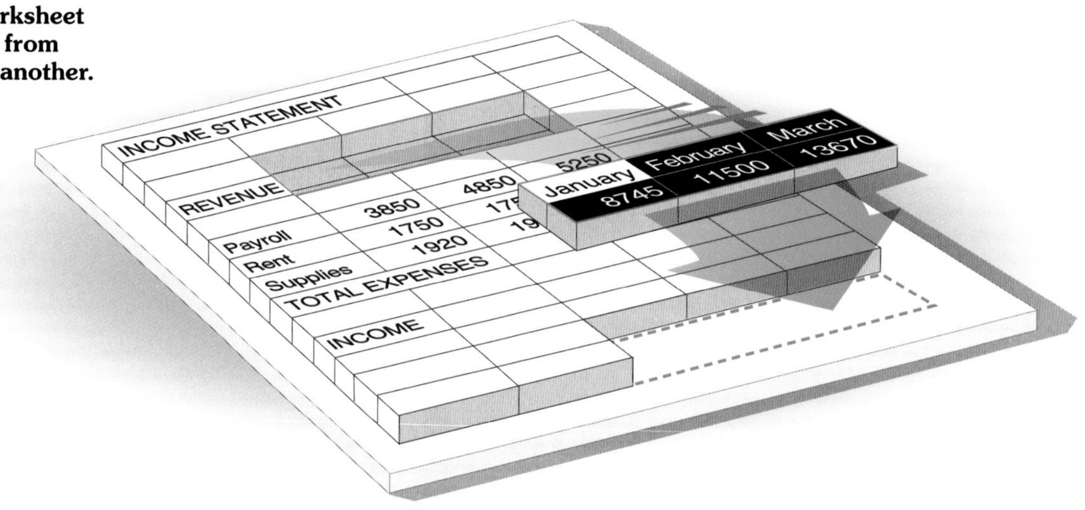

MOVE DATA

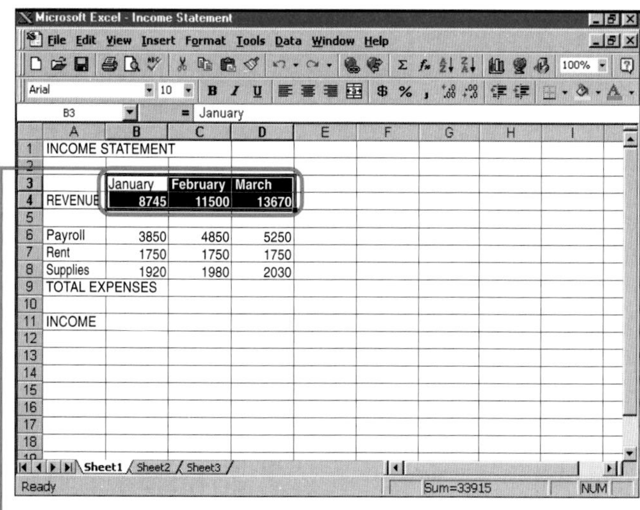

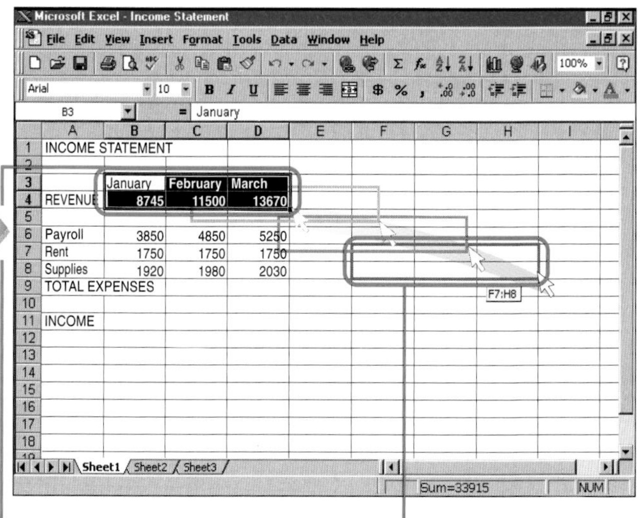

1 Select the cells containing the data you want to move. To select cells, refer to page 120.

2 Position the mouse ✥ over a border of the selected cells (✥ changes to ↖).

3 Drag the mouse ↖ to where you want to place the data.

Why does this message appear when I try to move data?

This message may appear when you try to move data to a location that already contains data.

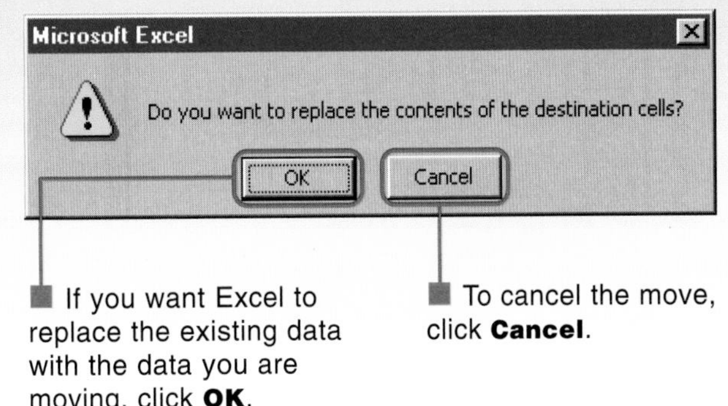

■ If you want Excel to replace the existing data with the data you are moving, click **OK**.

■ To cancel the move, click **Cancel**.

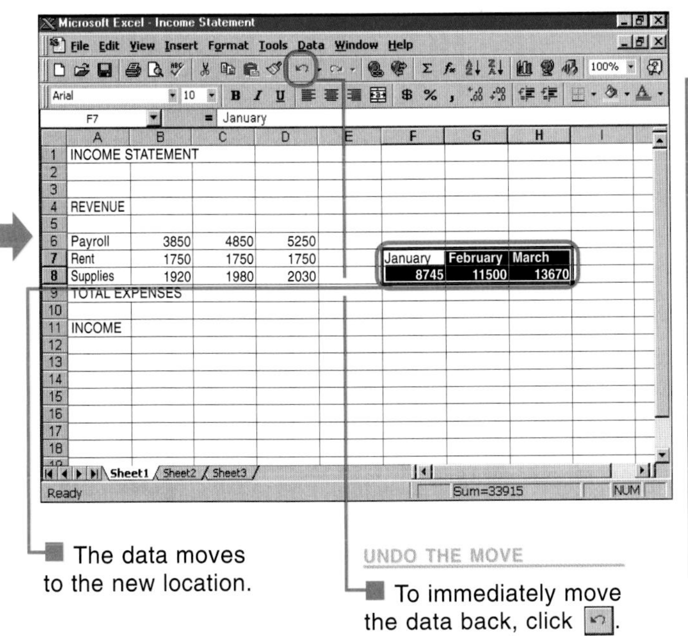

■ The data moves to the new location.

UNDO THE MOVE

■ To immediately move the data back, click ↶.

MOVE DATA USING TOOLBAR

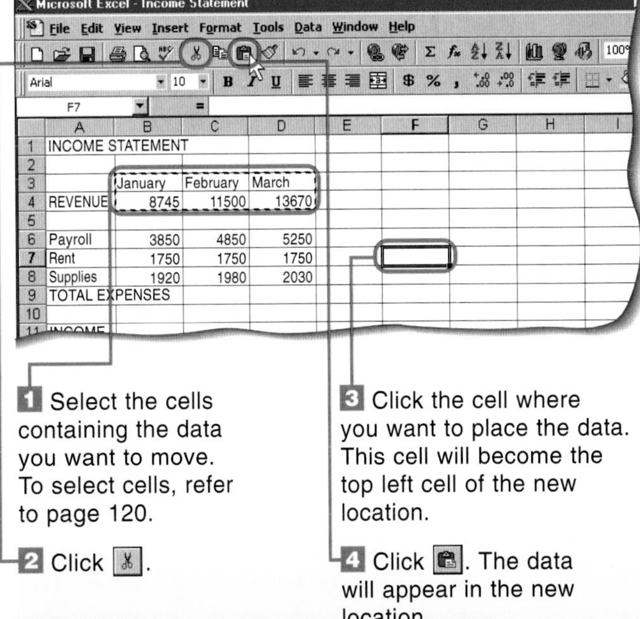

1 Select the cells containing the data you want to move. To select cells, refer to page 120.

2 Click ✂.

3 Click the cell where you want to place the data. This cell will become the top left cell of the new location.

4 Click 📋. The data will appear in the new location.

You can place a copy of data in a different location in your worksheet. This will save you time since you do not have to retype the data.

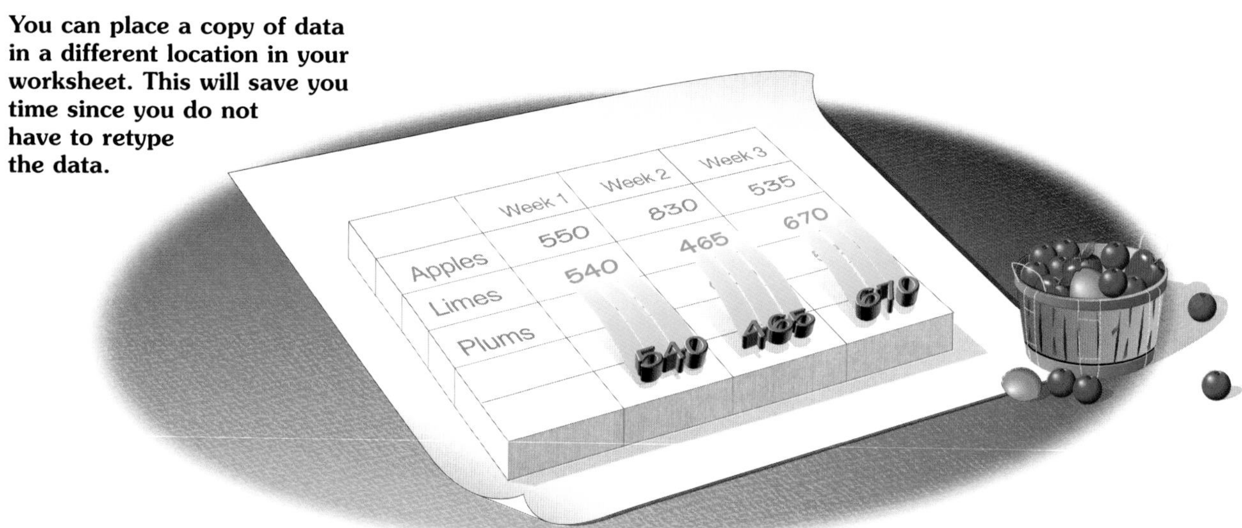

COPY DATA

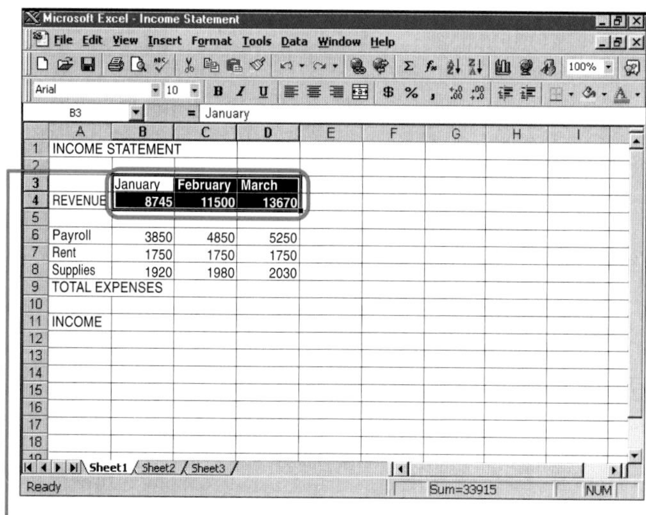

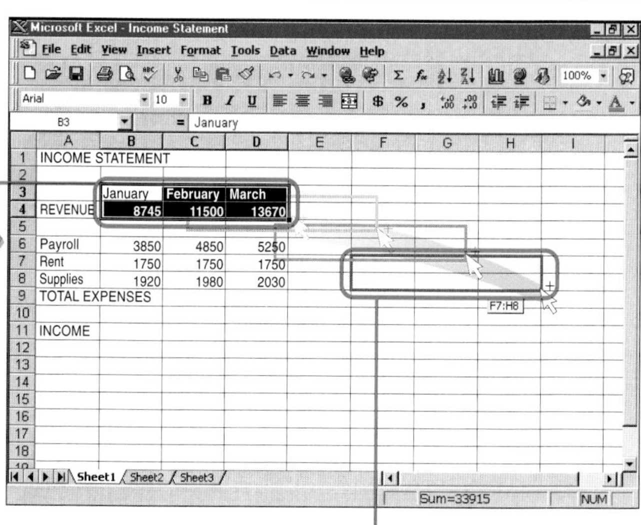

1 Select the cells containing the data you want to copy. To select cells, refer to page 120.

2 Position the mouse ✣ over a border of the selected cells (✣ changes to ↖).

3 Press and hold down Ctrl on your keyboard.

4 Still holding down Ctrl, drag the mouse ↖ to where you want to place the copy. Then release Ctrl.

How can I quickly copy data to the active cell?

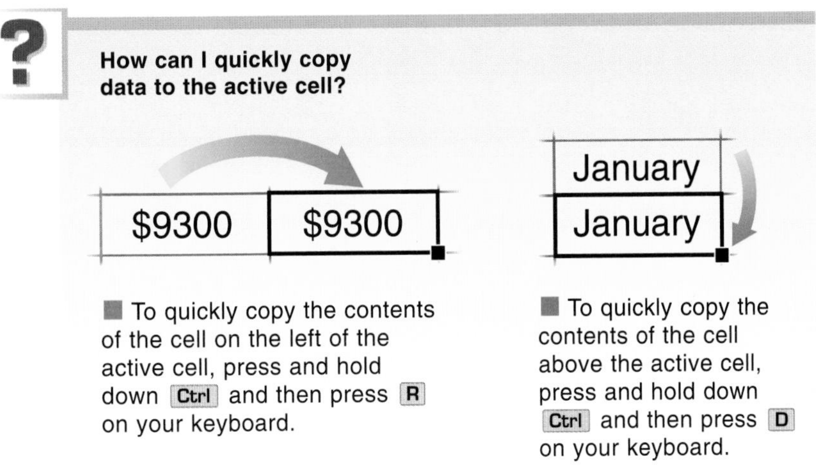

■ To quickly copy the contents of the cell on the left of the active cell, press and hold down Ctrl and then press R on your keyboard.

■ To quickly copy the contents of the cell above the active cell, press and hold down Ctrl and then press D on your keyboard.

COPY DATA USING TOOLBAR

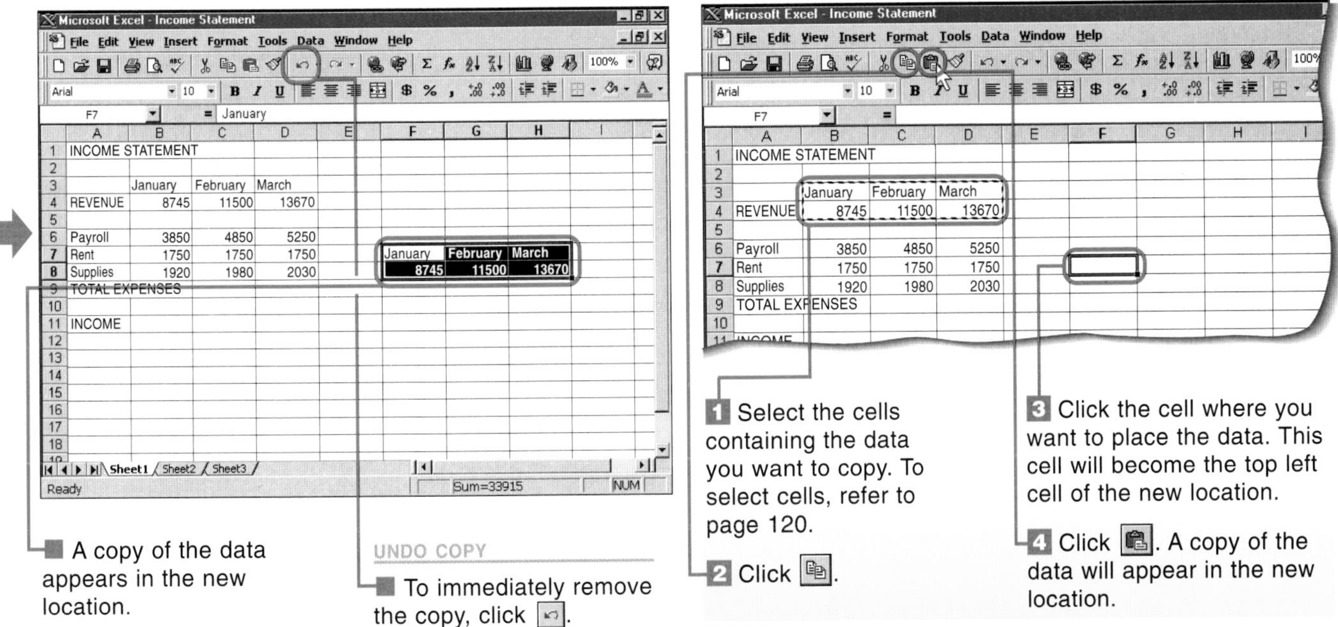

■ A copy of the data appears in the new location.

UNDO COPY

■ To immediately remove the copy, click ↶.

1 Select the cells containing the data you want to copy. To select cells, refer to page 120.

2 Click (Copy).

3 Click the cell where you want to place the data. This cell will become the top left cell of the new location.

4 Click (Paste). A copy of the data will appear in the new location.

INSERT A ROW OR COLUMN

You can add a row or column to your worksheet when you want to insert additional data.

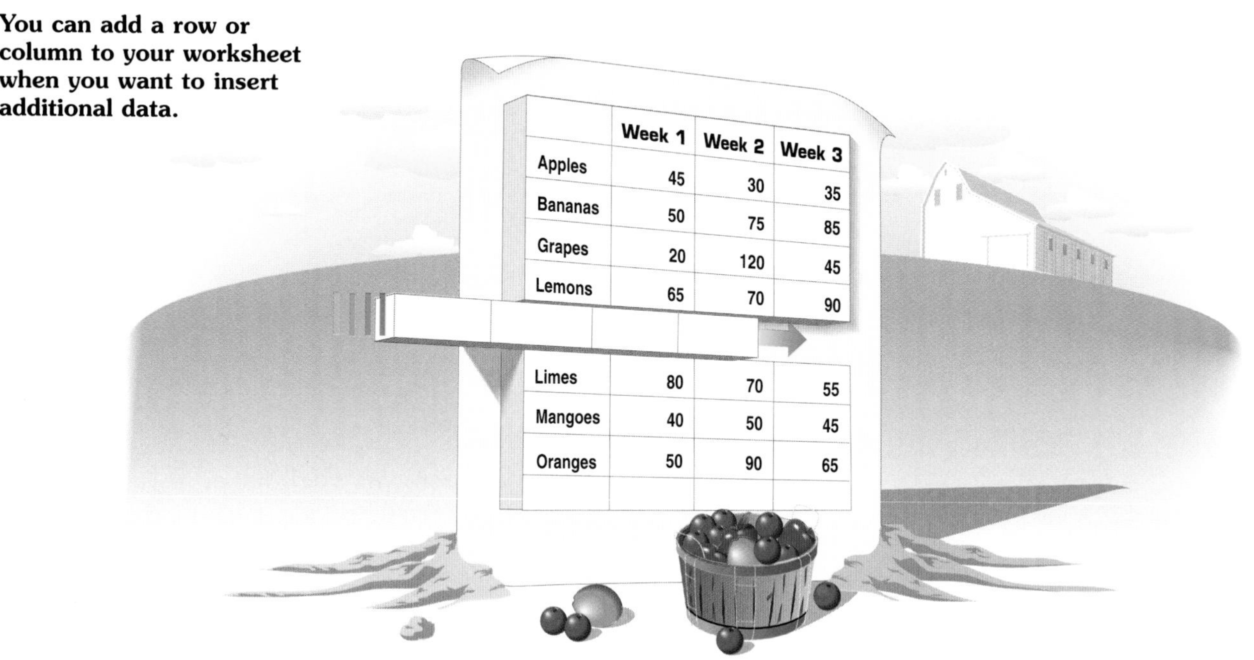

INSERT A ROW

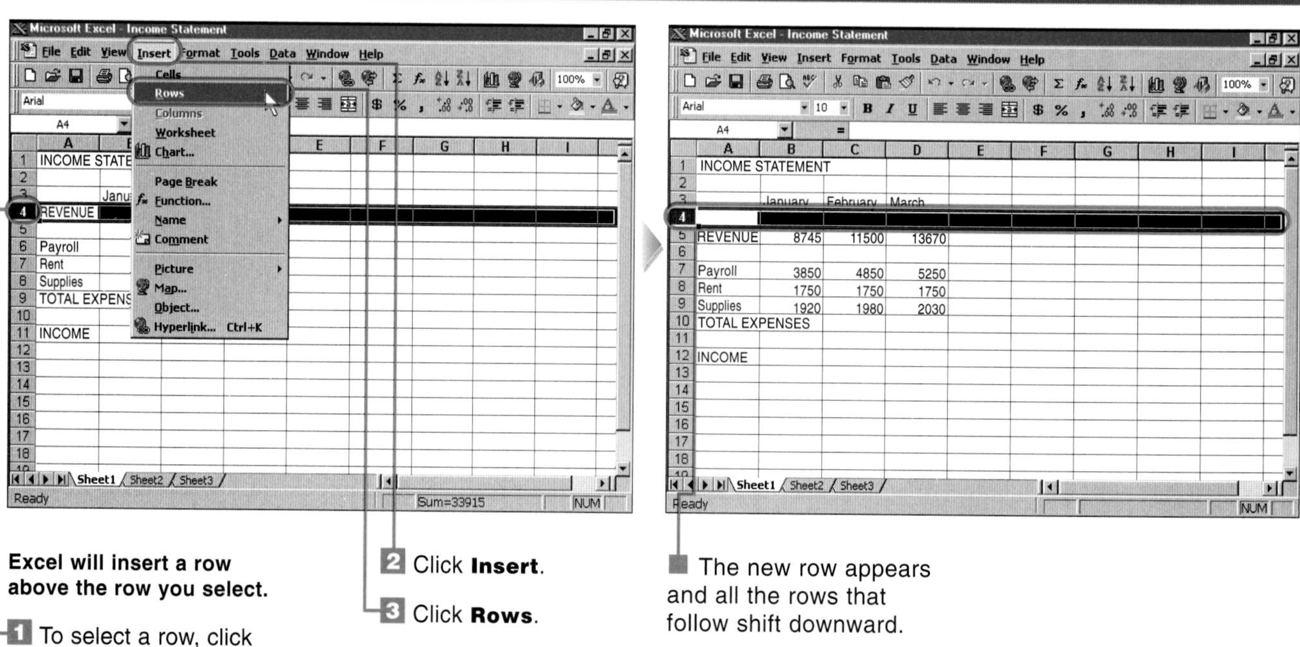

Excel will insert a row above the row you select.

1 To select a row, click the row number.

2 Click **Insert**.

3 Click **Rows**.

■ The new row appears and all the rows that follow shift downward.

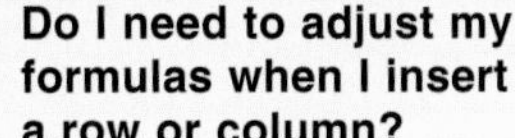

Do I need to adjust my formulas when I insert a row or column?

When you insert a row or column, Excel updates any formulas affected by the insertion.

Note: For information on formulas, refer to page 146.

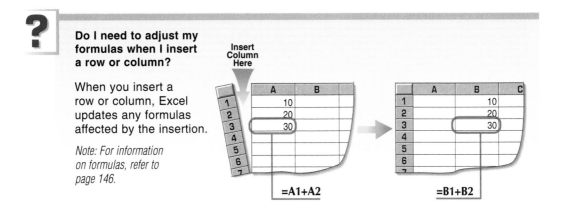

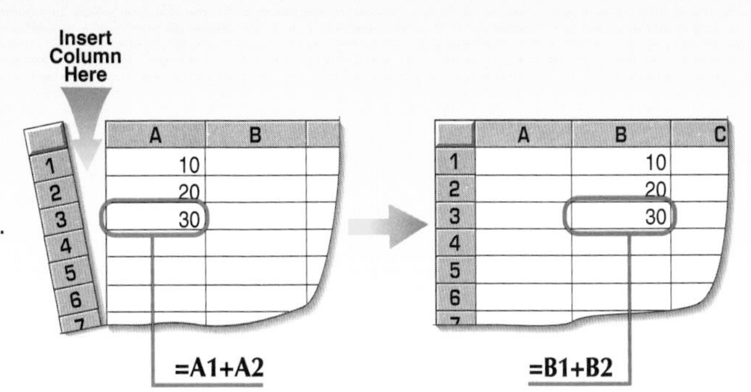

INSERT A COLUMN

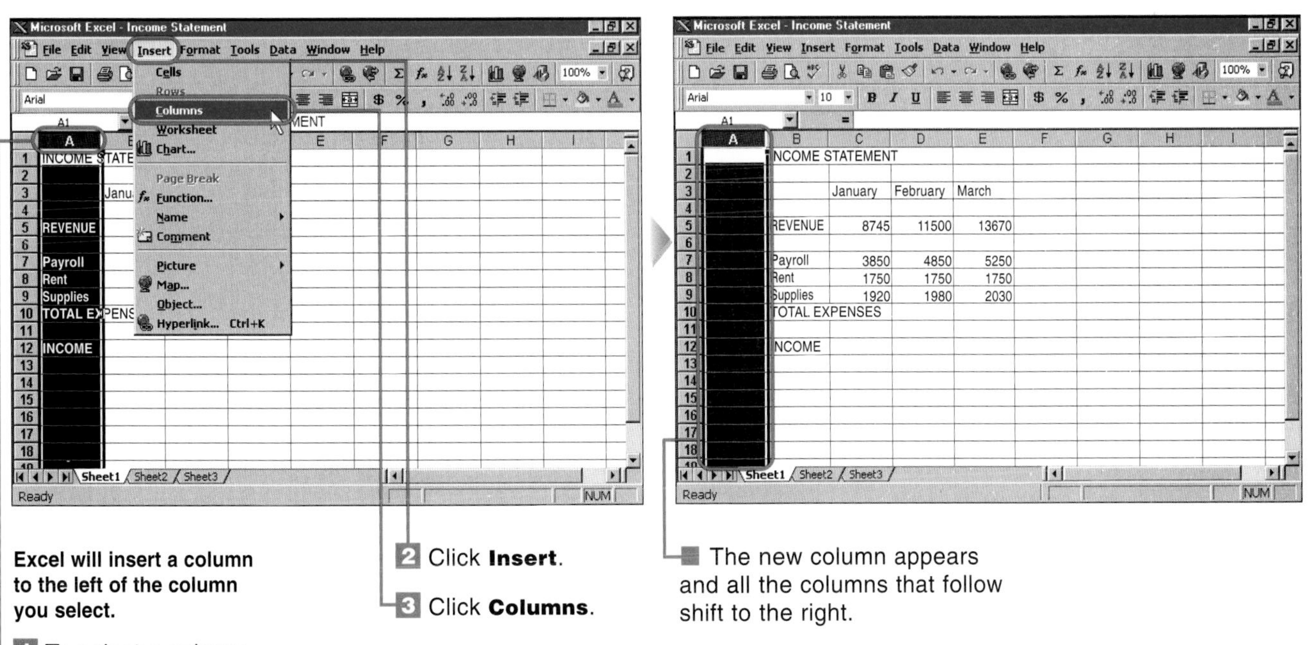

Excel will insert a column to the left of the column you select.

1 To select a column, click the column letter.

2 Click **Insert**.

3 Click **Columns**.

■ The new column appears and all the columns that follow shift to the right.

DELETE A ROW OR COLUMN

You can delete a row or column from your worksheet to remove cells you no longer need.

DELETE A ROW

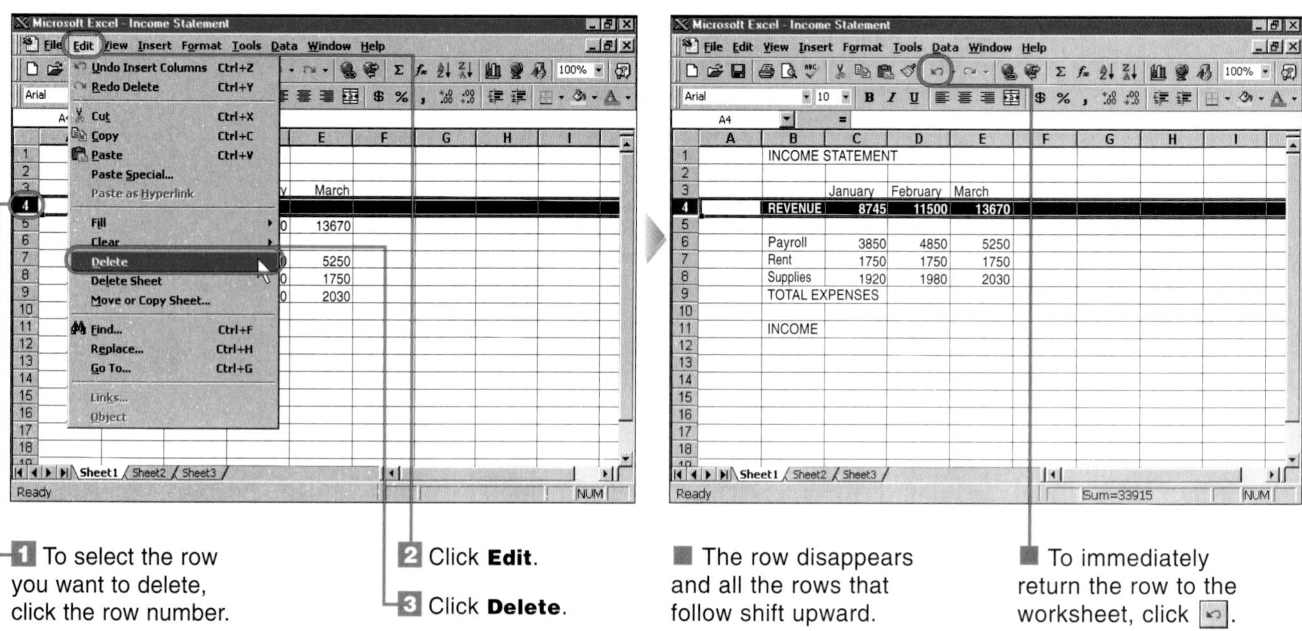

1 To select the row you want to delete, click the row number.

2 Click **Edit**.

3 Click **Delete**.

■ The row disappears and all the rows that follow shift upward.

■ To immediately return the row to the worksheet, click ↶.

Why did #REF! appear in a cell after I deleted a row or column?

If #REF! appears in a cell in your worksheet, you deleted data needed to calculate a formula.

Note: For information on formulas, refer to page 146.

DELETE A COLUMN

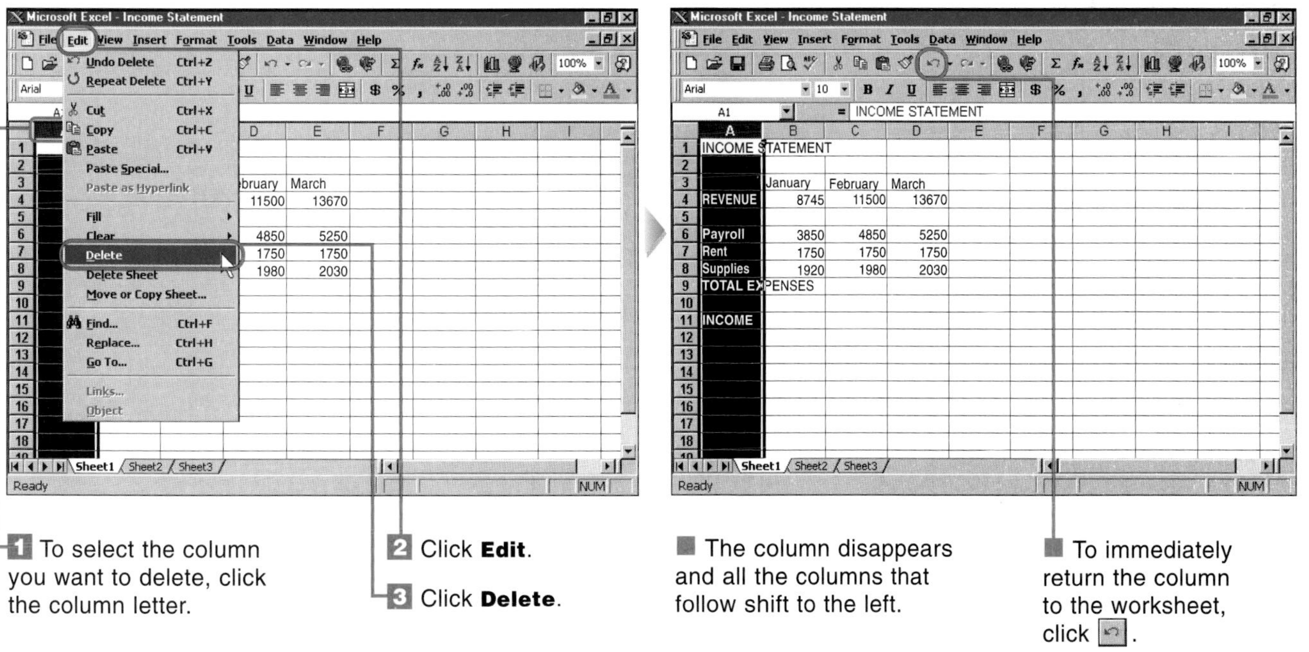

1 To select the column you want to delete, click the column letter.

2 Click **Edit**.

3 Click **Delete**.

■ The column disappears and all the columns that follow shift to the left.

■ To immediately return the column to the worksheet, click [undo button].

USING FORMULAS

A formula helps you calculate and analyze data in your worksheet.

A formula always begins with an equal sign (=).

INTRODUCTION TO FORMULAS

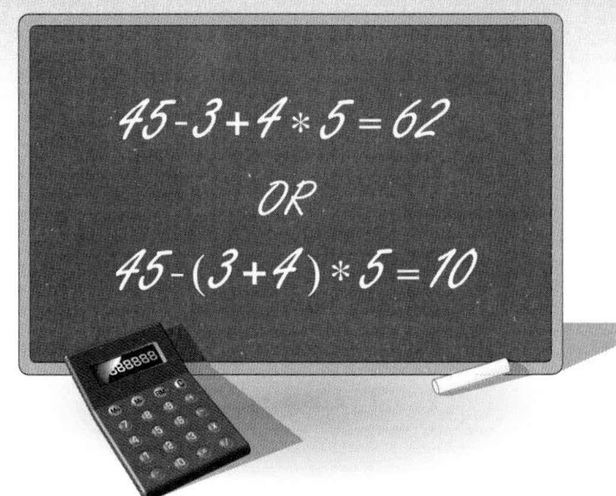

Order of Calculations

Excel performs calculations in the following order:

1 Exponents (^)

2 Multiplication (*) and Division (/)

3 Addition (+) and Subtraction (-)

You can use parentheses ( ) to change the order that Excel performs calculations. Excel will calculate the data inside the parentheses first.

Cell References

When entering formulas, use cell references (example: **=A1+A2**) instead of actual data (example: **=10+30**) whenever possible. When you use cell references and you change a number used in a formula, Excel will automatically redo the calculations for you.

EXAMPLES OF FORMULAS

	A	B
1	10	
2	20	
3	30	
4	40	
5		
6	1230	

■ This cell contains the formula:

=A1+A2+A3*A4

=10+20+30*40

=1230

	A	B
1	10	
2	20	
3	30	
4	40	
5		
6	2010	

■ This cell contains the formula:

=A1+(A2+A3)*A4

=10+(20+30)*40

=2010

	A	B
1	10	
2	20	
3	30	
4	40	
5		
6	320	

■ This cell contains the formula:

=A1*A3-A2+A4

=10*30-20+40

=320

	A	B
1	10	
2	20	
3	30	
4	40	
5		
6	140	

■ This cell contains the formula:

=A1*(A3-A2)+A4

=10*(30-20)+40

=140

	A	B
1	10	
2	20	
3	30	
4	40	
5		
6	63	

■ This cell contains the formula:

=A3/A1+A2+A4

=30/10+20+40

=63

	A	B
1	10	
2	20	
3	30	
4	40	
5		
6	41	

■ This cell contains the formula:

=A3/(A1+A2)+A4

=30/(10+20)+40

=41

You can enter a formula into any cell in your worksheet.

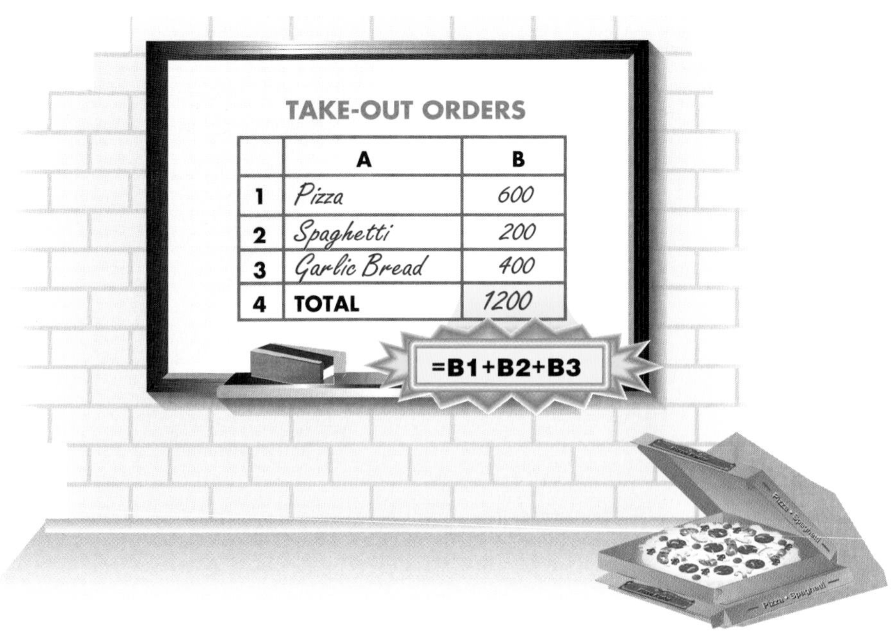

TAKE-OUT ORDERS
A
B
1 Pizza 600
2 Spaghetti 200
3 Garlic Bread 400
4 TOTAL 1200
=B1+B2+B3

ENTER A FORMULA

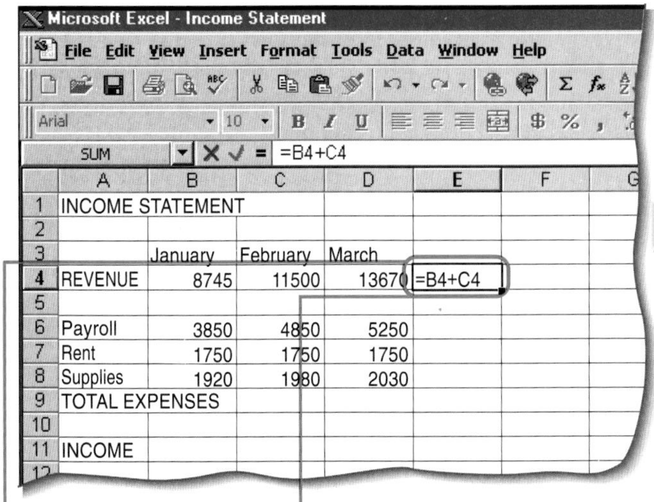

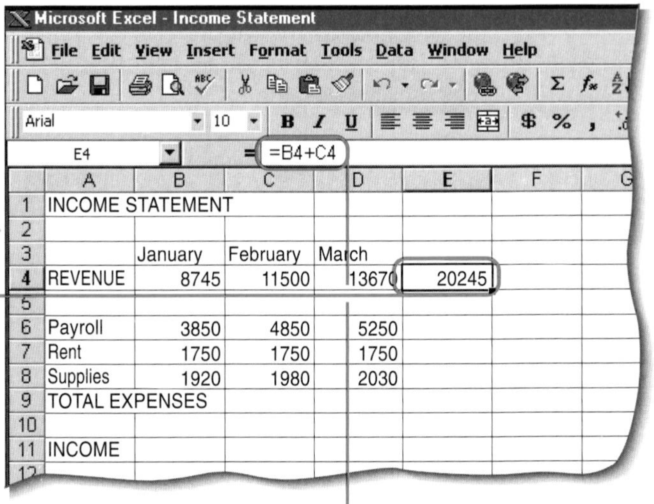

Microsoft Excel - Income Statement

SUM = =B4+C4

	A	B	C	D	E	F	G
1	INCOME STATEMENT						
2							
3		January	February	March			
4	REVENUE	8745	11500	13670	=B4+C4		
5							
6	Payroll	3850	4850	5250			
7	Rent	1750	1750	1750			
8	Supplies	1920	1980	2030			
9	TOTAL EXPENSES						
10							
11	INCOME						

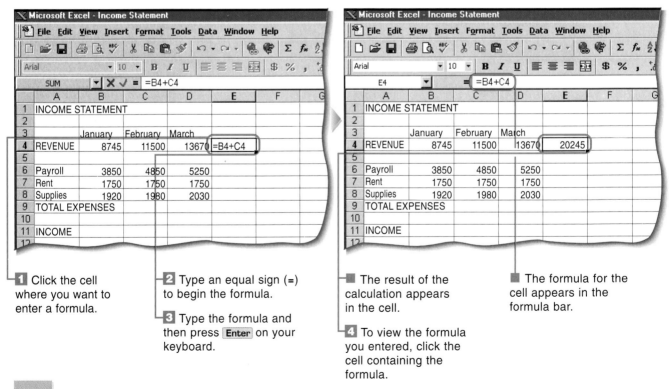

1 Click the cell where you want to enter a formula.

2 Type an equal sign (=) to begin the formula.

3 Type the formula and then press Enter on your keyboard.

Microsoft Excel - Income Statement

E4 = =B4+C4

	A	B	C	D	E	F	G
1	INCOME STATEMENT						
2							
3		January	February	March			
4	REVENUE	8745	11500	13670	20245		
5							
6	Payroll	3850	4850	5250			
7	Rent	1750	1750	1750			
8	Supplies	1920	1980	2030			
9	TOTAL EXPENSES						
10							
11	INCOME						

■ The result of the calculation appears in the cell.

4 To view the formula you entered, click the cell containing the formula.

■ The formula for the cell appears in the formula bar.

What happens if I change a number used in a formula?

If you change a number used in a formula, Excel will automatically calculate a new result.

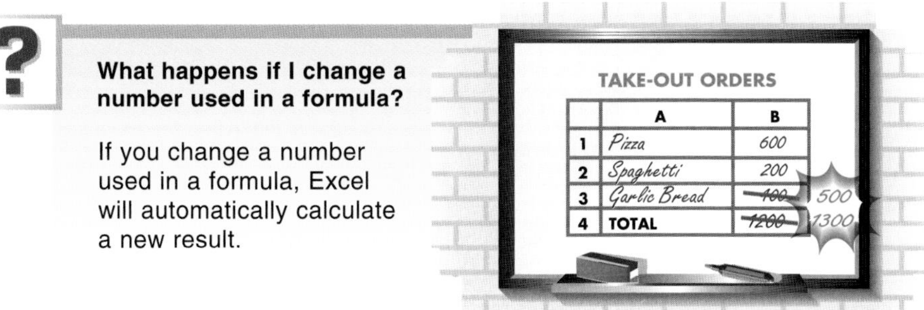

EDIT A FORMULA

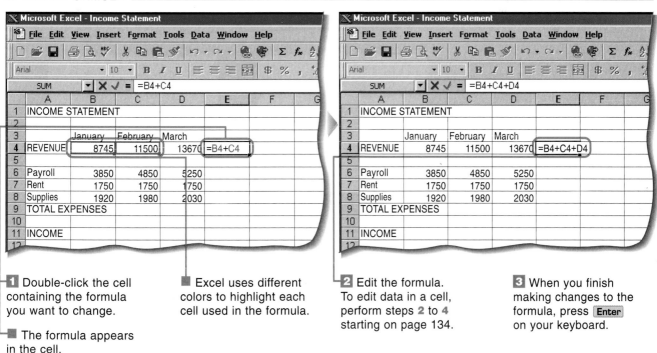

1 Double-click the cell containing the formula you want to change.

■ The formula appears in the cell.

■ Excel uses different colors to highlight each cell used in the formula.

2 Edit the formula. To edit data in a cell, perform steps **2** to **4** starting on page 134.

3 When you finish making changes to the formula, press **Enter** on your keyboard.

USING FUNCTIONS

A function is a ready-to-use formula that performs a specialized calculation on your worksheet data.

INTRODUCTION TO FUNCTIONS

- A function always begins with an equal sign (=).
- The data Excel will use to calculate a function is enclosed in parentheses ( ).

=SUM(A1,A2,A3)

=AVERAGE(C1,C2,C3)

=MAX(B7,C7,D7,E7)

=COUNT(D12,D13,D14)

Specify Individual Cells

When there is a comma (,) between cell references in a function, Excel uses each cell to perform the calculation.

For example, the function =SUM(A1,A2,A3) is the same as the formula =A1+A2+A3.

=SUM(A1:A3)

=AVERAGE(C1:C3)

=MAX(B7:E7)

=COUNT(D12:D14)

Specify Group of Cells

When there is a colon (:) between cell references in a function, Excel uses the specified cells and all cells between them to perform the calculation.

For example, the function =SUM(A1:A3) is the same as the formula =A1+A2+A3.

COMMON FUNCTIONS

	A	B
1	10	
2	20	
3	30	
4	40	
5		
6	25	

Average

Calculates the average value of a list of numbers.

■ This cell contains the function:

=AVERAGE(A1:A4)

=(A1+A2+A3+A4)/4

=(10+20+30+40)/4

=25

	A	B
1	10	
2	20	
3	30	
4	40	
5		
6	4	

Count

Calculates the number of values in a list.

■ This cell contains the function:

=COUNT(A1:A4)

=4

	A	B
1	10	
2	20	
3	30	
4	40	
5		
6	40	

Max

Finds the largest value in a list of numbers.

■ This cell contains the function:

=MAX(A1:A4)

=40

	A	B
1	10	
2	20	
3	30	
4	40	
5		
6	10	

Min

Finds the smallest value in a list of numbers.

■ This cell contains the function:

=MIN(A1:A4)

=10

	A	B
1	10	
2	20	
3	30	
4	40	
5		
6	100	

Sum

Adds a list of numbers.

■ This cell contains the function:

=SUM(A1:A4)

=A1+A2+A3+A4

=10+20+30+40

=100

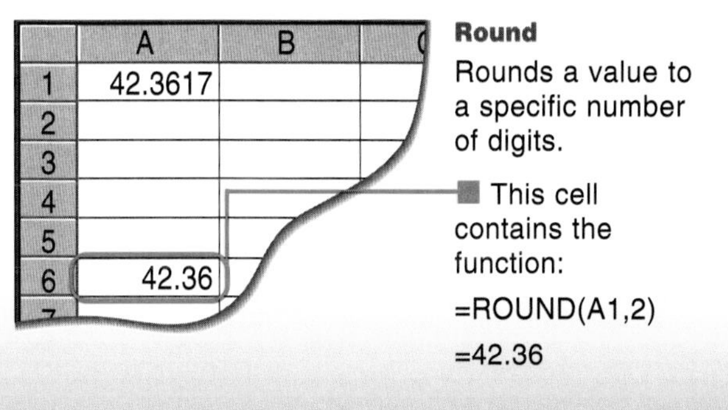

	A	B
1	42.3617	
2		
3		
4		
5		
6	42.36	

Round

Rounds a value to a specific number of digits.

■ This cell contains the function:

=ROUND(A1,2)

=42.36

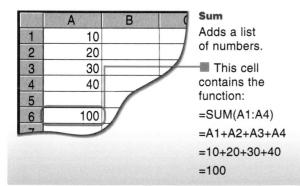

Excel helps you enter functions in your worksheet. This lets you perform calculations without typing long, complex formulas.

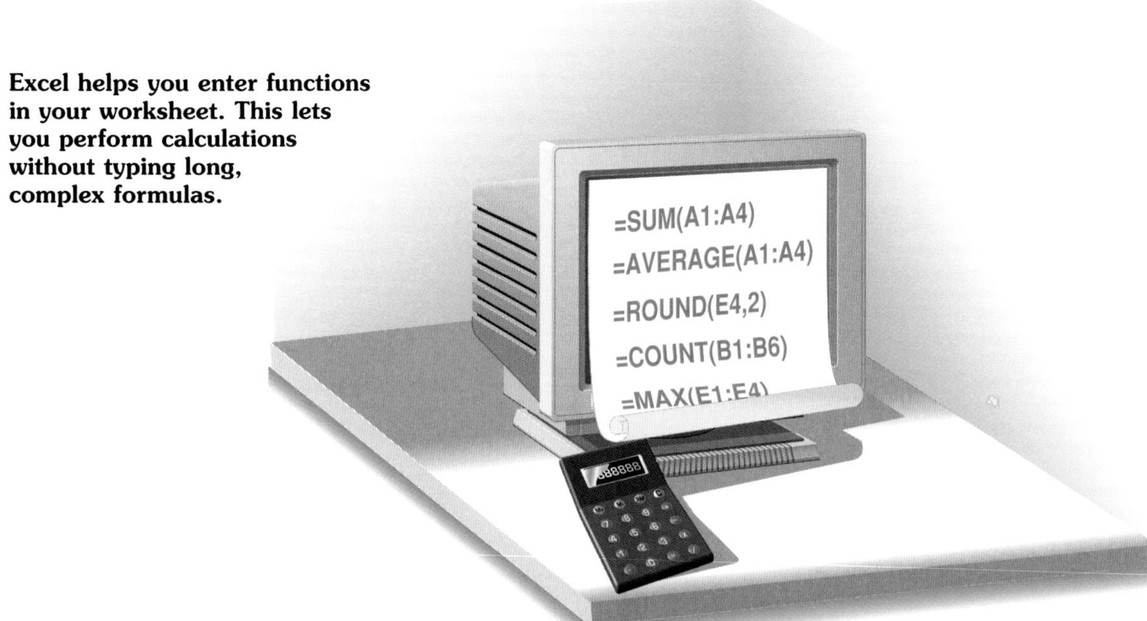

ENTER A FUNCTION

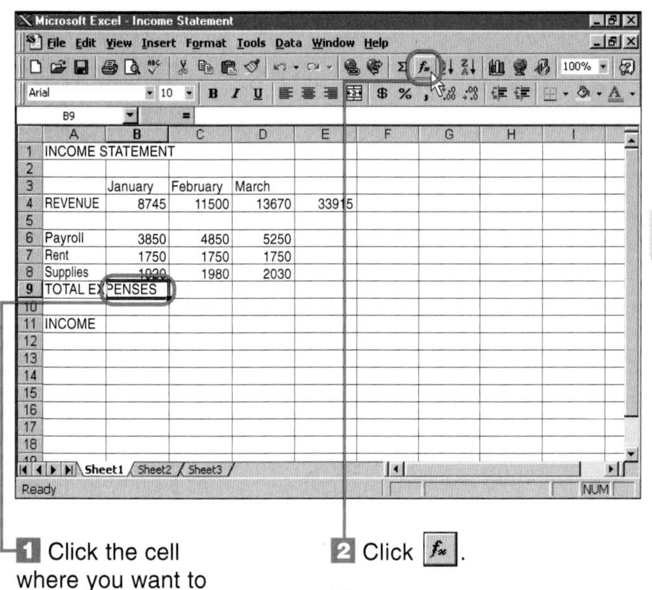

1 Click the cell where you want to enter a function.

2 Click [fx].

■ The **Paste Function** dialog box appears.

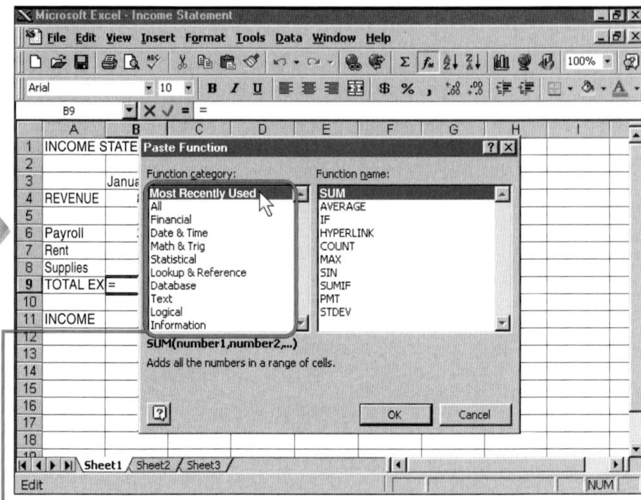

3 Click the category that contains the function you want to use.

Note: If you do not know which category contains the function you want to use, select ***All*** *to display a list of all the functions.*

How many functions does Excel offer?

Excel offers over 200 functions to help you analyze data in your worksheet. There are financial functions, math and trigonometry functions, date and time functions, statistical functions and many more.

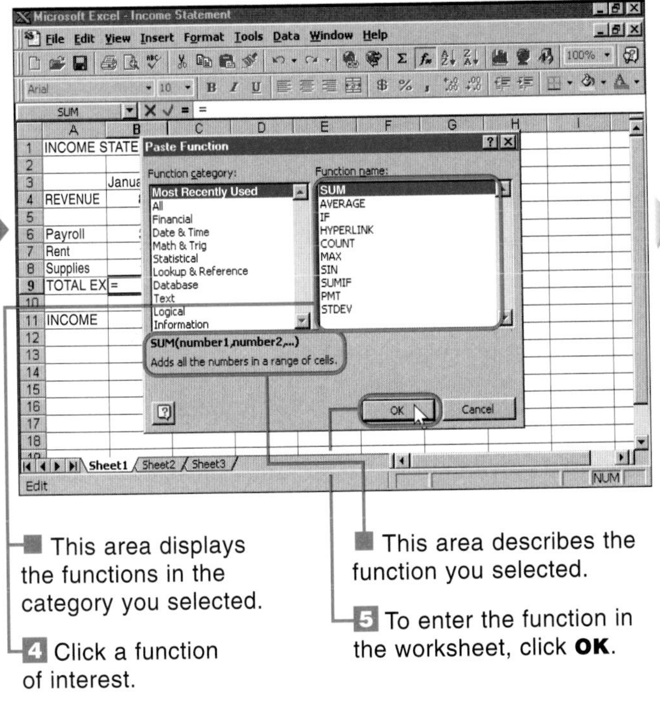

■ This area displays the functions in the category you selected.

4 Click a function of interest.

■ This area describes the function you selected.

5 To enter the function in the worksheet, click **OK**.

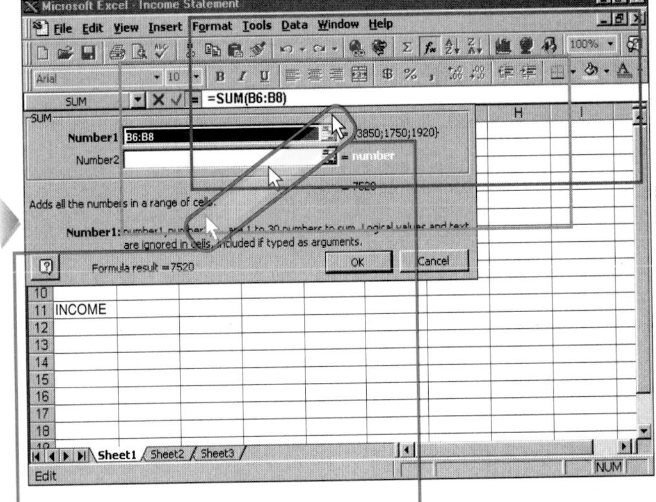

■ A dialog box appears. If the dialog box covers data you want to use in the calculation, you can move it to a new location.

6 To move the dialog box, position the mouse over a blank area in the dialog box.

7 Drag the dialog box to a new location.

CONTINUED

When entering a function, you must specify which numbers you want to use in the calculation.

= SUM(D1:D4)
A
B
C
D
1
100
12
128
20
2
200
22
601
60
3
400
68
288
80
4
800
21
204
97

ENTER A FUNCTION (CONTINUED)

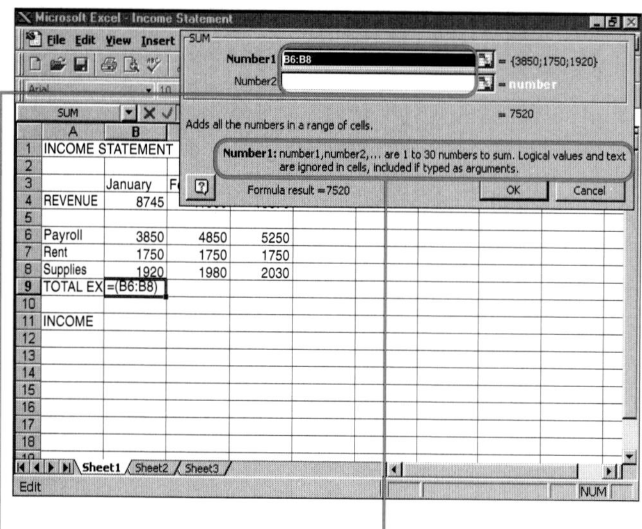

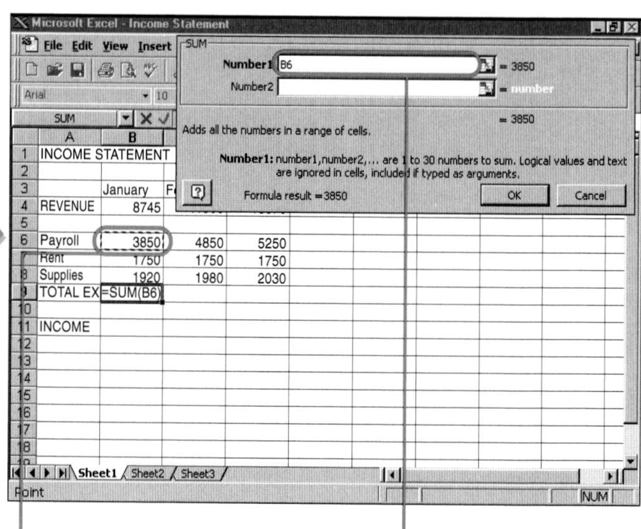

■ This area displays boxes where you enter the numbers you want to use in the calculation.

■ This area describes the number you need to enter.

8 To enter a number, click the cell in the worksheet that contains the number.

Note: If the number you want to enter does not appear in the worksheet, type the number.

■ The area now displays the cell you selected.

?

Can I enter a function by myself?

You can easily enter a function yourself by typing the entire function into a cell.

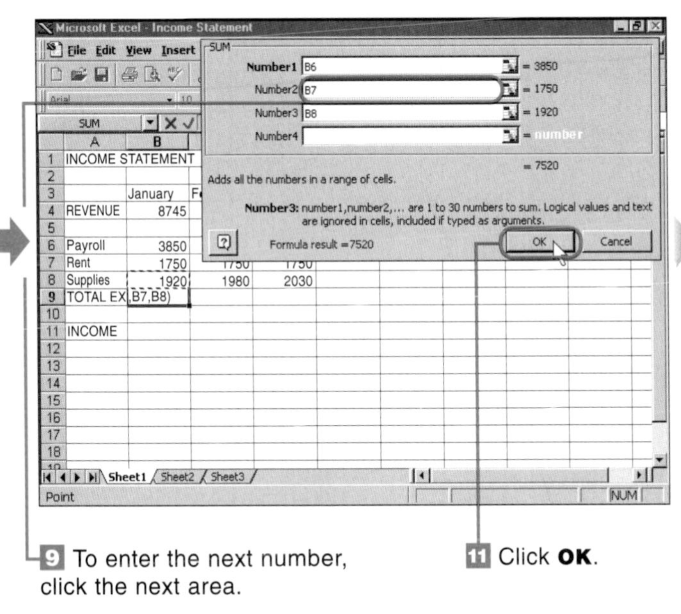

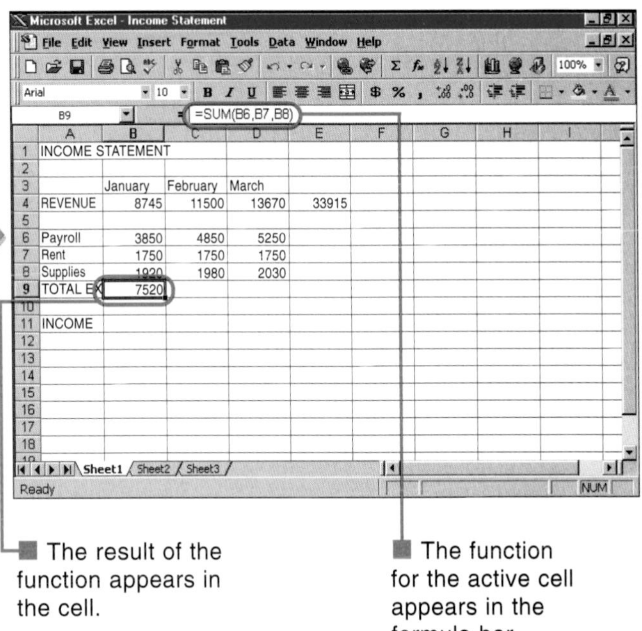

9 To enter the next number, click the next area.

10 Repeat steps 8 and 9 until you have entered all the numbers you want to use in the calculation.

11 Click **OK**.

■ The result of the function appears in the cell.

■ The function for the active cell appears in the formula bar.

You can quickly view the results of common calculations without entering a formula into your worksheet.

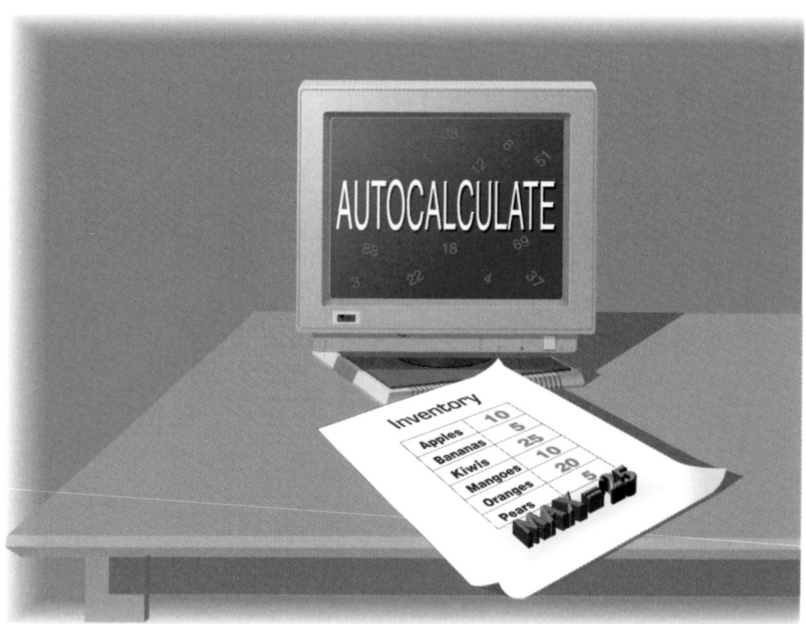

USING AUTOCALCULATE

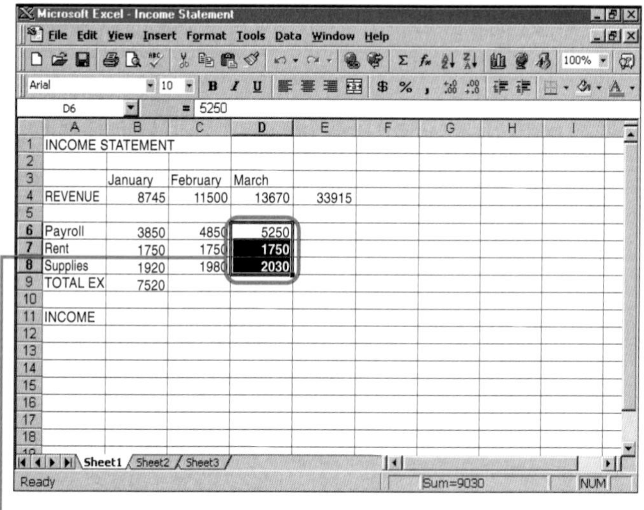

1 Select the cells you want to include in the calculation. To select cells, refer to page 120.

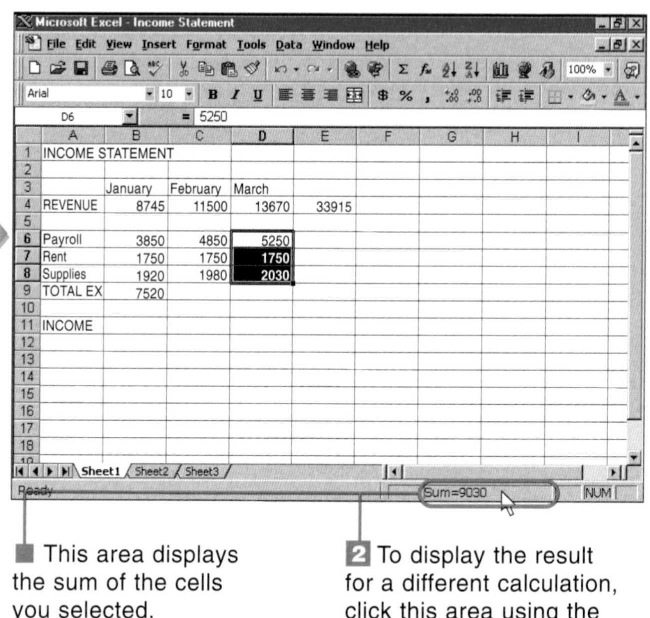

■ This area displays the sum of the cells you selected.

2 To display the result for a different calculation, click this area using the **right** mouse button.

?

What calculations can AutoCalculate perform?

Average
Calculates the average value of a list of numbers.

Count
Calculates the number of items in a list, including text.

Count Nums
Calculates the number of values in a list.

Max
Finds the largest value in a list.

Min
Finds the smallest value in a list.

Sum
Adds a list of numbers.

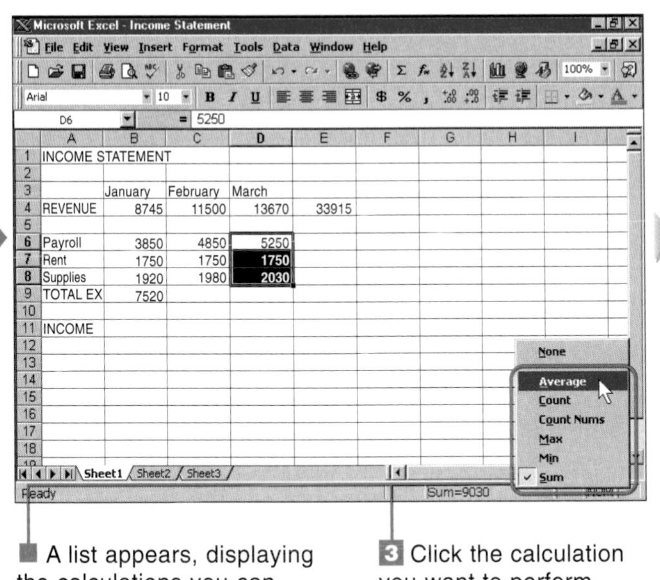

■ A list appears, displaying the calculations you can perform.

3 Click the calculation you want to perform.

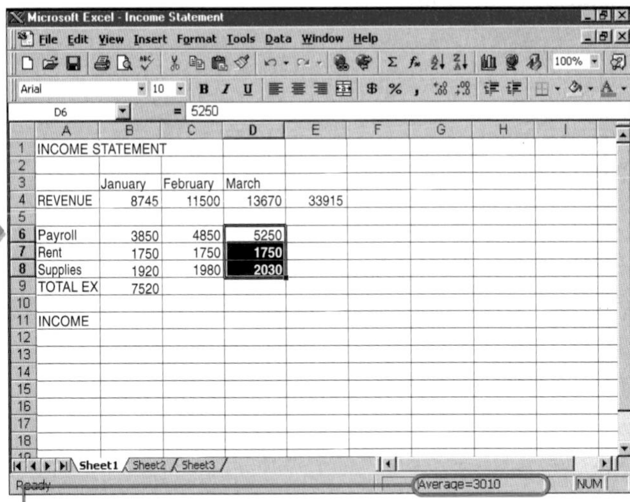

■ This area displays the result for the new calculation.

You can quickly calculate the sum of a list of numbers in your worksheet.

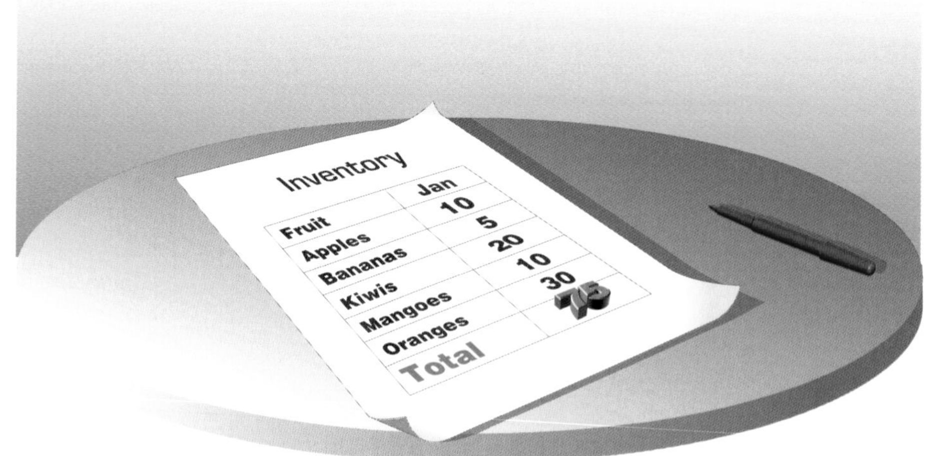

ADD NUMBERS

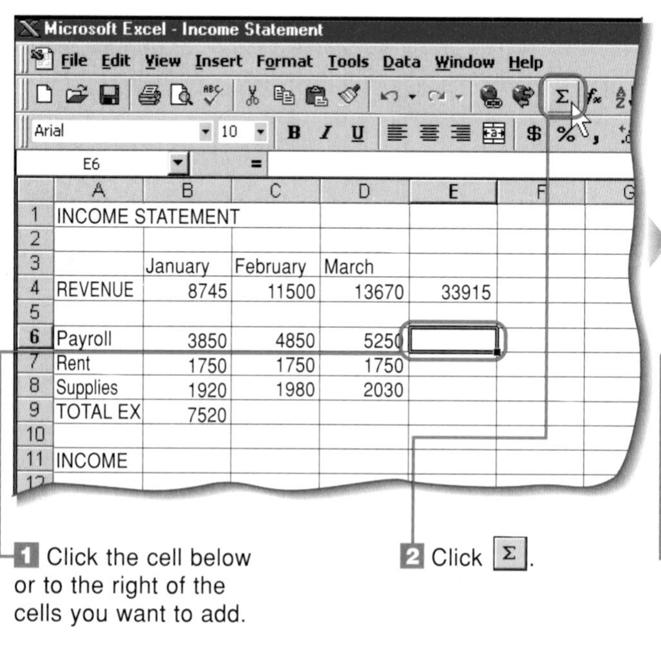

1 Click the cell below or to the right of the cells you want to add.

2 Click Σ.

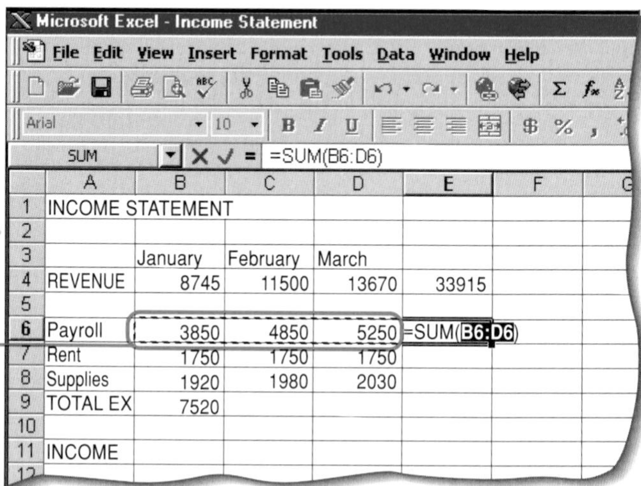

■ Excel outlines the cells it will use in the calculation with a dotted line.

■ If Excel does not outline the correct cells, select the cells containing the numbers you want to add. To select cells, refer to page 120.

?

Why did number signs (#) appear in a cell?

If number signs (#) appear in a cell, the result of a calculation is too long to fit in the cell. To display the result, you need to change the column width. To do so, refer to page 166.

Microsoft Excel - Income Statement

E7

	A	B	C	D	E	F
1	INCOME STATEMENT					
2						
3		January	February	March		
4	REVENUE	8745	11500	13670	33915	
5						
6	Payroll	3850	4850	5250	13950	
7	Rent	1750	1750	1750		
8	Supplies	1920	1980	2030		
9	TOTAL EX	7520				
10						
11	INCOME					

3 Press Enter on your keyboard to perform the calculation.

■ The result appears.

CALCULATE A GRAND TOTAL

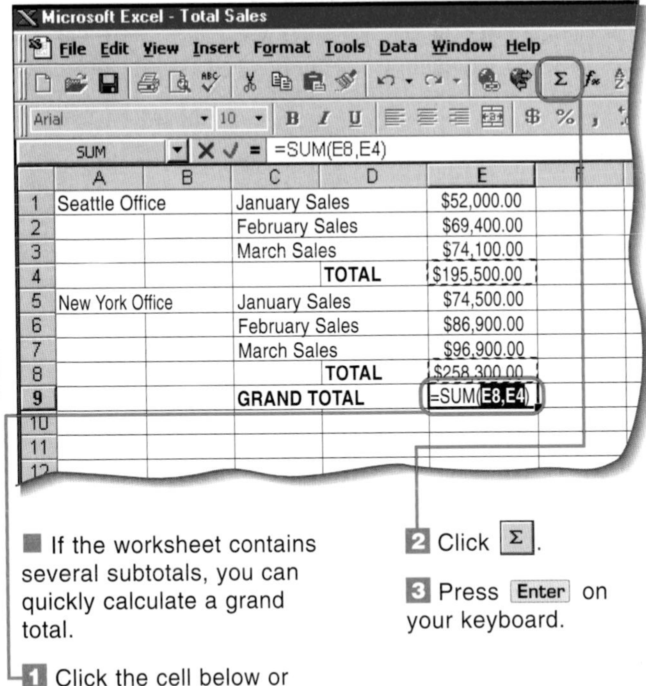

Microsoft Excel - Total Sales
File Edit View Insert Format Tools Data Window Help
SUM
=SUM(E8,E4)
Seattle Office
January Sales $52,000.00
February Sales $69,400.00
March Sales $74,100.00
TOTAL $195,500.00
New York Office
January Sales $74,500.00
February Sales $86,900.00
March Sales $96,900.00
TOTAL $258,300.00
GRAND TOTAL =SUM(E8,E4)

■ If the worksheet contains several subtotals, you can quickly calculate a grand total.

1 Click the cell below or to the right of the cells that contain the subtotals.

2 Click Σ.

3 Press Enter on your keyboard.

ERRORS IN FORMULAS

An error message appears when Excel cannot properly calculate a formula.

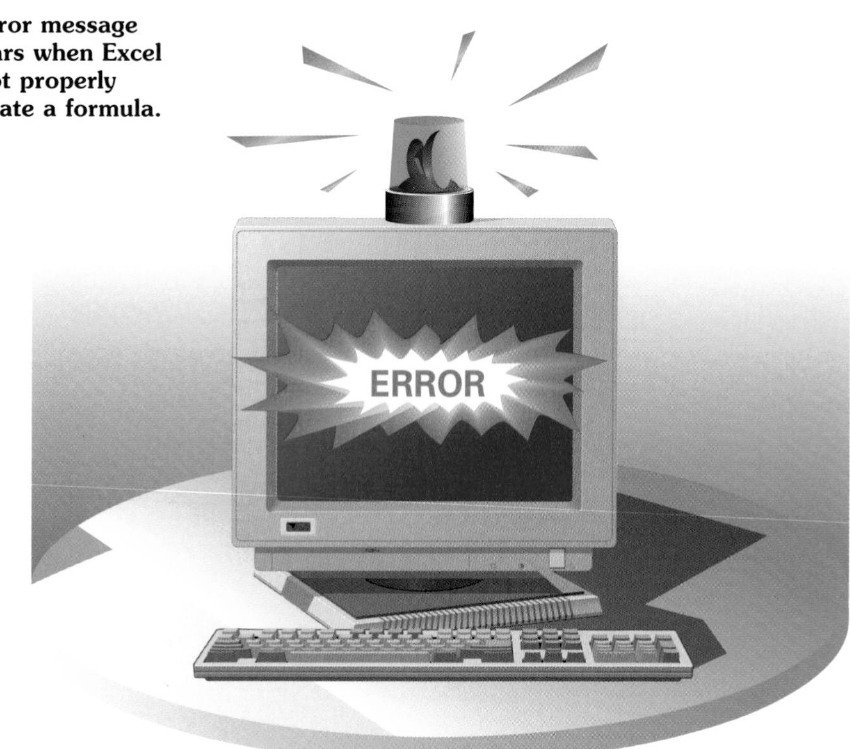

Errors in formulas are often the result of typing mistakes. You can correct an error by editing the cell containing the error. To edit data in a cell, refer to page 134.

#####

The column is too narrow to display the result of the calculation. To display the result, refer to page 166 to change the column width.

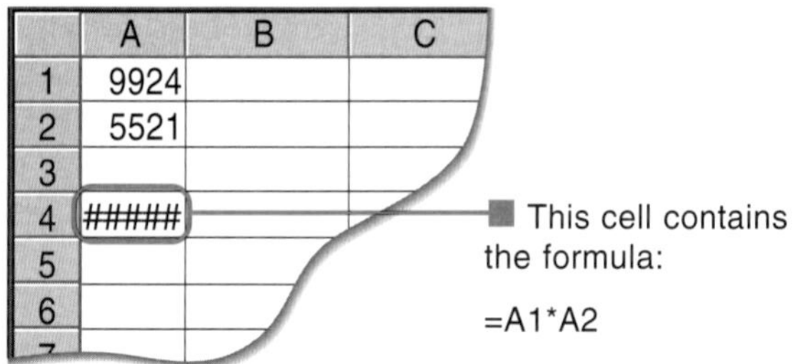

#DIV/0!

The formula divides a number by zero (0). Excel considers a blank cell to contain a value of zero.

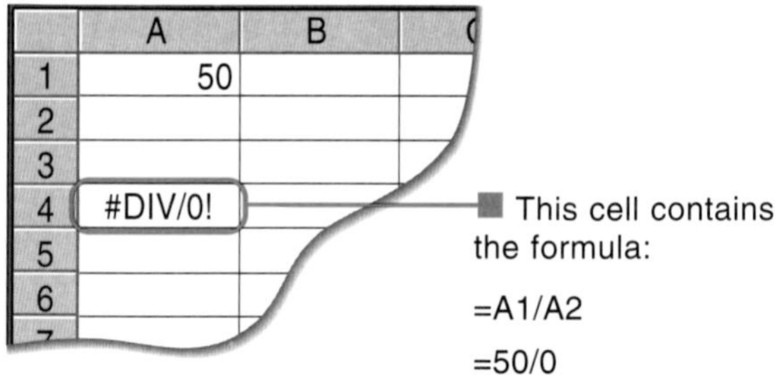

#NAME?

The formula contains a function name or cell reference Excel does not recognize.

■ This cell contains the formula:

=SUMM(A1:A3)

In this example, the name of the SUM function was misspelled.

#REF!

The formula refers to a cell that is not valid.

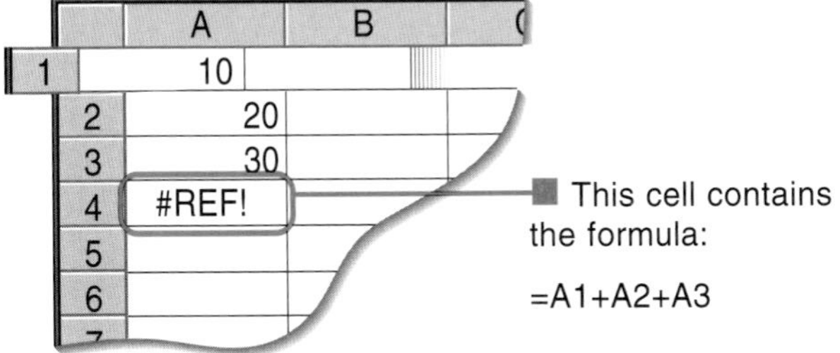

■ This cell contains the formula:

=A1+A2+A3

In this example, a row containing a cell used in the formula was deleted.

#VALUE!

The formula refers to a cell that Excel cannot use in a calculation.

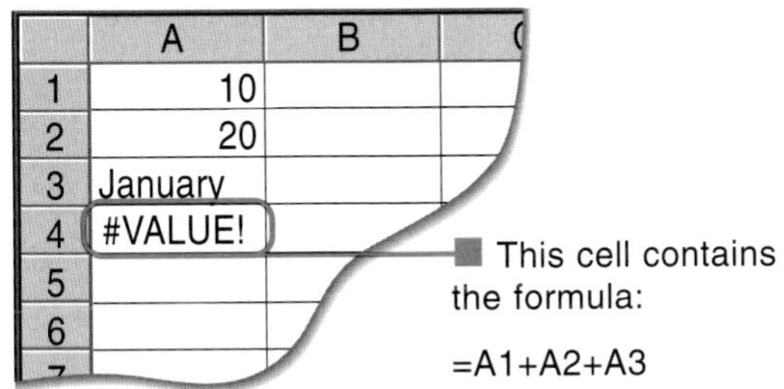

A
B
1 10
2 20
3 January
4 #VALUE!
5
6

■ This cell contains the formula:

=A1+A2+A3

In this example, a cell used in the formula contains text.

Circular Reference

A warning message appears when a formula refers to the cell that contains the formula. This is called a circular reference.

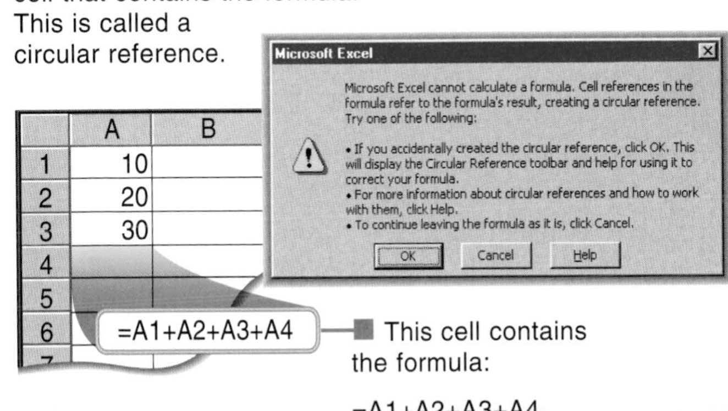

Microsoft Excel
Microsoft Excel cannot calculate a formula. Cell references in the formula refer to the formula's result, creating a circular reference. Try one of the following:
• If you accidentally created the circular reference, click OK. This will display the Circular Reference toolbar and help for using it to correct your formula.
• For more information about circular references and how to work with them, click Help.
• To continue leaving the formula as it is, click Cancel.
OK
Cancel
Help
A
B
1 10
2 20
3 30
4
5
6 =A1+A2+A3+A4

■ This cell contains the formula:

=A1+A2+A3+A4

If you want to use the same formula several times in your worksheet, you can save time by copying the formula.

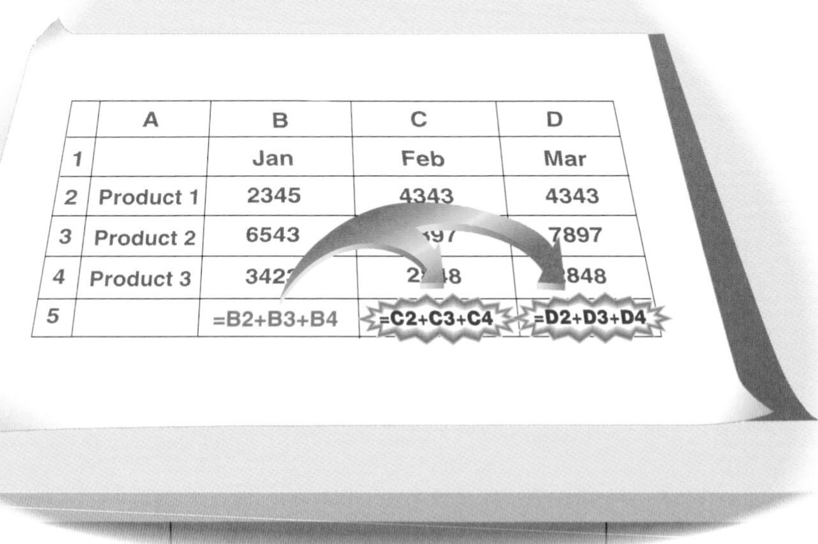

A
B
C
D
1
Jan
Feb
Mar
2
Product 1
2345
4343
4343
3
Product 2
6543
7897
4
Product 3
5
=B2+B3+B4
=C2+C3+C4
=D2+D3+D4

COPY A FORMULA—USING RELATIVE REFERENCES

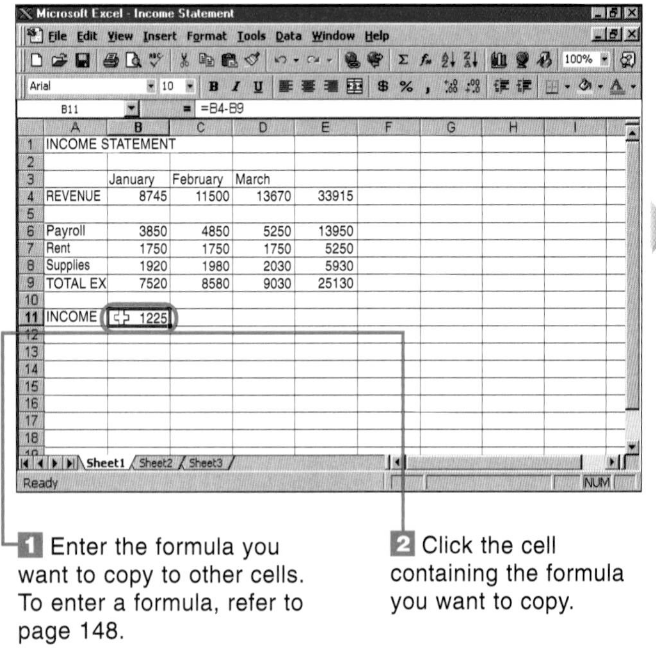

1 Enter the formula you want to copy to other cells. To enter a formula, refer to page 148.

*Note: In this example, enter the formula **=B4-B9** in cell **B11** to calculate INCOME.*

2 Click the cell containing the formula you want to copy.

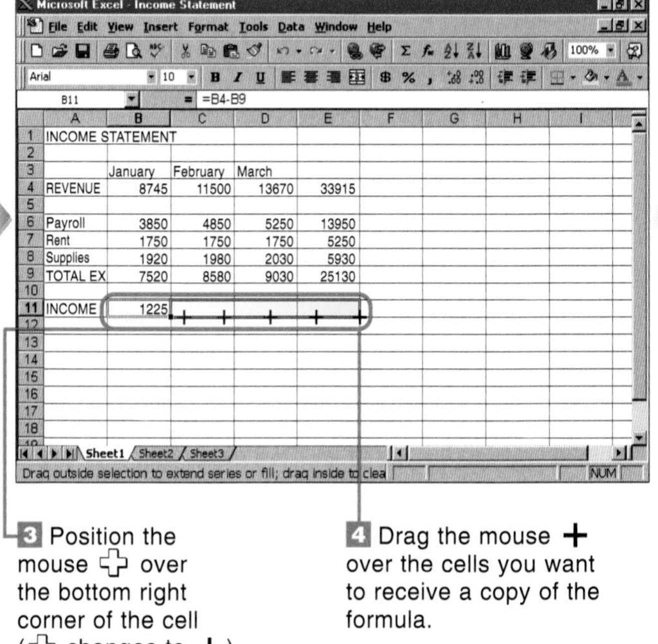

3 Position the mouse ✣ over the bottom right corner of the cell (✣ changes to +).

4 Drag the mouse + over the cells you want to receive a copy of the formula.

What is a relative reference?

A relative reference is a cell reference that changes when you copy a formula.

	A	B	C
1	10	20	5
2	20	30	10
3	30	40	20
4	60	90	35
5			

=A1+A2+A3 | =B1+B2+B3 | =C1+C2+C3

This cell contains the formula =A1+A2+A3

If you copy the formula to other cells in the worksheet, Excel automatically changes the cell references in the new formulas.

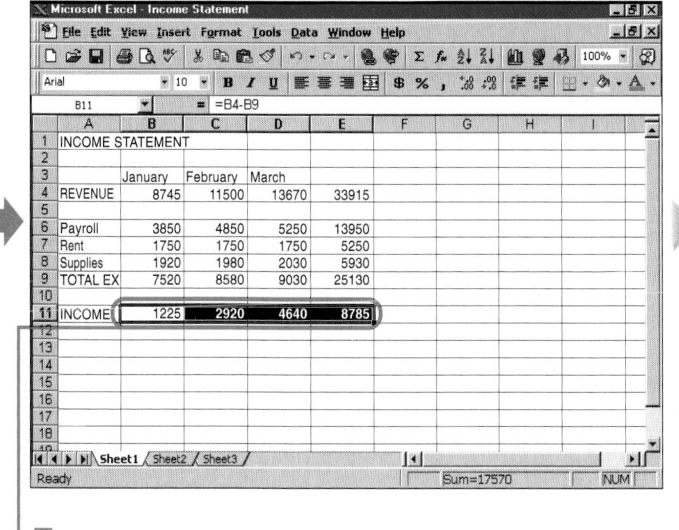

■ The results of the formulas appear.

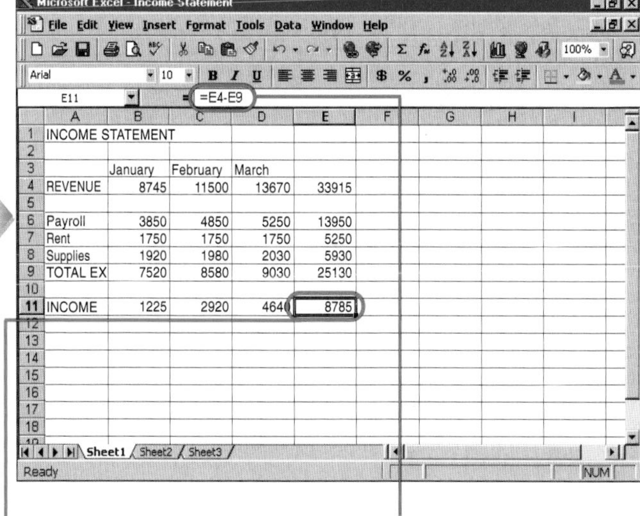

5 To see the new formulas, click a cell that received a copy of the formula.

■ The formula bar displays the formula with the new cell references.

COPY A FORMULA

You can copy a formula to other cells in your worksheet to save time. If you do not want Excel to change a cell reference when you copy a formula, you can use an absolute reference.

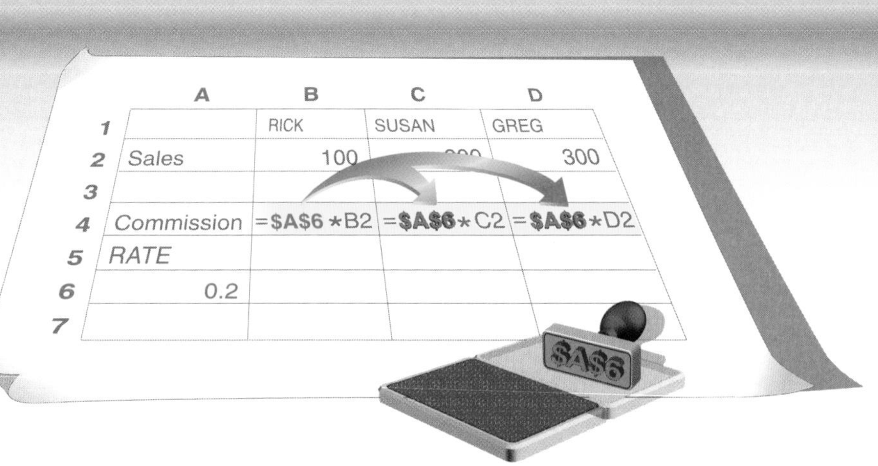

A B C D
1 RICK SUSAN GREG
2 Sales 100 300
3
4 Commission =$A$6 *B2 =$A$6 *C2 =$A$6 *D2
5 RATE
6 0.2
7
$A$6

COPY A FORMULA—USING ABSOLUTE REFERENCES

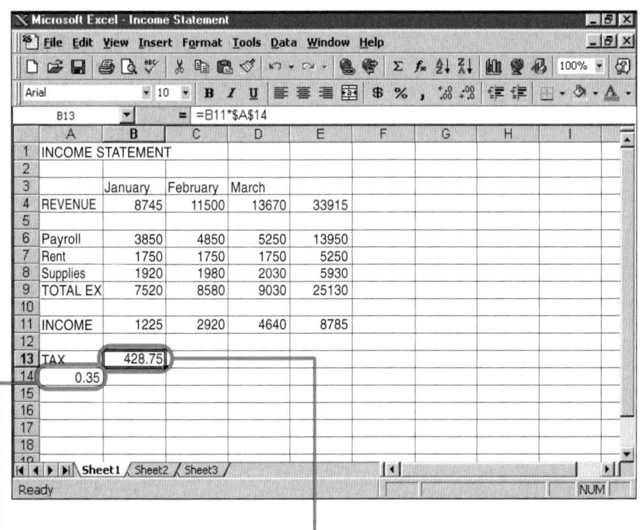

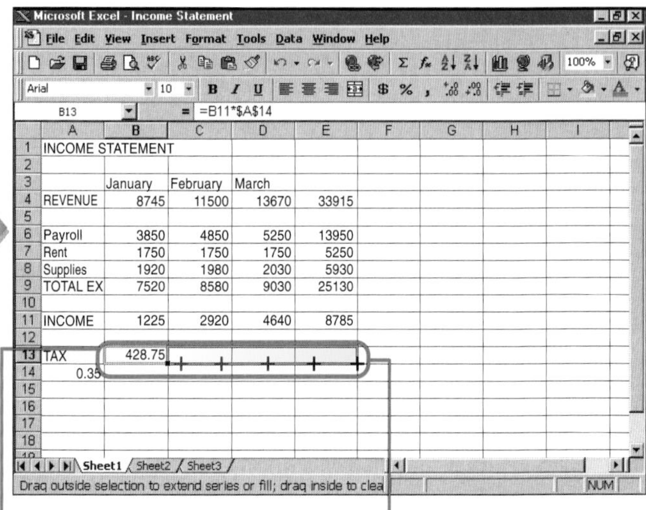

1 Enter the data you want to remain the same in all the formulas.

2 Enter the formula you want to copy to other cells. To enter a formula, refer to page 148.

Note: In this example, enter the formula ***=B11*$A$14*** *in cell* ***B13*** *to calculate TAX. For information on absolute references, refer to the top of page 165.*

3 Click the cell containing the formula you want to copy.

4 Position the mouse ✣ over the bottom right corner of the cell (✣ changes to +).

5 Drag the mouse + over the cells you want to receive a copy of the formula.

What is an absolute reference?

An absolute reference is a cell reference that does not change when you copy a formula. To make a cell reference absolute, type a dollar sign ($) before both the column letter and row number (example: $A$7).

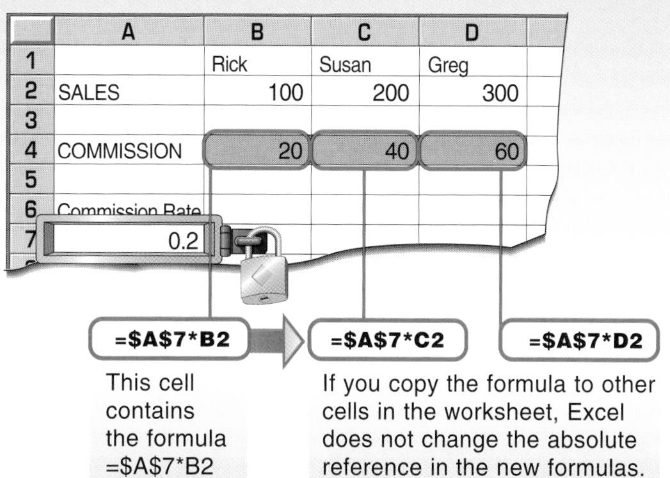

This cell contains the formula =$A$7*B2

If you copy the formula to other cells in the worksheet, Excel does not change the absolute reference in the new formulas.

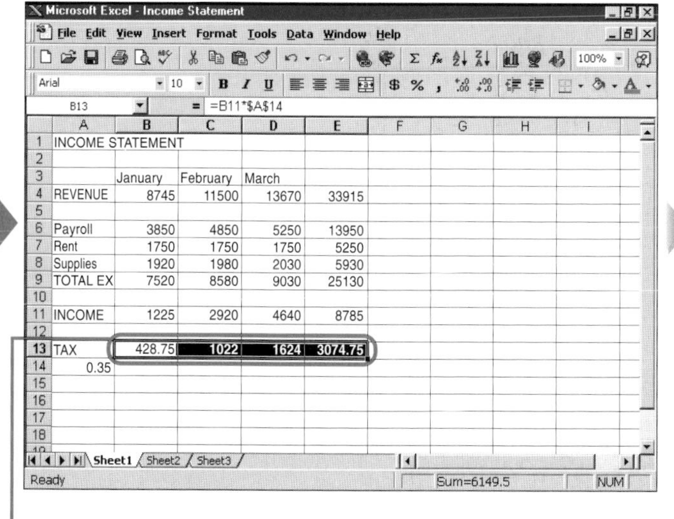

The results of the formulas appear.

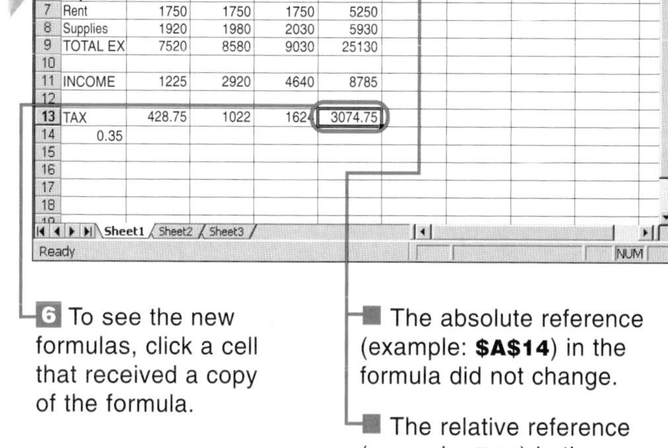

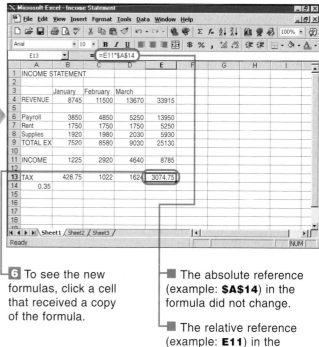

6 To see the new formulas, click a cell that received a copy of the formula.

■ The absolute reference (example: **$A$14**) in the formula did not change.

■ The relative reference (example: **E11**) in the formula did change.

CHANGE COLUMN WIDTH

You can improve the appearance of your worksheet and display hidden data by changing the width of columns.

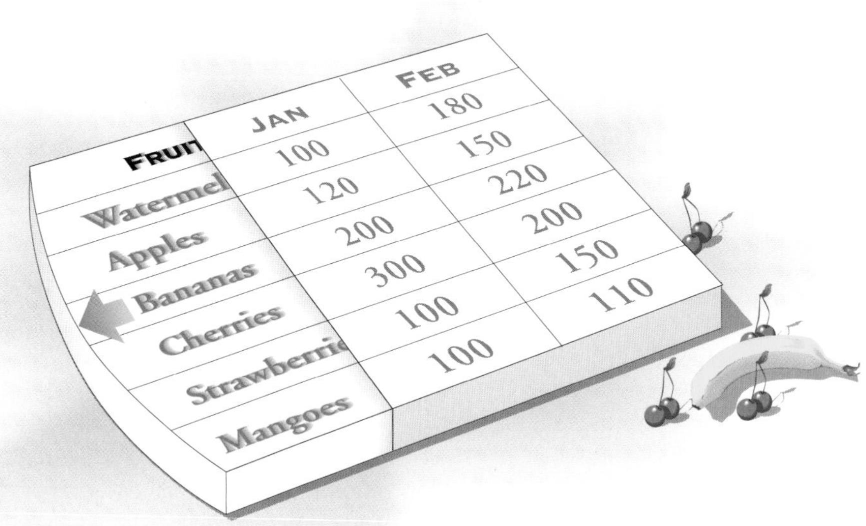

CHANGE COLUMN WIDTH

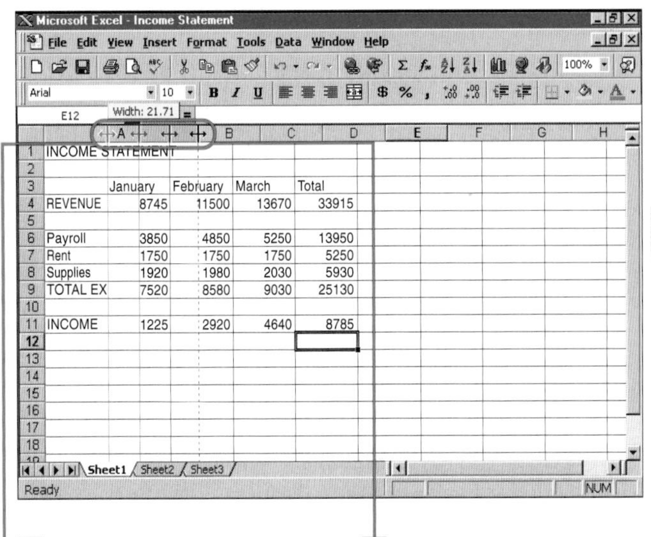

1 To change the width of a column, position the mouse ✚ over the right edge of the column heading (✚ changes to ↔).

2 Drag the column edge until the dotted line displays the column width you want.

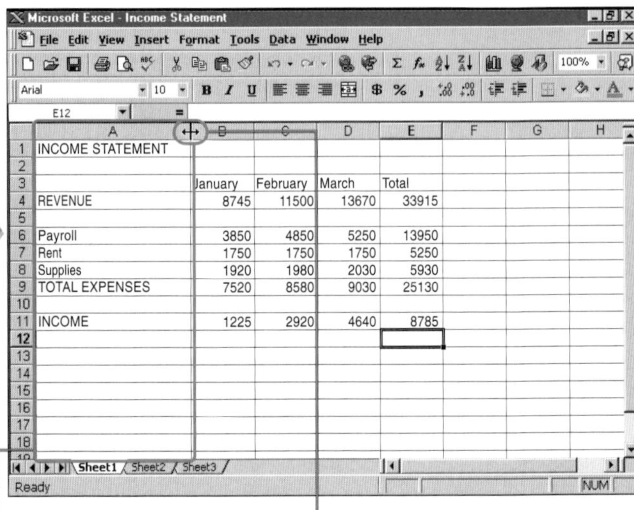

■ The column displays the new width.

FIT LONGEST ITEM

You can have Excel change a column width to fit the longest item in the column.

■ Double-click the right edge of the column heading.

CHANGE ROW HEIGHT

You can change the height of rows to add space between the rows of data in your worksheet.

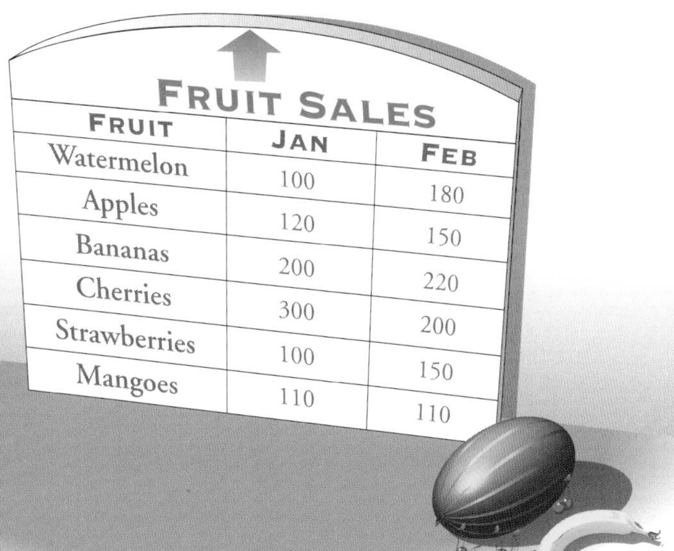

CHANGE ROW HEIGHT

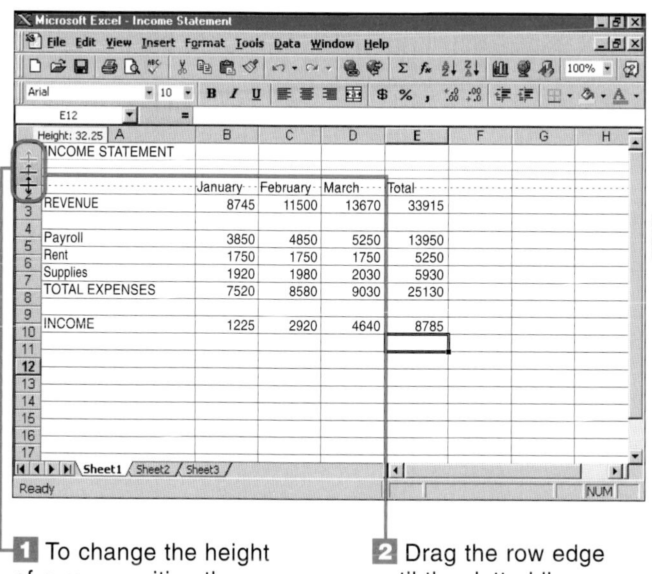

1 To change the height of a row, position the mouse ✥ over the bottom edge of the row heading (✥ changes to ✚).

2 Drag the row edge until the dotted line displays the row height you want.

■ The row displays the new height.

FIT TALLEST ITEM

You can have Excel change a row height to fit the tallest item in the row.

■ Double-click the bottom edge of the row heading.

CHANGE APPEARANCE OF NUMBERS

You can quickly change the appearance of numbers in your worksheet without retyping the numbers.

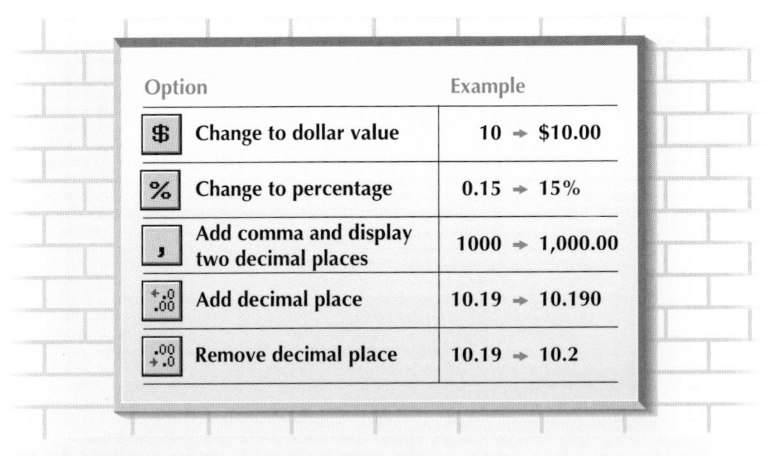

Option	Example
Change to dollar value	10 → $10.00
Change to percentage	0.15 → 15%
Add comma and display two decimal places	1000 → 1,000.00
Add decimal place	10.19 → 10.190
Remove decimal place	10.19 → 10.2

When you change the appearance of numbers, you do not change the value of the numbers.

CHANGE APPEARANCE OF NUMBERS

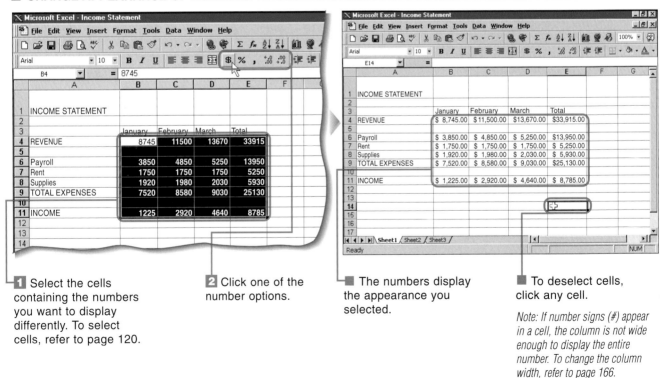

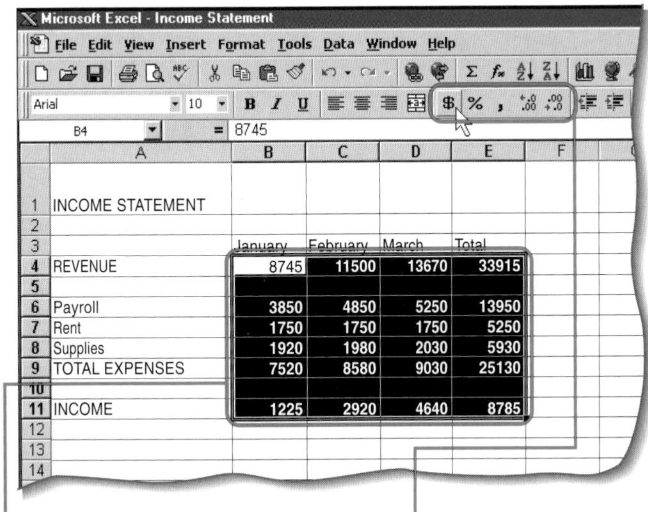

1 Select the cells containing the numbers you want to display differently. To select cells, refer to page 120.

2 Click one of the number options.

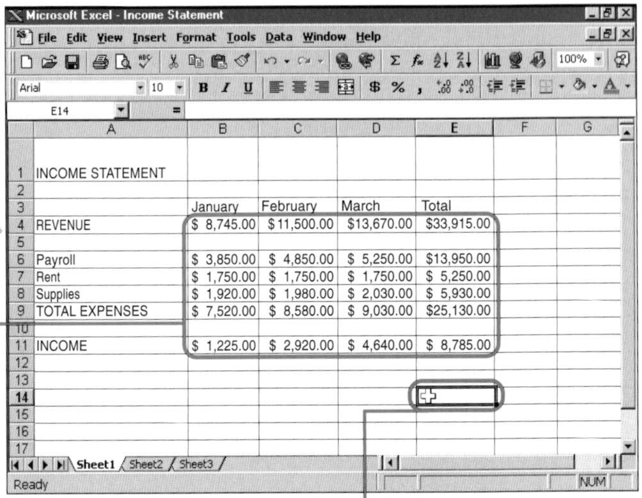

■ The numbers display the appearance you selected.

■ To deselect cells, click any cell.

Note: If number signs (#) appear in a cell, the column is not wide enough to display the entire number. To change the column width, refer to page 166.

You can use the bold, italic and underline styles to emphasize data in your worksheet.

BOLD, ITALIC AND UNDERLINE

Microsoft Excel - Income Statement

	A	B	C	D	E
1	INCOME STATEMENT				
2					
3		January	February	March	Total
4	REVENUE	$ 8,745.00	$ 11,500.00	$13,670.00	$33,915.00
5					
6	Payroll	$ 3,850.00	$ 4,850.00	$ 5,250.00	$13,950.00
7	Rent	$ 1,750.00	$ 1,750.00	$ 1,750.00	$ 5,250.00
8	Supplies	$ 1,920.00	$ 1,980.00	$ 2,030.00	$ 5,930.00
9	TOTAL EXPENSES	$ 7,520.00	$ 8,580.00	$ 9,030.00	$25,130.00
10					
11	INCOME	$ 1,225.00	$ 2,920.00	$ 4,640.00	$ 8,785.00

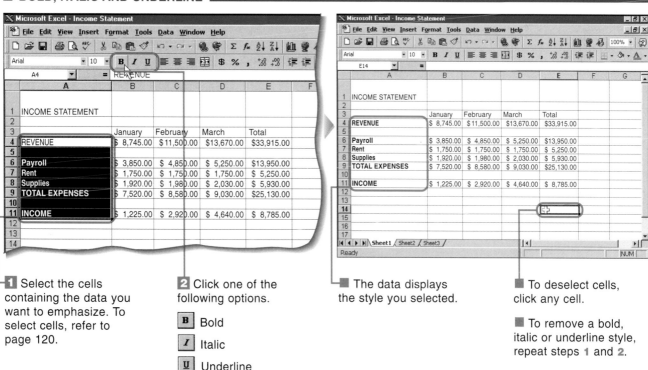

1 Select the cells containing the data you want to emphasize. To select cells, refer to page 120.

2 Click one of the following options.

- **B** Bold
- *I* Italic
- U Underline

■ The data displays the style you selected.

■ To deselect cells, click any cell.

■ To remove a bold, italic or underline style, repeat steps **1** and **2**.

You can enhance the appearance of your worksheet by changing the font of data.

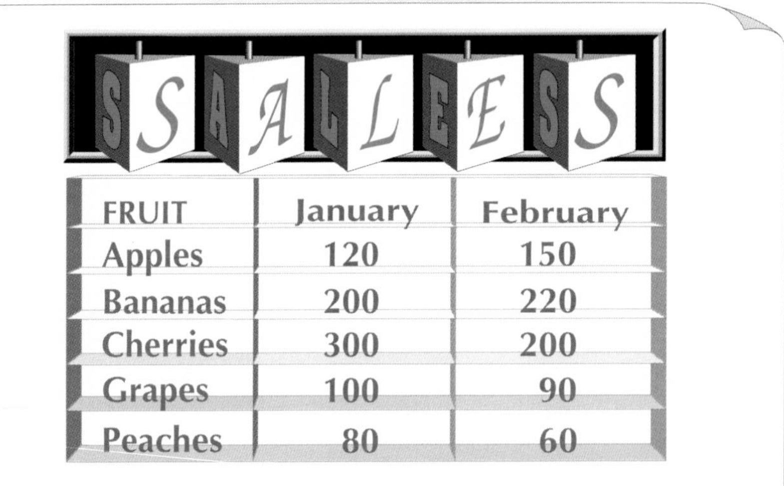

CHANGE FONT OF DATA

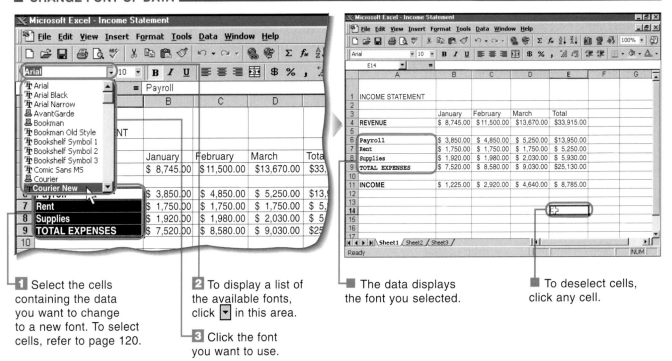

1 Select the cells containing the data you want to change to a new font. To select cells, refer to page 120.

2 To display a list of the available fonts, click ▾ in this area.

3 Click the font you want to use.

■ The data displays the font you selected.

■ To deselect cells, click any cell.

CHANGE SIZE OF DATA

You can increase or decrease the size of data in your worksheet.

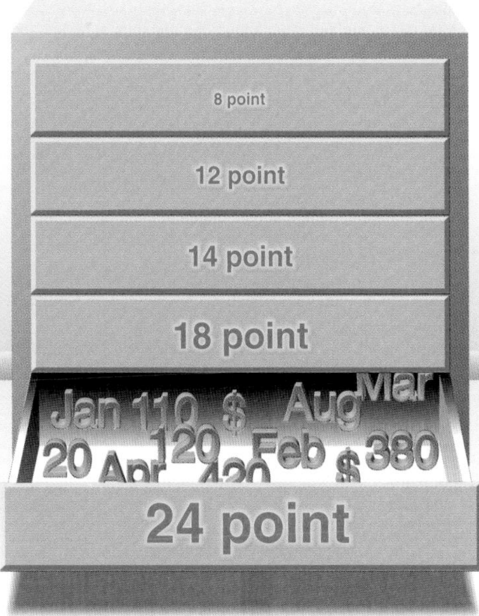

CHANGE SIZE OF DATA

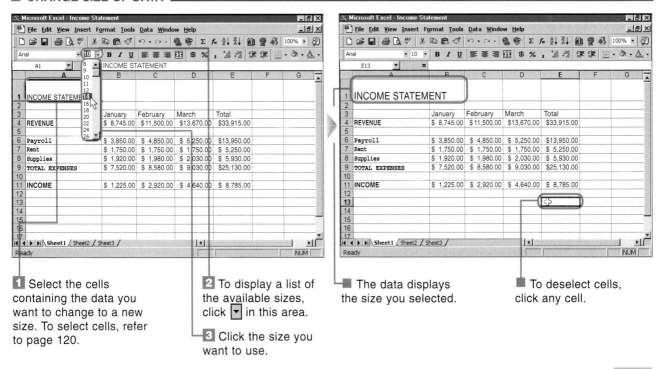

1 Select the cells containing the data you want to change to a new size. To select cells, refer to page 120.

2 To display a list of the available sizes, click ▾ in this area.

3 Click the size you want to use.

■ The data displays the size you selected.

■ To deselect cells, click any cell.

CHANGE ALIGNMENT OF DATA

You can change the position of data in each cell of your worksheet.

CHANGE ALIGNMENT OF DATA

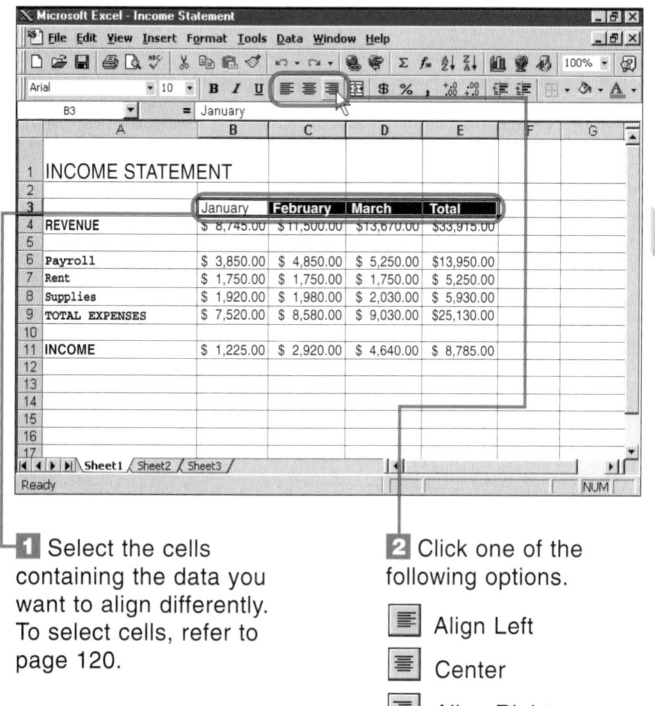

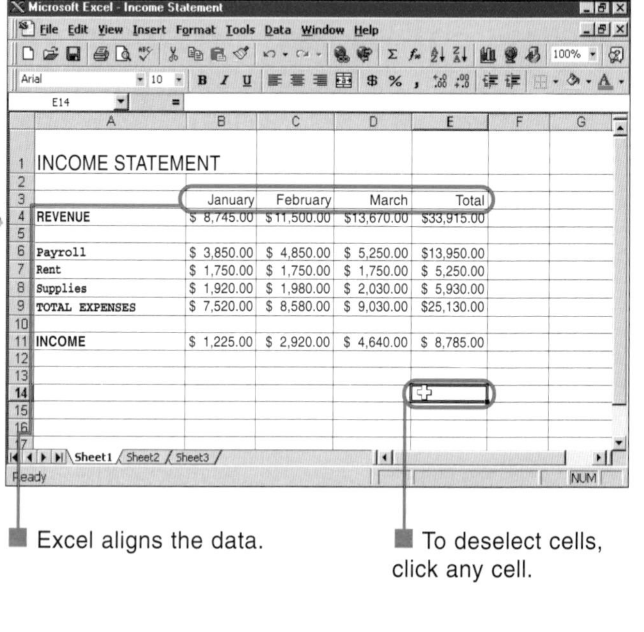

1 Select the cells containing the data you want to align differently. To select cells, refer to page 120.

2 Click one of the following options.

- Align Left
- Center
- Align Right

■ Excel aligns the data.

■ To deselect cells, click any cell.

INDENT DATA

You can use the Indent feature to move data away from the left edge of a cell.

INDENT DATA

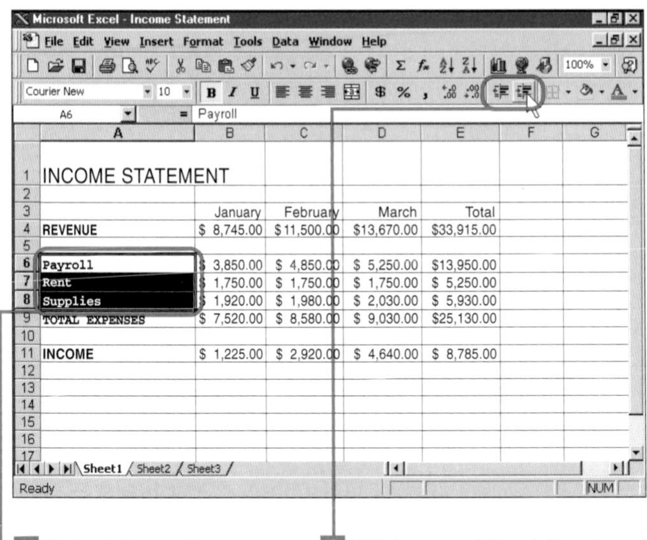

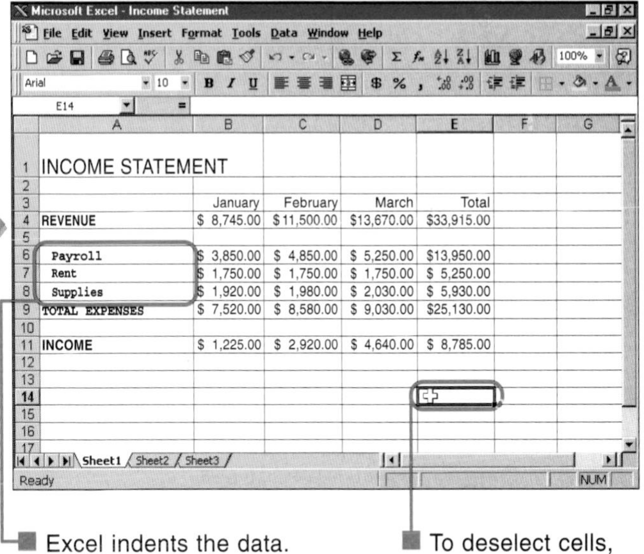

1 Select the cells containing the data you want to indent. To select cells, refer to page 120.

2 Click one of the following options.

- Move data to the left
- Move data to the right

■ Excel indents the data.

■ To deselect cells, click any cell.

ADD BORDERS

You can add borders to enhance the appearance of your worksheet.

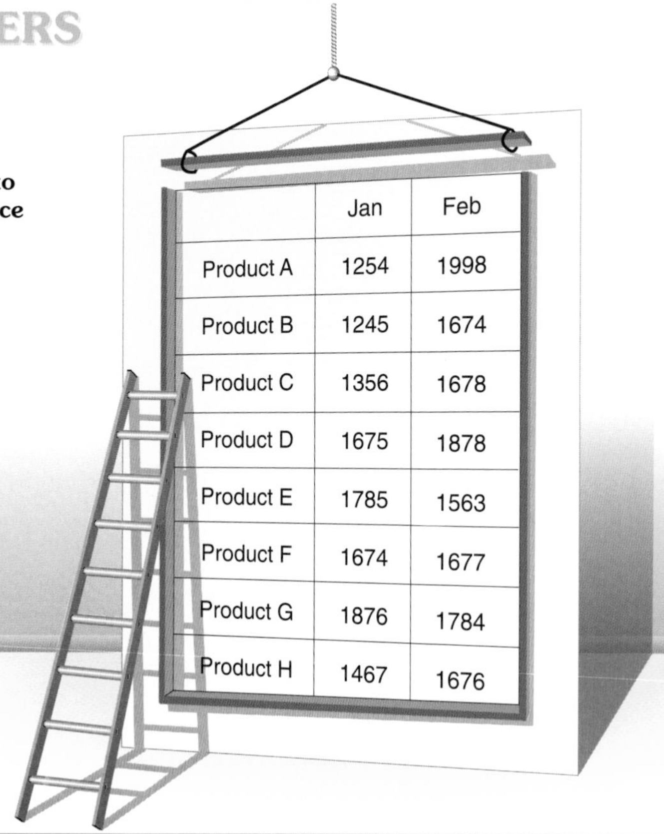

	Jan	Feb
Product A	1254	1998
Product B	1245	1674
Product C	1356	1678
Product D	1675	1878
Product E	1785	1563
Product F	1674	1677
Product G	1876	1784
Product H	1467	1676

ADD BORDERS

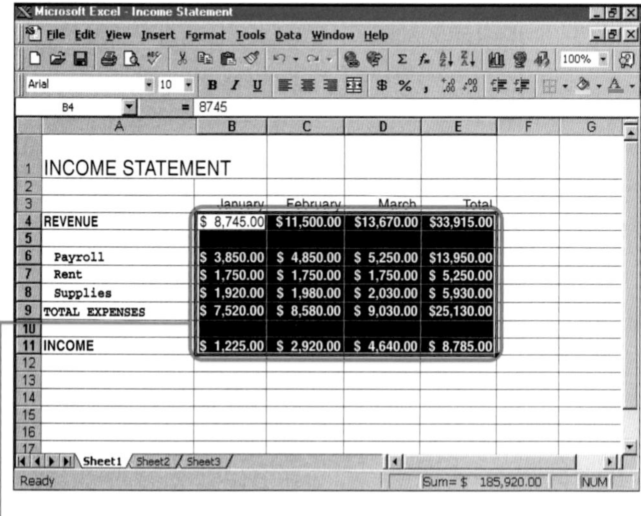

	A	B	C	D	E
1	INCOME STATEMENT				
2					
3		January	February	March	Total
4	REVENUE	$ 8,745.00	$11,500.00	$13,670.00	$33,915.00
5					
6	Payroll	$ 3,850.00	$ 4,850.00	$ 5,250.00	$13,950.00
7	Rent	$ 1,750.00	$ 1,750.00	$ 1,750.00	$ 5,250.00
8	Supplies	$ 1,920.00	$ 1,980.00	$ 2,030.00	$ 5,930.00
9	TOTAL EXPENSES	$ 7,520.00	$ 8,580.00	$ 9,030.00	$25,130.00
10					
11	INCOME	$ 1,225.00	$ 2,920.00	$ 4,640.00	$ 8,785.00

1 Select the cells you want to display borders. To select cells, refer to page 120.

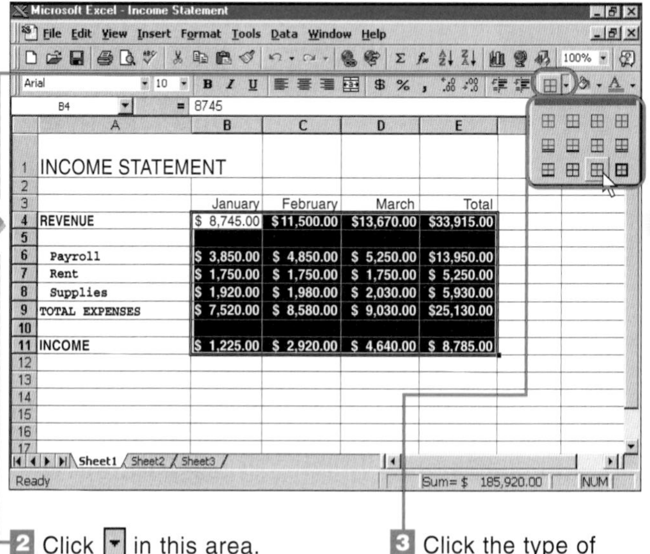

	A	B	C	D	E
1	INCOME STATEMENT				
2					
3		January	February	March	Total
4	REVENUE	$ 8,745.00	$11,500.00	$13,670.00	$33,915.00
5					
6	Payroll	$ 3,850.00	$ 4,850.00	$ 5,250.00	$13,950.00
7	Rent	$ 1,750.00	$ 1,750.00	$ 1,750.00	$ 5,250.00
8	Supplies	$ 1,920.00	$ 1,980.00	$ 2,030.00	$ 5,930.00
9	TOTAL EXPENSES	$ 7,520.00	$ 8,580.00	$ 9,030.00	$25,130.00
10					
11	INCOME	$ 1,225.00	$ 2,920.00	$ 4,640.00	$ 8,785.00

2 Click ▼ in this area.

3 Click the type of border you want to add.

Can I print lines in my worksheet without adding borders?

Instead of adding borders to your worksheet, you can have Excel automatically print light lines, called gridlines, around each cell. To print gridlines, refer to page 190.

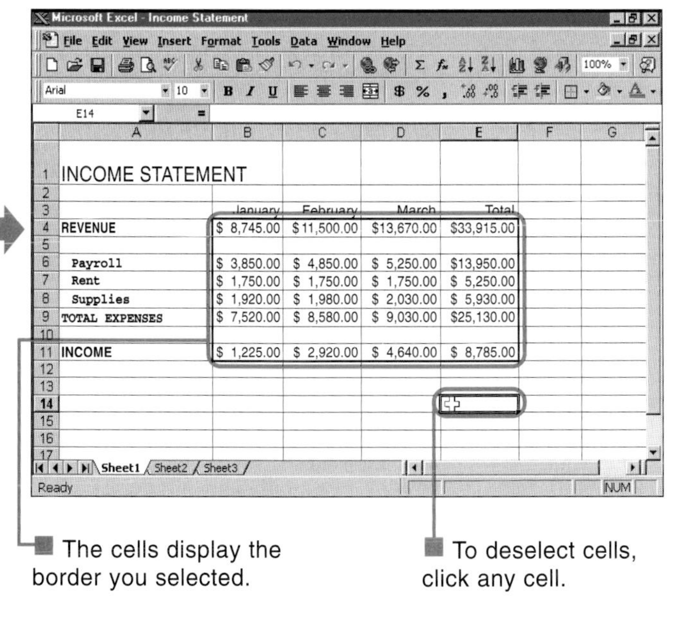

■ The cells display the border you selected.

■ To deselect cells, click any cell.

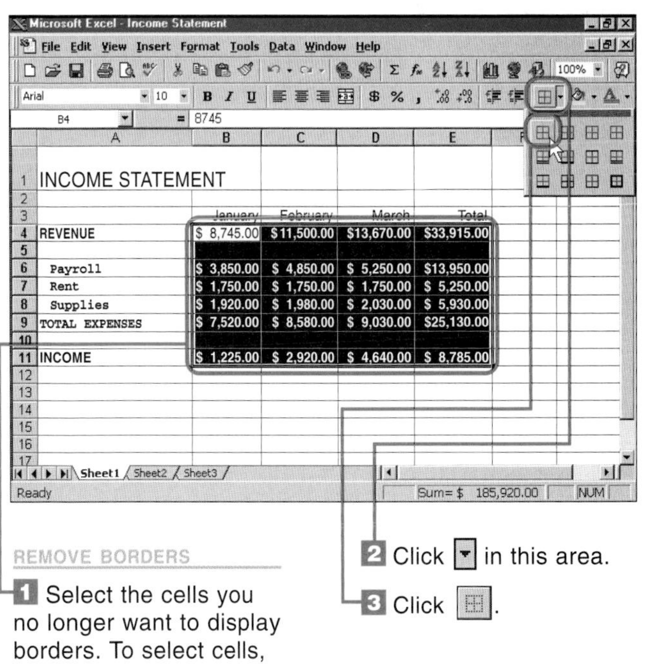

REMOVE BORDERS

1 Select the cells you no longer want to display borders. To select cells, refer to page 120.

2 Click ▾ in this area.

3 Click ⊞.

You can make your worksheet more attractive by adding color.

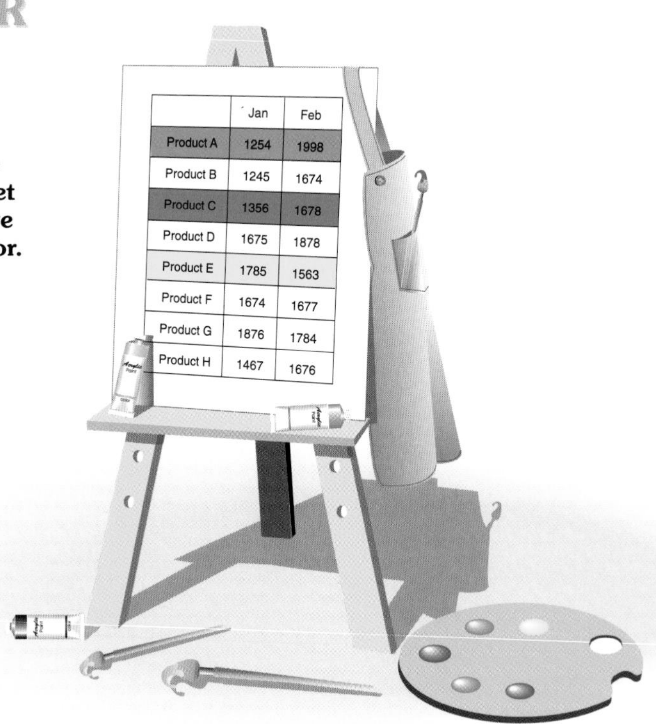

CHANGE CELL COLOR

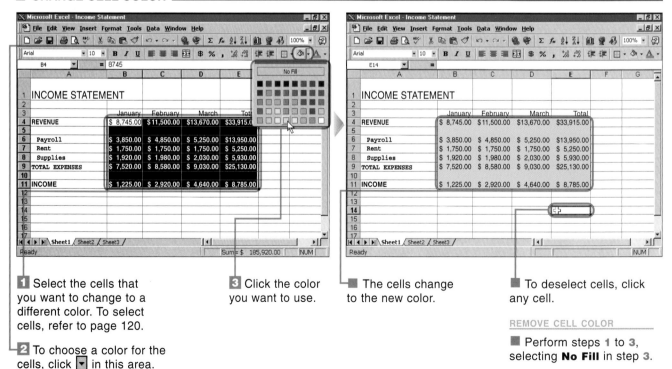

1 Select the cells that you want to change to a different color. To select cells, refer to page 120.

2 To choose a color for the cells, click ▾ in this area.

3 Click the color you want to use.

■ The cells change to the new color.

■ To deselect cells, click any cell.

REMOVE CELL COLOR

■ Perform steps 1 to 3, selecting **No Fill** in step 3.

What colors should I choose?

When adding color to a worksheet, make sure you choose cell and data colors that work well together. For example, red text on a blue background is difficult to read. To choose from many ready-to-use designs offered by Excel, refer to page 180.

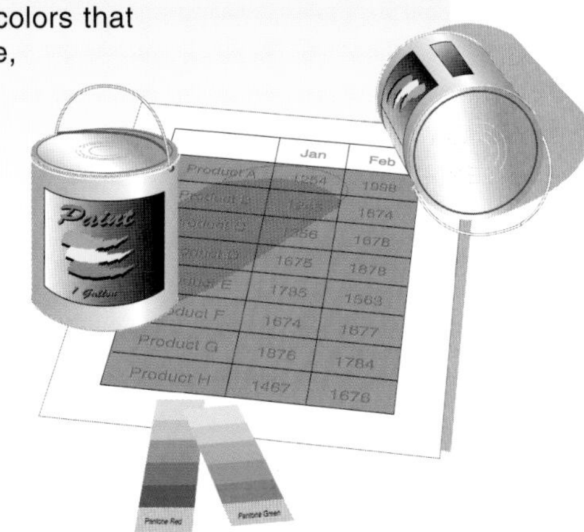

CHANGE DATA COLOR

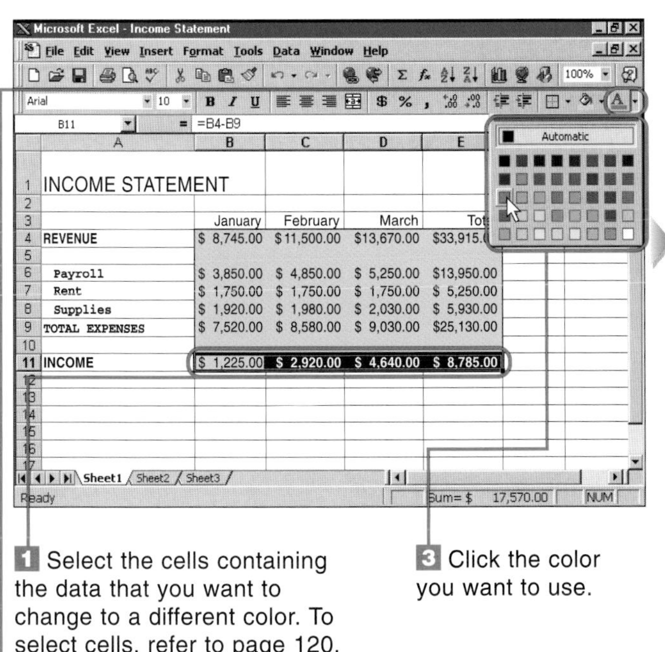

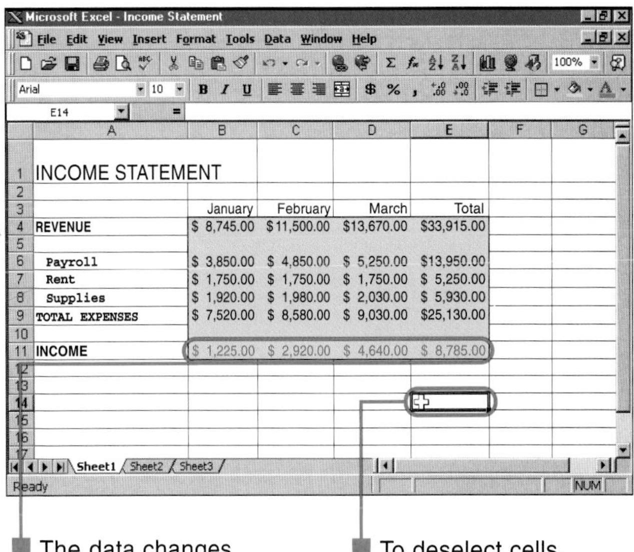

1 Select the cells containing the data that you want to change to a different color. To select cells, refer to page 120.

2 To choose a color for the data, click ▾ in this area.

3 Click the color you want to use.

■ The data changes to the new color.

■ To deselect cells, click any cell.

REMOVE DATA COLOR

■ Perform steps 1 to 3, selecting **Automatic** in step 3.

If you like the appearance of a cell in your worksheet, you can make other cells look exactly the same.

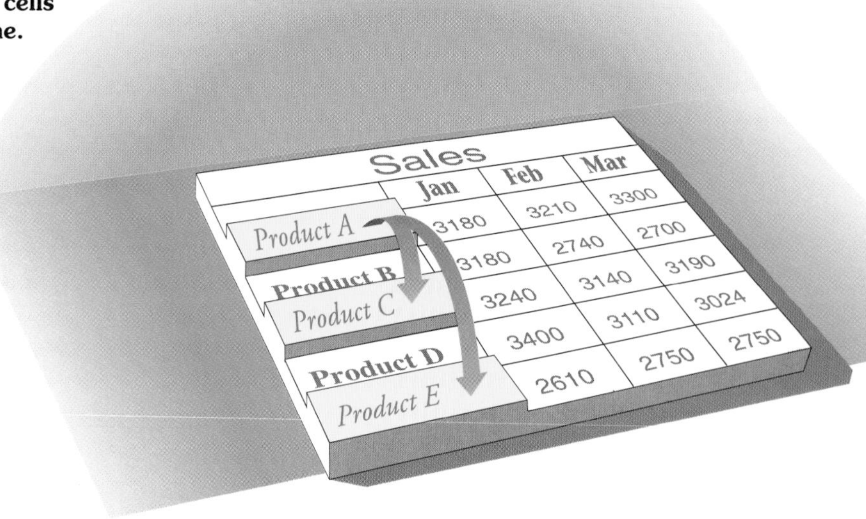

COPY FORMATTING

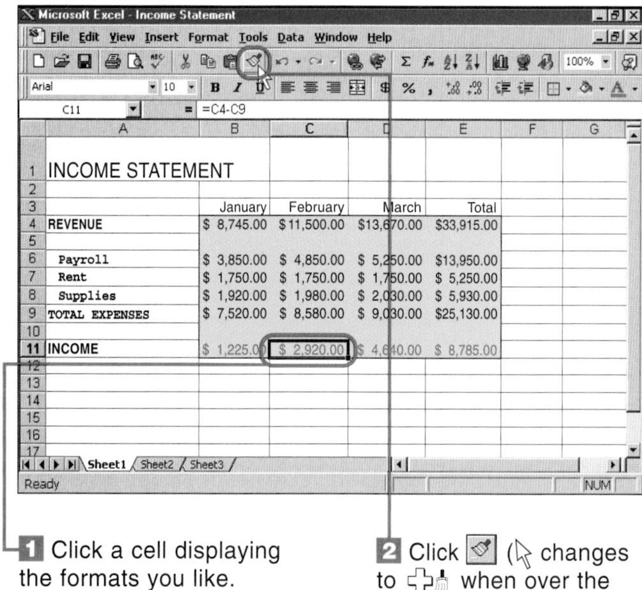

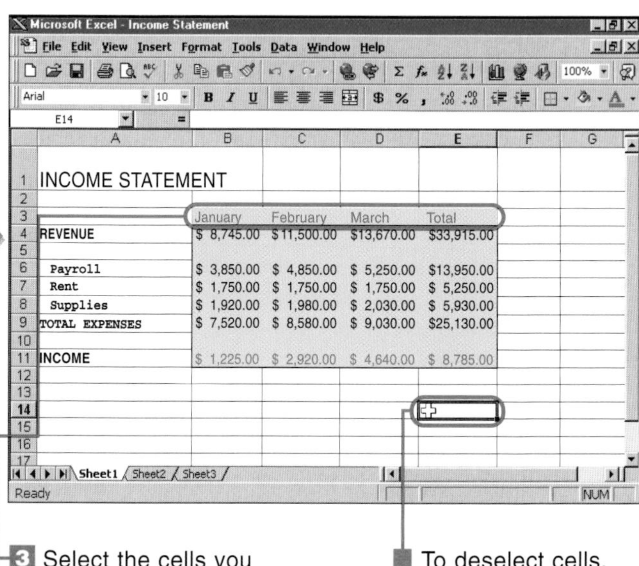

1 Click a cell displaying the formats you like.

2 Click the Format Painter button (the mouse pointer changes to a paintbrush pointer when over the worksheet).

3 Select the cells you want to display the same formats. To select cells, refer to page 120.

■ The cells display the formats.

■ To deselect cells, click any cell.

Note: If number signs (#) appear in a cell, the column is too narrow to fit the data. To change the column width, refer to page 166.

CENTER DATA ACROSS COLUMNS

You can center data across several columns in your worksheet. This is useful for centering titles over your data.

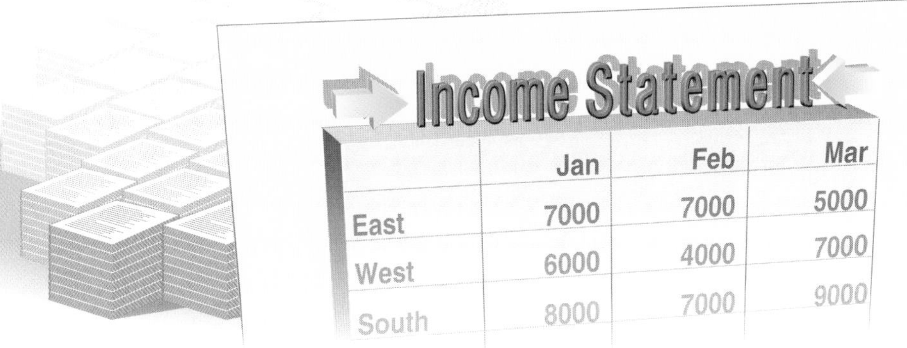

CENTER DATA ACROSS COLUMNS

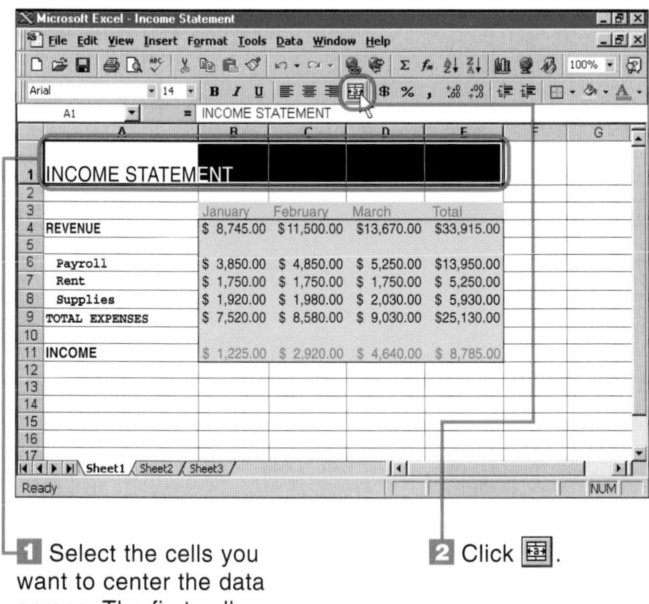

1 Select the cells you want to center the data across. The first cell you select should contain the data you want to center.

2 Click the Merge and Center button.

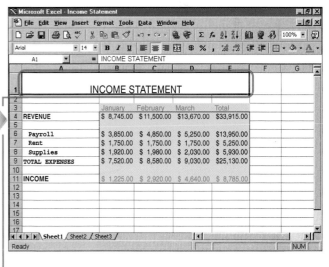

■ Excel centers the data across the cells you selected.

QUICKLY APPLY A DESIGN

Excel offers many ready-to-use designs that you can choose from to give your worksheet a new appearance.

QUICKLY APPLY A DESIGN

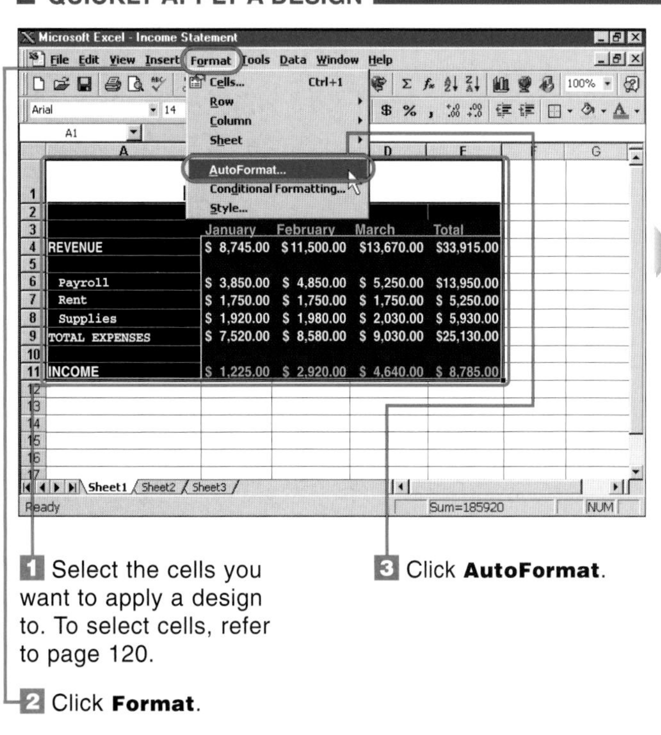

1 Select the cells you want to apply a design to. To select cells, refer to page 120.

2 Click **Format**.

3 Click **AutoFormat**.

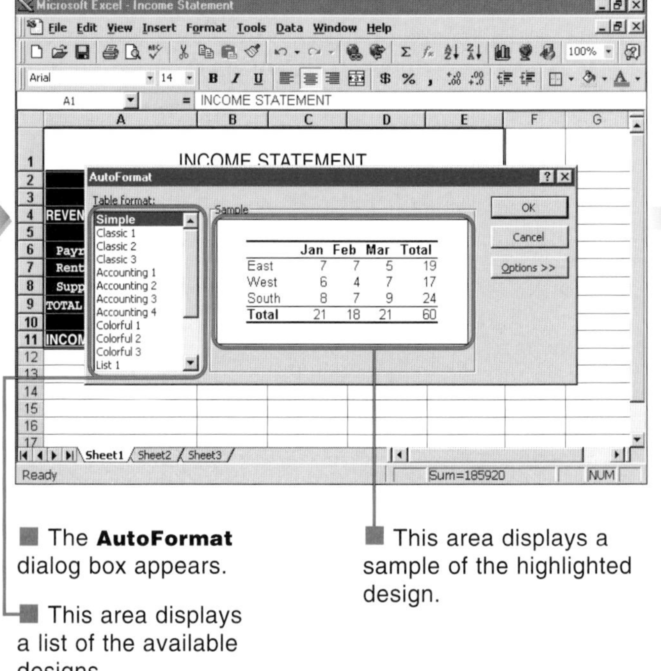

■ The **AutoFormat** dialog box appears.

■ This area displays a list of the available designs.

■ This area displays a sample of the highlighted design.

?

What are some designs offered by Excel?

	Jan	Feb	Mar	Total
East	7	7	5	19
West	6	4	7	17
South	8	7	9	24
Total	21	18	21	60

List 2

	Jan	Feb	Mar	Total
East	$ 7	$ 7	$ 5	$ 19
West	6	4	7	17
South	8	7	9	24
Total	$ 21	$ 18	$ 21	$ 60

Accounting 2

	Jan	Feb	Mar	**Total**
East	7	7	5	19
West	6	4	7	17
South	8	7	9	24
Total	21	18	21	60

Classic 2

	Jan	Feb	Mar	Total
East	7	7	5	19
West	6	4	7	17
South	8	7	9	24
Total	21	18	21	60

3D Effects 1

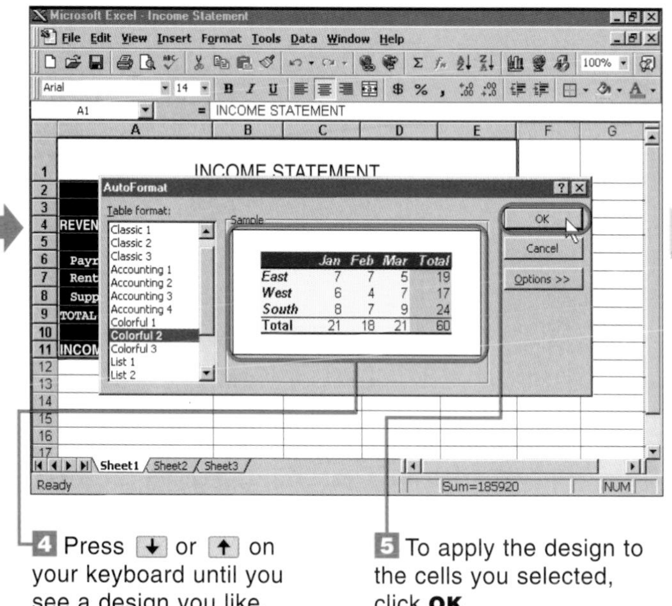

4 Press ↓ or ↑ on your keyboard until you see a design you like.

5 To apply the design to the cells you selected, click **OK**.

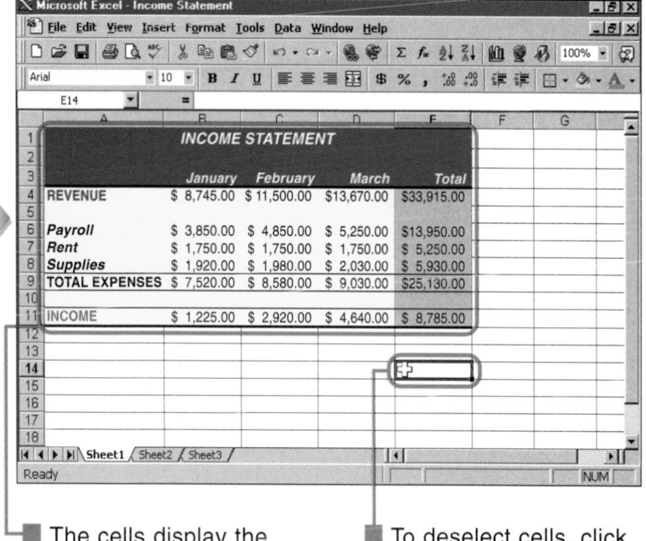

■ The cells display the design you selected.

■ To deselect cells, click any cell.

REMOVE AUTOFORMAT

■ Perform steps 1 to 5, selecting **None** in step 4.

You can see on the screen how your worksheet will look when printed.

PREVIEW A WORKSHEET

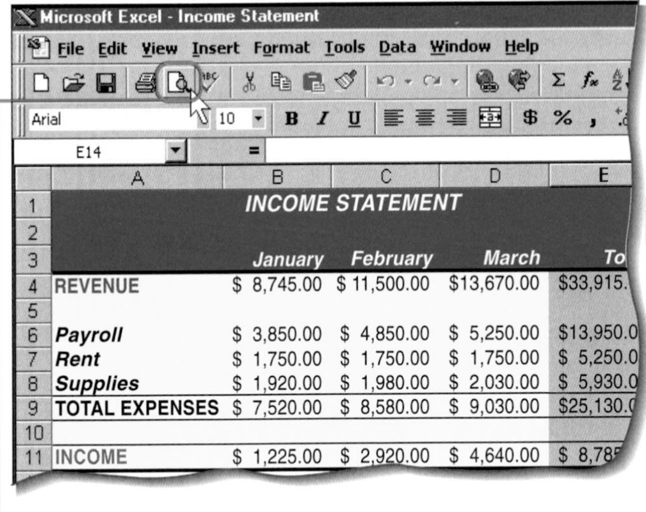

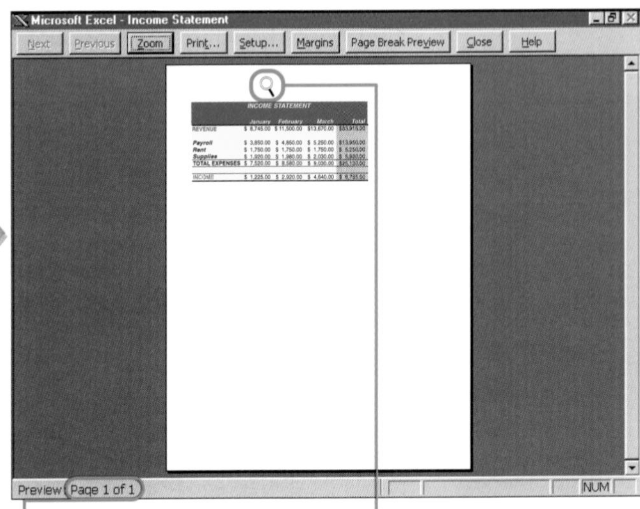

1 Click .

■ The Print Preview window appears.

■ This area tells you which page is displayed and the total number of pages in the worksheet.

Note: If you have a black-and-white printer, Excel displays the page in black and white.

2 To magnify an area of the page, click the area (changes to).

What should I do before printing my worksheet?

Before printing your worksheet, preview the worksheet to ensure it will print the way you want. Also make sure the printer is turned on and contains paper.

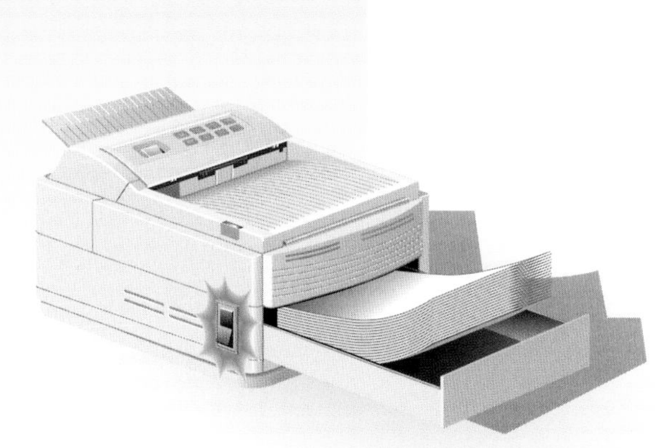

INCOME STATEMENT				
	January	February	March	Total
REVENUE	$ 8,745.00	$ 11,500.00	$13,670.00	$33,915.00
Payroll	$ 3,850.00	$ 4,850.00	$ 5,250.00	$13,950.00
Rent	$ 1,750.00	$ 1,750.00	$ 1,750.00	$ 5,250.00
Supplies	$ 1,920.00	$ 1,980.00	$ 2,030.00	$ 5,930.00
TOTAL EXPENSES	$ 7,520.00	$ 8,580.00	$ 9,030.00	$25,130.00
INCOME	$ 1,225.00	$ 2,920.00	$ 4,640.00	$ 8,785.00

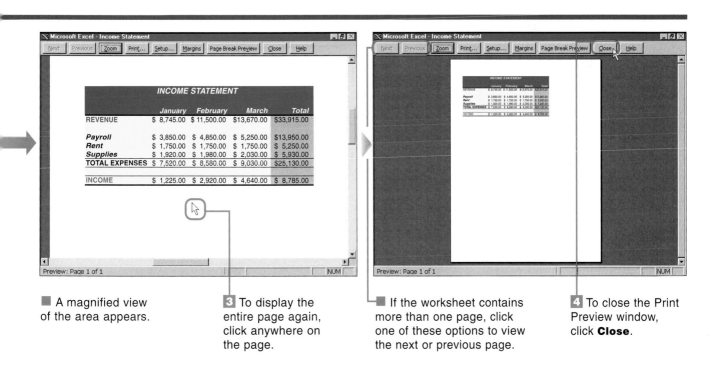

■ A magnified view of the area appears.

3 To display the entire page again, click anywhere on the page.

■ If the worksheet contains more than one page, click one of these options to view the next or previous page.

4 To close the Print Preview window, click **Close**.

A margin is the amount of space between data and an edge of your paper. You can easily change the margins.

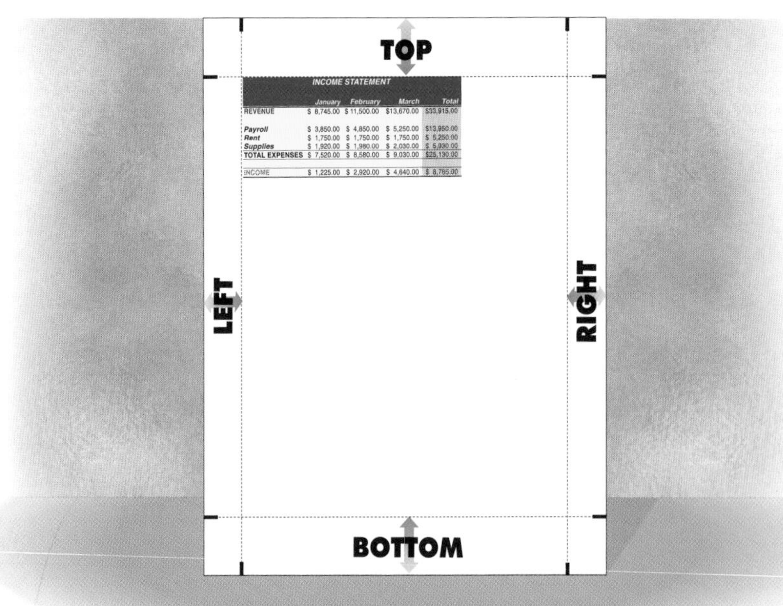

CHANGE MARGINS

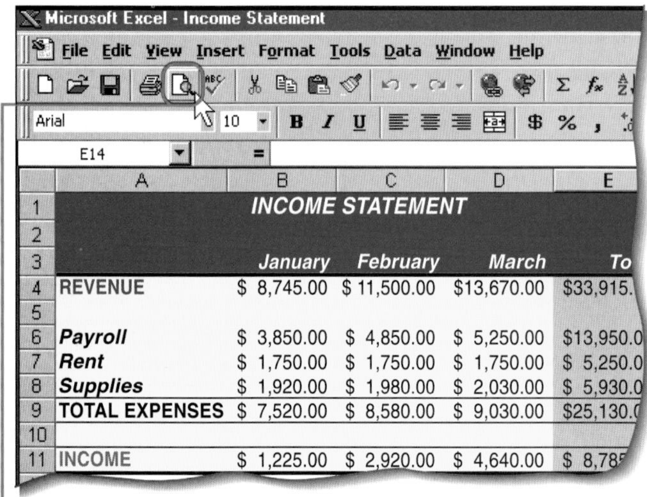

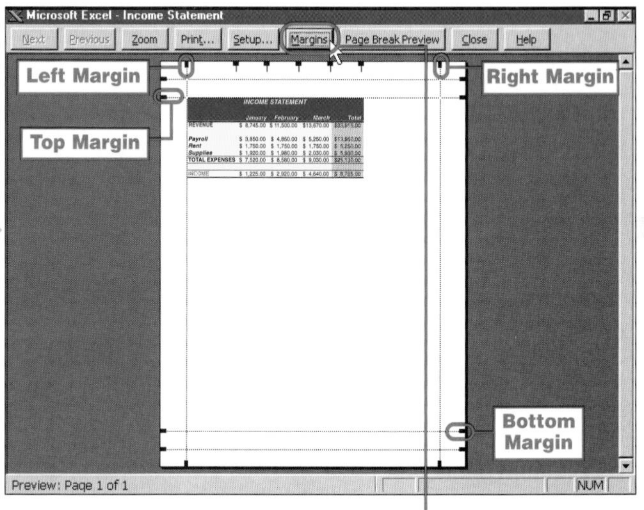

1 To display the worksheet in the Print Preview window, click [Print Preview button].

■ The worksheet appears in the Print Preview window. For information on previewing a worksheet, refer to page 182.

2 If the margins are not displayed, click **Margins**.

Why would I change the margins?

Changing the margins lets you accommodate letterhead and other specialty paper.

You can also change the the margins to fit more or less information on a page.

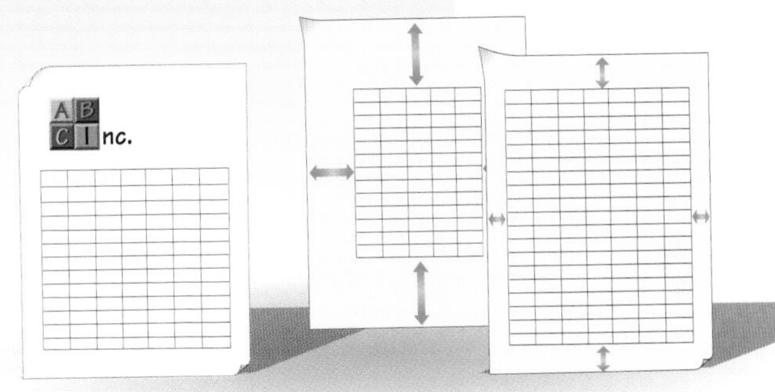

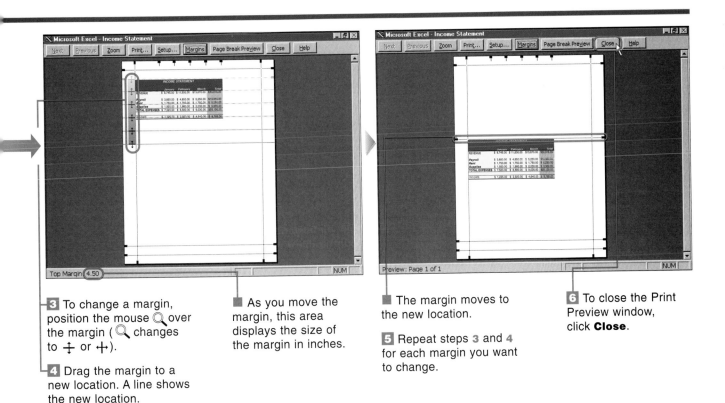

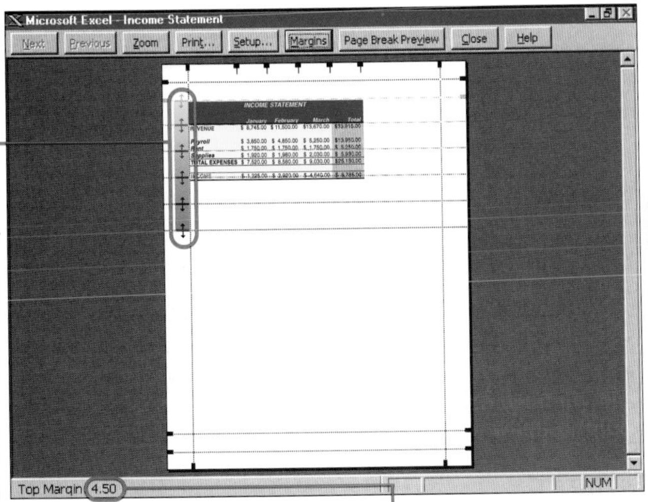

3 To change a margin, position the mouse over the margin (changes to ⌖ or ⌖).

4 Drag the margin to a new location. A line shows the new location.

■ As you move the margin, this area displays the size of the margin in inches.

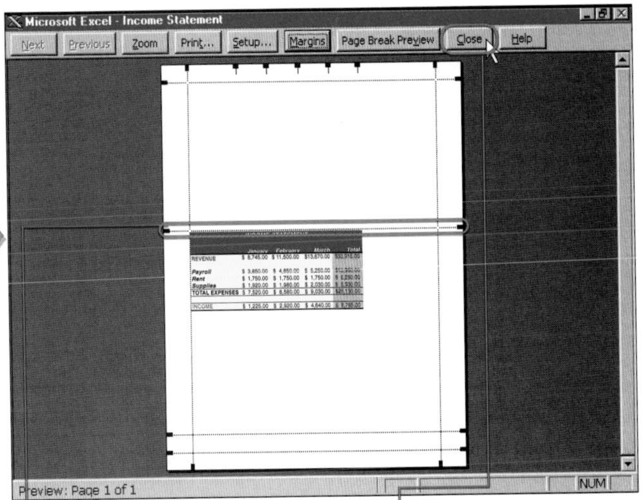

■ The margin moves to the new location.

5 Repeat steps 3 and 4 for each margin you want to change.

6 To close the Print Preview window, click **Close**.

You can produce a paper copy of the worksheet displayed on your screen.

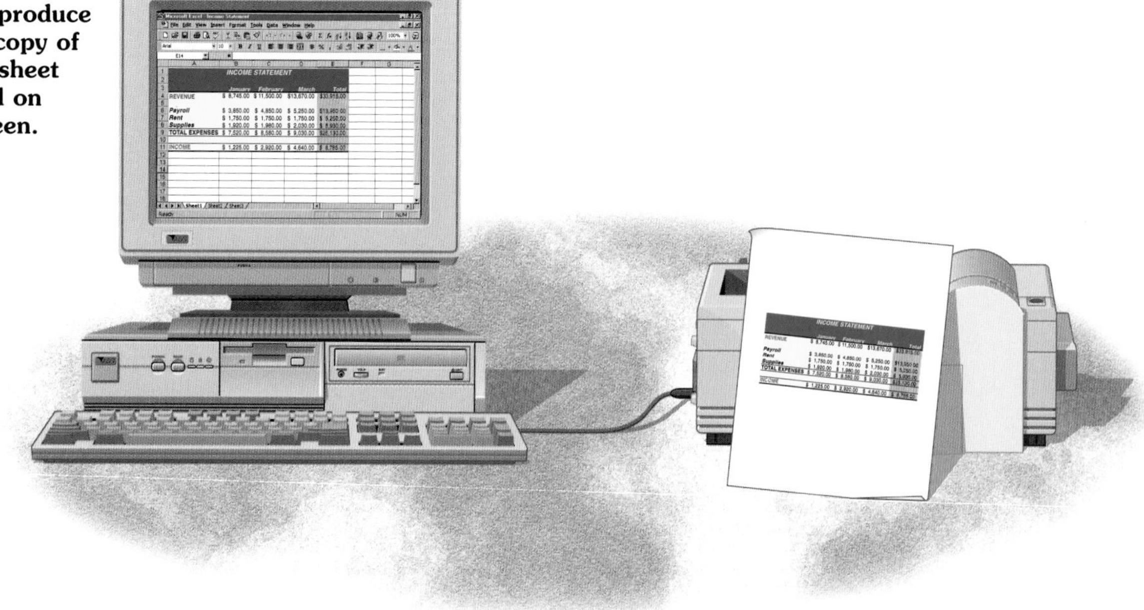

PRINT A WORKSHEET

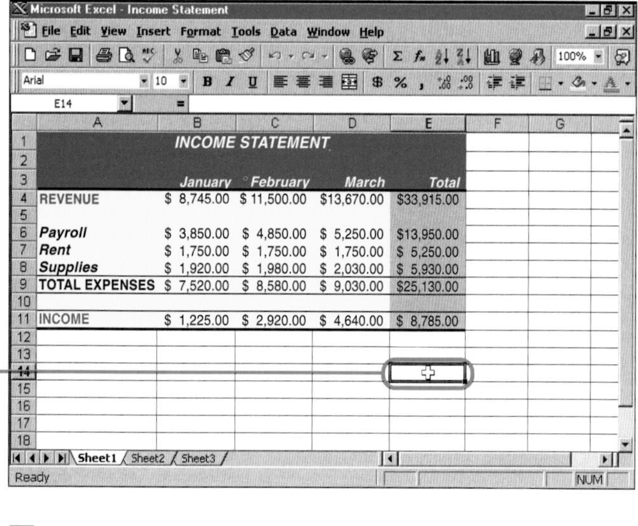

1 To print a worksheet, click any cell in the worksheet.

■ To print only part of the worksheet, select the cells you want to print. To select cells, refer to page 120.

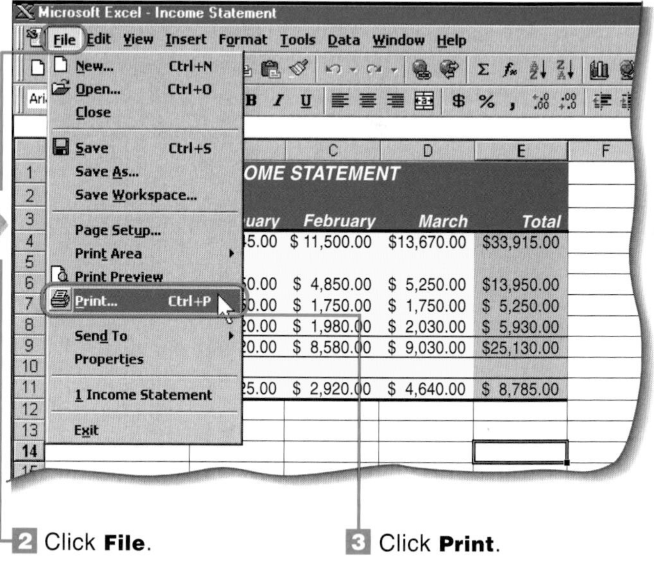

2 Click **File**.

3 Click **Print**.

■ The **Print** dialog box appears.

What can I print?

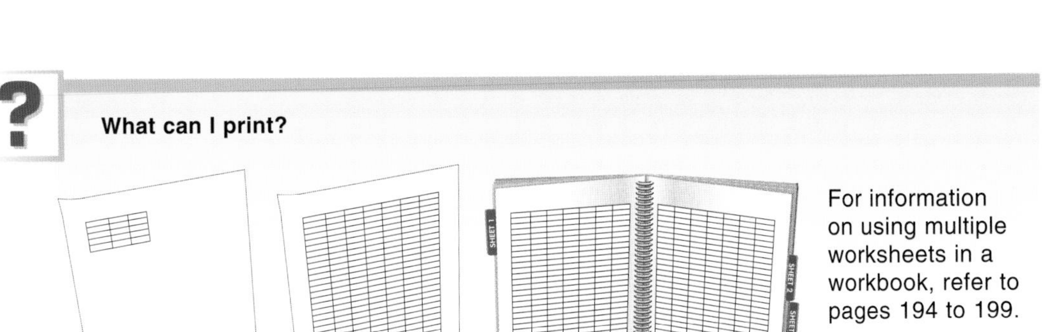

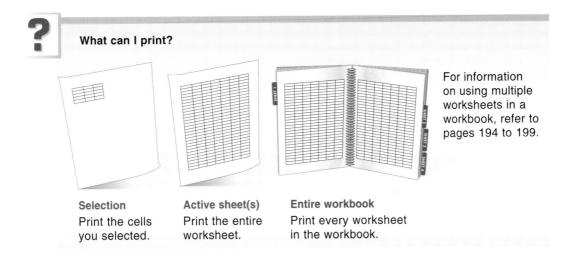

For information on using multiple worksheets in a workbook, refer to pages 194 to 199.

Selection
Print the cells you selected.

Active sheet(s)
Print the entire worksheet.

Entire workbook
Print every worksheet in the workbook.

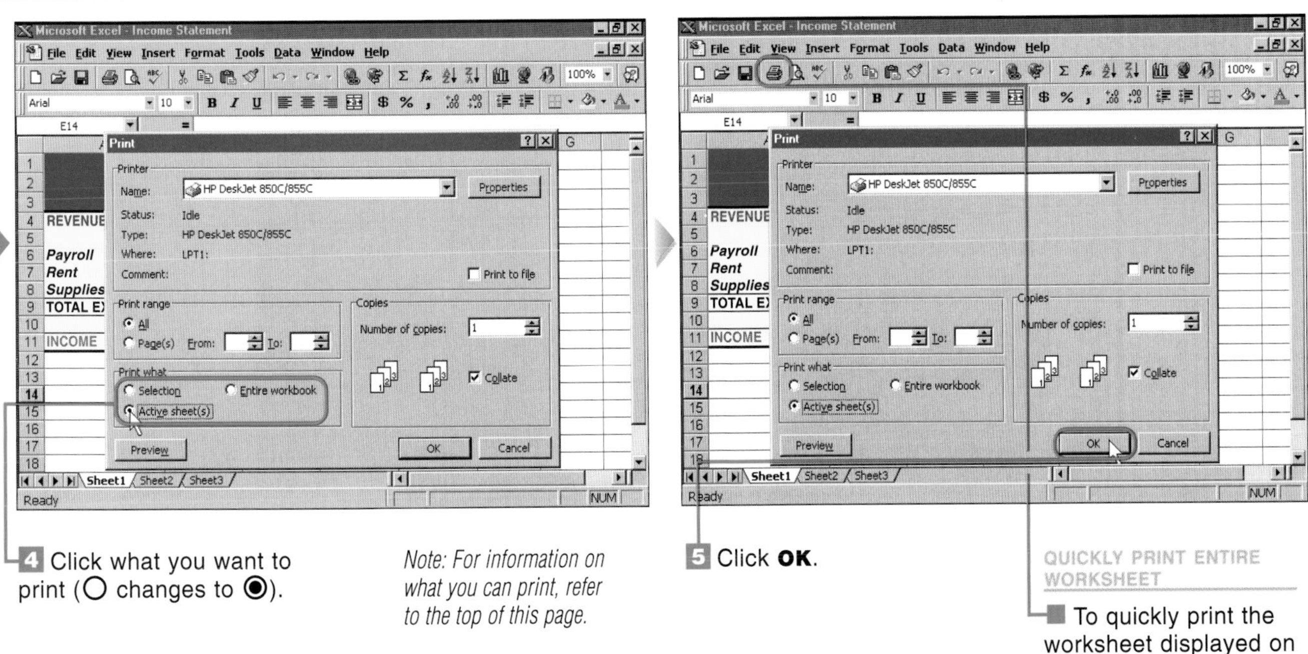

4 Click what you want to print (○ changes to ◉).

Note: For information on what you can print, refer to the top of this page.

5 Click **OK**.

QUICKLY PRINT ENTIRE WORKSHEET

■ To quickly print the worksheet displayed on the screen, click 🖶.

CENTER DATA ON A PAGE

You can center data horizontally and vertically between the margins on a page.

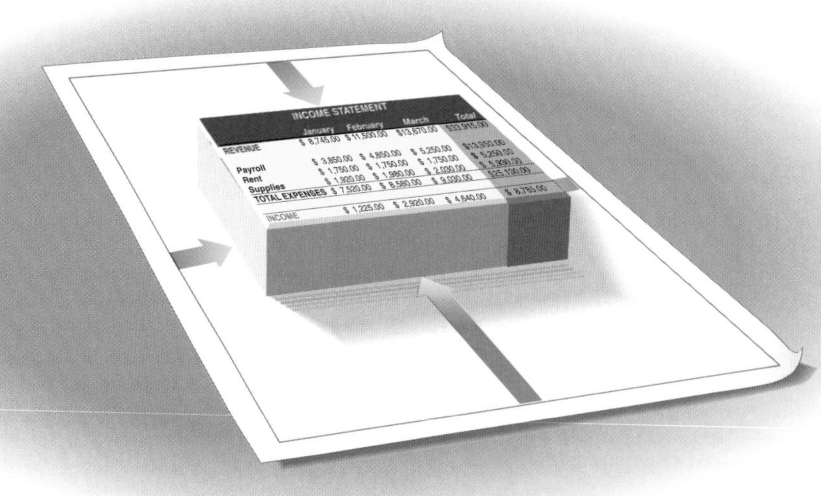

CENTER DATA ON A PAGE

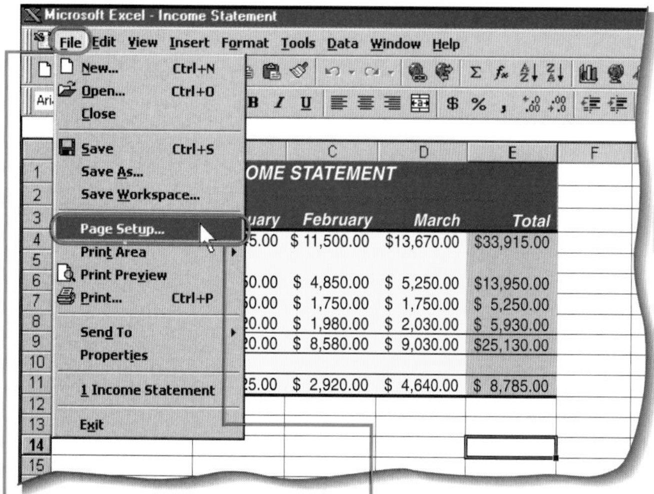

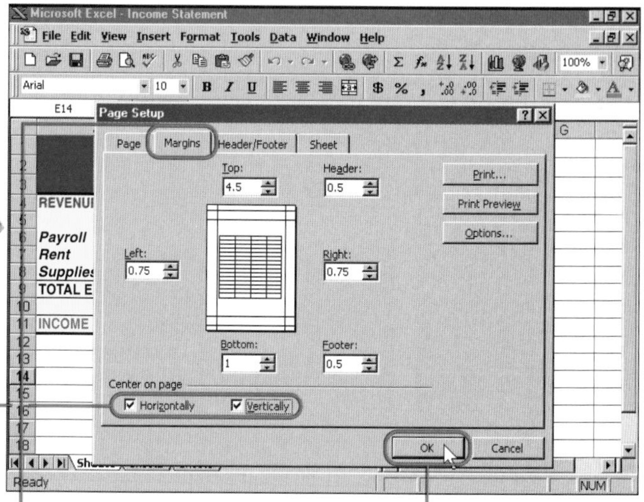

1 Click **File**.

2 Click **Page Setup**.

■ The **Page Setup** dialog box appears.

3 Click the **Margins** tab.

4 Click the way you want to center the data (☐ changes to ☑). You can select both center options if you wish.

5 Click **OK**.

CHANGE PAGE ORIENTATION

You can change the orientation of your printed worksheet.

The landscape orientation is ideal if you want a wide worksheet to fit on one page.

CHANGE PAGE ORIENTATION

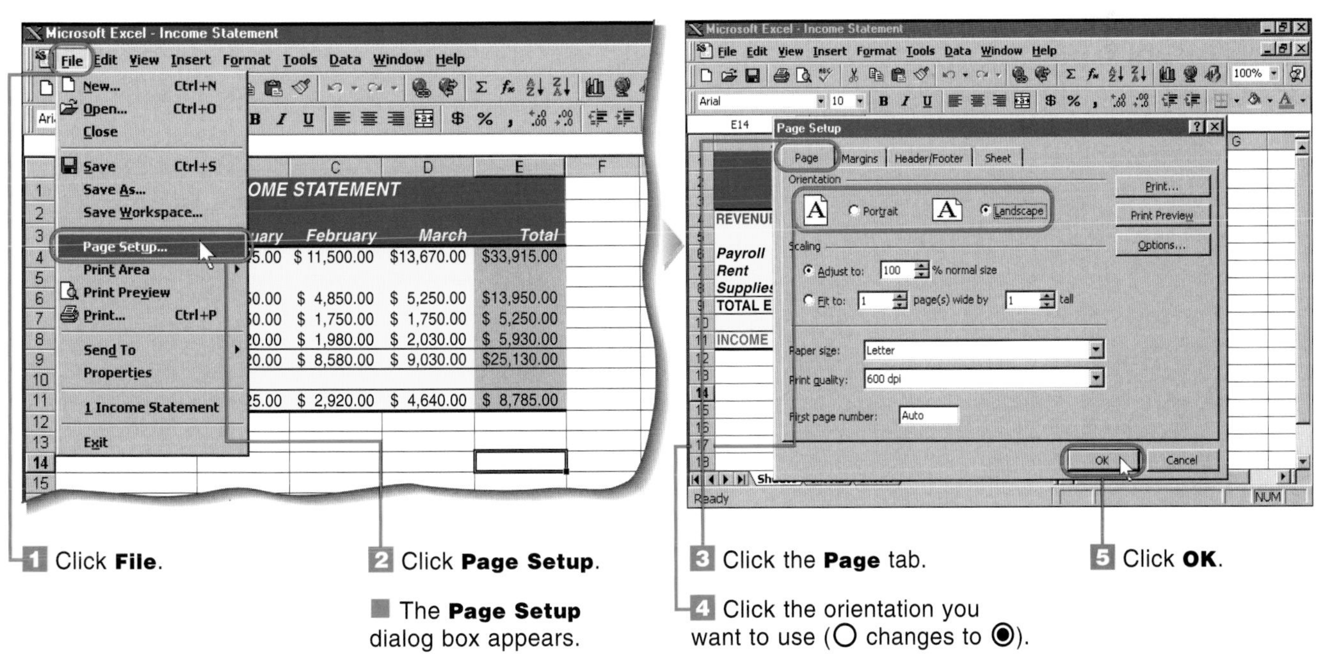

1 Click **File**.

2 Click **Page Setup**.

■ The **Page Setup** dialog box appears.

3 Click the **Page** tab.

4 Click the orientation you want to use (○ changes to ◉).

5 Click **OK**.

You can change the way your worksheet appears on a printed page.

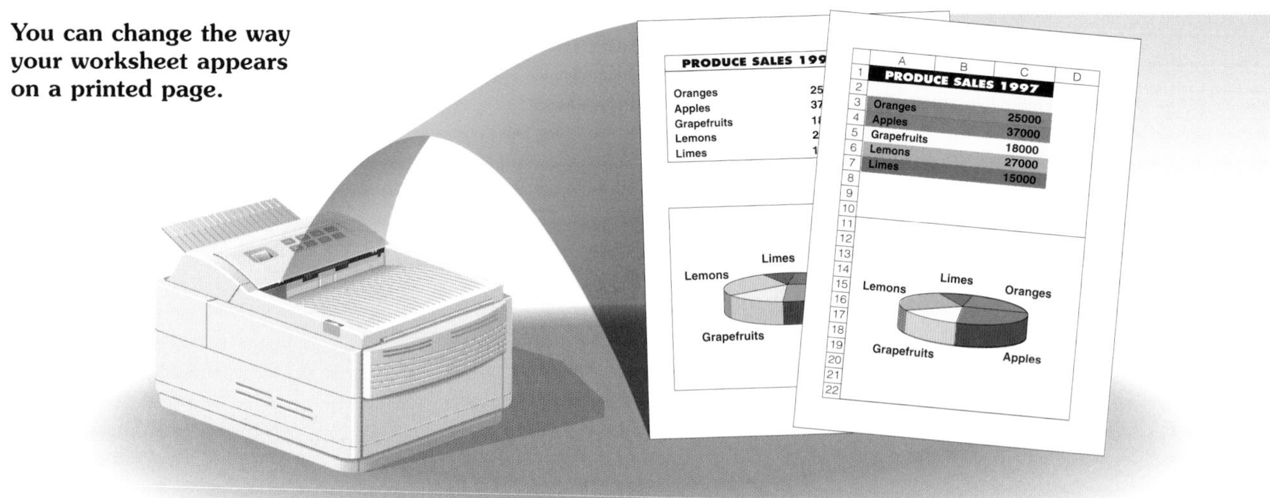

CHANGE PRINT OPTIONS

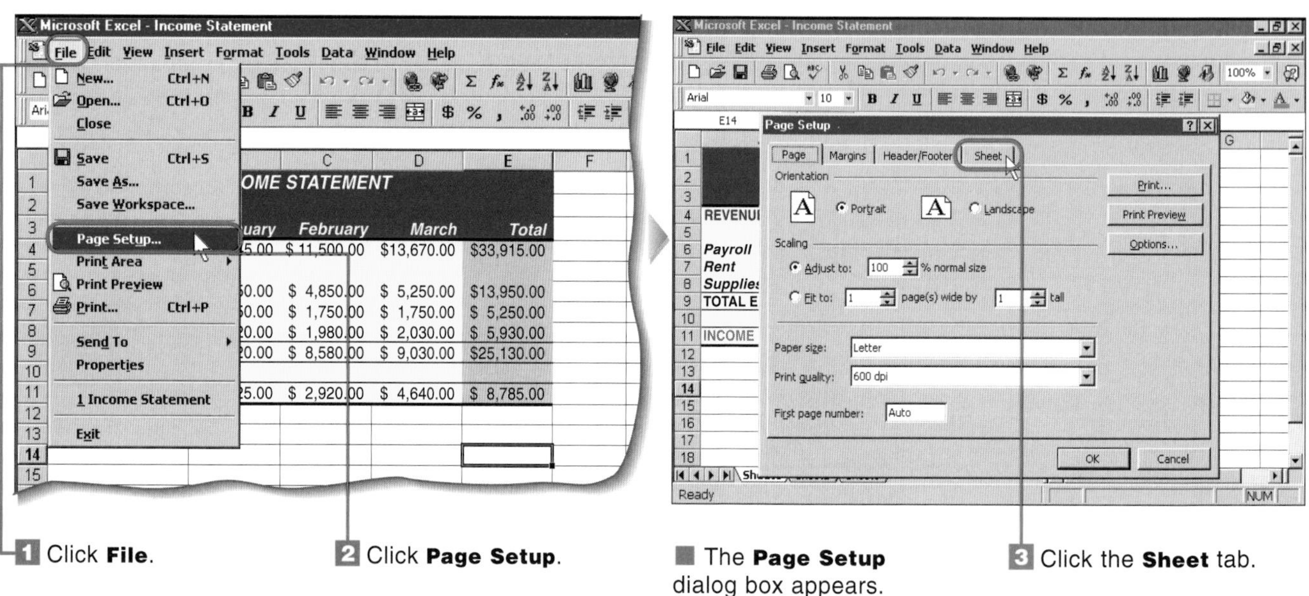

1 Click **File**.

2 Click **Page Setup**.

■ The **Page Setup** dialog box appears.

3 Click the **Sheet** tab.

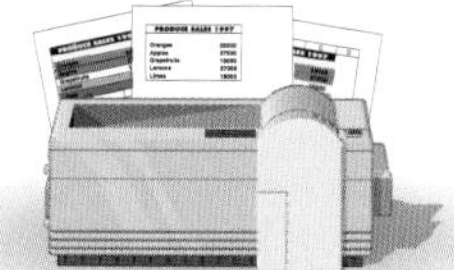

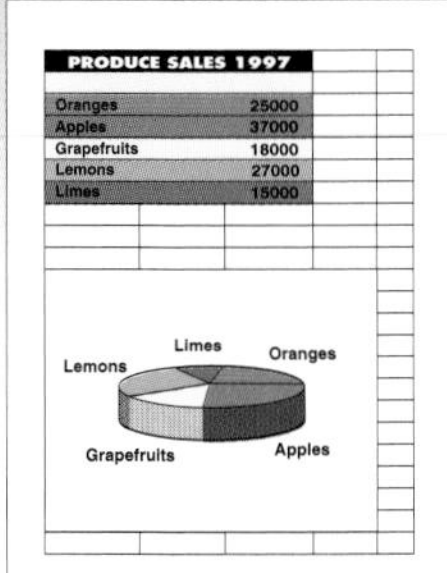

Gridlines
Prints lines around each cell in your worksheet.

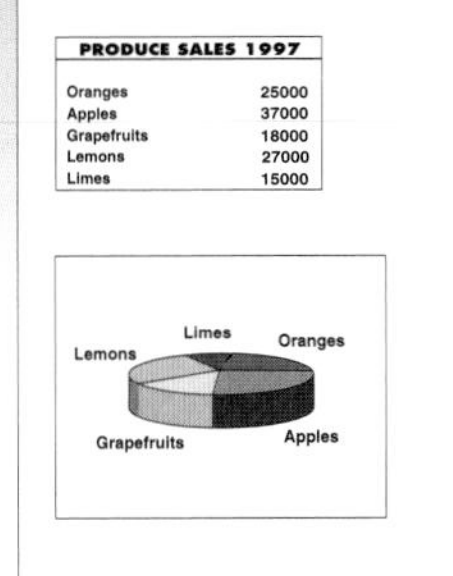

Black and white
Prints the worksheet in black and white. This can make a colored worksheet printed on a black-and-white printer easier to read.

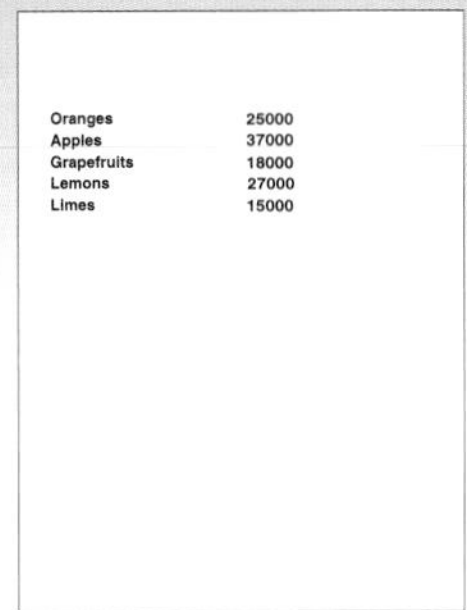

Draft quality
Does not print gridlines or most graphics to reduce printing time.

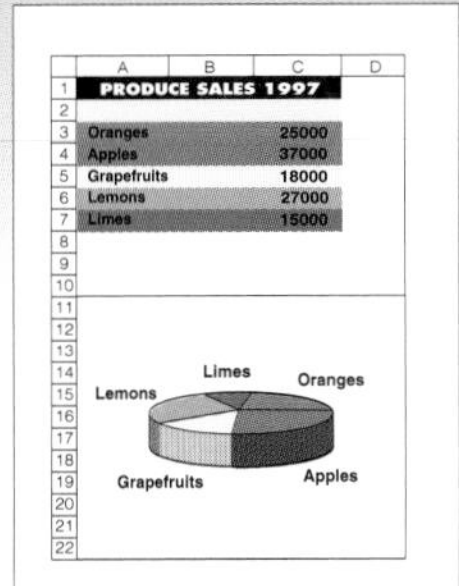

Row and column headings
Prints the row numbers and column letters.

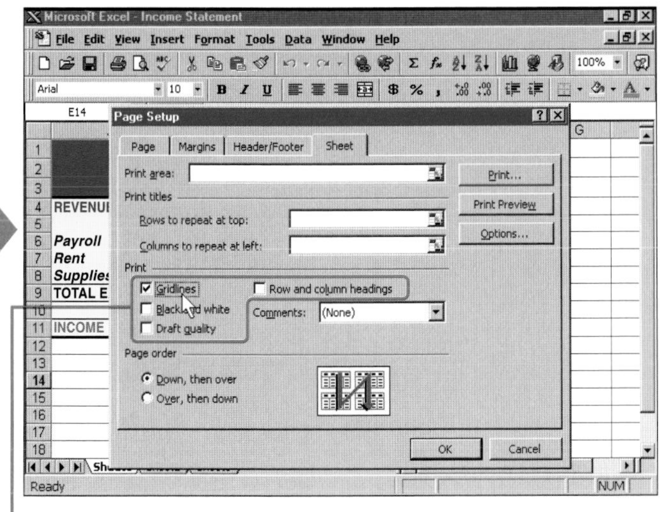

4 Click the print option you want to select (☐ changes to ☑).

Note: For information on the print options, refer to the top of this page.

5 Repeat step 4 for each print option you want to select.

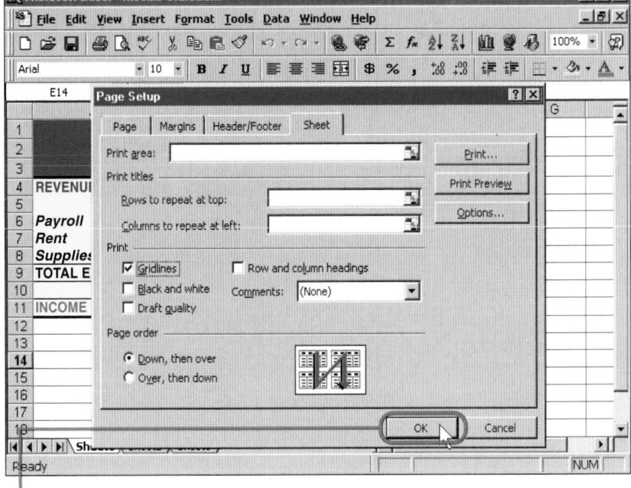

6 Click **OK**.

■ The print options you selected only change the way the worksheet appears on a printed page. The print options do not affect the way the worksheet appears on your screen.

INSERT A PAGE BREAK

If you want to start a new page at a specific place in your worksheet, you can add a page break. A page break defines where one page ends and another begins.

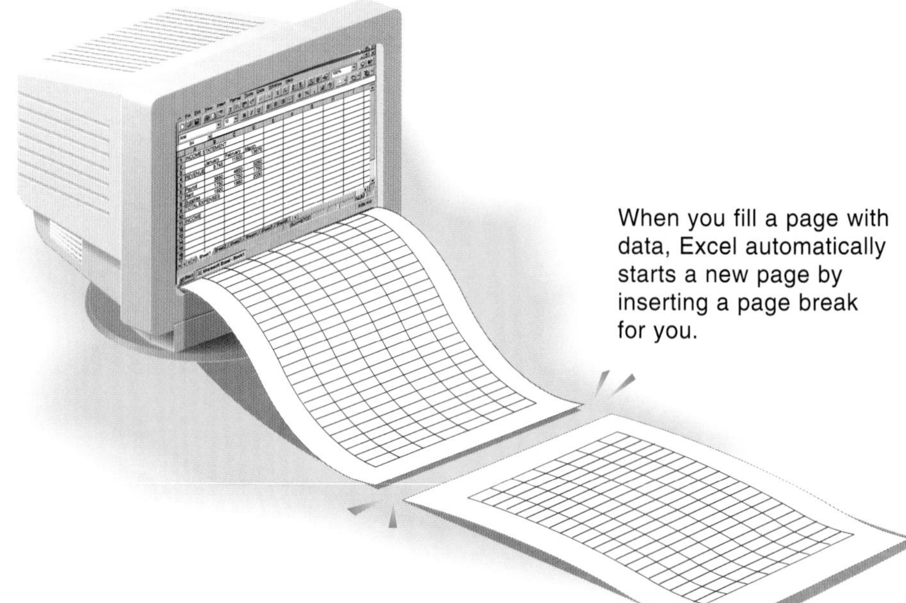

When you fill a page with data, Excel automatically starts a new page by inserting a page break for you.

INSERT A PAGE BREAK

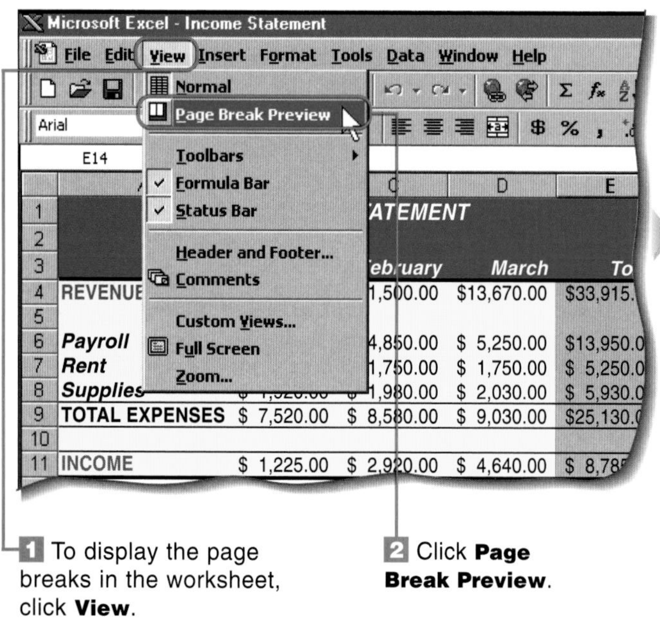

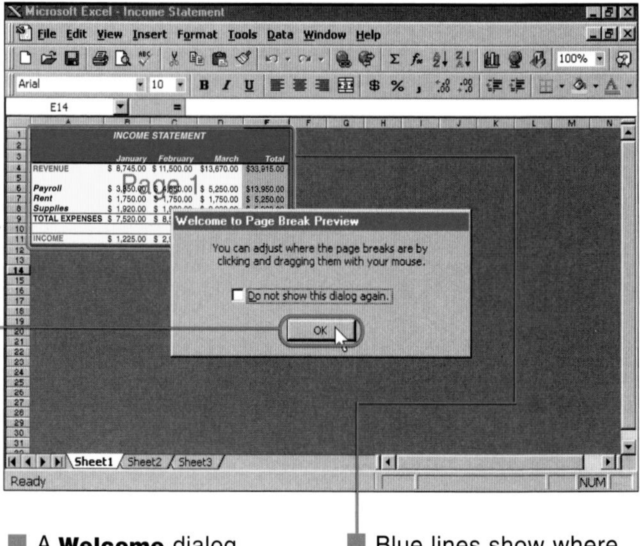

1 To display the page breaks in the worksheet, click **View**.

2 Click **Page Break Preview**.

■ A **Welcome** dialog box appears.

3 To close the dialog box, click **OK**.

■ Blue lines show where page breaks currently occur in the worksheet.

*Note: To return to the Normal view at any time, repeat steps 1 and 2, selecting **Normal** in step 2.*

How can I move a page break?

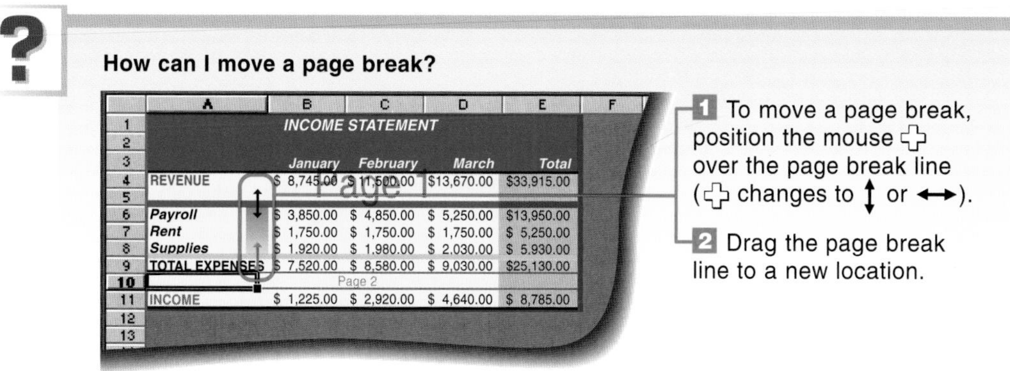

1 To move a page break, position the mouse ✥ over the page break line (✥ changes to ↕ or ↔).

2 Drag the page break line to a new location.

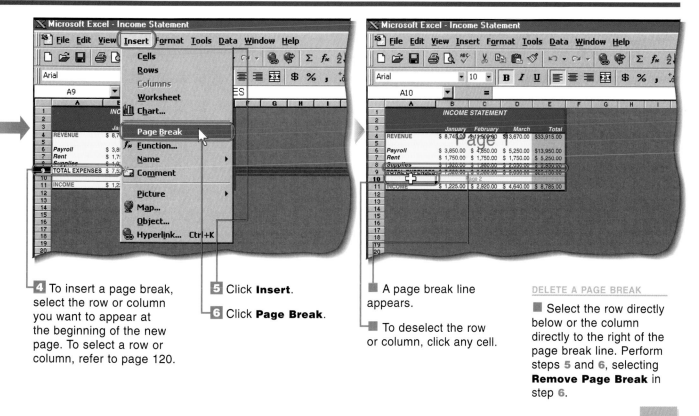

4 To insert a page break, select the row or column you want to appear at the beginning of the new page. To select a row or column, refer to page 120.

5 Click **Insert**.

6 Click **Page Break**.

■ A page break line appears.

■ To deselect the row or column, click any cell.

DELETE A PAGE BREAK

■ Select the row directly below or the column directly to the right of the page break line. Perform steps 5 and 6, selecting **Remove Page Break** in step 6.

SWITCH BETWEEN WORKSHEETS

The worksheet displayed on your screen is one of several worksheets in a workbook. You can easily switch between the worksheets.

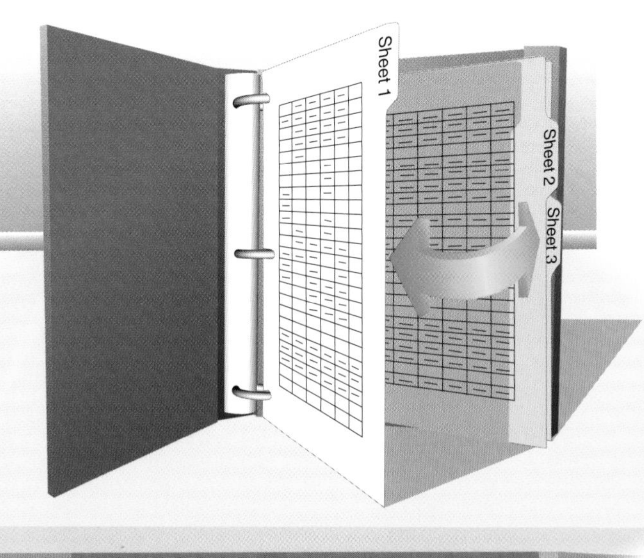

SWITCH BETWEEN WORKSHEETS

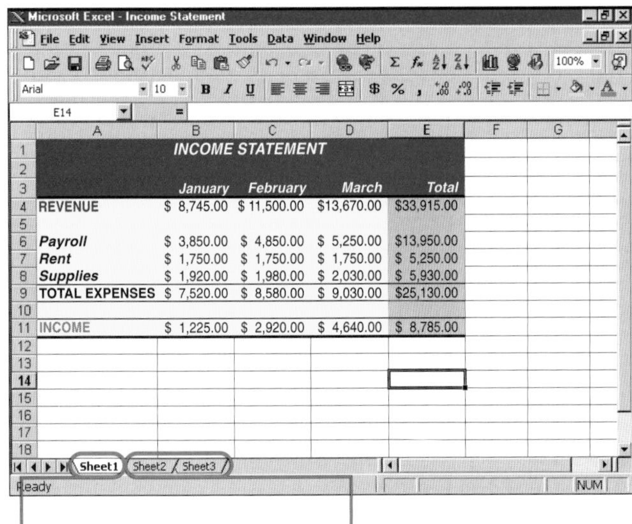

■ The worksheet displayed on the screen has a white tab.

■ The other worksheets in the workbook have gray tabs. The contents of these worksheets are hidden.

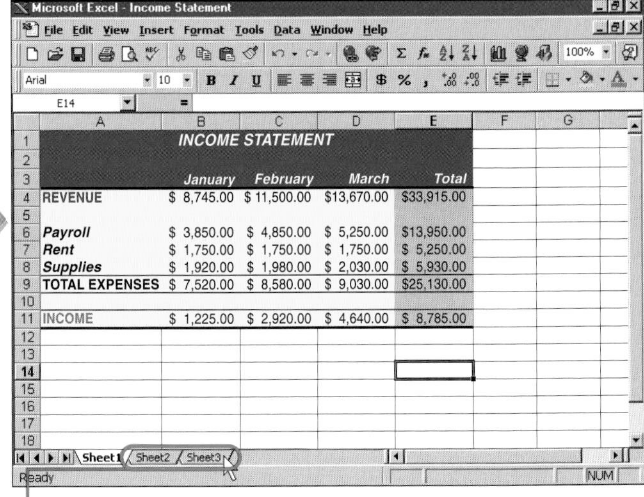

1 To display the contents of a worksheet, click the tab of the worksheet.

? Why would I need more than one worksheet?

Worksheets allow you to keep related information in a single file, called a workbook. For example, information for each division of a company can be stored on a separate worksheet in one workbook.

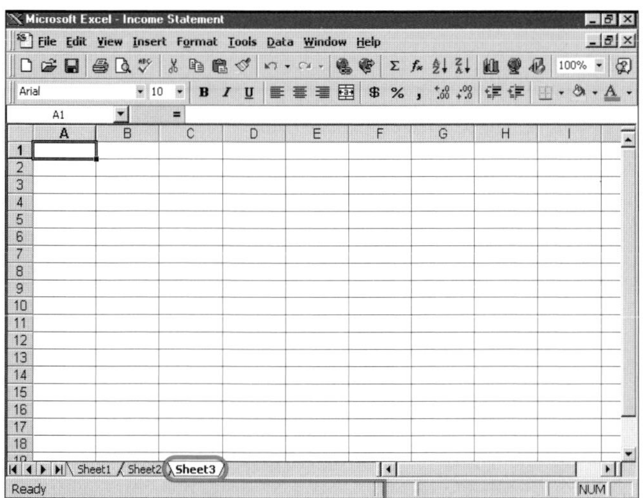

■ The contents of the worksheet appear. The contents of the other worksheets in the workbook are hidden.

■ The worksheet you selected now has a white tab.

BROWSE THROUGH TABS

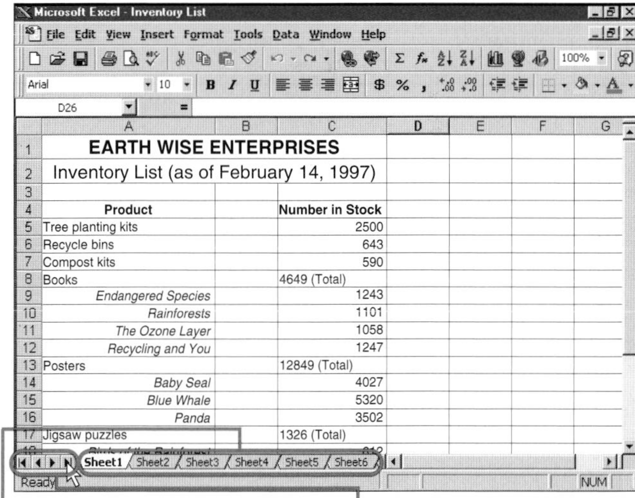

■ If you have many worksheets in your workbook, you may not be able to see all the tabs.

Note: To insert additional worksheets, refer to page 196.

1 To browse through the tabs, click one of the following options.

- Display first tab
- Display tab to the left
- Display tab to the right
- Display last tab

INSERT A WORKSHEET

You can easily insert a new worksheet to add related information to a workbook.

INSERT A WORKSHEET

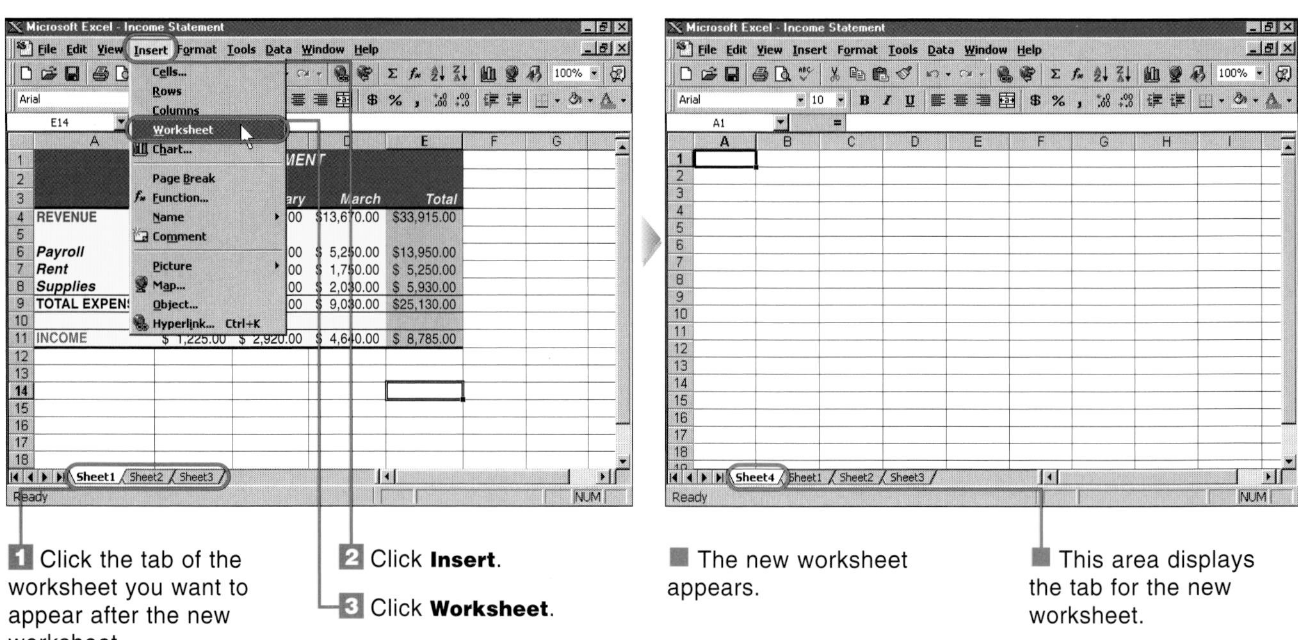

1 Click the tab of the worksheet you want to appear after the new worksheet.

2 Click **Insert**.

3 Click **Worksheet**.

■ The new worksheet appears.

■ This area displays the tab for the new worksheet.

DELETE A WORKSHEET

You can permanently remove a worksheet you no longer need.

DELETE A WORKSHEET

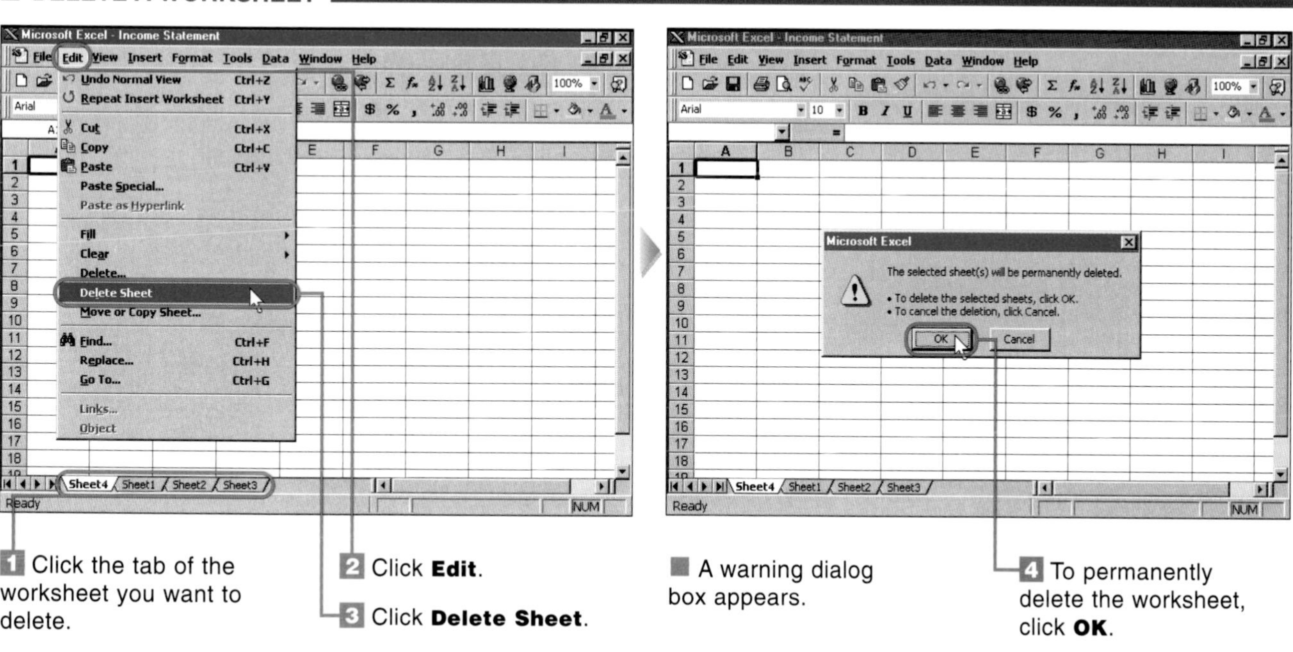

1 Click the tab of the worksheet you want to delete.

2 Click **Edit**.

3 Click **Delete Sheet**.

■ A warning dialog box appears.

4 To permanently delete the worksheet, click **OK**.

RENAME A WORKSHEET

You can give each worksheet in a workbook a descriptive name. This helps you remember where you stored your data.

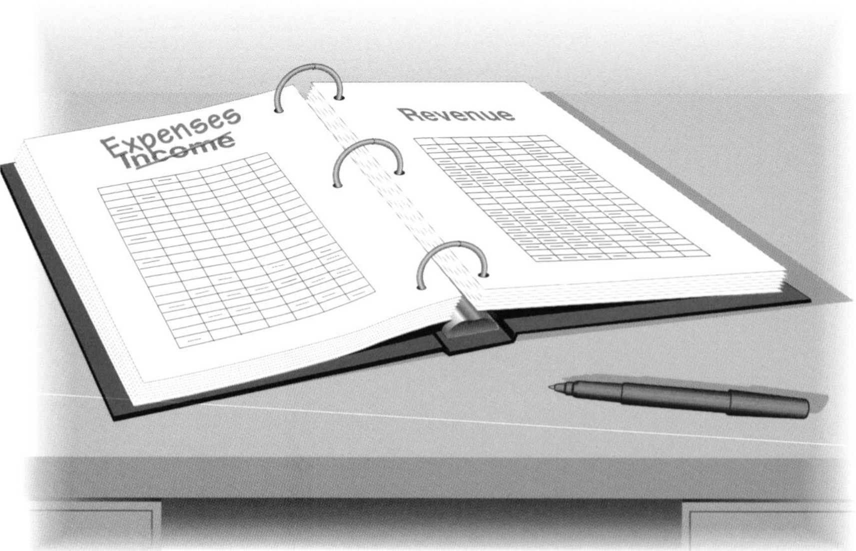

RENAME A WORKSHEET

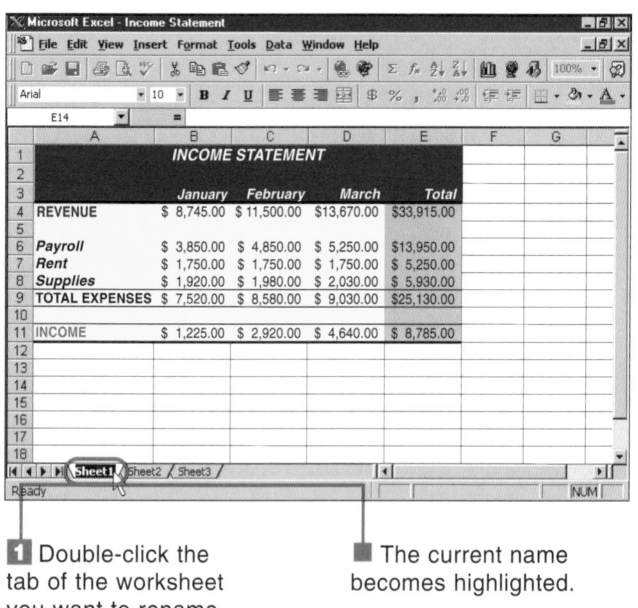

1 Double-click the tab of the worksheet you want to rename.

■ The current name becomes highlighted.

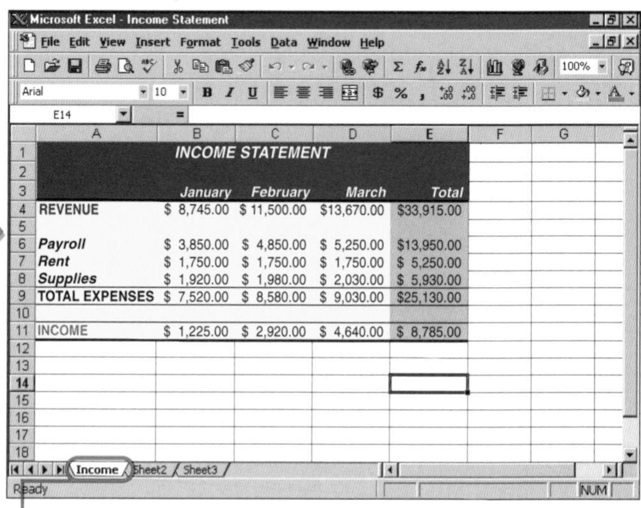

2 Type a new name and then press Enter on your keyboard. A worksheet name can contain up to 31 characters, including spaces.

MOVE A WORKSHEET

You can reorganize information by moving a worksheet to a new location in a workbook.

MOVE A WORKSHEET

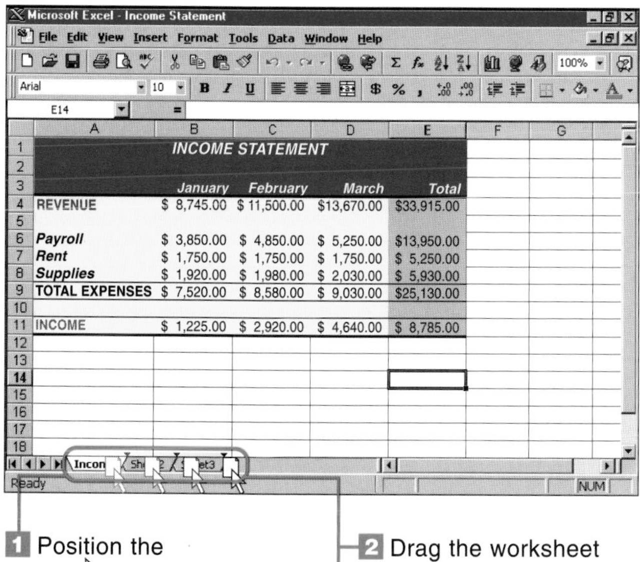

1 Position the mouse over the tab of the worksheet you want to move.

2 Drag the worksheet to a new location.

■ An arrow (▾) shows where the worksheet will appear.

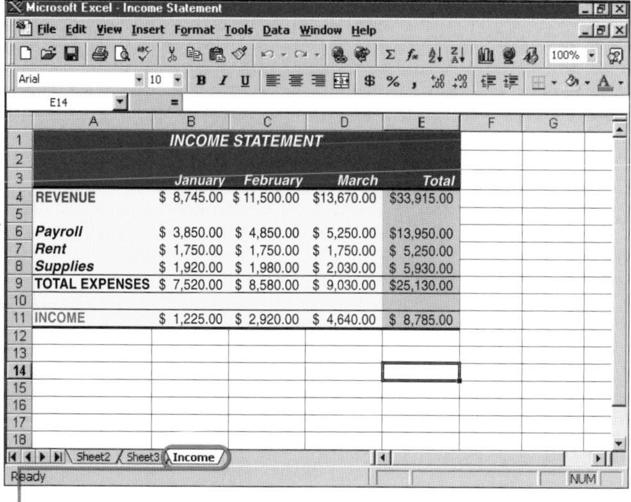

■ The worksheet appears in the new location.

CREATE A CHART

You can graphically display your worksheet data in a chart.

CREATE A CHART

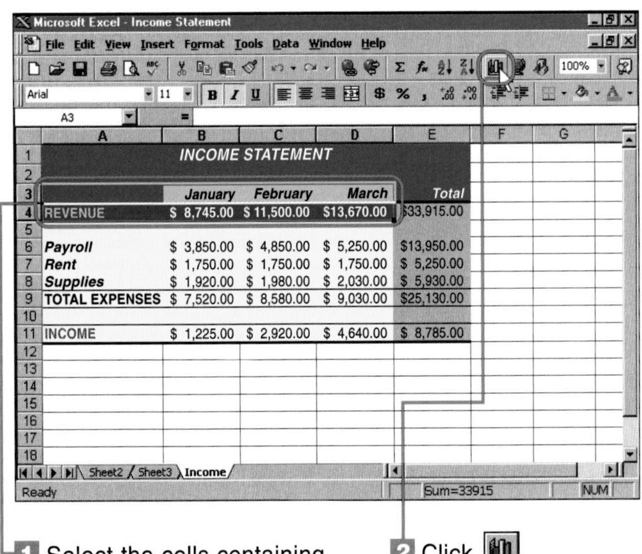

1 Select the cells containing the data you want to display in a chart, including the text that describes the data. To select cells, refer to page 120.

2 Click [chart wizard button].

■ The **Chart Wizard** dialog box appears.

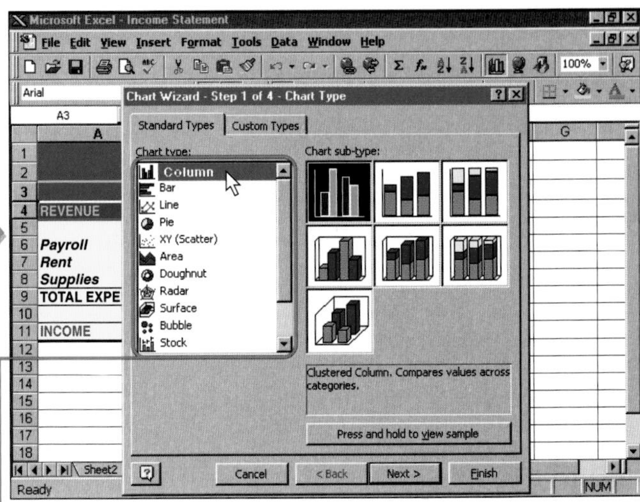

3 Click the type of chart you want to create.

Note: You can easily change the type of chart later on. For information, refer to page 204.

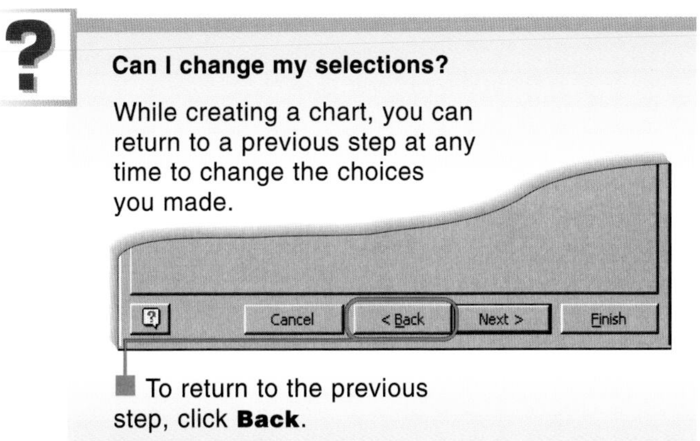

Can I change my selections?

While creating a chart, you can return to a previous step at any time to change the choices you made.

■ To return to the previous step, click **Back**.

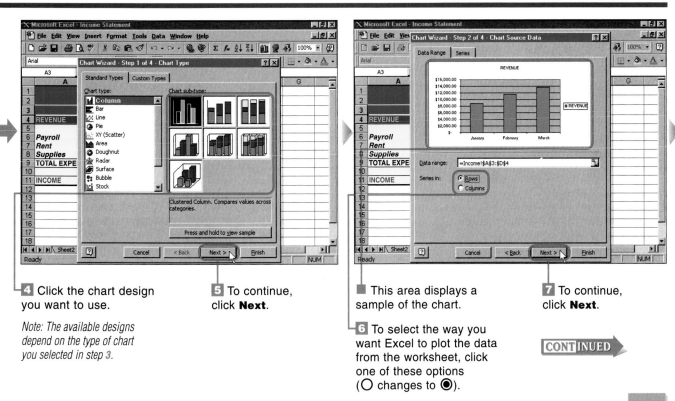

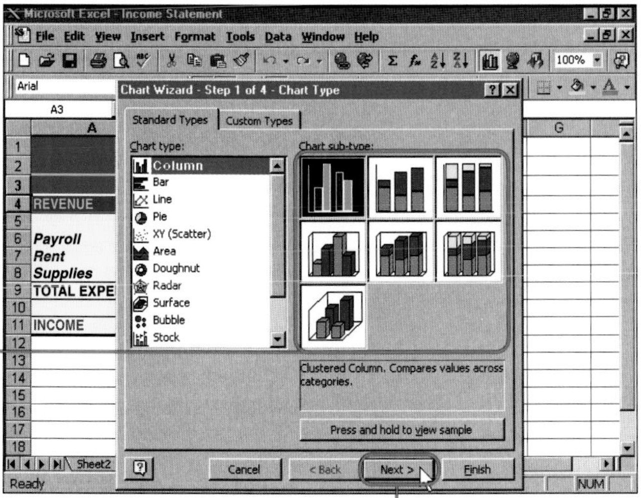

4 Click the chart design you want to use.

Note: The available designs depend on the type of chart you selected in step 3.

5 To continue, click **Next**.

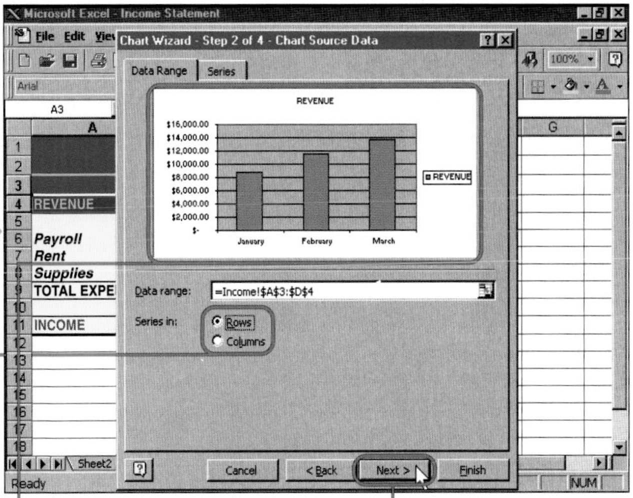

■ This area displays a sample of the chart.

6 To select the way you want Excel to plot the data from the worksheet, click one of these options (○ changes to ◉).

7 To continue, click **Next**.

CONTINUED

You can add titles to the chart to make the chart easier to understand.

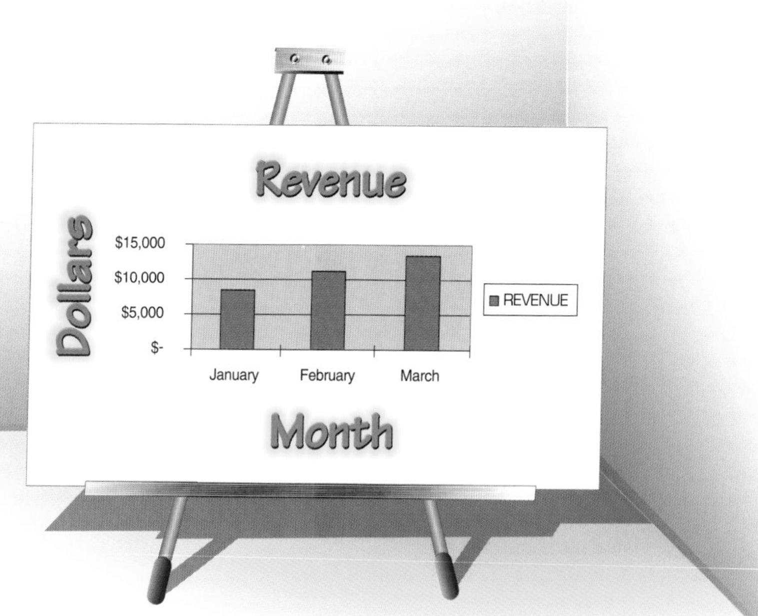

CREATE A CHART (CONTINUED)

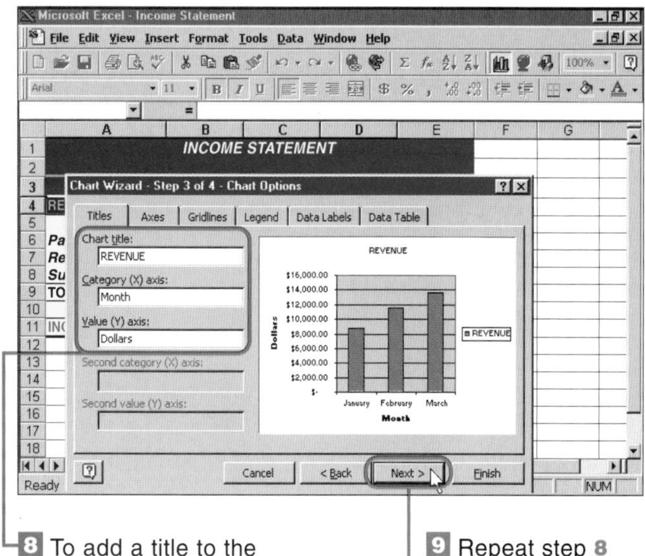

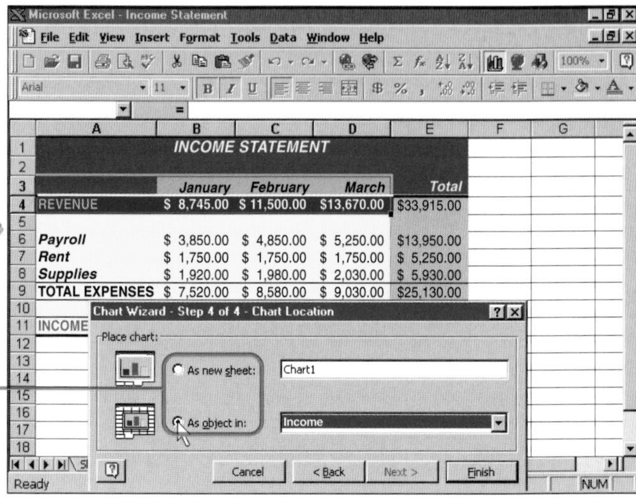

8 To add a title to the chart, click the box for the title you want to add. Then type the title.

9 Repeat step 8 for each title you want to add.

10 To continue, click **Next**.

11 To choose where you want to display the chart, click one of these options (○ changes to ◉).

As new sheet

Display chart on its own sheet, called a chart sheet.

As object in

Display chart on the same worksheet as the data.

What happens if I change data used in a chart?

If you change data used in a chart, Excel will automatically update the chart.

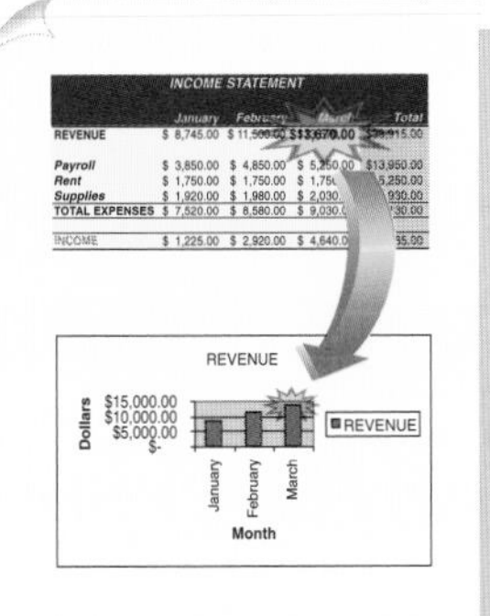

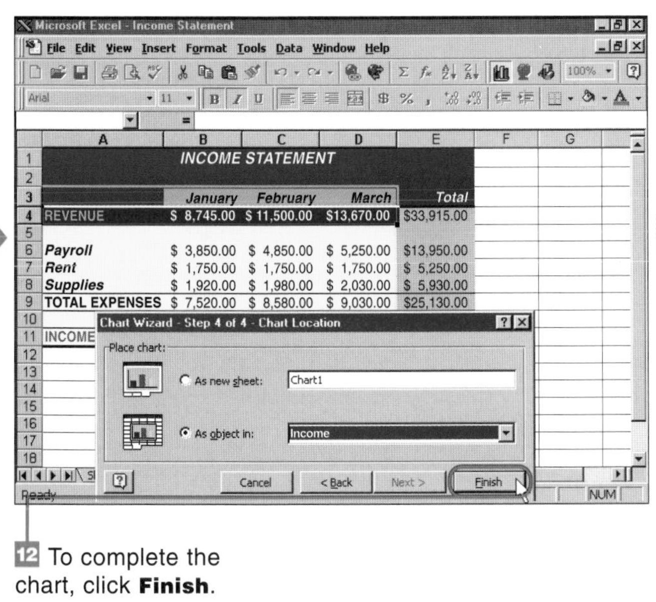

12 To complete the chart, click **Finish**.

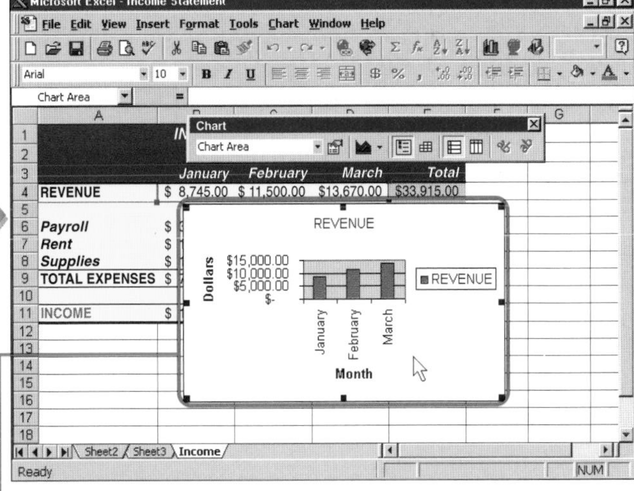

■ The chart appears.

DELETE A CHART

1 Click a blank area in the chart. Handles (■) appear around the chart.

2 Press Delete on your keyboard.

Note: To delete a chart displayed on a chart sheet, follow the steps to delete a worksheet. To delete a worksheet, refer to page 197.

CHANGE CHART TYPE

After you create a chart, you can select a different type of chart that will better suit your data.

CHANGE CHART TYPE

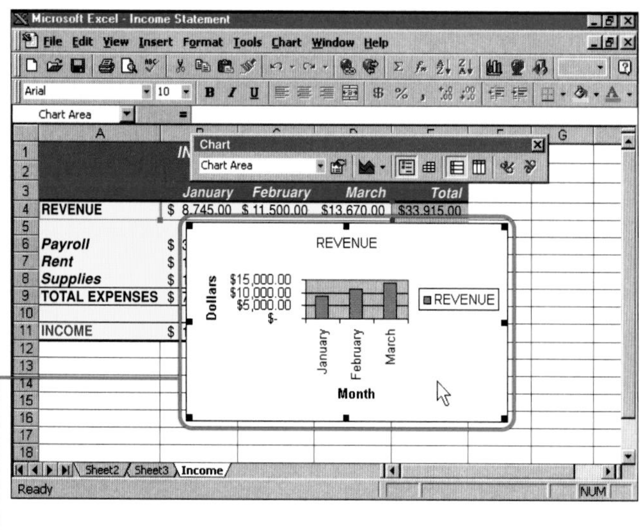

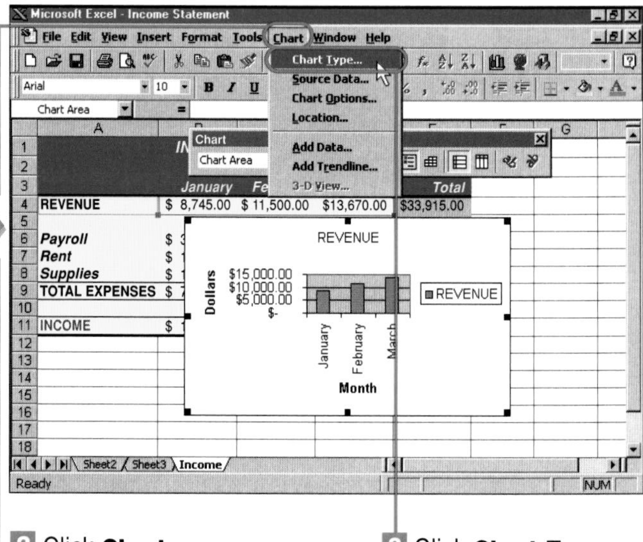

1 To change a chart on a worksheet, click a blank area in the chart. Handles (■) appear around the chart.

■ To change a chart on a chart sheet, click the tab for the chart sheet.

2 Click **Chart**.

3 Click **Chart Type**.

■ The **Chart Type** dialog box appears.

What type of chart should I choose?

The type of chart you should choose depends on your data. For example, area, column and line charts are ideal for showing changes to values over time, whereas pie charts are ideal for showing percentages.

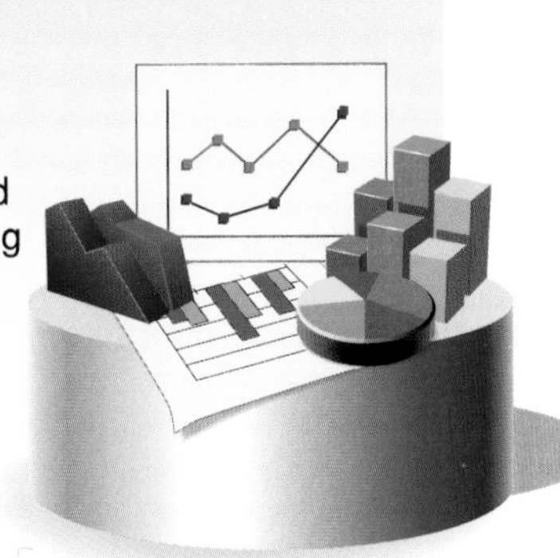

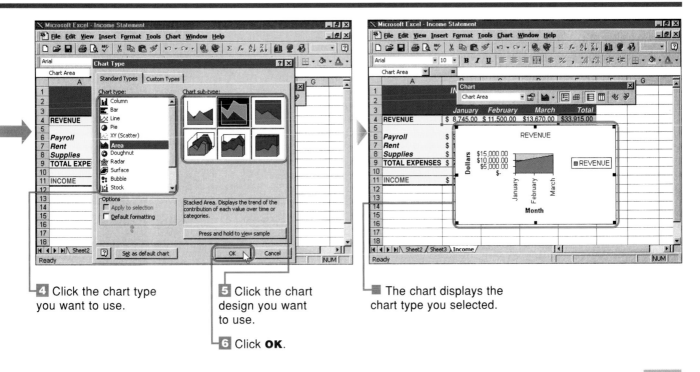

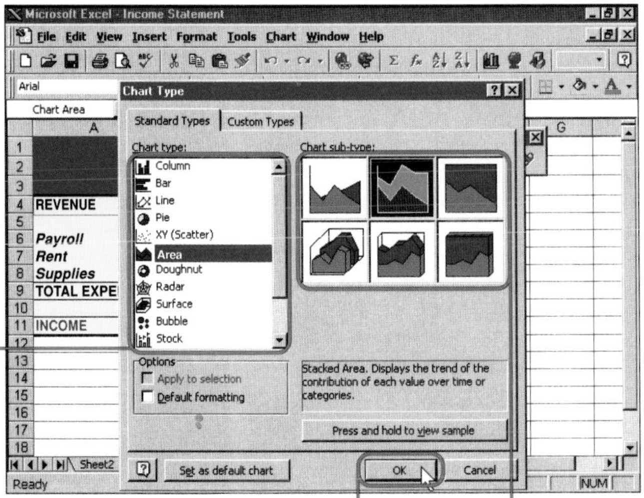

4 Click the chart type you want to use.

5 Click the chart design you want to use.

6 Click **OK**.

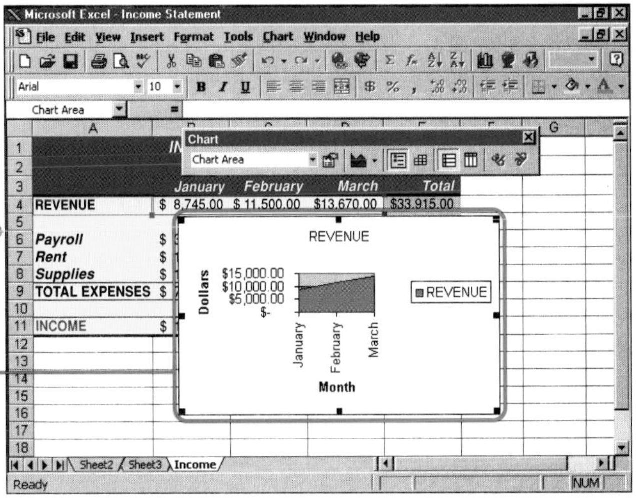

■ The chart displays the chart type you selected.

MOVE OR RESIZE A CHART

After you create a chart, you can change the location and size of the chart.

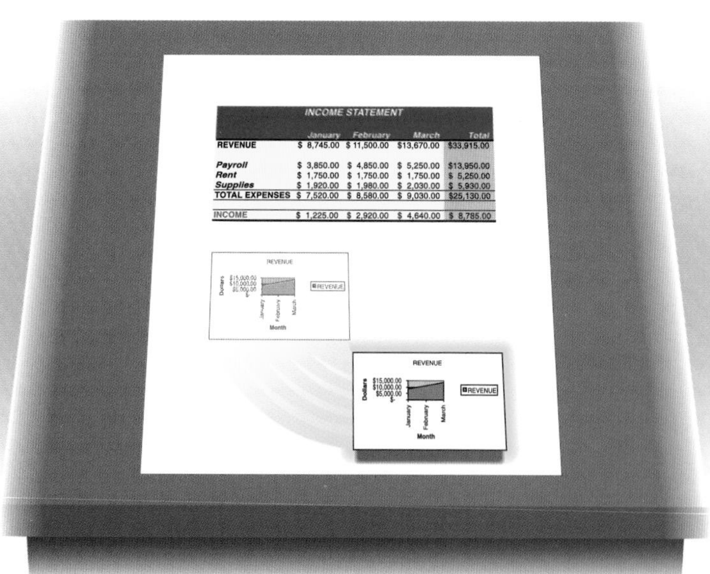

MOVE A CHART

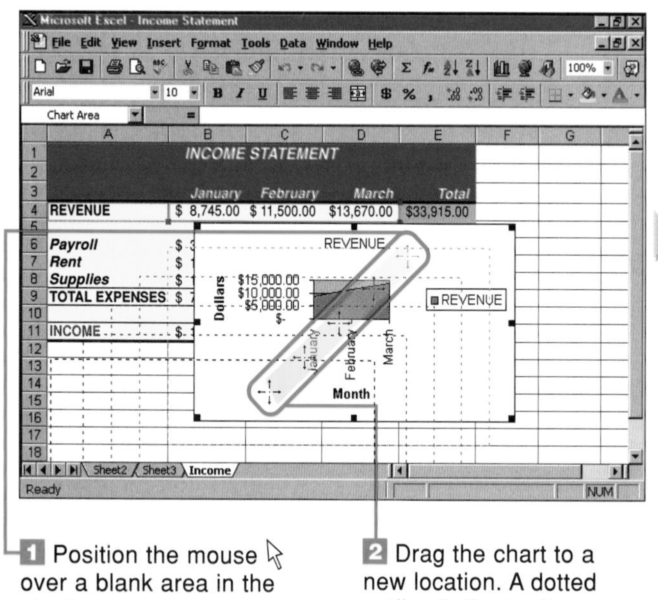

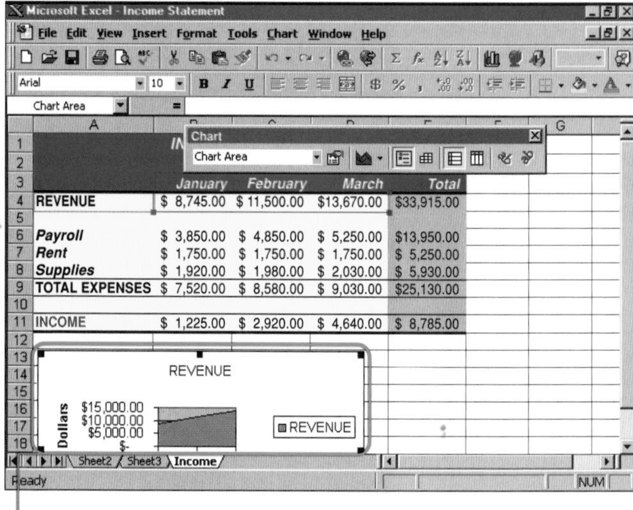

1 Position the mouse over a blank area in the chart.

2 Drag the chart to a new location. A dotted outline indicates the new location.

■ The chart appears in the new location.

What are the handles (■) that appear around a chart?

The handles around a chart let you change the size of the chart.

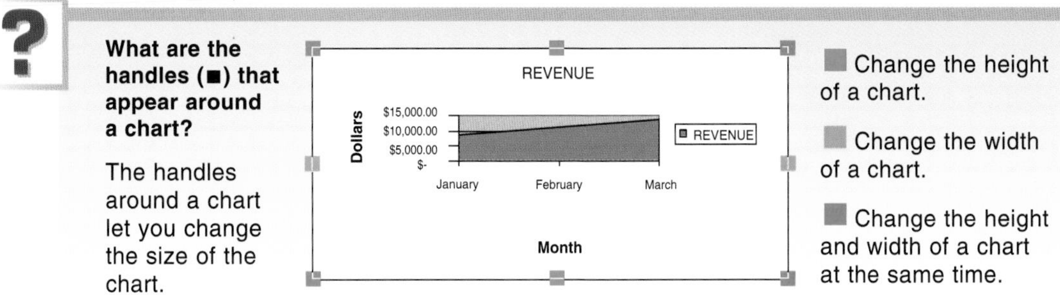

■ Change the height of a chart.

■ Change the width of a chart.

■ Change the height and width of a chart at the same time.

RESIZE A CHART

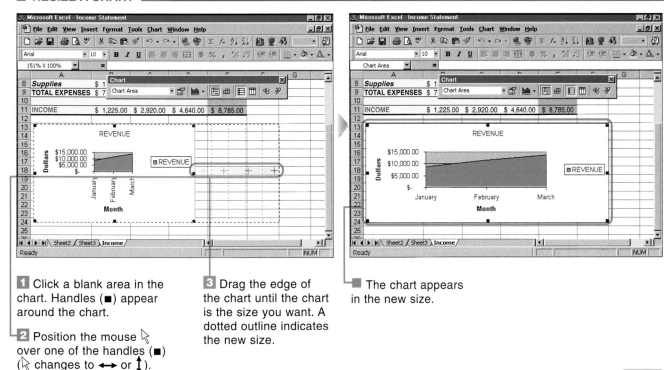

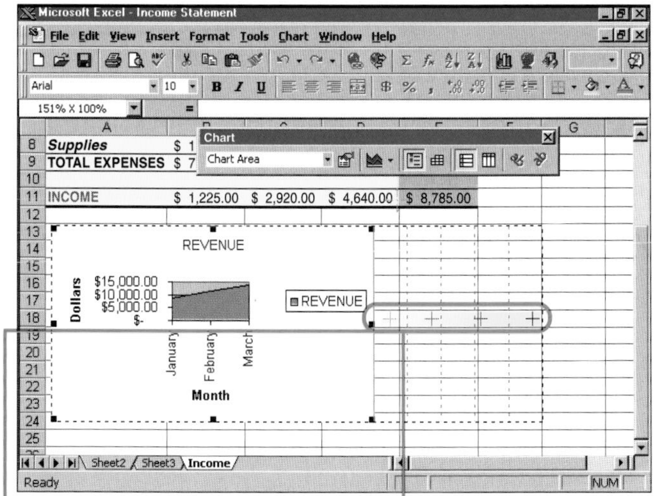

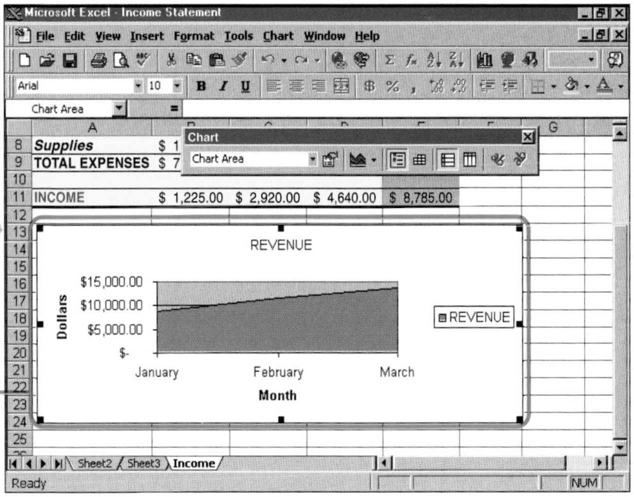

1 Click a blank area in the chart. Handles (■) appear around the chart.

2 Position the mouse over one of the handles (■) (changes to ↔ or ↕).

3 Drag the edge of the chart until the chart is the size you want. A dotted outline indicates the new size.

■ The chart appears in the new size.

PRINT A CHART

You can print your chart with the worksheet data or on its own page.

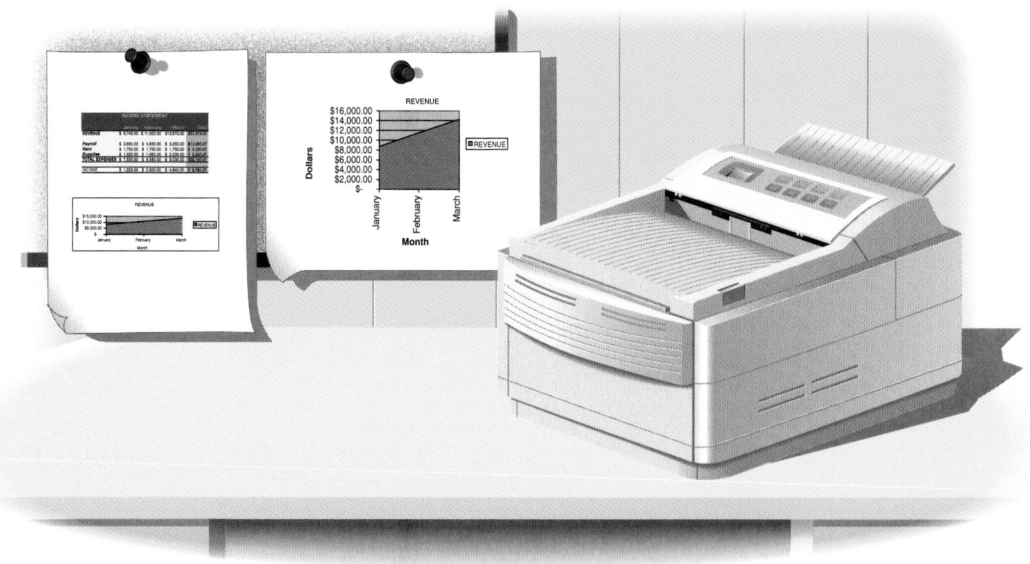

PRINT A CHART WITH WORKSHEET DATA

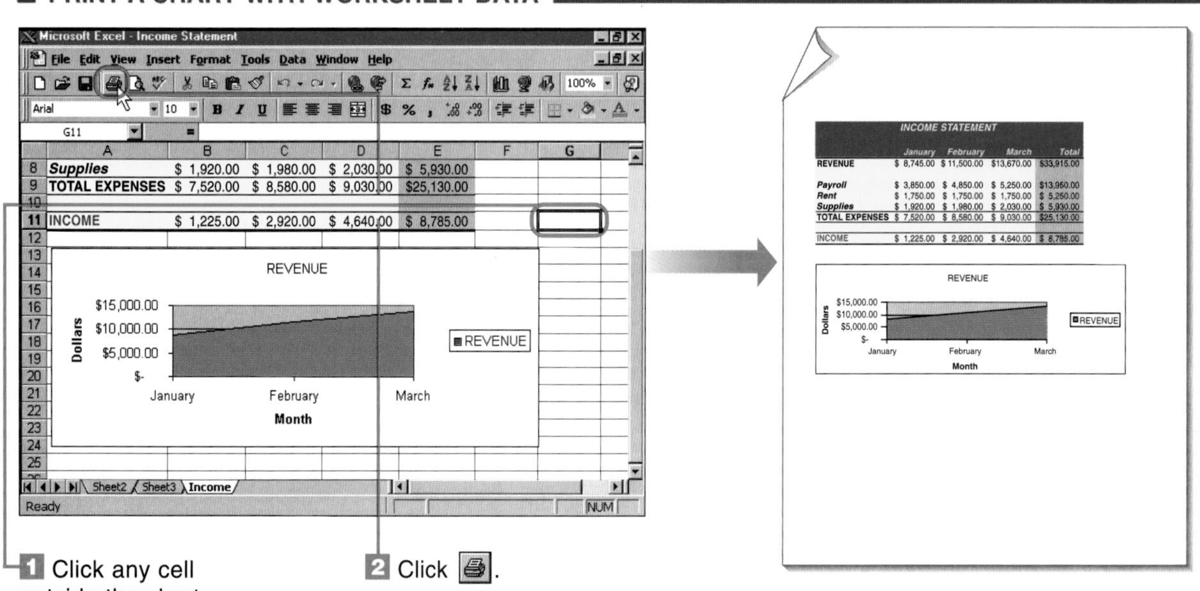

1 Click any cell outside the chart.

2 Click the print button.

Note: For more information on printing, refer to pages 182 to 193.

Can I see what my chart will look like when printed?

You can preview your chart to see what the chart will look like when printed. To preview a chart, refer to page 182.

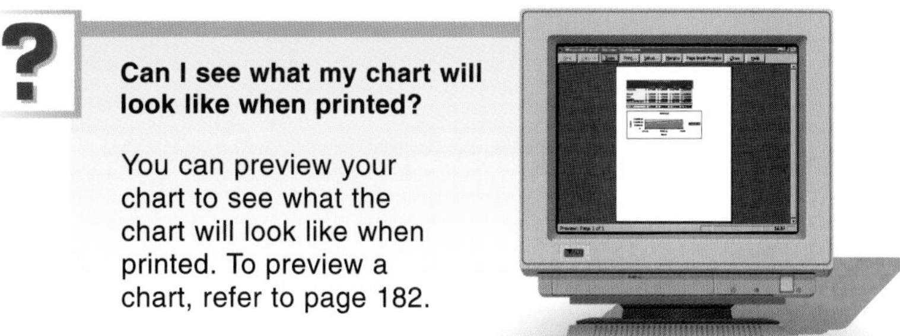

PRINT A CHART ON ITS OWN PAGE

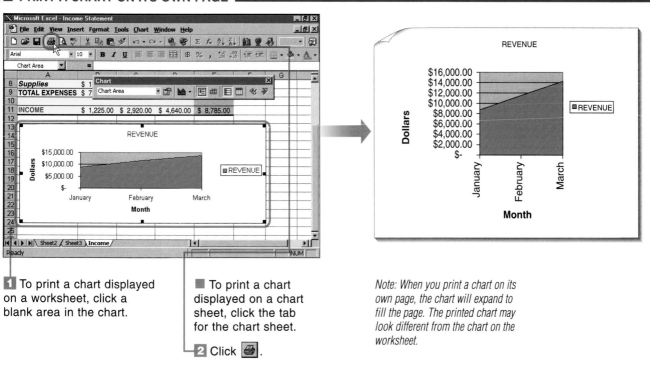

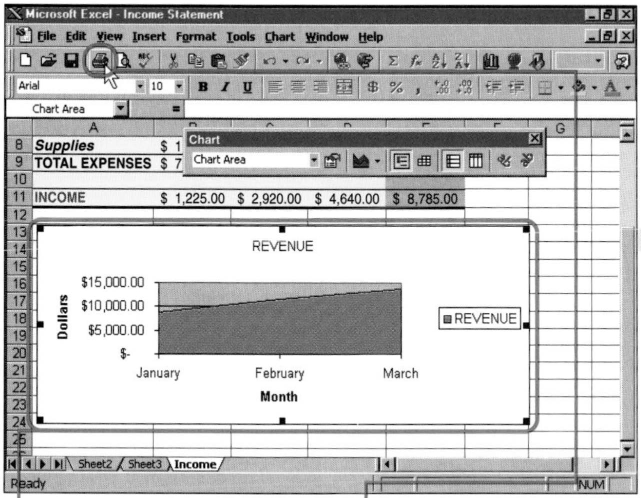

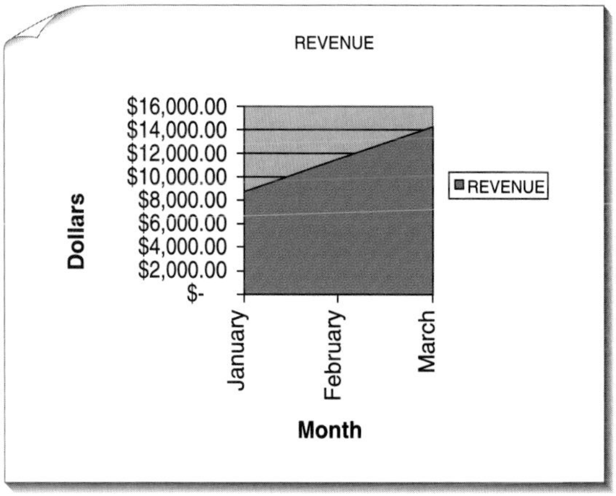

1 To print a chart displayed on a worksheet, click a blank area in the chart.

■ To print a chart displayed on a chart sheet, click the tab for the chart sheet.

2 Click 🖨.

Note: When you print a chart on its own page, the chart will expand to fill the page. The printed chart may look different from the chart on the worksheet.

Marketing Plan
• Advertising
– television
– Internet
• In-store Displays
• International Toy Trac

PowerPoint

Includes:

1 Getting Started
This chapter teaches you the basic skills you need to organize and design professional presentations.

2 Edit Slides
Learn how to edit the text in your presentation.

3 Add Objects to Slides
Make your presentation more interesting and entertaining by adding clip art, pictures and charts to your slides.

4 Enhance a Presentation
PowerPoint offers many ways to enhance your presentation, from emphasizing text to animating objects on your slides.

5 Fine-Tune a Presentation
This chapter will help you add the final touches to your presentation before you deliver it to an audience.

INTRODUCTION TO POWERPOINT

PowerPoint helps you to organize and design professional presentations.

WAYS TO USE POWERPOINT

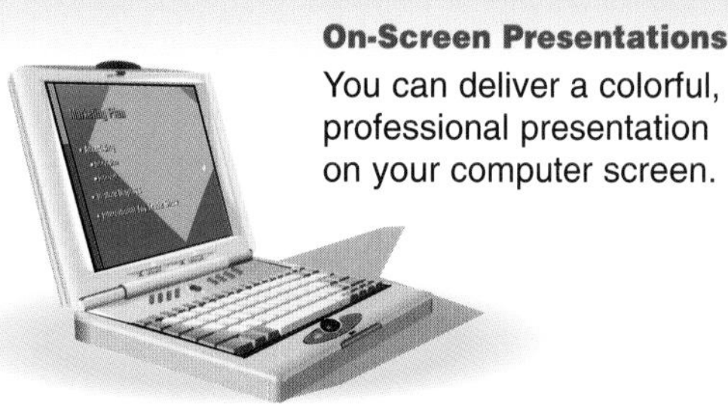

On-Screen Presentations

You can deliver a colorful, professional presentation on your computer screen.

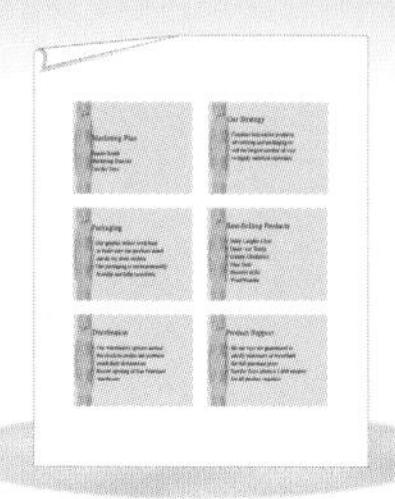

Handouts

You can print handouts to help the audience follow your presentation. Handouts contain copies of your slides.

35mm Slides or Overheads

You can create 35mm slides or overhead transparencies for presenting your ideas to a large audience.

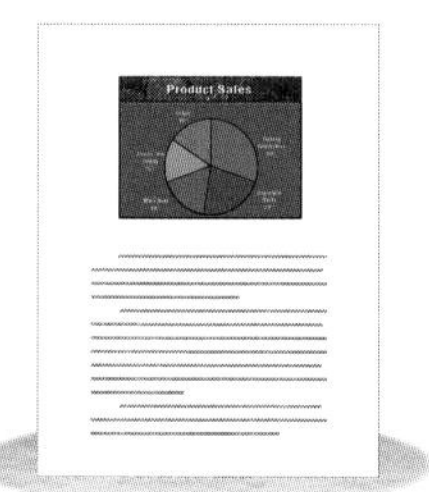

Speaker Notes

You can create speaker notes to help you deliver your presentation. Speaker notes contain copies of your slides along with all the ideas you want to discuss.

START POWERPOINT

You can start PowerPoint to create a professional presentation.

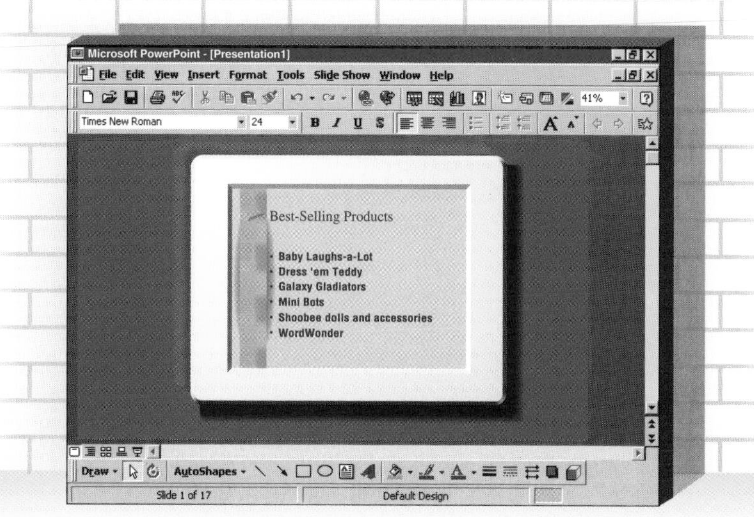

START POWERPOINT

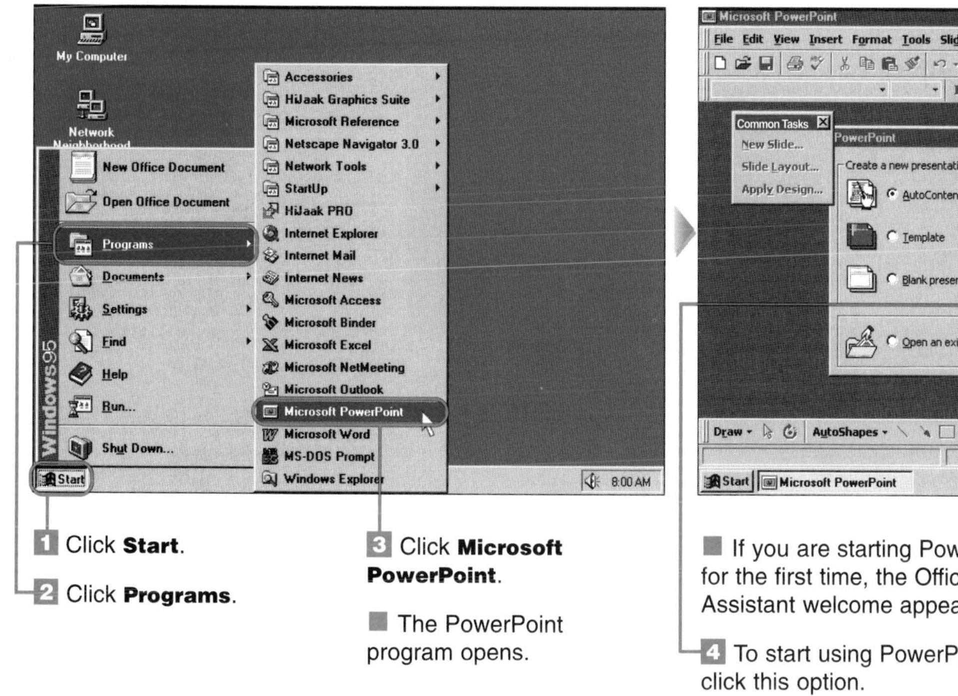

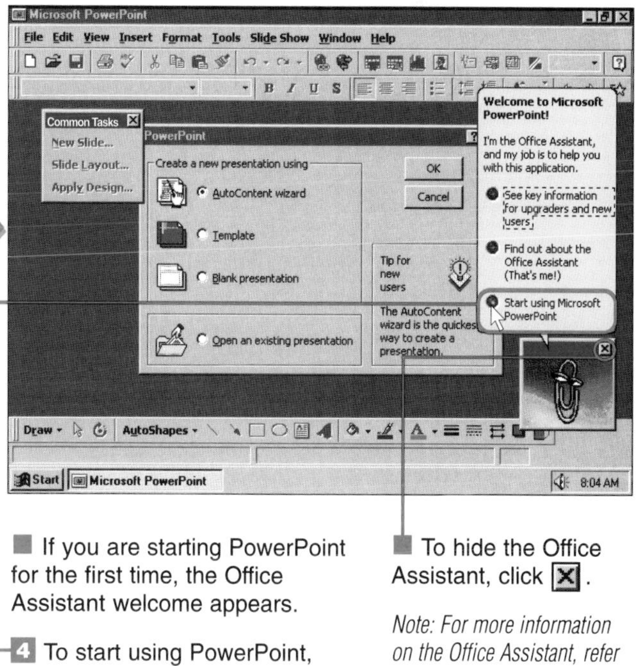

1 Click **Start**.

2 Click **Programs**.

3 Click **Microsoft PowerPoint**.

■ The PowerPoint program opens.

■ If you are starting PowerPoint for the first time, the Office Assistant welcome appears.

4 To start using PowerPoint, click this option.

■ To hide the Office Assistant, click ☒.

Note: For more information on the Office Assistant, refer to page 12.

CREATE A PRESENTATION

You can use the AutoContent wizard to quickly create a presentation.

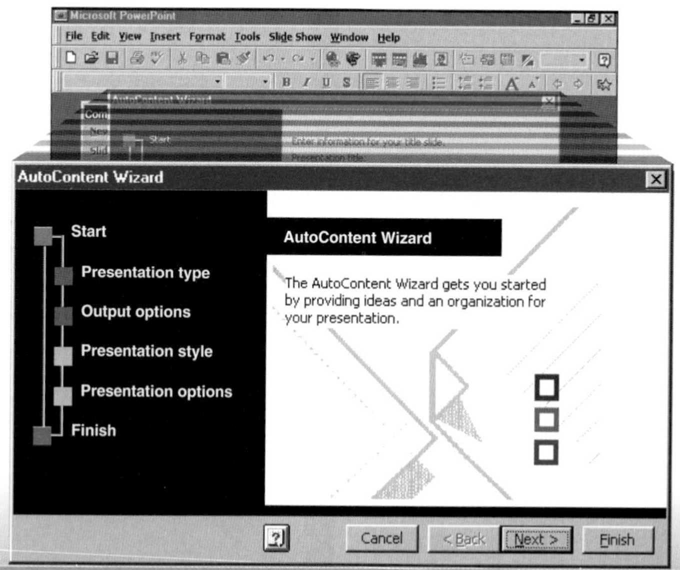

The wizard will ask you a series of questions and then set up a presentation based on your answers.

CREATE A PRESENTATION

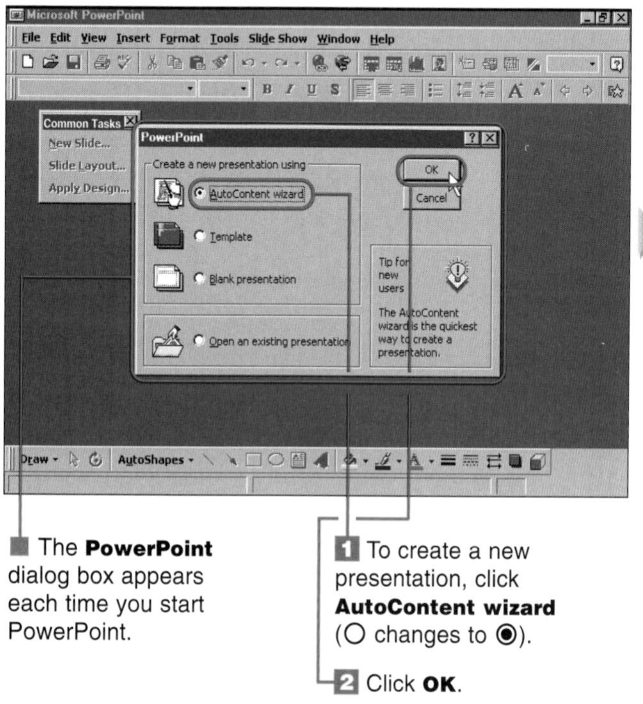

■ The **PowerPoint** dialog box appears each time you start PowerPoint.

1 To create a new presentation, click **AutoContent wizard** (○ changes to ◉).

2 Click **OK**.

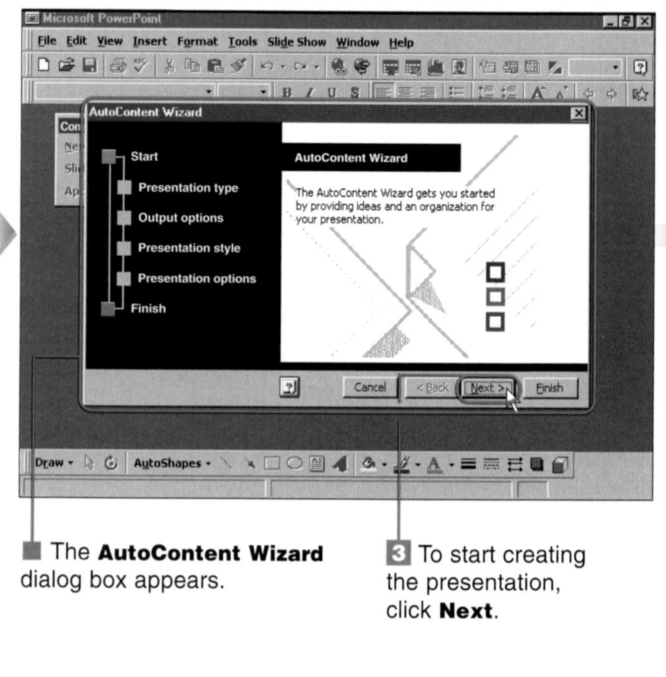

■ The **AutoContent Wizard** dialog box appears.

3 To start creating the presentation, click **Next**.

What types of presentations can I create?

The AutoContent wizard provides ideas and an organization for many types of presentations. You can select the type of presentation that best suits your needs.

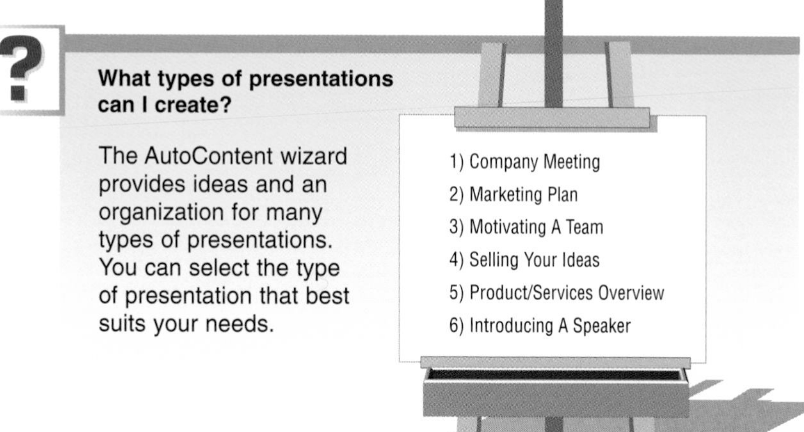

1) Company Meeting
2) Marketing Plan
3) Motivating A Team
4) Selling Your Ideas
5) Product/Services Overview
6) Introducing A Speaker

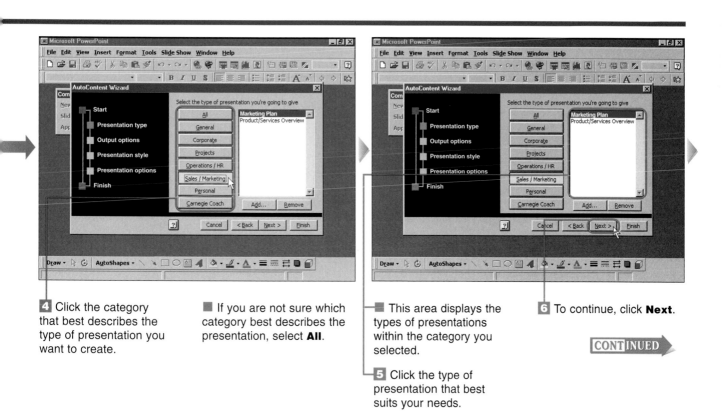

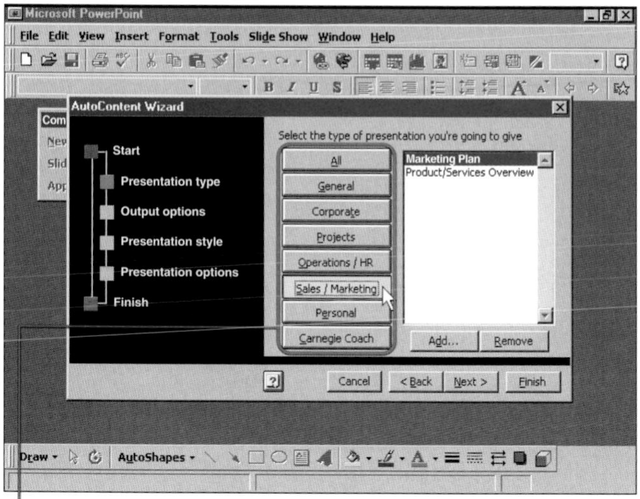

4 Click the category that best describes the type of presentation you want to create.

■ If you are not sure which category best describes the presentation, select **All**.

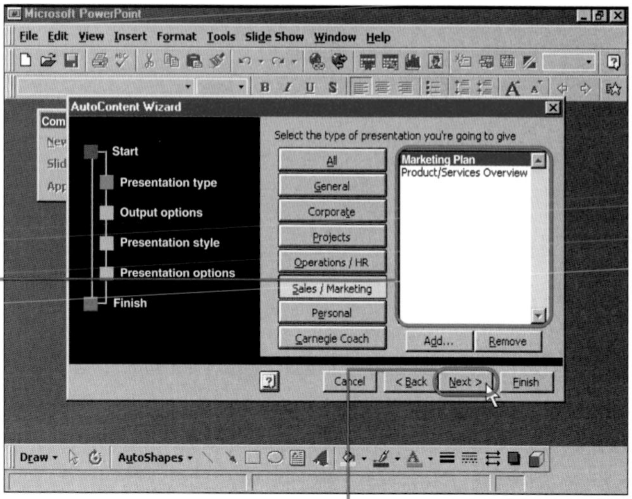

■ This area displays the types of presentations within the category you selected.

5 Click the type of presentation that best suits your needs.

6 To continue, click **Next**.

CONTINUED

CREATE A PRESENTATION

You can choose to deliver a presentation to an audience or have people view the presentation on their own.

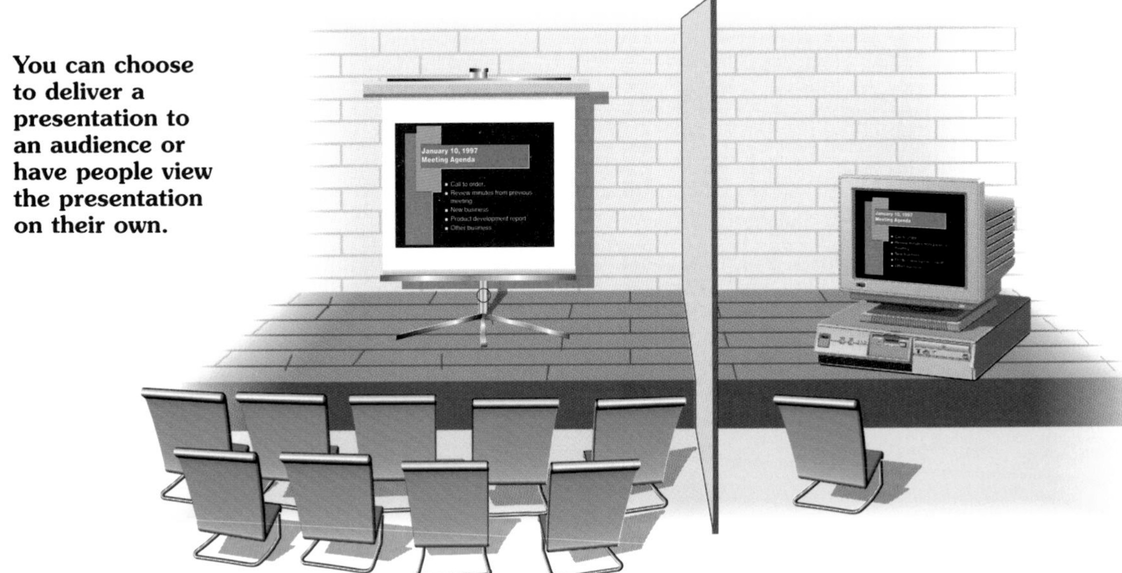

CREATE A PRESENTATION (CONTINUED)

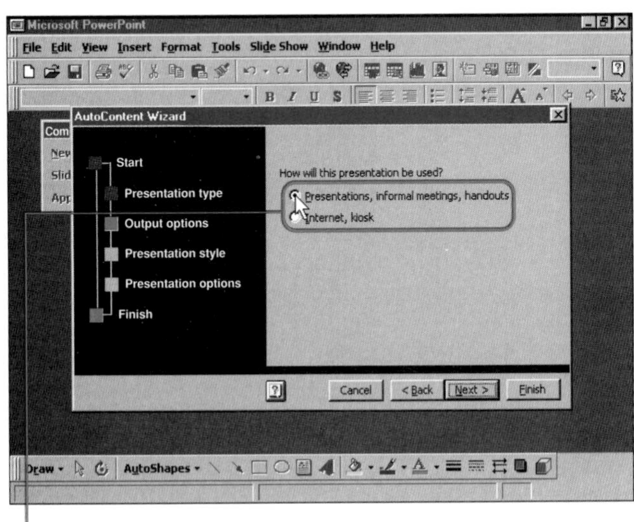

7 Click the way you plan to use the presentation (○ changes to ◉).

Presentations

You will deliver the presentation to an audience.

Internet

People will view the presentation on their own.

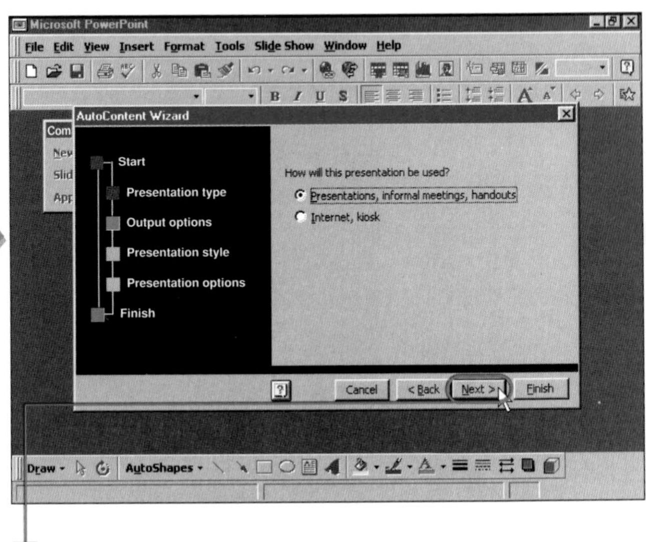

8 To continue, click **Next**.

How can I output my presentation?

There are four ways you can output your presentation.

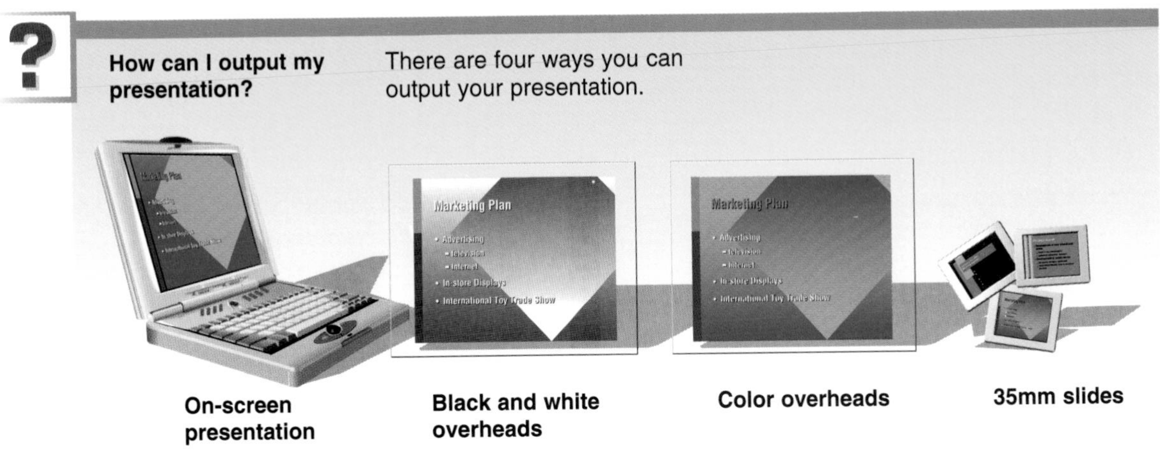

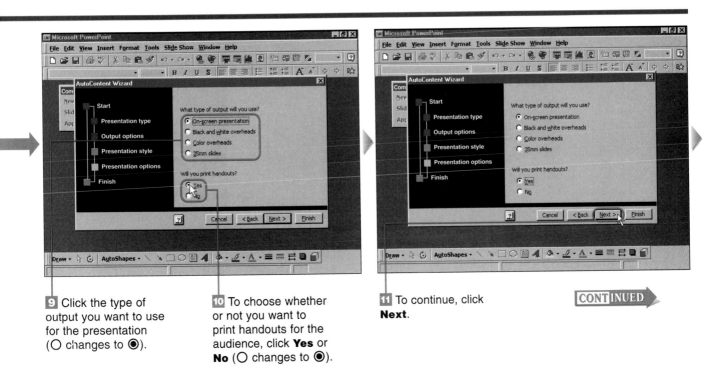

9 Click the type of output you want to use for the presentation (○ changes to ◉).

10 To choose whether or not you want to print handouts for the audience, click **Yes** or **No** (○ changes to ◉).

11 To continue, click **Next**.

CONTINUED

The AutoContent wizard asks you what information you want to appear on your first slide.

CREATE A PRESENTATION (CONTINUED)

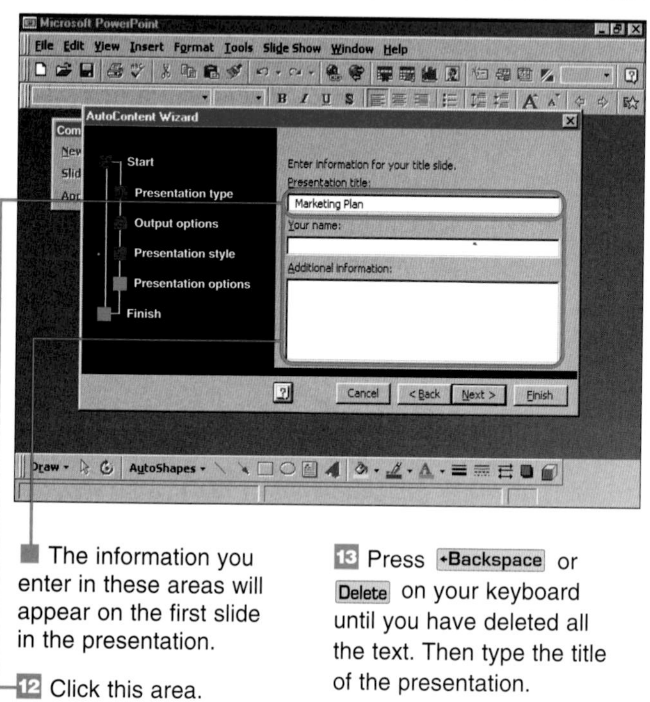

■ The information you enter in these areas will appear on the first slide in the presentation.

12 Click this area.

13 Press ←Backspace or Delete on your keyboard until you have deleted all the text. Then type the title of the presentation.

14 Press Tab on your keyboard to move to the next area.

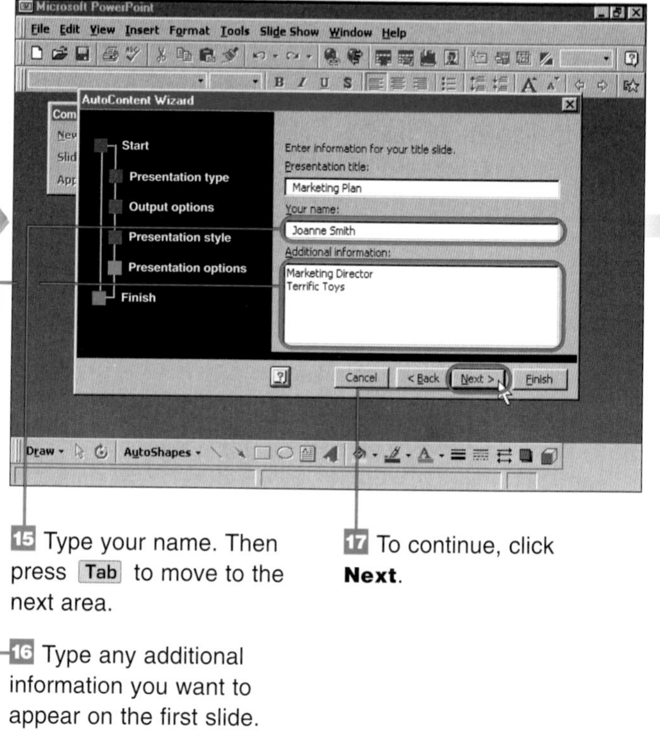

15 Type your name. Then press Tab to move to the next area.

16 Type any additional information you want to appear on the first slide.

17 To continue, click **Next**.

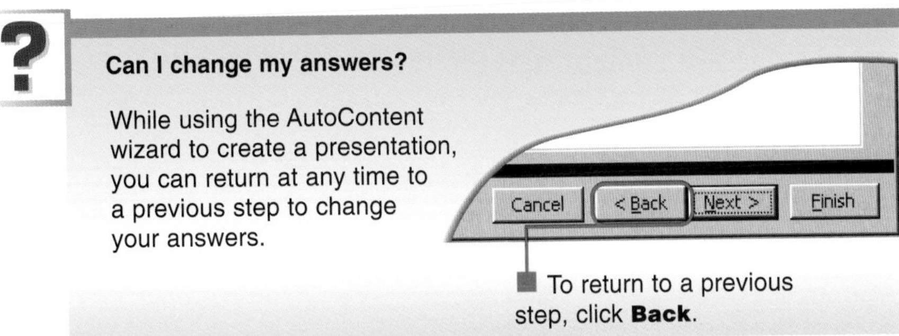

Can I change my answers?

While using the AutoContent wizard to create a presentation, you can return at any time to a previous step to change your answers.

■ To return to a previous step, click **Back**.

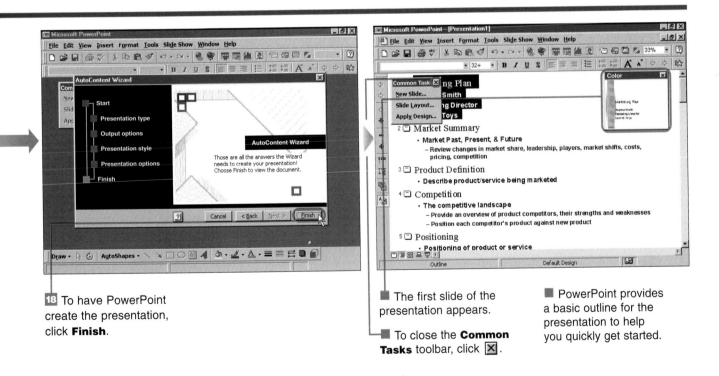

18 To have PowerPoint create the presentation, click **Finish**.

■ The first slide of the presentation appears.

■ To close the **Common Tasks** toolbar, click ☒.

■ PowerPoint provides a basic outline for the presentation to help you quickly get started.

CHANGE THE VIEW

PowerPoint offers four different ways that you can view a presentation on your screen.

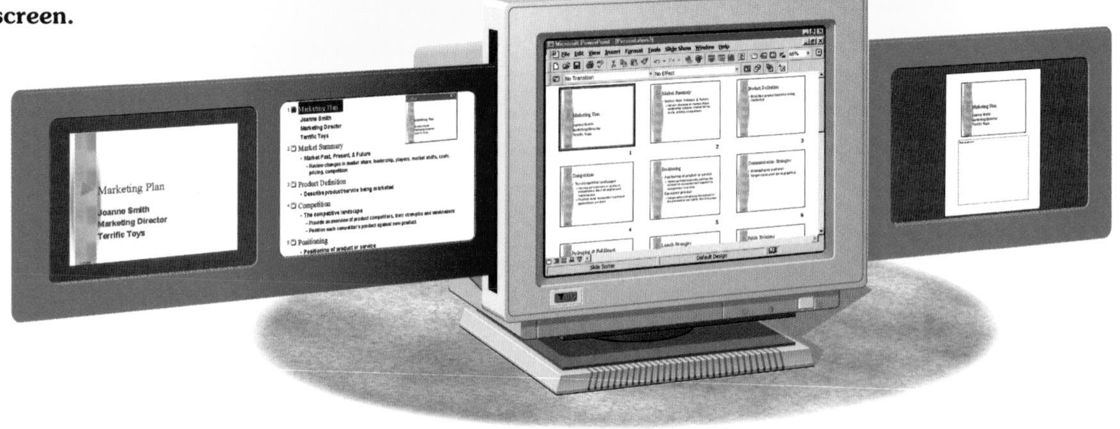

CHANGE THE VIEW

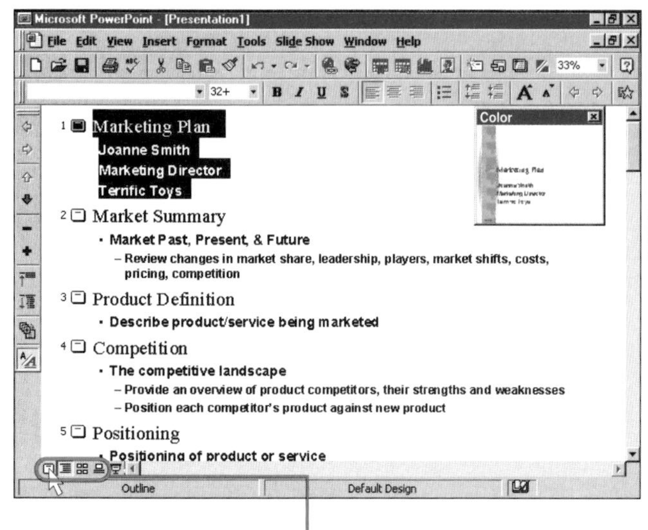

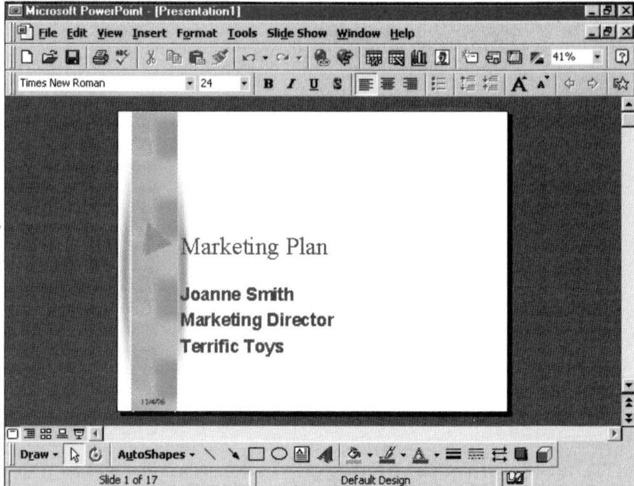

■ When you first create a presentation, PowerPoint displays the presentation in the Outline view.

1 To display the presentation in a different view, click one of the following options.

- Slide
- Outline
- Slide Sorter
- Notes Page

■ PowerPoint displays the presentation in the new view.

■ All views display the same presentation. If you make changes to a slide in one view, the other views will also change.

THE FOUR VIEWS

Slide

The Slide view displays one slide at a time. This view is useful for changing the layout or design of your slides.

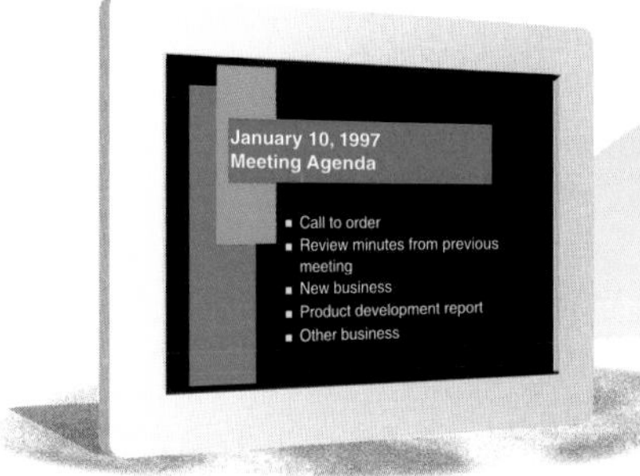

Slide Sorter

The Slide Sorter view displays a miniature version of each slide. This view lets you see a general overview of your presentation.

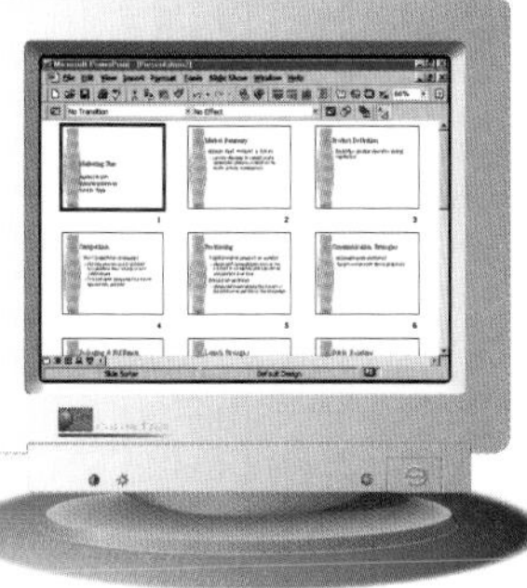

Outline

The Outline view displays the text on all the slides. This view lets you develop the content and organization of your presentation.

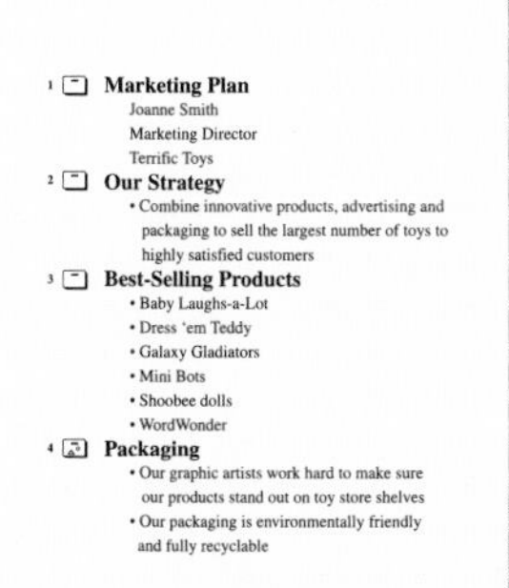

Notes Page

The Notes Page view displays one slide at a time, with space to type comments. You can use these comments as a guide when delivering your presentation.

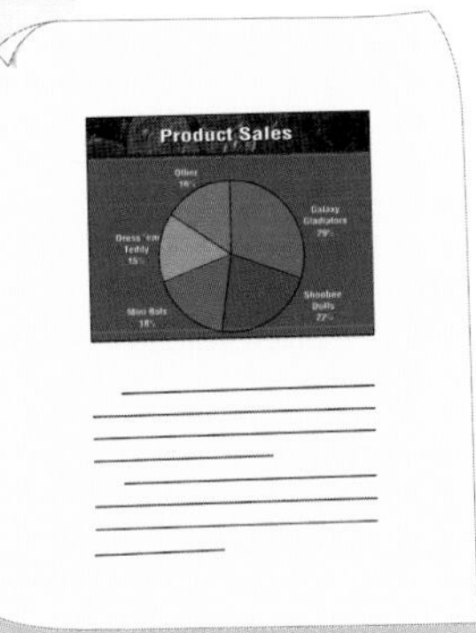

BROWSE THROUGH A PRESENTATION

Your computer screen cannot display your entire presentation at once. You must browse through the presentation to view slides or text not displayed on your screen.

SLIDE OR NOTES PAGE VIEW

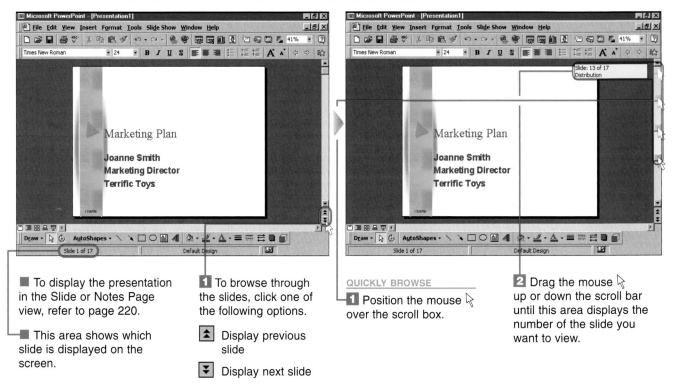

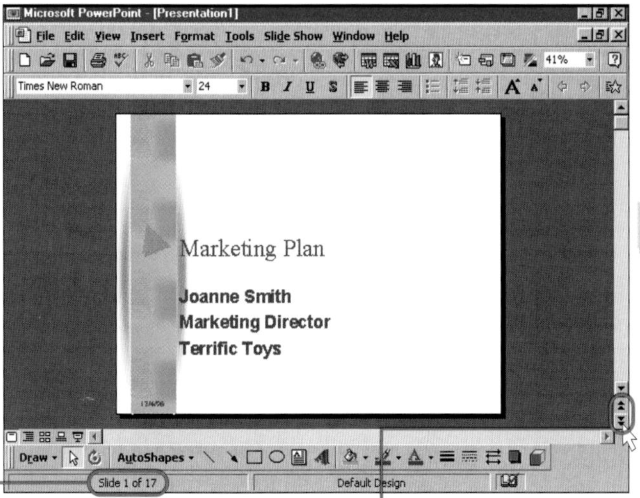

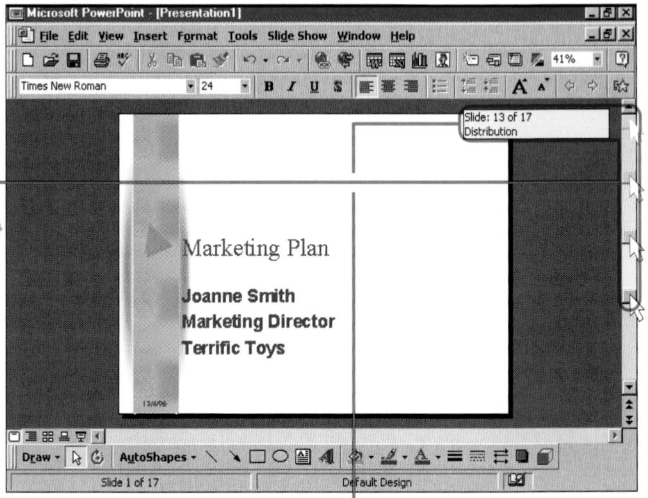

■ To display the presentation in the Slide or Notes Page view, refer to page 220.

■ This area shows which slide is displayed on the screen.

1 To browse through the slides, click one of the following options.

- Display previous slide
- Display next slide

QUICKLY BROWSE

1 Position the mouse over the scroll box.

2 Drag the mouse up or down the scroll bar until this area displays the number of the slide you want to view.

Which views let me see more than one slide at a time?

These views display one slide at a time.

These views display more than one slide at a time.

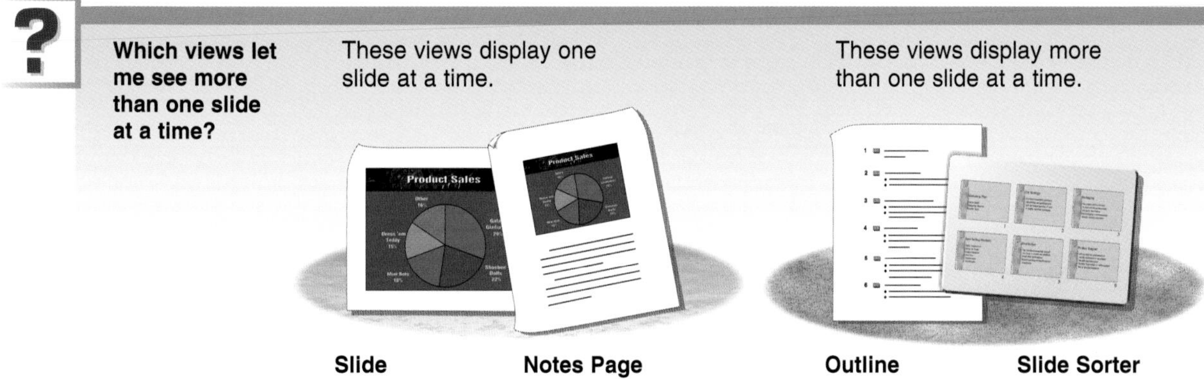

OUTLINE OR SLIDE SORTER VIEW

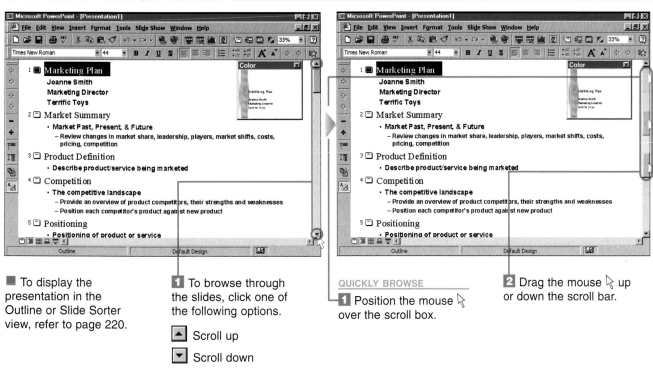

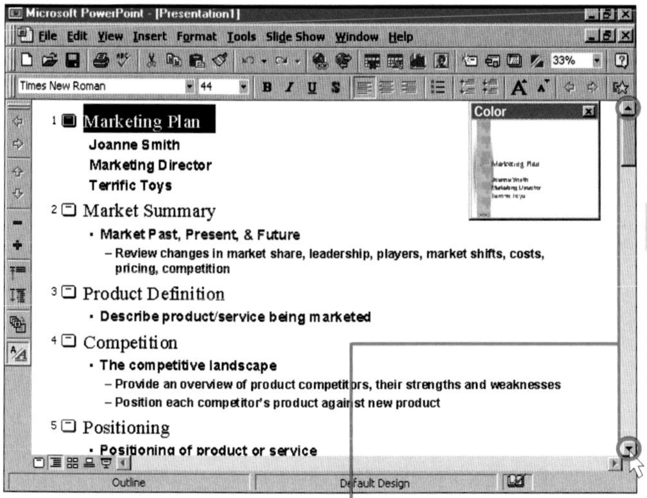

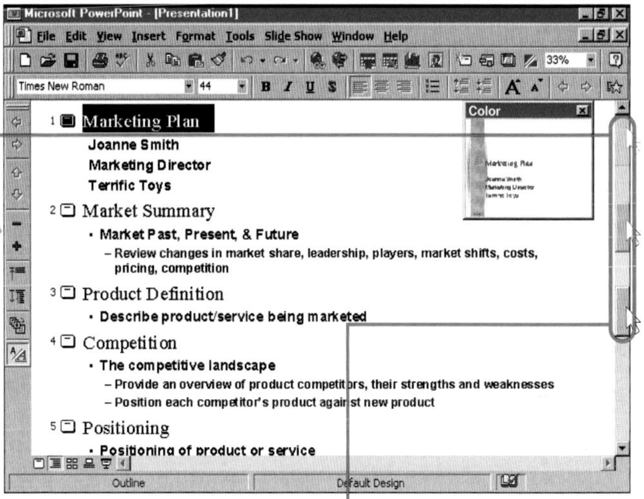

■ To display the presentation in the Outline or Slide Sorter view, refer to page 220.

1 To browse through the slides, click one of the following options.

▲ Scroll up

▼ Scroll down

QUICKLY BROWSE

1 Position the mouse over the scroll box.

2 Drag the mouse up or down the scroll bar.

You should save your presentation to store it for future use. This allows you to later review and make changes to the presentation.

SAVE A PRESENTATION

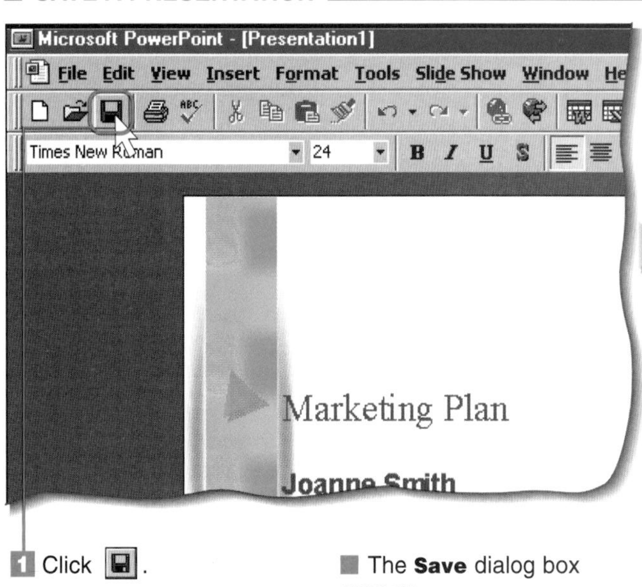

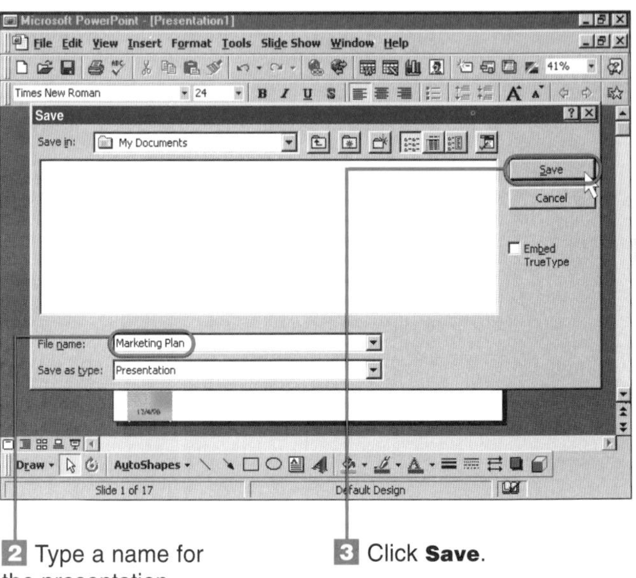

1 Click 💾.

■ The **Save** dialog box appears.

Note: If you previously saved the presentation, the ***Save*** *dialog box will not appear since you have already named the presentation.*

2 Type a name for the presentation.

Note: You can use up to 255 characters to name a presentation.

3 Click **Save**.

When you finish using PowerPoint, you can exit the program.

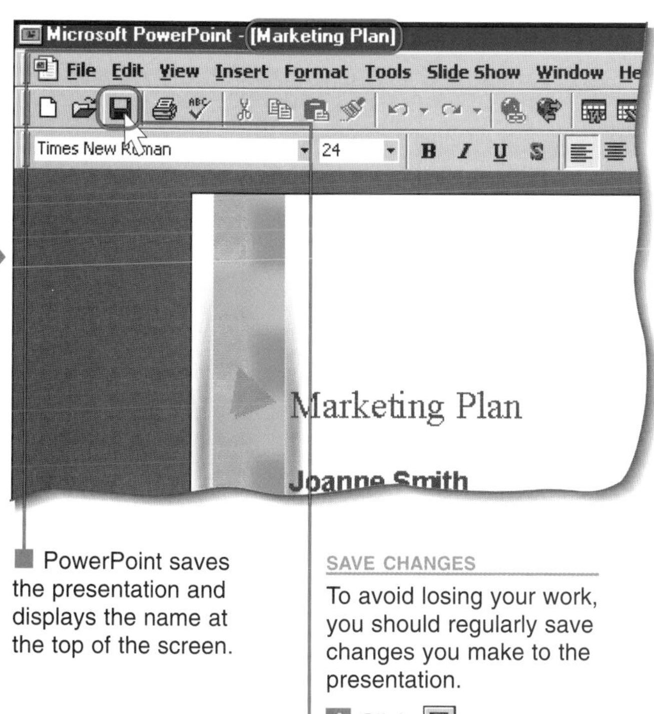

■ PowerPoint saves the presentation and displays the name at the top of the screen.

SAVE CHANGES

To avoid losing your work, you should regularly save changes you make to the presentation.

1 Click 💾.

EXIT POWERPOINT

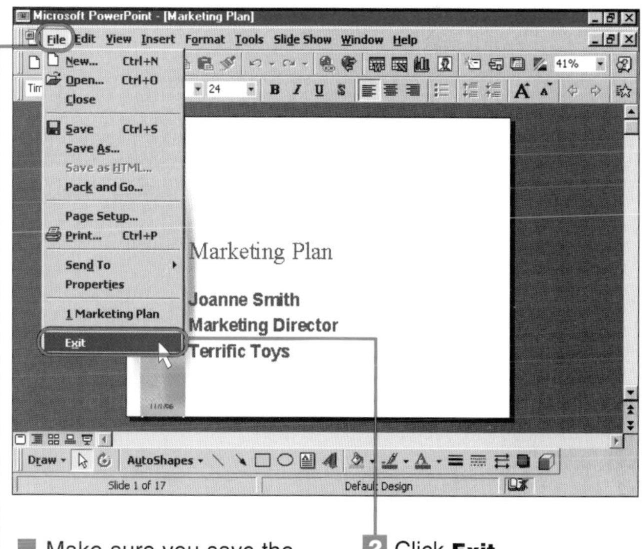

■ Make sure you save the presentation before exiting PowerPoint.

1 Click **File**.

2 Click **Exit**.

Note: To restart PowerPoint, refer to page 213.

OPEN A PRESENTATION

You can open a saved presentation and display it on your screen. This lets you review and make changes to the presentation.

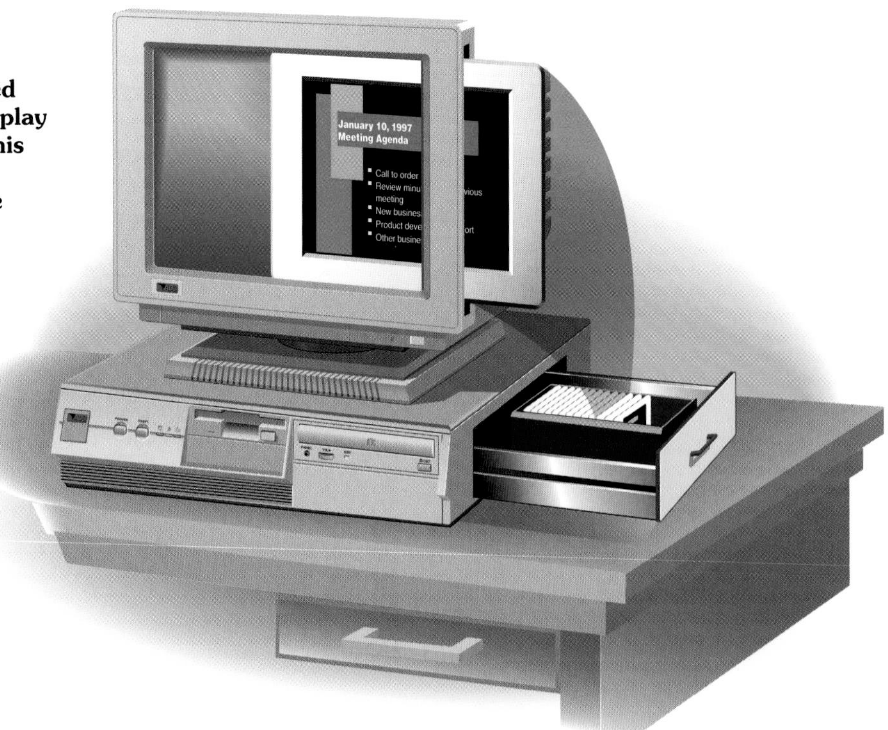

OPEN A PRESENTATION

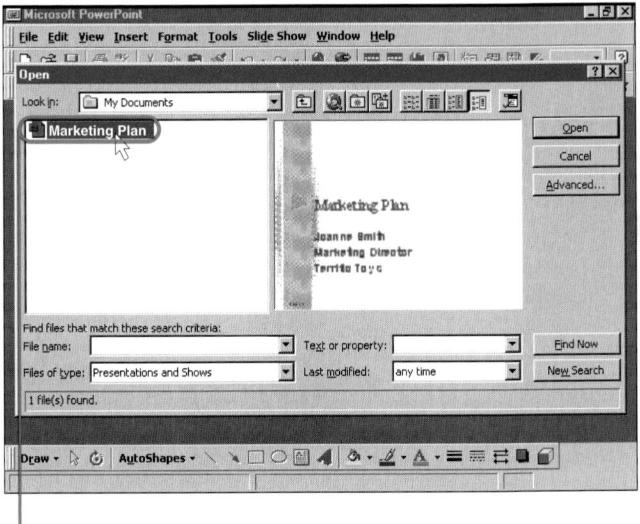

1 Click [Open button].

■ The **Open** dialog box appears.

2 Click the name of the presentation you want to open.

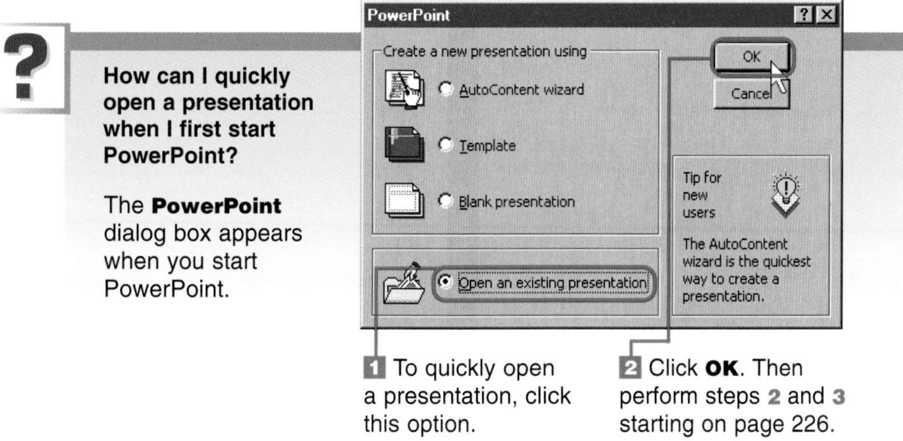

How can I quickly open a presentation when I first start PowerPoint?

The **PowerPoint** dialog box appears when you start PowerPoint.

1 To quickly open a presentation, click this option.

2 Click **OK**. Then perform steps 2 and 3 starting on page 226.

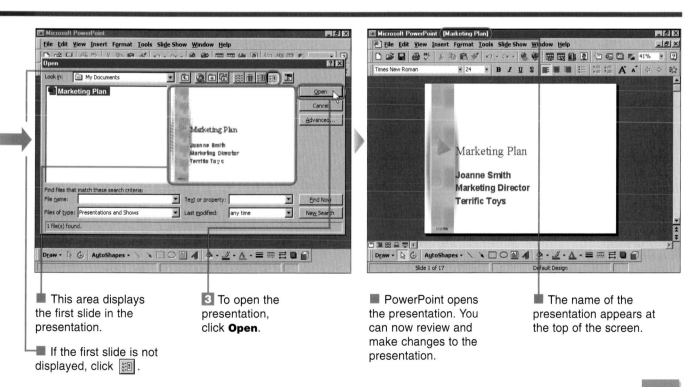

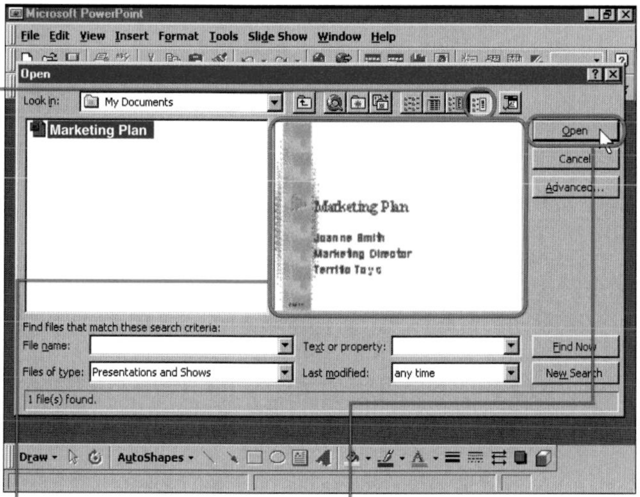

■ This area displays the first slide in the presentation.

■ If the first slide is not displayed, click [icon].

3 To open the presentation, click **Open**.

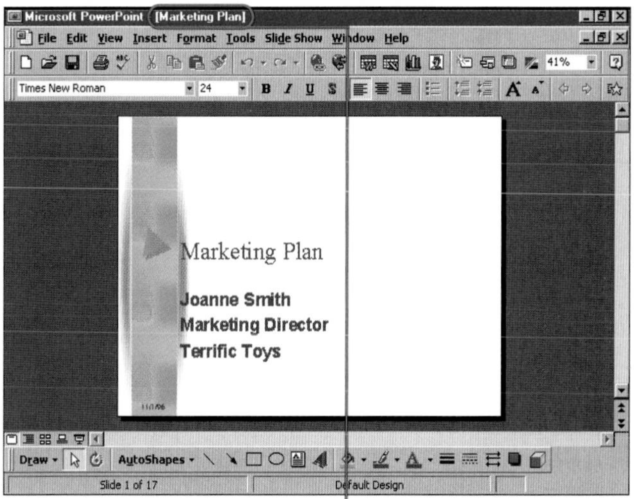

■ PowerPoint opens the presentation. You can now review and make changes to the presentation.

■ The name of the presentation appears at the top of the screen.

SELECT TEXT

Before changing text in a presentation, you will often need to select the text you want to work with. Selected text appears highlighted on your screen.

SELECT TEXT

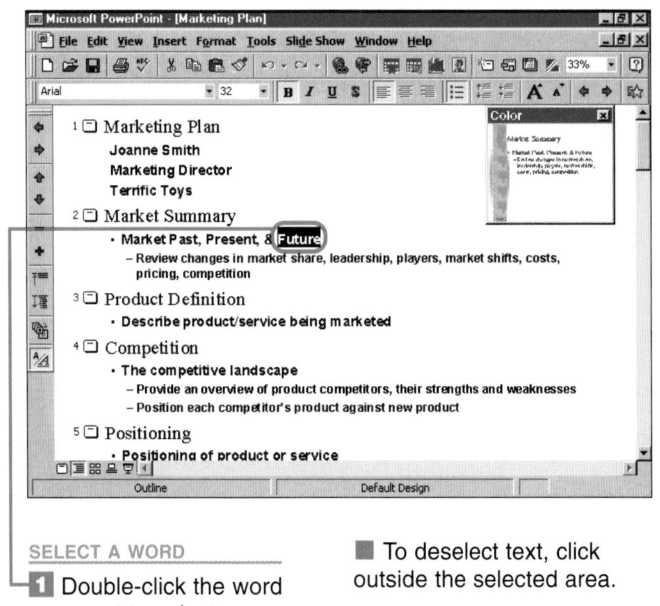

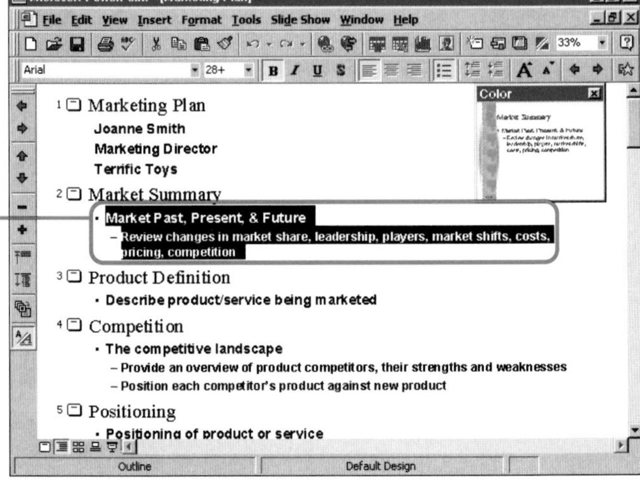

SELECT A WORD

1 Double-click the word you want to select.

■ To deselect text, click outside the selected area.

SELECT A POINT

1 Click the bullet (■) beside the point you want to select.

How do I select all the text in my presentation?

To quickly select all the text in your presentation, press and hold down **Ctrl** and then press **A** on your keyboard. Then release both keys.

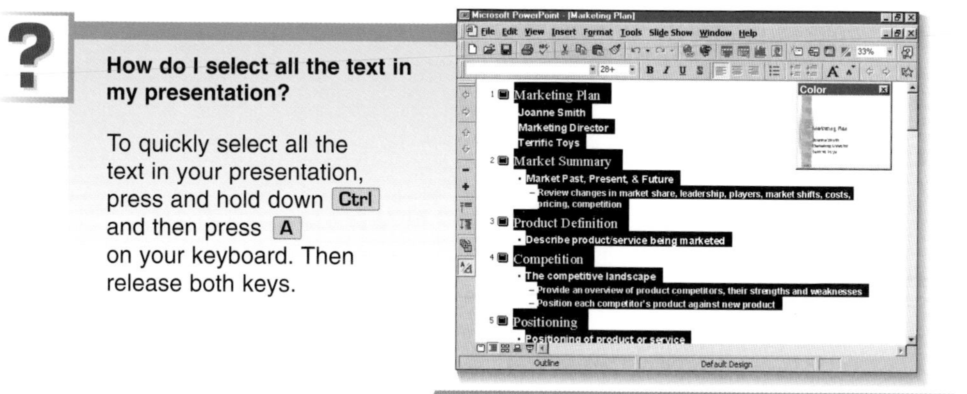

SELECT A SLIDE

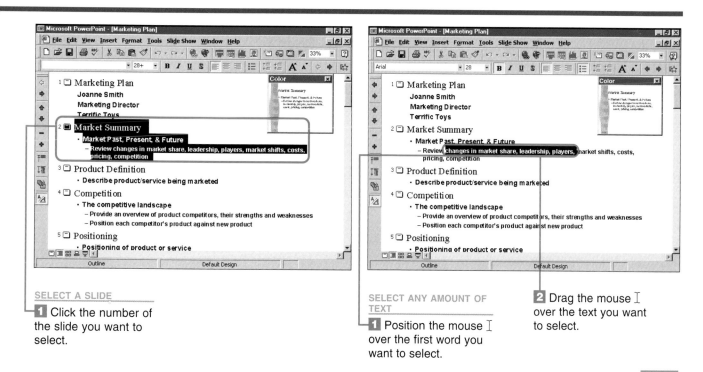

1 Click the number of the slide you want to select.

SELECT ANY AMOUNT OF TEXT

1 Position the mouse I over the first word you want to select.

2 Drag the mouse I over the text you want to select.

REPLACE TEXT

You can easily replace text in your presentation with new text.

REPLACE TEXT

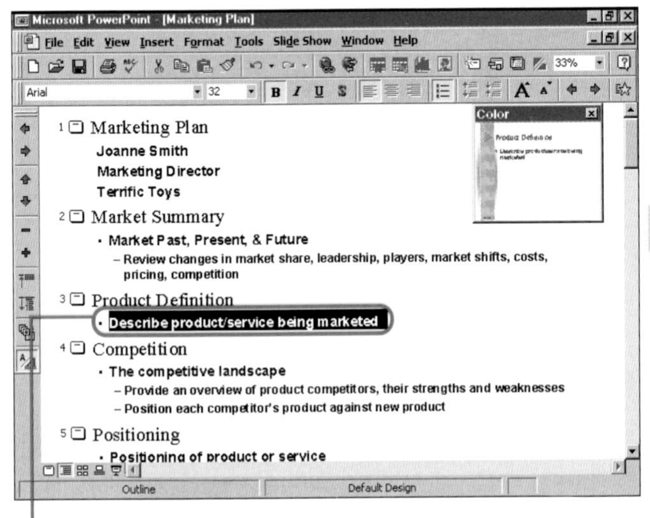

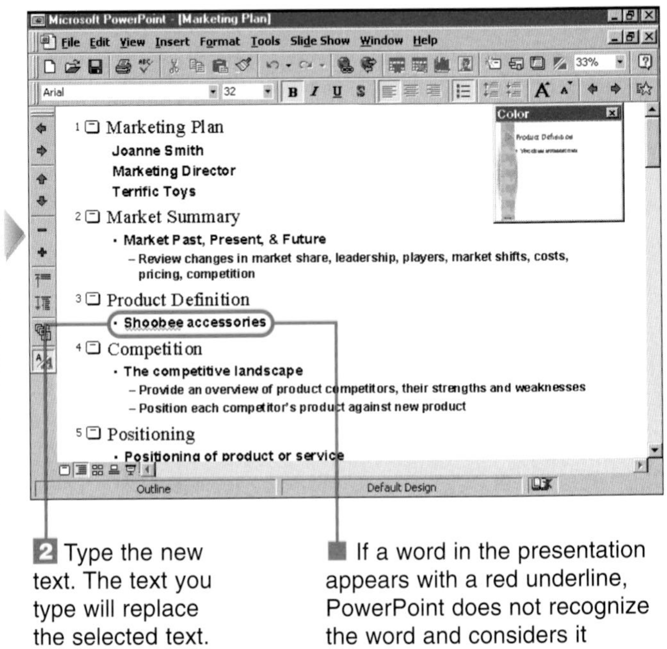

1 Select the text you want to replace with new text. To select text, refer to page 228.

2 Type the new text. The text you type will replace the selected text.

■ If a word in the presentation appears with a red underline, PowerPoint does not recognize the word and considers it misspelled. To spell check the presentation, refer to page 238.

UNDO LAST CHANGE

PowerPoint remembers the last changes you made to your presentation. If you regret these changes, you can cancel them by using the Undo feature.

UNDO LAST CHANGE

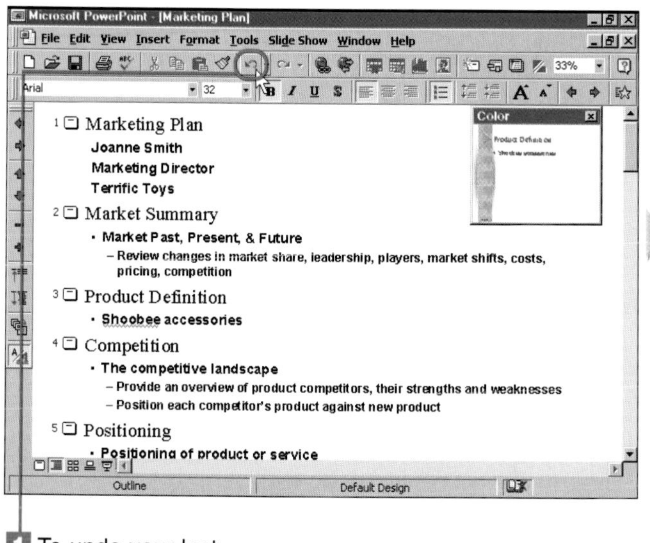

1 To undo your last change, click [undo icon].

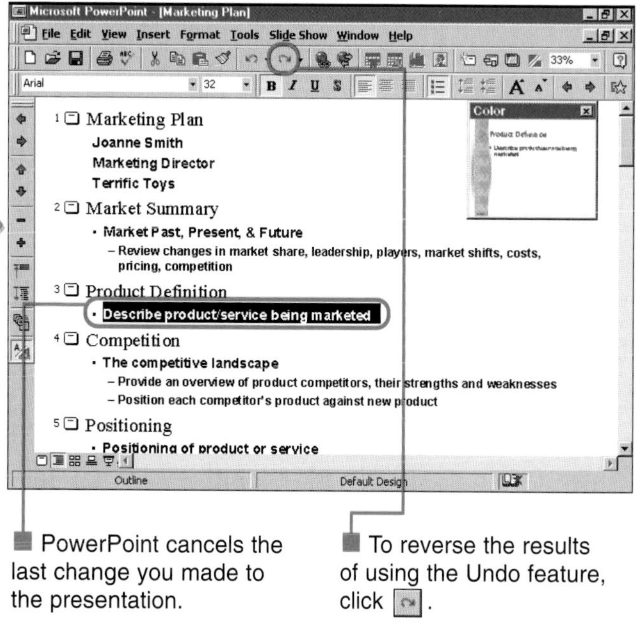

■ PowerPoint cancels the last change you made to the presentation.

■ You can repeat step 1 to cancel previous changes you made.

■ To reverse the results of using the Undo feature, click [redo icon].

INSERT TEXT

You can easily add new text to your presentation.

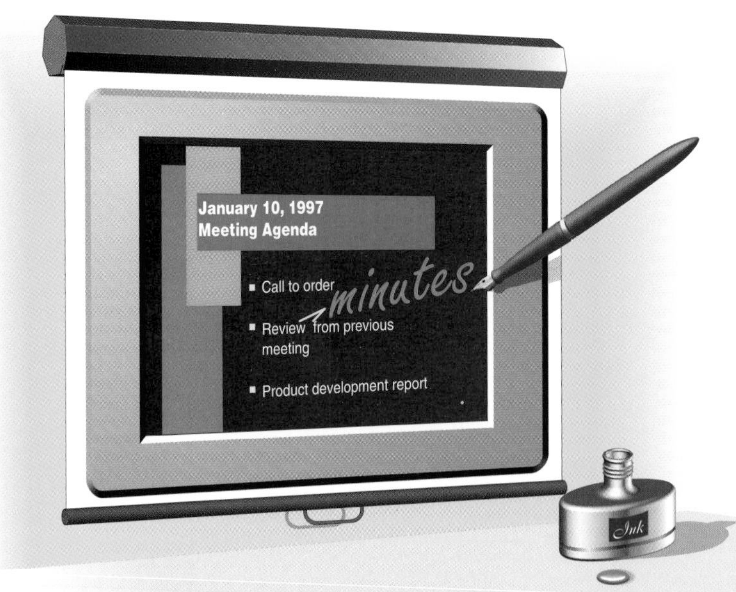

INSERT CHARACTERS

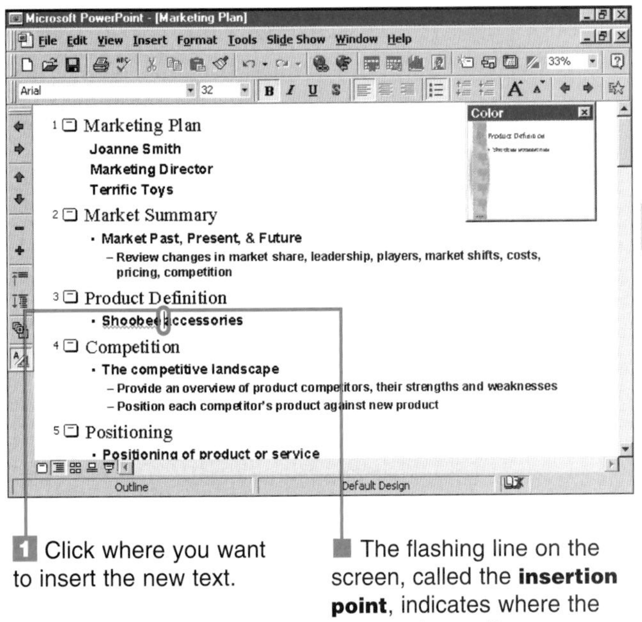

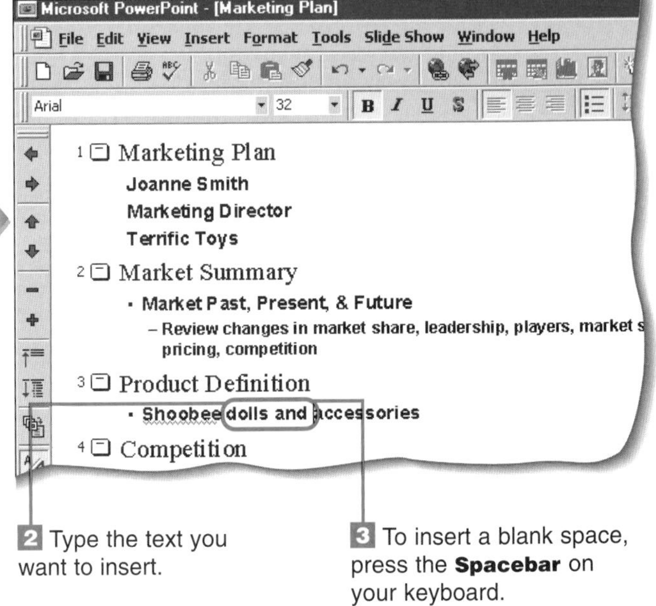

1 Click where you want to insert the new text.

■ The flashing line on the screen, called the **insertion point**, indicates where the text you type will appear.

Note: You can also use the →, ←, ↑ and ↓ keys on your keyboard to move the insertion point on the screen.

2 Type the text you want to insert.

3 To insert a blank space, press the **Spacebar** on your keyboard.

?

Why are some words in my presentation underlined with a wavy, red line?

If PowerPoint does not recognize a word in your presentation and considers it misspelled, the word will display a wavy, red underline. To spell check your presentation, refer to page 238.

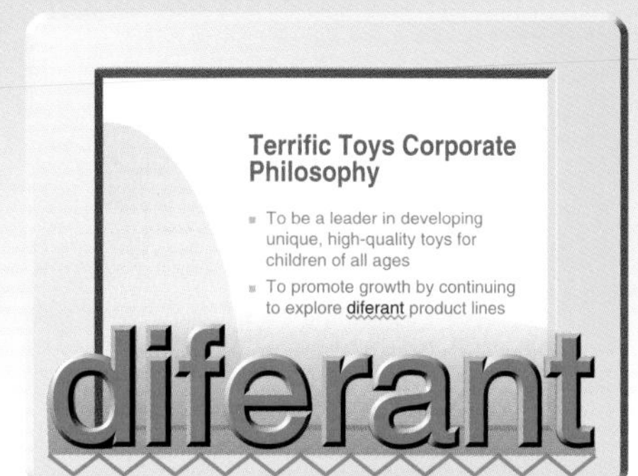

INSERT A NEW POINT

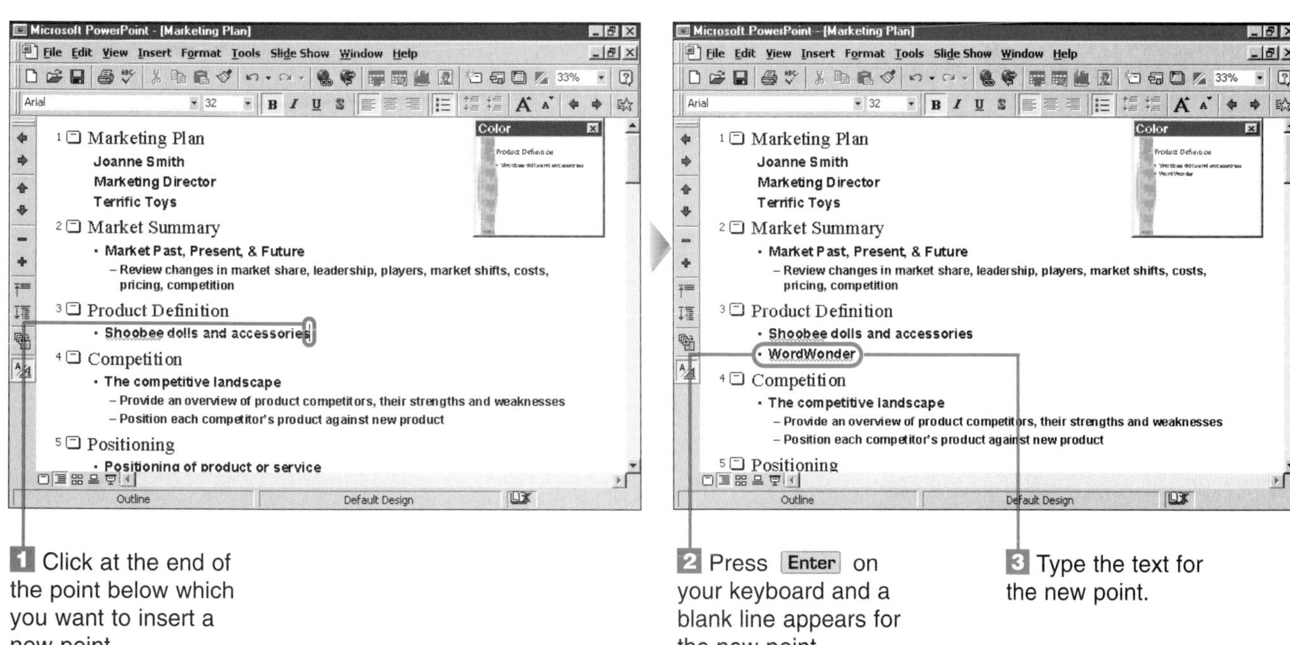

1 Click at the end of the point below which you want to insert a new point.

2 Press Enter on your keyboard and a blank line appears for the new point.

3 Type the text for the new point.

DELETE TEXT

You can easily remove text you no longer need from your presentation.

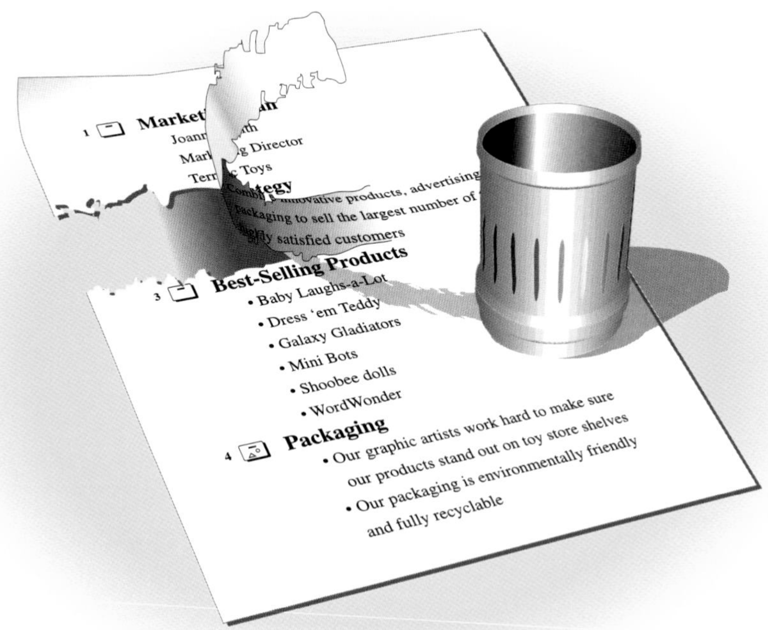

DELETE CHARACTERS

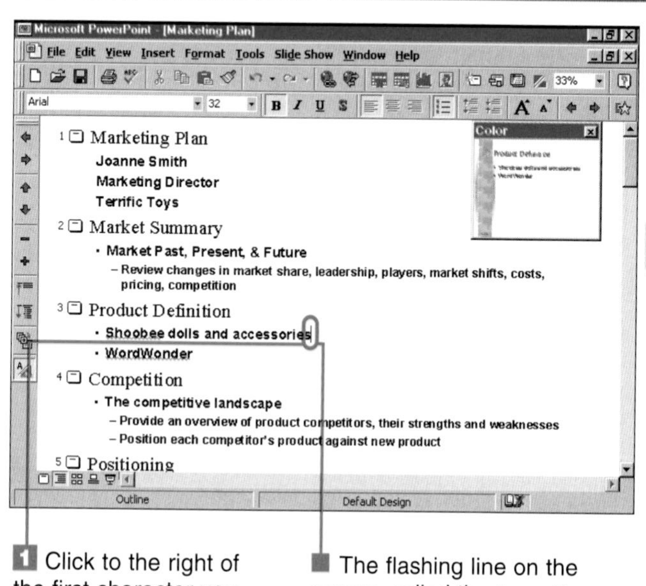

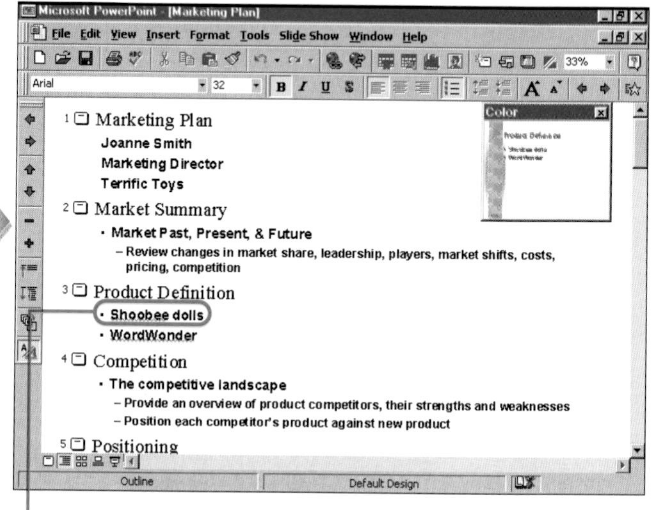

1 Click to the right of the first character you want to delete.

■ The flashing line on the screen, called the **insertion point**, moves to the location you selected.

Note: You can also use the →, ←, ↑ and ↓ keys on your keyboard to move the insertion point on the screen.

2 Press Backspace on your keyboard once for each character or space you want to delete.

?

Can I delete text in the Slide view?

You can delete, insert and change text when viewing your slides in the Slide view. To change to the Slide view, refer to page 220.

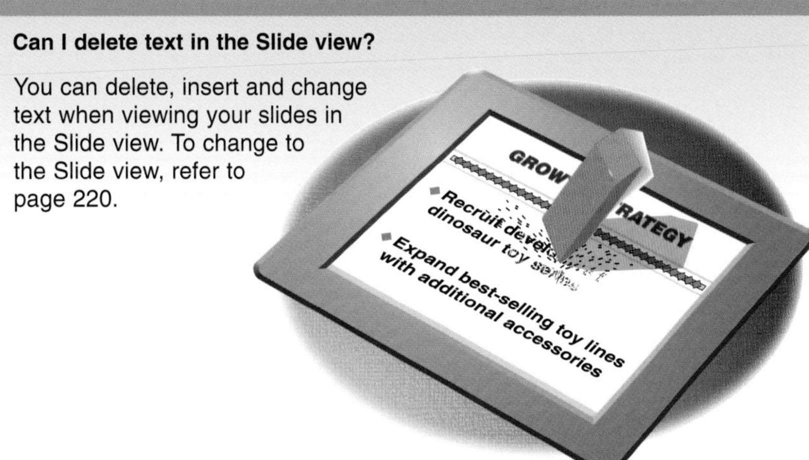

DELETE SELECTED TEXT

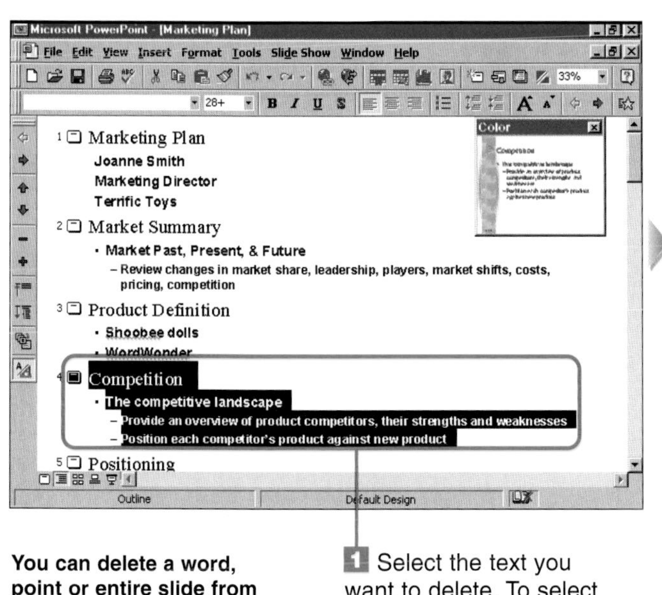

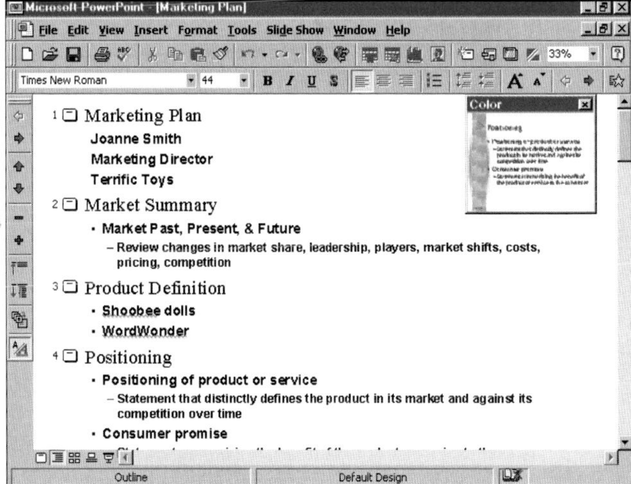

You can delete a word, point or entire slide from a presentation.

1 Select the text you want to delete. To select text, refer to page 228.

2 Press ←Backspace on your keyboard to remove the text.

MOVE TEXT

You can move text in your presentation to reorganize your ideas.

MOVE TEXT

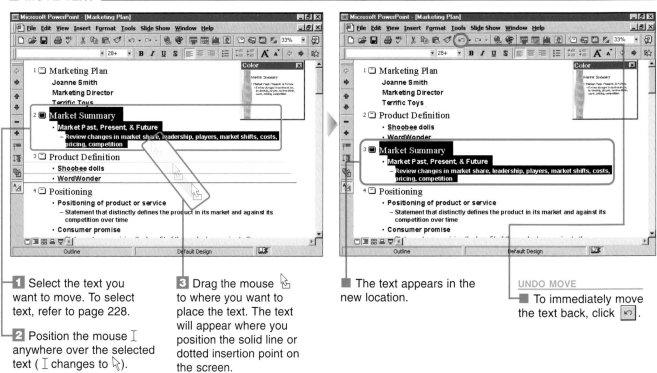

1 Select the text you want to move. To select text, refer to page 228.

2 Position the mouse I anywhere over the selected text (I changes to ↖).

3 Drag the mouse ↖ to where you want to place the text. The text will appear where you position the solid line or dotted insertion point on the screen.

■ The text appears in the new location.

UNDO MOVE

■ To immediately move the text back, click ↶.

CHANGE IMPORTANCE OF TEXT

You can increase or decrease the importance of text in your presentation.

CHANGE IMPORTANCE OF TEXT

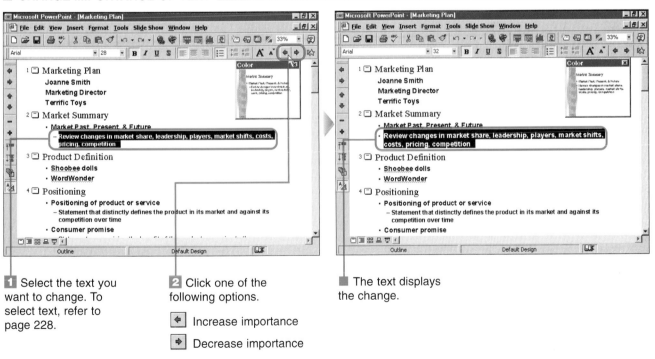

1 Select the text you want to change. To select text, refer to page 228.

2 Click one of the following options.

- Increase importance
- Decrease importance

■ The text displays the change.

CHECK SPELLING

You can quickly find and correct spelling errors in your presentation.

PowerPoint compares every word in your presentation to words in its dictionary. If a word does not exist in the dictionary, PowerPoint considers it misspelled.

CHECK SPELLING

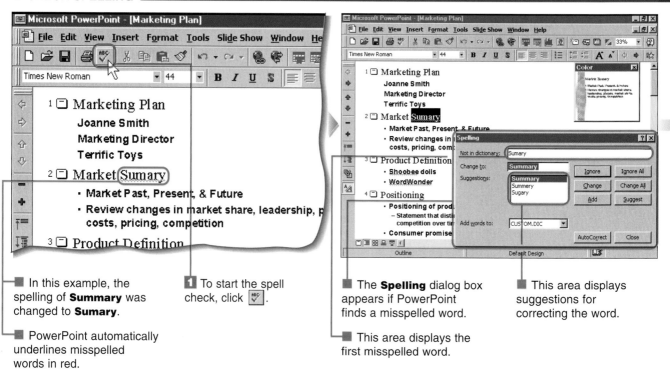

■ In this example, the spelling of **Summary** was changed to **Sumary**.

■ PowerPoint automatically underlines misspelled words in red.

1 To start the spell check, click the ABC (spelling) button.

■ The **Spelling** dialog box appears if PowerPoint finds a misspelled word.

■ This area displays the first misspelled word.

■ This area displays suggestions for correcting the word.

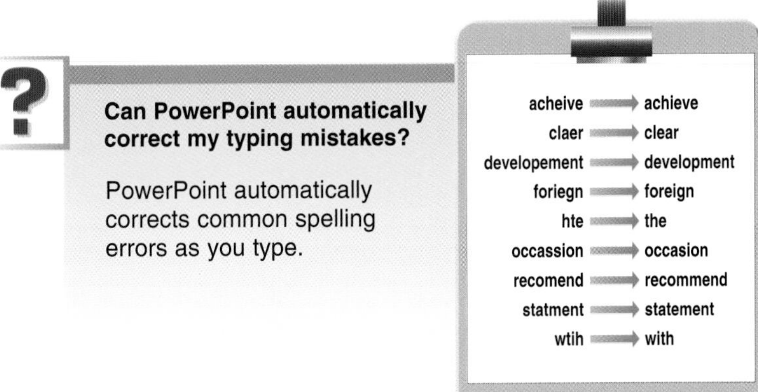

acheive → achieve
claer → clear
developement → development
foriegn → foreign
hte → the
occassion → occasion
recomend → recommend
statment → statement
wtih → with

Can PowerPoint automatically correct my typing mistakes?

PowerPoint automatically corrects common spelling errors as you type.

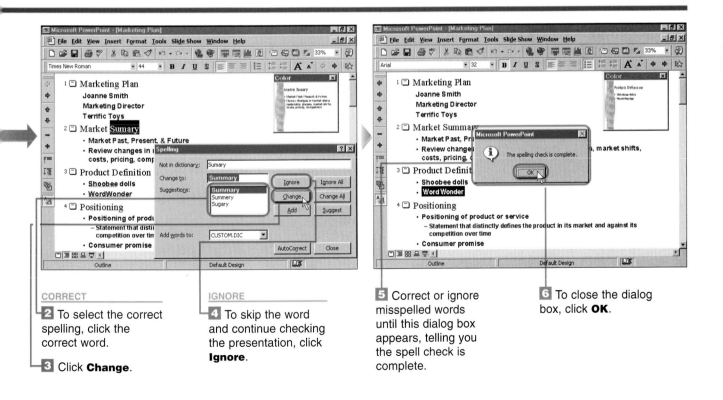

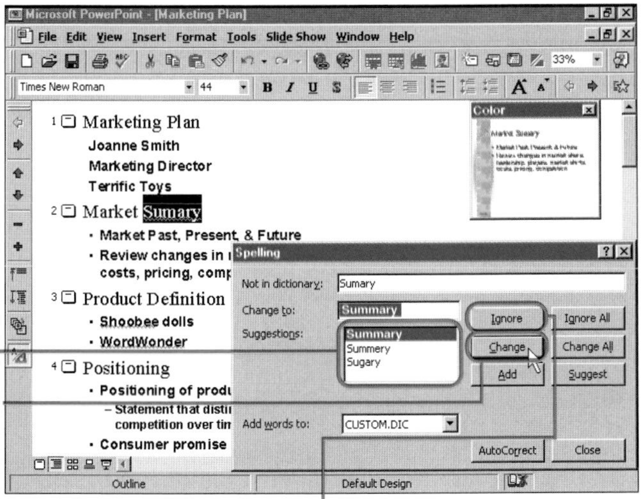

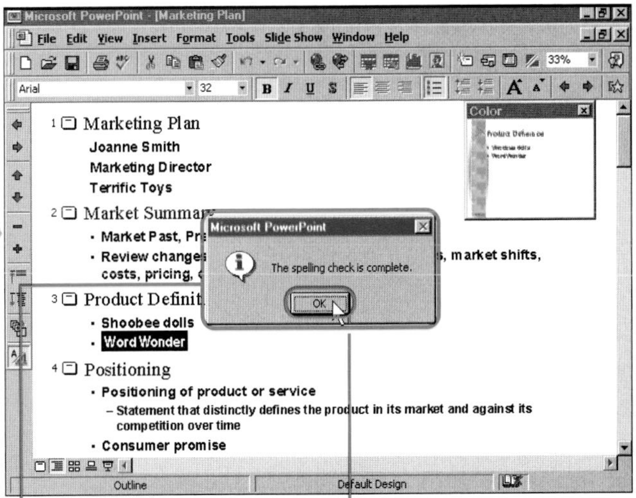

CORRECT

2 To select the correct spelling, click the correct word.

3 Click **Change**.

IGNORE

4 To skip the word and continue checking the presentation, click **Ignore**.

5 Correct or ignore misspelled words until this dialog box appears, telling you the spell check is complete.

6 To close the dialog box, click **OK**.

CHANGE THE SLIDE LAYOUT

You can have PowerPoint arrange text and objects on a slide for you.

CHANGE THE SLIDE LAYOUT

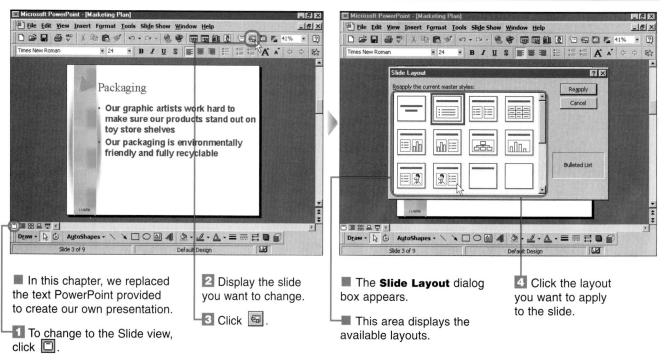

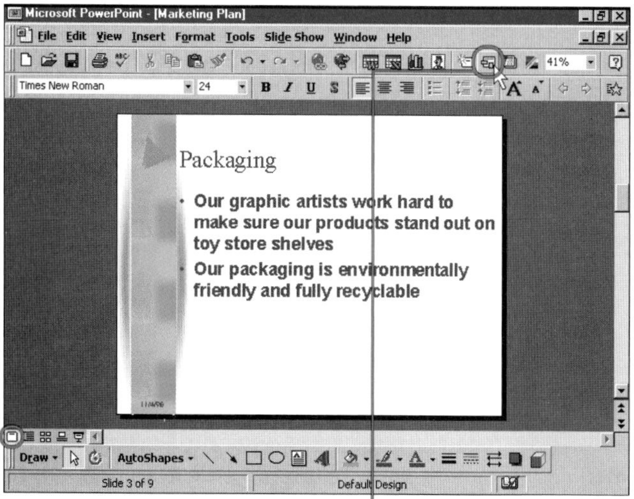

■ In this chapter, we replaced the text PowerPoint provided to create our own presentation.

1 To change to the Slide view, click .

2 Display the slide you want to change.

3 Click .

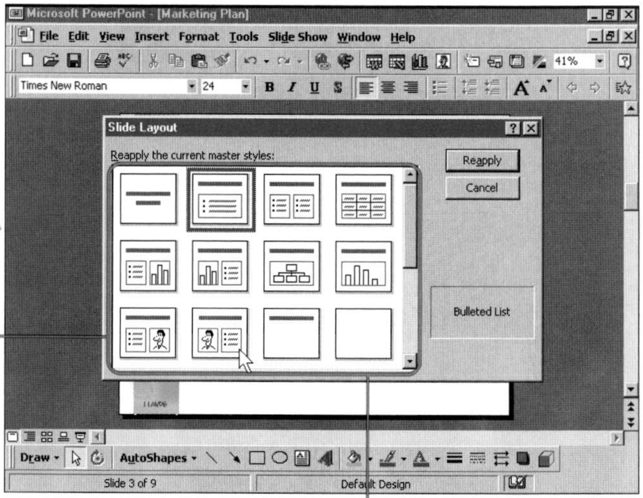

■ The **Slide Layout** dialog box appears.

■ This area displays the available layouts.

4 Click the layout you want to apply to the slide.

How can changing the slide layout help me add objects to my slides?

PowerPoint offers slide layouts that allow you to easily add objects such as a bulleted list, a chart or clip art to your slides.

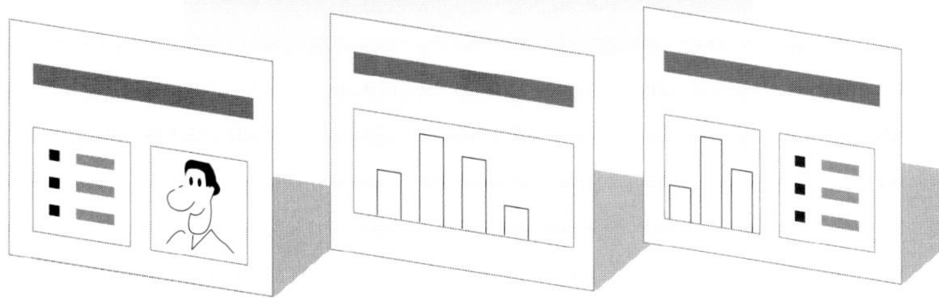

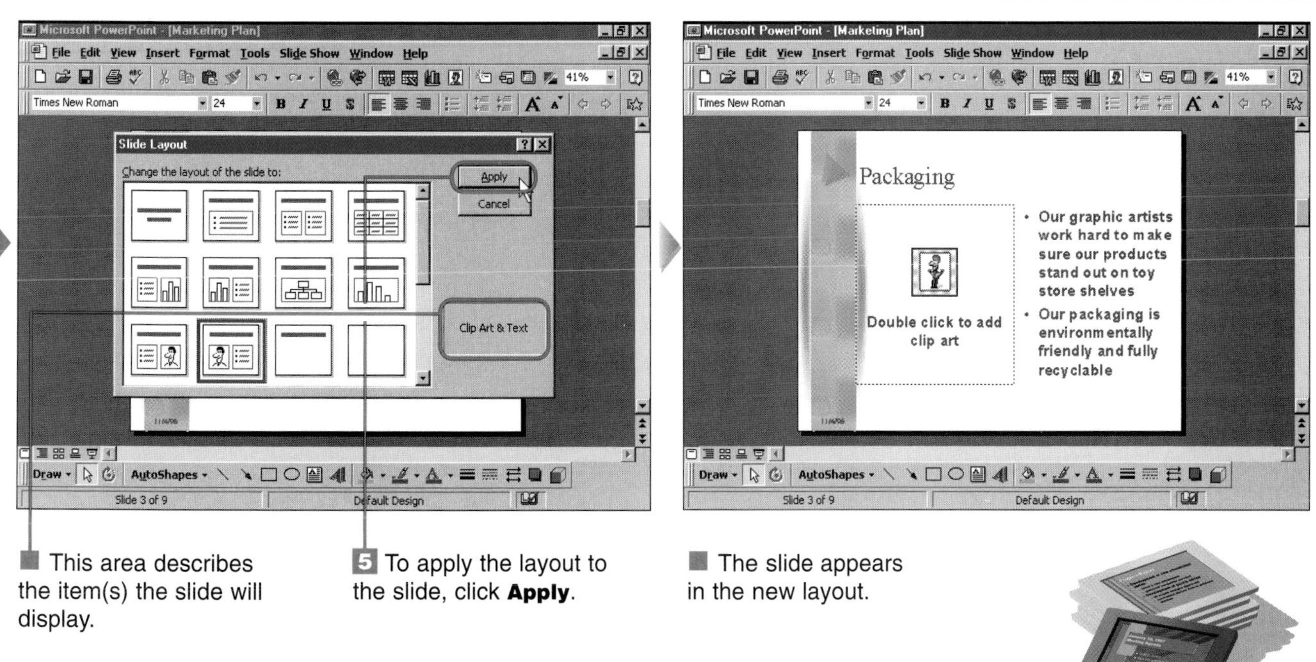

■ This area describes the item(s) the slide will display.

5 To apply the layout to the slide, click **Apply**.

■ The slide appears in the new layout.

ADD A NEW SLIDE

You can insert a new slide into your presentation to add a new topic you want to discuss.

ADD A NEW SLIDE

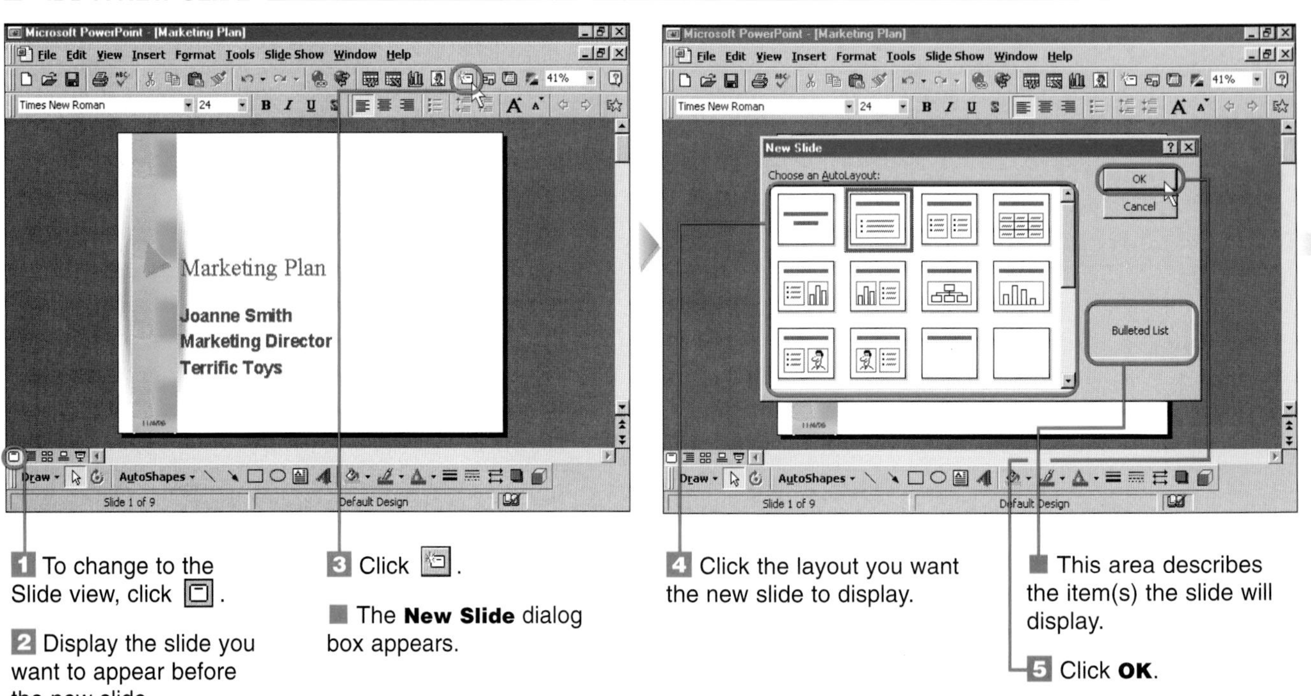

1 To change to the Slide view, click ▭.

2 Display the slide you want to appear before the new slide.

3 Click ▭.

■ The **New Slide** dialog box appears.

4 Click the layout you want the new slide to display.

■ This area describes the item(s) the slide will display.

5 Click **OK**.

How much text should I display on one slide?

Too many words on a slide can minimize the impact of important ideas. If a slide contains too much text, place the text on two or three slides.

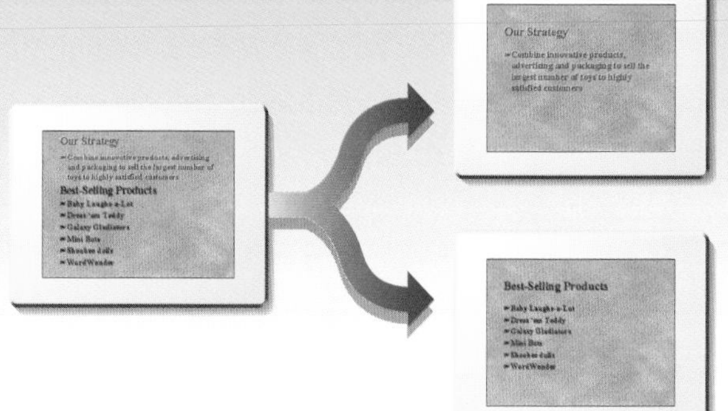

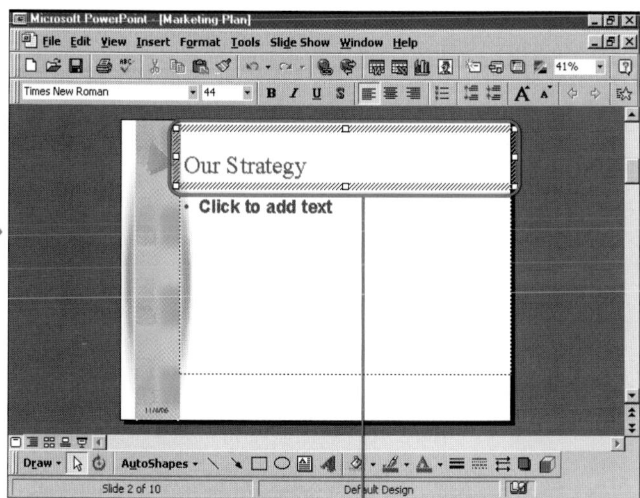

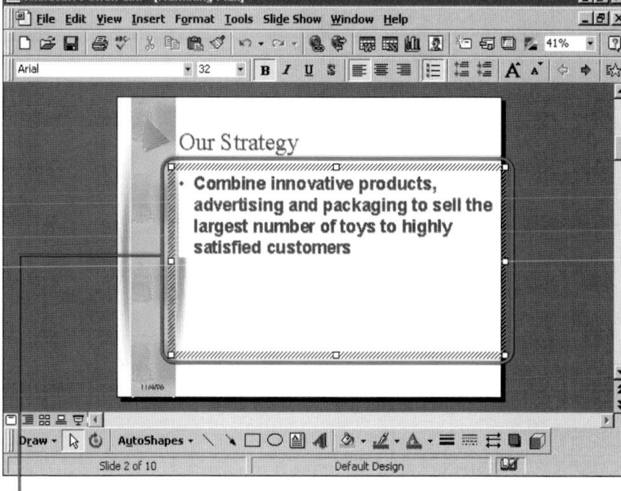

■ The new slide appears, displaying the layout you selected.

Note: You can change the layout at any time. To change the slide layout, refer to page 240.

6 If the layout you selected displays an area for a title, click the title area. Then type the title.

7 If the layout you selected displays an area for text, click the text area. Then type the text.

■ Press Enter on your keyboard each time you want to start a new point.

ADD CLIP ART OR PICTURES

You can add images to slides to make your presentation more interesting and entertaining.

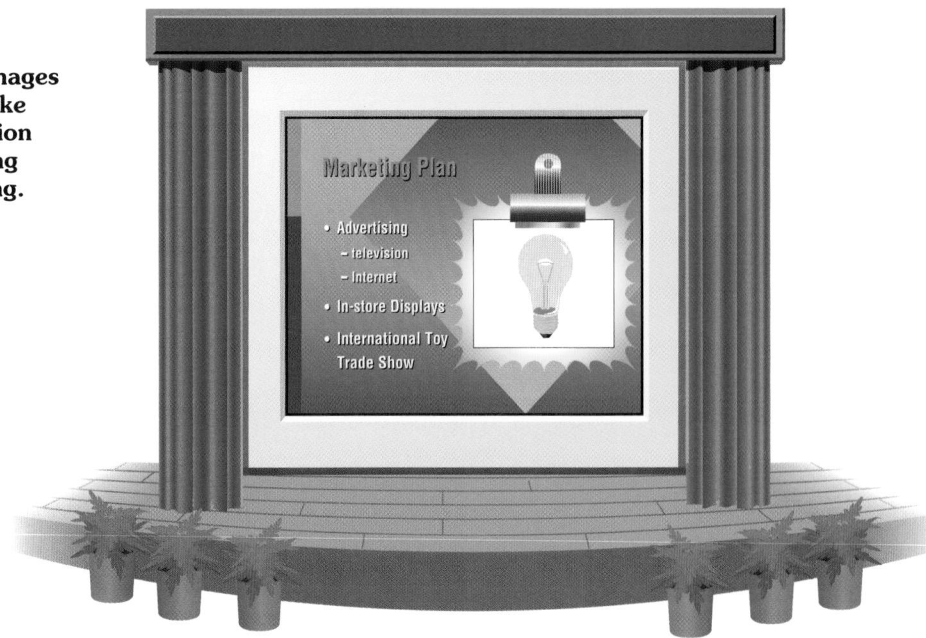

ADD CLIP ART OR PICTURES

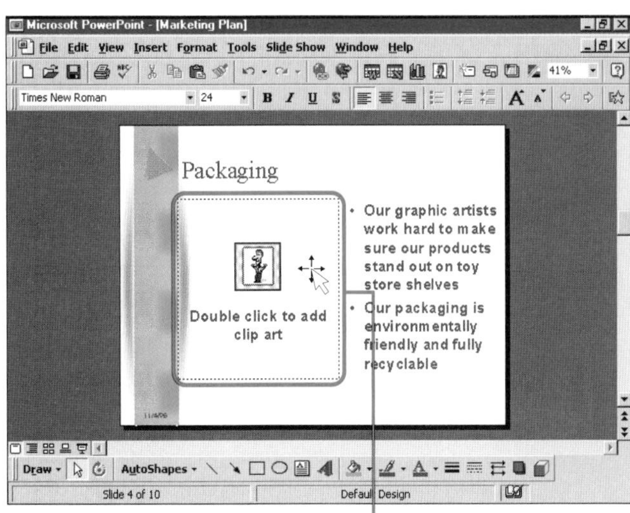

1 Display the slide you want to add an image to.

2 Change the layout of the slide to one that includes space for a clip art image. To change the slide layout, refer to page 240.

3 To add an image, double-click the clip art area.

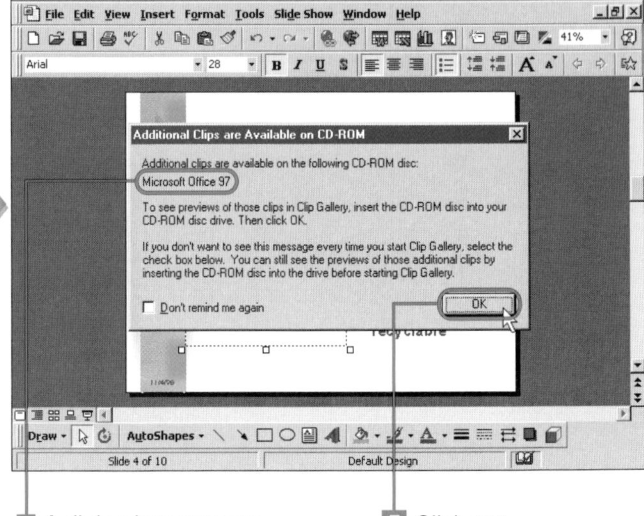

■ A dialog box appears if additional images are available on the CD-ROM disc identified in this area.

4 To view the additional images, insert the CD-ROM disc into your CD-ROM drive.

5 Click **OK**.

■ The **Microsoft Clip Gallery** dialog box appears.

How do I delete an image from a slide?

To delete an image from a slide in your presentation, click the image. Then press Delete on your keyboard.

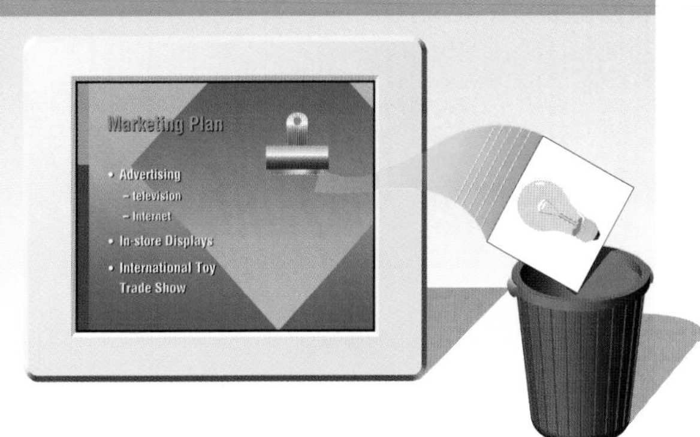

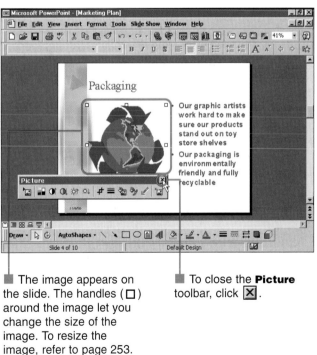

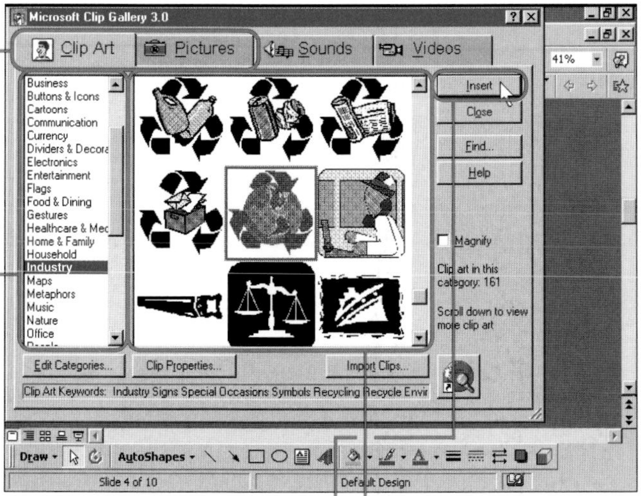

6 Click the **Clip Art** or **Pictures** tab.

7 Click the category of images you want to display.

8 Click the image you want to add to the slide.

9 To add the image to the slide, click **Insert**.

■ The image appears on the slide. The handles (□) around the image let you change the size of the image. To resize the image, refer to page 253.

■ To close the **Picture** toolbar, click ☒.

ADD A CHART

You can add a chart to a slide to show trends and compare data.

ADD A CHART

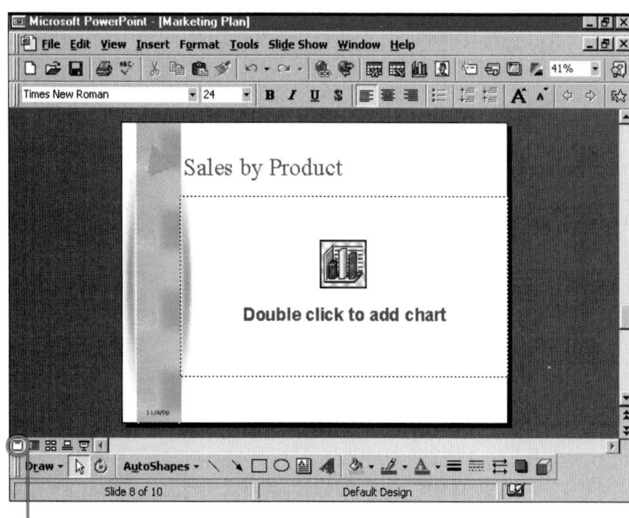

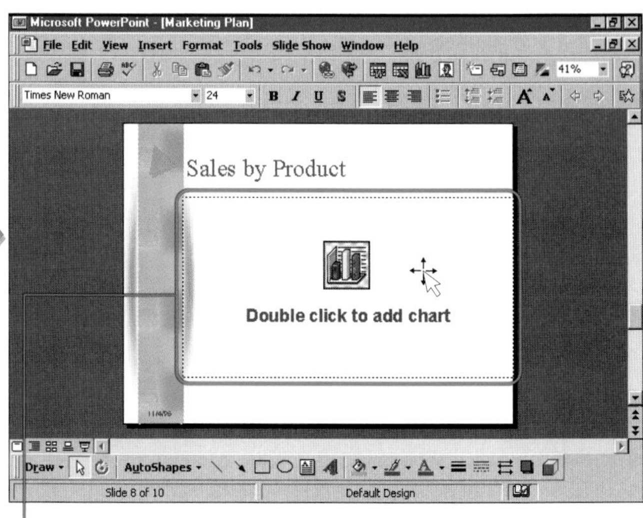

1 To change to the Slide view, click ☐.

2 Display the slide you want to add a chart to.

3 Change the layout of the slide to one that includes space for a chart. To change the slide layout, refer to page 240.

4 To add a chart, double-click the chart area.

?

Why should I use a chart in my presentation?

A chart is more appealing and often easier to understand than a list of numbers.

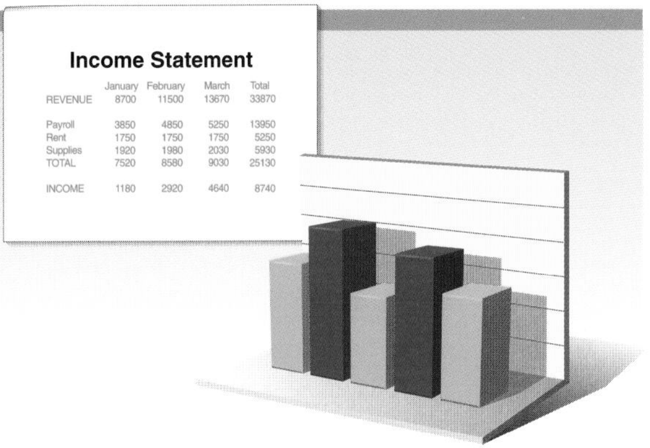

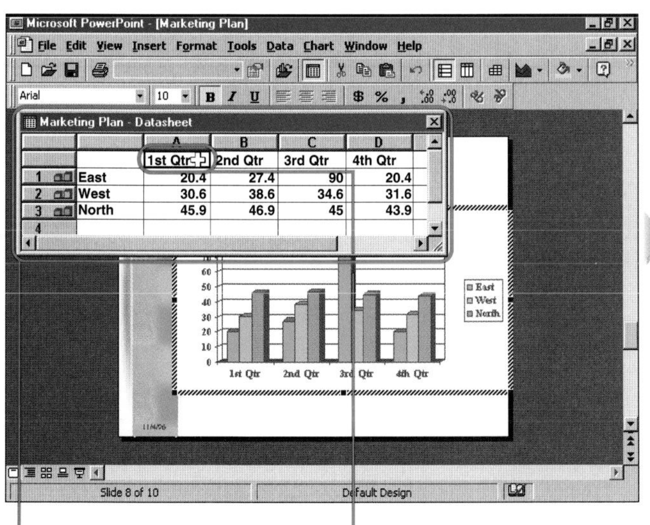

■ A datasheet appears, displaying sample data to show you where to enter your information.

5 To change the data in a cell, click the cell. A thick border appears around the cell.

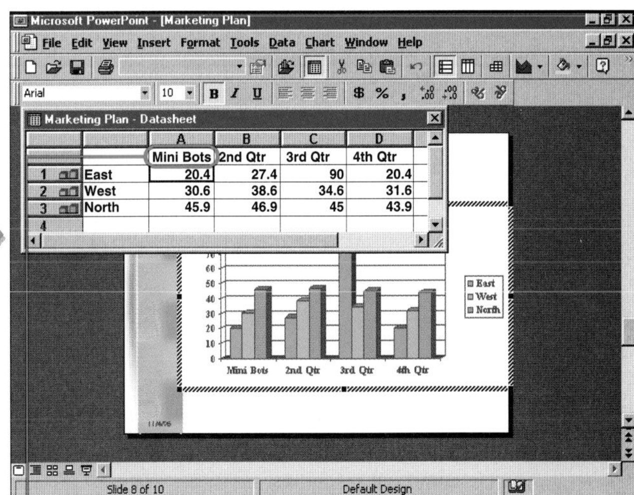

6 Type your data and then press Enter on your keyboard.

Note: To delete the text PowerPoint provides, click the cell containing the text and then press Delete on your keyboard.

7 Repeat steps 5 and 6 until you finish entering all your data.

CONTINUED

You can choose the type of chart you want to create.

ADD A CHART (CONTINUED)

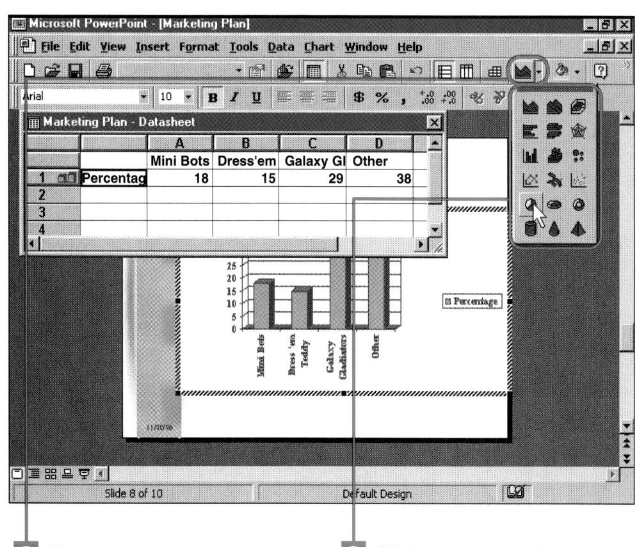

8 To select the type of chart you want to create, click ▾ in this area.

9 Click the type of chart you want to use.

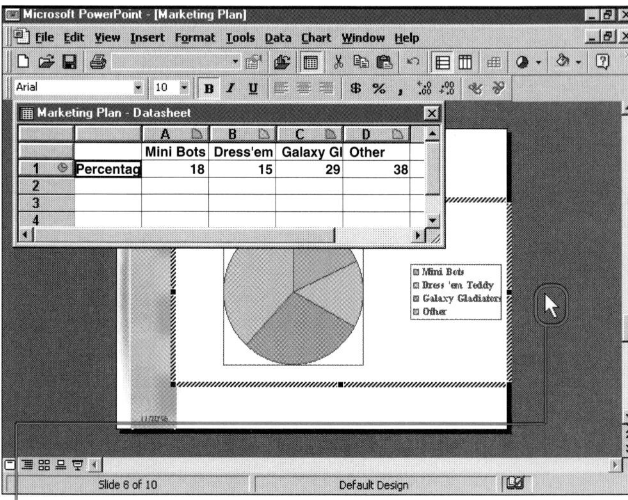

10 To hide the datasheet, click a blank area on the screen.

?

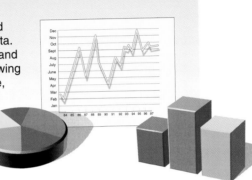

What type of chart should I choose?

The type of chart you should choose depends on your data. For example, area, column and line charts are ideal for showing changes to values over time, whereas pie charts are ideal for showing percentages.

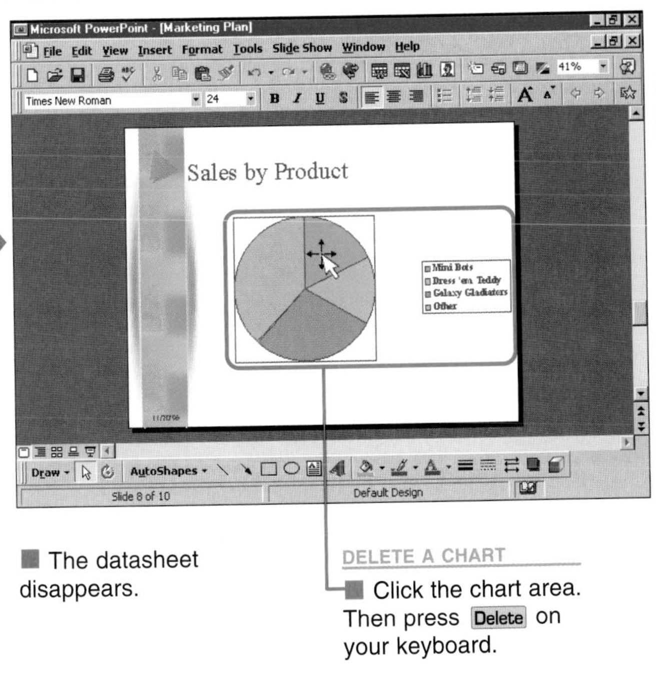

■ The datasheet disappears.

DELETE A CHART

■ Click the chart area. Then press Delete on your keyboard.

EDIT A CHART

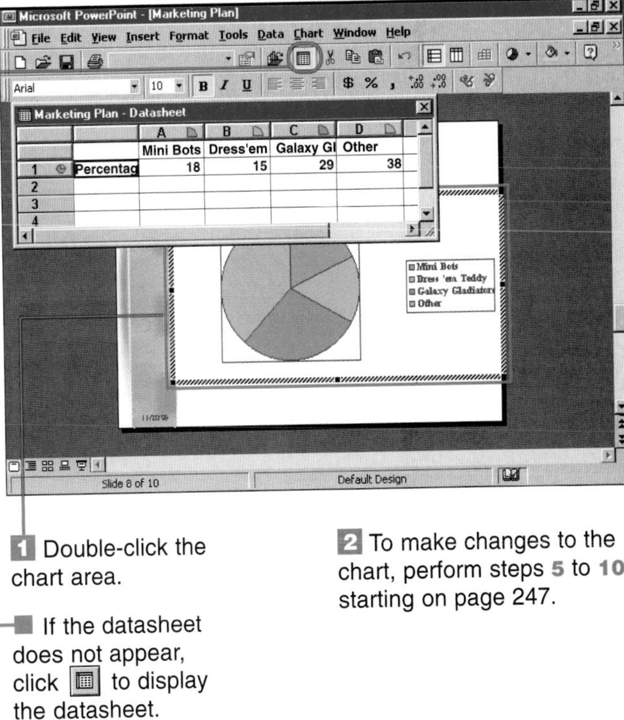

1 Double-click the chart area.

■ If the datasheet does not appear, click ▦ to display the datasheet.

2 To make changes to the chart, perform steps 5 to 10 starting on page 247.

ADD AN AUTOSHAPE

You can add simple shapes such as arrows and stars to the slides in your presentation.

ADD AN AUTOSHAPE

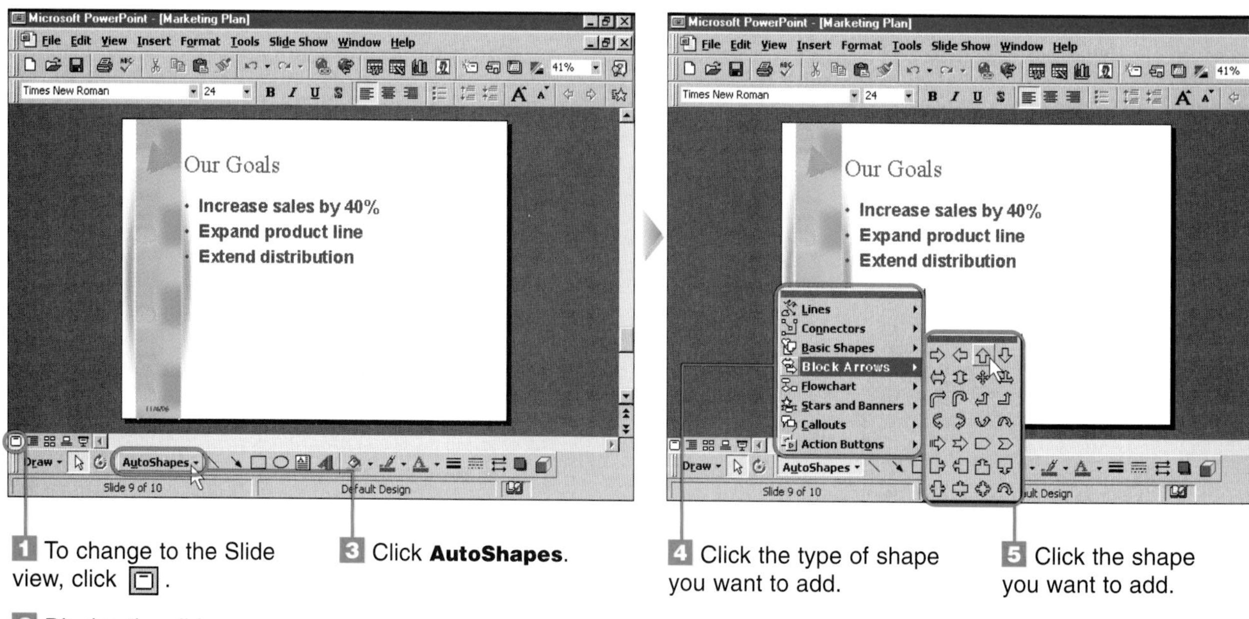

1 To change to the Slide view, click ▢.

2 Display the slide you want to add a shape to.

3 Click **AutoShapes**.

4 Click the type of shape you want to add.

5 Click the shape you want to add.

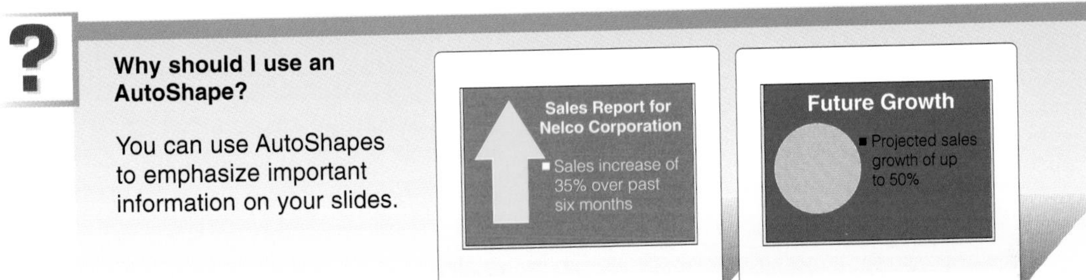

Why should I use an AutoShape?

You can use AutoShapes to emphasize important information on your slides.

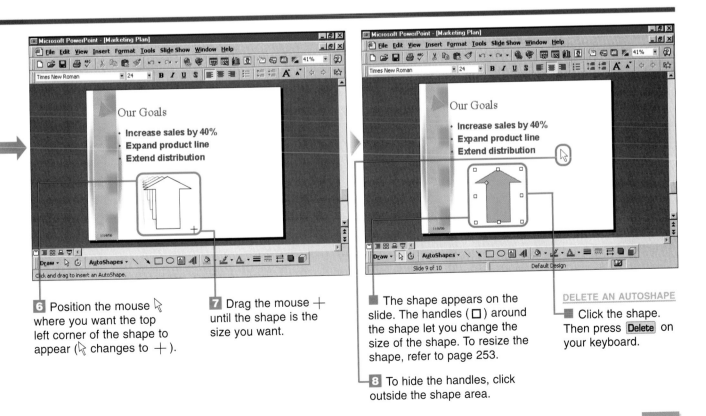

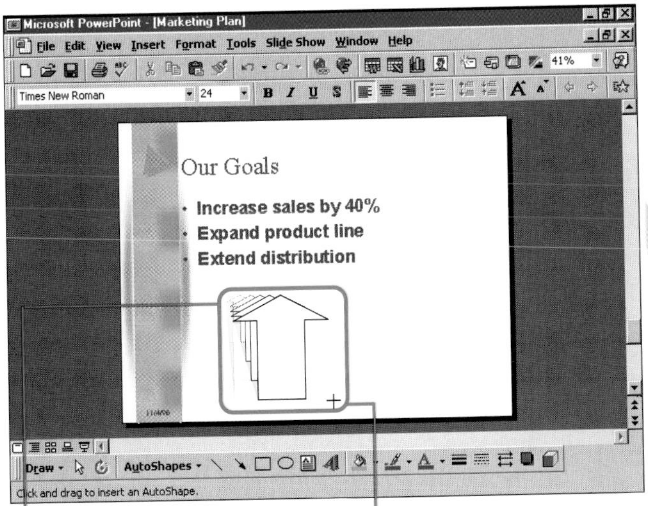

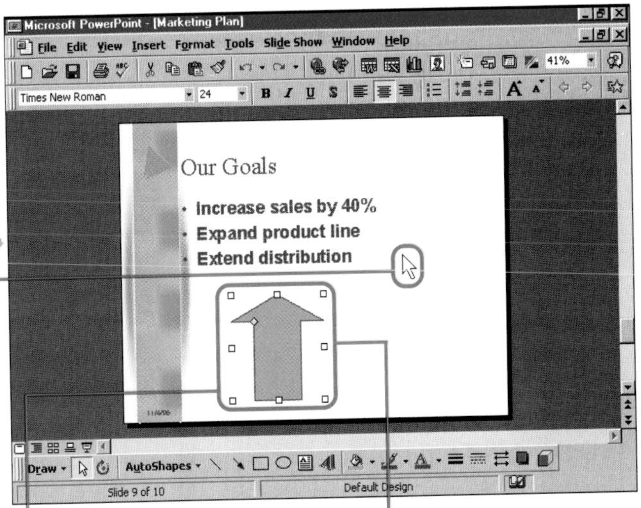

6 Position the mouse where you want the top left corner of the shape to appear (changes to +).

7 Drag the mouse + until the shape is the size you want.

■ The shape appears on the slide. The handles (□) around the shape let you change the size of the shape. To resize the shape, refer to page 253.

8 To hide the handles, click outside the shape area.

DELETE AN AUTOSHAPE

■ Click the shape. Then press Delete on your keyboard.

MOVE OR RESIZE AN OBJECT

You can easily change the location or size of any object on a slide.

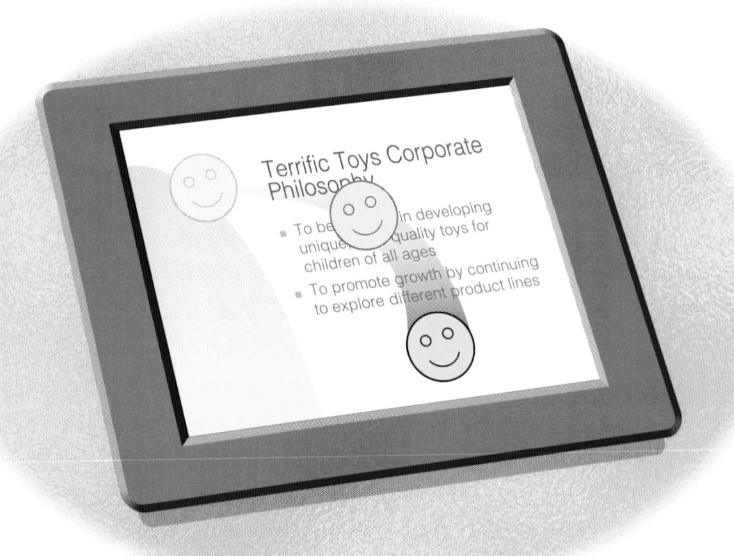

An object can include text, a clip art image, a chart or an AutoShape.

MOVE AN OBJECT

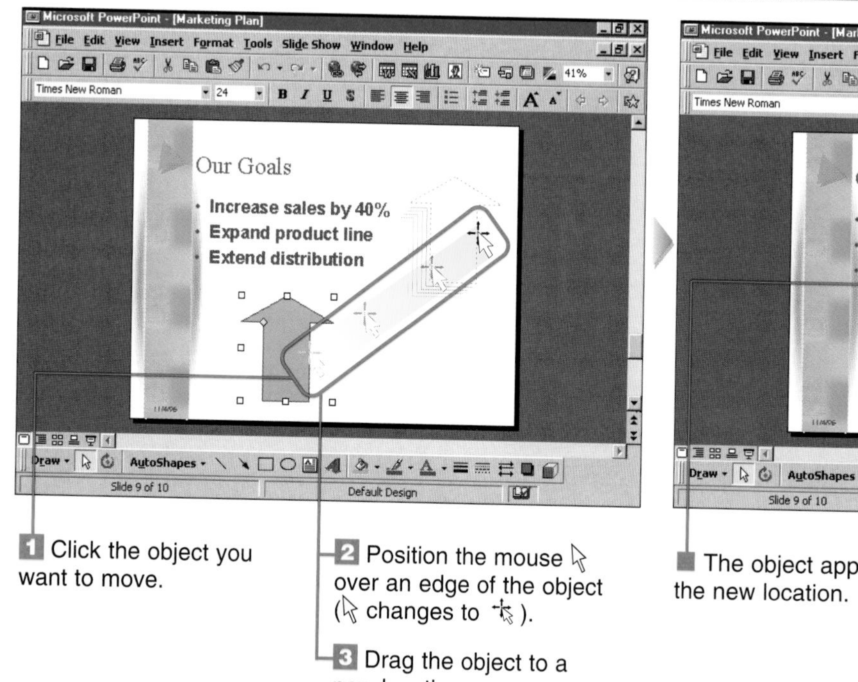

1 Click the object you want to move.

2 Position the mouse over an edge of the object (changes to).

3 Drag the object to a new location.

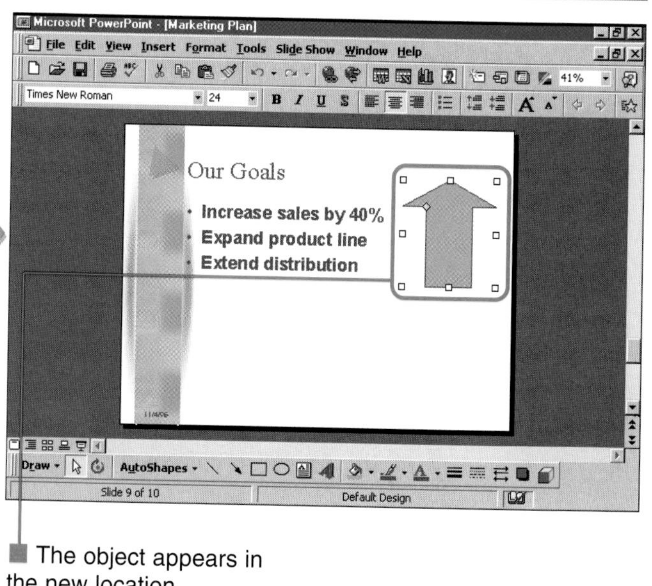

■ The object appears in the new location.

?

How can I use the handles (□) that appear around a selected object?

The handles around an object let you change the size of the object.

■ Changes the height of an object.

■ Changes the width of an object.

■ Changes the height and width of an object at the same time.

RESIZE AN OBJECT

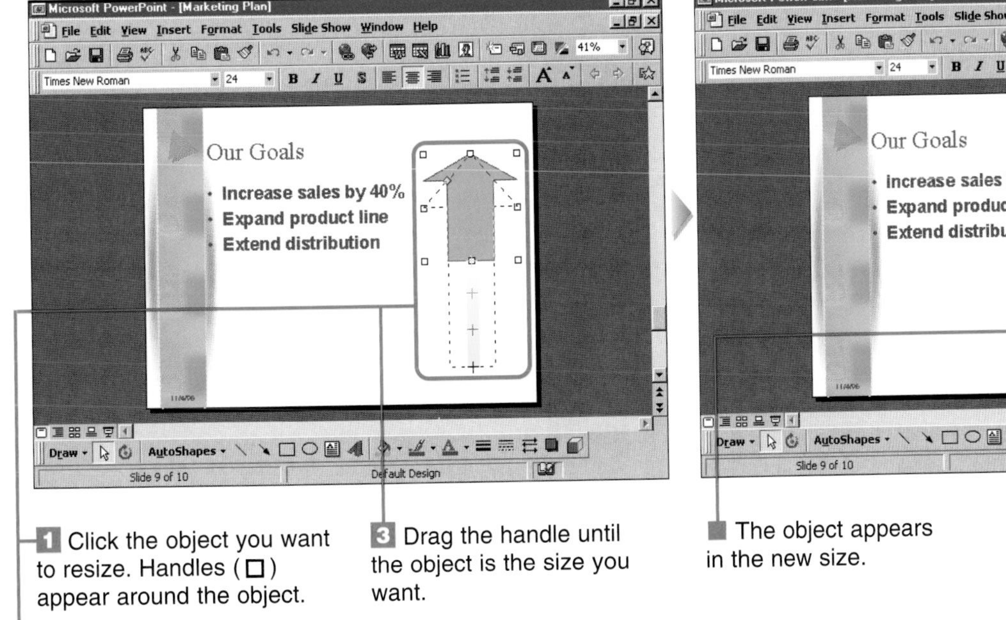

1 Click the object you want to resize. Handles (□) appear around the object.

2 Position the mouse ↖ over one of the handles (↖ changes to ↕ or ↔).

3 Drag the handle until the object is the size you want.

■ The object appears in the new size.

PowerPoint offers many ready-to-use designs that you can choose from to give the slides in your presentation a new appearance.

CHANGE SLIDE DESIGN

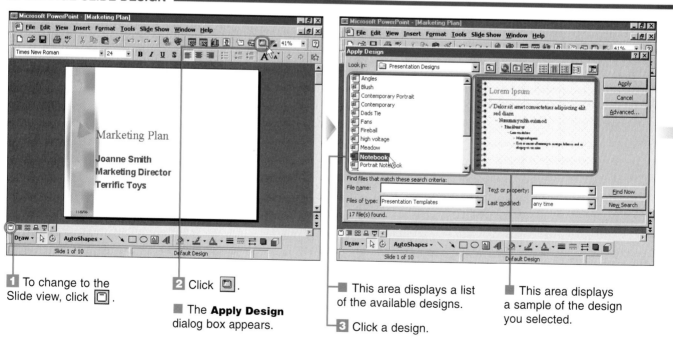

1 To change to the Slide view, click ▢.

2 Click ▢.

■ The **Apply Design** dialog box appears.

■ This area displays a list of the available designs.

3 Click a design.

■ This area displays a sample of the design you selected.

?

What slide designs does PowerPoint offer?

Here are some of the designs that PowerPoint offers.

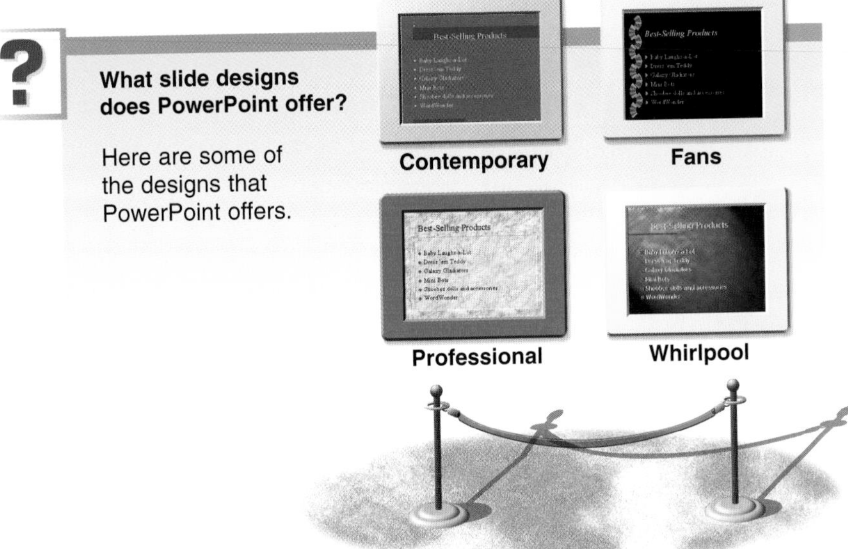

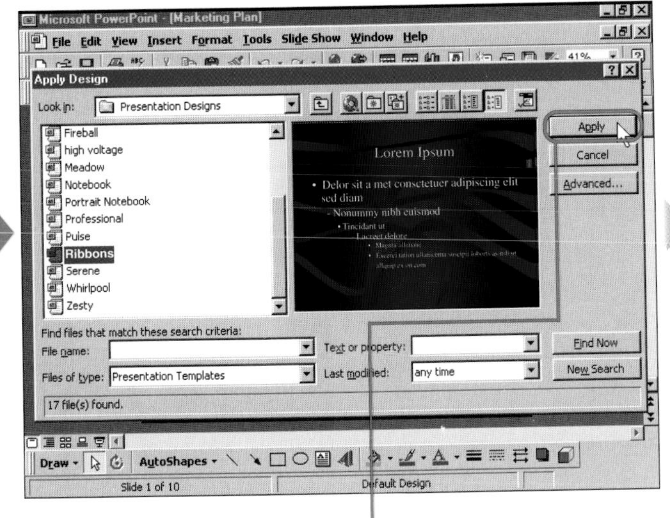

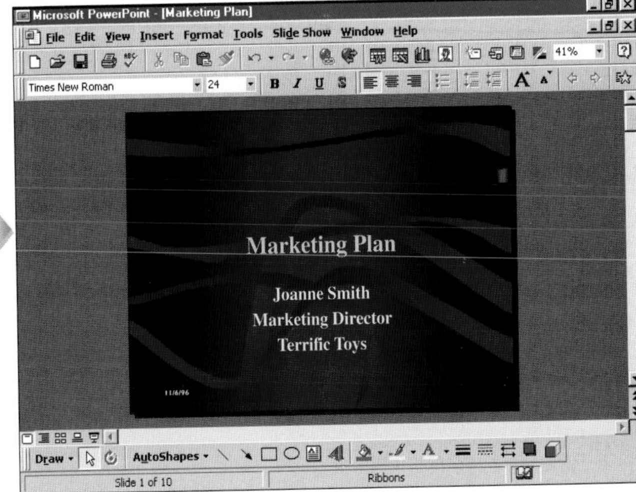

4 Repeat step 3 until the design you want to use appears.

5 To apply the design to all the slides in the presentation, click **Apply**.

■ The slides in the presentation display the new design.

■ The design you selected only changes the appearance of the slides. The content of the slides does not change.

CHANGE COLOR SCHEME

You can select a different color scheme for your entire presentation.

CHANGE COLOR SCHEME

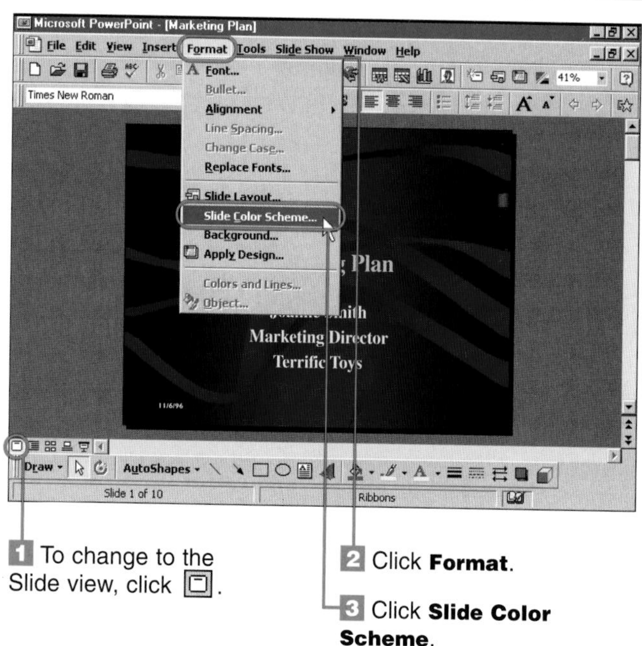

1 To change to the Slide view, click [icon].

2 Click **Format**.

3 Click **Slide Color Scheme**.

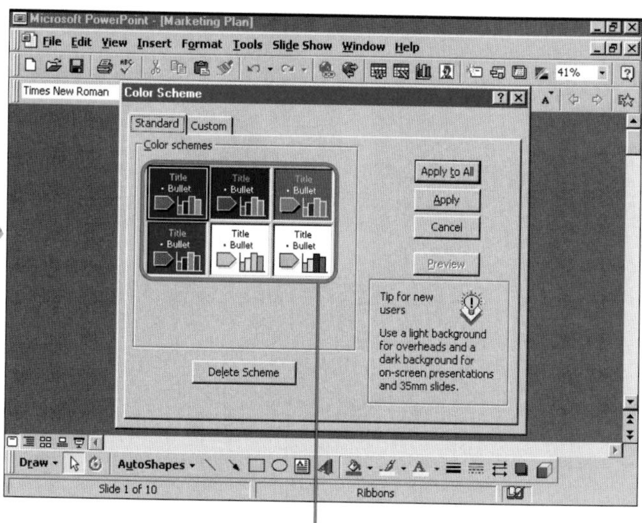

■ The **Color Scheme** dialog box appears.

■ This area displays samples of the color schemes that PowerPoint offers for the presentation.

Note: The color schemes offered depend on the slide design. To change the slide design, refer to page 254.

?

How can I emphasize one slide in my presentation?

You can make an important slide stand out from the rest of your presentation by changing the color scheme for only that slide.

To change the color scheme for only one slide, display the slide you want to change. Then perform steps **1** to **5** starting on page 256, selecting **Apply** in step **5**.

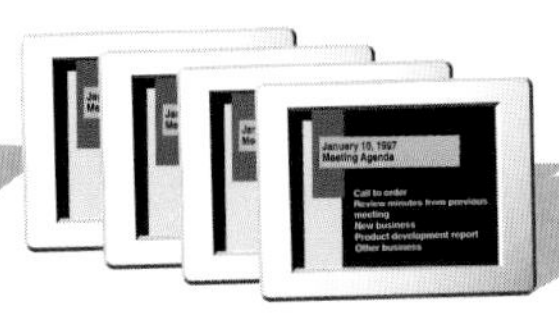

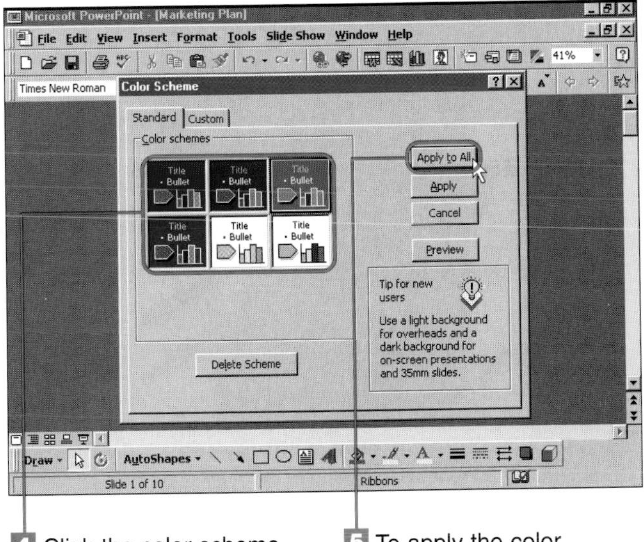

4 Click the color scheme you want to use.

5 To apply the color scheme to all the slides in the presentation, click **Apply to All**.

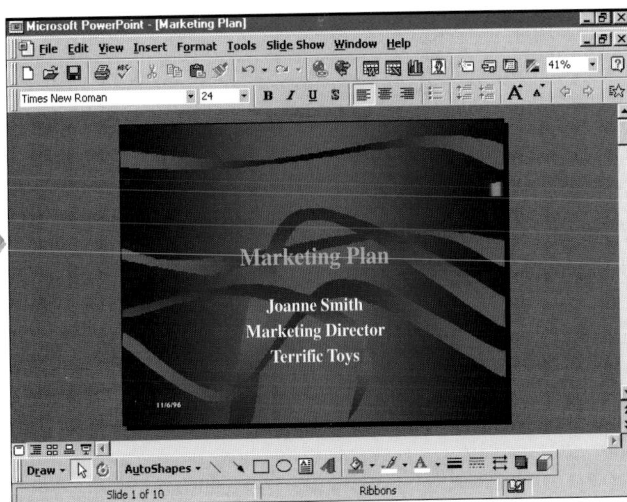

■ All the slides in the presentation display the new color scheme.

EMPHASIZE TEXT

PowerPoint offers several styles that you can use to emphasize information on your slides.

EMPHASIZE TEXT

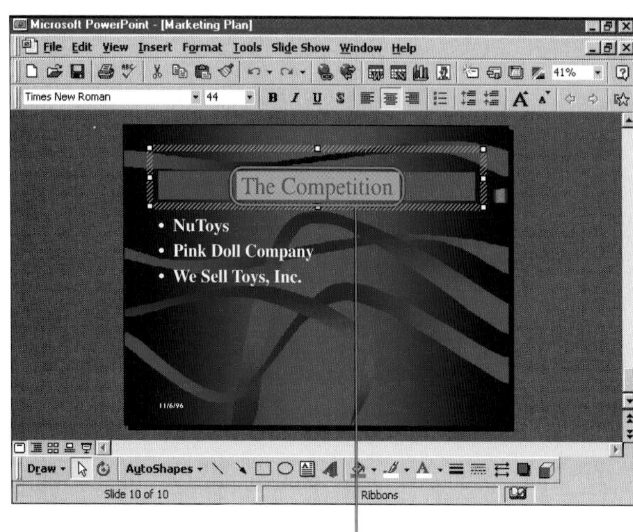

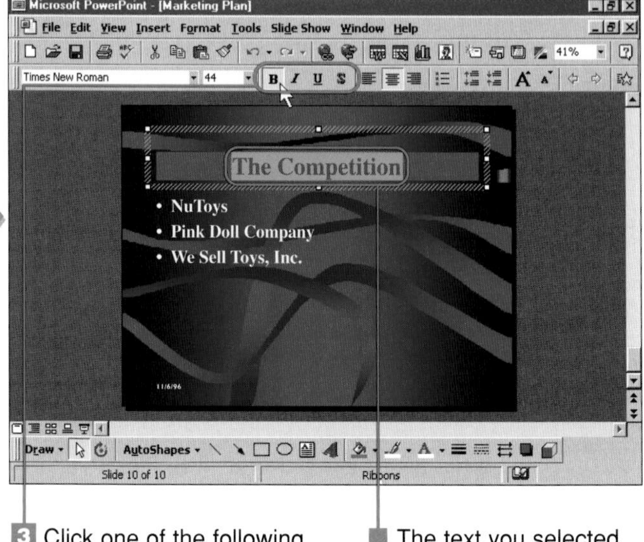

1 Display the slide containing the text you want to change.

2 Select the text you want to change. To select text, refer to page 228.

3 Click one of the following options.

B Bold

I Italic

U Underline

S Shadow

■ The text you selected appears in the new style. To remove the style, repeat steps 2 and 3.

CHANGE ALIGNMENT OF TEXT

You can enhance the appearance of your slides by aligning text in different ways.

CHANGE ALIGNMENT OF TEXT

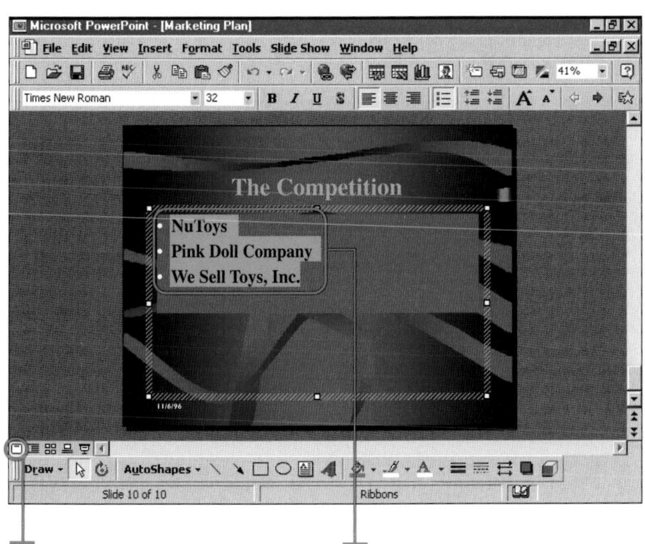

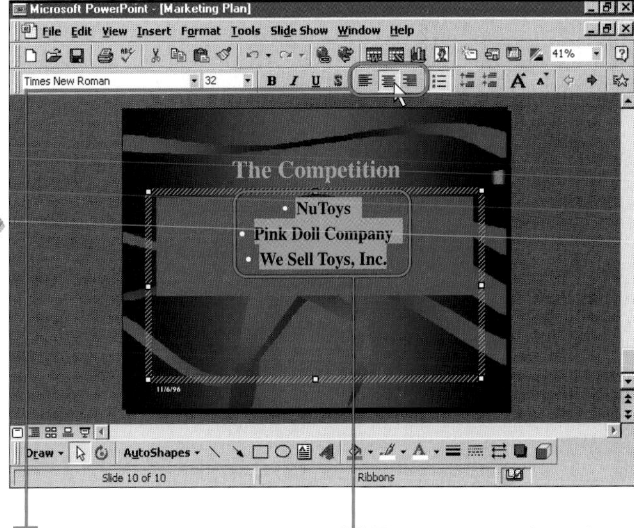

1 To change to the Slide view, click ▢.

2 Display the slide containing the text you want to align differently.

3 Select the text you want to align differently. To select text, refer to page 228.

4 Click one of the following options.

- ≡ Left Align
- ≡ Center
- ≡ Right Align

■ The text you selected displays the new alignment.

You can enhance the appearance of slides in your presentation by changing the design of the text.

CHANGE FONT OF TEXT

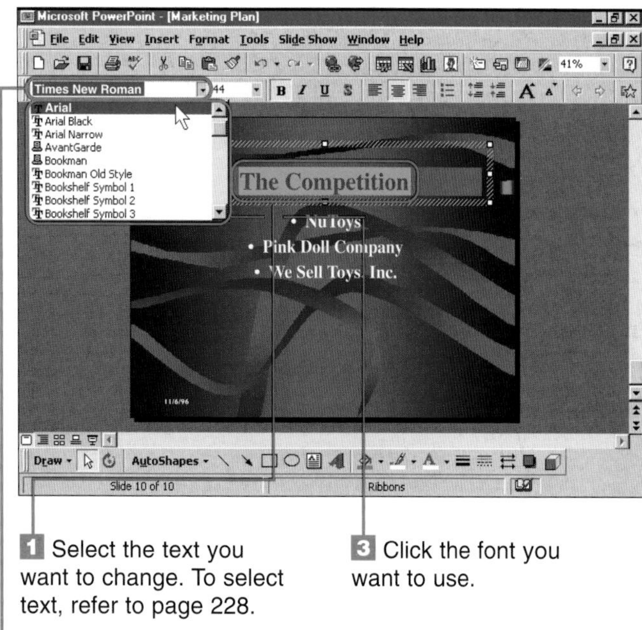

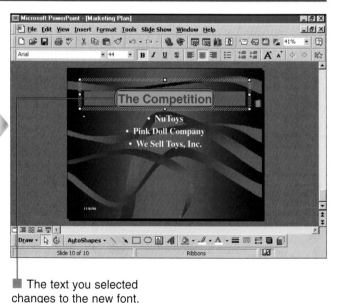

1 Select the text you want to change. To select text, refer to page 228.

2 To display a list of the available fonts, click ▾ in this area.

3 Click the font you want to use.

■ The text you selected changes to the new font.

CHANGE SIZE OF TEXT

You can increase or decrease the size of text in your presentation.

CHANGE SIZE OF TEXT

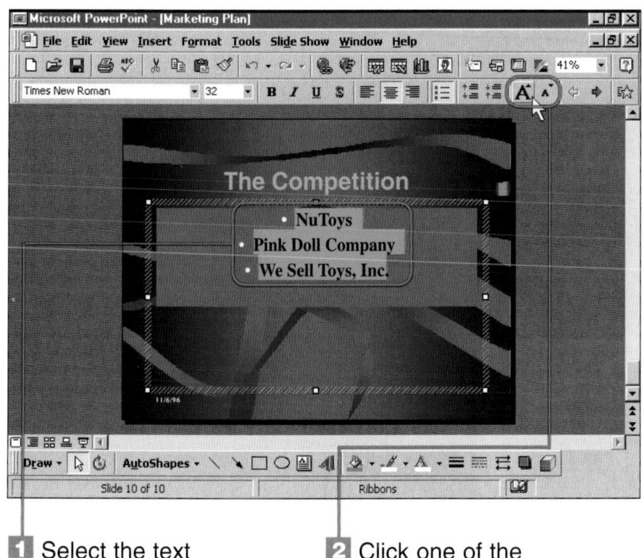

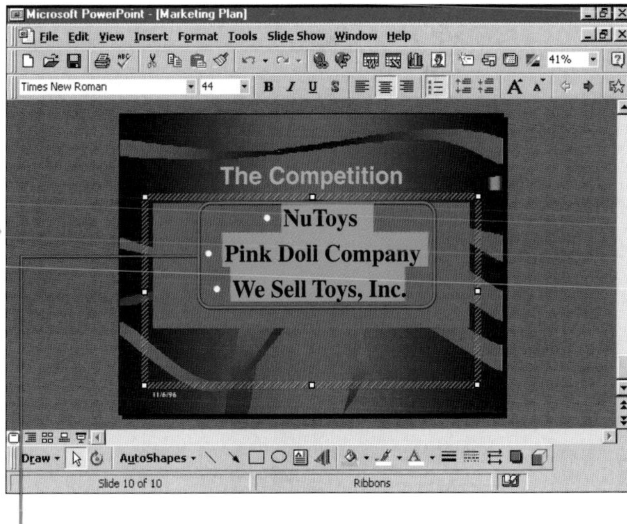

1 Select the text you want to change. To select text, refer to page 228.

2 Click one of the following options until the text is the size you want.

A Increase size of text

A Decrease size of text

■ The text you selected changes to the new size.

You can change the color of text on a slide.

CHANGE TEXT COLOR

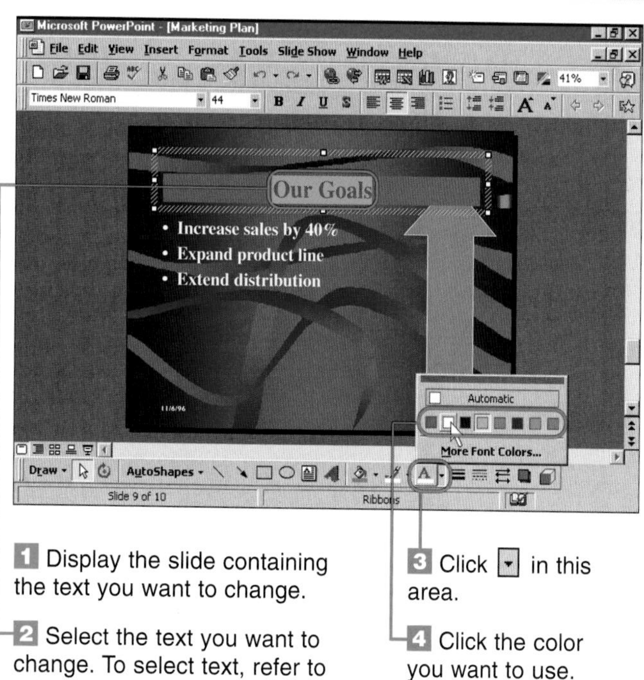

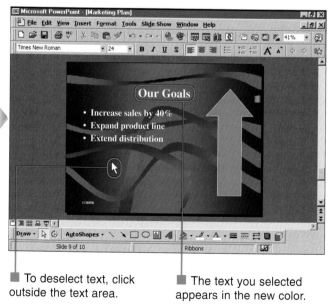

1 Display the slide containing the text you want to change.

2 Select the text you want to change. To select text, refer to page 228.

3 Click ▾ in this area.

4 Click the color you want to use.

■ To deselect text, click outside the text area.

■ The text you selected appears in the new color.

CHANGE OBJECT COLOR

You can change the color of an object on a slide.

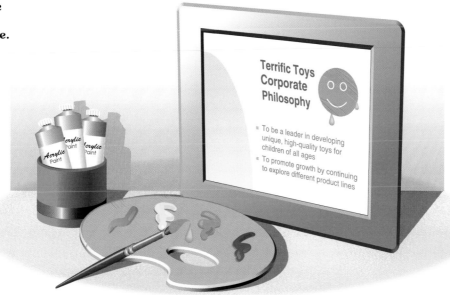

CHANGE OBJECT COLOR

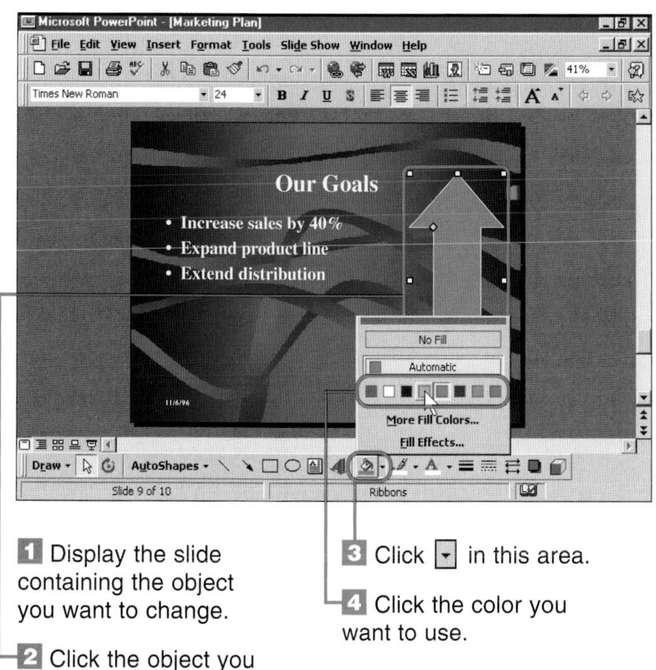

1 Display the slide containing the object you want to change.

2 Click the object you want to change.

3 Click ▾ in this area.

4 Click the color you want to use.

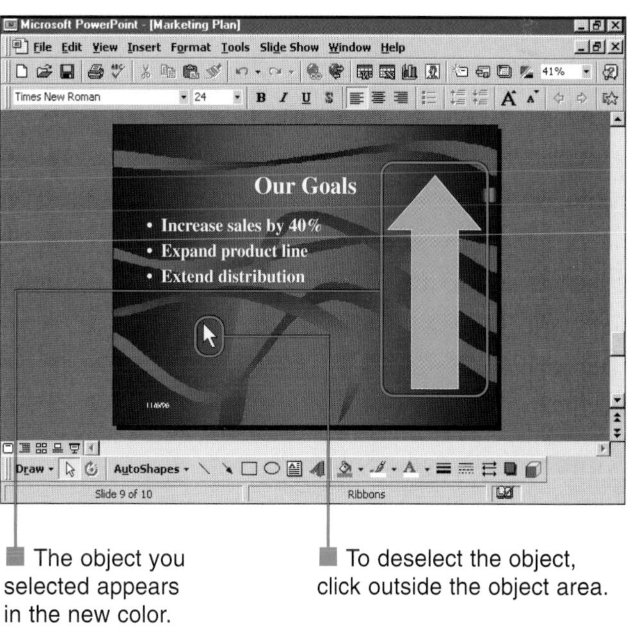

■ The object you selected appears in the new color.

■ To deselect the object, click outside the object area.

ADD A HEADER AND FOOTER

You can add information to every slide or page in your presentation.

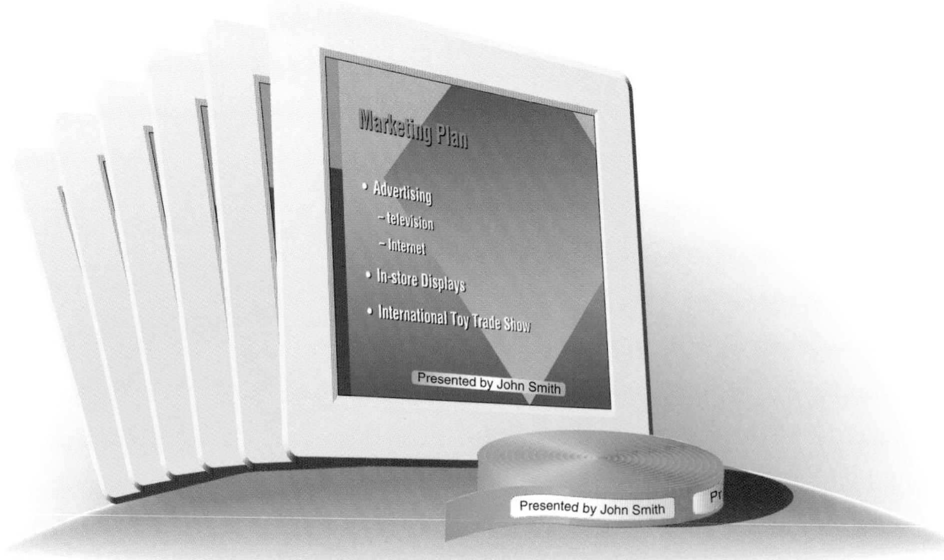

ADD A HEADER AND FOOTER

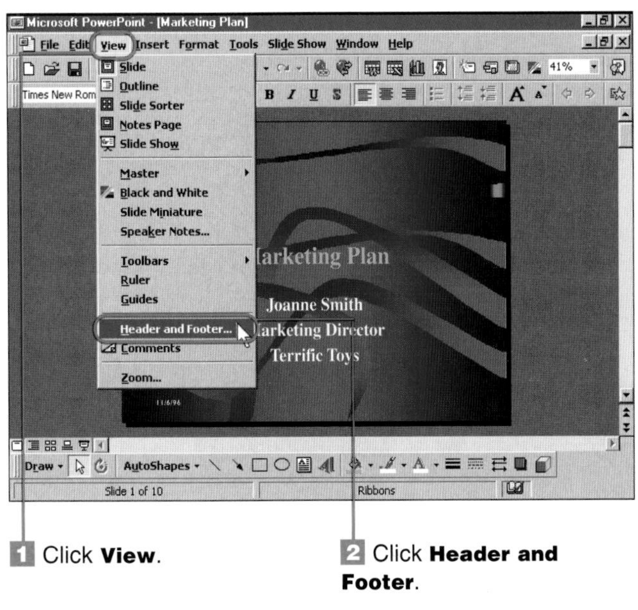

1 Click **View**.

2 Click **Header and Footer**.

■ The **Header and Footer** dialog box appears.

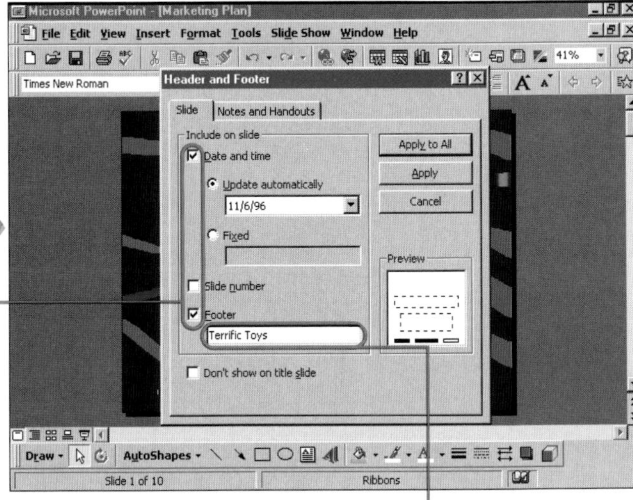

■ Each option that displays a check mark (✔) will appear on all the slides in the presentation.

3 To add or remove a check mark (✔) for an option, click the check box beside the option.

4 To type the footer text you want to appear at the bottom of each slide, click this area. Then type the footer text.

What information can I add to my presentation?

Slides can include a date, footer and slide number.

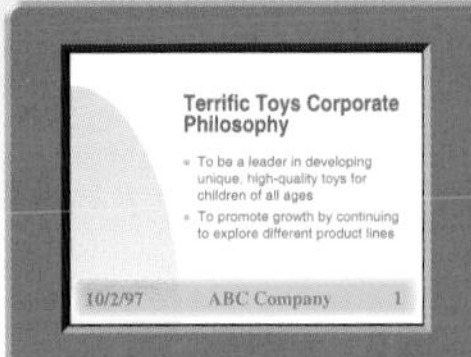

Notes and handouts can include a header, date, footer and page number.

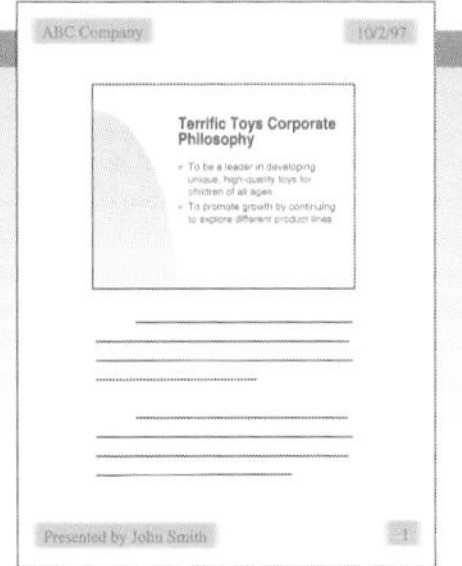

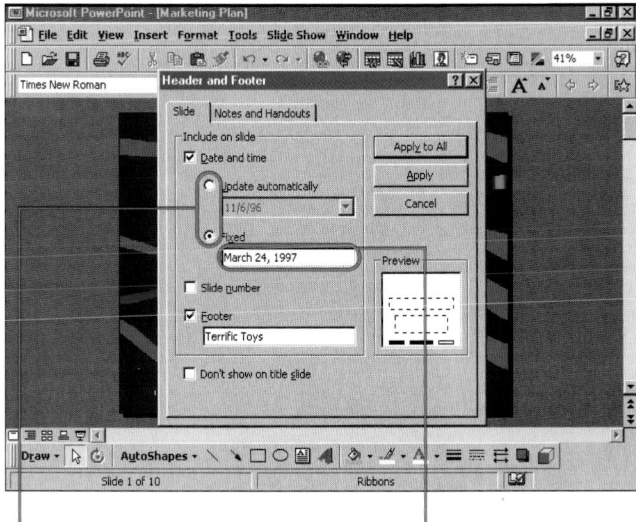

5 To select the date you want each slide to display, click one of these options (○ changes to ◉).

Update automatically - Display the current date.

Fixed - Display the date you specify.

6 If you selected **Fixed** in step 5, type the date.

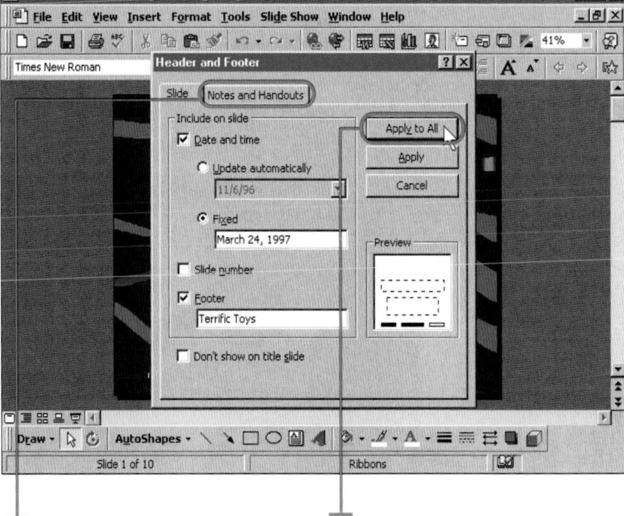

■ To specify the information you want to appear on the notes and handout pages, click this tab. Then repeat steps 3 to 6 to specify the information.

7 To apply the changes to all the slides and pages, click **Apply to All**.

ANIMATE SLIDES

You can add movement and sound effects to the objects on your slides.

ANIMATE SLIDES

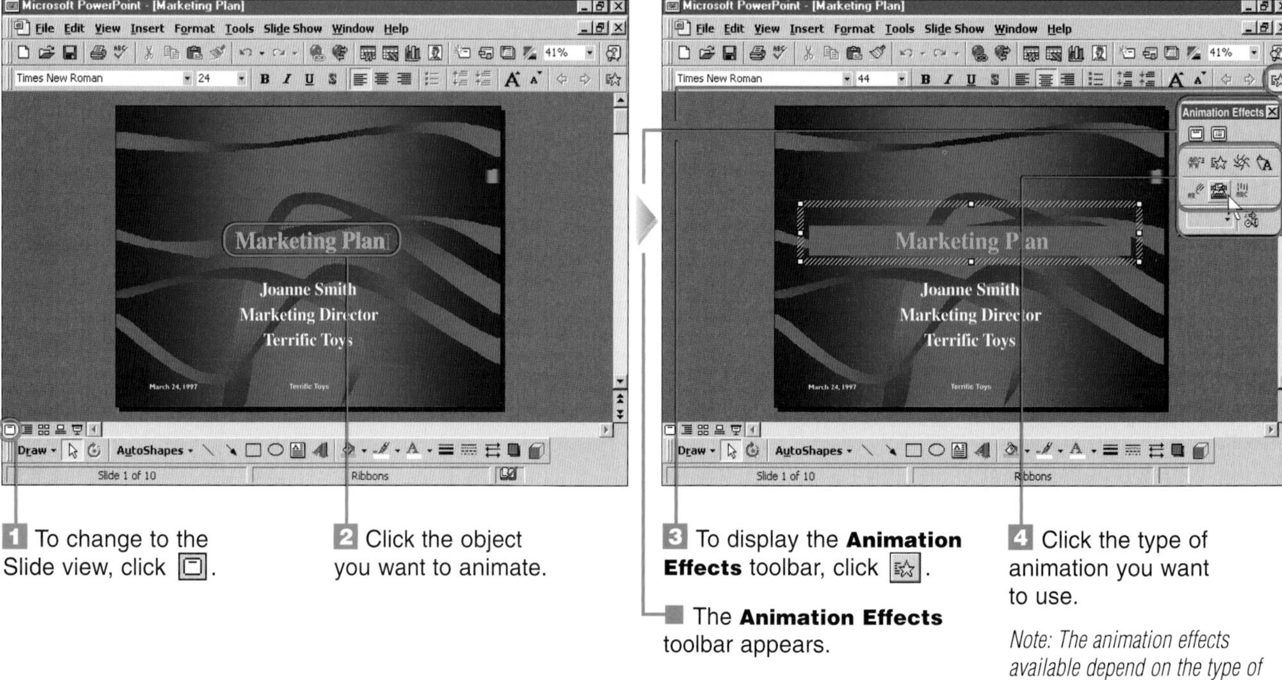

1 To change to the Slide view, click [Slide view icon].

2 Click the object you want to animate.

3 To display the **Animation Effects** toolbar, click [Animation Effects icon].

■ The **Animation Effects** toolbar appears.

4 Click the type of animation you want to use.

Note: The animation effects available depend on the type of object you selected in step ***2****.*

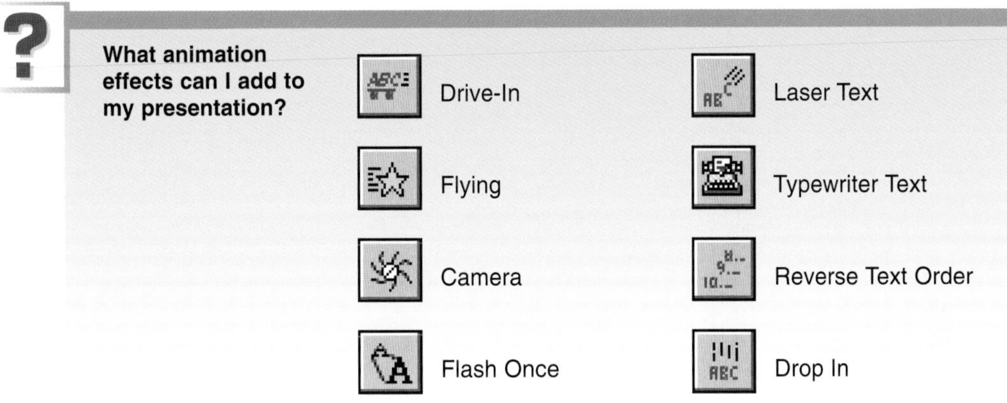

? **What animation effects can I add to my presentation?**

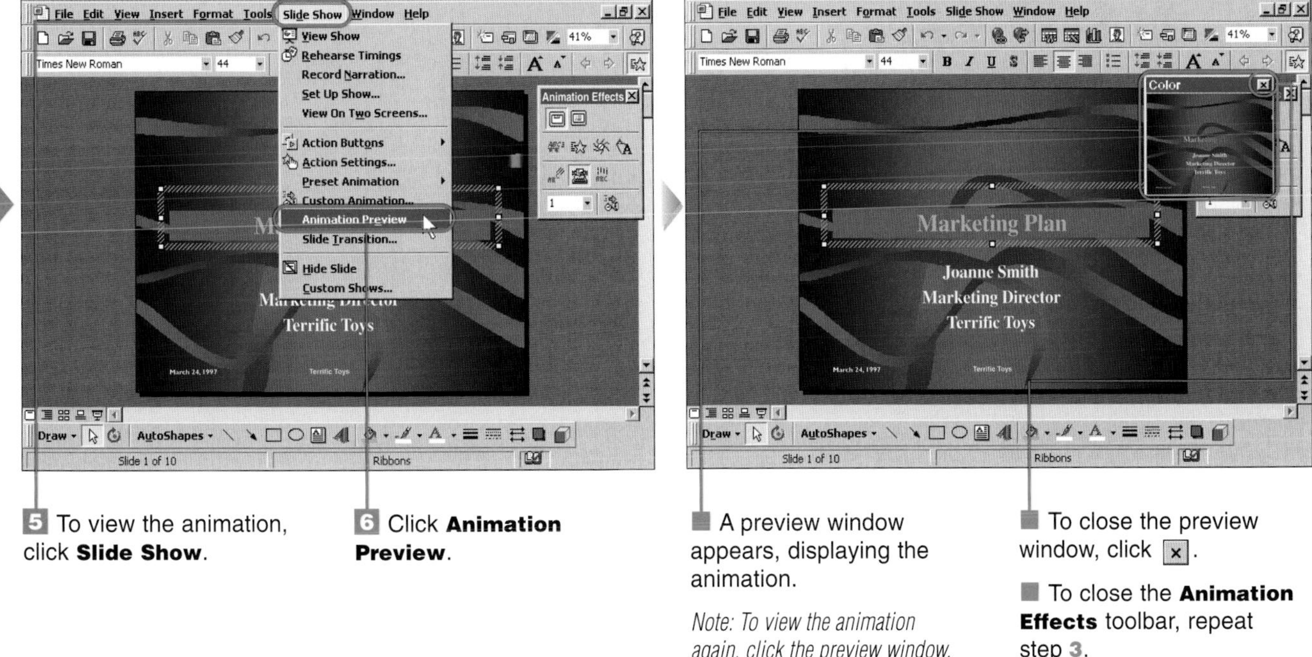

5 To view the animation, click **Slide Show**.

6 Click **Animation Preview**.

■ A preview window appears, displaying the animation.

Note: To view the animation again, click the preview window.

■ To close the preview window, click ☒.

■ To close the **Animation Effects** toolbar, repeat step **3**.

REORDER SLIDES

You can easily change the order of the slides in your presentation.

REORDER SLIDES

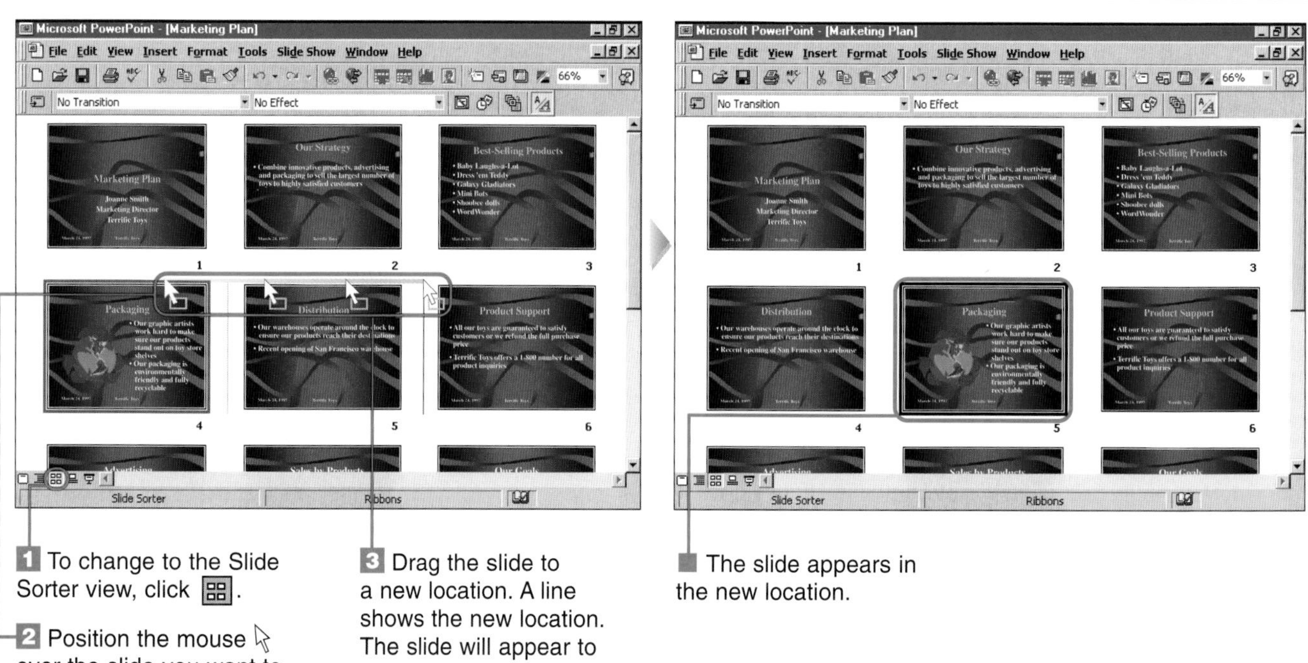

1 To change to the Slide Sorter view, click .

2 Position the mouse over the slide you want to move.

3 Drag the slide to a new location. A line shows the new location. The slide will appear to the left of the line.

■ The slide appears in the new location.

DELETE A SLIDE

You can remove a slide you no longer need.

DELETE A SLIDE

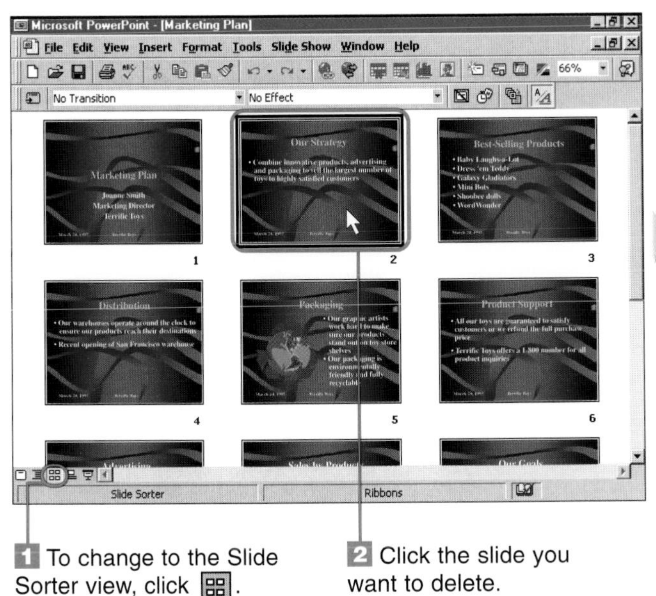

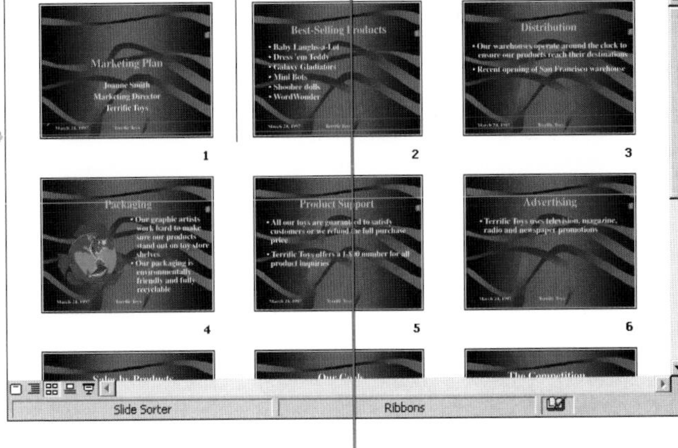

1 To change to the Slide Sorter view, click ⊞.

2 Click the slide you want to delete.

3 Press Delete on your keyboard.

■ The slide disappears.

■ To immediately return the slide to the presentation, click ↶.

CREATE SPEAKER NOTES

You can create speaker notes that contain copies of your slides with all the ideas you want to discuss. These notes will help you deliver your presentation.

CREATE SPEAKER NOTES

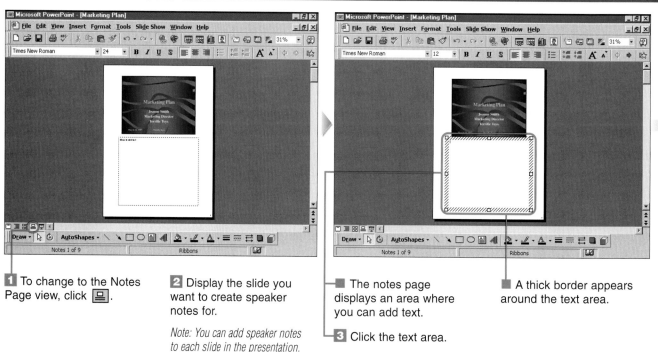

1 To change to the Notes Page view, click .

2 Display the slide you want to create speaker notes for.

Note: You can add speaker notes to each slide in the presentation.

■ The notes page displays an area where you can add text.

3 Click the text area.

■ A thick border appears around the text area.

What should I include in my speaker notes?

When creating speaker notes, include the key points you want to discuss during your presentation.

Speaker notes can also include statistics or additional information that will support your ideas and help you to answer questions from the audience.

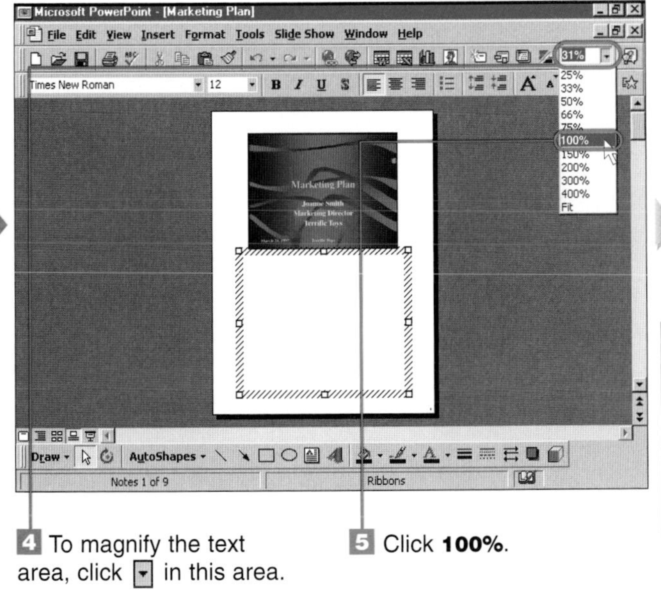

4 To magnify the text area, click ▾ in this area.

5 Click **100%**.

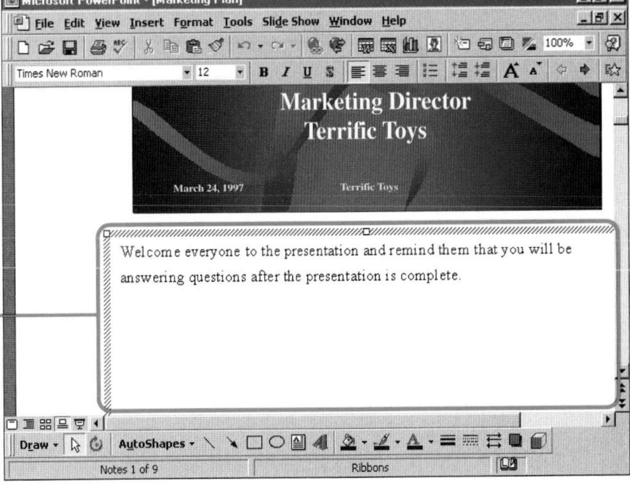

■ The text area is magnified.

6 Type the ideas you want to discuss when you display the slide during the presentation.

7 To once again display the entire notes page, repeat steps 4 and 5, selecting **Fit** in step 5.

VIEW A SLIDE SHOW

You can view a slide show of your presentation on a computer screen.

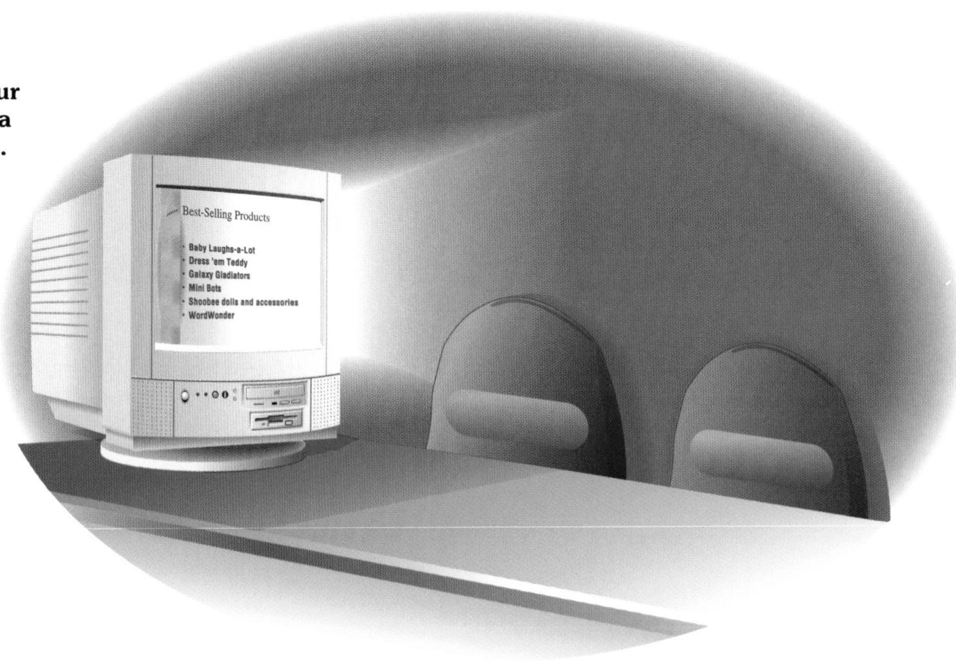

VIEW A SLIDE SHOW

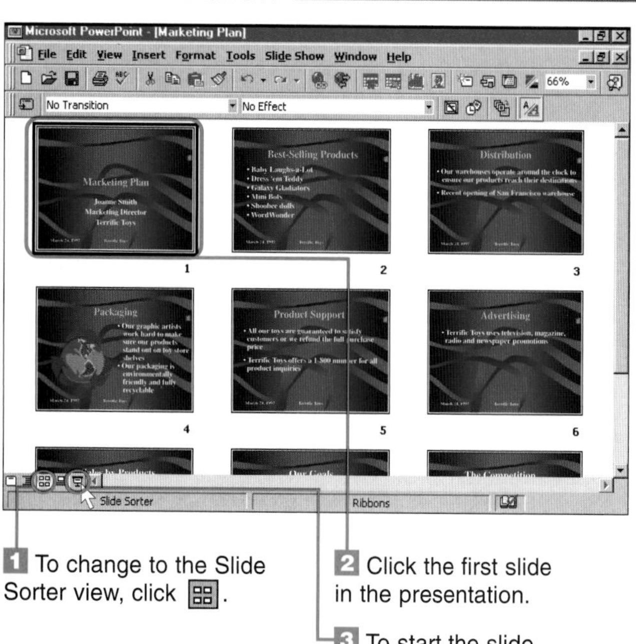

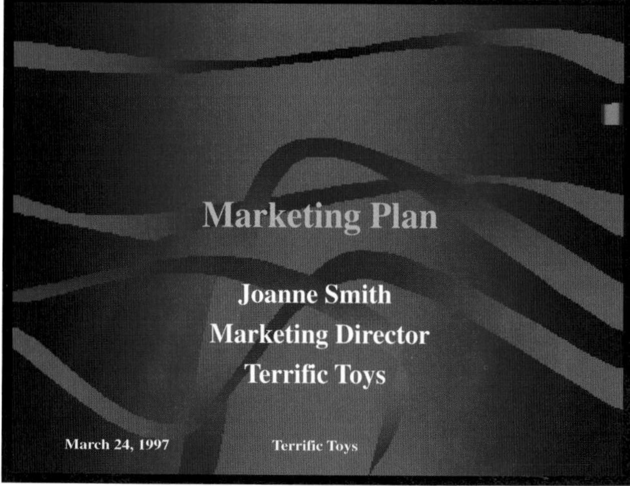

1 To change to the Slide Sorter view, click [Slide Sorter button].

2 Click the first slide in the presentation.

3 To start the slide show, click [Slide Show button].

■ The first slide fills the screen.

4 To display the next slide, press the **Spacebar** on your keyboard or click anywhere over the slide.

Is the speed at which I deliver a presentation important?

Make sure you rehearse the pace of your presentation before delivering it to an audience. A fast pace can overwhelm an audience whereas a slow pace may put the audience to sleep.

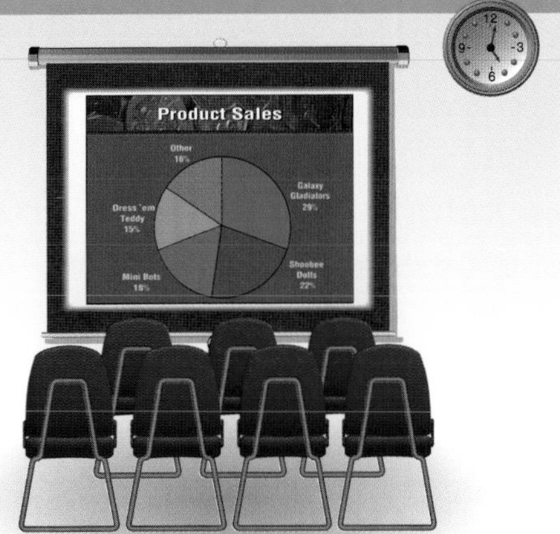

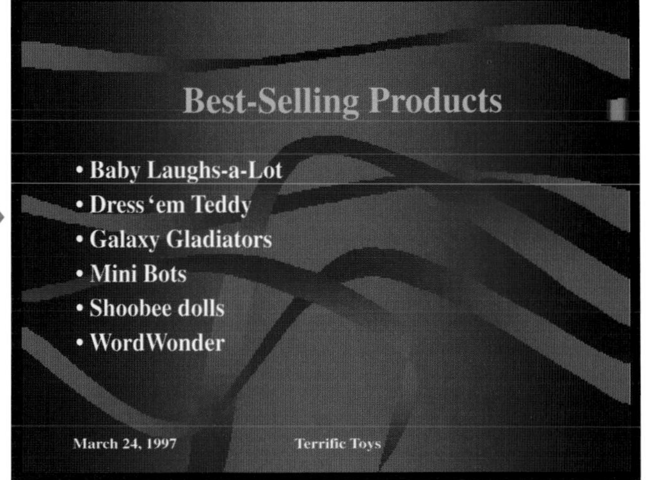

■ The next slide appears.

5 Repeat step 4 until you finish viewing all the slides in the presentation.

QUICK REFERENCE

You can use the keyboard to help you move through your presentation.

Display the next slide	Press the **Spacebar**.
Display the previous slide	Press ←Backspace .
Display any slide	Press the number of the slide on your keyboard and then press Enter .
End the presentation	Press Esc .

ADD SLIDE TRANSITIONS

You can use special effects, called transitions, to help you move from one slide to the next. Transitions help to introduce each slide during an on-screen slide show.

ADD SLIDE TRANSITIONS

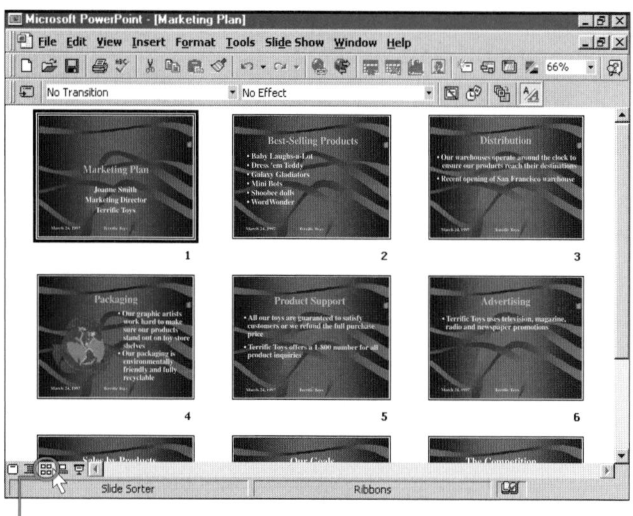

1 To change to the Slide Sorter view, click ▦.

Note: PowerPoint automatically adds transitions to slides for some types of presentations. A symbol ( ) appears below every slide with a transition.

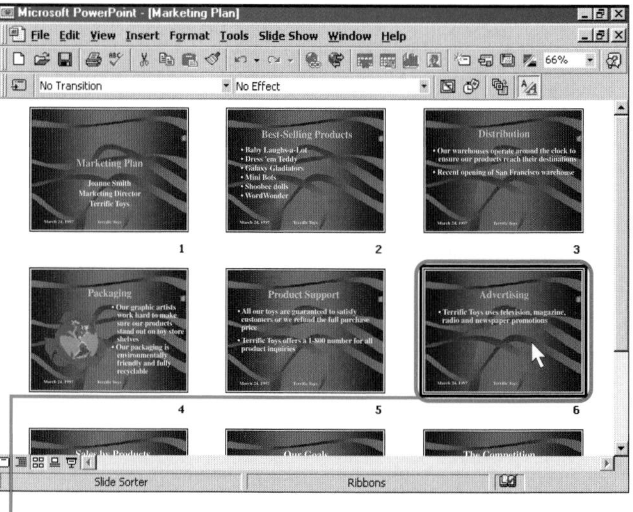

2 To add or change a transition for a slide, click the slide.

What slide transitions does PowerPoint offer?

These are a few of the slide transitions PowerPoint offers.

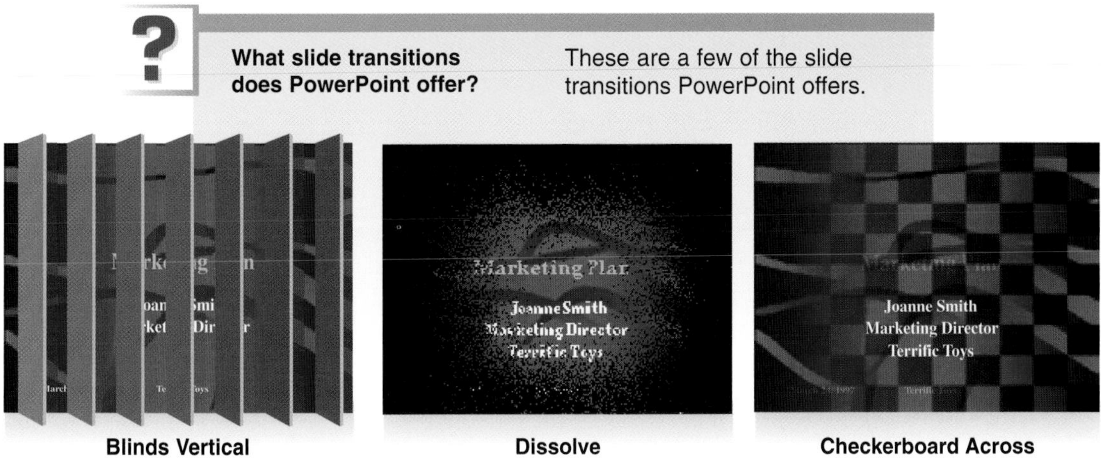

Blinds Vertical **Dissolve** **Checkerboard Across**

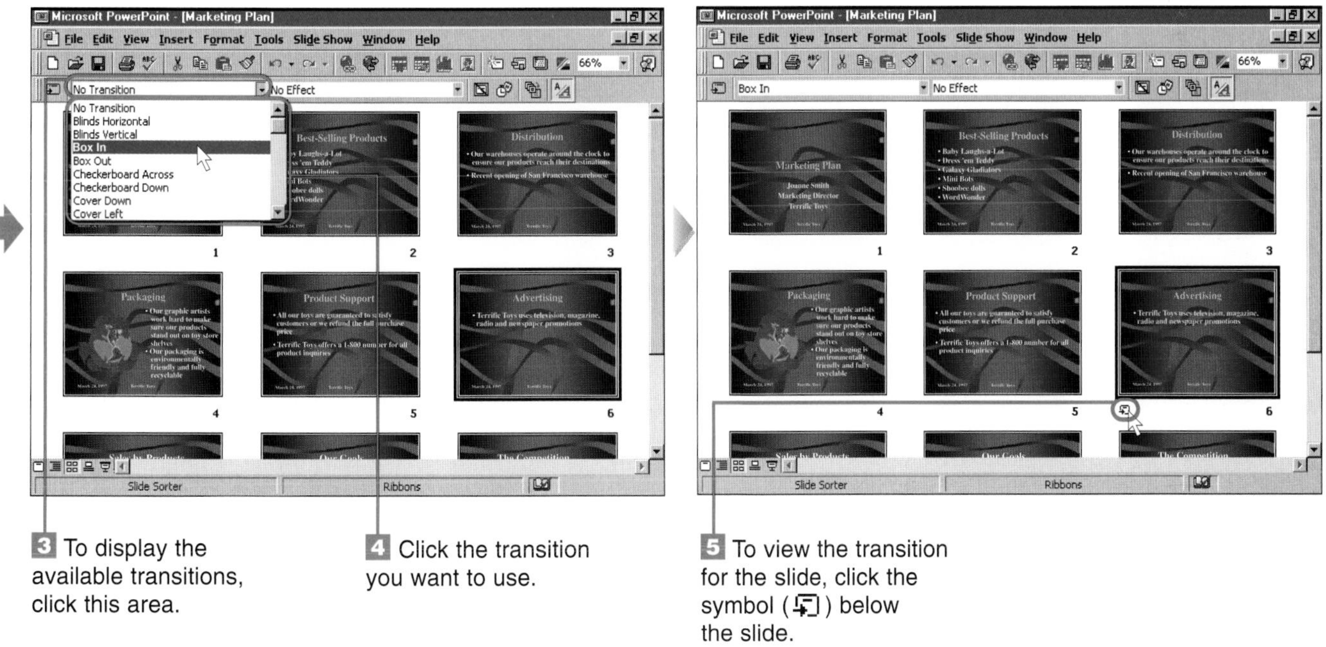

3 To display the available transitions, click this area.

4 Click the transition you want to use.

5 To view the transition for the slide, click the symbol ( ) below the slide.

PRINT A PRESENTATION

You can produce a paper copy of a presentation for your own use or to hand out to an audience.

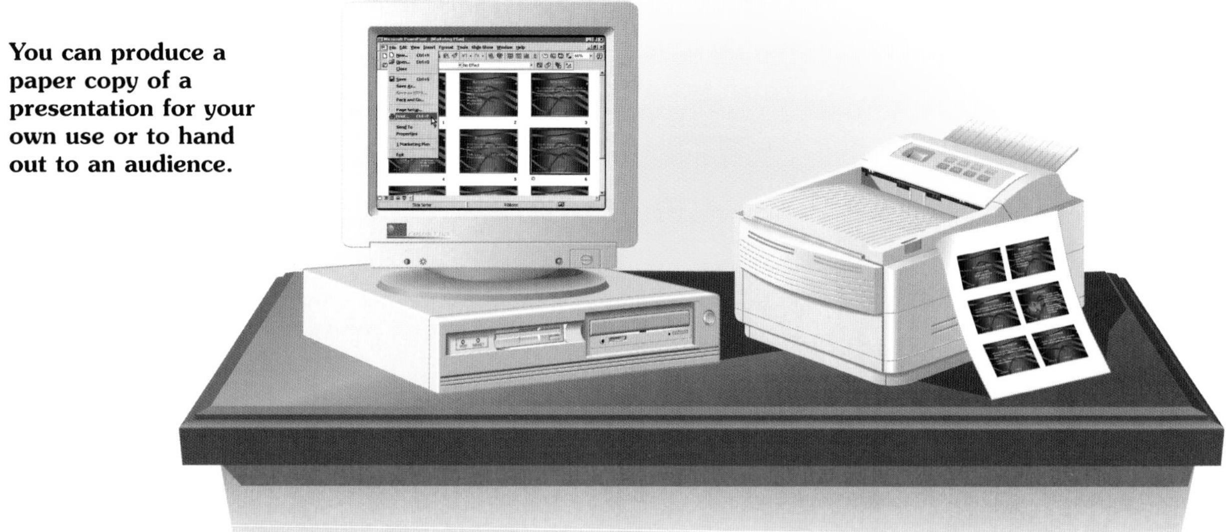

PRINT A PRESENTATION

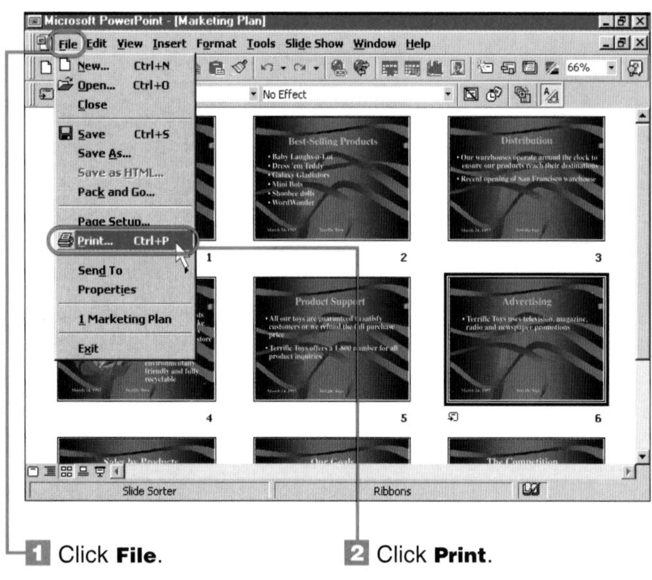

1 Click **File**.

2 Click **Print**.

■ The **Print** dialog box appears.

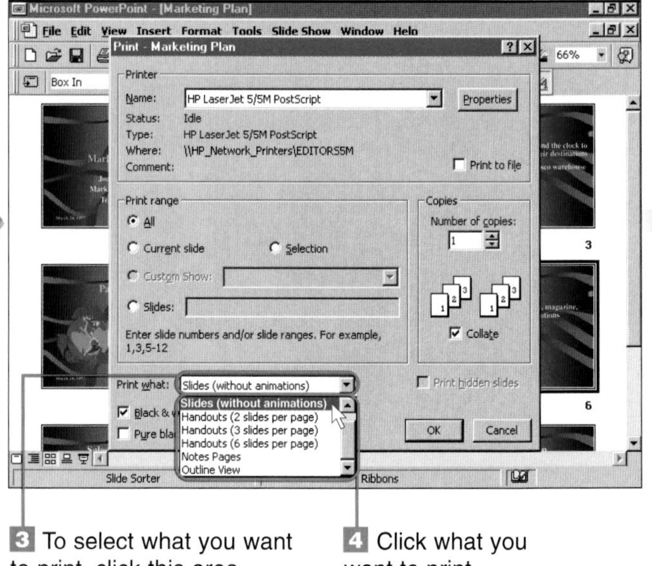

3 To select what you want to print, click this area.

4 Click what you want to print.

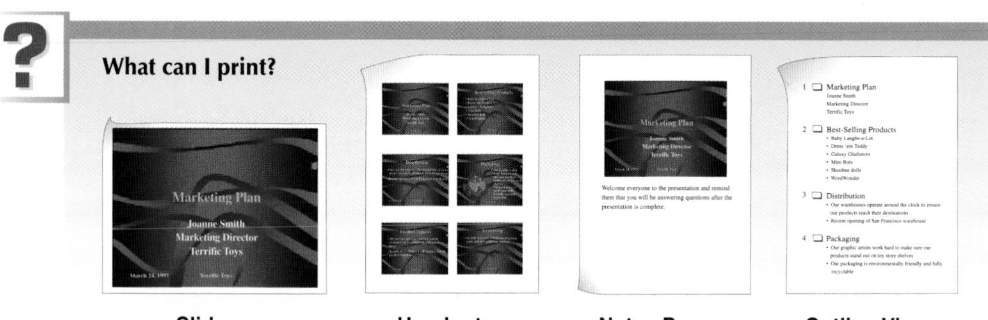

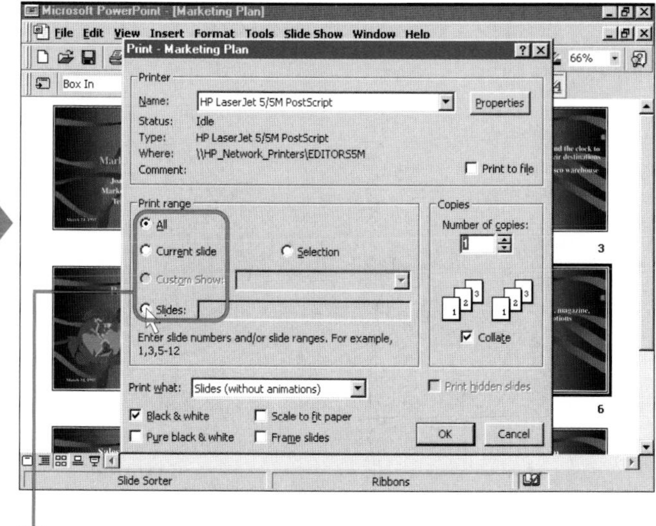

5 Click one of these options (○ changes to ◉).

All - Prints every slide in the presentation.

Current slide - Prints the selected slide or the slide displayed on the screen.

Slides - Prints the slides you specify.

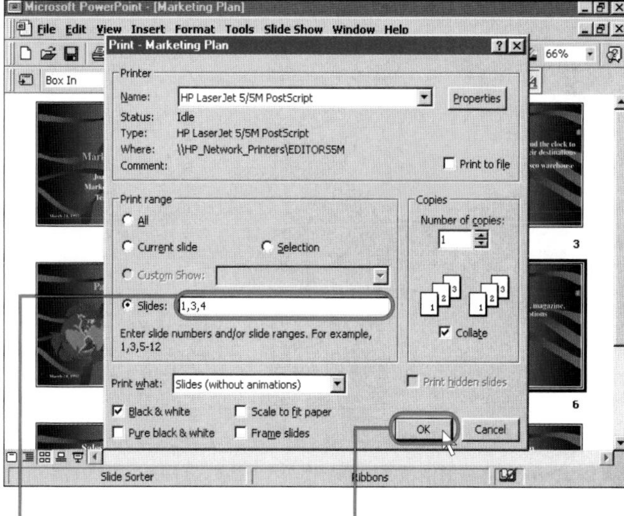

6 If you selected **Slides** in step **5**, type the slide numbers you want to print (example: 1,3,4 or 2-4).

7 Click **OK**.

Calendar
June 1997
1 2 3 4 5 6 7
8 9 10 11 12 13 14
15 16 17 18 19 20 21
27 28
6
Time
Activities
12:30 Lunch with Tim
2:00 Marketing meeting
3:50 Presentation at ABC Company
6:30 Dinner with the Smiths
7
Time
Activities
9:00 Sales meeting
12:15 Dentist Appointment
1:00 Test prototype
3:15 Meet with Ad Reps.
1
2
3
4
5
6

Outlook

Includes:

1 Start Outlook
Learn how to start Outlook and find out what features the program offers.

2 Using Inbox
Learn how to exchange electronic mail messages with friends, family members, colleagues and clients.

3 Using Notes
Learn how to use Notes to store information such as reminders, questions and ideas.

4 Using Tasks
Learn how to keep track of your tasks using Outlook.

5 Using Calendar
Find out how to use the Calendar to keep track of your appointments and plan your schedule.

6 Using Contacts
The Contacts feature lets you store detailed information about your friends, family members, colleagues and clients.

7 Using Journal
Learn how to use the Journal to keep track of your activities.

8 Print
Learn how to produce a paper copy of the information stored in Outlook.

9 Using Deleted Items
Learn how to work with items you have deleted in Outlook.

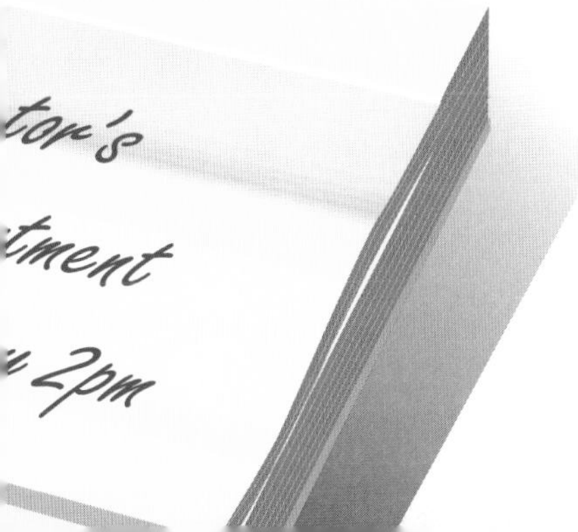

START OUTLOOK

Outlook can help you manage your messages, appointments, contacts, tasks and activities.

START OUTLOOK

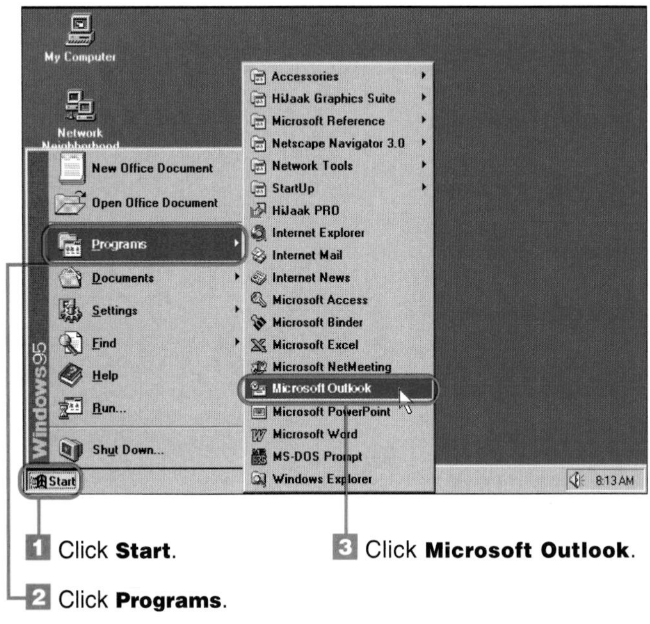

1 Click **Start**.

2 Click **Programs**.

3 Click **Microsoft Outlook**.

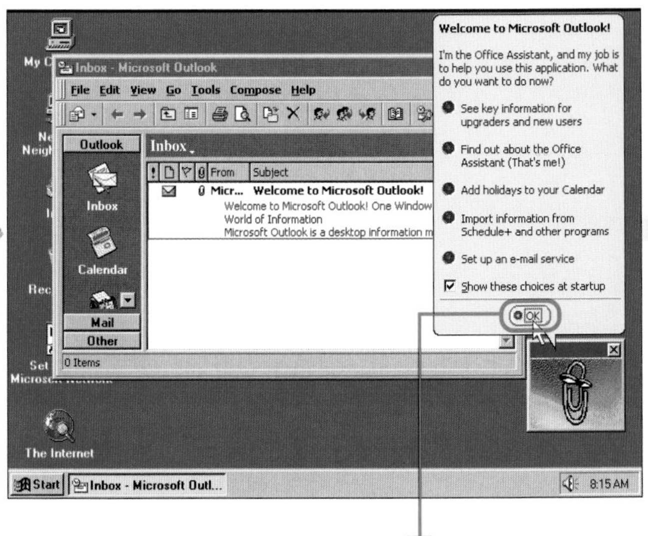

■ The Microsoft Outlook window and the Office Assistant welcome appear.

Note: For information on the Office Assistant, refer to page 12.

4 To start using Outlook, click **OK**.

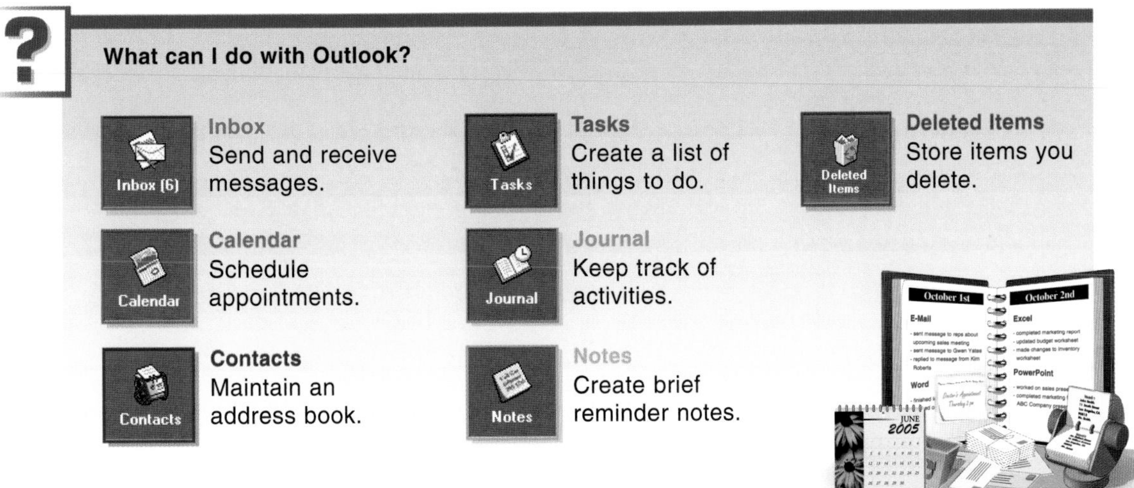

What can I do with Outlook?
Inbox (6)
Inbox
Send and receive messages.
Tasks
Tasks
Create a list of things to do.
Deleted Items
Deleted Items
Store items you delete.
Calendar
Calendar
Schedule appointments.
Journal
Journal
Keep track of activities.
Contacts
Contacts
Maintain an address book.
Notes
Notes
Create brief reminder notes.

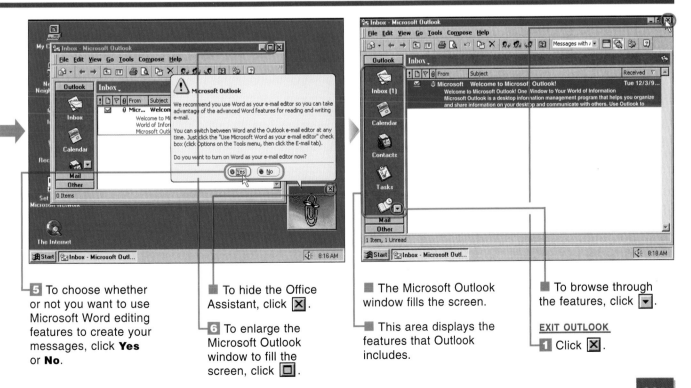

5 To choose whether or not you want to use Microsoft Word editing features to create your messages, click **Yes** or **No**.

■ To hide the Office Assistant, click ☒.

6 To enlarge the Microsoft Outlook window to fill the screen, click ☐.

■ The Microsoft Outlook window fills the screen.

■ This area displays the features that Outlook includes.

■ To browse through the features, click ▼.

EXIT OUTLOOK

1 Click ☒.

VIEW INBOX

The Inbox lets you exchange electronic mail (e-mail) messages with friends, family members, colleagues and clients.

VIEW INBOX

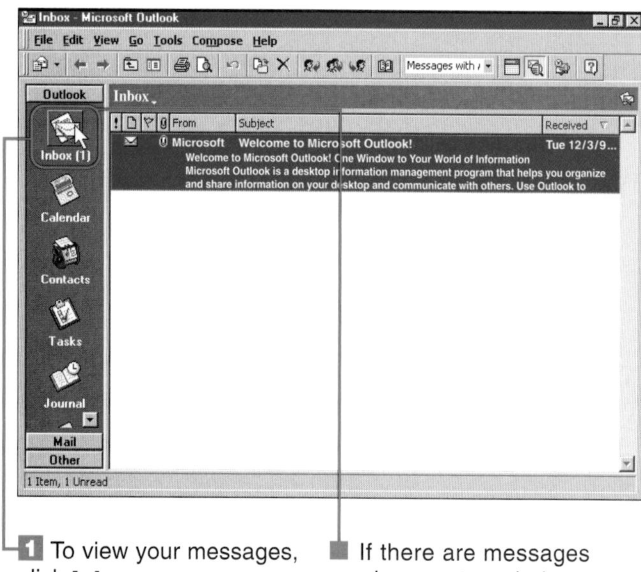

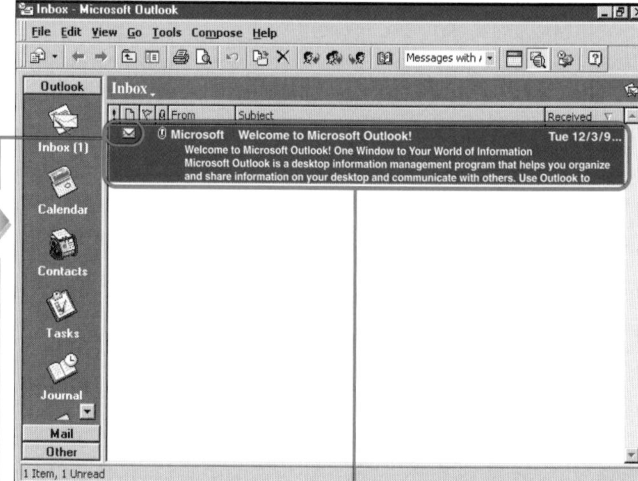

1 To view your messages, click **Inbox**.

■ If there are messages you have not read, the number of unread messages will appear in brackets beside **Inbox**.

■ This area shows you whether or not you have read each message.

Unread message

Read message

■ This area displays the author, subject and date of each message along with a few lines of text from each unread message.

Note: To view all the text in a message, refer to page 284 to open the message.

USING THE MAIL FOLDERS

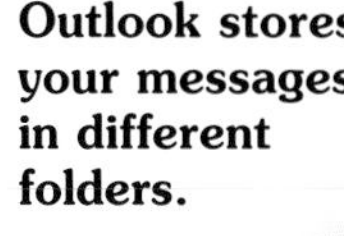

Outlook stores your messages in different folders.

Inbox
Stores messages sent to you.

Sent Items
Stores messages you have sent.

Outbox
Stores messages that have not yet been sent.

Deleted Items
Stores messages you have deleted.

USING THE MAIL FOLDERS

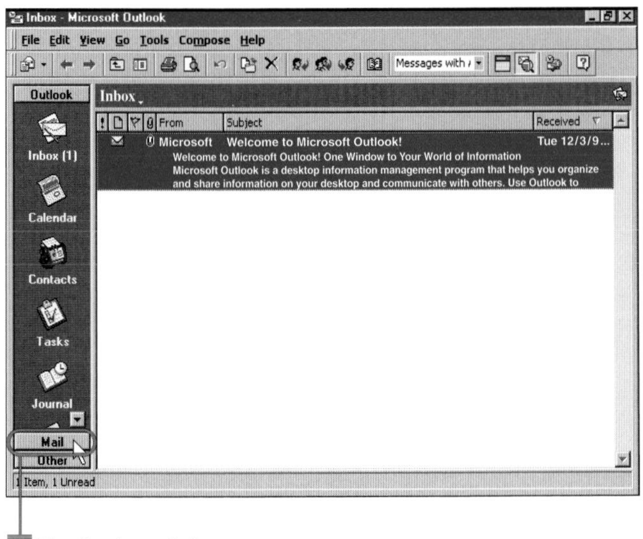

1 To display all the Mail folders, click **Mail**.

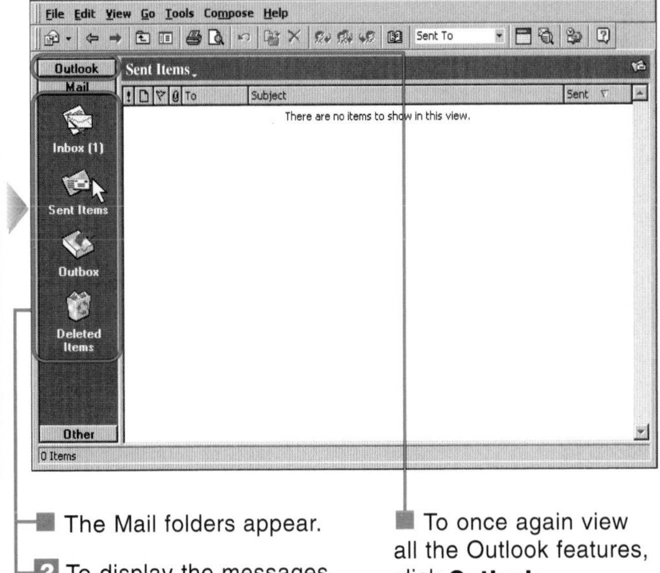

■ The Mail folders appear.

2 To display the messages in a specific folder, click the folder.

■ To once again view all the Outlook features, click **Outlook**.

OPEN A MESSAGE

You can easily open a message to view its contents.

Joanne,
The drafts for next month's advertising campaign are ready. Will you be free at 2:00 p.m. tomorrow to discuss them?
Jill

OPEN A MESSAGE

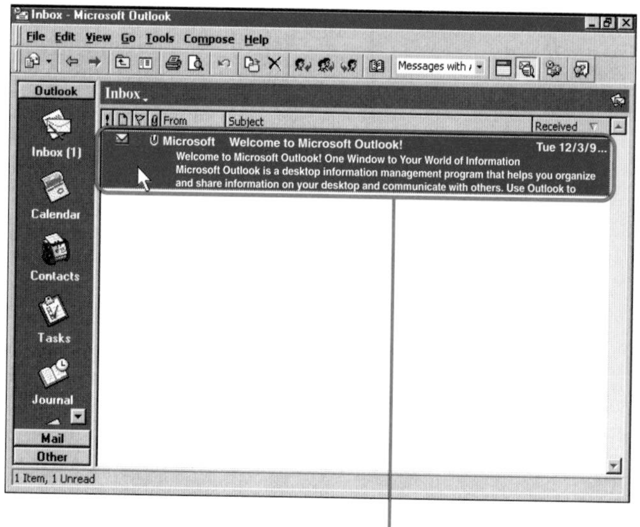

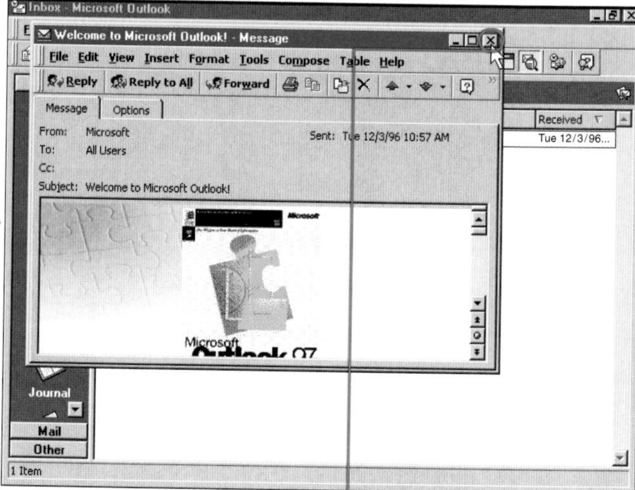

Note: To display a message in a specific folder, refer to page 283.

1 Double-click the message you want to open.

■ The contents of the message appear on the screen.

2 To close the message, click ☒.

DELETE A MESSAGE

You can delete a message you no longer need. This prevents your folders from becoming cluttered with messages.

DELETE A MESSAGE

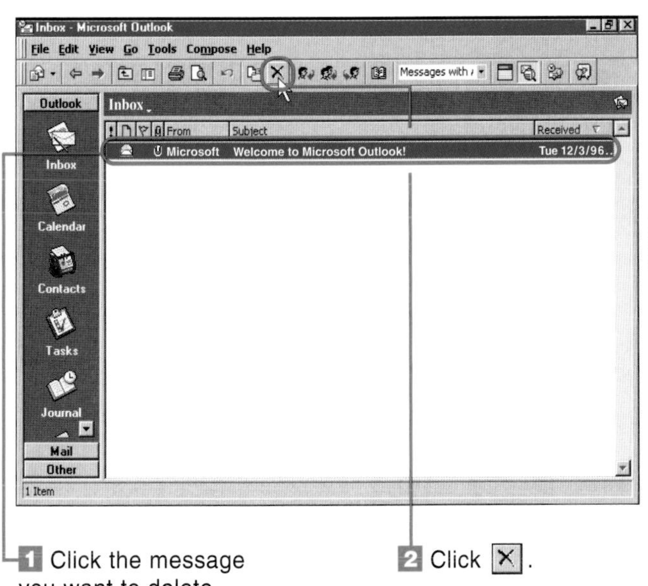

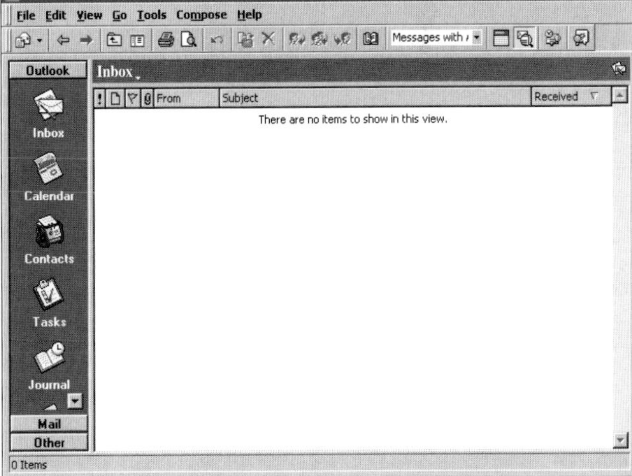

1 Click the message you want to delete.

2 Click 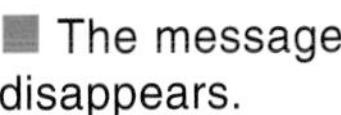.

■ The message disappears.

■ Outlook places the deleted message in the **Deleted Items** folder.

*Note: To display the messages in the **Deleted Items** folder, refer to page 283.*

SEND A MESSAGE

You can send a message to exchange ideas or request information.

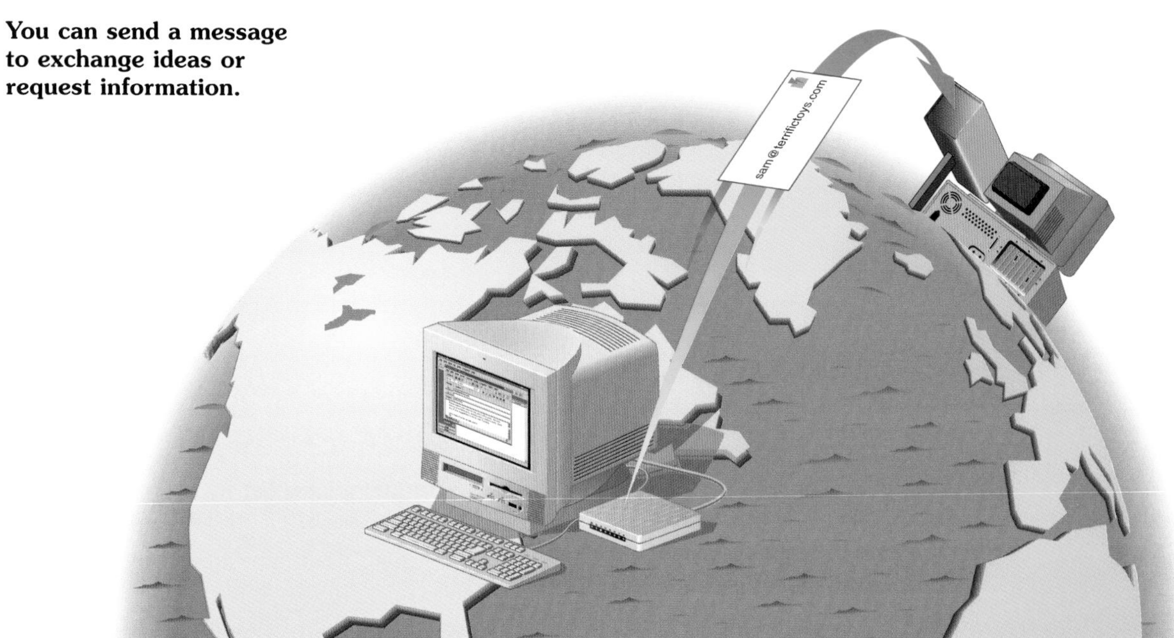

SEND A MESSAGE

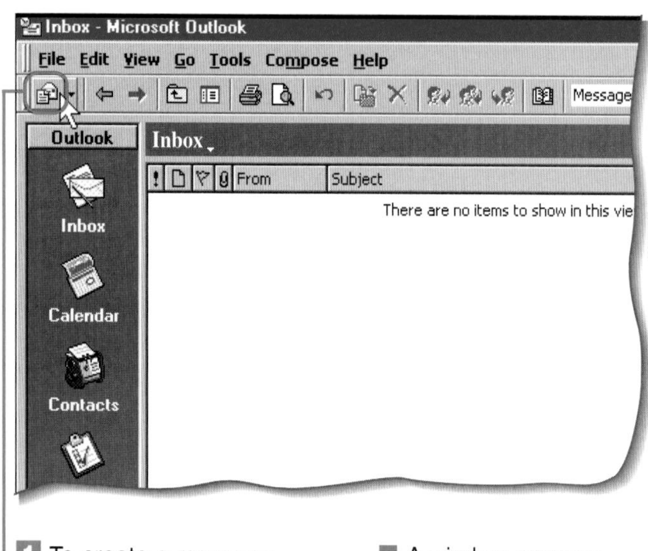

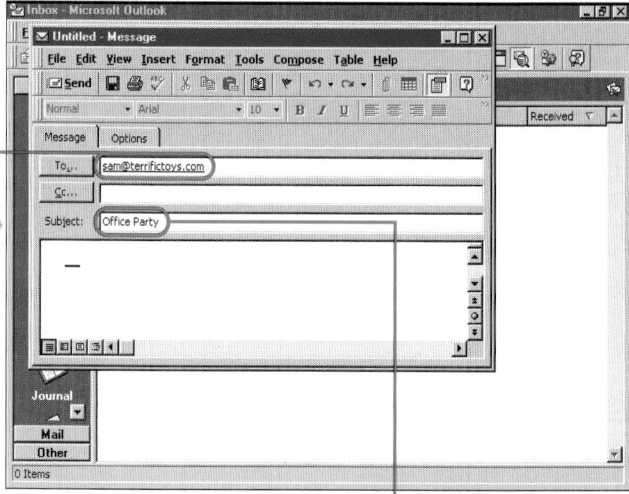

1 To create a message, click .

■ A window appears.

2 Type the e-mail address of the person you want to receive the message.

Note: You can practice sending a message by sending a message to yourself.

3 To enter a subject, press Tab twice on your keyboard. Then type the subject.

Why can't I send or receive messages?

Before you can send and receive messages, you must be connected to a service that allows you to exchange messages. These services include an office network, a commercial online service or an Internet service provider.

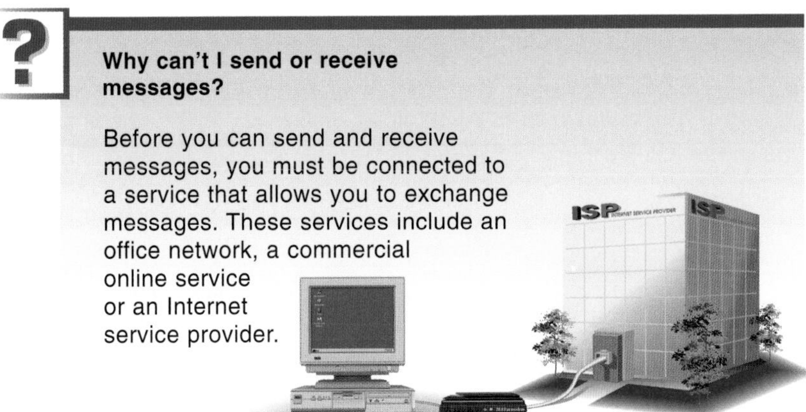

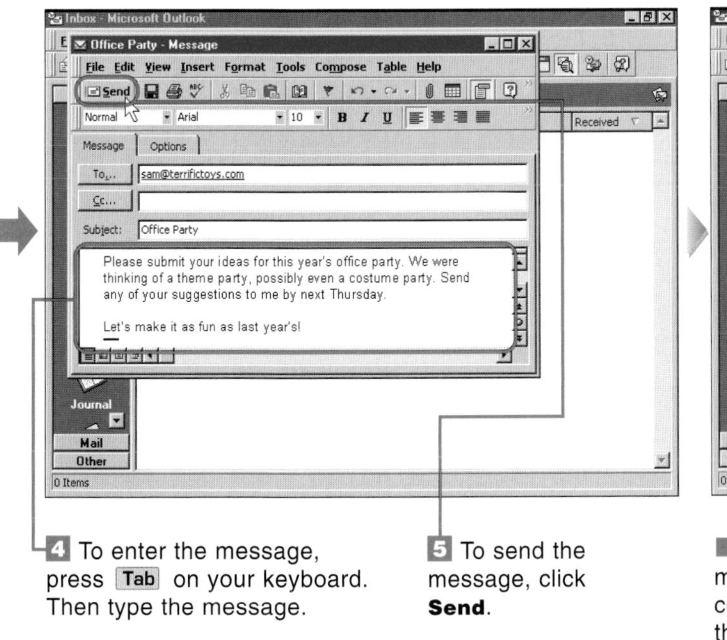

4 To enter the message, press Tab on your keyboard. Then type the message.

5 To send the message, click **Send**.

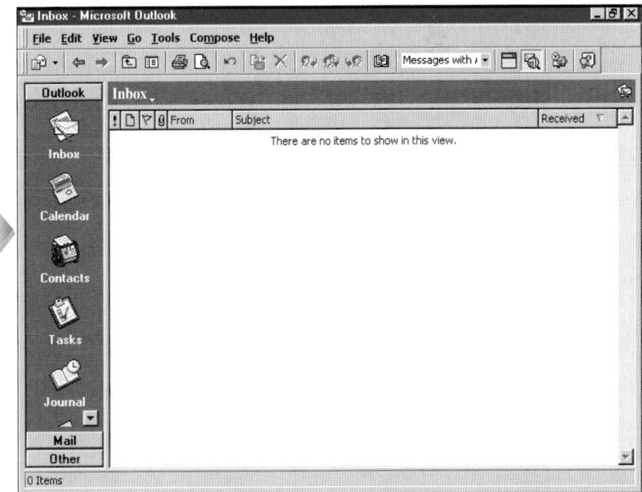

■ Outlook sends the message and stores a copy of the message in the **Sent Items** folder.

*Note: To display the messages in the **Sent Items** folder, refer to page 283.*

REPLY TO A MESSAGE

You can reply to a message to answer a question, express an opinion or supply additional information.

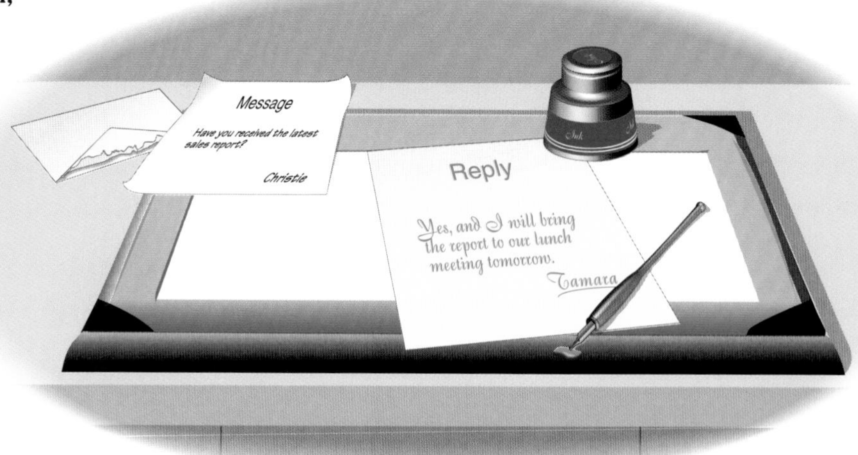

REPLY TO A MESSAGE

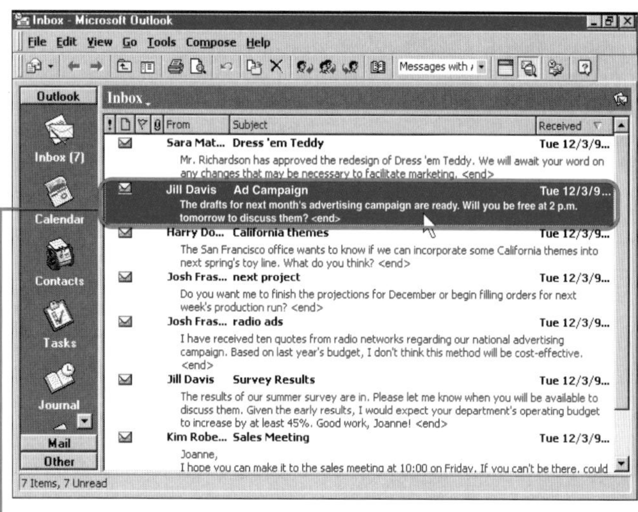

1 Click the message you want to reply to.

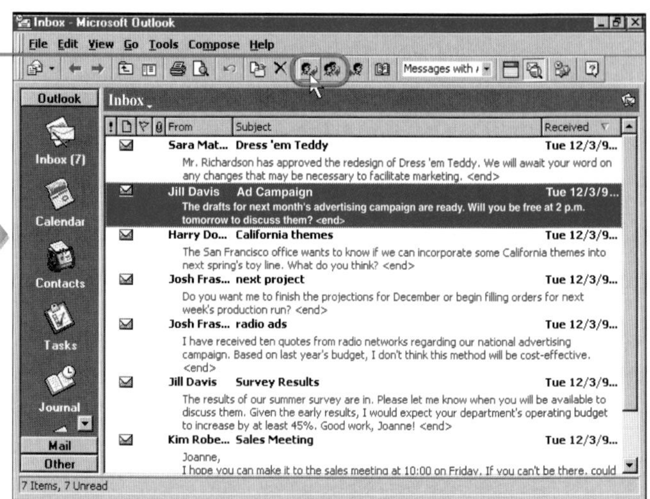

2 Click one of the following reply options.

Reply to sender

Reply to sender and everyone who received the original message

Why haven't I received a response to my message?

When you send a message, do not assume the person receiving the message will read it right away. Some people may not regularly check their e-mail.

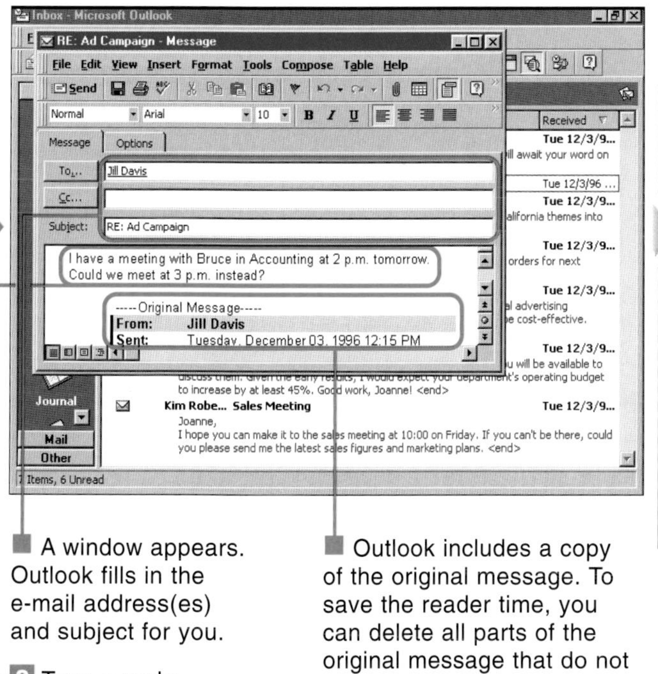

■ A window appears. Outlook fills in the e-mail address(es) and subject for you.

3 Type a reply to the message.

■ Outlook includes a copy of the original message. To save the reader time, you can delete all parts of the original message that do not directly relate to your reply.

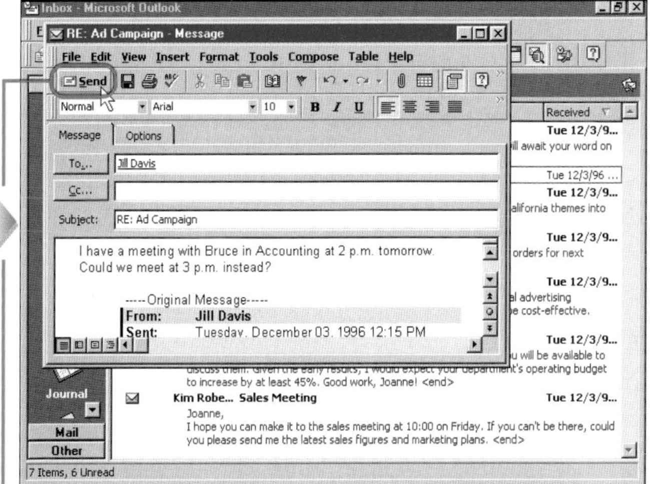

4 To send the reply, click **Send**.

■ Outlook sends the reply and stores a copy of the reply in the **Sent Items** folder.

Note: To display the messages in the ***Sent Items*** *folder, refer to page 283.*

FORWARD A MESSAGE

After reading a message, you can add comments and then send the message to a friend or colleague.

FORWARD A MESSAGE

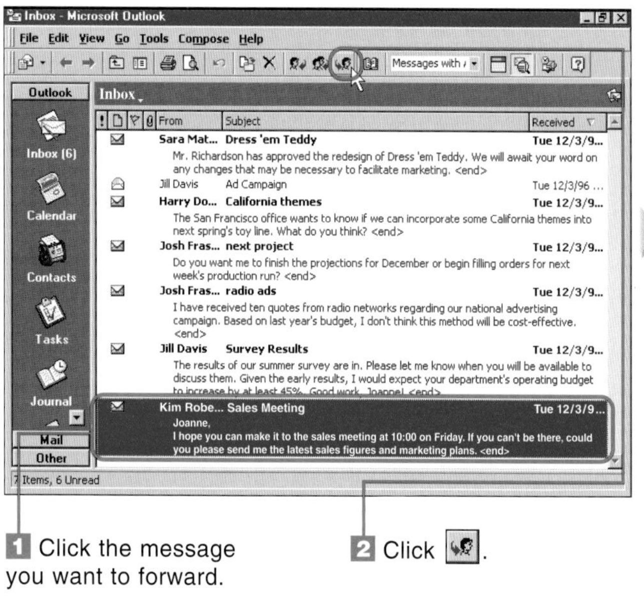

1 Click the message you want to forward.

2 Click .

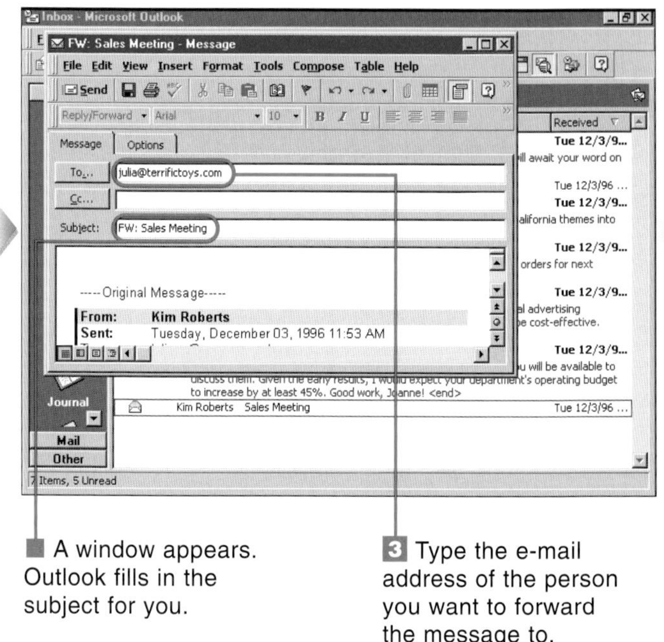

■ A window appears. Outlook fills in the subject for you.

3 Type the e-mail address of the person you want to forward the message to.

Can exchanging e-mail save me money?

Using e-mail can save you money on long distance calls to colleagues, friends and family. The next time you are about to use the telephone, consider sending an e-mail message instead.

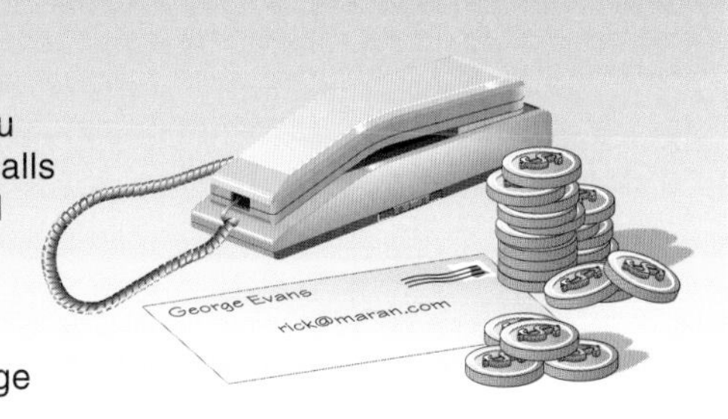

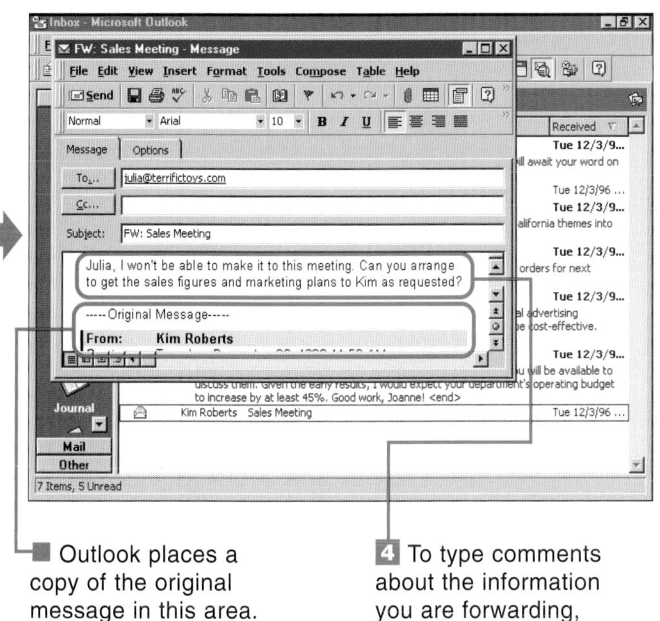

■ Outlook places a copy of the original message in this area.

4 To type comments about the information you are forwarding, click this area. Then type your comments.

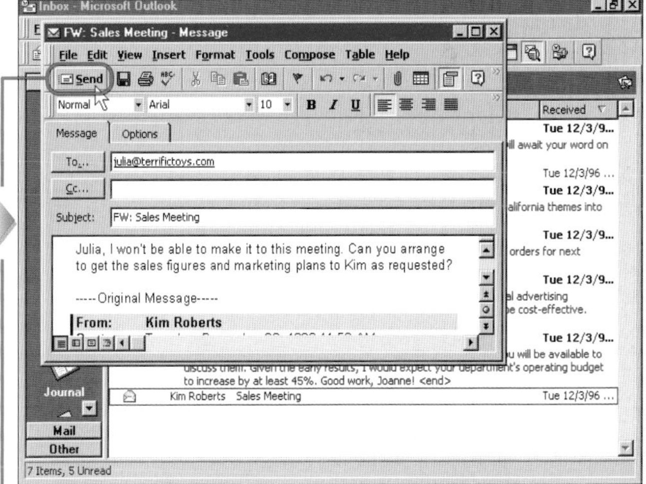

5 To forward the message, click **Send**.

■ Outlook sends the message and stores a copy of the message in the **Sent Items** folder.

Note: To display the messages in the ***Sent Items*** *folder,* *refer to page 283.*

CREATE A NOTE

You can create electronic notes that are similar to paper sticky notes.

CREATE A NOTE

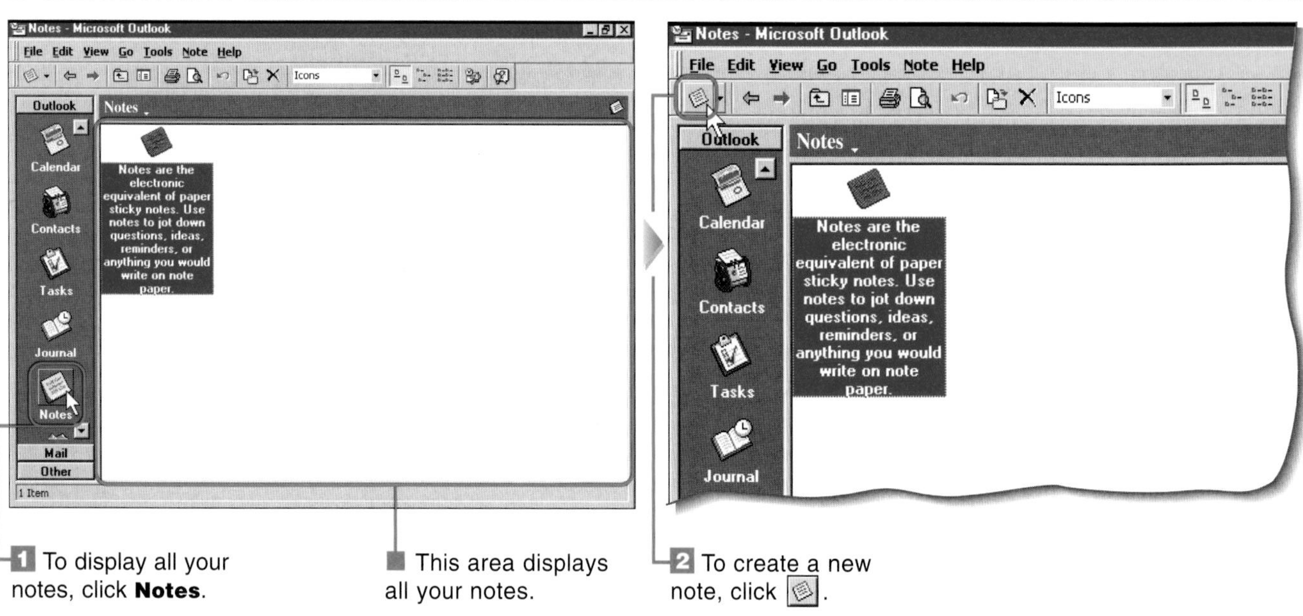

1 To display all your notes, click **Notes**.

■ This area displays all your notes.

2 To create a new note, click .

What can I use notes for?

Notes are ideal for storing bits of information such as reminders, questions, ideas and anything else you would record on note paper.

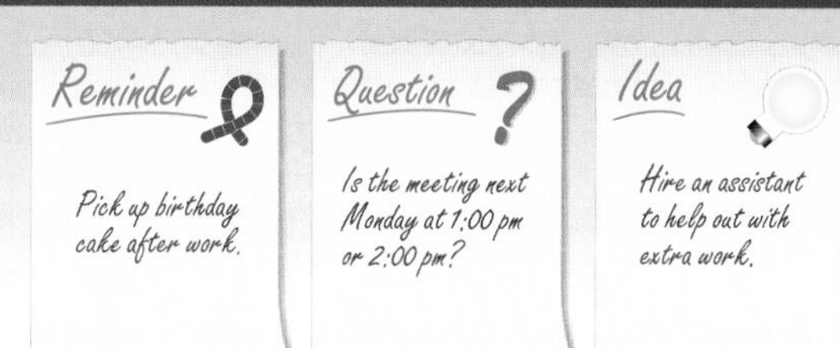

Reminder
Pick up birthday cake after work.
Question
Is the meeting next Monday at 1:00 pm or 2:00 pm?
Idea
Hire an assistant to help out with extra work.

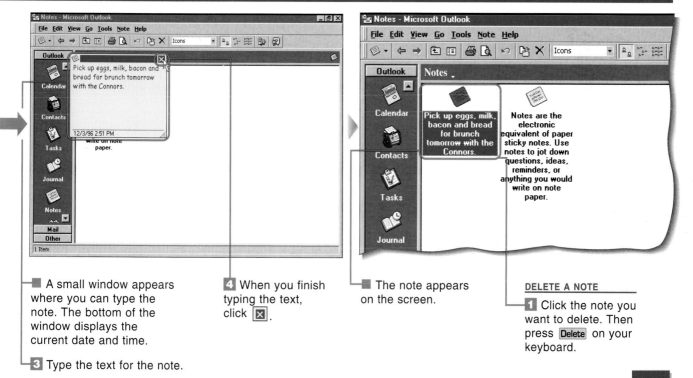

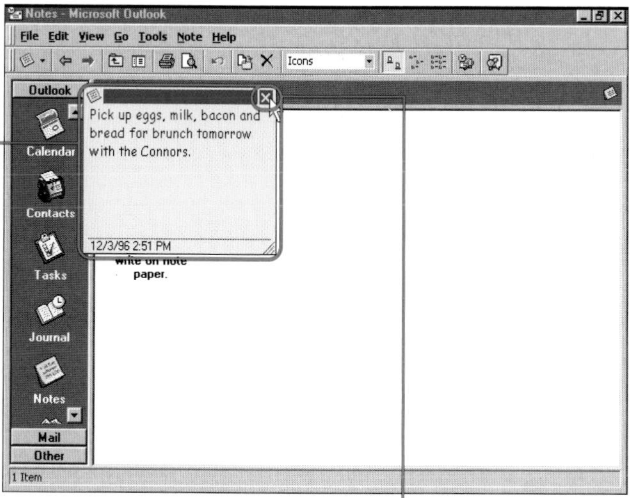

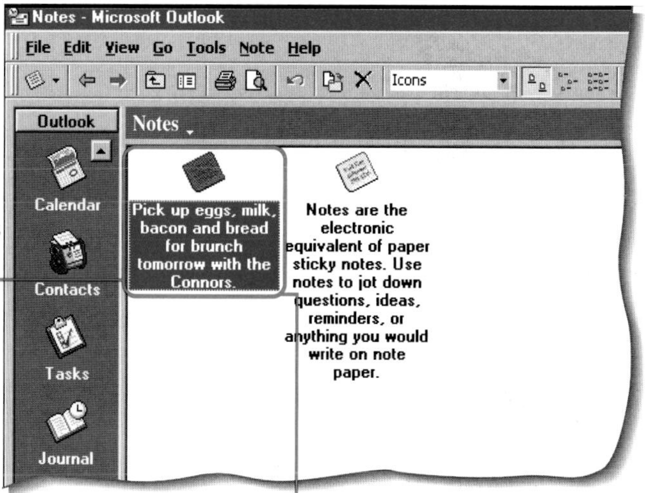

■ A small window appears where you can type the note. The bottom of the window displays the current date and time.

3 Type the text for the note.

4 When you finish typing the text, click ☒.

■ The note appears on the screen.

DELETE A NOTE

1 Click the note you want to delete. Then press Delete on your keyboard.

OPEN A NOTE

You can easily open a note to view its contents.

OPEN A NOTE

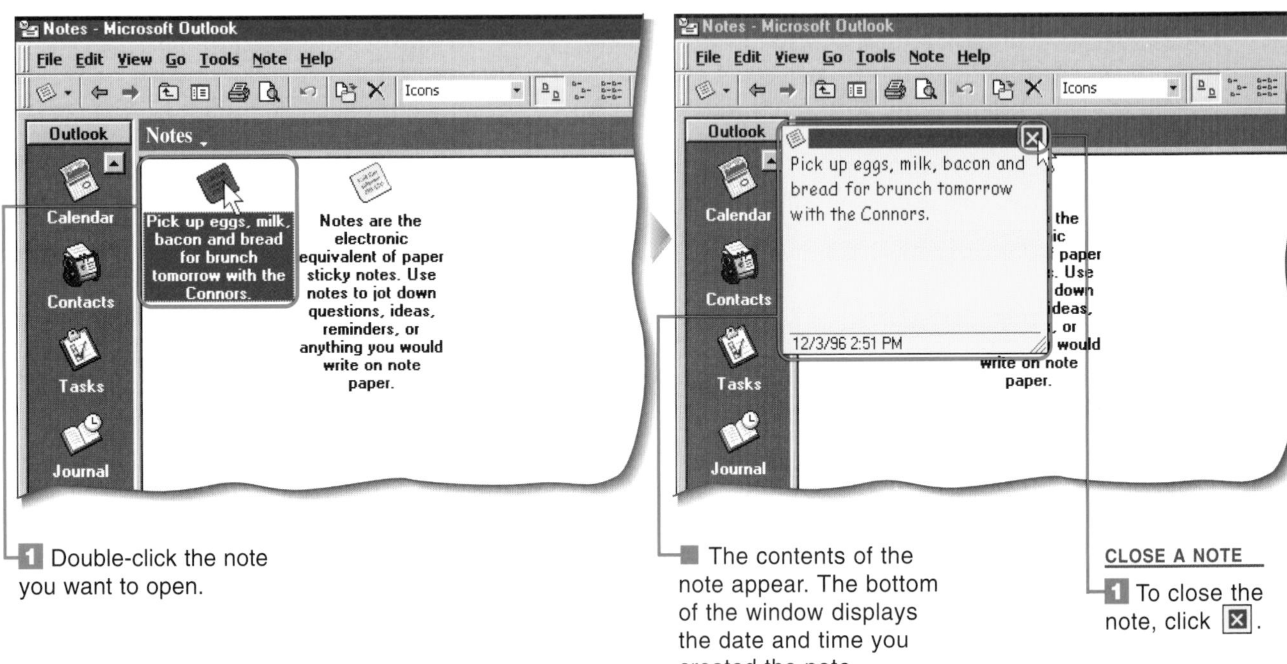

1 Double-click the note you want to open.

■ The contents of the note appear. The bottom of the window displays the date and time you created the note.

CLOSE A NOTE

1 To close the note, click ☒.

RESIZE A NOTE

You can change the size of a note. This is useful when the window is too small to display all the text.

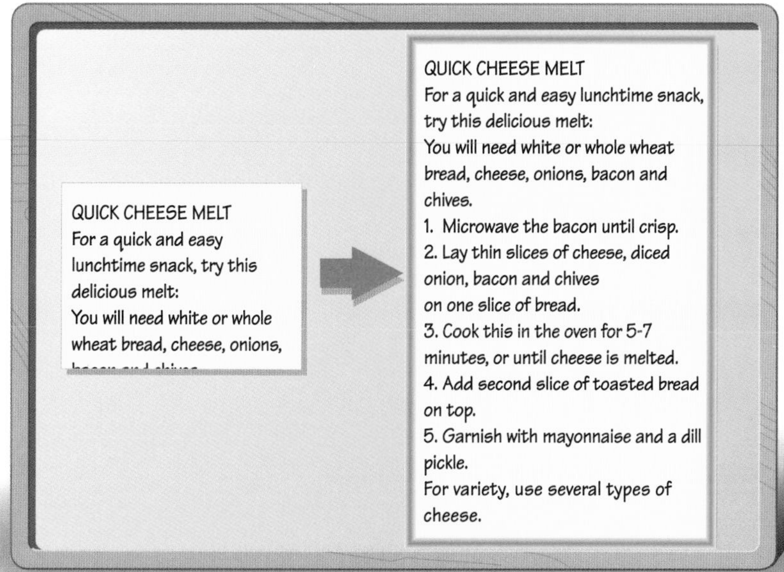

RESIZE A NOTE

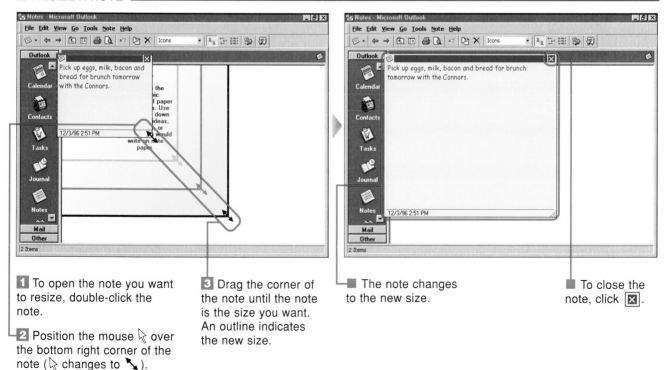

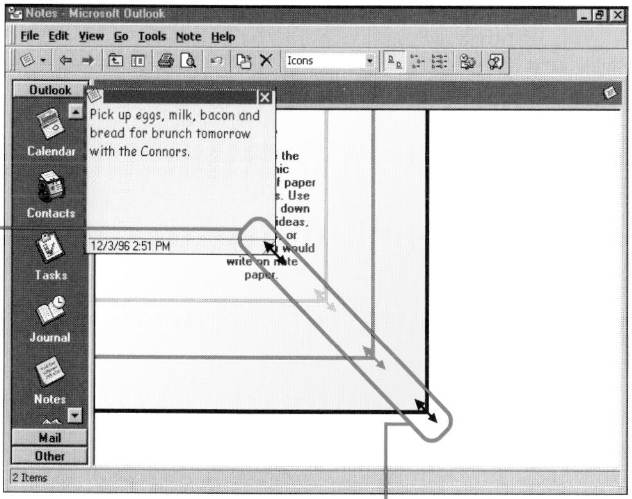

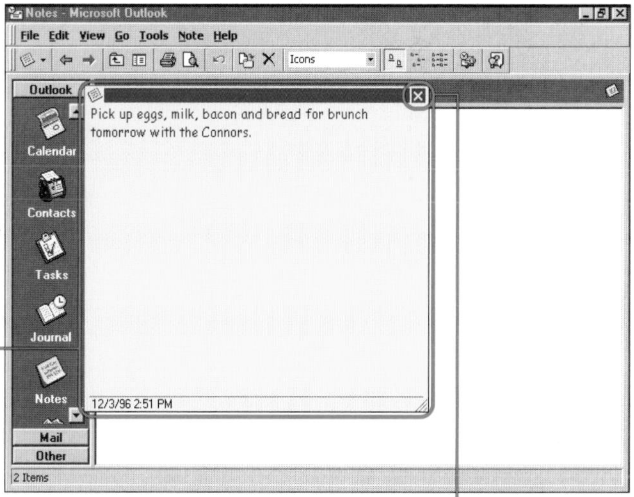

1. To open the note you want to resize, double-click the note.

2. Position the mouse over the bottom right corner of the note (changes to ↘).

3. Drag the corner of the note until the note is the size you want. An outline indicates the new size.

- The note changes to the new size.

- To close the note, click ☒.

CREATE A TASK

You can create a list of personal and work-related tasks that you want to accomplish.

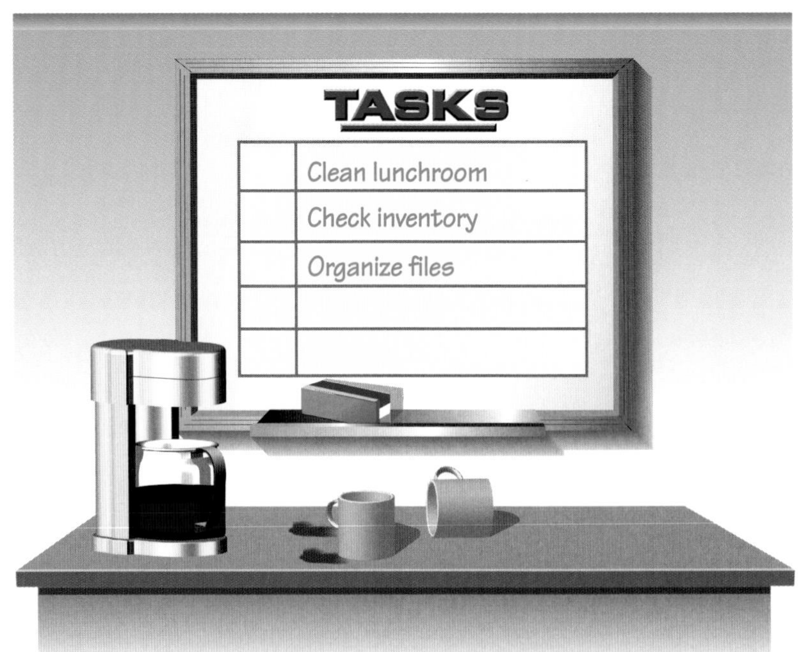

CREATE A TASK

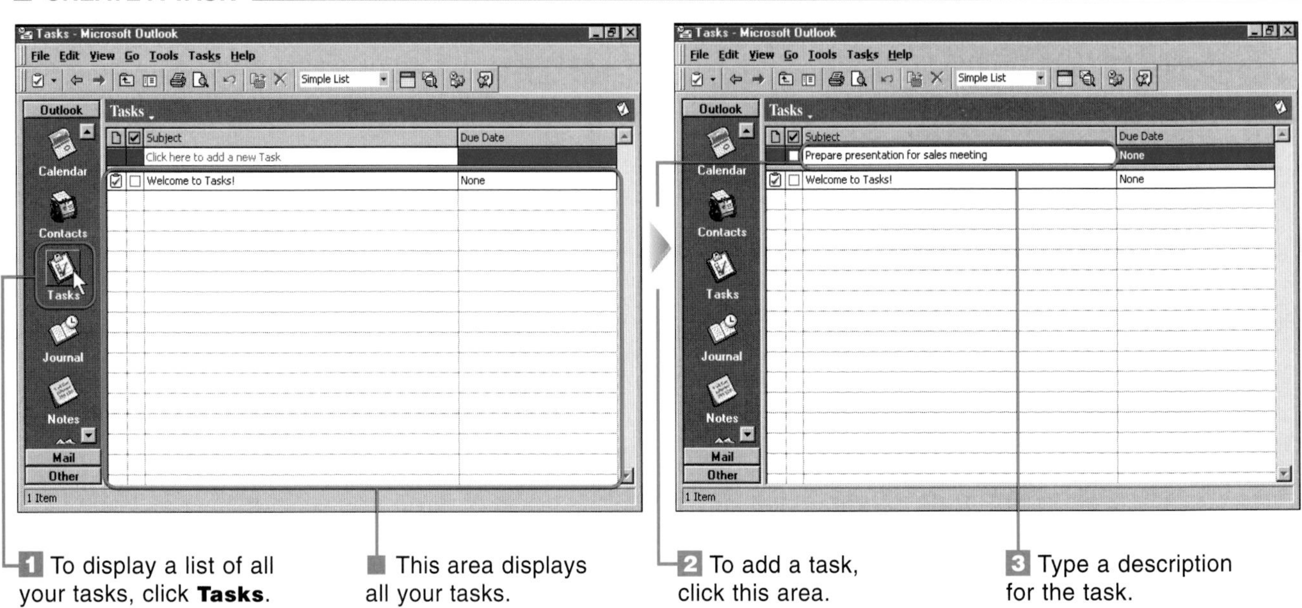

1 To display a list of all your tasks, click **Tasks**.

■ This area displays all your tasks.

2 To add a task, click this area.

3 Type a description for the task.

Where else can I see a list of my tasks?

There is a small area in the Calendar that displays a list of your tasks.

Note: For information on the Calendar, refer to page 300.

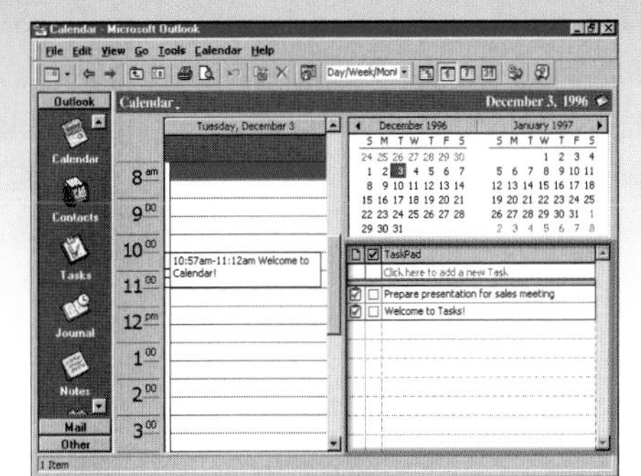

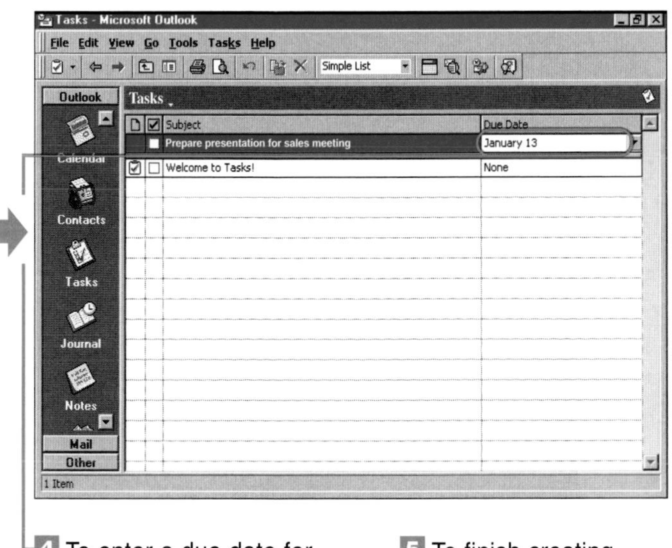

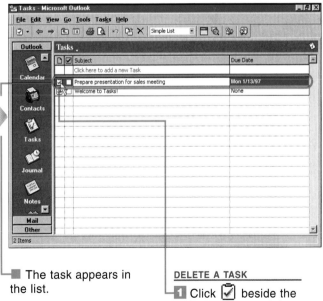

4 To enter a due date for the task, click this area. Then type the due date.

5 To finish creating the task, press Enter on your keyboard.

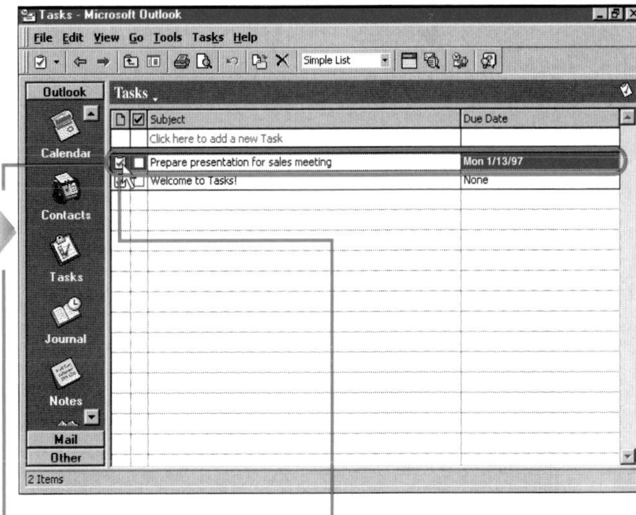

■ The task appears in the list.

DELETE A TASK

1 Click ☑ beside the task you want to delete.

2 Press Delete on your keyboard.

MARK A TASK AS COMPLETE

When you complete a task, you can place a line through the task to remind you that it is complete.

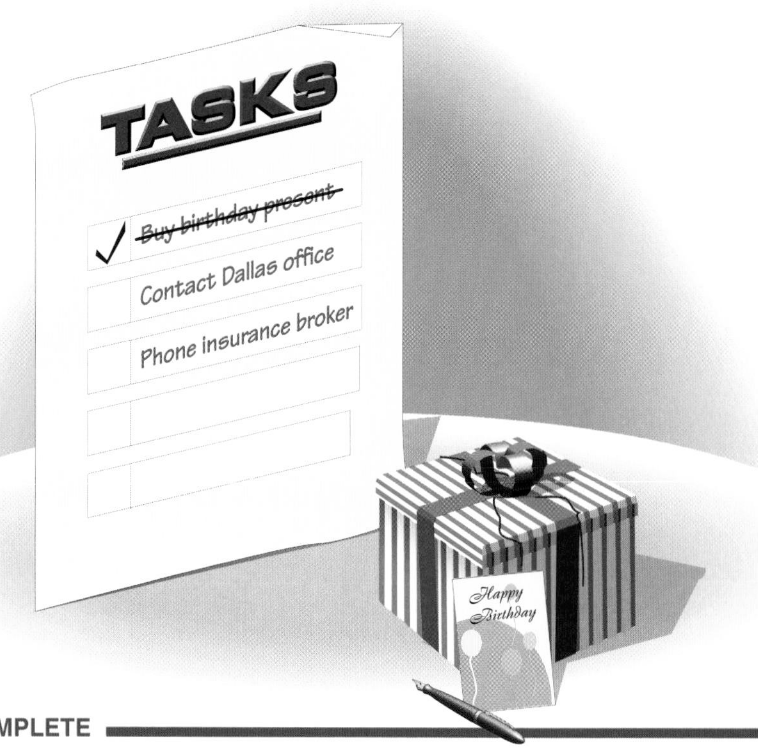

MARK A TASK AS COMPLETE

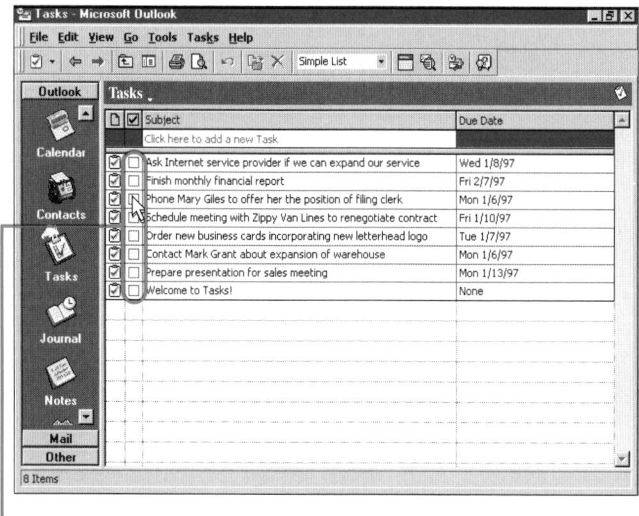

1 To mark a task as complete, click ☐ beside the task (☐ changes to ☑).

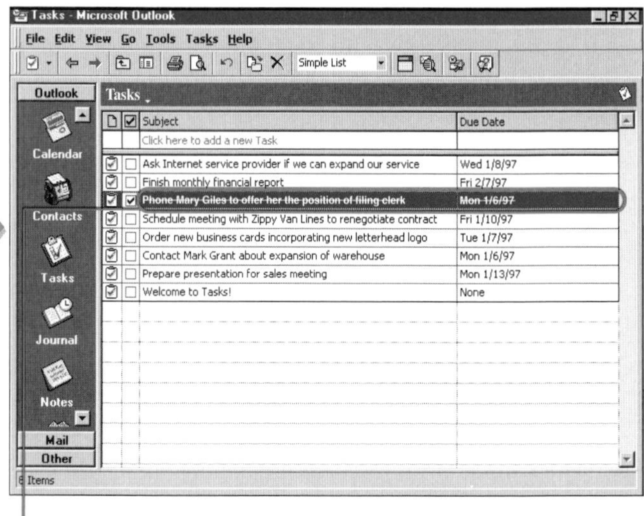

■ A line appears through the task to show that the task is complete.

■ To remove the line through a task, repeat step 1.

SORT TASKS

You can sort your tasks alphabetically by subject or by due date to help you quickly find tasks of interest.

SORT TASKS

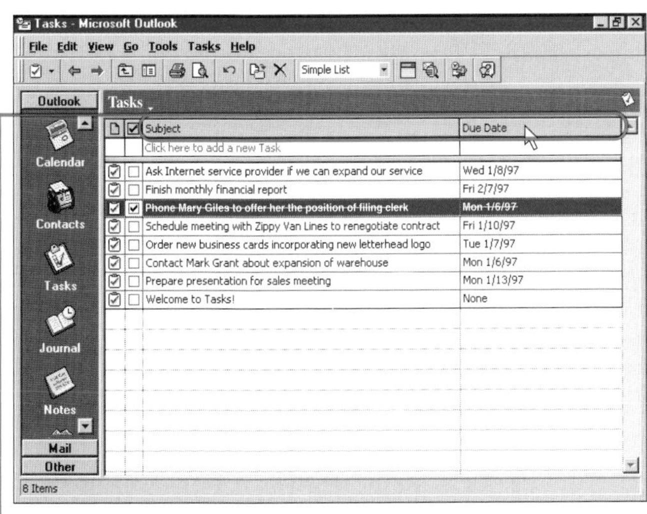

1 Click the heading of the column you want to sort by.

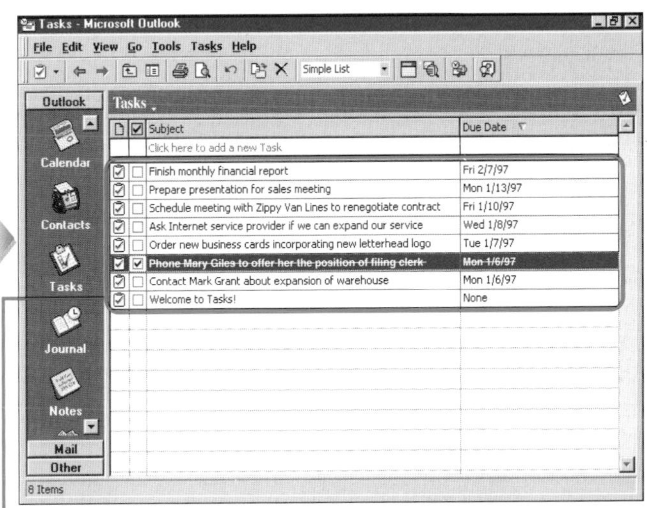

■ The tasks are sorted.

■ To sort the tasks in the opposite order, repeat step 1.

VIEW CALENDAR

The Calendar helps you keep track of your appointments.

VIEW CALENDAR

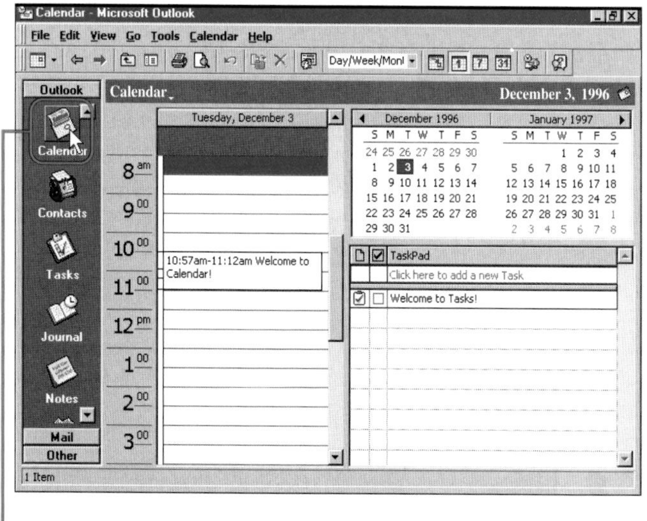

1 To display the Calendar, click **Calendar**.

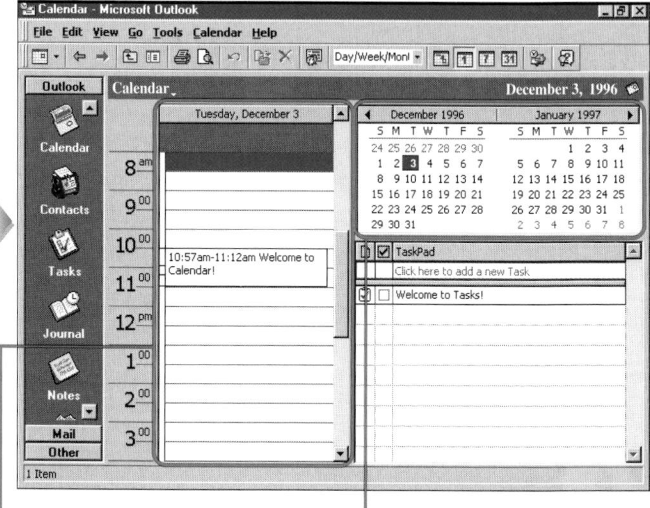

■ This area displays the appointments for the current day.

■ This area displays the days in the current month and the next month. Days with appointments are shown in **bold**.

Note: To add an appointment, refer to page 302.

? How does Outlook know what day it is?

Outlook uses the date and time set in your computer to determine today's date. To change the date and time set in your computer, refer to your Windows manual.

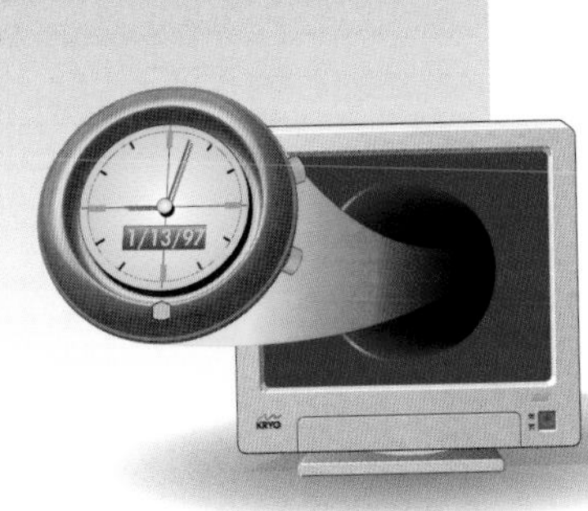

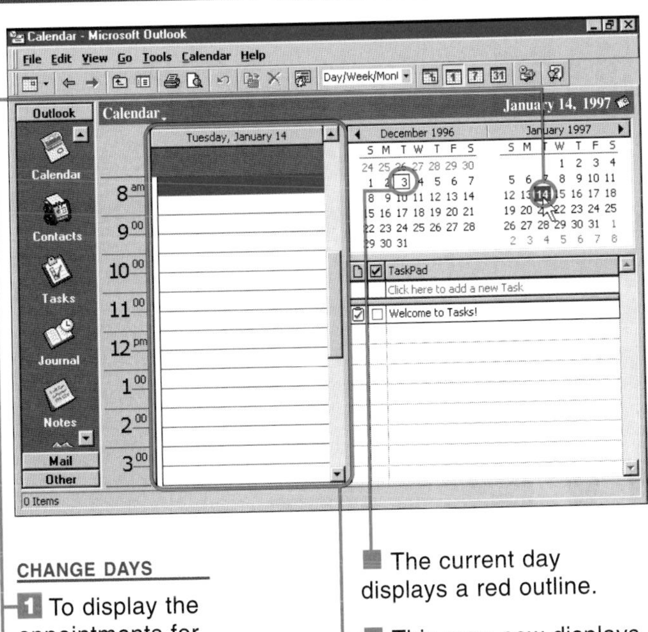

CHANGE DAYS

1 To display the appointments for another day, click the day.

■ The day you selected is highlighted.

■ The current day displays a red outline.

■ This area now displays the appointments for the day you selected.

CHANGE MONTHS

1 To display the days in another month, click one of the following options.

◀ Display previous month

▶ Display next month

2 Repeat step 1 until the month you want to display appears.

ADD AN APPOINTMENT

You can add appointments to the Calendar to remind you of activities such as meetings, lunch dates and doctor's appointments.

ADD AN APPOINTMENT

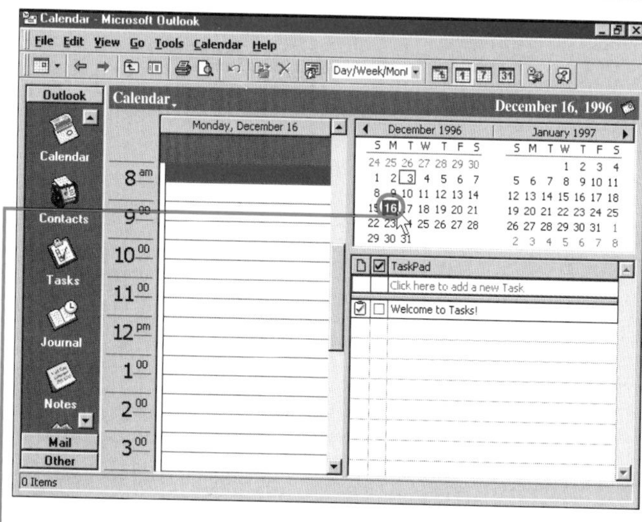

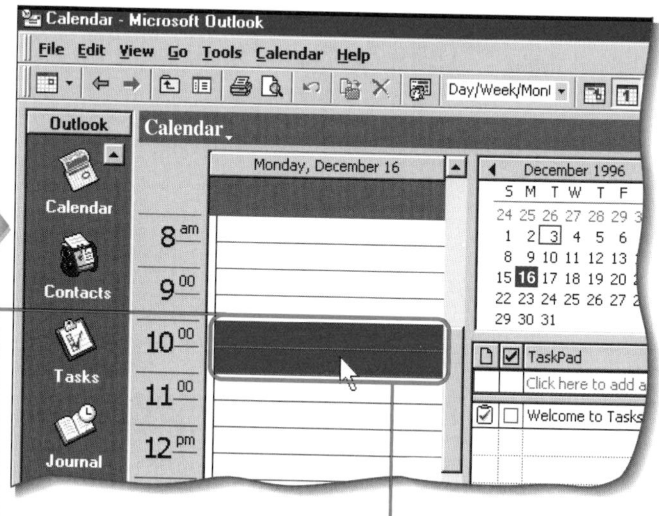

1 Click the day when you want to add an appointment.

Note: To view the days in other months, refer to page 301.

2 Position the mouse over the starting time for the appointment.

3 Drag the mouse to select the time you want to set aside for the appointment.

Outlook will play a brief sound and display a dialog box 15 minutes before a scheduled appointment.

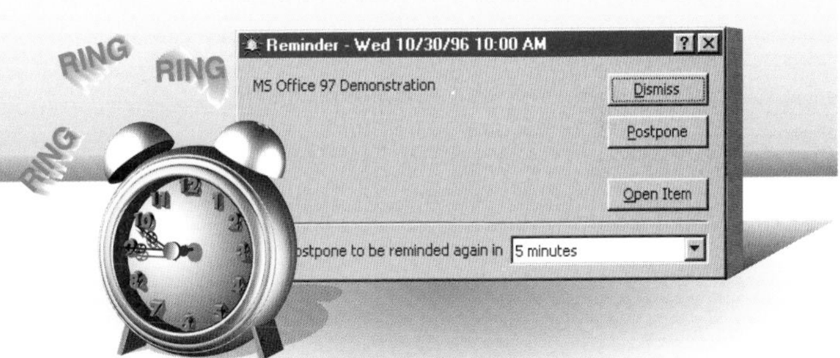

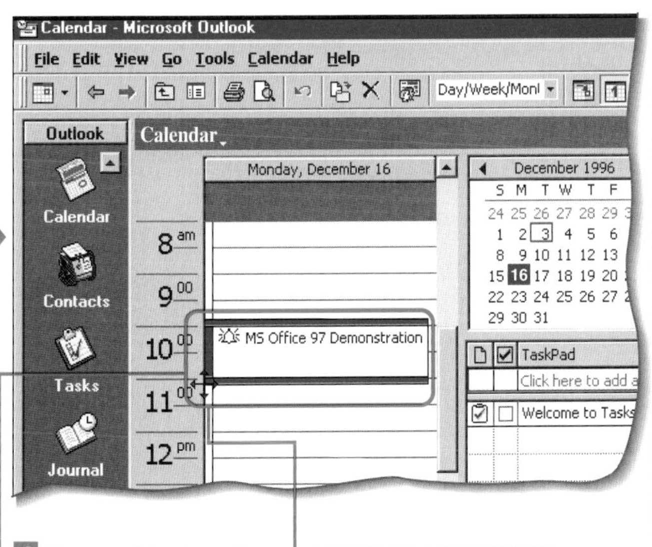

4 Type text to describe the appointment and then press Enter on your keyboard.

DELETE AN APPOINTMENT

1 To select the appointment you want to delete, click the left edge of the appointment.

2 Press Delete on your keyboard.

APPOINTMENT REMINDER

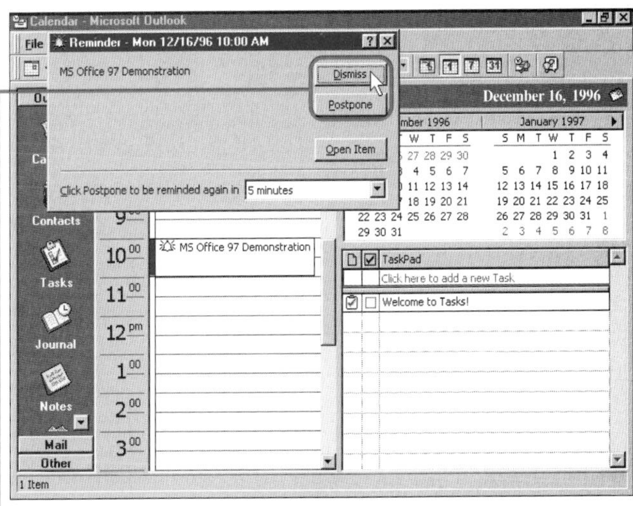

1 To close the **Reminder** dialog box, click one of the following options.

Dismiss - Close the reminder

Postpone - Remind again in 5 minutes

DAY, WEEK AND MONTH VIEWS

You can view your appointments by day, week or month.

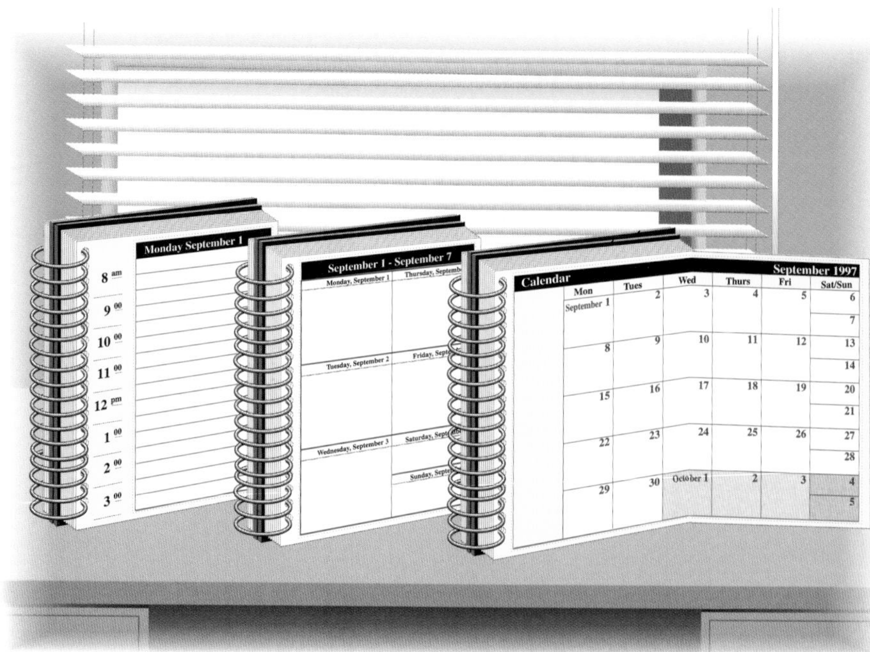

DAY, WEEK AND MONTH VIEWS

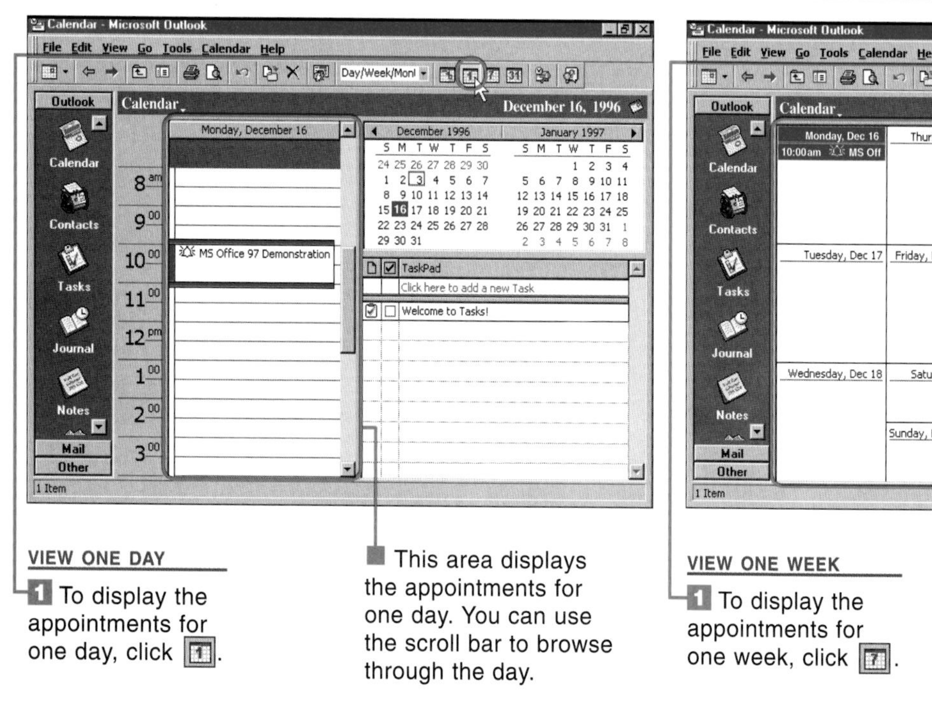

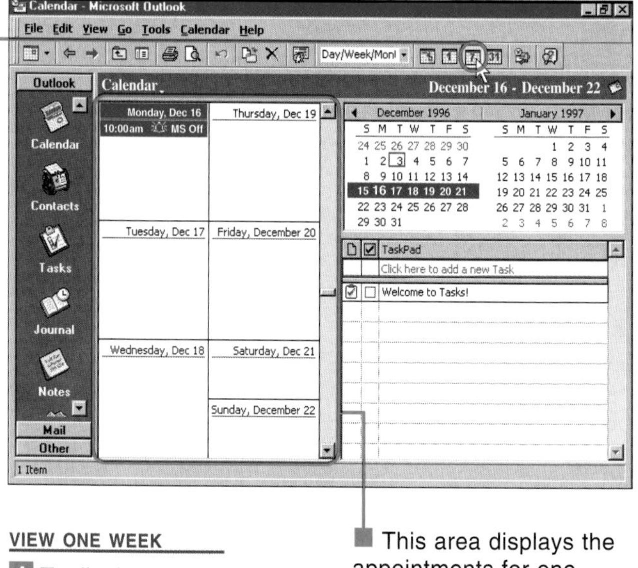

VIEW ONE DAY

1 To display the appointments for one day, click [1].

■ This area displays the appointments for one day. You can use the scroll bar to browse through the day.

VIEW ONE WEEK

1 To display the appointments for one week, click [7].

■ This area displays the appointments for one week. You can use the scroll bar to browse through other weeks.

Can I schedule appointments months in advance?

You can schedule appointments months or even years in advance. Outlook will keep track of all your appointments no matter how far in advance you schedule them.

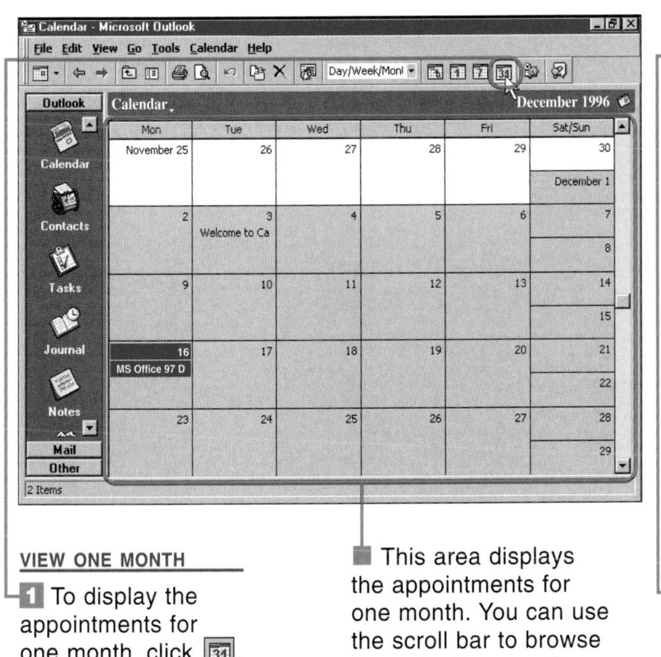

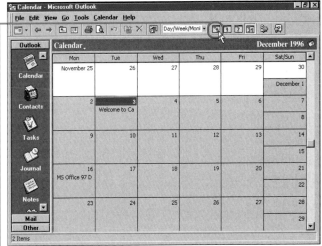

VIEW ONE MONTH

1 To display the appointments for one month, click 31.

■ This area displays the appointments for one month. You can use the scroll bar to browse through other months.

VIEW TODAY

1 To display the appointments for today in any view, click the Go to Today button.

■ Today's date is highlighted on your screen.

ADD A CONTACT

Outlook supplies an address book where you can keep detailed information about your friends, family members, colleagues and clients.

ADD A CONTACT

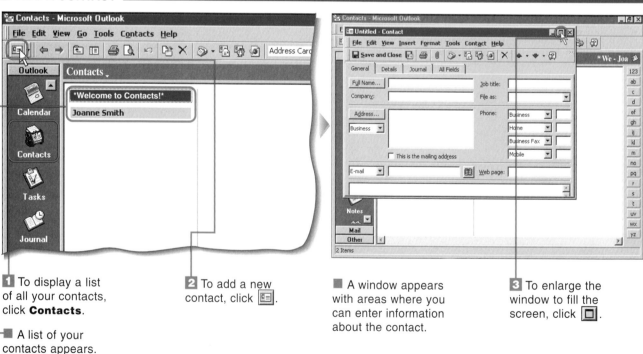

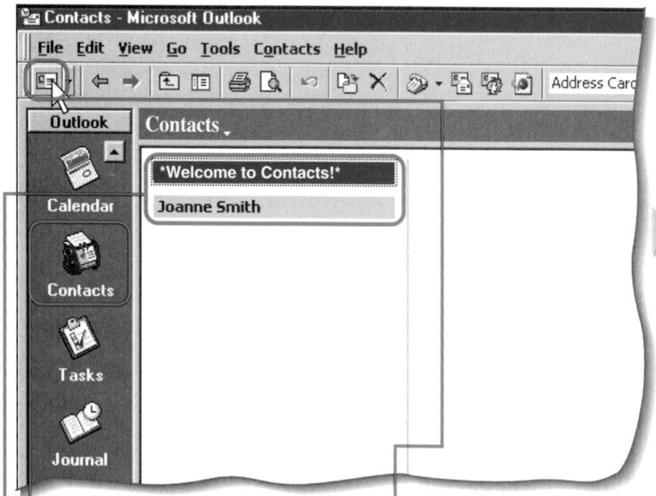

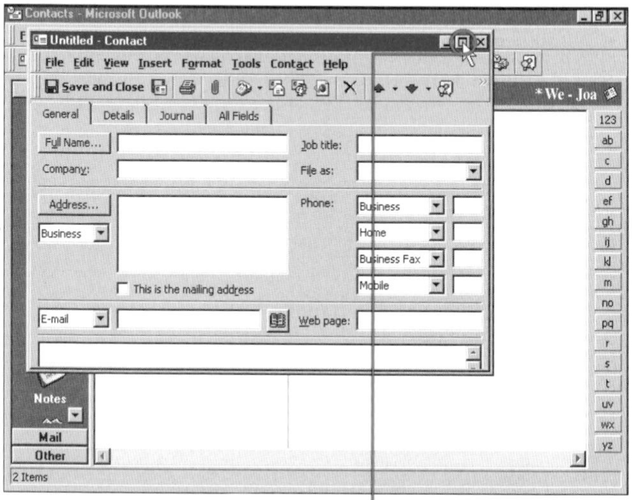

1 To display a list of all your contacts, click **Contacts**.

■ A list of your contacts appears.

2 To add a new contact, click the New Contact button.

■ A window appears with areas where you can enter information about the contact.

3 To enlarge the window to fill the screen, click the Maximize button.

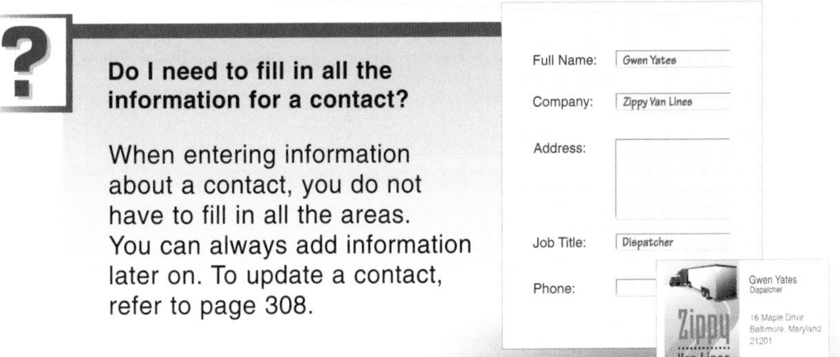

Do I need to fill in all the information for a contact?

When entering information about a contact, you do not have to fill in all the areas. You can always add information later on. To update a contact, refer to page 308.

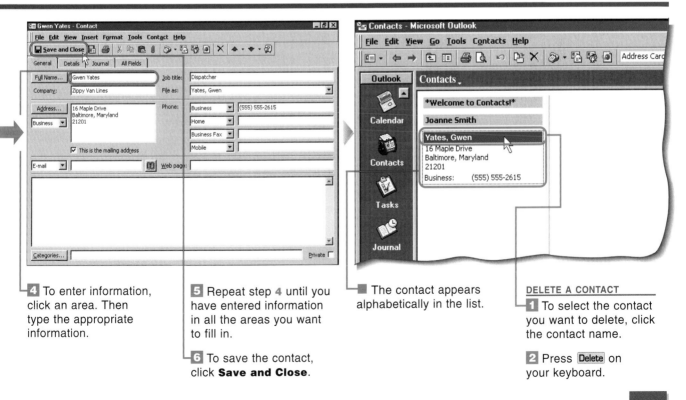

4 To enter information, click an area. Then type the appropriate information.

5 Repeat step 4 until you have entered information in all the areas you want to fill in.

6 To save the contact, click **Save and Close**.

■ The contact appears alphabetically in the list.

DELETE A CONTACT

1 To select the contact you want to delete, click the contact name.

2 Press Delete on your keyboard.

UPDATE A CONTACT

You can easily update or add additional information to a contact in your list.

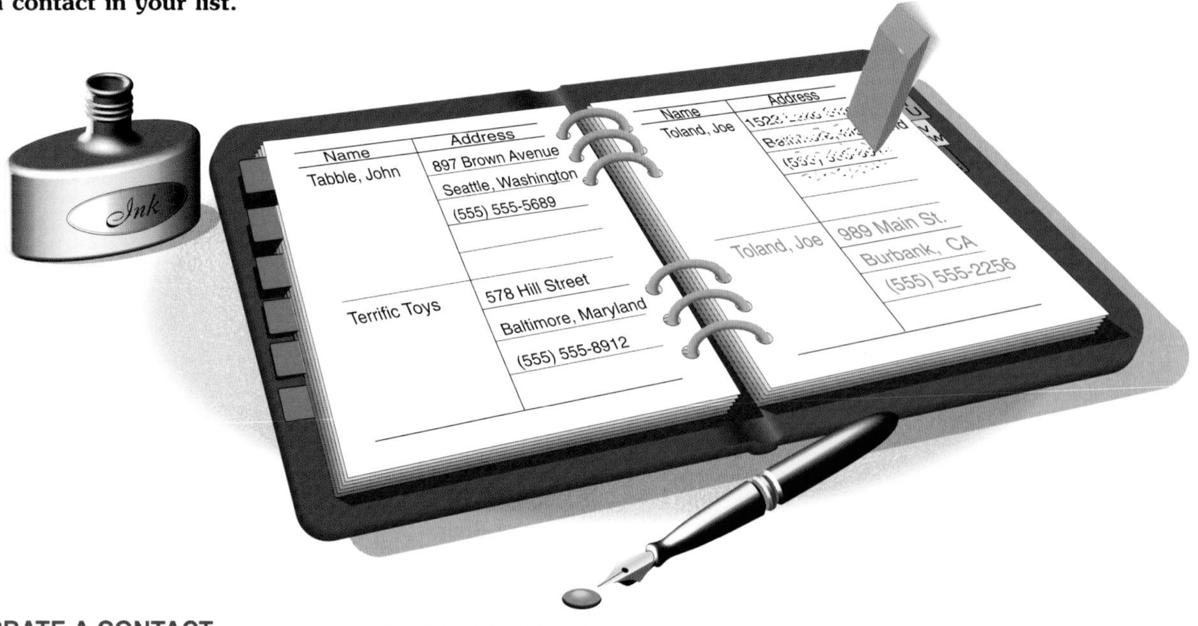

UPDATE A CONTACT

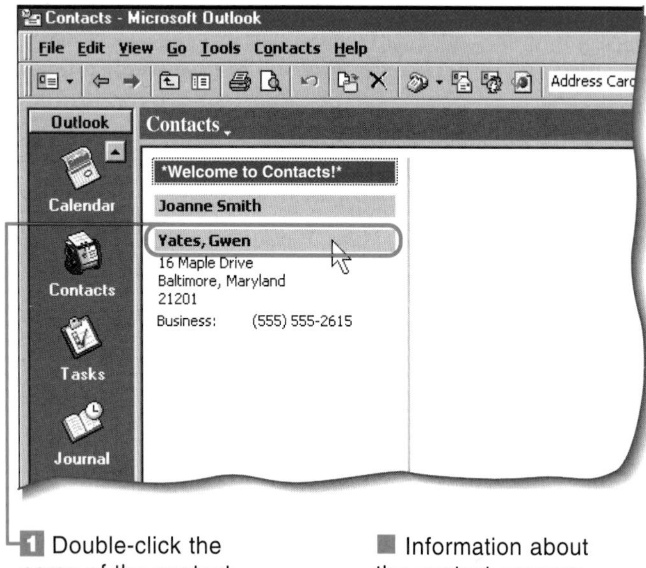

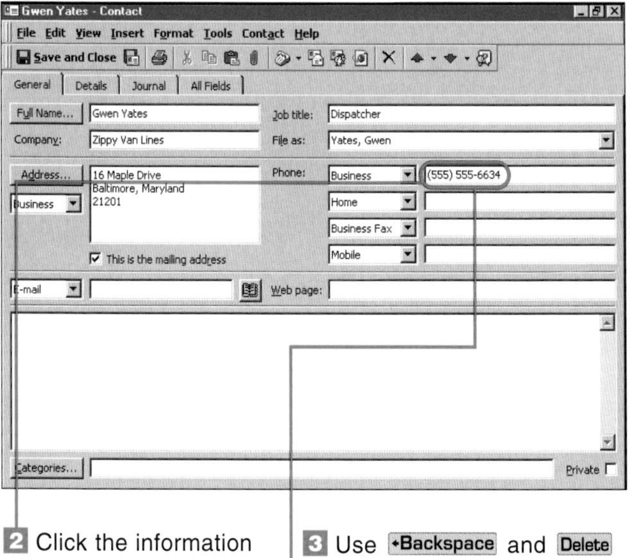

1 Double-click the name of the contact you want to update.

■ Information about the contact appears.

2 Click the information you want to change.

3 Use ←Backspace and Delete on your keyboard to remove the existing text.

4 Type the new information.

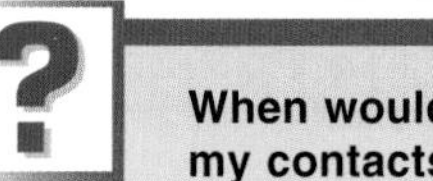

When would I need to update my contacts?

Over time, friends and colleagues may move and you will need to record their new addresses.

Also, as you learn more about your contacts, you can add information such as directions to their house or the names of their children.

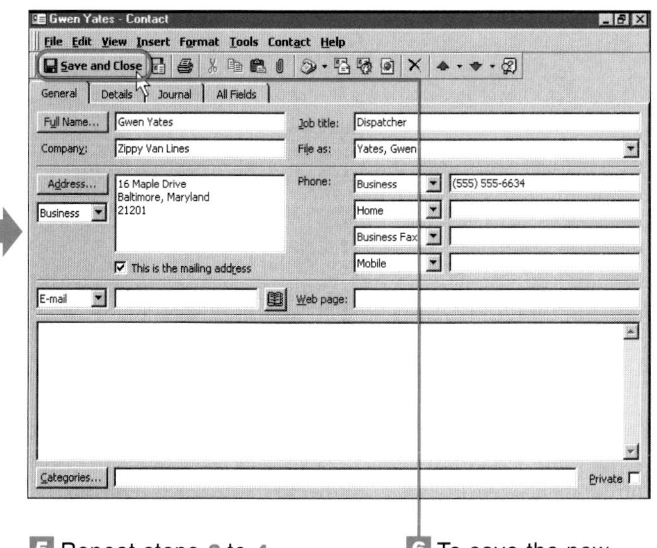

5 Repeat steps 2 to 4 for all the information you want to change.

6 To save the new information, click **Save and Close**.

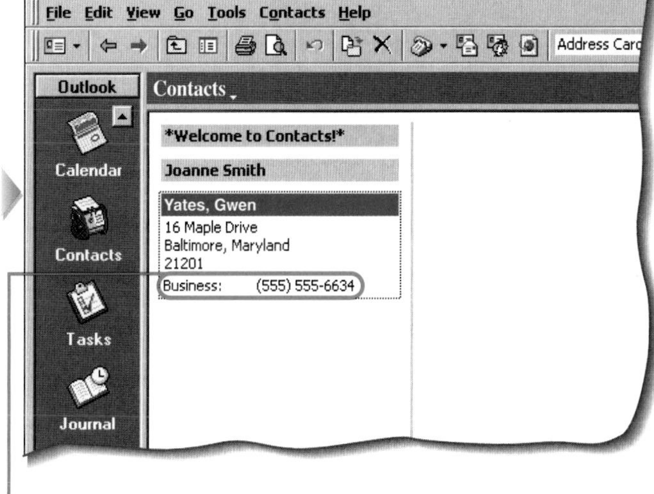

■ The information is updated.

BROWSE THROUGH CONTACTS

You can easily browse through your contacts to find information of interest.

BROWSE THROUGH CONTACTS

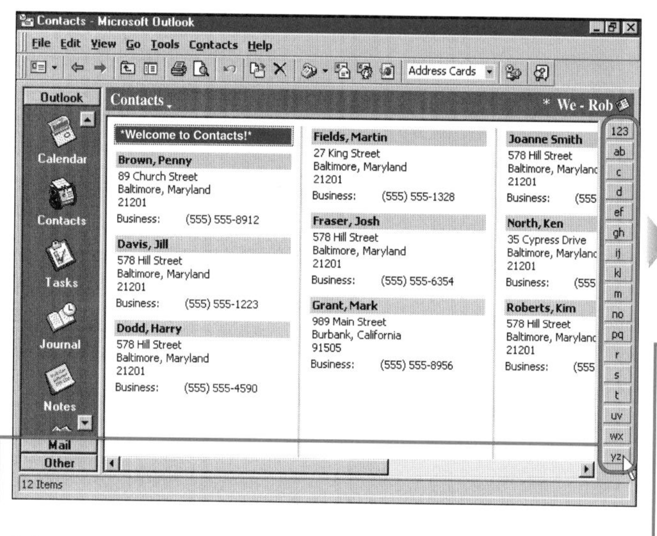

1 Click the first letter of the contact you want to view.

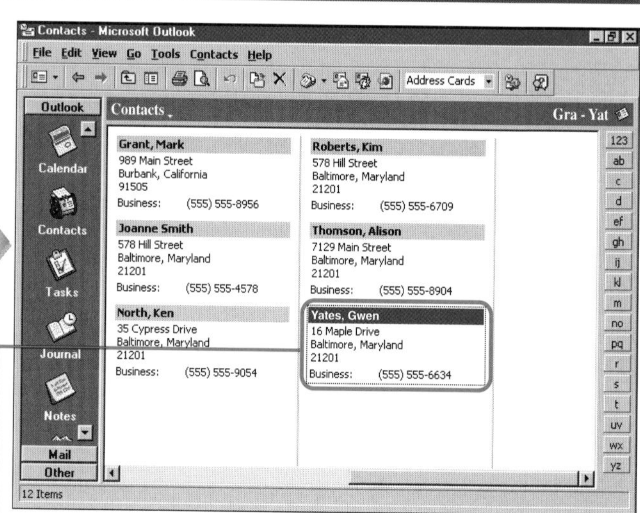

■ Contacts beginning with the letter you selected appear.

CHANGE VIEWS

You can change the way you view your contacts.

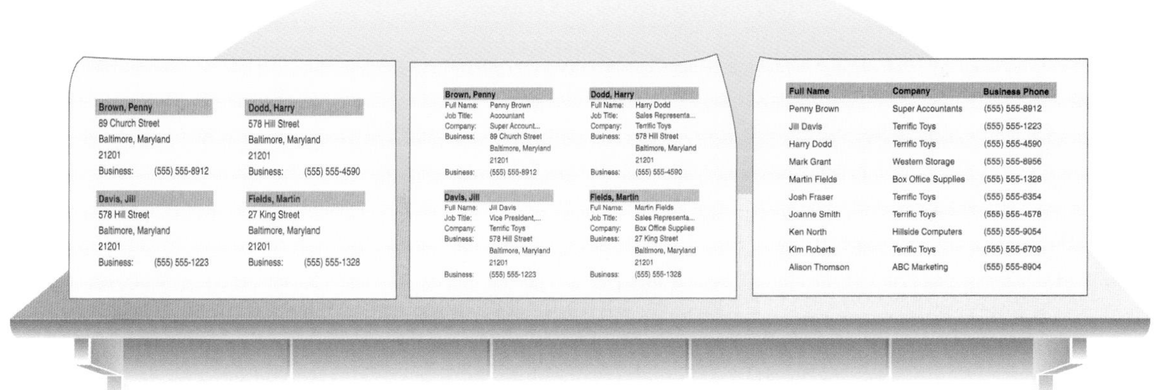

CHANGE VIEWS

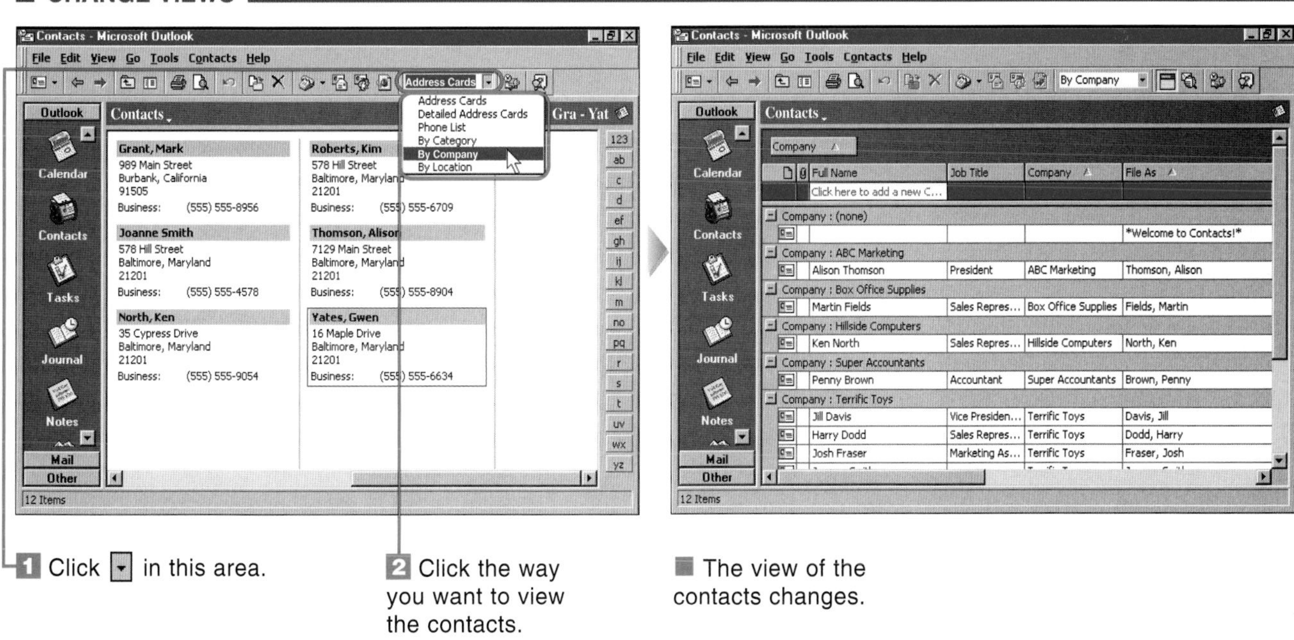

1 Click ▾ in this area.

2 Click the way you want to view the contacts.

■ The view of the contacts changes.

VIEW JOURNAL ENTRIES

The Journal helps you keep track of all your activities. You can easily view the activities you accomplished on any day.

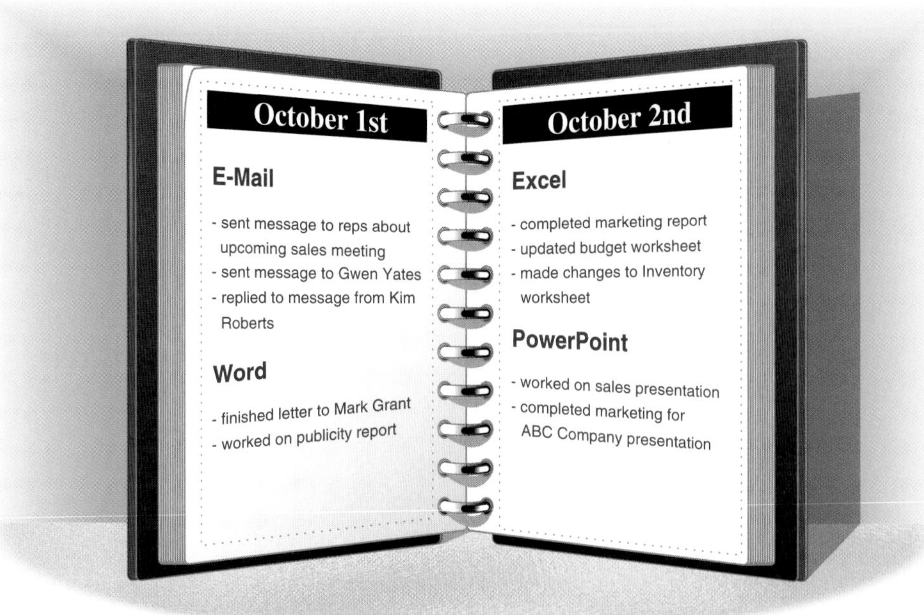

October 1st
E-Mail
- sent message to reps about upcoming sales meeting
- sent message to Gwen Yates
- replied to message from Kim Roberts
Word
- finished letter to Mark Grant
- worked on publicity report
October 2nd
Excel
- completed marketing report
- updated budget worksheet
- made changes to Inventory worksheet
PowerPoint
- worked on sales presentation
- completed marketing for ABC Company presentation

VIEW JOURNAL ENTRIES

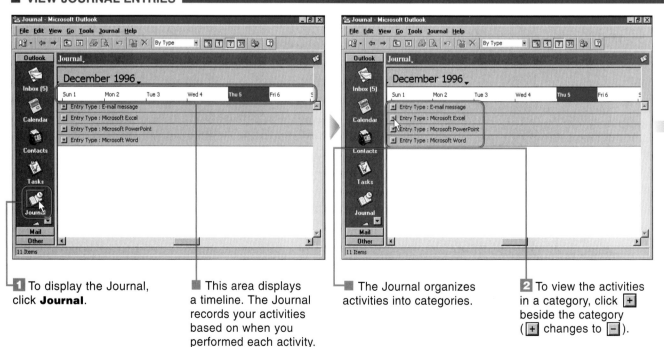

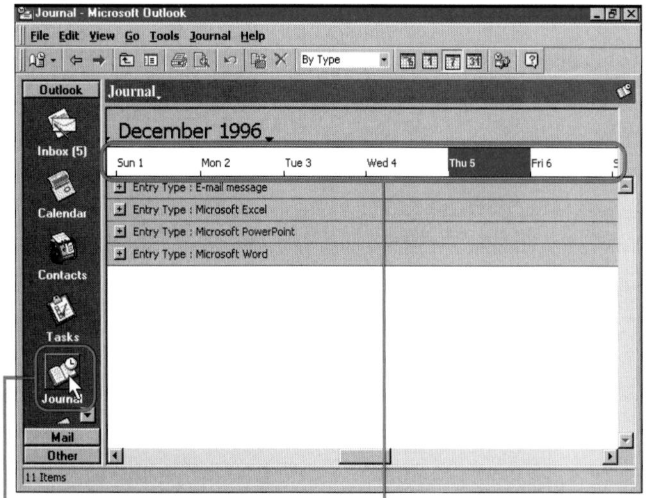

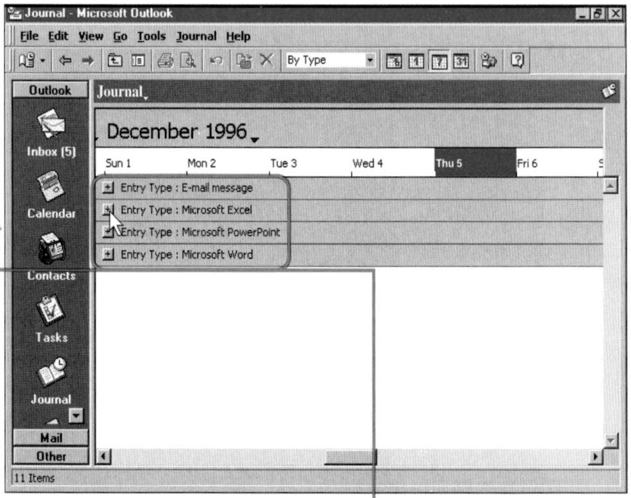

1 To display the Journal, click **Journal**.

This area displays a timeline. The Journal records your activities based on when you performed each activity.

The Journal organizes activities into categories.

2 To view the activities in a category, click ⊞ beside the category (⊞ changes to ⊟).

Can the Journal help me locate documents?

The Journal keeps track of the documents you work with each day. If you cannot remember where you stored a document, you can locate the document by looking in the Journal.

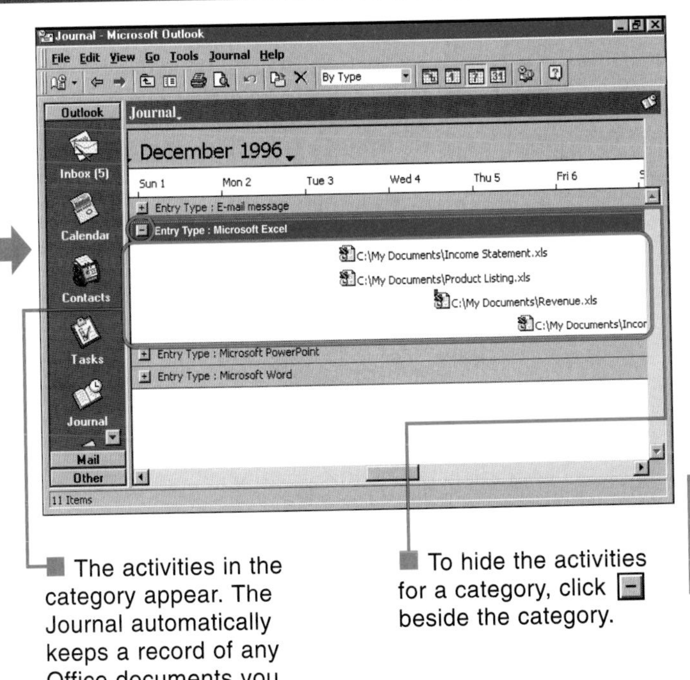

■ The activities in the category appear. The Journal automatically keeps a record of any Office documents you have saved.

■ To hide the activities for a category, click ⊟ beside the category.

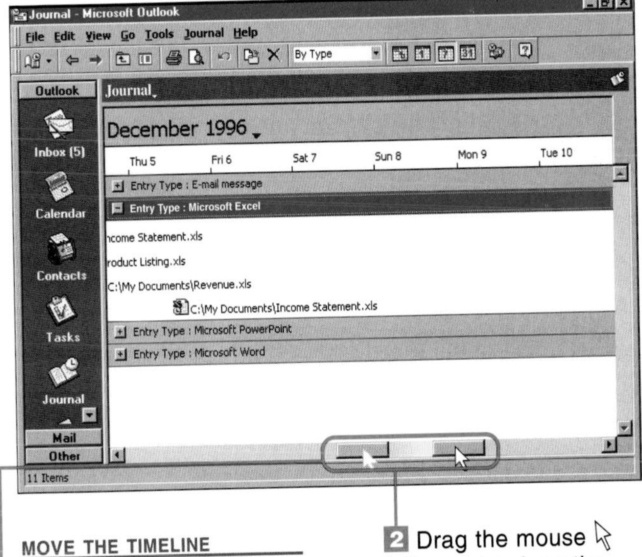

MOVE THE TIMELINE

1 To move the timeline to display the activities for a different day, position the mouse over the scroll box.

2 Drag the mouse left or right along the scroll bar until the day you want to view appears.

OPEN A JOURNAL ENTRY

You can open a journal entry to view details about the activity or to open the document or item the entry refers to.

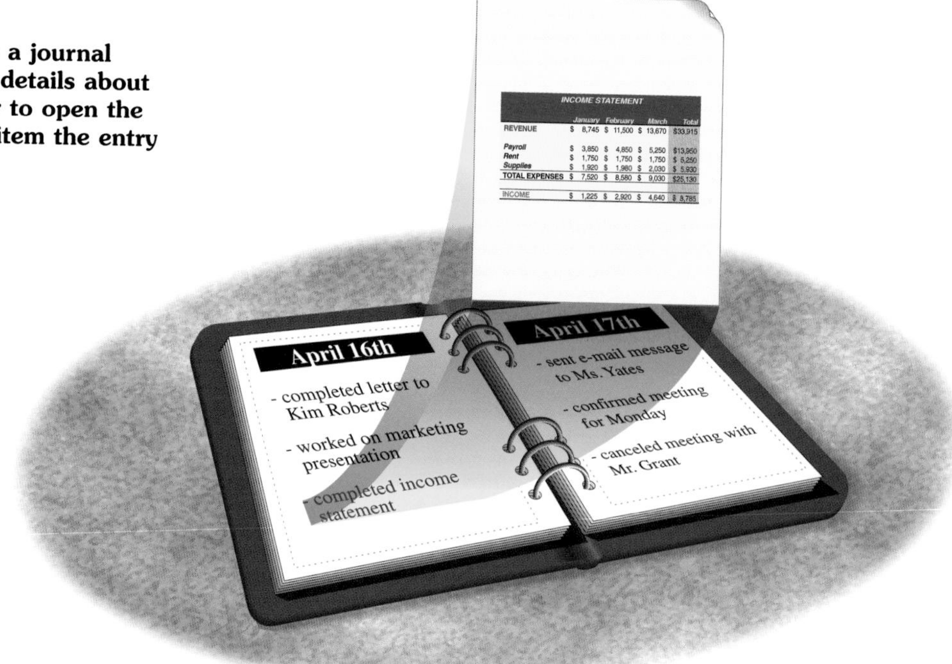

OPEN A JOURNAL ENTRY

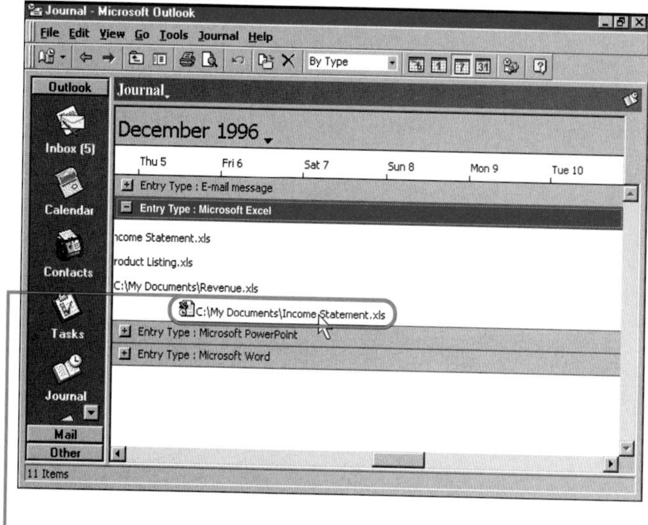

1 Double-click the journal entry you want to open.

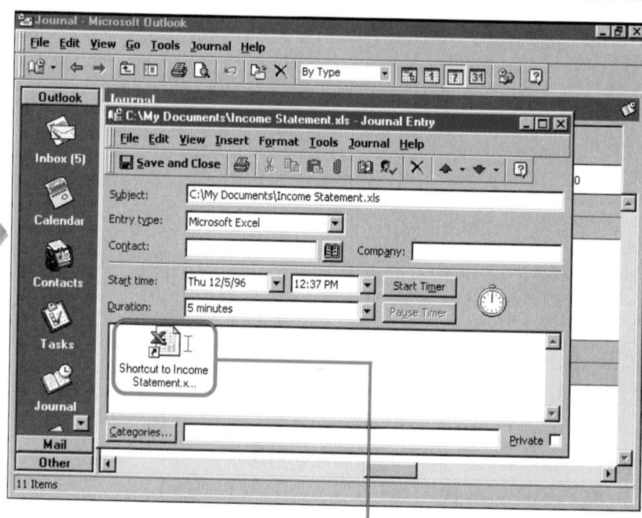

■ A window appears, displaying information about the journal entry.

2 To open the document or item, double-click the picture representing the document or item.

What is removed from my computer when I delete a journal entry?

When you delete a journal entry, you do not delete the item or document the journal entry refers to. Only the entry itself is deleted.

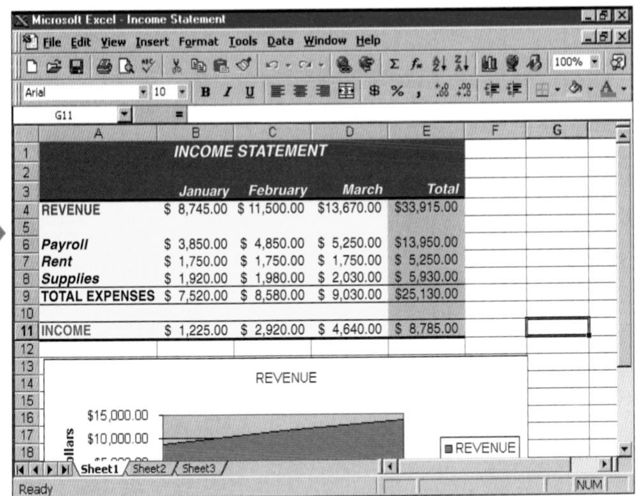

■ The document or item appears on the screen.

Note: To return to the Journal, refer to page 10 to switch between programs.

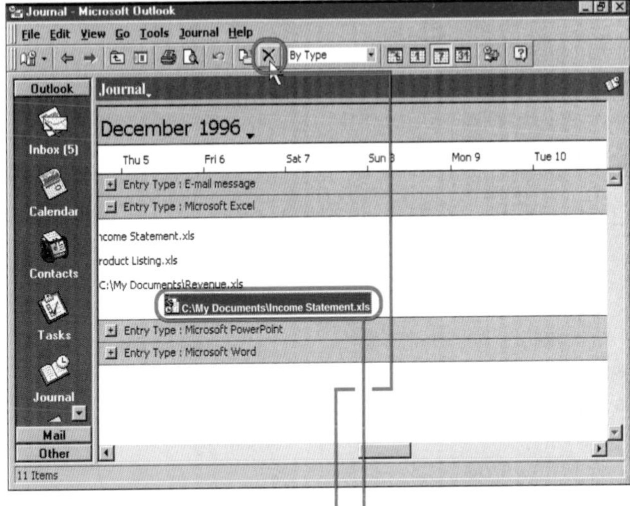

DELETE A JOURNAL ENTRY

You can delete a journal entry to make the Journal less cluttered.

1 Click the journal entry you want to delete.

2 Click ☒.

SELECT ACTIVITIES TO RECORD

You can choose which activities you want the Journal to record.

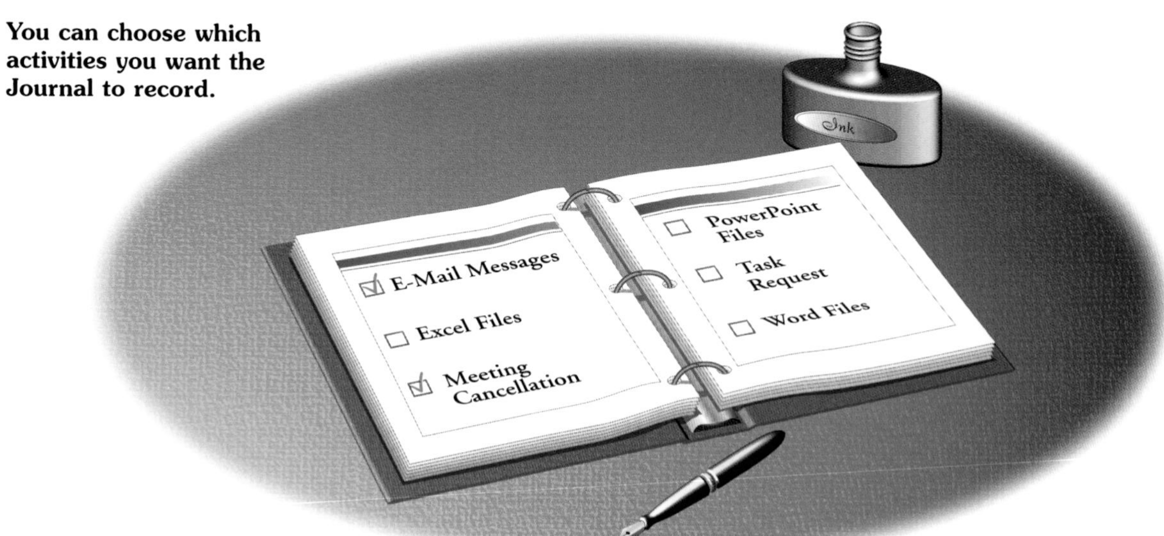

SELECT ACTIVITIES TO RECORD

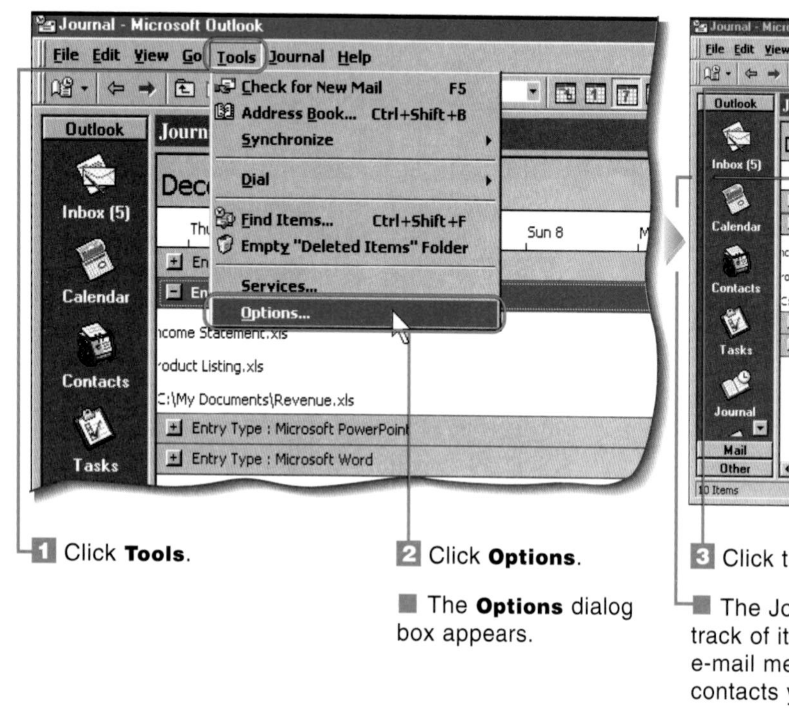

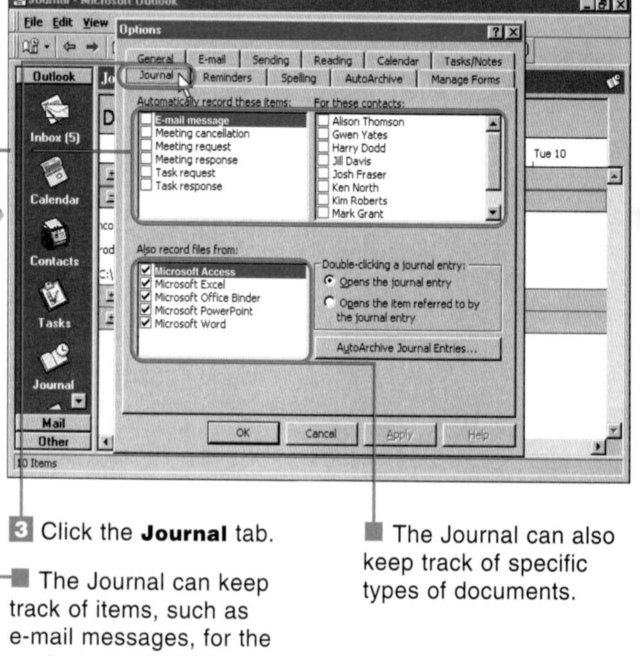

1 Click **Tools**.

2 Click **Options**.

■ The **Options** dialog box appears.

3 Click the **Journal** tab.

■ The Journal can keep track of items, such as e-mail messages, for the contacts you select.

Note: For information on contacts, refer to pages 306 to 311.

■ The Journal can also keep track of specific types of documents.

?

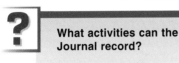

What activities can the Journal record?

The Journal can record communication with important contacts and work done in programs such as Word or Excel.

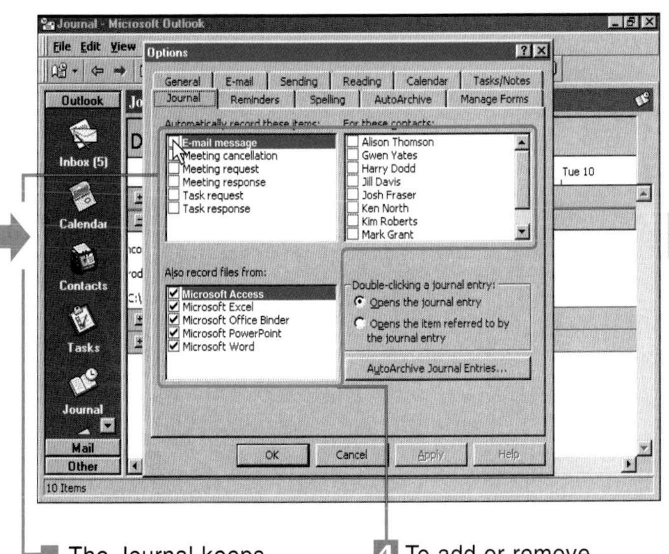

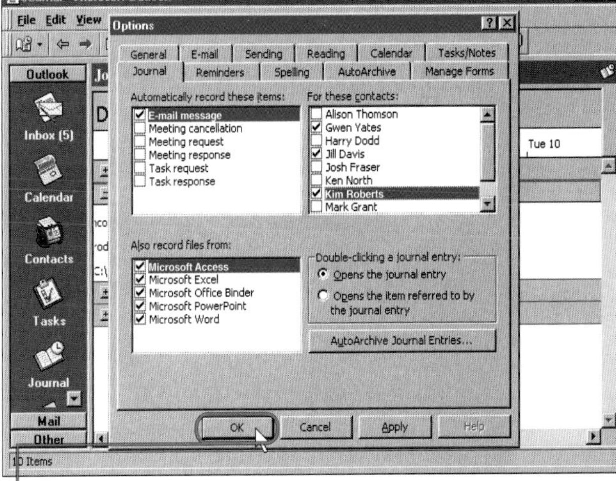

■ The Journal keeps track of each item that displays a check mark (☑).

4 To add or remove a check mark (☑), click the box (☐) beside an item.

5 When all the items you want the Journal to keep track of display a check mark (☑), click **OK**.

You can produce a paper copy of your e-mail messages, contacts, tasks, notes, journal and calendar.

PRINT

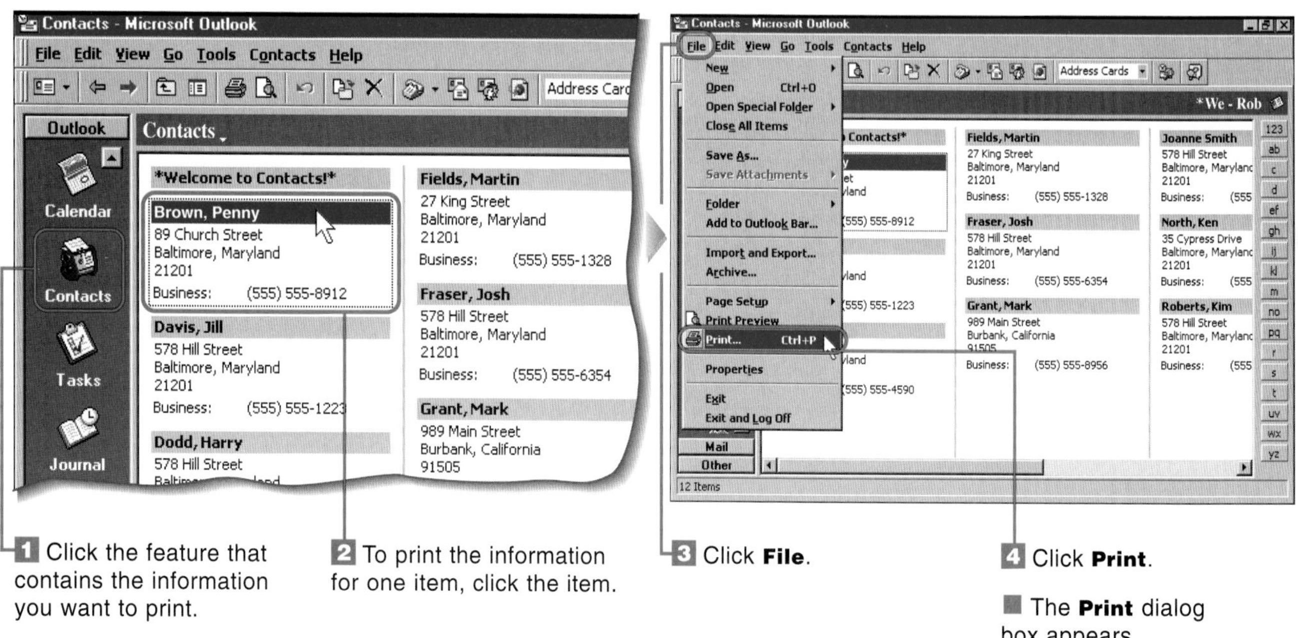

1 Click the feature that contains the information you want to print.

2 To print the information for one item, click the item.

3 Click **File**.

4 Click **Print**.

■ The **Print** dialog box appears.

What are print styles?

Outlook lets you select the way you want to print information.

For example, you can print your calendar for one day, week or month.

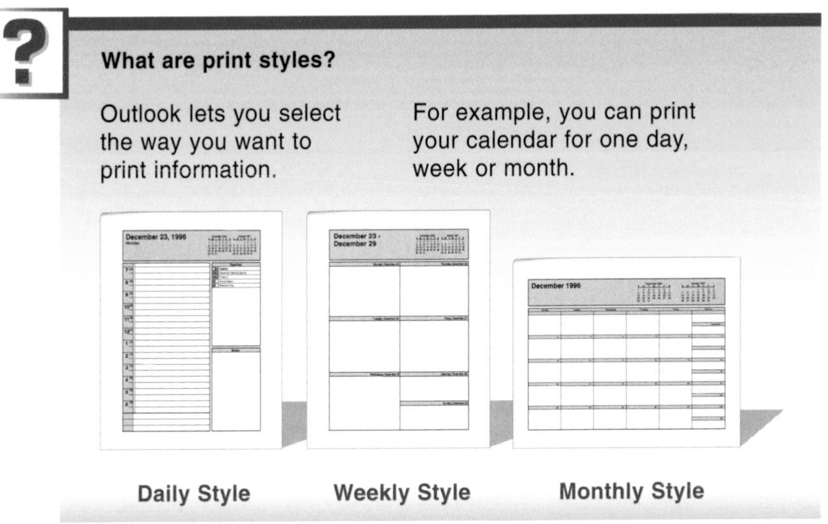

Daily Style Weekly Style Monthly Style

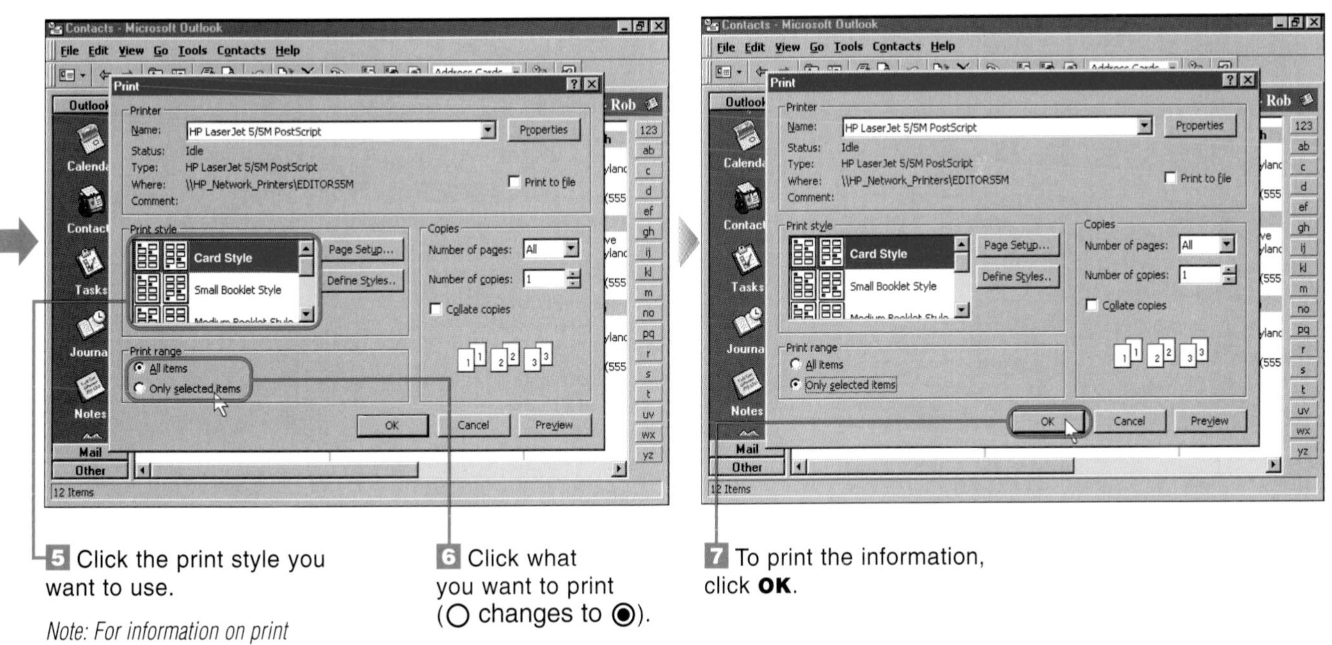

5 Click the print style you want to use.

Note: For information on print styles, refer to the top of this page.

6 Click what you want to print (○ changes to ◉).

7 To print the information, click **OK**.

RECOVER A DELETED ITEM

The Deleted Items folder stores all the items you have deleted in Outlook. You can easily recover any of these items.

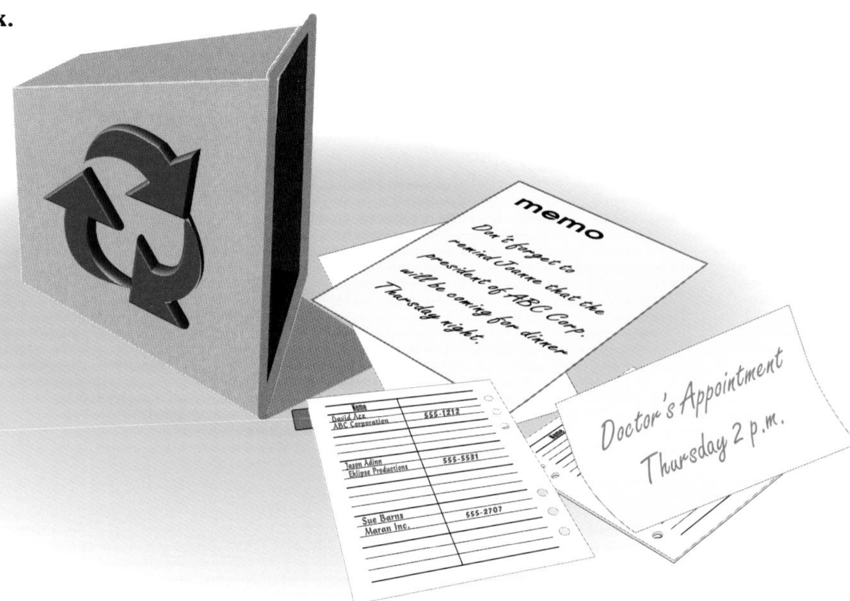

RECOVER A DELETED ITEM

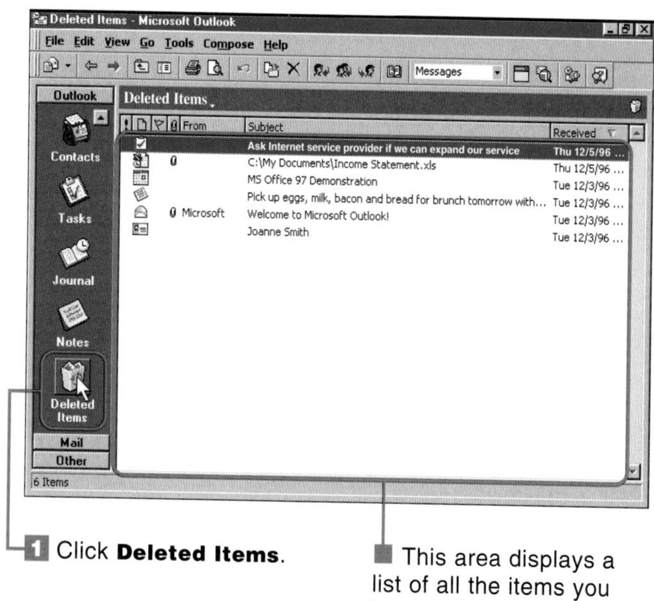

1 Click **Deleted Items**.

■ This area displays a list of all the items you have deleted in Outlook.

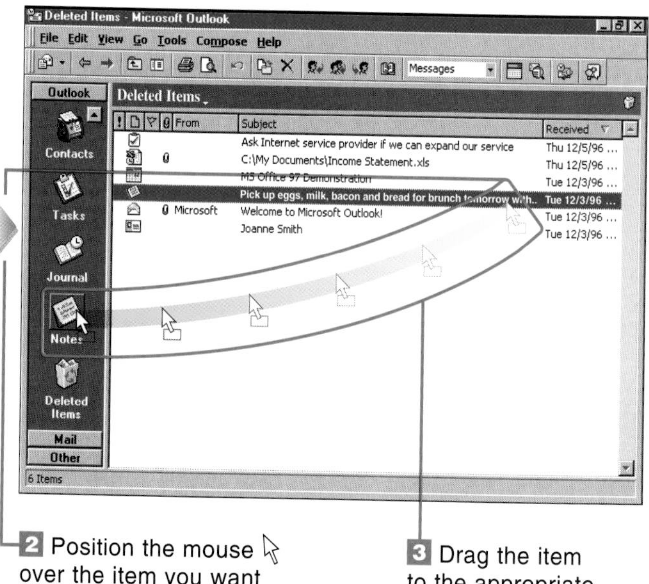

2 Position the mouse over the item you want to recover.

3 Drag the item to the appropriate Outlook feature.

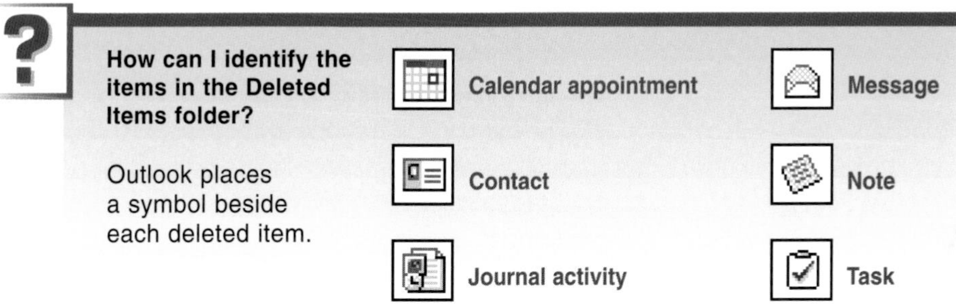

?
How can I identify the items in the Deleted Items folder?
Outlook places a symbol beside each deleted item.
Calendar appointment
Message
Contact
Note
Journal activity
Task

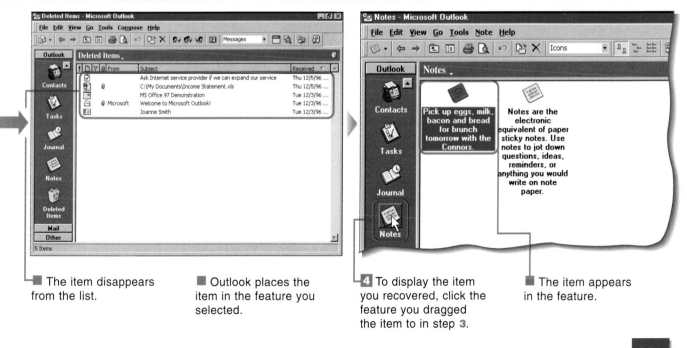

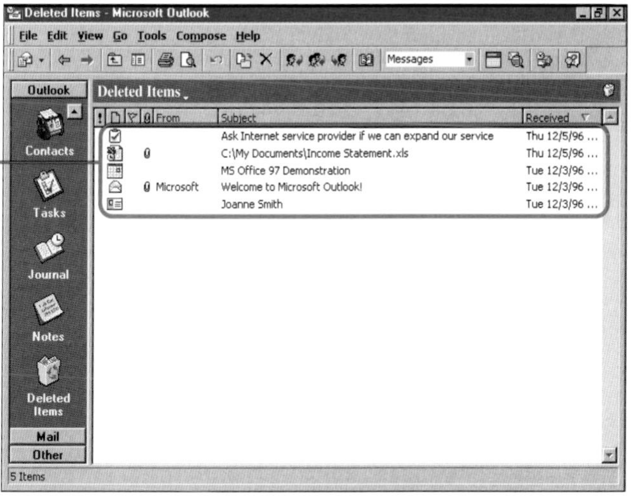

■ The item disappears from the list.

■ Outlook places the item in the feature you selected.

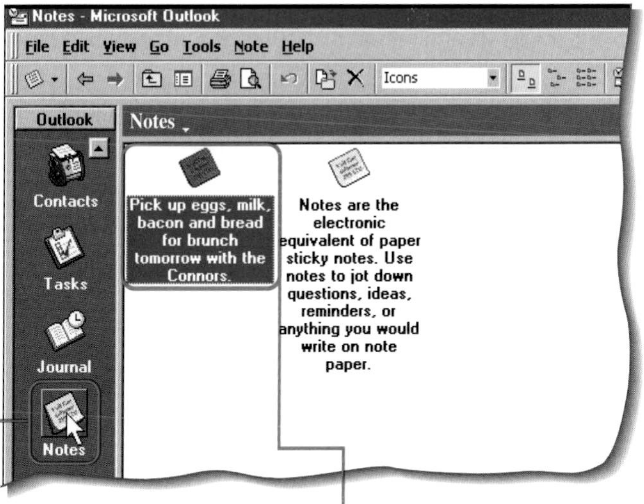

4 To display the item you recovered, click the feature you dragged the item to in step 3.

■ The item appears in the feature.

EMPTY DELETED ITEMS FOLDER

You should regularly empty the Deleted Items folder to save space on your computer.

EMPTY DELETED ITEMS FOLDER

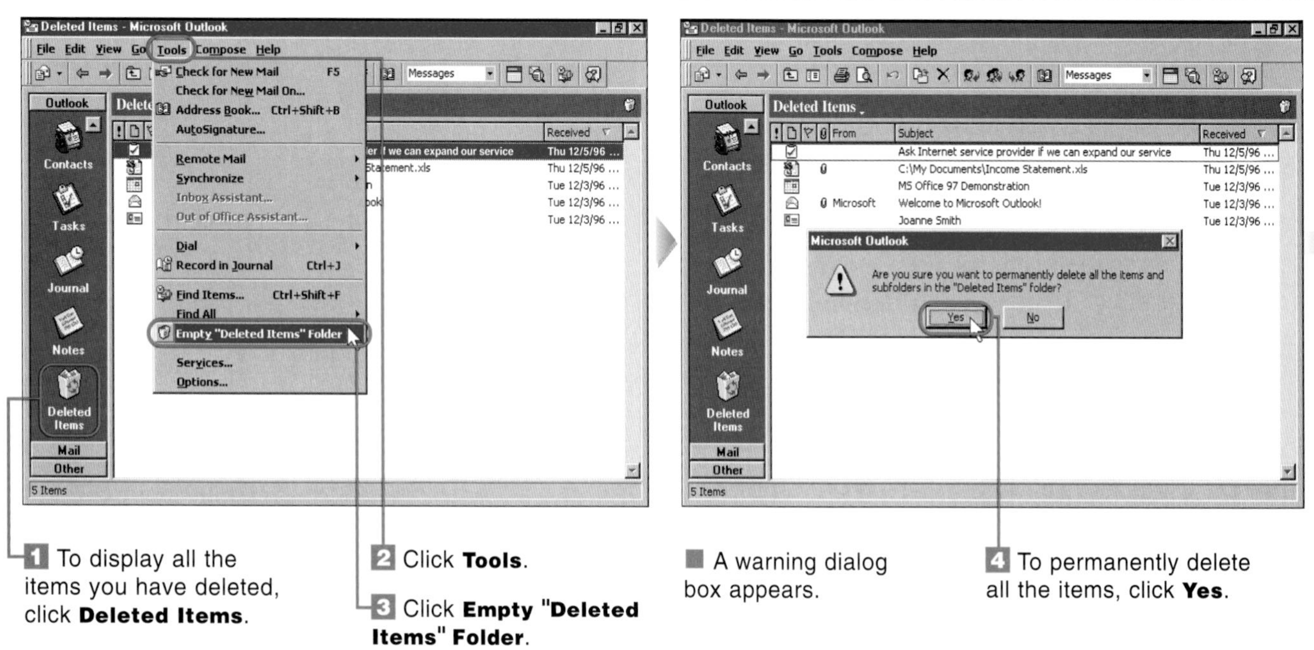

1 To display all the items you have deleted, click **Deleted Items**.

2 Click **Tools**.

3 Click **Empty "Deleted Items" Folder**.

■ A warning dialog box appears.

4 To permanently delete all the items, click **Yes**.

?

What if I may need an item in the future?

Deleting an item from the Deleted Items folder will permanently remove the item from your computer. Do not delete an item you may need in the future.

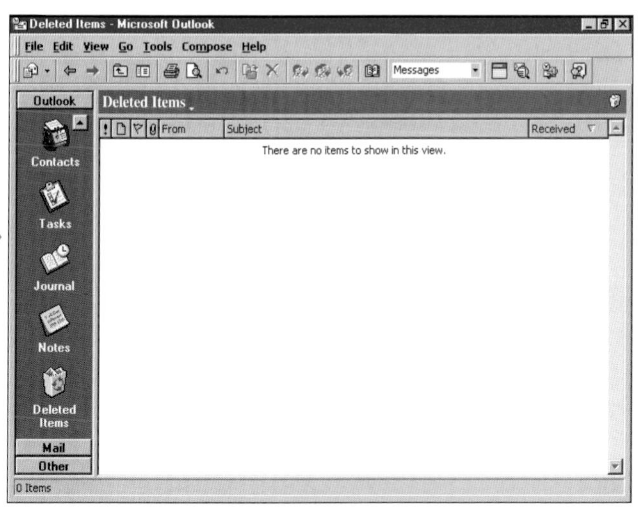

■ The items are permanently deleted.

DELETE ONE ITEM

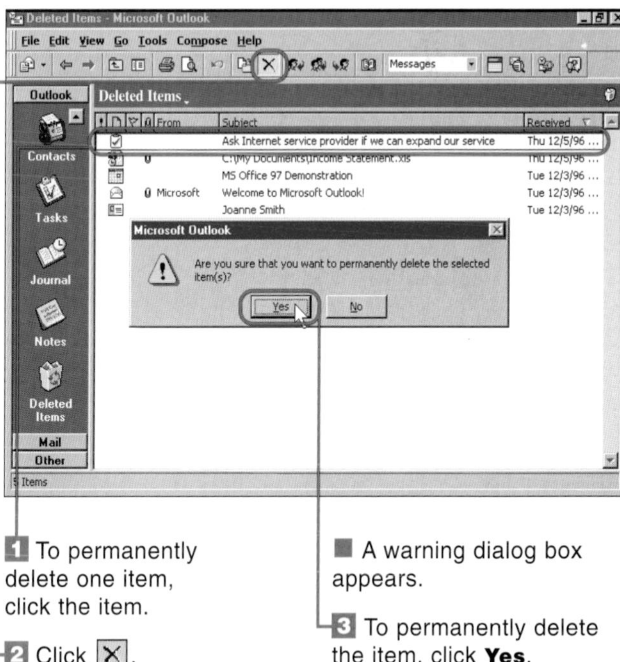

1 To permanently delete one item, click the item.

2 Click ☒.

■ A warning dialog box appears.

3 To permanently delete the item, click **Yes**.

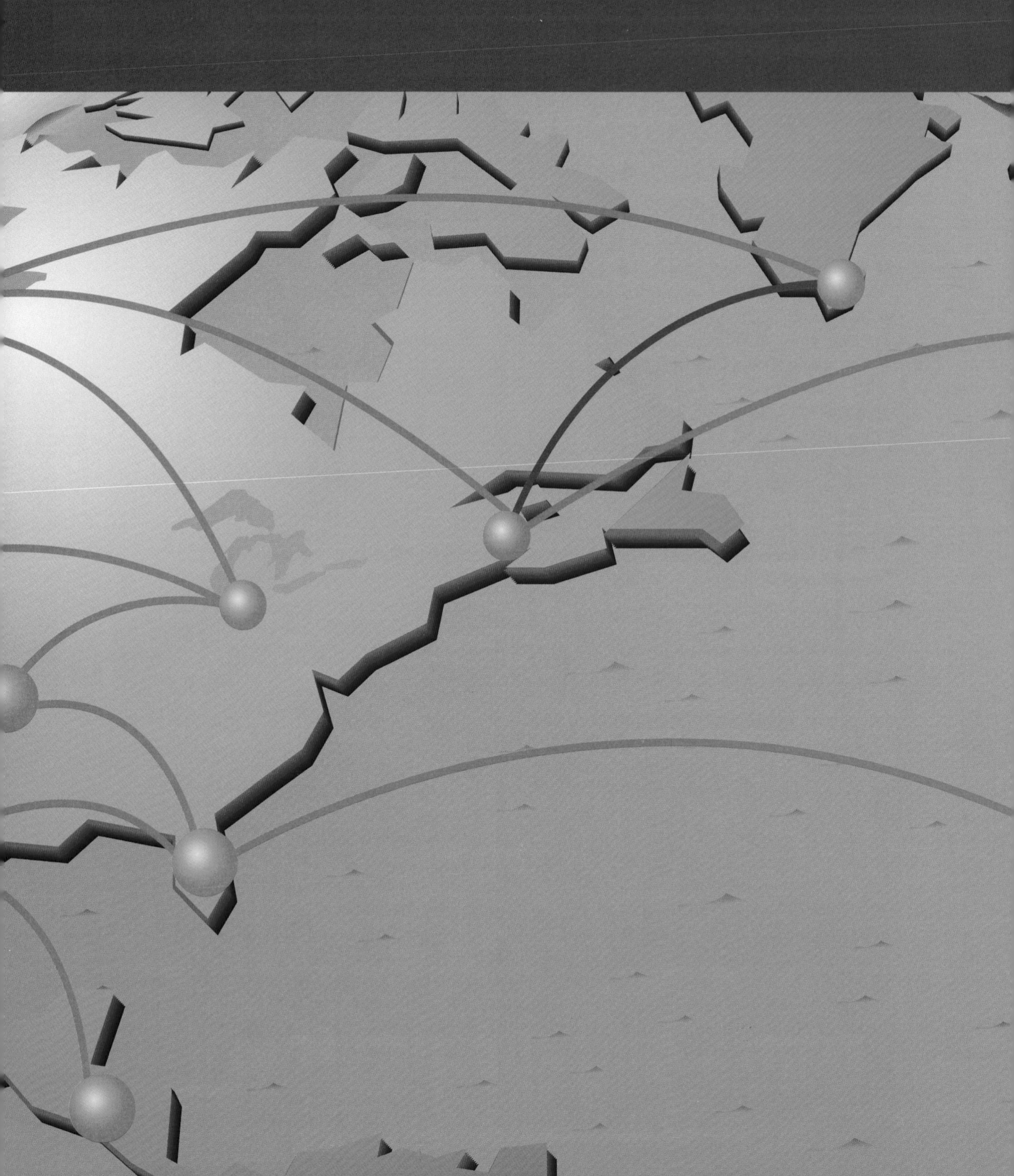

Office and the Internet

This chapter shows you how to use features offered in Office to take advantage of the Internet and World Wide Web.

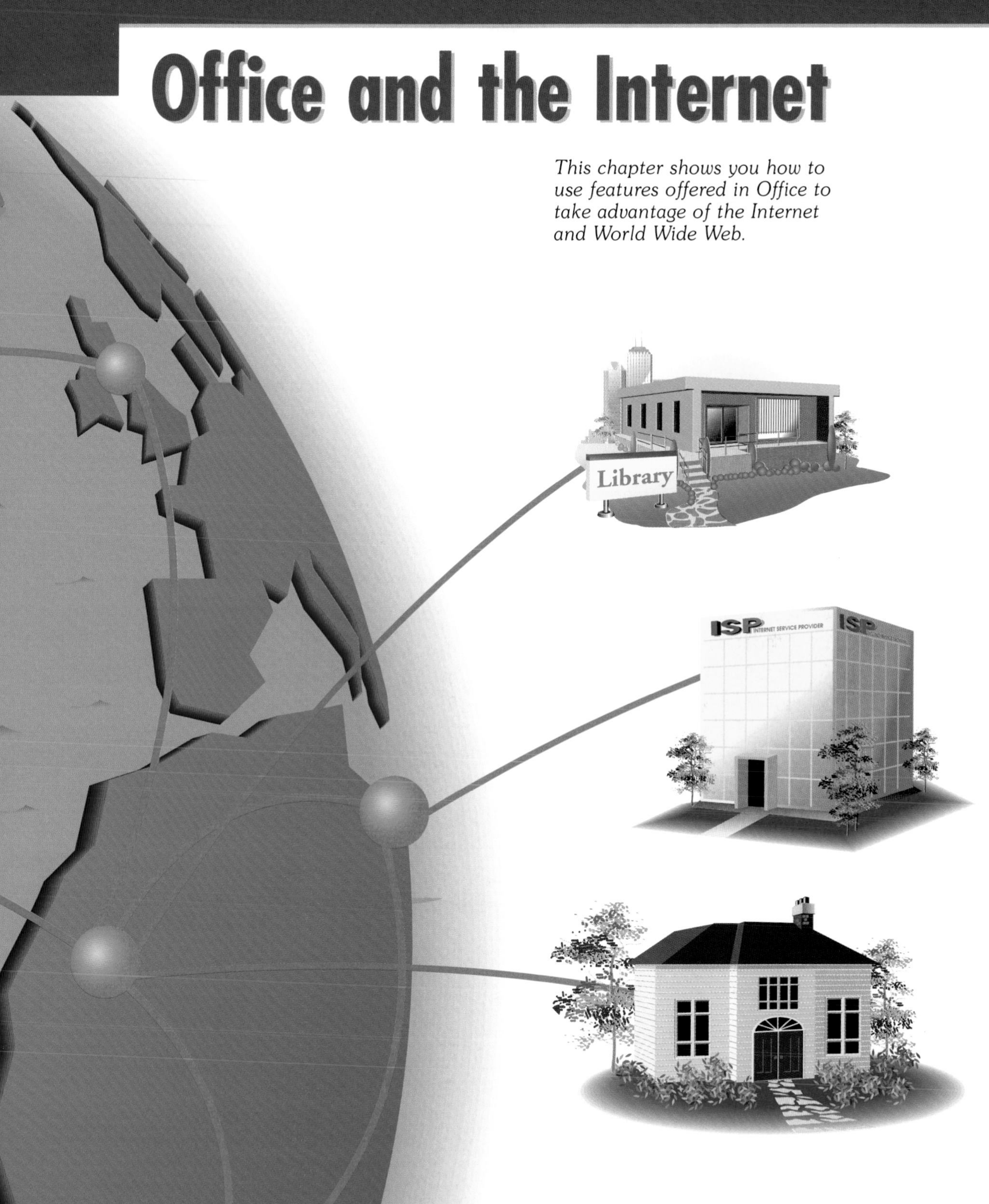

CREATE A HYPERLINK

You can create a hyperlink to connect a word or phrase in one document to another document or Web page. When you select the word or phrase, the other document appears.

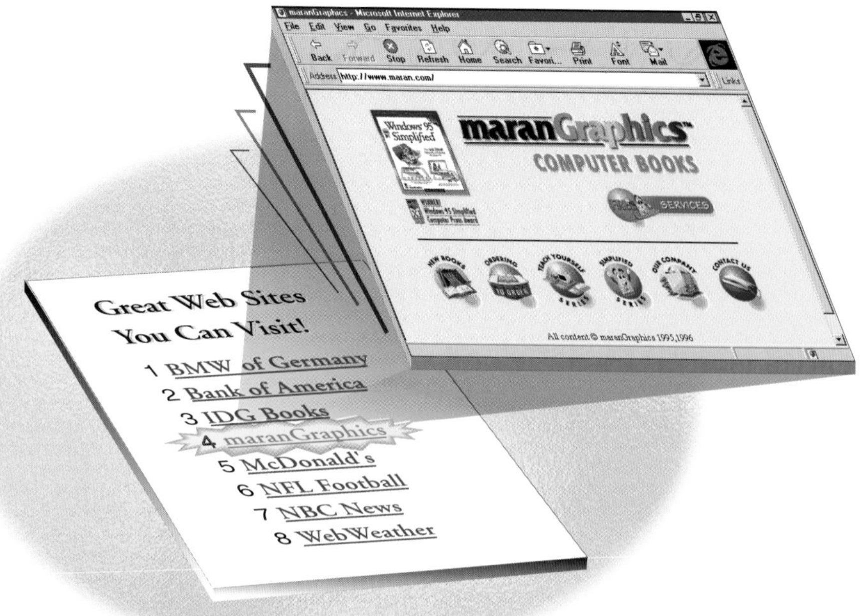

CREATE A HYPERLINK

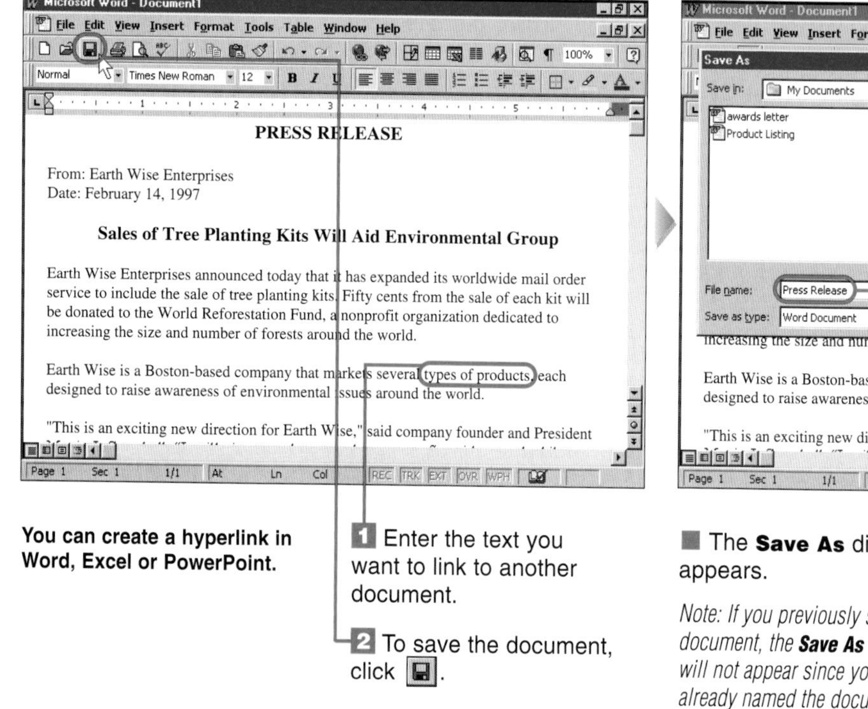

You can create a hyperlink in Word, Excel or PowerPoint.

1 Enter the text you want to link to another document.

2 To save the document, click 💾.

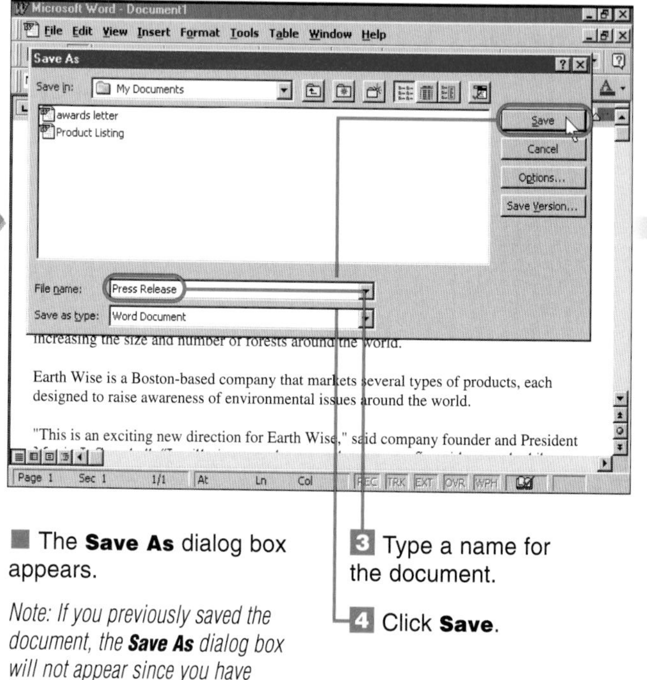

■ The **Save As** dialog box appears.

Note: If you previously saved the document, the ***Save As*** *dialog box will not appear since you have already named the document.*

3 Type a name for the document.

4 Click **Save**.

? **Where can a hyperlink take me?**

You can create a hyperlink that takes you to another document on your computer, network, corporate intranet or the Internet.

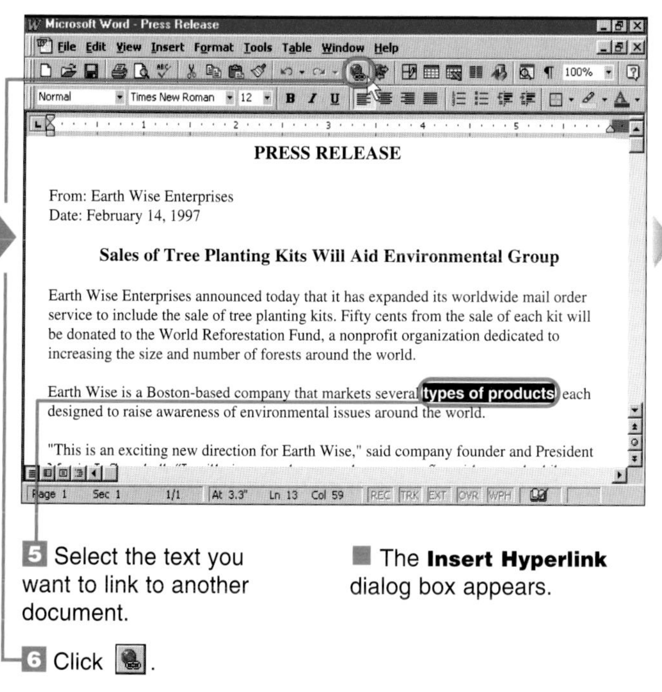

5 Select the text you want to link to another document.

6 Click [icon].

■ The **Insert Hyperlink** dialog box appears.

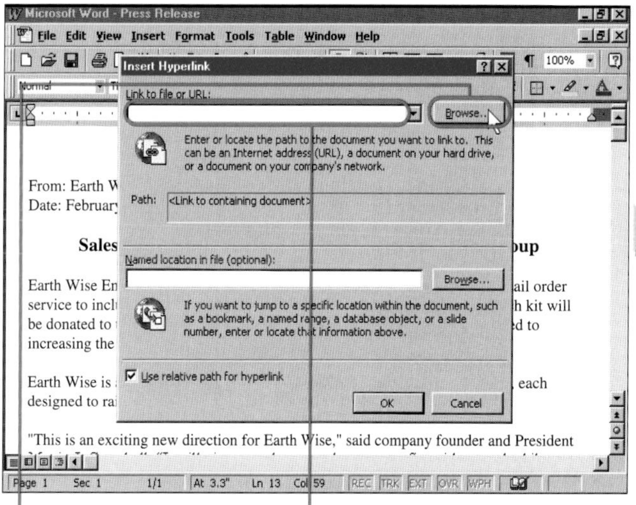

7 To link the text to a document on your computer or network, click **Browse**.

■ To link the text to a Web page, type the address of the Web page (example: http://www.maran.com). Then skip to step **10** on page 328.

CONTINUED

CREATE A HYPERLINK

You can easily see hyperlinks in a document. Hyperlinks appear underlined and in color.

EARTH WISE ENTERPRISES
We care about the environment.
All products created and marketed by Earth Wise Enterprises are designed to increase awareness of environmental issues around the world.
A list of our main types of products is presented below. To find out more about the products in any category, select the category name.
Tree planting kits
Recycle bins
Compost kits

CREATE A HYPERLINK (CONTINUED)

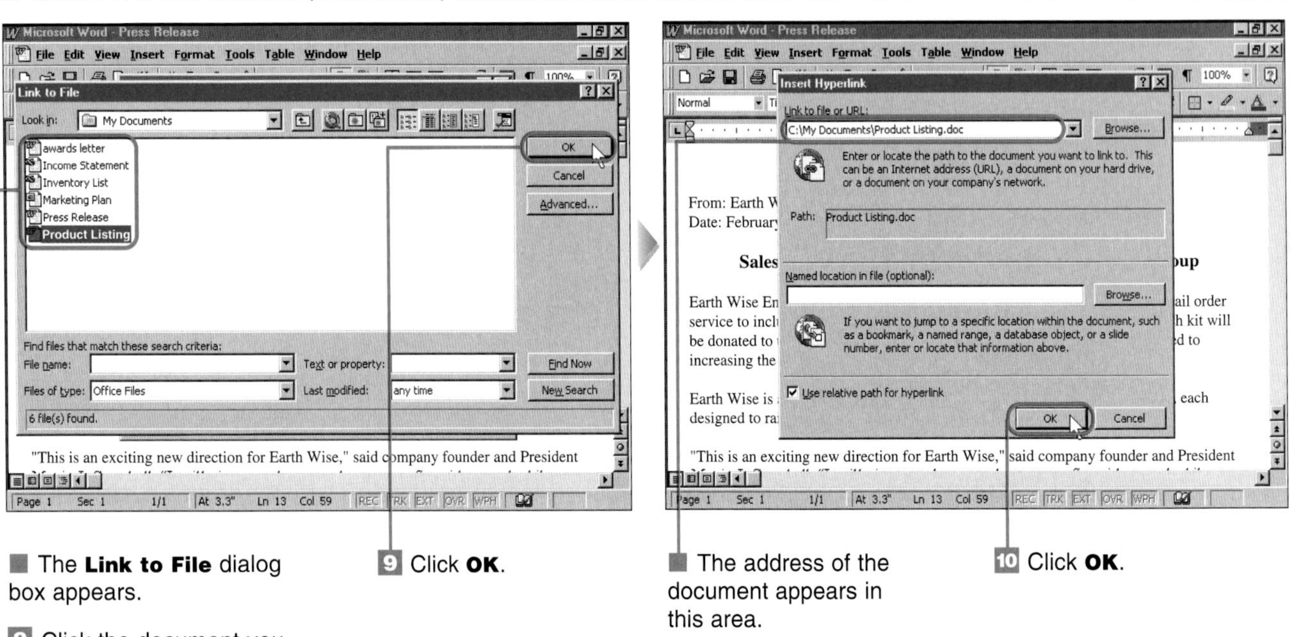

■ The **Link to File** dialog box appears.

8 Click the document you want to link to.

9 Click **OK**.

■ The address of the document appears in this area.

10 Click **OK**.

?

Can Word automatically create hyperlinks for me?

When you type the address of a document located on a network or on the Internet, Word automatically changes the address to a hyperlink.

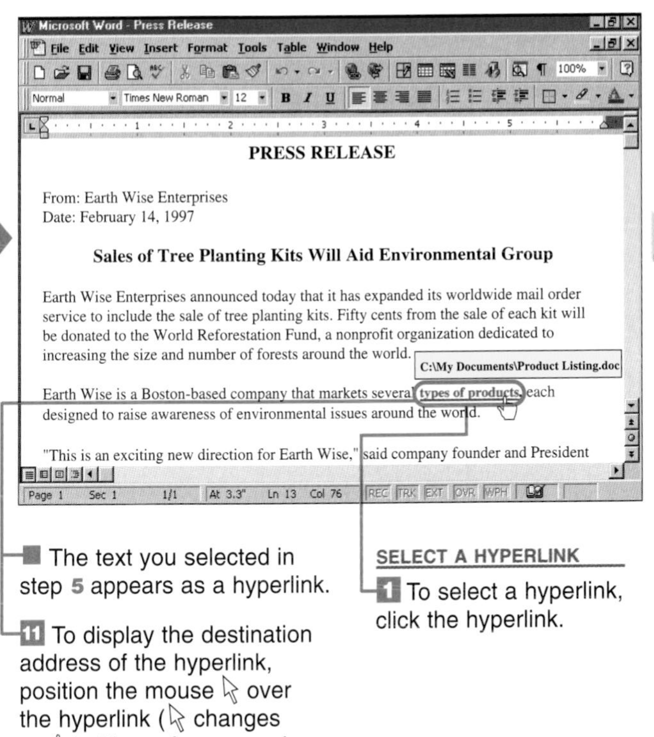

■ The text you selected in step **5** appears as a hyperlink.

11 To display the destination address of the hyperlink, position the mouse ↖ over the hyperlink (↖ changes to ☝). After a few seconds, the address appears.

SELECT A HYPERLINK

1 To select a hyperlink, click the hyperlink.

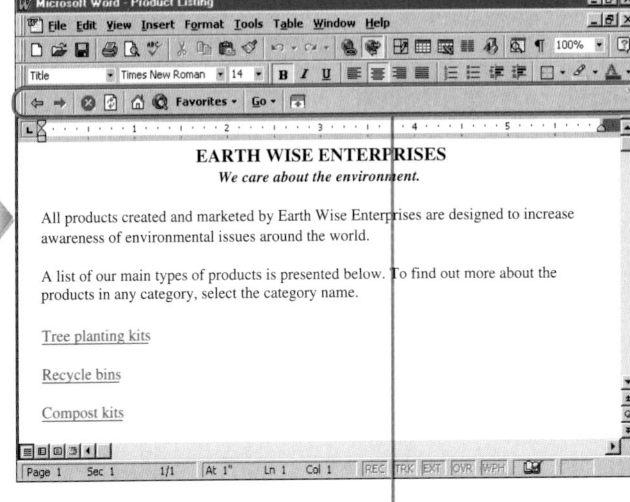

■ The document connected to the hyperlink appears.

■ If the hyperlink is connected to a Web page, your Web browser opens and displays the Web page.

■ When you select a hyperlink, the Web toolbar may appear on the screen. For more information on the Web toolbar, refer to page 330.

DISPLAY THE WEB TOOLBAR

You can display the Web toolbar to help you browse through documents containing hyperlinks.

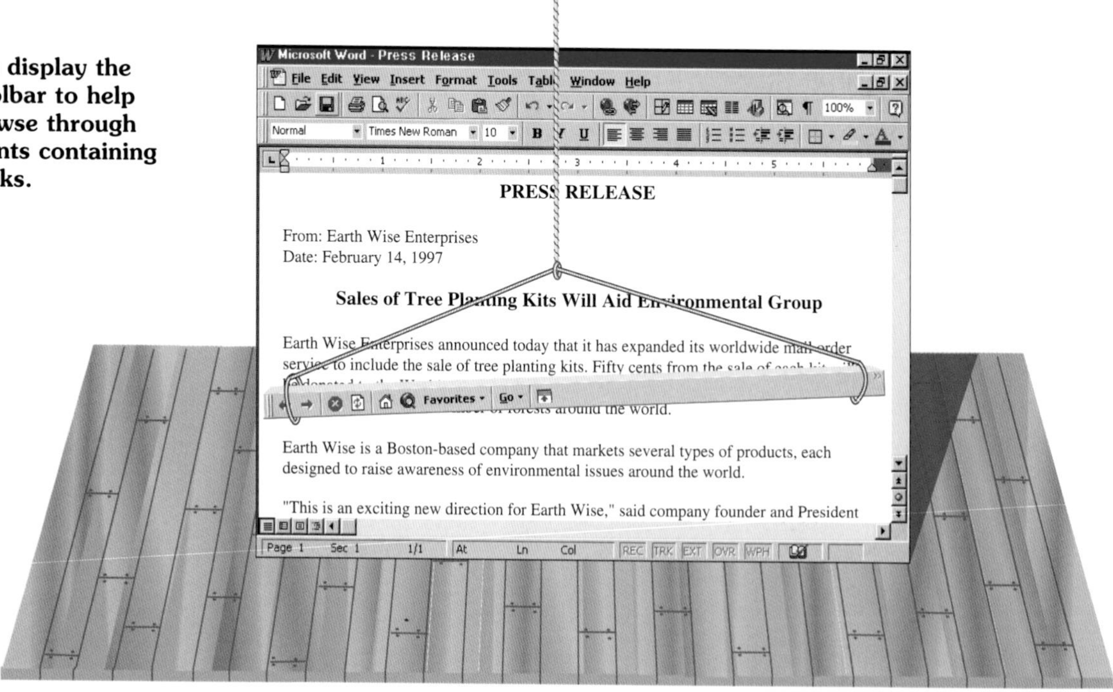

DISPLAY THE WEB TOOLBAR

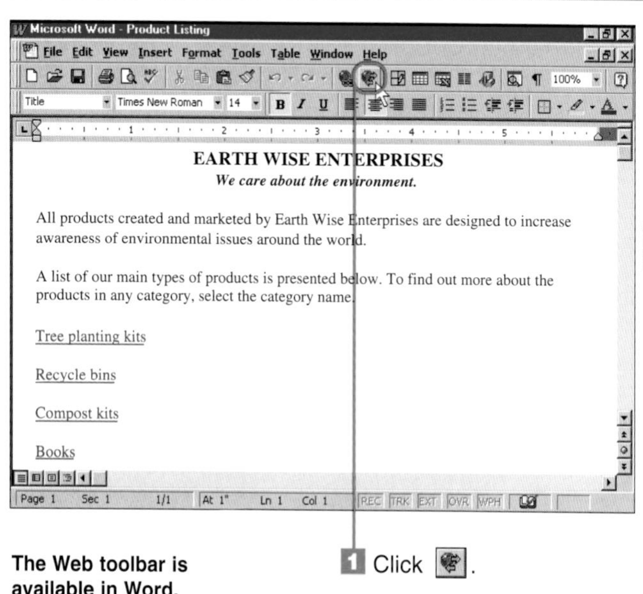

The Web toolbar is available in Word, Excel and PowerPoint.

1 Click .

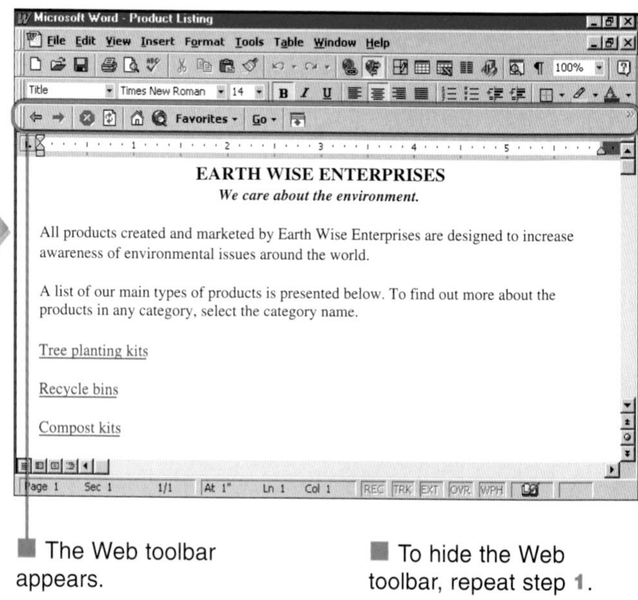

■ The Web toolbar appears.

■ To hide the Web toolbar, repeat step 1.

MOVE BETWEEN DOCUMENTS

After selecting hyperlinks in documents, you can easily move back and forth between these documents.

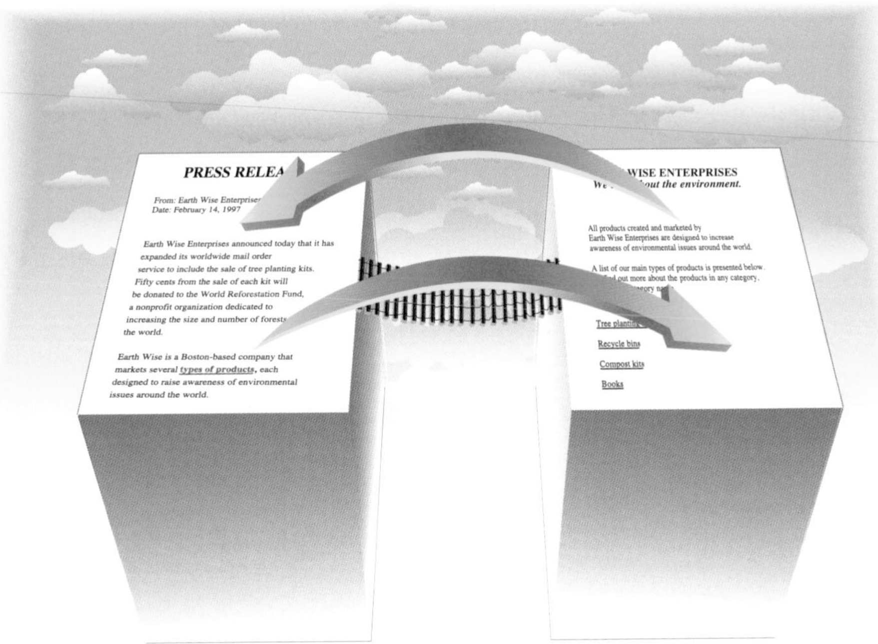

MOVE BETWEEN DOCUMENTS

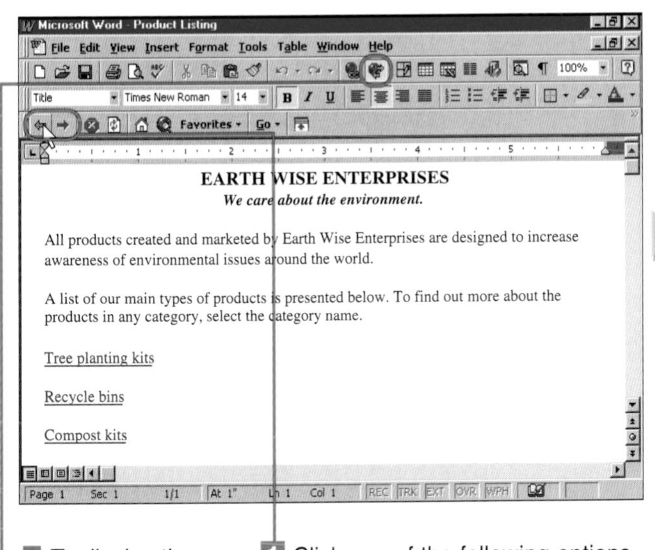

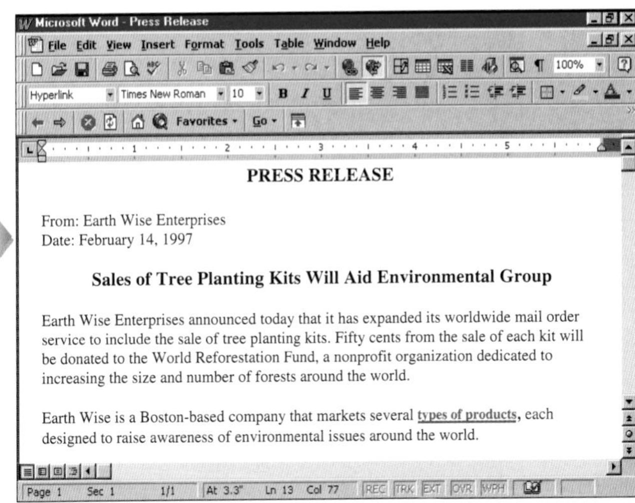

■ To display the Web toolbar, click [icon].

1 Click one of the following options.

[←] Display the previous document

[→] Display the next document

■ The document you selected appears.

OPEN A DOCUMENT

You can quickly open a document that is on your computer, network, corporate intranet or the Internet.

OPEN A DOCUMENT

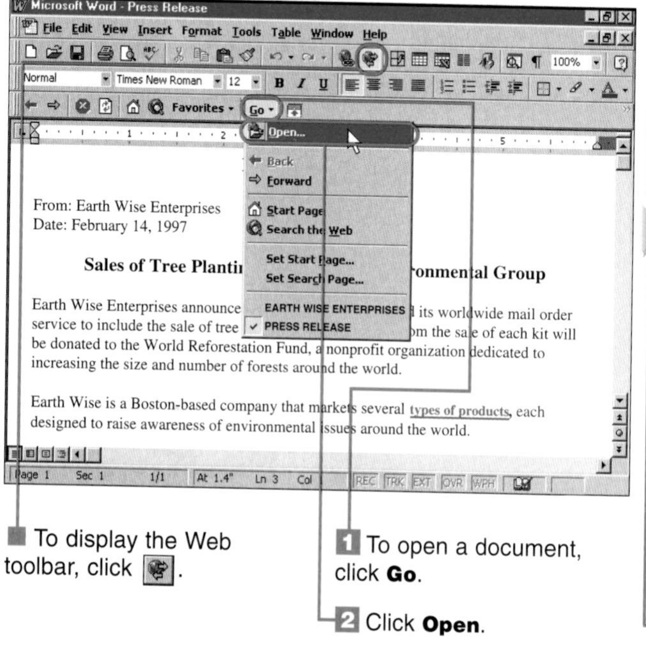

■ To display the Web toolbar, click [icon].

1 To open a document, click **Go**.

2 Click **Open**.

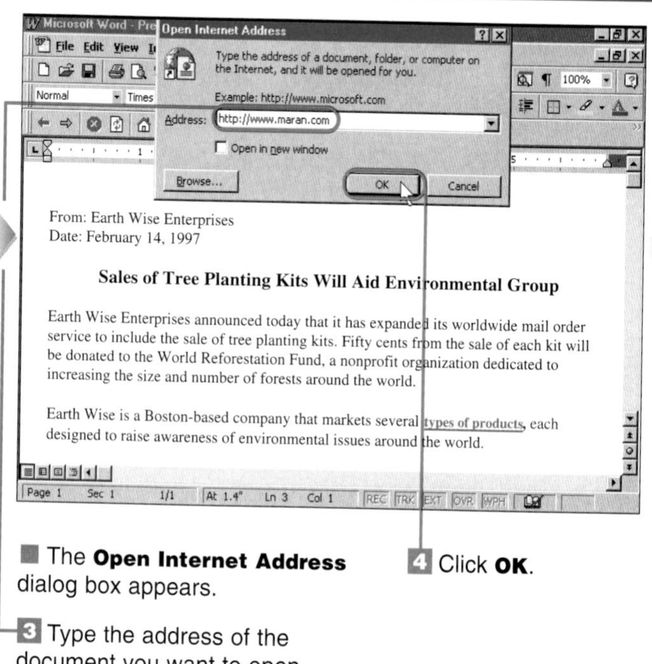

■ The **Open Internet Address** dialog box appears.

3 Type the address of the document you want to open.

4 Click **OK**.

Microsoft Office remembers the last documents you visited. You can quickly return to any of these documents.

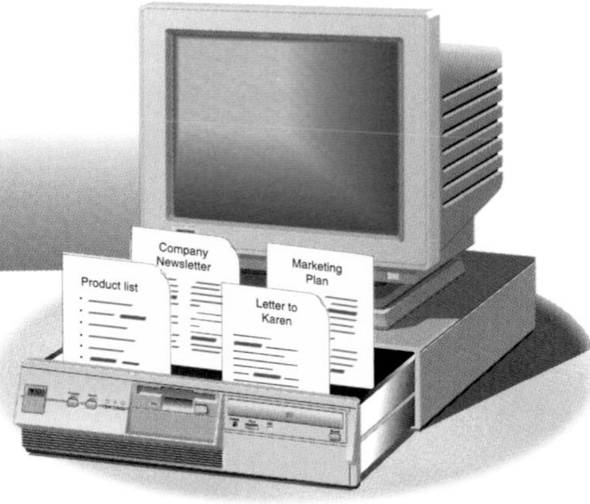

RETURN TO A DOCUMENT

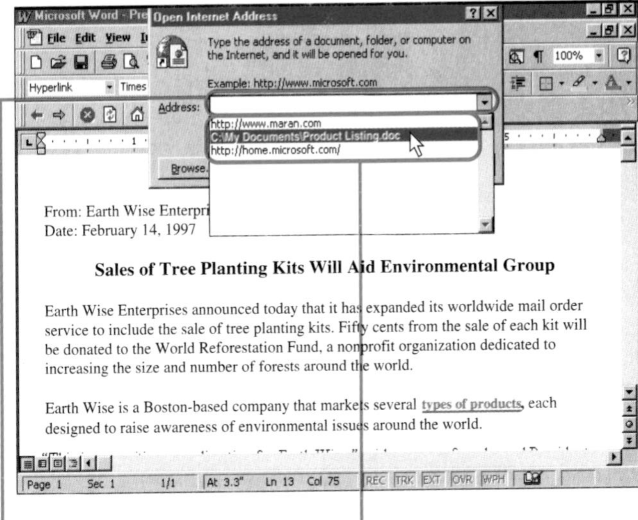

1 To open the **Open Internet Address** dialog box, perform steps 1 and 2 on page 332.

2 Click ▾ in this area.

3 Click the document you want to open.

4 Press Enter on your keyboard to open the document.

■ The document appears.

■ If the document you opened is a Web page, your Web browser opens and displays the Web page.

STOP THE CONNECTION

If a Web page is taking a long time to appear, you can stop the transfer of information.

STOP THE CONNECTION

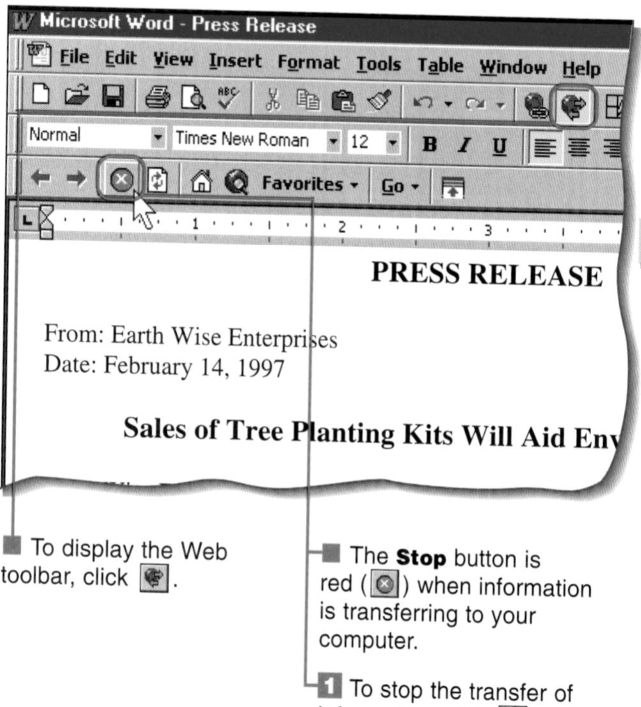

■ To display the Web toolbar, click .

■ The **Stop** button is red ( ) when information is transferring to your computer.

1 To stop the transfer of information, click .

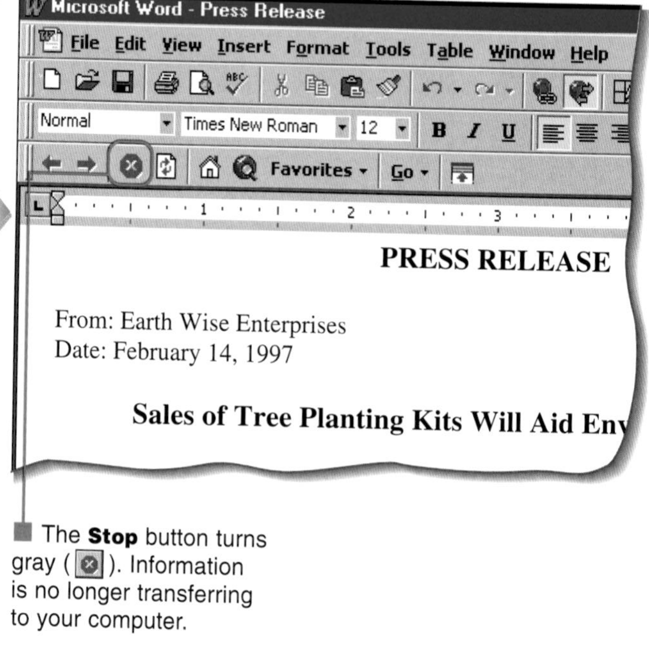

■ The **Stop** button turns gray ( ). Information is no longer transferring to your computer.

REFRESH A DOCUMENT

While you are viewing a document, the author may make changes to the document. You can easily transfer a fresh copy of the document to your computer.

REFRESH A DOCUMENT

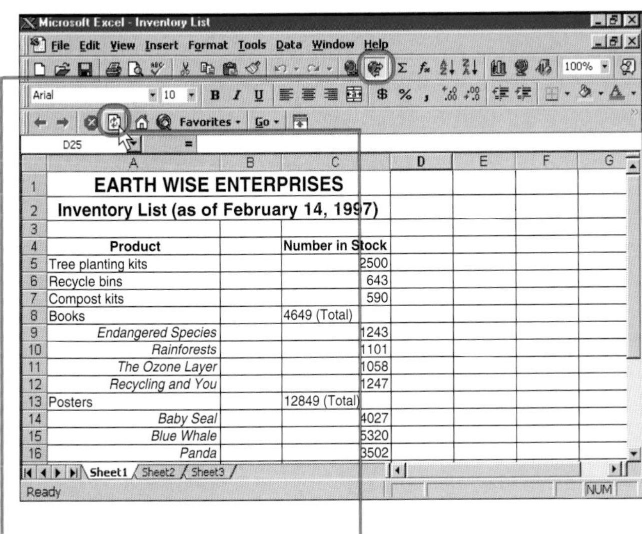

■ To display the Web toolbar, click [icon].

1 To refresh the document, click [icon].

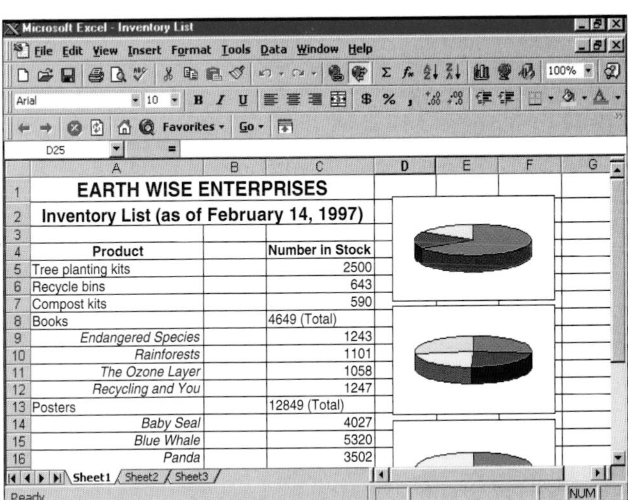

■ An up-to-date copy of the document appears.

DISPLAY THE START PAGE

The start page is the first page that appears when you start a Web browser.

The start page often includes instructions and hyperlinks that let you quickly connect to interesting documents.

DISPLAY THE START PAGE

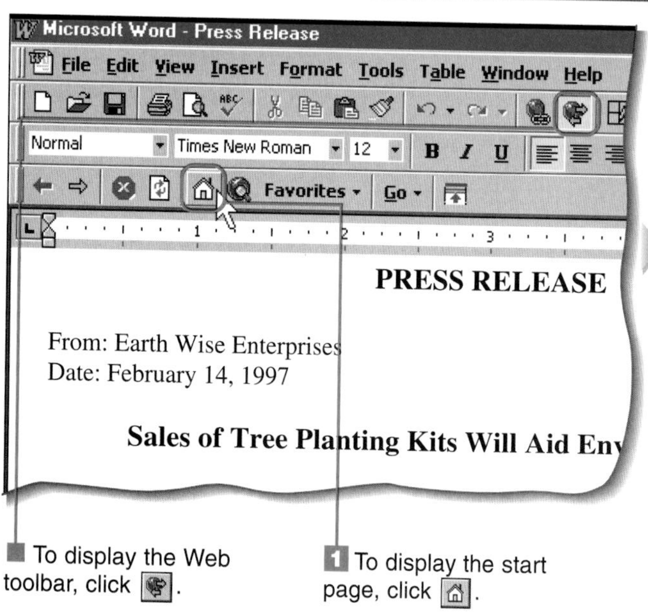

■ To display the Web toolbar, click [icon].

1 To display the start page, click [icon].

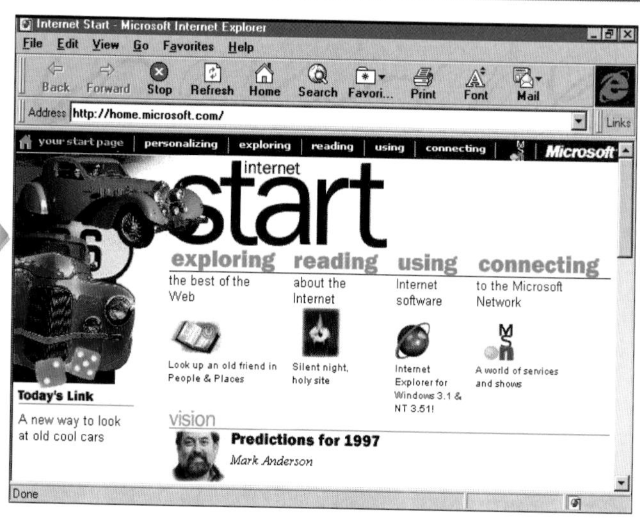

■ The Web browser opens and displays the start page.

DISPLAY THE SEARCH PAGE

The search page helps you find information of interest.

DISPLAY THE SEARCH PAGE

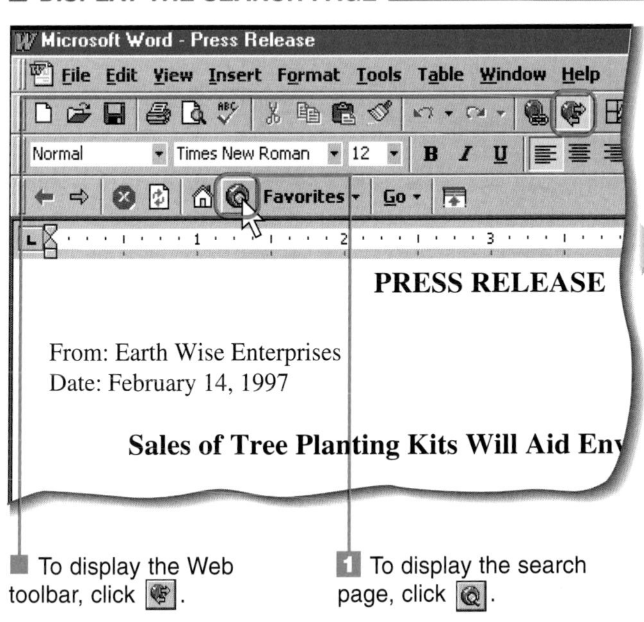

■ To display the Web toolbar, click [icon].

1 To display the search page, click [icon].

■ The Web browser opens and displays the search page.

ADD DOCUMENT TO FAVORITES

You can add documents you frequently use to the Favorites folder. This lets you quickly open these documents at any time.

ADD DOCUMENT TO FAVORITES

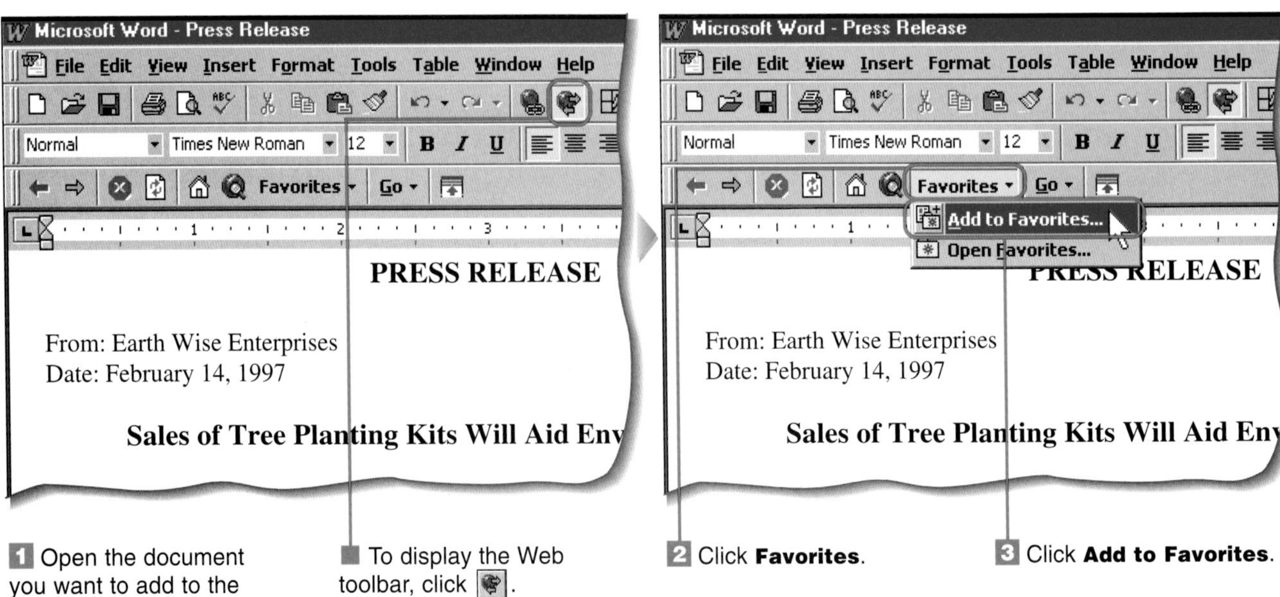

1 Open the document you want to add to the Favorites folder.

■ To display the Web toolbar, click .

2 Click **Favorites**.

3 Click **Add to Favorites**.

When I add a document to the Favorites folder, does the document change locations?

When you add a document to the Favorites folder, you create a shortcut to the original document. The original document does not change its location on your computer.

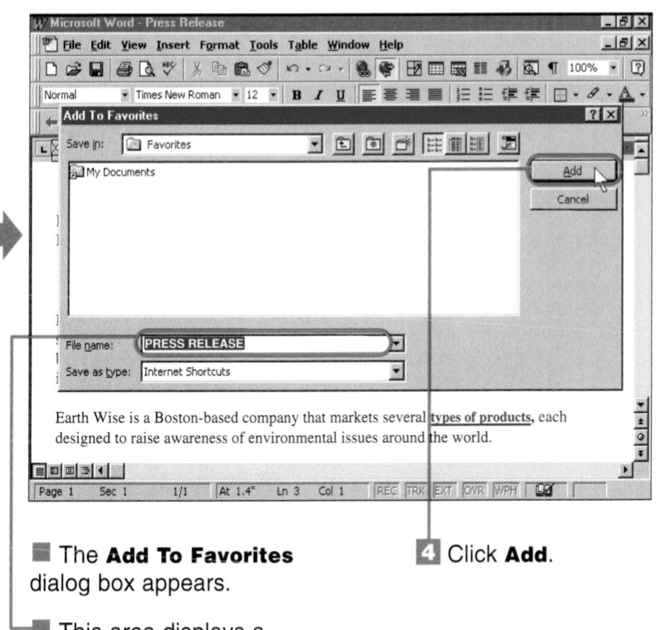

■ The **Add To Favorites** dialog box appears.

■ This area displays a name for the document. To change the name, type a new name.

4 Click **Add**.

OPEN DOCUMENT IN FAVORITES

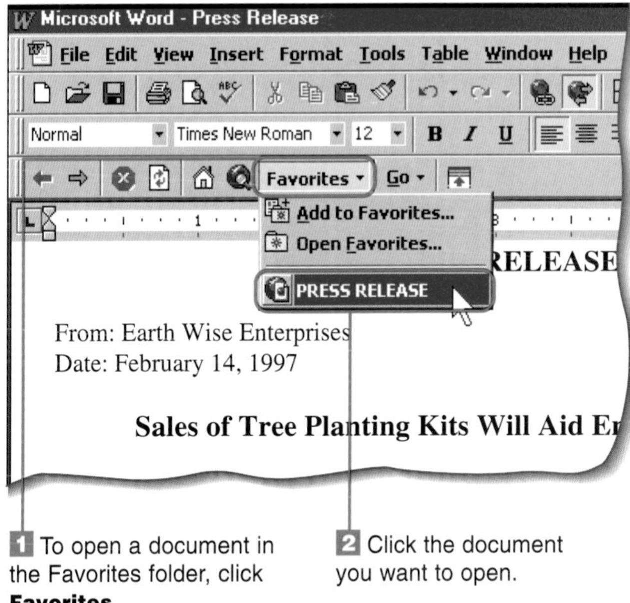

1 To open a document in the Favorites folder, click **Favorites**.

2 Click the document you want to open.

SAVE A DOCUMENT AS A WEB PAGE

You can save a document as a Web page. This lets you place the document on the company intranet or the Web.

SAVE A DOCUMENT AS A WEB PAGE

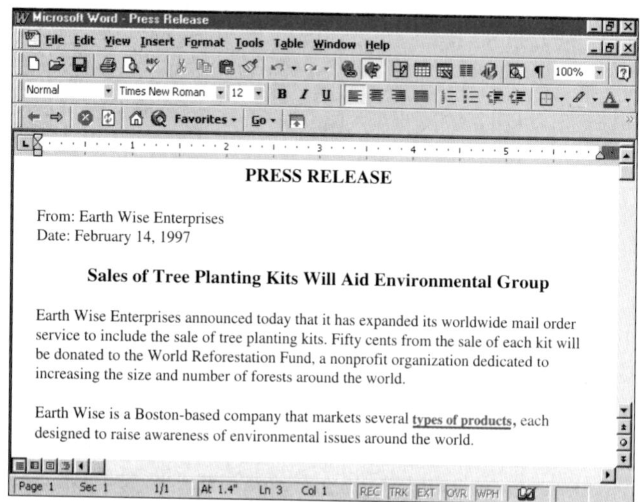

You can save a Word, Excel or PowerPoint document as a Web page.

1 Open the document you want to save as a Web page.

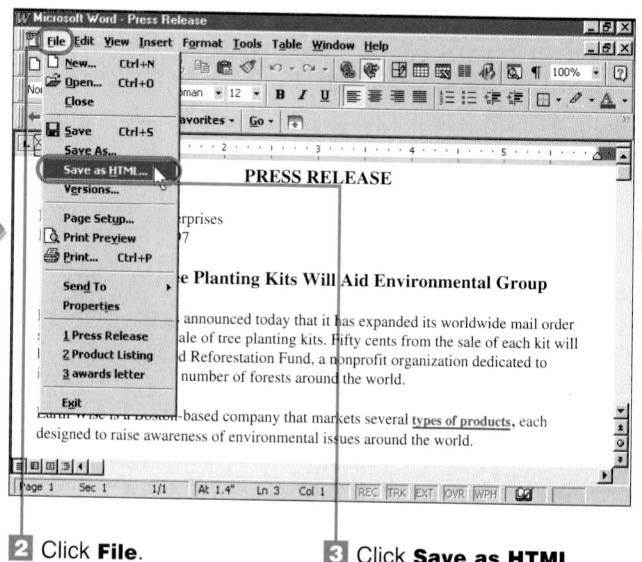

2 Click **File**.

3 Click **Save as HTML**.

*Note: If the **Save as HTML** command is not available, you need to add the Web Page Authoring (HTML) component of Microsoft Office to your computer.*

Why do Excel and PowerPoint ask me a series of questions?

When you save an Excel or PowerPoint document as a Web page, you will be asked a series of questions. Your answers help customize the resulting Web page to suit your needs.

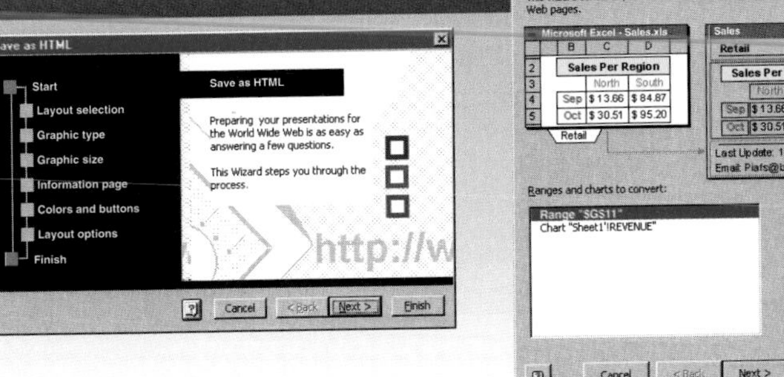

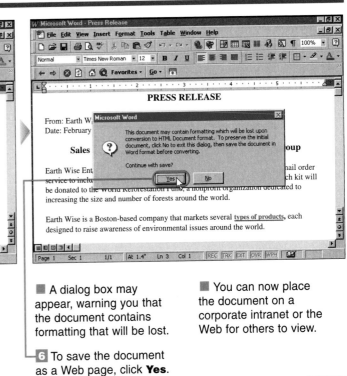

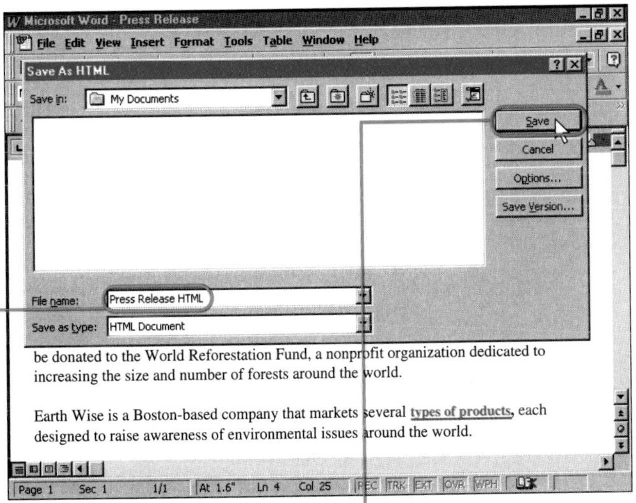

■ The **Save As HTML** dialog box appears.

4 Type a name for the document.

5 Click **Save**.

■ A dialog box may appear, warning you that the document contains formatting that will be lost.

6 To save the document as a Web page, click **Yes**.

■ You can now place the document on a corporate intranet or the Web for others to view.

INDEX

D

Inbox
Sent Items
Outbox
Deleted Items

E

F

G

H

INDEX

R

S

Reminder
Pick up birthday cake after work.

Question
Is the meeting next Monday at 1:00 pm or 2:00 pm?

Idea
Hire an assistant to help out with extra work.

INBOX

T

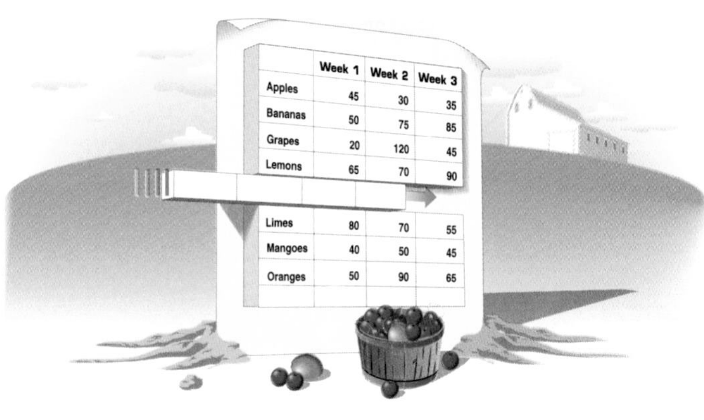

Week 1
Week 2
Week 3
Apples 45 30 35
Bananas 50 75 85
Grapes 20 120 45
Lemons 65 70 90
Limes 80 70 55
Mangoes 40 50 45
Oranges 50 90 65